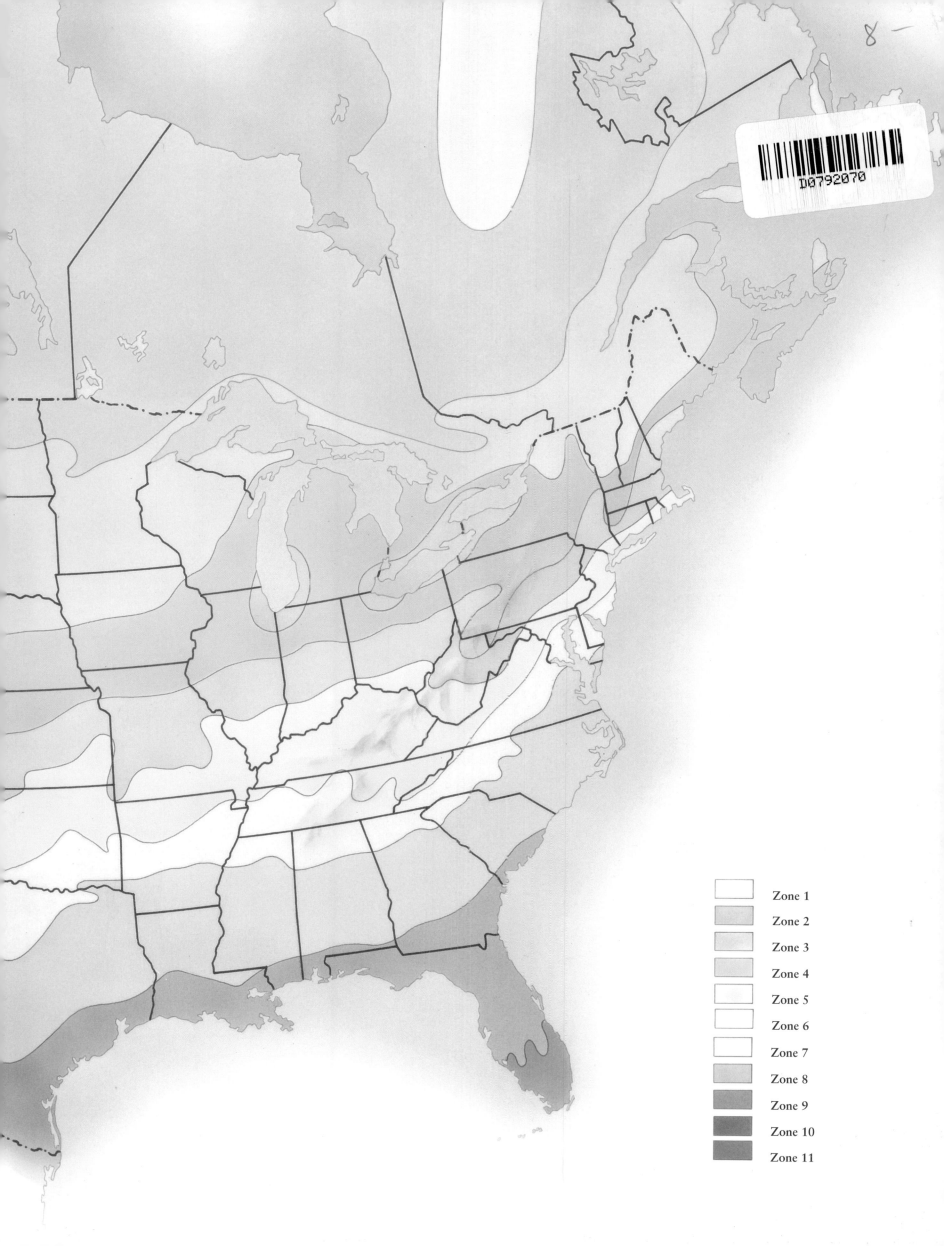

Zone 1
Zone 2
Zone 3
Zone 4
Zone 5
Zone 6
Zone 7
Zone 8
Zone 9
Zone 10
Zone 11

THE ILLUSTRATED ENCYCLOPEDIA OF

Perennials

THE ILLUSTRATED ENCYCLOPEDIA OF

Perennials

A unique reference guide to more than 1500 plants with comprehensive descriptions and planting information

PROFESSOR MARSHALL CRAIGMYLE

PUBLISHED BY

SALAMANDER BOOKS LIMITED

LONDON

DEDICATED TO SADIE

A Salamander Book

Published by Salamander Books Ltd.
8 Blenheim Court
Brewery Road
London N7 9NY
United Kingdom

3 5 7 9 8 6 4
Text © Salamander Books 2002

A member of the Chrysalis Group plc

ISBN 1 84065 393 0

Credits
Managing Editor: Charlotte Davies
Editor: Candida Frith-MacDonald
Designers: John Heritage, Mark Holt
Indexer: Amanda O'Neill
Film set: SX Composing Ltd, England
Reproduction: Studio Tec, England
Printed in China

Acknowledgements
I am indebted to many persons and establishments for help or encouragement, or both, in the preparation of this book, in particular Mr Michael Upward, past secretary of the Alpine Garden Society. My thanks go to Martin Rickard, Rickard's Hardy Ferns, Kyre Park, Tenbury Wells for advising me on ferns. I am indebted to Gryaza Ajilvski for help in identifying the Flora of Texas, to C. Ritchie Bell for help with the Flora of North Carolina, and to Rod Saunders for help with the South African Flora. I owe a substantial debt of gratitude to those members of the Hardy Plant Society in whose gardens many of the photographs were taken, and to the members in particular of the South Wales Group, and those groups which hosted Hardy Plant Society Autumn Weekends which I attended, viz. The Worcester Group, the Hampshire Group and the Hertfordshire Group; but for these the project would not have been possible.
In addition I owe much gratitude for photographic opportunities in many nurseries, and in particular Messrs. Blooms of Bressingham, Cotswold Garden Flowers (Bob Brown), Apple Court Nursery (Diana Grenfell and Roger Grounds), Bernie Stevens, the Nursery, St. David's, Pembrokeshire, the Perennial Nursery, St. David's, Pembrokeshire (Mrs. P. Symons), Wye Valley Plants, Tintern (Adrian and Elsa Wood). I am indebted to the Director of The Royal Botanic Garden, Edinburgh for permission to use the following illustrations taken in Logan Botanic Garden: *Aciphylla aurea*; *Aciphylla glaucescens*; *Celmisia coriacea*; *Erysimum* 'Bowles Mauve'; *Fuchsia splendens*; *Kniphofia thompsonii* var. *snowdenii*; *Meconopsis betonicifolia*; *Meconopsis x sheldonii* 'Slieve Donard'; *Ranunculus lyalii*; *Rodgersia aesculifolia*; *Salvia leucantha*; and *Salvia microphylla*.
I am indebted also to the Director, Sissinghurst Castle Garden, Kent for permission to use several photographs taken in the garden; to Dr Smart for permission to use the picture of the bog garden in Marwood Hill Garden , Barnstaple (p.17). I am also indebted to several nurseries for supplying me with catalogues on request and in particular Jacques Amand, Harrow, Middlesex, Blooms of Bressingham, Diss, Norfolk, and Messrs Parkers, Dutch Bulbs Ltd. I owe many thanks to successive librarians of Pershore College of Horticulture for extending the use of the College Library to me over the years.
My final thanks go to Ms Anne McDowall, formerly of Salamander Books Ltd, for her enthusiasm for the project, and with whom the basic plan of the book was devised, to the staff of Salamander Books for all their help and encouragement, and to Ms Candida Frith-Macdonald. Last, but by no means least, my thanks go to my wife for tolerating for several years, many long winter evenings alone while I sat at the computer.

M.B.L. CRAIGMYLE M.B. Ch. B. M.D.

Additional Pictures
Page 1 *Dicentra spectabilis* forma *alba* A.G.M, Page 2 *Allium cristophii* 'Star of Persia', Page 4 Iris 'Tinkerbell', Page 5 *Paeonia officinalis* Common Peony

CONTENTS

PERENNIALS IN THE GARDEN

❦

PERENNIALS GIVE A GARDEN ITS CHARACTER. While trees and shrubs form the permanent backbone of a garden, providing form and structure that endure for years and can not easily be changed, many of them are primarily background plants, contributing little in the way of showy flowers or extravagant foliage. At the other extreme, annuals provide seasonal color and variety but must be renewed each year, letting the gardener ring the changes but increasing the labor involved in the garden. Perennials provide color and a variety of form that last for years, and it is worth choosing them carefully. Fortunately, this is a wide and varied group of plants. While many of the world's most interesting annuals come from warm, Mediterranean-type climates, and require some help and care to grow in other conditions, perennials are well-represented in the flora of diverse habitats in all regions of the world. There is a range of perennial plants to suit every situation in the garden, from a dry stone wall to a bog garden or pond. Perennials have been important in garden design for centuries. Their influence stretches from the notorious tulip mania, in which fortunes were made and lost, to the humble cottage garden. Classic garden design featured the herbaceous border, its selection of perennials carefully graded with taller plants at the back and shorter specimens at the front, shown against the backdrop of an immaculately clipped evergreen hedge or a mellow brick wall, and appreciated from an expanse of smooth lawn. Since the end of the nineteenth century, this approach has been giving way to island beds and less regimented plantings. Increased travel means that modern gardens often show the influences of exotic locations and foreign styles. Gardens today are also often designed with concern for water conservation and other environmental issues, and so look to the natural landscape and wild plant groupings for inspiration. These considerations affect small gardens as well as great ones: even the modest size suburban plot may now revolve around a gravel garden, miniature wildflower meadow, or wildlife pond. Such gardens have the great advantage to the modern gardener of being less labor-intensive, and here the perennial comes into its own, returning to bloom again year after year.

A fine example of the traditional deep herbaceous border, here at Packwood House, in Warwickshire, England.

7

A PERENNIAL PLANT is one that lives for three or more years, with some perennials living for many more than that. They are distinct from annual plants, which live for one year, and biennials, which live for two, but some very beautiful perennials are short-lived (see p.295), and our gardens would be all the poorer were they restricted to plants of the long-lived variety.

Perennials have developed different strategies for surviving over winter. A perennial plant may disappear below ground completely in winter, in which case it is described as herbaceous, or it may retain some of its leaves throughout the year, in which case it is described as semi-evergreen, or all of them, in which case it is described as evergreen. The great majority of perennial plants are herbaceous. Most of them are also fibrous-rooted, but some have a swollen underground stem in the form of a bulb, a corm, a rhizome, or a tuber. These are all devices for storing energy, enabling a plant to overwinter underground, where it is protected from cold. For the average gardener, the subtle botanical differences between bulbs, corms, rhizomes, or tubers are unlikely to be important, although the particular techniques used in dividing them vary (see p.22). Subshrubs are also included in this book because they associate well with perennials in mixed borders; they produce woody mature growth that survives the cold, as well as some soft growth, which dies back in the winter.

Perennial plants come from many different regions of the world, and as a result they vary enormously in their tolerance of cold. The term "hardy" is used to describe a plant that can survive through the winter outside, and "tender" to describe a plant that requires protection under glass, but these constrictions vary from place to place. In temperate climates, many less hardy or tender perennials are treated as annuals and discarded in the autumn; conversely, in many countries of the world, plants that the Americans think of as tender can be left to overwinter in the open ground. As a result, it is necessary to define the terms whenever they are used. The Royal Horticultural Society uses a scale from H1 (needs heated protection under glass) to H4 (generally hardy in the British Isles), but its publications also give specific minimum temperatures for plants. In mainland Europe, systems with more bands, with narrower ranges, are used, but all of these remain fairly general and so provide necessarily limited help. In this book, a system of climatic zones based on minimum winter temperates has been used (see p.10), as this gives the most reliable and universal guide to a plant's needs.

HOW PLANTS ARE NAMED

The world of plant nomenclature can be complex and may seem confusing at first. Plant names are liable to change as botanical study advances, and many out-of-date names remain in common use for some years. All plants described in the plant directory include the plant's name in binominal nomenclature – that is, a generic name followed by a specific name. The plants are listed alphabetically by species name. The authority for the terminology is *The Plant Finder*, 1999–2000 Edition, published by the Royal Horticultural Society, London, England. The terms used can be defined as follows:

Division The broadest categories, for example, Pteridophyta (ferns) or Angiospermae (flowering plants).

Order For example, Ranunculales, which includes three families. The name of an order always ends with the suffix "-ales".

Family This term is used to classify plants into groups exhibiting similar characteristics such as flower and foliage form. These names usually end in "-aceae," for example, Liliaceae. The family name is given for every plant in the plant directory. In some cases, names have changed, and both are given, as with Asteraceae/Compositae.

Genus A genus is a group of similar species. Each genus has a Latin name, which has its first letter in capitals and which also forms the first half of the binominal nomenclature system, by which all plants are identified, and which is always written in italics, for example *Lilium formosanum*, in which *Lilium* is the genus or generic name.

Species The basic unit of plant nomenclature is a species: a group of plants with the same characteristics, interbreeding freely, usually in a distinct geographical range. The specific name forms the second word of the binominal nomenclature, and is written in italics, but without an initial capital letter. It usually indicates a characteristic of the plant, for example, *lancifolia*, meaning that the leaves are lance-shaped, or the origin of the plant, as in *formosanum*, meaning "as found in Formosa." A species grows in the wild somewhere in the world, and usually all plants are of fairly uniform appearance and habit, and can be propagated by seed. Further adaptation of the system of nomenclature divides species into lesser categories as described below.

Subspecies This denotes naturally occurring plants that have subtle differences from the species. The name is written in italics, with the word subspecies usually abbreviated as "subsp." and not given in italics, for example, *Aconitum napellus* subsp. *vulgare*.

Variety This describes a variation, between a subspecies and a form, that is sufficiently distinct to have its own name. The word variety is not written in italics, and is abbreviated to "var.," for example *Agapanthus campanulatus* var. *albidus*.

Forma This lowest of the subclassifications, is not italicized and is abbreviated to "f.," for example, *Allium carinatum* subsp. *pulchellum* f. *album*. It denotes characteristics that may be important to a gardener but which are genetically minor, such as flower color.

Hybrids These are the result of a sexual union between two species or two genera, and are distinguished by having an "x" in their name. An interspecific hybrid is expressed with the "x" before the specific name, for example, *Potentilla* x *tonguei*, while an intergeneric hybrid is expressed with the "x" before the generic name, for example, x *Solidaster luteus*. Hybrids must be propagated vegetatively from cuttings if they are to come true to type. It is possible to take seed, but only a percentage of the progeny will be true to type.

Cultivars An abbreviation of the description "cultivated variety," this is a plant raised deliberately in cultivation. Cultivar names are not given in italics, but are put in inverted commas, for example *Agapanthus* 'Bressingham Blue'. A cultivar may be a hybrid, but the name is also used generally to cover sports; these are spontaneous genetic mutations of a portion of a plant, producing atypical foliage or flowers, or both. Some sports are unstable, and revert rapidly to the parent type. Many variegated plants originated as sports. Due to their origins, most cultivars need to be propagated vegetatively, rather than from seed. The rules that govern cultivar names have

Above: *The much-hybridized genus Crocosmia has given rise to cultivars such as Crocosmia x crocosmiiflora 'Emily McKenzie', which has large, bright orange flowers with deeper-colored markings in the throats. Plants bred for the garden are often more lush in habit than the species, or have larger, bolder flowers.*

been considerably tightened over the years, excluding proper names and Latin words for new cultivars. Some breeders now register trade names for their plants that are more marketable than the true cultivar names; such plants are marked "Regd." in this and other books, and the name is legally controlled.

HARDINESS ZONES

The first consideration when choosing a perennial to be grown in the garden all year round is whether it is hardy in your area. The United States Department of Agriculture (USDA) has developed a system of temperature zones as a basis for assessing which plants can be grown in different areas. The zones are based on the annual average minimum temperature in an area, and are illustrated on the maps below and opposite of Europe, North America, Australia, New Zealand, and South Africa. The maps have been divided into the USDA climatic zones, numbered from Zone 1, the coldest, with a winter minimum of -50°F (-44°C), up to Zone 11, the warmest, with a minimum of +40°F (+5°C). Every entry in the directory section of this book cites the plant's hardiness zone. To establish whether a perennial will be hardy in your garden, refer to the map of hardiness zones and find the rating for your area. Any plant with a zonal rating equal to or lower than the rating for your area will be hardy in your garden. Thus if your

area is rated Zone 7, all plants graded from Zone 1 to Zone 7 will survive and flower at the average minimum winter temperature there and plants graded Zone 8 to Zone 11 will not. However, Zone 8 plants may be grown outside provided they are given protection in the form of a deep mulch of bracken or leaves, a pane of glass or a cloche, all of which keep the plants dry and help them substantially in surviving the winter. Zone 9 to Zone 11 plants can be grown out of doors in summer in a Zone 7 area, but will have to be lifted and kept under glass in winter or, alternatively, grown in containers and brought into a conservatory or greenhouse over winter.

Another consideration is that every garden has a number of microclimates – that is, some parts of the garden are warmer than others. It may be that the zonal rating for your area does not apply to all of your garden. So if your garden is rated Zone 7, the warmest corner, such as at the foot of a south-facing wall, may well be Zone 8. The only way to find out is to experiment by growing Zone 8-rated plants in that site.

Temperature ranges

ZONE 1: Below -50°F (Below -45°C)

ZONE 2: -50 to -35°F (-45 to -37°C)

ZONE 3: -35 to -20°F (-37 to 29°C)

ZONE 4: -20 to -10°F (-29 to 23°C)

ZONE 5: -10 to-5°F (-23 to -21°C)

ZONE 6: -5 to 5°F (-21 to -15°C)

ZONE 7: 5 to 10°F (-15 to -12°C)

ZONE 8: 10 to 20°F (-12 to -7°C)

ZONE 9: 20 to 30°F (-7 to -1°C)

ZONE 10: 30 to 40°F (-I to 4°C)

ZONE 11: Above +40°F (Above +5°C)

Zone 1
Zone 2
Zone 3
Zone 4
Zone 5
Zone 6
Zone 7
Zone 8
Zone 9
Zone 10
Zone 11

Western Europe

North America

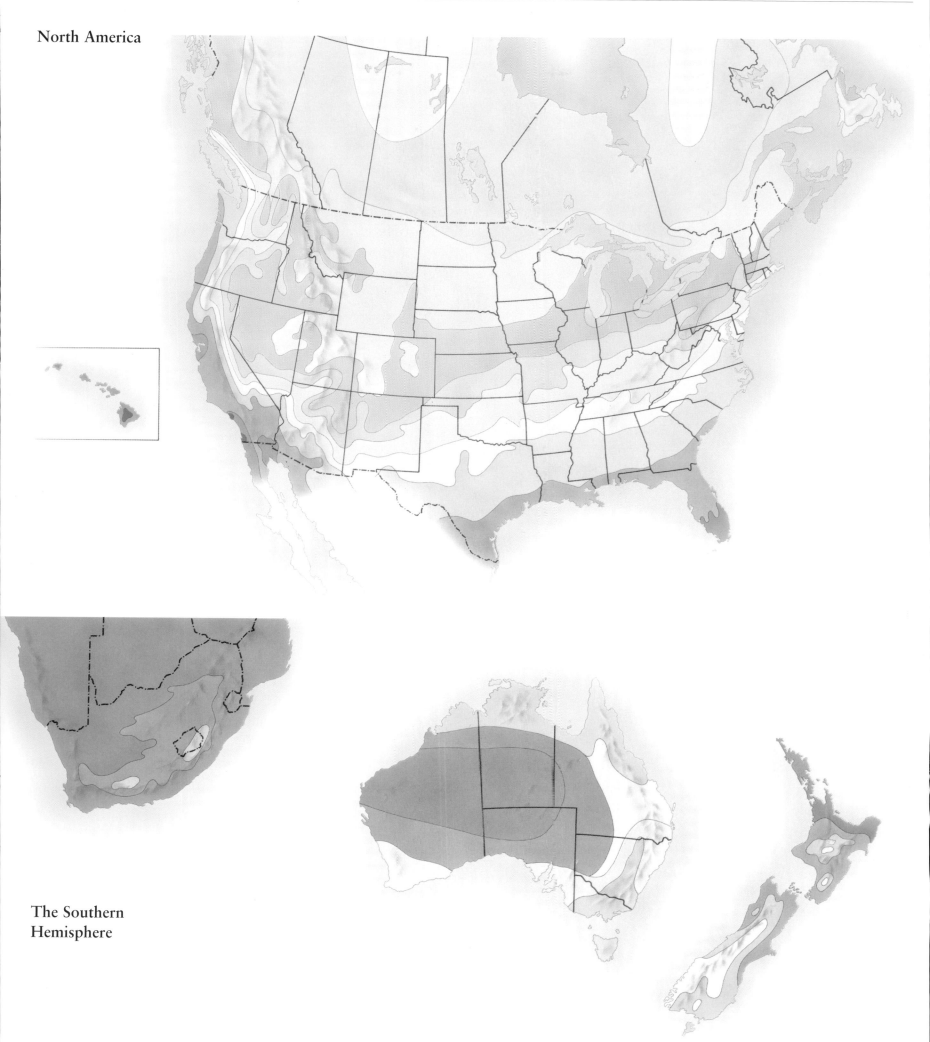

The Southern
Hemisphere

Leaf Shapes and Inflorescences

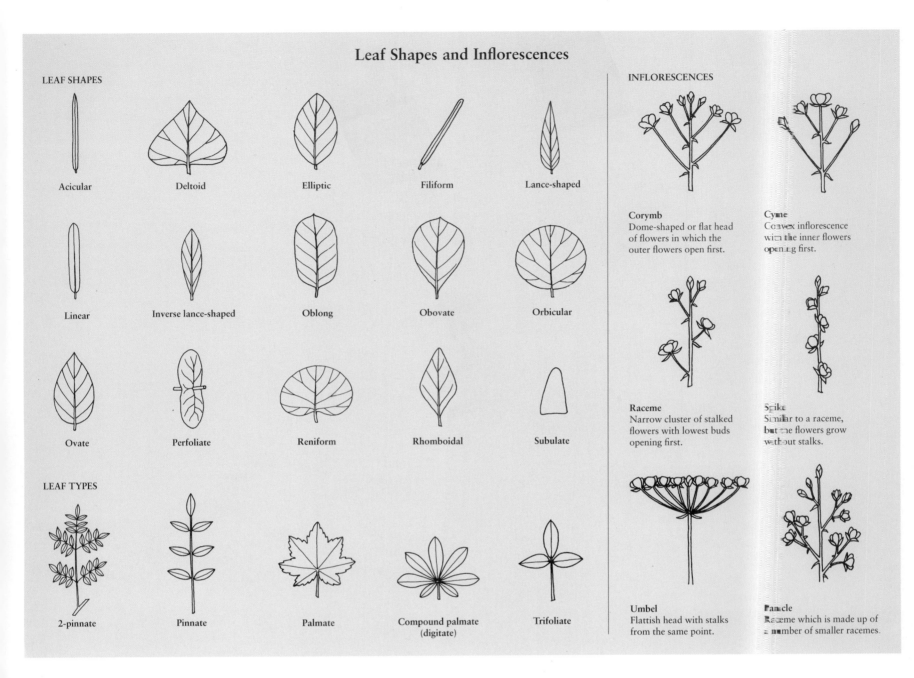

LEAF SHAPES

Acicular · Deltoid · Elliptic · Filiform · Lance-shaped

Linear · Inverse lance-shaped · Oblong · Obovate · Orbicular

Ovate · Perfoliate · Reniform · Rhomboidal · Subulate

LEAF TYPES

2-pinnate · Pinnate · Palmate · Compound palmate (digitate) · Trifoliate

INFLORESCENCES

Corymb
Dome-shaped or flat head of flowers in which the outer flowers open first.

Cyme
Convex inflorescence with the inner flowers opening first.

Raceme
Narrow cluster of stalked flowers with lowest buds opening first.

Spike
Similar to a raceme, but the flowers grow without stalks.

Umbel
Flattish head with stalks from the same point.

Panicle
Raceme which is made up of a number of smaller racemes.

PLANNING A PERENNIAL GARDEN

In the past, the main way in which perennials were grown was in conventional herbaceous borders. These were frequently mixed, in the sense that shrubs were included. These borders were long and needed to be deep to be effective. They usually had a high wall or hedge behind, with the result that the plants grew at an angle toward the light. Wind then tended to cascade over the wall and flatten the plants, and much time-consuming staking was required.

Island beds, pioneered by the famous nurseryman Alan Bloom in his garden in Bressingham, in Norfolk, England, have several advantages over herbaceous borders. Provided the bed is not underneath overhanging trees or in the shade of buildings, the plants grow vertically, and much less staking is required. Another great advantage of the narrow island bed is that the plants are much more accessible for general maintenance such as deadheading, cutting, or staking, and unless the bed is very large, it is not necessary to trample through it for such purposes. Shrubs are less likely to be incorporated into island beds of perennials, but it is not unusual to see

subshrubs, such as *Fuchsia, Helianthemum, Phygelius,* and others included in these beds, as they are so akin to perennials in many respects, and thus many are included in this book. Island beds of shade-loving perennials can of course be created in densely shaded areas, or in dappled shade for those which prefer half-shade. Island beds are also better suited to the small garden.

A development that has been spearheaded on mainland Europe is the inclusion of grasses in beds and borders, and along with this a "loosening up" of the planting, with plants of different heights being more intermingled, so that tall plants with an open, airy habit may be grown at the edge of a bed, with plants behind seen as if through a veil. Such plantings may be strongly architectural, or may tend toward a wilder, more natural look: they are perhaps not for all gardens, but they do provide a lower-maintenance option.

Above: *A visual guide to the different leaf shapes and types of inflorescence described in the plant directory section.*

Right: *Exuberant planting spills onto the path from these double borders at Crathes Castle in Grampian, owned by the National Trust for Scotland.*

Above: *Tender plants, such as some fuchsias, are best grown in containers that can be moved in winter. Here, Fuchsia 'Gartenmeister Bonstedt' grows in a sandstone basket urn on the main terrace at Powis Castle, in Wales.*
Right: Aubrieta, Alyssum, *and* Iberis *cascading down a stone wall show the opportunity for varied planting afforded by a change in levels or a raised bed.*

Conditions in the garden can affect planting as much as stylistic preferences. Containers can be used for perennial plants, and this is a useful method for gardens in temperate climes, because tender plants grown in this way can easily be brought under cover or indoors for the winter. However, it is not necessary to restrict their use to tender plants. All perennials may be grown in this way, but the containers of those that are to be left in the open garden all year round must not be small, or the plant may either dry out in summer or succumb to frost in winter because the roots are too near the cold sides of the container. For the older or wheelchair-bound gardener, containers allow plants to be raised up to levels where they can more easily be tended, smelled, and viewed close at hand. Planting in raised beds has many of the same advantages as using containers. The flowers are brought nearer and can therefore be more readily appreciated, and maintenance is easier. Raised beds have the added advantage that trailing plants can be grown on and in their walls, increasing both the selection of plant types that can be grown and the area that is available for planting, both of which are important considerations in small gardens.

You might design either part or the whole of the garden specifically to attract and support local wildlife. Labor-intensive lawns may quickly be turned into something resembling a wildflower meadow (although a true meadow takes time and care to establish), and plants chosen to feed beneficial insects incorporated (see p.294 for suitable plants). A wildlife-friendly garden will usually succeed better in its aims if it includes a pond or a bog garden. These can both be created with pond liners. In a garden that is naturally waterlogged, it is better not to fight the prevailing conditions, but to make a virtue of necessity. There are plenty of attractive, even dramatic plants that will thrive in bog conditions (see page 292).

At the opposite end of the spectrum, the need to conserve water has resulted in a rise in recent years in the popularity of gardens designed to cope with dry summers without the need for constant watering. Thirsty lawns are replaced by paving with planting pockets or mulches of gravel, at best laid over weed-suppressing membranes, options that reduce both maintenance and evaporation. Such gravel gardens often feature tough perennials from Mediterranean climates. Perhaps the most famous gravel planting is in Beth Chatto's garden at Elmstead Market in Essex, England, a planting developed specifically to explore and show the diverse and beautiful range of plants that will survive naturally with little or no watering in a low-rainfall area (see p.291 for drought-tolerant plants).

Perennials that actively dislike wet, particularly winter wet, can be grown in scree beds. These have a covering of several inches of coarse grit, and have several advantages. They keep the neck of a plant, where it is most likely to rot in a wet winter, dry, and they provide excellent drainage, minimizing plant losses in wet winters. Scree beds are also relatively maintenance-free, and the scree garden planted up with perennials is almost totally maintenance-free.

Below: These alpine plants growing in a scree bed were photographed in Hartpury, Gloucestershire, where they survive the winters in spite of the high level of winter wet in the area. It is necessary to plan such a bed carefully to create a natural look. Larger pieces of stone in the design here help in this. Always ensure that the stone does not come from environmentally sensitive areas.

COMBINING PERENNIALS

There are many possible arrangements for planting perennials in any garden. The usual way of combining perennials is simply to grow all kinds – flowering, foliage, bulbs, ferns, grasses, and sub-shrubs – together, intermingling plants with differing contours to give a pleasant architectural outline. This has many advantages, mainly that it offers points of interest throughout the seasons. Also, since many bulbs are spring-flowering, the gaps they leave as their foliage dies down are soon filled by herbaceous perennials coming into leaf. This sort of mixed planting also helps to guard against pests or diseases associated with one plant type gaining a hold.

Below: This planting of moisture-loving perennials, in Marwood Hill Garden, Barnstaple, in Devon, shows what can be achieved by gardening with the prevailing circumstances. The area, at the bottom of a slope, is a damp location that provides many bog plants with the reliably moist conditions that they require throughout the year to flourish.

There are however, many other interesting possibilities for those who would like to take a more structured or thematic approach. Some gardeners prefer to create very specific mixed plantings using "companion planting," holding that certain plant combinations benefit the health of the plants; this is a subject for a specialist book.

Those with the luxury of space may plant a one-season garden or bed. There are enough perennials of interest in each season for this to be a possibility for any one of them. The drawback, especially of a summer border is that the planting lacks interest for the rest of the year. Other seasonal beds can be planted with annuals in summer.

Many gardeners combine plants on the basis of color. The all-white garden, as in the famous example at Sissinghurst, is popular, but any color can be accommodated in a planting of perennials. A scheme of two colors broadens the range of plants. Blue and gold make a very pleasing combination, as do red and yellow, but not all colors mix, so they must be chosen carefully. In a looser approach, hot-colored flowers complement each other and will have great impact, while cool-colored flowers create a restful atmosphere.

Another approach is to combine plants according to their type. Gardeners usually have their favorite genera, and often choose to grow only these. Beds composed entirely of tulips, narcissi, irises, lilies, hostas, pinks, geraniums, columbines, cannas, campanulas, or New York daisies are all common sights. A less restrictive theme would be to use one class of plant, such as grasses, flowering plants, or ferns – ferneries were very popular in the 19th century.

Other groupings may be suggested by the area of the garden and its use. In an area directly outside a door or window, highly visible all year, a bed of evergreens (see p.290) may be appropriate. In part of the garden used mainly in fine summer weather, an abundance of flowers over a long season (see p.290) may be a priority. For a low-maintenance garden, ground-cover planting (see pp.292–93) will be essential. And in difficult, shady areas, only a grouping of shade-lovers (see pp.290–91) will succeed.

Left: *Bold red* Crocosmia *combines with yellow* Ligularia *and* Kniphofia *in a high-impact hot border.*
Below: *This well-planned combination of spires, rounded shapes, and trailing plants is at the National Trust's Packwood House, in Warwickshire.*

CHOOSING PERENNIALS

When choosing perennials, whether they suit your conditions is one of the most important considerations. Do not assume that if a plant is bought locally, it will be hardy in that area: a sales center may have brought the plants from a long way off, even from another country. Many smaller nurseries do their own propagating, and so their plants may well be hardy locally; but always check first. Also, it is easiest to garden with the soil type and moisture level; there is little to be gained from trying to grow acid-loving plants in chalky soil or moisture-loving plants in a dry, free-draining soil. If some favorites must be included, be prepared to grow them in either containers or specially prepared beds, and to take extra care of them.

Another factor is the space available. The width of a plant has to be known to decide how many are needed to make a good-sized clump; for some, as many as five may be required. Also consider how far they spread. This is especially important in small gardens, and must be established beforehand. Some perennials, such as *Geranium* 'Ann Folkard', may spread several feet. Some perennials spread rapidly and invasively by underground stolons (see p.296).

Even in a large garden, invasive perennials can be a nuisance: they spread through neighboring plants, grow up through them, and can cause them to die off, so are best avoided. Some perennials also seed themselves so freely that they become a nuisance (see p.295). At the other end of the scale, some perennials are very short-lived, (see p.295) and while there are many beautiful garden plants in this category, the gaps they leave behind need to be filled.

It is also important to look ahead to flowering time to ensure that color clashes do not occur. It is useful to draw a plan of the area in each season before planting to ensure that these points are taken into account, and when planting out, start by placing the plants on the bed in their pots to ensure they are well-spaced before planting.

There are also practical human needs to consider. Allergies and asthma are on the increase, and our understanding of which plants trigger reactions is improving. Plants in the Asteraceae/Compositae family are the worst, but by no means the only, offenders in this.

Above: Careful planning has produced this spectacular flowering display in a border at Jenkyn Place, near Bentley in Hampshire. It is best to see the plants in flower and compare colors before planning such a planting: even within a single color the range of shades and tones can be surprisingly wide.

Gardeners who suffer should avoid plants that cause skin irritation (see p.295), or which may trigger an allergic reaction (see p.293), and choose those plants which are least likely to cause a reaction (see p.293). In gardens that will be used by young children, it is best to avoid plants that are harmful if eaten, and in particular those plants with berries or poisonous swollen roots (see p.295). Some perennials need to be lifted and divided every few years to keep them in healthy trim, (see p.296) and should be avoided by infirm gardeners, or those with little time to spare. By avoiding perennials which are likely to be troublesome to them, any gardener can plant a garden that will be a pleasure for many years

PLANTING AND MAINTAINING PERENNIALS

Since the advent of "containerization", it has become possible to buy perennials all year round. This does not mean, however, that they can be planted all year round. Spring and autumn are good times to plant; spring is preferable in cold countries, giving the plant time to establish a root system before the onset of winter. Grasses and gray-leaved perennials transplant best in spring. Summer planting is possible, but there is the risk of the plant drying out, with disastrous results. Winter planting should be avoided if the ground is, or may become, frozen or waterlogged.

When planting perennials, keep in mind that the plants are likely to remain *in situ* for a number of years, and so thorough preparation of the ground is vital. This entails making sure that the drainage is good, removing all perennial weeds, digging over the site and incorporating as much humus as possible, and in particular, matter that is slow to disintegrate, such as bark.

Some perennials are taprooted, and resent transplantation (see p.296) so these should be placed with particular care: plant according to their needs, rather than taking a chance, and note the height when fully grown, so that it is not awkwardly placed. All plants should be allowed sufficient room for growth, and not surrounded too closely with others.

Once they are established, perennials are remarkably low-maintenance plants; nevertheless any garden requires a certain amount of work. The following tasks will all need to be carried out on a regular basis.

Weeding It is impossible to prevent annual grasses and perennial weeds such as dandelions from seeding into beds. Weeding can be performed either by hand or by hoe. The former is preferable, because hoeing can damage root systems, but is more tiring. Some plants, such as *Eremurus*, are surface-rooting, and should never be hoed around.

Mulching The most desirable, albeit expensive, way of keeping weeds to a minimum is to mulch on a regular basis, say once or twice a season. An organic mulch will also nourish plants as it disintegrates. A mulch should be applied only when the ground is wet; if it is not possible to wait for rain, water beforehand.

Staking The most important consideration here is to provide the support early, before the plants have flopped over. After that the task is twice as difficult. Many of the commercially available staking devices are designed on the principle that the plant grows up through a circular grid, so the device should be in place early in the growth cycle. However, there are many others that are designed to be put in place only after the plant has made considerable growth; all are vastly superior to the old-fashioned bamboo cane and string method. One favored method is to use Christmas trees; the side branches of these can be cut off and put in place early, letting the plant grow up through them, or later, to provide support around the edges of the plants.

Deadheading This is a very important task for three reasons. Firstly, it prevents energy going into the setting of seed and instead lets the plant to put its effort into building up reserves for the winter. Secondly, for some plants, it will result in a second flush of flowers later in the season. Thirdly, it will prevent many plants from self-seeding too freely.

Feeding Beds of perennials that lie undisturbed for many years will require feeding on a regular basis. The more mulching they receive, the less feeding they will require, since organic mulches decompose and feed the soil in the long run. However, nitrogen-rich fertilizers early in the growing season will help to build up a strong plant, and phosphate-rich feeds at flowering time will help to improve the quality of bloom.

Watering To water is tedious, time-consuming, and sometimes expensive, but necessary at times. The first golden rule of watering is to water thoroughly, or not at all, since repeated surface watering encourages plants to form surface roots at the expense of deep ones, which is courting disaster. The second golden rule is to do so late in the day, and not in the morning, as during the day much of the water will be lost by transpiration. It is always worth conserving water by diverting down-pipes into water butts.

Combating pests and diseases The number of pests and diseases affecting plants is extensive, but perennials suffer less than most other plants, one reason for their increasing popularity. No category of plant, however, is entirely problem-free.

The major pest of perennials is the snail or slug. Common slug and snail killers contain metaldehyde, a potent poison. The dead slugs will be eaten by hedgehogs and birds (especially in suburban areas where every garden may be laced), and the poison may get into the hands of children. Slug and snail killers that are aluminum-sulphate based do not harm wildlife, but are more readily rendered ineffective by rain, needing to be renewed after each shower. Bell cloches are very useful in protecting new growth in spring, because the cloche prevents the slug killer from becoming ineffective after rain. The cloches should be removed when a healthy plant has been established. Slug traps, which are filled with beer, milk, or other suitably tempting liquids, and in which the slugs drown, are also effective: be sure to place them with the edge a little above ground level so that beneficial beetles do not fall in. Biological controls, in the form of nematodes that parasitize slugs, are a more expensive, but effective and environmentally friendly alternative. Hedgehogs are the most natural solution of all, hence the importance of not endangering them with metaldehyde.

As regards disease, the problem common to many perennials is powdery mildew, which is particularly prevalent in very wet areas. It is disfiguring, debilitating, and often fatal. Chemical fungicides barely control it, and some plants, such as *Phlox paniculata* and *Aster novi-belgii*, are untreatable. Affected growth should be cut down and disposed of, but not composted or burned. It is often best simply to grow something else if the problem persists.

PROPAGATING PERENNIALS

Perennials can be propagated by seed, by division, and by cuttings.
Seed Species will come true from seed, but even these will show some variation in the progeny. Varieties, forms, sports, and most cultivars can not be propagated by seed if they are required to come true. The seedlings will vary widely, with only a few similar to the parent plant. Seed of *Gentiana*, *Helleborus*, and *Primula* must be sown fresh; be patient, as the seed will germinate the following spring, or even the spring after that. *Pulsatilla* must also be sown fresh, but germinates at once, as will seeds of the Ranunculaceae family. Most other seeds should be sown in spring. Use sterile seed compost and leave fine seeds on the surface, but lightly cover larger seeds. The largest seeds, such as *Lupinus* and *Baptisia*, have tough coats that must be chipped or abraded before sowing.

Cuttings These can be of stems or basal growth, generally taken in spring, or of roots, taken in late winter. A sandy soil should be used for rooting, preferably with bottom heat.

Division Most perennials can be increased easily by lifting and dividing established, congested plants. For herbaceous perennials, this should be carried out during the dormant period, and as a rule, division should take place in spring or autumn. The roots of the plants determine the best method of dividing the plant. Plants with fibrous roots, such as *Aster novae-angliae* (New England daisy), *Aster novi-belgii* (New York daisy), *Leucanthemum × superbum* (shasta daisy), *Rudbeckia* (coneflower), and *Helenium* (sneezeweed), can be increased by lifting and carefully dividing the complete roots. Plants with fleshy roots and woody crowns, such as *Delphinium* and *Lupinus* (lupines), can be propagated by lifting the crowns and using a sharp knife to cut through them, or by taking cuttings from young shoots in spring. Rhizomatous plants, such as *Iris germanica*, have thick, tough roots; these can be lifted and, using a sharp knife, the young roots around the outside of the clump divided into pieces 2–3in (5–7.5cm) long, each containing a few strong leaves. Dust the cut surfaces with fungicide, then replant them to the same depth,

Below: *Division is an easy and inexpensive way to increase many herbaceous perennials. Once a border is established with these plants it is easy to lift and divide them every three or four years. Helenium autumnale 'Pumilum magnificum', a yellow autumn daisy, offers a sunny splash of bright yellow blooms from late summer through to the end of autumn. Congested clumps should be divided by division after flowering in autumn or in spring.*

using the dark mark on the stem indicating the previous level as a guide. Discard the old, woody, central parts. Tuberous genera such as *Paeonia* should also be divided using a sharp knife, ensuring that each section of the tuber has good growing points. Both cormous and bulbous perennials increase freely at the root, and all that is necessary is separation of the offsets, best done when the plant is dormant. Only taprooted perennials can not be propagated by division and must be increased by seed or cuttings.

Most perennials are fibrous-rooted, so the method of division for these is worth describing in more detail; all fibrous-rooted plants can be increased in this way, either by pulling the outer shoots apart with roots attached, or by dividing the root ball with a spade or with garden forks held back-to-back (as below). They can be divided at any time between early autumn and midspring, as long as the soil is not frozen or waterlogged. Usually this means in autumn when the weather is mild, but it is advisable to wait until spring in extremely cold and frost-prone areas.

When dividing fibrous-rooted plants, first cut down all stems to within a few inches of the ground. Clear these away and make sure that the soil is free from debris, including weeds. Use a garden fork to dig up the clump, taking care not to sever too many roots.

To divide the plant, push two garden forks back-to-back down through the center of the clump, then lever the handles together to force the roots apart. Ensure that the forks are both pushed in fully; otherwise the upper part of the clump will tear away from the base. Select and pull away young parts from the outside of the clump for replanting. Discard the woody, central area, which is the oldest part, and remove the roots of perennial weeds at the same time.

If the roots are extremely matted, wash them in water and part them gently with a plant label or a pointed stick. Replant the pieces before their roots become dry; if they cannot be replanted at once, wrap them in wet sacking. Ensure that the soil into which they are to be planted is also moist; water thoroughly several days before planting, so that excess moisture has time to drain away. Water again after planting and regularly through the growing season.

If the divided parts are particularly small, increase their size by planting them in a nursery bed for one or two years before putting them in their permanent positions in a border. If the parent plant is especially fine and a large number of new plants are wanted, pot very small pieces into 3in (7.5cm) pots and place in a cold frame until they are large enough to be planted into a garden. This is most important if the clump is divided in autumn.

1 Cut down all stems so that the crown of the plant can be seen. Use a garden fork to dig up the clump, taking care not to damage the roots.

2 Insert two garden forks into the clump back-to-back, and lever their handles together. Small plants are best divided with handforks.

3 Gently pull the clump into small pieces, but not very small unless a large number of plants are required. Discard the old, woody central part.

4 Replant the young pieces soon after the clump has been divided. Do not let the roots become dry; cover them with damp sacking if planting is delayed.

THE PLANT DIRECTORY

❦

MORE THAN 1500 plant entries are featured in the directory. Each entry is illustrated with a color picture of the plant *in situ*, and gives the botanical and common name or names; the height and spread of the plant in imperial and metric measures; the required aspect and type of soil; hardiness rating; and suitable propagation methods. There is a brief description of the plant, giving any appropriate information about the root system or the area in which the plant originated, and detailing the the form and color of the flower and the foliage. The Royal Horticultural Society in the UK carries out extensive trials of all categories of plants, and the accolade of the Award of Garden Merit is given to the most outstanding plants. A plant which has the Award of Garden Merit will have the letters A.G.M. after its name. Positive and negative attributes of each plant are given in the form of symbols, explained below and on the bookmark.

KEY TO SYMBOLS

Positive Attribute Symbols	**Negative Attribute Symbols**
Long flowering	Insignificant flowers
Repeat flowering	Short-lived plant
Aromatic/perfumed	Requires staking
Evergreen	Invasive plant
Architectural plant	Seeds everywhere
Good cut flower	Prone to slug/snail damage
Good for winter drying	Regular lifting and dividing
Drought-tolerant	Resents disturbance
Attracts butterflies/bees	Prone to powdery mildew
Attractive seedheads/berries	Highly allergenic
Low allergen	Poisonous/skin irritant
Attractive foliage	

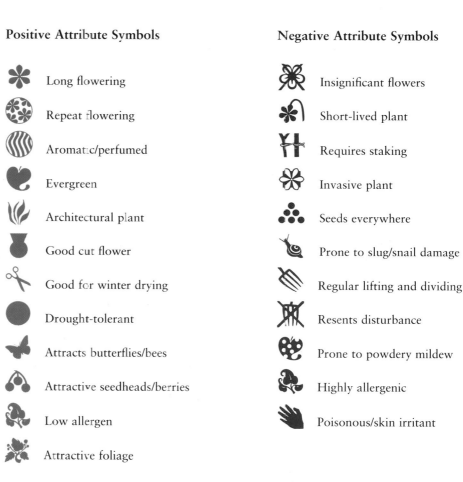

Herbaceous border at Bramdean House, in midsummer.

Acaena caesiiglauca
(Rosaceae)

Common name: Sheepburr
Height: 5in (12cm)
Spread: To 3ft (1m)
Aspect: Sun or half-shade
Soil: Well-drained
Hardiness: Zone 6
Propagation: Seed, in
autumn; softwood cuttings,
in spring; division, in spring
or autumn

Semi-prostrate, evergreen subshrub. Leaves
glaucous, pinnate, with 7–13 obovate
leaflets. Flowerheads spherical, followed by
reddish-brown burrs in late summer.

Acaena microphylla
'Kupferteppich'
(Rosaceae)

Common name: Redspine
sheepburr
Height: 2in (5cm)
Spread 24in (60cm)
Aspect: Sun or half shade
Soil: Must not be waterlogged
Hardiness: Zone 6
Propagation: Seed, in autumn;
softwood cuttings, in spring;
division, in spring or autumn

Prostrate, evergreen subshrub. Leaves
bronze, pinnate, with 9–15 rounded leaflets.
Flowerheads spherical, small, followed by
red burrs. Good for rock garden or wall.

Acanthus dioscoridis
var. *perringii*
(Acanthaceae)

Common name: Bear's-breech
Height: 16in (40cm)
Spread: 24in (60cm)
Aspect: Sun or half shade
Soil: Well-drained
Hardiness: Zone 8
Propagation: Seed, in spring;
division, in spring or autumn;
root cuttings, in winter

Evergreen with running, fleshy rootstalk.
Leaves spiny, pinnatifid, gray-green, rosetted.
Racemes of pink flowers with green bracts,
late spring to late summer. Shy-flowering.

Acanthus hungaricus
(Acanthaceae)

Common name: Bear's-breech
Height: 4ft (1.2m)
Spread: 3ft (90cm)
Aspect: Sun or half shade
Soil: Well-drained
Hardiness: Zone 8
Propagation: Seed, in spring;
division, in spring or autumn;
root cuttings, in winter

Clump-forming evergreen. Leaves oblong-
obovate, dark green, deeply lobed.
Racemes of pale pink or white flowers,
bracts tinged purple, early to midsummer.

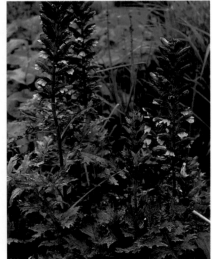

Acanthus mollis
(Acanthaceae)

Common name: Bear's-breech
Height: To 5ft (1.5m)
Spread: 3ft (90cm)
Aspect: Sun or half shade
Soil: Well-drained
Hardiness: Zone 6
Propagation: Seed, in spring;
division, in spring or autumn;
root cuttings, in winter

Clump-forming, architectural evergreen
with obovate, dark green, deeply lobed,
shiny leaves. Flowers in racemes, white,
with purple-shaded bracts, in late summer.

Acanthus spinosus
A.G.M.
(Acanthaceae)

Common name: Bear's-breech
Height: To 4ft (1.2m)
Spread: 2ft (60cm)
Aspect: Sun or half shade
Soil: Well-drained
Hardiness: Zone 6
Propagation: Seed, in spring;
division, in spring or autumn;
root cuttings, in winter

Clump-forming, architectural evergreen.
Leaves spiny, oblong, deeply cut, arching,
dark green. Tall raceme of soft mauve
flowers and purple bracts, from late spring.

ACHILLEA (Compositae)
Yarrow • Milfoil • Sneezewort

A genus of some 80 species, from various habitats in the
temperate northern hemisphere. The daisylike flowerheads
usually lack ray petals, so have only disc florets, and are
closely packed in tight corymbs, borne on stout stems. They
exhibit a wide range of color. All are attractive to both bees
and butterflies. The foliage is feathery, save for that of
A. ptarmica (Zone 5), and some are evergreen. The
flowerheads last a long time, and are good for cutting and
drying for the winter, and suitable for flower arrangements in
both fresh and dry states. *Achillea* do best in full sun with
good drainage, but they are only reasonably tolerant of
drought, so a moisture-retentive soil is best. Drawbacks are
that they are prone to powdery mildew, and some forms
require staking. *A. millefolium* (Zone 2) and *A. ptarmica*,
both rhizomatous, can be as invasive as weeds. All the rest
are well-behaved, except that they may die out in the center
and usually have to be lifted and divided every few years, and
the healthy outer edges replanted. Many species and cultivars
hold an Award of Garden Merit; some not illustrated here are
A. ageratifolia (Zone 3), *A.* x *lewisii* 'King Edward' (Zone 5),
and *A. tomentosa* (Zone 3).

Achillea
'Coronation Gold' A.G.M.
(Asteraceae/Compositae)

Common name: Yarrow
Height: 36in (90cm)
Spread: 18in (45cm)
Aspect: Sun
Soil: Humus-rich
Hardiness: Zone 6
Propagation: Division,
in spring

Clump-forming evergreen with pinnatifid, oblong, gray-green leaves. Corymbs 4in (10cm) across of golden-yellow flowerheads, from midsummer. Good for small gardens.

Achillea
'Credo'
(Asteraceae/Compositae)

Common names: Milfoil;
yarrow
Height: 4ft (1.2m)
Spread: 2ft (60cm)
Aspect: Sun
Soil: Humus-rich
Hardiness: Zone 6
Propagation: Division,
in spring

Clump-forming perennial with feathery, pale green leaves and corymbs of pale yellow flowerheads, aging to cream, in summer.

Achillea
'Fanal'
(Asteraceae/Compositae)

Common name: Yarrow
Height: 30in (75cm)
Spread: 24in (60cm)
Aspect: Sun
Soil: Humus-rich
Hardiness: Zone 2
Propagation: Division,
in spring

Mat-forming hybrid with linear, 2-pinnate, gray-green leaves. Corymbs 6in (15cm) across of bright red flowerheads with yellow discs. Flowers fade as they age.

Achillea filipendula
'Gold Plate' A.G.M.
(Asteraceae/Compositae)

Common name: Fernleaf
yarrow
Height: 4ft (1.2m)
Spread: 18in (45cm)
Aspect: Sun
Soil: Humus-rich
Hardiness: Zone 3
Propagation: Division,
in spring

Clump-forming evergreen. Rosettes of mid- to gray-green, oblong, 1- or 2-pinnate leaves. Bright yellow flowerheads in corymbs 6in (15cm) across, early summer to early autumn.

Achillea
'Forncett Candy'
(Asteraceae/Compositae)

Common name: Yarrow
Height: 36in (90cm)
Spread: 18in (45cm)
Aspect: Sun
Soil: Humus-rich
Hardiness: Zone 6
Propagation: Division,
in spring

Clump-forming evergreen, with fernlike, gray-green leaves. Abundant pale pink flowerheads, fading to almost white in corymbs 6in (15cm) across, in summer.

Achillea
'Huteri'
(Asteraceae/Compositae)

Common name: Yarrow
Height: 24in (60cm)
Spread: 12in (30cm)
Aspect: Sun
Soil: Humus-rich
Hardiness: Zone 6
Propagation: Division,
in spring

A bushy cultivar, with linear, pinnate leaves of silver-gray. Flowerheads with white ray florets are borne in corymbs in summer.

Achillea millefolium
'Cerise Queen'
(Asteraceae/Compositae)

Common names: Yarrow;
milfoil
Height: 2ft (60cm)
Spread: 2ft (60cm)
Aspect: Sun
Soil: Humus-rich
Hardiness: Zone 2
Propagation: Division,
in spring

Rhizomatous, mat-forming cultivar. Leaves linear to lance-shaped, pinnatisect, dark green. Corymbs of magenta flowerheads with white discs in summer. Highly invasive.

Achillea
'Moonshine' A.G.M.
(Asteraceae/Compositae)

Common name: Yarrow
Height: 2ft (60cm)
Spread: 2ft (60cm)
Aspect: Sun
Soil: Humus-rich
Hardiness: Zone 7
Propagation: Division,
in spring

Clump-forming evergreen with linear to lance-shaped, gray-green, pinnatifid leaves. Corymbs 6in (15cm) across of light yellow flowerheads, early summer to early autumn.

Achillea ptarmica
'Nana Compacta'
(Asteraceae/Compositae)

Common name: Sneezewort
Height: 12in (30cm)
Spread: 24in (60cm)
Aspect: Sun
Soil: Humus-rich
Hardiness: Zone 5
Propagation: Division,
in spring

Achillea ptarmica
'Stephanie Cohen'
(Asteraceae/Compositae)

Common name: Sneezewort
Height: 30in (75cm)
Spread: 32in (80cm)
Aspect: Sun
Soil: Any
Hardiness: Zone 5
Propagation: Division,
in spring

Aciphylla aurea
(Apiaceae/Umbelliferae)

Common names: None
Height: 3ft (1m)
Spread: 3ft (1m)
Aspect: Full sun
Soil: Moist but well-drained,
humus-rich
Hardiness: Zone 5
Propagation: Seed, when ripe

Aciphylla glaucescens
(Apiaceae/Umbelliferae)

Common names: None
Height: 3ft (1m)
Spread: 3ft (1m)
Aspect: Full sun
Soil: Moist but well-drained,
humus-rich
Hardiness: Zone 5
Propagation: Seed, when ripe

Rhizomatous perennial. Leaves linear to lance-shaped, toothed, dark green. Corymbs of off-white flowers with gray-green centers in summer. Too invasive for borders.

A handsome but invasive cultivar. Foliage linear to lance-shaped, toothed, green. Pale pink flowers with darker centers, borne in corymbs from early to late summer.

Rosettes of straplike, 2-pinnate, gray-green leaves with spiny tips and gold edges. Many golden-brown, star-shaped flowers. Needs both sexes and warm summers to fruit.

Rosettes of narrow, 3-pinnate, straplike leaves, silver-gray, spiny-tipped and edged. Yellow-green, star-shaped flowers. Needs both sexes and a warm climate to fruit.

ACONITUM (Ranunculaceae)
Monkshood • Aconite • Wolfsbane

A genus of about 100 species from woodlands, grasslands, and scrub in the northern hemisphere. They are tuberous-rooted, except for *A. lycotonum* subsp. *vulparia*. The distinctive flowers have hoods composed of sepals, so providing one of the common names, which provide the shape and color and hide the petals. They are carried in tall panicles or racemes, well above the foliage. The leaves are generally of a rich green, and ovate, round, palmately lobed, or kidney-shaped. All *Aconitum* need to be lifted and divided every few years; the taller forms, although good architectural plants for woodland or border, will also require staking. It is important to note that all parts of these plants are highly poisonous if eaten. There are no particularly tempting-looking fruits, but it is still safest to say that the genus should not be grown in a garden where there are children. Contact with the foliage may also cause skin irritation, but handled with care they make good cut flowers, and are popular with flower-arrangers. The flowers are not allergenic. Other Award of Garden Merit varieties that have not been illustrated here are *A.* 'Bressingham Spire' (Zone 4), *A. carmichaelii* 'Kelmscott' (Zone 3), and *A.* 'Spark's Variety' (Zone 4).

Aconitum x *cammarum*
'Bicolor' A.G.M.
(Ranunculaceae)

Common name: Monkshood
Height: 4ft (1.2m)
Spread: 4ft (1.2m)
Aspect: Sun or half shade
Soil: Moist, fertile,
humus-rich
Hardiness: Zone 3
Propagation: Division,
in autumn

Aconitum septentrionale
'Ivorine'
(Ranunculaceae)

Common name: Monkshood
Height: 36in (90cm)
Spread: 18in (45cm)
Aspect: Sun or half shade
Soil: Moist, fertile, cool
Hardiness: Zone 5
Propagation: Division,
in autumn

A very hardy perennial. Foliage ovate to round, deeply lobed, glossy, dark green. Blue and white flowers in loose arching panicles from midsummer.

Very attractive perennial with deeply lobed, rounded, rich green leaves. Ivory flowers in spikelike racemes in late spring and early summer; largest in a cool, moist climate.

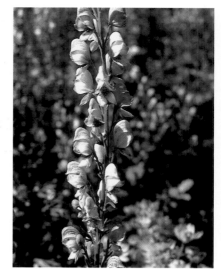

Aconitum lycoctonum subsp. *vulparia* (Ranunculaceae)

Common name: Wolfsbane monkshood
Height: To 5ft (1.5m)
Spread: 1ft (30cm)
Aspect: Sun or half shade
Soil: Moist, fertile, humus-rich
Hardiness: Zone 3
Propagation: Seed, in spring; division, in autumn

An erect, very hardy perennial with round, lobed, rich green leaves. Panicles of hooded, pale yellow flowers are borne from mid- to late summer.

Aconitum lycoctonum, subsp. *vulparia* 'Albidum' (Ranunculaceae)

Common name: Wolfsbane monkshood
Height: To 5ft (1.5m)
Spread: 1ft (30cm)
Aspect: Sun or half shade
Soil: Moist, fertile, humus-rich
Hardiness: Zone 3
Propagation: Division, in autumn

A very hardy, handsome perennial. Erect stems. Leaves dark green, rounded, with 5 to 9 lobes. Flowers in panicles, hooded, pure white.

Aconitum napellus (Ranunculaceae)

Common name: Aconite monkshood
Height: To 5ft (1.5m)
Spread: 1ft (30cm)
Aspect: Sun or half shade
Soil: Moist, fertile, humus-rich
Hardiness: Zone 6
Propagation: Seed, in spring; division, in autumn

Erect, with rounded, deeply lobed, often toothed, dark green leaves. Panicles of flowers are intense indigo-blue in the best forms. Very variable; buy in bloom.

Aconitum napellus subsp. *vulgare* 'Albidum' (Ranunculaceae)

Common name: Aconite monkshood
Height: To 5ft (1.5m)
Spread: 1ft (30cm)
Aspect: Sun or half shade
Soil: Moist, fertile, humus-rich
Hardiness: Zone 6
Propagation: Division, in autumn

Erect, with handsome foliage of rounded, deeply lobed, toothed, dark green leaves. Panicles of gray-white flowers in mid- to late summer.

Actaea alba A.G.M. (Ranunculacae)

Common name: White baneberry
Height: 3ft (90cm)
Spread: 2ft (60cm)
Aspect: Half shade
Soil: Cool, moist, fertile, humus-rich
Hardiness: Zone 3
Propagation: Seed, in autumn; division, in spring

Rhizomatous woodland plant with 2-, 3-, or 5-ternate, toothed, green leaves. Tiny white flowers in spherical racemes are followed by clusters of extremely toxic white berries.

Actaea rubra A.G.M. (Ranunculaceae)

Common name: Red baneberry
Height: 18in (45cm)
Spread: 12in (30cm)
Aspect: Half shade
Soil: Cool, moist, fertile, humus-rich
Hardiness: Zone 3
Propagation: Seed, in autumn; division, in spring

Woodlander with 2- or 3-pinnate leaves of up to 15 ovate leaflets. Small racemes of white, ovoid flowers in spring to summer, followed by shiny, red, highly toxic berries.

Adenophora asiatica (Campanulaceae)

Common name: Ladybell
Height: 12in (30cm)
Spread: 6in (15cm)
Aspect: Sun or half shade
Soil: Moist, well-drained, humus-rich
Hardiness: Zone 5
Propagation: Seed, in autumn; cuttings in spring; no division

A charming fleshy-rooted perennial. Leaves ovate, toothed, midgreen. Flowers bell-shaped, pendent, pale lavender-blue, in terminal racemes, in mid- to late summer.

Adenophora potaninii (Campanulaceae)

Common name: Bush ladybell
Height: To 3ft (90cm)
Spread: 1ft (30cm)
Aspect: Sun or half shade
Soil: Moist, well-drained, humus-rich
Hardiness: Zone 3
Propagation: Seed, in autumn; cuttings, in spring

Reliable perennial with lax stems and ovate to lance-shaped, toothed leaves. Racemes of pendent, open, bell-shaped, violet-blue flowers in mid- to late summer.

Adiantum aleuticum
A.G.M.
(Adiantaceae/Pteridaceae)

Common name: Aleutian
maidenhair fern
Height: 30in (75cm)
Spread: 30in (75cm)
Aspect: Sun or half shade
Soil: Moist, well-drained,
humus-rich
Hardiness: Zone 4
Propagation: Spores, in
warmth when ripe; division, in spring

Rhizomatous, deciduous fern. Fronds pale
to midgreen, kidney-shaped to broadly
ovate, pedate, with oblong segments and
black stalks and midribs.

Adiantum capillus-veneris
(Adiantaceae/Pteridaceae)

Common name: True
maidenhair fern
Height: 12in (30cm)
Spread: 18in (45cm)
Aspect: Half shade
Soil: Moist, well-drained,
alkaline, fertile
Hardiness: Zone 8
Propagation: Spores, in
warmth when ripe; division, in spring

Creeping, rhizomatous fern, evergreen down
to 28°F (-2°C). Fronds arching, bronze-
pink, turning green, 2- or 3-pinnate,
triangular. Pinnae fan-shaped, stems black.

Adiantum pedatum
A.G.M.
(Adiantaceae/Pteridaceae)

Common name: Five-fingered
maidenhair fern
Height: 16in (40cm)
Spread: 16in (40cm)
Aspect: Half-shade
Soil: Moist, well drained,
fertile
Hardiness: Zone 5
Propagation: Spores, in
warmth in autumn; division, in spring

Deciduous, creeping, rhizomatous fern.
Fronds ovate to kidney-shaped, pinnate,
midgreen. Segments oblong or triangular,
upper edges lobed or toothed. Stems black.

Aegopodium podagraria
'Variegatum'
(Apiaceae/Umbelliferae)

Common names: Goutweed;
Bishop's-weed
Height: 2ft (60cm)
Spread: Indefinite
Aspect: Full or half shade
Soil: Any
Hardiness: Zone 2
Propagation: Division,
in spring

Invasive rhizomatous plant. Leaves ovate,
green, cream-edged. Insignificant white
flowers. Grow in dry shade or in a
container; deadhead before it sets seed.

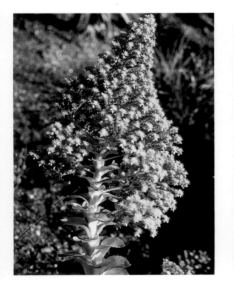

Aeonium cuneatum
(Crassulaceae)

Common names: None
Height: 6ft (2m)
Spread: 20in (50cm)
Aspect: Half shade
Soil: Well-drained, fertile
Hardiness: Zone 9
Propagation: Seed, in warmth
in spring; cuttings, in spring

Showy, evergreen succulent. Tidy rosettes
of fleshy leaves on clustered, basal shoots.
Spikelike panicle of star-shaped, yellow
flowers in spring and summer.

Aethionema schistosum
(Brassicaceae/Cruciferae)

Common name: Stonecress
Height: 4in (10cm)
Spread: 12in (30cm)
Aspect: Sun
Soil: Well-drained
Hardiness: Zone 6
Propagation: Seed,
in spring

Upright, free-flowering; for border front or
rock garden. Narrow, linear, acuminate,
crowded leaves. Tight raceme of 4-petalled,
tiny pink flowers in spring. From Turkey.

Aethionema
'Warley Rose' A.G.M.
(Brassicaceae/Cruciferae)

Common name: Stonecress
Height: 8in (20cm)
Spread: 8in (20cm)
Aspect: Sun
Soil: Well-drained
Hardiness: Zone 7
Propagation: Softwood
cuttings, in spring or autumn

Free-flowering but short-lived dwarf
subshrub. Leaves linear, blue-gray. Small
pink flowers in tight racemes in spring and
early summer. Good wall plant.

Agapanthus
'Blue Imp'
(Alliaceae/Liliaceae)

Common name: African
blue lily
Height: 12in (30cm)
Spread: 8in (20cm)
Aspect: Full sun
Soil: Moist, well-drained,
fertile
Hardiness: Zone 7
Propagation: Division,
in late spring

Choice dwarf form, ideal for small
gardens. Deciduous, strap-shaped, dark
green leaves. Large umbels of deep blue
flowers in late summer.

AGAPANTHUS (Alliaceae/Liliaceae)
African blue lily

A genus of about 10 perennials from southern Africa. They are vigorous, and form large clumps. The foliage is strap-shaped, often arching, and of a deep green; some species are evergreen, but the hybrid forms are all deciduous. The inflorescence is an umbel, which may be rounded, pendent, or intermediate between the two. The individual flowers may be tubular, trumpet-shaped, or bell-shaped, and are usually blue in color, although white forms exist. They are followed by attractive seed heads. The roots are very brittle, so the genus does not transplant well: they should be moved while in growth, if at all. *Agapanthus* are generally fairly hardy, but in cold areas they should be mulched over winter if left in the open ground; they make excellent container plants that can be moved under some protection in winter. The evergreen species, originating in coastal areas, are tender and should have winter protection. All make good flowers for cutting; the seed heads also dry well, and are liked by flower-arrangers. Other Award of Garden Merit forms not included in this selection are *A. africanus* and *A. africanus* 'Albus' (both Zone 9), *A. caulescens* (Zone 7), *A.* 'Loch Hope' (Zone 7), and *A. praecox* 'Variegatus' (Zone 9).

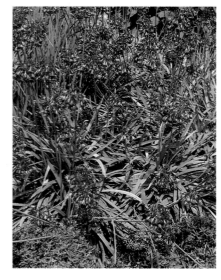

Agapanthus
'Bressingham Blue'
(Alliaceae/Liliaceae)

Common name: African
blue lily
Height: 36in (90cm)
Spread: 18in (45cm)
Aspect: Full sun
Soil: Moist, well-drained,
fertile
Hardiness: Zone 7
Propagation: Division,
in late spring

Very robust cultivar. Trumpet-shaped, intensely amethyst-blue flowers in huge, rounded umbels in mid- to late summer. Straplike, deep green leaves

Agapanthus campanulatus
(Alliaceae/Liliaceae)

Common name: African
blue lily
Height: 4ft (1.2m)
Spread: 18in (45cm)
Aspect: Full sun
Soil: Moist, well-drained,
fertile
Hardiness: Zone 7
Propagation: Division,
in late spring

Vigorous, clump-forming species. Narrow, straplike, gray-green leaves. Bell-shaped flowers of pale or dark blue in rounded umbels on strong stems.

Agapanthus campanulatus
var. *albidus*
(Alliaceae:Liliaceae)

Common name: African
blue lily
Height: To 4ft (1.2m)
Spread: 18in (45cm)
Aspect: Full sun
Soil: Moist, well-drained,
fertile
Hardiness: Zone 7
Propagation: Division,
in late spring

A white-flowered form of the species. Vigorous and clump-forming, with narrow, straplike, gray-green leaves. Rounded umbels of bell-shaped flowers.

Agapanthus
'Lilliput'
(Alliaceae/Liliaceae)

Common name: African
blue lily
Height: 16in (40cm)
Spread: 16in (40cm)
Aspect: Full sun
Soil: Moist, well-drained,
fertile
Hardiness: Zone 7
Propagation: Division,
in late spring

Clump-forming dwarf form, ideal for small gardens. Umbels rounded or intermediate, flowers trumpet-shaped and deep blue, in mid- to late summer.

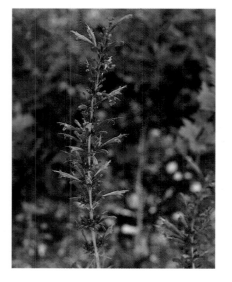

Agastache
'Firebird'
(Labiatae/Lamiaceae)

Common name: Hyssop
Height: 2ft (60cm)
Spread: 1ft (30cm)
Aspect: Full sun
Soil: Well-drained, fertile
Hardiness: Zone 8
Propagation: Semiripe
cuttings, in late summer

A short-lived cultivar with lance-shaped to ovate, gray-green, aromatic leaves. Spikes of tubular, two-lipped, long-lasting, copper-red flowers from midsummer to early autumn.

Agastache foeniculum
(Labiatae/Lamiaceae)

Common names: Giant
hyssop; anise hyssop
Height: 5ft (1.5m)
Spread: 1ft (30cm)
Aspect: Full sun
Soil: Well-drained, fertile
Hardiness: Zone 8
Propagation: Semiripe
cuttings, in late summer

Upright, aniseed-scented plant. Veined, ovate to lance-shaped leaves, downy beneath. Blue flowers with lilac bracts and calyces, in spikes from midsummer to early autumn.

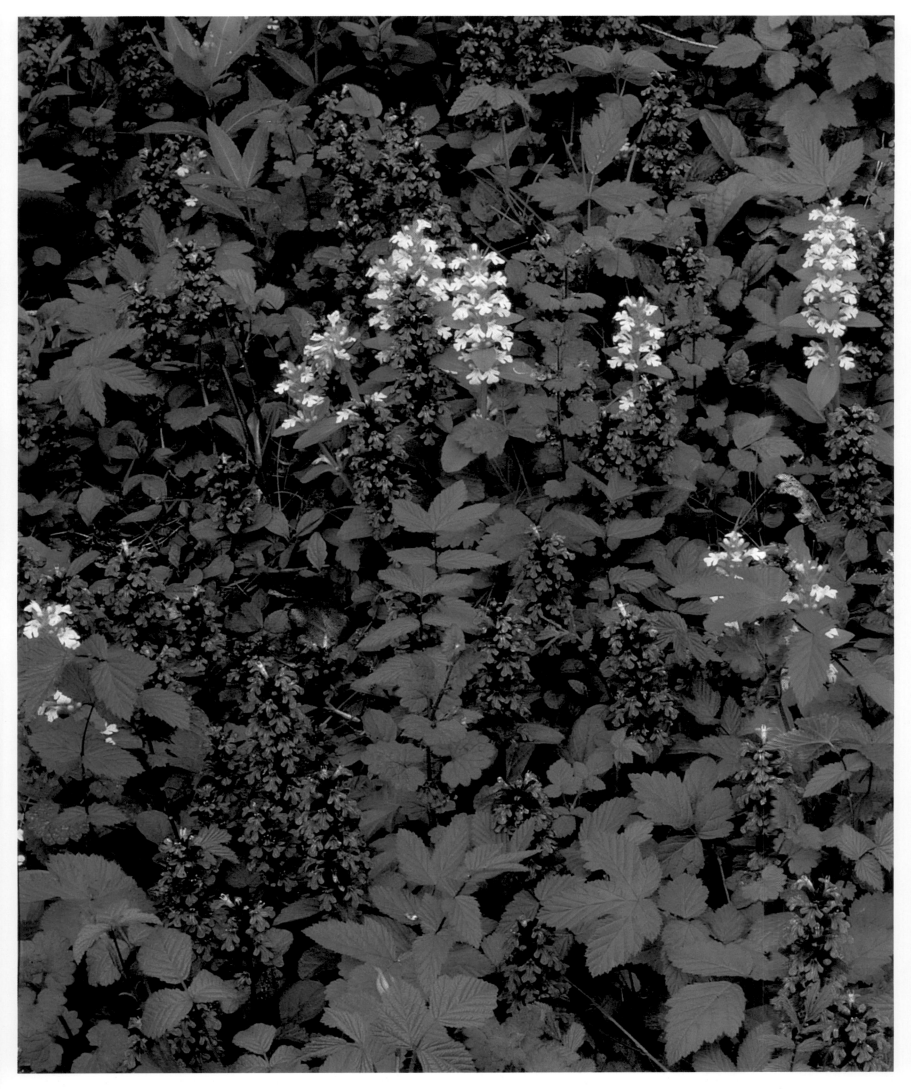

Carpet bugle (Ajuga reptans) *flowering in an oak wood in Monkswood, UK.*

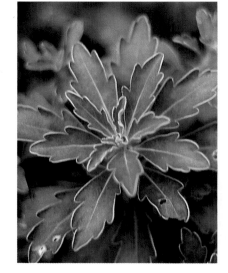

Agastache mexicana
(Labiatae/Lamiaceae)

Common name: Mexican
hyssop
Height: 3ft (90cm)
Spread: 1ft (30cm)
Aspect: Full sun
Soil: Well-drained, fertile
Hardiness: Zone 9
Propagation: Semiripe
cuttings, in early summer

Short-lived, bushy perennial with aromatic
foliage. Ovate to lance-shaped, green
leaves. Flowers rosy-red, in tall spikes,
from mid- to late summer.

Agave americana
'Marginata'
(Agavaceae)

Common name: Century
plant
Height: 6ft (2m)
Spread: 10ft (3m)
Aspect: Full sun
Soil: Sharply drained, acidic
Hardiness: Zone 9
Propagation: Seed, in warmth
in spring; offsets, in spring
or autumn

Succulent from Central America. Rosette of
lance-shaped, gray-green leaves with spiny
yellow edges. May produce panicles of
yellow flowers in summer; monocarpic.

Ajania pacifica
(Asteraceae/Compositae)

Common names: None
Height: 1ft (30cm)
Spread: 3ft (90cm)
Aspect: Full sun
Soil: Well-drained, poor
Hardiness: Zone 6
Propagation: Seed, cuttings,
or division, all in spring

Mound-forming Asian subshrub, spreading
by runners. Leaves ovate, lobed, silky,
gray-green, edged white. Flowers yellow
buttons, in corymbs in autumn.

Ajuga reptans
'Atropurpurea' A.G.M.
(Labiatae: Lamiaceae)

Common names: Carpet
bugle; Bugleweed
Height: 6in (15cm)
Spread: 36in (90cm)
Aspect: Half shade; protect
from midday sun
Soil: Moist
Hardiness: Zone 6
Propagation: Softwood
cuttings, in spring

Rhizomatous, creeping ground cover. Ovate
to oblong-spoon-shaped, dark purple
leaves. Whorled spikes of dark blue flowers
in spring and early summer.

Ajuga reptans
'Burgundy Glow' A.G.M.
(Labiatae/Lamiaceae)

Common names: Carpet
bugle; Bugleweed
Height: 6in (15cm)
Spread: To 36in (90cm)
Aspect: Half shade; protect
from midday sun
Soil: Moist
Hardiness: Zone 6
Propagation: Softwood
cuttings, in spring

Rhizomatous, creeping ground cover. Ovate
to spoon-shaped leaves are silvery green,
flushed dark red. Blue flowers in hairy-
stemmed spikes in spring to early summer.

Ajuga reptans
'Multicolor' syn. 'Rainbow'
(Labiatae/Lamiaceae)

Common names: Carpet
bugle; Bugleweed
Height: 6in (15cm)
Spread: 3ft (1m)
Aspect: Half shade; protect
from midday sun
Soil: Moist
Hardiness: Zone 6
Propagation: Softwood
cuttings, in spring

Rhizomatous, creeping ground cover. Ovate
to spoon-shaped leaves, reddish-bronze and
green, splashed pink and cream. Spikes of
dark blue flowers in spring to early summer.

Albuca altissima
(Hyacinthaceae/Liliaceae)

Common names: None
Height: 18in (45cm)
Spread: 12in (30cm)
Aspect: Full sun
Soil: Well-drained, fertile
Hardiness: Zone 9
Propagation: Seed, in spring;
bulbils, in autumn

Bulbous plant from South Africa. Glabrous,
green, lanceolate leaves. Trumpet-shaped,
white flowers, with a broad green median
stripe, in a loose raceme in late summer.

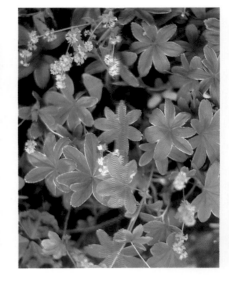

Albuca humilis
(Hyacintheae/Liliaceae)

Common names: None
Height: 4in (10cm)
Spread: 2in (5cm)
Aspect: Sun
Soil: Well-drained, fertile
Hardiness: Zone 7
Propagation: Seed, in warmth
in spring; offsets, in autumn

Bulbous perennial. Leaves narrow, linear,
green, basal. Flowers narrow, white bells,
outer tepals striped green, inner ones tipped
yellow, in late spring and early summer.

Alcea rosea
(Malvaceae)

Common name: Hollyhock
Height: 6ft (2m)
Spread: 3ft (1m)
Aspect: Sun
Soil: Well-drained, fertile
Hardiness: Zone 3
Propagation: Seed, *in situ*
in summer

Well-loved perennial. Leaves rounded,
hairy, lobed, green. Long terminal racemes
of yellow, white, pink, or purple, single
flowers in early and midsummer. Dries well.

Alcea rosea
'Chater's Double'
(Malvaceae)

Common name: Hollyhock
Height: 8ft (2.5m)
Spread: 2ft (60cm)
Aspect: Sun
Soil: Well-drained, fertile
Hardiness: Zone 3
Propagation: Seed, *in situ*
in summer

Race with fully double, peonylike flowers
in many shades in early and midsummer.
Leaves round, hairy, green. Grow as
annuals if hollyhock rust is a problem.

Alchemilla alpina
(Rosaceae)

Common name: Mountain
lady's-mantle
Height: 5in (12cm)
Spread: 20in (50cm)
Aspect: Sun or half shade
Soil: Moist, humus-rich
Hardiness: Zone 3
Propagation: Seed, in spring;
division, in spring or autumn

Creeping, mat-forming, woody perennial.
Kidney-shaped or rounded, lobed, white-
edged green leaves, silver beneath. Straggly
cymes of tiny, yellow flowers in summer.

Alchemilla mollis
A.G.M.
(Rosaceae)

Common name: Lady's-
mantle
Height: 2ft (60cm)
Spread: 3ft (90cm)
Aspect: Sun or half shade
Soil: Moist, humus-rich
Hardiness: Zone 3
Propagation: Seed, in spring;
division, in spring or autumn

Handsome, clump-forming ground cover.
Leaves rounded, lobed, toothed, pale green,
softly hairy. Tiny greenish-yellow flowers
in lax cymes from spring to autumn.

Alisma plantago-aquatica
(Alismataceae)

Common name: Water-
plantain
Height: 30in (75cm)
Spread: 30in (75cm)
Aspect: Sun
Soil: Marginal or in water
6–12in (15–30cm) deep
Hardiness: Zone 6
Propagation: Seed, when ripe;
division, in spring

Rhizomatous, deciduous aquatic marginal.
Basal rosettes of elliptic to lance-shaped,
gray-green leaves. Huge, branched panicle of
tiny white flowers in mid- and late summer.

ALLIUM (Liliaceae)
Onion

Huge genus of some 700 species from a wide range of
habitats in the northern hemisphere. They may be bulbous or
rhizomatous, and are grown for culinary or ornamental
value, or both. All enjoy full sun, and most prefer well-
drained soil. Hardiness varies: many are reliably hardy, but
there are some tender species. Most are deciduous. The
flowerheads are umbels, which may be ovoid, round, or
pendent in shape; individual flowers are cup-, bell-, or star-
shaped. All alliums make good cut flowers, although the
onion odor may not be to everyone's liking, and they are
much used fresh and dried by flower-arrangers. Contact with
the bulbs may cause skin irritation, or exacerbate existing
allergic skin disease. Many alliums are well-behaved garden
plants, and twenty-one carry an Award of Garden Merit as
ornamental plants. Others spread like pernicious weeds: those
that carry bulbils in the flowerhead, such as *A. carinatum*
(Zone 7), *A. vineale* (Zone 5), and *A. scorodoprasum*
(Zone 7), should be avoided in most situations. Other
promiscuous alliums to be treated with caution are
A. canadense (Zone 4), *A. ampeloprasum* var. *bulbiferum*
(Zone 6), *A. paradoxum* (Zone 8), and *A. roseum* (Zone 8).

Allium angulosum
(Alliaceae/Liliaceae)

Common name: Mouse garlic
Height: 18in (45cm)
Spread: 12in (30cm)
Aspect: Sun
Soil: Moist, fertile
Hardiness: Zone 5
Propagation: Seed, in spring;
offsets, in autumn

Bulbous onion with linear to straplike, rich, shiny, green basal leaves, sharply keeled underneath. Flowers are pale lilac, in hemispherical umbels on stout stems.

Allium carinatum
subsp. *pulchellum* A.G.M.
(Alliaceae/Liliaceae)

Common name: Keeled garlic
Height: 24in (60cm)
Spread: 4in (10cm)
Aspect: Sun
Soil: Well-drained, fertile
Hardiness: Zone 7
Propagation: Seed, in spring;
offsets, in autumn

Bulbous evergreen perennial with midgreen, linear, basal leaves. Rich purple, bell-shaped flowers in elongated, dense umbel. Slowly forms clumps. From southern Europe.

Allium cernuum
(Alliaceae/Liliaceae)

Common name: Nodding onion
Height: 24in (60cm)
Spread: 4in (10cm)
Aspect: Sun
Soil: Well-drained, fertile
Hardiness: Zone 6
Propagation: Seed, in spring;
offsets, in autumn

An easy-going, vigorous, bulbous plant with deep pink, bell-shaped flowers in a drooping umbel. The leaves are narrow, dark green basal straps.

Allium cristophii
A.G.M.
(Alliaceae/Liliaceae)

Common name: Star-of-Persia
Height: 24in (60cm)
Spread: 8in (20cm)
Aspect: Sun
Soil: Well-drained, fertile
Hardiness: Zone 5
Propagation: Seed, in spring;
offsets, in autumn

Popular bulbous perennial. Leaves basal, straplike, gray-green. Bears purplish-pink, star-shaped flowers with a metallic sheen in large, spherical umbels in early summer.

Allium flavum
A.G.M.
(Alliaceae/Liliaceae)

Common name: Yellow onion
Height: 16in (40cm)
Spread: 4in (10cm)
Aspect: Sun
Soil: Well-drained, fertile
Hardiness: Zone 7
Propagation: Seed, in spring;
offsets, in autumn

Very variable, bulbous onion. Leaves strap-shaped, glaucous, green. Up to 60 bright yellow, bell-shaped, pendent flowers in a loose umbel in summer.

Allium giganteum
A.G.M.
(Alliaceae/Liliaceae)

Common name: Giant onion
Height: 6ft (2m)
Spread: 8in (20cm)
Aspect: Sun
Soil: Well-drained, fertile
Hardiness: Zone 5
Propagation: Seed, in spring;
offsets, in autumn

Bulbous allium with pale green, straplike basal leaves that wither before flowering. Large, dense umbel of up to 60 lilac-pink, star-shaped flowers in summer.

Allium
'Globemaster' A.G.M.
(Alliaceae/Liliaceae)

Common names: None
Height: 32in (80cm)
Spread: 8in (20cm)
Aspect: Sun
Soil: Well-drained, fertile
Hardiness: Zone 7
Propagation: Offsets,
in autumn

Very desirable hybrid with strap-shaped, gray-green basal leaves. Numerous dark violet, star-shaped flowers in an umbel 6–8in (15–20cm) across, in summer.

Allium karataviense
A.G.M.
(Alliaceae/Liliaceae)

Common name: Turkestan onion
Height: 10in (25cm)
Spread: 4in (10cm)
Aspect: Sun
Soil: Well-drained, fertile
Hardiness: Zone 4
Propagation: Seed, in spring;
offsets, in autumn

Bulbous species from Central Asia. Paired, elliptic, gray-green or gray-purple, horizontal basal leaves. Large umbel of many pale pink, star-shaped flowers in summer.

Allium moly
A.G.M.
(Alliaceae/Liliaceae)

Common names: Golden
garlic; lily leek
Height: 10in (25cm)
Spread: 4in (10cm)
Aspect: Sun or half shade
Soil: Well-drained, fertile
Hardiness: Zone 3
Propagation: Seed, in spring;
offsets, in autumn

Bulbous woodland plant with gray-green,
lance-shaped basal leaves. The umbel is
dense, with up to 30 star-shaped golden-
yellow flowers in summer. From Europe.

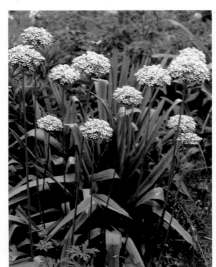

Allium nigrum
(Alliaceae/Liliaceae)

Common names: None
Height: 14in (35cm)
Spread: 3in (8cm)
Aspect: Sun
Soil: Well-drained, fertile
Hardiness: Zone 4
Propagation: Seed, in spring;
offsets, in autumn

Bulbous Mediterranean perennial with gray-
green, lance-shaped, basal leaves. Off-white,
cup-shaped flowers with prominent, dark
green ovaries, in a flattened umbel, summer.

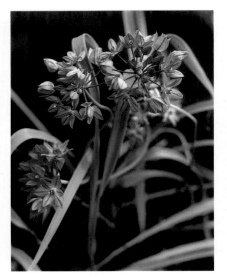

Allium oreophilum
A.G.M.
(Alliaceae/Liliaceae)

Common names: None
Height: 8in (20cm)
Spread: 2in (5cm)
Aspect: Sun
Soil: Well-drained, fertile
Hardiness: Zone 4
Propagation: Seed, in spring;
offsets, in autumn

Bulbous perennial. Leaves basal, linear,
mid-green. Umbel very loose, with some
15 long-lasting, bell-shaped, strong pink
flowers, each tepal with a dark midrib.

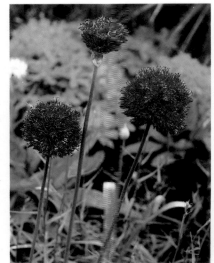

Allium
'Purple Sensation' A.G.M.
(Alliaceae/Liliaceae)

Common names: None
Height: 36in (1m)
Spread: 3in (8cm)
Aspect: Sun
Soil: Well-drained, fertile
Hardiness: Zone 2
Propagation: Offsets
in autumn

Free-flowering, bulbous hybrid of unknown
parentage. Basal, gray-green, strap-shaped
leaves. Tight, spherical umbel of over 50
star-shaped, dark violet flowers in summer.

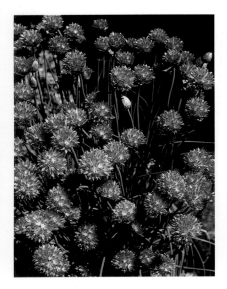

Allium schoenoprasum
'Forescate'
(Alliaceae/Liliaceae)

Common name: Chives
Height: 24in (60cm)
Spread: 3in (8cm)
Aspect: Sun
Soil: Well-drained, fertile
Hardiness: Zone 1
Propagation: Offsets,
in autumn

Rhizomatous allium grown for its edible
leaves, which are hollow, dark green
cylinders, and for its dense umbels of
bright pinkish-purple flowers in summer.

Allium schubertii
(Alliaceae/Liliaceae)

Common names: None
Height: 24in (60cm)
Spread: 8in (20cm)
Aspect: Sun
Soil: Well, drained, fertile
Hardiness: Zone 5
Propagation: Seed, in spring;
offsets, in autumn

Bulbous allium. The straplike, bright green
basal leaves die back before early-summer
flowering. Pale lilac flowers have pedicels of
unequal length, so umbel appears shaggy.

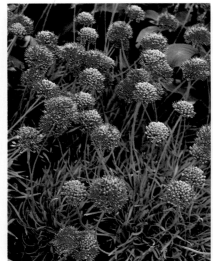

Allium senescens
(Alliaceae/Liliaceae)

Common names: None
Height: 24in (60cm)
Spread: 2in (5cm)
Aspect: Sun
Soil: Well-drained, fertile
Hardiness: Zone 1
Propagation: Seed, in spring;
offsets, in autumn

Vigorous, bulbous perennial. Strap-shaped,
short, midgreen basal leaves. Pink, cup-
shaped, long-lasting flowers in a dense
umbel of 30 in early and midsummer.

Allium sphaerocephalon
(Alliaceae/Liliaceae)

Common name: Ballhead
onion
Height: 36in (90cm)
Spread: 3in (8cm)
Aspect: Sun
Soil: well-drained, fertile
Hardiness: Zone 1
Propagation: Seed, in spring;
offsets, in autumn

Bulbous allium. Leaves are basal, linear,
midgreen. Flowers are bell-shaped, dark
pink or red-brown, in dense, ovoid umbel
in summer. Bulbils may form in the umbel.

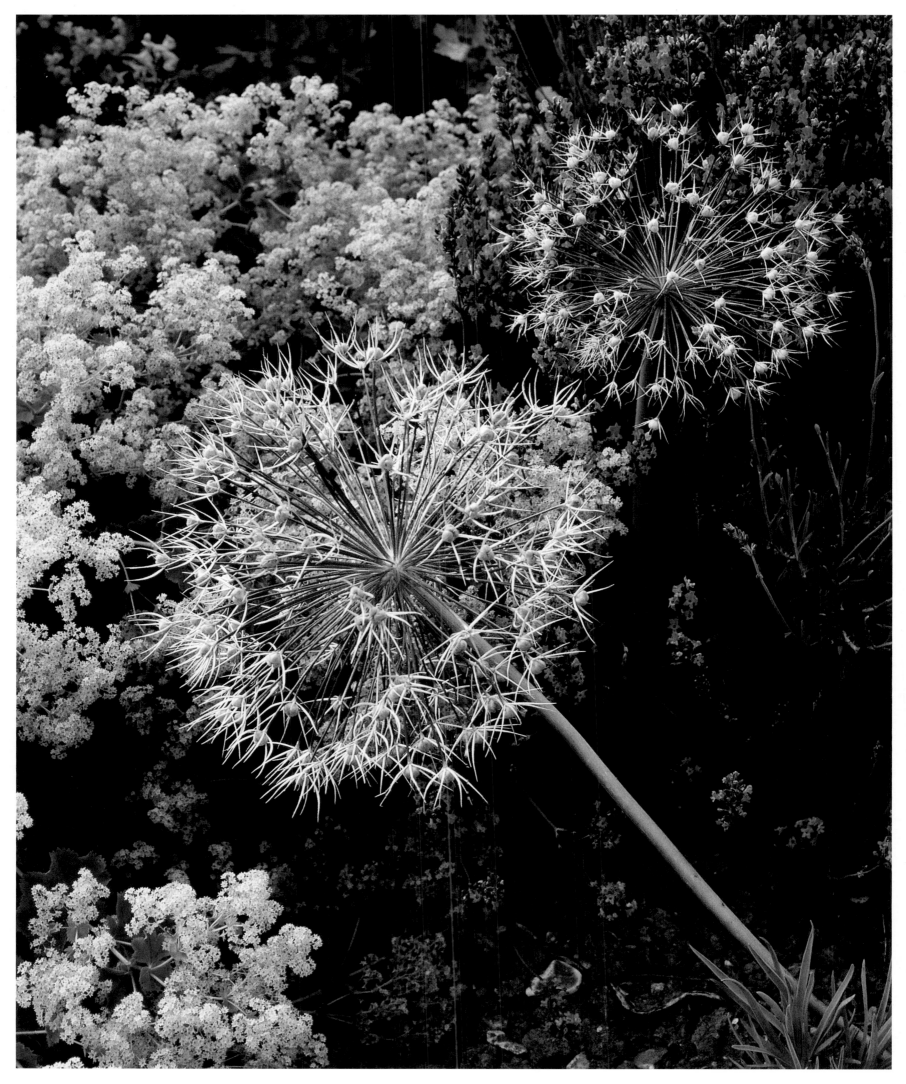

The rounded umbels of Star-of-Persia (Allium christophii) *against Lady's-mantle* (Alchemilla mollis) *and Lavandula.*

Allium unifolium
(Alliaceae/Liliaceae)

Common name: One-leaved
onion
Height: 10in (25cm)
Spread: 2in (5cm)
Aspect: Sun
Soil: Well-drained, fertile
Hardiness: Zone 4
Propagation: Seed, in spring;
offsets, in autumn

Bulbous North American perennial. Short,
linear, gray-green basal leaves die back
before flowering in spring. Flowers clear
pink, large, open, bell-shaped, in umbels.

ALOES with an A.G.M.

A. aristata (Zone 9)

A. bakeri (Zone 10)

A. melanocantha (Zone 9)

A. rauhii (Zone 10)

A. somaliensis (Zone 10)

A. 'Variegata' (Zone 9)

A. vera (Zone 8)

ADDITIONAL ALLIUMS
with an A.G.M.

A. 'Beau Regard' (Zone 8)

A. beesianum (Zone 8)

A. caeruleum (Zone 7)

A. carinatum subsp. pulchellum
(Zone 7)

A. 'Gladiator' (Zone 7)

A. hollandicum (Zone 8)

A. hollandicum 'Purple Sensation'
(Zone 8)

A. insubricum (Zone 8)

**Alonsoa warscewiczii
A.G.M.**
(Scrophulariaceae)

Common names: Heartleaf
muskflower
Height: 2ft (60cm)
Spread: 1ft (30cm)
Aspect: Full sun
Soil: Well-drained, fertile
Hardiness: Zone 9
Propagation: Seed, in warmth
in spring or late summer

Evergreen, bushy subshrub. Leaves ovate to
lance-shaped, toothed, dark green. Spurred,
deep pink flowers in loose racemes, summer
to autumn. Treat as annual in cold areas.

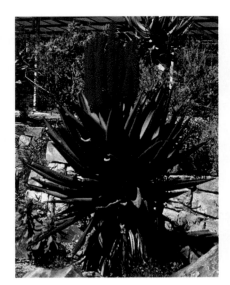

Aloe ferox
(Aloeaceae/Liliaceae)

Common name: Cape aloe
Height: 10ft (3m)
Spread: 5ft (1.5m)
Aspect: Full sun
Soil: Well-drained, fertile
Hardiness: Zone 9
Propagation: Seed, when ripe;
offsets, in late spring,
early summer

Evergreen succulent with a rosette of dull-
green, fleshy, lance-shaped leaves with red
teeth. Large, erect panicle of scarlet flowers
in summer. Conservatory plant in cold areas.

**Alopecurus pratensis
'Aureovariegatus'**
(Graminae/Poaceae)

Common name: Meadow
foxtail grass
Height: 4ft (1.2m)
Spread: 2ft (60cm)
Aspect: Sun or half shade
Soil: Well-drained, fertile
Hardiness: Zone 5
Propagation: Seed, when ripe;
division, in spring or autumn

Perennial grass that clumps up rapidly.
Leaves basal, linear, striped yellow and
green. Long, dense panicles of green or
purple spikelets in spring to midsummer.

Aloe tenuior
(Aloeaceae/Liliaceae)

Common names: None
Height: 10ft (3m)
Spread: 2ft (60cm)
Aspect: Full sun
Soil: Well-drained, fertile
Hardiness: Zone 9
Propagation: Seed, when ripe;
offsets in late spring to
early summer

Evergreen, succulent perennial from South
Africa. Forms a rosette of linear, glaucous,
toothed leaves. Bears orange-yellow
flowers in a panicle in summer.

Alstroemeria aurea
(Alstroemeriaceae)

Common names: None
Height: 3ft (1m)
Spread: 18in (45cm)
Aspect: Sun or partial shade
Soil: Moist, well-drained,
fertile
Hardiness: Zone 7
Propagation: Seed, when ripe;
division, in spring or autumn

Tuberous perennial. Leaves linear to lance-
shaped, midgreen. Terminal 3- to 7-rayed
umbels, each with up to 3 yellow or orange
flowers, in summer. Can be invasive.

ALSTROEMERIA (Alstroemeriaceae)
Peruvian Lily

A genus of some 50 species of perennials from South America, found in mountains and grasslands. *Alstroemeria* are tuberous, and will spread rapidly to form large clumps; they can even become invasive if the conditions suit them. The tubers should be handled carefully, and are best left undisturbed once planted. They have extremely handsome flowers, and a long flowering season, making them valuable border plants. They also make excellent cut flowers, and are popular with flower-arrangers and grown commercially for florists. A few species are tender, but many are marginally hardy in most areas, and can be grown outside if they are given a sunny spot and covered with a dry mulch through winter. Contact with the foliage may cause exacerbation of a skin allergy. The tubers should be planted 8in (20cm) deep. Thirty forms have an Award of Garden Merit, including the popular Ligtu Hybrids, a name covering many crosses, principally of *A. ligtu* and *A. haemantha*. Also holding an A.G.M. are the 'Princess' strain: this is a registered name, and the botanically preferred name is given as a synonym in the panel at right; the plants are most likely to be sold under the former, but may be found in books under the latter.

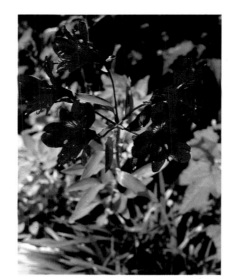

Alstroemeria
Ligtu Hybrids A.G.M.
(Alstroemeriaceae)

Common name: Peruvian lily
Height: 3ft (1m)
Spread: 18in (45cm)
Aspect: Sun or half shade
Soil: Moist, well-drained, fertile
Hardiness: Zone 7
Propagation: Seed, when ripe; division, in spring or autumn

Vigorous hybrids with a wide range of colors, such as this deep red. Leaves linear to lance-shaped, midgreen. Flowers in terminal, 3- to 7-rayed racemes, summer.

Alstroemeria
Ligtu Hybrids A.G.M.
(Alstroemeriaceae)

Common name: Peruvian lily
Height: 3ft (1m)
Spread: 18in (45cm)
Aspect: Sun or half shade
Soil: Moist, well-drained, fertile
Hardiness: Zone 7
Propagation: Seed, when ripe; division, in spring or autumn

Two-tone yellow and cream color break in the Ligtu Hybrid range. Leaves linear to lance-shaped, midgreen. Terminal, 3- to 7-rayed racemes of flowers in summer.

Alstroemeria psittacina
(Alstroemeriaceae)

Common name: Peruvian lily
Height: 3ft (1m)
Spread: 18in (45cm)
Aspect: Sun or half shade
Soil: Moist, well-drained, fertile
Hardiness: Zone 7
Propagation: Seed, when ripe; division, in spring or autumn

Tuberous species with gray-green, linear to lance-shaped leaves. Flowers in 4- to 6-rayed panicles, each ray having up to 3 green and red flowers, in summer.

Alstroemeria
'Solent Wings'
(Alstroemeriaceae)

Common name: Peruvian lily
Height: 3ft (1m)
Spread: 18in (45cm)
Aspect: Sun or half shade
Soil: Moist, well-drained, fertile
Hardiness: Zone 7
Propagation: Division, in spring or autumn

Tuberous, hybrid Peruvian lily, with linear to lance-shaped leaves of gray-green. Panicles of rosy-red flowers, edged with white, in summer.

Alstroemeria
'White Apollo'
(Alstroemeriaceae)

Common name: Peruvian lily
Height: 3ft (1m)
Spread: 18in (45cm)
Aspect: Sun or half shade
Soil: Moist, well-drained,
fertile
Hardiness: Zone 7
Propagation: Division,
in spring or autumn

Very handsome hybrid with terminal
clusters of pure white, orange-throated
flowers, streaked brown, in summer.
Leaves linear to lance-shaped.

Althaea cannabina
(Malvaceae)

Common name: Mallow
Height: 6ft (2m)
Spread: 30in (75cm)
Aspect: Any, but best in sun
Soil: Moist, well-drained,
fertile
Hardiness: Zone 4
Propagation: Seed, in summer

Erect, woody-stemmed plant for the larger
garden. Leaves dark green, paler beneath,
hairy, round, lobed. Small, pink flowers in
axillary clusters, summer to early autumn.

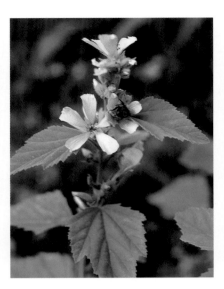

Althaea officinalis
(Malvaceae)

Common name:
Marshmallow
Height: 6ft (2m)
Spread: 5ft (1.5m)
Aspect: Any, but best in sun
Soil: Moist, well-drained,
fertile
Hardiness: Zone 3
Propagation: Seed, in summer

Erect plant, sometimes grown for culinary
use. Leaves lobed, toothed, oval, pointed,
softly hairy, green. Flowers pale pink, in
terminal or axillary clusters. From Europe.

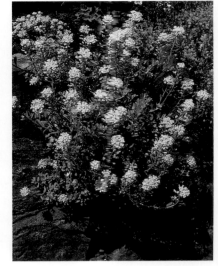

Alyssum montanum
'Berggold'
(Brassicaceae/Cruciferae)

Common name: Madwort
Height: 6in (15cm)
Spread: 24in (60cm) or more
Aspect: Sun
Soil: Well-drained,
humus-rich
Hardiness: Zone 6
Propagation: Seed, in spring
or autumn; cuttings, in
summer

Prostrate, mat-forming evergreen with gray,
oblong-obovate leaves in rosettes. Bears
racemes of yellow, fragrant flowerheads in
early summer. An excellent wall plant.

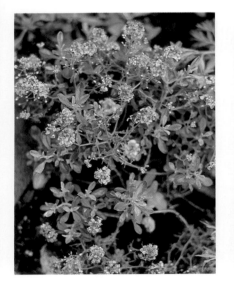

Alyssum spinosum
'Roseum' A.G.M.
(Brassicaceae/Cruciferae)

Common names: None
Height: 16in (40cm)
Spread: 20in (50cm)
Aspect: Sun
Soil: Well-drained,
humus-rich
Hardiness: Zone 6
Propagation: Seed, in autumn
or spring; cuttings, in summer

Rounded, compact, evergreen subshrub;
spiny and densely branched. Leaves small,
obovate, gray-green. Flowers cross-shaped,
4-petalled, pale or dark pink, in racemes.

Amaryllis belladonna
(Amaryllidaceae)

Common name: Belladonna
lily
Height: 24in (60cm)
Spread: 4in (10cm)
Aspect: Full sun
Soil: Well-drained
Hardiness: Zone 9
Propagation: Seed, in warmth
when ripe; offsets, in spring

Bulbous perennial. Umbels of funnel-shaped,
scented, purplish-pink flowers in autumn;
strap-shaped, fleshy leaves in early winter.
Protect from frost. Needs a dry dormancy.

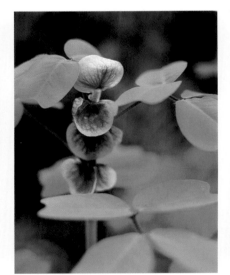

Amicia zygomeris
(Leguminosae/Papilionaceae)

Common names: None
Height: 6ft (2m)
Spread: 4ft (1.2m)
Aspect: Full sun
Soil: Well-drained, fertile
Hardiness: Zone 9
Propagation: Seed, in warmth
in spring; cuttings, in spring
and summer

Unusual perennial, not for a small garden.
Leaves inversely heart-shaped, large, with
pale green stipules. Flowers cream with
purple keels, pealike, in autumn.

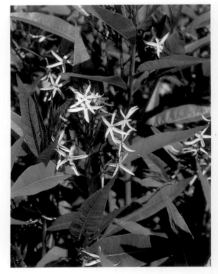

Amsonia tabernaemontana
(Apocynaceae)

Common names: None
Height: 24in (60cm)
Spread: 18in (45cm)
Aspect: Sun
Soil: Moist, well-drained
Hardiness: Zone 8
Propagation: Seed or division,
in spring

Clump-forming perennial. Small, ovate or
elliptic, matt, dark green leaves. Pale blue
flowers in dense panicles from spring to
midsummer. Milky sap may irritate skin.

Anagallis monellii
A.G.M.
(Primulaceae)

Common name: Blue
pimpernel
Height: 8in (20cm)
Spread: 16in (40cm)
Aspect: Full sun
Soil: Moist, well-drained,
fertile
Hardiness: Zone 7
Propagation: Seed or division,
both in spring

Sprawling, short-lived perennial with midgreen, lance-shaped to elliptic, stalkless
leaves. Open, 5-petalled, deep blue flowers
in summer. From southeast Europe.

Anaphalis triplinervis
A.G.M.
(Asteraceae/Compositae)

Common name: Pearly
everlasting
Height: 3ft (90cm)
Spread: 2ft (60cm)
Aspect: Sun or half shade
Soil: Well-drained, fertile,
humus-rich
Hardiness: Zone 5
Propagation: Seed or division,
both in spring

Perennial with spoon-shaped, pale gray-
green leaves, white-woolly underneath.
Corymbs of yellow flowers with white
bracts in summer. From S.W. China.

Anchusa azurea
(Boraginaceae)

Common name: Alkanet
Height: 5ft (1.5m)
Spread: 2ft (60cm)
Aspect: Full sun
Soil: Moist, well-drained,
fertile
Hardiness: Zone 3
Propagation: Seed or basal
cuttings, both in spring

Clump-forming, Mediterranean perennial.
Leaves linear to lance-shaped, hairy, dark
green. Panicles of open, gentian-blue
flowers in early summer.

Anchusa azurea
'Feltham Pride'
(Boraginaceae)

Common name: Alkanet
Height: 3ft (90cm)
Spread: 2ft (60cm)
Aspect: Full sun
Soil: Moist, well-drained,
fertile
Hardiness: Zone 3
Propagation: Basal cuttings,
in spring; root cuttings,
in winter

A compact cultivar, sometimes grown as a
biennial, with linear to lance-shaped leaves
of mid- to dark green. Clear, bright blue
flowers in early summer.

Anchusa
'Loddon Royalist' A.G.M.
(Boraginaceae)

Common name: Alkanet
Height: 3ft (90cm)
Spread: 2ft (60cm)
Aspect: Full sun
Soil: Moist, well-drained,
fertile
Hardiness: Zone 3
Propagation: Basal cuttings,
in spring; root cuttings,
in winter

Sturdy hybrid, but it may still need to be
staked in exposed areas. Leaves linear to
lance-shaped, midgreen. Panicle of deep
blue flowers in early summer.

ANEMONE (Ranunculaceae)
Windflower

This large genus contains some 120 species of perennials,
with open, saucer- to cup-shaped flowers, with a prominent
boss of stamens, and lobed, dissected foliage. They originate
in a wide range of habitats across both the northern and
southern hemispheres, and they vary widely in their character
and in cultural requirements as a result. Some are good
specimens for the border, others are more suitable for rock
gardens or naturalizing in woodlands. For the purposes of
cultivation requirements, anemones can be divided into three
broad groups:

Spring-flowering, tuberous or rhizomatous species that come
from Alpine or woodland areas.

Spring- or early summer-flowering, tuberous species from
the Mediterranean and regions of Central Asia that have
hot, dry summers.

Summer- or autumn-flowering, fibrous-rooted, tall,
herbaceous species from open sites.

All these types are covered here, but the third category will
form the main group. Some anemones are poisonous, and the
sap of all may cause skin irritation. All are unfortunately
prone to powdery mildew, and slug damage.

Anemone blanda
A.G.M.
(Ranunculaceae)

Common name: Windflower
Height: 6in (15cm)
Spread: 6in (15cm)
Aspect: Sun or half shade
Soil: Well-drained,
humus-rich
Hardiness: Zone 5
Propagation: Seed, when ripe;
offsets, in summer

Tuberous, woodland perennial from
Turkey. Leaves 3-palmate, triangular or
oval, deep green. Flowers solitary, single,
with deep blue tepals, in spring.

This lovely white form was a "sport" from a red-flowered variety in the garden of M. Jobert in 1858.

Anemone blanda
'White Splendour' A.G.M.
(Ranunculaceae)

Common name: Greek
anemone
Height: 6in (15cm)
Spread: 6in (15cm)
Aspect: Full sun or half shade
Soil: Well-drained,
humus-rich
Hardiness: Zone 5
Propagation: Seed, when ripe;
offsets, in summer

Spring flowers have pure white tepals with
pinkish reverse. Leaves oval or triangular,
3-palmate, dark green. One of a few
A.G.M. cultivars of this species.

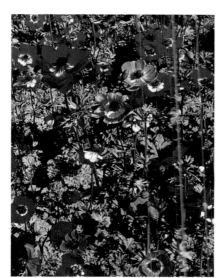

Anemone coronaria
De Caen Group
(Ranunculaceae)

Common names: Florists'
poppy anemone; windflower
Height: 18in (45cm)
Spread: 6in (15cm)
Aspect: Full sun
Soil: Porous, sandy
Hardiness: Zone 8
Propagation: Seed, when ripe;
offsets, in summer

Clones with single, long-stemmed flowers
with 5–8 tepals in a wide range of colors.
Oval, 3-palmate, midgreen basal and stem
leaves. Tuberous; keep dry after flowering.

Anemone coronoria
St. Brigid Group
(Ranunculaceae)

Common names: Florists'
poppy anemone; windflower
Height: 18in (45cm)
Spread: 6in (15cm)
Aspect: Full sun
Soil: Porous
Hardiness: Zone 8
Propagation: Seed, when ripe;
offsets, in summer

Leaves midgreen, 3-palmate, round or
oval. Solitary, fully double flowers in a
wide range of colors, on long stems in
spring. Tuberous; keep dry after flowering.

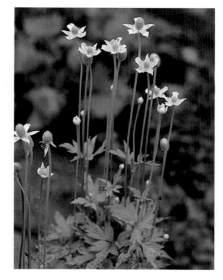

Anemone cylindrica
(Ranunculaceae)

Common names: None
Height: 24in (60cm)
Spread: 4in (10cm)
Aspect: Half shade
Soil: Well-drained,
humus-rich
Hardiness: Zone 6
Propagation: Seed, when ripe

Fibrous-rooted, cushion-forming, rosetted
perennial. Leaves linear to elliptic, glossy
green. Flowers in early spring, white with
a yellow-green eye, on long stems.

Anemone hupehensis
'Hadspen Abundance'
A.G.M. (Ranunculaceae)

Common name: Dwarf
Japanese anemone
Height: 36in (90cm)
Spread: 16in (40cm)
Aspect: Sun or half shade
Soil: Moist, fertile,
humus-rich
Hardiness: Zone 6
Propagation: Division,
in spring or autumn

Fibrous-rooted, suckering perennial. Oval,
3-palmate, long-stalked, basal, dark green
leaves. Umbels of up to 15 flowers, each
with 5 or 6 deep pink tepals, in autumn.

Anemone hupehensis var.
japonica 'Prinz Heinrich'
A.G.M. (Ranunculaceae)

Common name: Japanese
anemone
Height: 36in (90cm)
Spread: 16in (40cm)
Aspect: Sun or half shade
Soil: Moist, fertile,
humus-rich
Hardiness: Zone 6
Propagation: Division,
in spring or autumn

Fibrous-rooted, suckering hybrid. Leaves
oval, 3-palmate, basal, dark green. Umbels
of up to 15 flowers, each with 5 or 6 dark
pink tepals, in mid- to late summer.

Anemone x _hybrida_
'Honorine Jobert' A.G.M.
(Ranunculaceae)

Common name: Japanese
anemone
Height: 4ft (1.2m)
Spread: Indefinite
Aspect: Sun or half shade
Soil: Moist, fertile,
humus-rich
Hardiness: Zone 6
Propagation: Division,
in spring or autumn

Vigorous, suckering, woody hybrid. Oval,
3-palmate, toothed, midgreen leaves.
Umbel of up to 20 pure white flowers, the
reverse pinkish, in autumn.

Anemone x _hybrida_
'Elegans'
(Ranunculaceae)

Common name: Japanese
anemone
Height: 4ft (1.2m)
Spread: Indefinite
Aspect: Sun or half shade
Soil: Moist, well-drained,
humus-rich
Hardiness: Zone 6
Propagation: Division,
in spring or autumn

A cloned selection of this popular, vigorous
plant. Leaves 3-palmate, oval, midgreen.
Single pink flowers in umbels of up to 20
over a long period in autumn.

Anemone x *hybrida*
'Margarete'
(Ranunculaceae)

Common name: Japanese
anemone
Height: 36in (90cm)
Spread: Indefinite
Aspect: Sun or half shade
Soil: Moist, fertile,
humus-rich
Hardiness: Zone 6
Propagation: Division,
in spring or autumn

A vigorous, cloned selection of this
popular perennial. Umbels of semidouble,
deep pink flowers in autumn. Leaves oval,
3-palmate, midgreen.

Anemone x *hybrida*
'Pamina'
(Ranunculaceae)

Common name: Japanese
anemone
Height: 32in (80cm)
Spread: Indefinite
Aspect: Sun or half shade
Soil: Moist, fertile,
humus-rich
Hardiness: Zone 6
Propagation: Division,
in spring or autumn

Cloned selection, slightly smaller than
most, with oval, 3-palmate, midgreen
leaves and umbels of single, lilac-pink
flowers with rounded tepals.

Anemone x *hybrida*
'Whirlwind'
(Ranunculaceae)

Common name: Japanese
anemone
Height: 4ft (1.2m)
Spread: Indefinite
Aspect: Sun or half shade
Soil: Moist, fertile,
humus-rich
Hardiness: Zone 6
Propagation: Division,
in spring or autumn

Cloned selection of the popular Japanese
anemone with umbels of semidouble, white
flowers, sometimes with a center of
greenish, whorled tepals.

Anemone x *lesseri*
(Ranunculaceae)

Common names: None
Height: 16in (40cm)
Spread: 12in (30cm)
Aspect: Sun or half shade
Soil: Well-drained,
humus-rich
Hardiness: Zone 3
Propagation: Seed, when ripe

Fibrous-rooted hybrid. Large, round, 3- to
5-palmate leaves; leaflets lobed, toothed.
Reddish-pink, purple, yellow, or white
flowers, singly or in umbels, in summer.

Anemone leveillei
(Ranunculaceae)

Common names: None
Height: 24in (60cm)
Spread: 12in (30cm)
Aspect: Half shade
Soil: Moist, humus-rich
Hardiness: Zone 6
Propagation: Seed, when ripe

Fibrous-rooted perennial. Leaves kidney-
shaped, 3-lobed, deeply divided, toothed,
midgreen. Flowers white, with 8 tepals, the
reverse hairy and pink, in summer.

Anemone multifida
(Ranunculaceae)

Common names: None
Height: 12in (30cm)
Spread: 6in (15cm)
Aspect: Sun or half shade
Soil: Well-drained,
humus-rich
Hardiness: Zone 2
Propagation: Seed, when ripe

Sturdy, vigorous, rhizomatous perennial.
Handsome, rounded, palmate, midgreen
stem and basal leaves. Umbels of 2 or 3
creamy yellow flowers with 5–9 tepals.

Anemone nemorosa
A.G.M.
(Ranunculaceae)

Common names: Windflower;
wood anemone
Height: 6in (15cm)
Spread: 12in (30cm) or more
Aspect: Half shade
Soil: Moist, well-drained,
humus-rich
Hardiness: Zone 5
Propagation: Seed, when ripe;
offsets, in autumn

Creeping, rhizomatous woodlander. Leaves
round, 3-palmate; leaflets lobed and toothed,
midgreen. Flowers are solitary, white, with
6–8 tepals, in spring and early summer.

Anemone nemorosa
'Robinsoniana' A.G.M.
(Ranunculaceae)

Common names: Windflower;
wood anemone
Height: 6in (15cm)
Spread: 12in (30cm)
Aspect: Half shade
Soil: Well-drained,
humus-rich
Hardiness: Zone 5
Propagation: Division,
in spring or autumn

Cloned selection of the species, with large,
pale lavender-pink flowers with creamy
gray undersides. One of a few cultivars of
A. nemorosa to carry an A.G.M.

Anemone rivularis
(Ranunculaceae)

Common names: None
Height: 36in (90cm)
Spread: 12in (30cm)
Aspect: Sun or half shade
Soil: Well-drained,
humus-rich
Hardiness: Zone 7
Propagation: Seed, when ripe

Fibrous-rooted, clump-forming anemone.
Long-stalked, round, 3-palmate or 3-lobed,
hairy, toothed basal and stem leaves. Umbels
of white flowers in spring and autumn.

Anemonella thalictroides
(Ranunculaceae)

Common name: Rue
anemone
Height: 4in (10cm)
Spread: 12in (30cm)
Aspect: Half shade
Soil: Moist, well-drained,
humus-rich
Hardiness: Zone 4
Propagation: Seed, when ripe

Clump-forming, tuberous woodlander. Blue-
green, fernlike, 3-ternate leaves. Pale pink,
cup-shaped flowers in loose umbels, spring
to early summer. Hates waterlogged soil.

Anemonopsis macrophylla
(Ranunculaceae)

Common names: None
Height: 32in (80cm)
Spread: 18in (45cm)
Aspect: Half shade
Soil: Moist, acidic,
humus-rich
Hardiness: Zone 4
Propagation: Seed, when ripe;
division, in summer

Woodlander with glossy leaves, 3-ternate;
toothed lobes ovate-oblong. Loose racemes
of nodding, cup-shaped flowers, sepals lilac
and petals violet, mid- to late summer.

Angelica archangelica
(Apiaceae/Umbelliferae)

Common name: Garden
angelica
Height: 6ft (2m)
Spread: 3ft (1m)
Aspect: Full or half shade
Soil: Moist, deep, fertile,
humus-rich
Hardiness: Zone 4
Propagation: Seed, when ripe;
plant out when small

Herbaceous, monocarpic herb. Leaves midgreen, 2- or 3-pinnate, with lance-shaped,
toothed leaflets. Umbels of greenish-yellow
flowers on stiff stems, early to midsummer.

Angelica gigas
(Apiaceae/Umbelliferae)

Common names: None
Height: to 6ft (2m)
Spread: 4ft (1.2m)
Aspect: Full or half shade
Soil: Moist, deep, fertile,
humus-rich
Hardiness: Zone 4
Propagation: Seed, when ripe

Large perennial for damp sites. Leaves very
large, 3-ternate; leaflets lobed, diamond-
ovate. Dense umbel of purple flowers and
bracts with red stems, summer to autumn.

Anigozanthos manglesii
A.G.M.
(Haemodoraceae)

Common names: None
Height: 4ft (1.2m)
Spread: 2ft (60cm)
Aspect: Full sun
Soil: Moist, well-drained,
sandy, humus-rich
Hardiness: Zone 9
Propagation: Seed, in warmth
when ripe

Clump-forming evergreen. Leaves lance- to
strap-shaped, gray-green. Flowers 2-lipped,
tubular, yellow-green, with dense, pale green
hairs outside, red inside, spring to summer.

Anisodontea capensis
(Malvaceae)

Common names: None
Height: 36in (90cm)
Spread: 32in (80cm)
Aspect: Full sun
Soil: Well-drained, fertile
Hardiness: Zone 9
Propagation: Seed, in warmth
in spring; semiripe cuttings,
in summer

Woody evergreen. Leaves ovate-triangular,
hairy, midgreen, shallowly lobed. Flowers
solitary or in racemes of 2 or 3, pale pink,
cup-shaped, in summer to autumn.

Anomatheca laxa
var. *alba*
(Iridaceae)

Common names: None
Height: 12in (30cm)
Spread: 2in (5cm)
Aspect: Full sun
Soil: Sandy, fertile
Hardiness: Zone 8
Propagation: Seed, in warmth
in spring; division, in spring

Cormous perennial. Leaves lance-shaped,
flat, midgreen. Flowers in racemes, open,
pure white, followed by brown capsules of
red seeds. Self-seeds, but not invasively.

Antennaria dioica
(Asteraceae/Compositae)

Common name: Common
pussy-toes
Height: 4in (10cm)
Spread: 16in (40cm)
Aspect: Full sun
Soil: Well-drained, fertile
Hardiness: Zone 5
Propagation: Seed, in spring
or autumn

Mat-forming, stoloniferous ground cover.
Spoon-shaped, gray-green leaves, very hairy
beneath. Corymbs of fluffy, pink or white,
everlasting flowers in late spring to summer.

ANTHEMIS (Asteraceae/Compositae)
Camomile

Genus of some 100 mat- or clump-forming species
originating in Europe, northern Africa, Turkey, the Caucasus,
and Iran. *Anthemis* make very useful border plants, with a
long flowering season extending from late spring to the end
of summer, and beautiful, filigree, aromatic, evergreen foliage
when they are not in flower. Smaller types also suit rock
gardens. The flowerheads are daisylike, with white or yellow
ray florets and yellow disc florets, and some of the species
will make good cut flowers. Although the genus as a whole is
not long-lived (*A. tinctoria* in particular is notable for this),
all are easily propagated from seed or cuttings. A plant's life
can also be extended by shearing it over in autumn just after
flowering is over. This will ensure that new basal growth is
encouraged, which will take the plant through the winter.
Shearing also helps to keep the plants from becoming
mildewed, a particular problem of *Anthemis*; they come from
sunny, well-drained sites in the wild, and wet winters are
greatly disliked by all species. They do not transplant well,
but should nevertheless be divided regularly in spring. Despite
these drawbacks, these plants provide the gardener with
rewards that make them well worth all the effort.

Anthemis puncteta subsp.
cupaniana A.G.M.
(Asteraceae/Compositae)

Common names: None
Height: 1ft (30cm)
Spread: 3ft (90cm)
Aspect: Full sun
Soil: Well-drained, sandy
Hardiness: Zone 6
Propagation: Seed, division or
basal cuttings, all in spring

Evergreen with aromatic, ovate-obovate,
pinnatisect, silver-gray leaves, gray-green in
winter. Flowers daisylike, white, long-
lasting, in early summer. From Sicily.

Anthemis tinctoria
'E.C. Buxton'
(Asteraceae/Compositae)

Common name: Golden
marguerite
Height: 28in (70cm)
Spread: 24in (60cm)
Aspect: Full sun
Soil: Well-drained, sandy
Hardiness: Zone 6
Propagation: Division or
basal cuttings, both in spring

A selected form with lemon-yellow,
daisylike flowerheads above aromatic,
evergreen, handsome foliage. Leaves are
ovate-obovate, pinnatisect, gray-green.

Anthemis 'Grallagh Gold'
(Asteraceae/Compositae)

Common name: Golden
marguerite
Height: 32in (80cm)
Spread: 24in (60cm)
Aspect: Full sun
Soil: Well-drained, sandy
Hardiness: Zone 6
Propagation: Division or
basal cuttings, both in spring

A selected form with intense gold,
daisylike flowerheads. Leaves are
evergreen, aromatic, ovate-obovate,
pinnatisect, and gray-green.

Anthemis tinctoria
'Sauce Hollandaise'
(Asteraceae/Compositae)

Common name: Golden
marguerite
Height: 2ft (60cm)
Spread: 2ft (60cm)
Aspect: Full sun
Soil: Well-drained, sandy
Hardiness: Zone 6
Propagation: Division or
basal cuttings, both in spring

Cloned selection. Flowers have near-white
ray petals, contrasting with yellow boss.
Foliage is evergreen, ovate-obovate,
aromatic, pinnatisect, and gray-green.

Anthemis tinctoria
'Wargrave'
(Asteraceae/Compositae)

Common name: Golden
marguerite
Height: 2ft (60cm)
Spread: 2ft (60cm)
Aspect: Full sun
Soil: Well-drained, sandy
Hardiness: Zone 6
Propagation: Division or
basal cuttings, both in spring

Cultivar with daisylike flowerheads of
pale, soft yellow. Leaves are aromatic,
evergreen, ovate-obovate, pinnatisect,
and gray-green.

Anthemis tinctoria 'Wargrave', a fine variety with lemon yellow flowers on long stems.

Anthericum liliago
(Anthericaceae/Liliaceae)

Common name:
St. Bernard-lily
Height: 36in (90cm)
Spread: 12in (30cm)
Aspect: Full sun
Soil: Well-drained, fertile
Hardiness: Zone 7
Propagation: Seed, in spring
or autumn; division, in spring

Clump-forming, rhizomatous perennial.
Leaves grassy, midgreen. Panicles of open,
lilylike, white flowers in late spring, early
summer, followed by attractive seed heads.

Anthriscus sylvestris
(Apiaceae/Umbelliferae)

Common names: None
Height: 3ft (1m)
Spread: 1ft (30cm)
Aspect: Sun or half shade
Soil: Well-drained
Hardiness: Zone 7
Propagation: Seed, in spring
or autumn

Short-lived, clump-forming perennial.
Leaves 3-pinnate, with ovate, pinnatifid
leaflets. Umbels of tiny white flowers from
midspring to summer.

Anthriscus sylvestris
'Ravenswing'
(Apiaceae/Umbelliferae)

Common names: None
Height: 3ft (1m)
Spread: 1ft (30cm)
Aspect: Sun or half shade
Soil: Well-drained
Hardiness: Zone 7
Propagation: Seed, in spring
or autumn

A dark-leaved form of the species. Leaves
lacy, dark purple-brown, 3-pinnate; leaflets
ovate, pinnatifid. Loose umbels of small,
white flowers in spring to early summer.

Antirrhinum hispanicum
(Scrophulariaceae)

Common name: Snapdragon
Height: 8in (20cm)
Spread: 12in (30cm)
Aspect: Full sun
Soil: Sharply drained, fertile
Hardiness: Zone 7
Propagation: Softwood
cuttings, in summer

Short-lived subshrub. Leaves lance-shaped
to orbicular, green. Flowers white or pale
pink, lip streaked red, perfumed, 2-lipped,
in loose racemes, late summer. From Spain.

Antirrhinum majus
'Taff's White'
(Scrophulariaceae)

Common name: Common
snapdragon
Height: 2ft (60cm)
Spread: 2ft (60cm)
Aspect: Full sun
Soil: Sharply drained
Hardiness: Zone 7
Propagation: Softwood
cuttings, in summer

Cloned selection of the garden snapdragon,
grown as an annual. Leaves lance-shaped,
glossy green, edged cream. Flowers fragrant,
2-lipped, white, in summer to autumn.

AQUILEGIA (Ranunculaceae)
Columbine

A genus of some 70 species from a wide range of habitats,
from mountain to woodland, widely distributed across the
northern hemisphere. The larger species and their cultivars,
covered here, are popular garden plants and an almost
indispensable element of the classic cottage garden. Their
flowering season forms a useful bridge over the gap between
the spring- and summer-flowering genera, and a wide range
of colors is available. The flowers are distinctive, often
bicolored, with hooked spurs, and carried either singly or in
panicles. The basal leaves are also distinctive and attractive.
Some enthusiasts have beds devoted entirely to columbines,
and later in the season dig them out to replace them with
summer bedding. They do have the drawback of being short-
lived, but this is mitigated by their tendency to grow very
readily from seed; they will also self-seed abundantly in the
garden, and any seedling with poor flowers can be taken out,
as there will be plenty of better examples. Columbines do not
transplant well, so seed should be sown *in situ*, or the
seedlings should be planted out when they are still small.
Contact with the sap may cause skin irritation, and all
members of the genus are poisonous.

Aquilegia canadensis
A.G.M.
(Ranunculaceae)

Common name: American
columbine
Height: 3ft (90cm)
Spread: 1ft (30cm)
Aspect: Sun or half shade
Soil: Moist, well-drained
Hardiness: Zone 3
Propagation: Seed, when ripe
or in spring

Clump-forming, with 2-ternate, fernlike,
green leaves. Racemes of up to 20 nodding
flowers, sepals scarlet, petals lemon, spurs
red, from midspring to early summer.

Aquilegia chrysantha
'Yellow Queen'
(Ranunculaceae)

Common name: Golden
columbine
Height: 3ft (90cm)
Spread: 2ft (60cm)
Aspect: Sun or half shade
Soil: Moist, well-drained
Hardiness: Zone 3
Propagation: Division,
in spring

Cloned selection with fernlike, 3-ternate
leaves, of ovate, green leaflets. Racemes of
4–12 flowers with pale yellow petals and
golden-yellow sepals in spring to summer.

Aquilegia
Mrs Scott-Elliot Hybrids
(Ranunculaceae)

Common name: Columbine
Height: 3ft (90cm)
Spread: 2ft (60cm)
Aspect: Sun or half shade
Soil: Moist, well-drained
Hardiness: Zone 3
Propagation: Seed, in autumn
or spring

Robust hybrid strain. Leaves 2-ternately
lobed, midgreen. Flowers in racemes, in a
range of colors and bicolors, from spring
to midsummer.

Aquilegia
Music Series A.G.M.
(Ranunculaceae)

Common name: Columbine
Height: 18in (45cm)
Spread: 18in (45cm)
Aspect: Sun or half shade
Soil: Moist, well-drained
Hardiness: Zone 3
Propagation: Seed, in autumn
or spring

Hybrid strain of compact and robust
plants with 2-ternate, midgreen leaves.
Long-spurred flowers in a range of colors
and bicolors in spring to summer.

Aquilegia vulgaris
(Ranunculaceae)

Common name: European
columbine
Height: 3ft (90cm)
Spread: 2ft (60cm)
Aspect: Sun or half shade
Soil: Moist, well-drained
Hardiness: Zone 3
Propagation: Seed, in spring
or autumn

Stiff, upright plant with 2-ternately lobed,
midgreen leaves. Terminal racemes of 5–15
pendent or horizontal, blue, pink, white,
or violet flowers in spring to early summer.

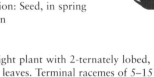

**ADDITIONAL AQUILEGIAS
with an A.G.M.**

A. bertolonii (Zone 5)

A. caerulea (Zone 3)

A. flabellata (Zone 3)

A. flabellatea var. *pumila* (Zone 3)

A. flabellata var. *pumila* f. *alba*
(Zone 3)

A. 'Hensol Harebell' (Zone 5)

A. vulgaris 'Nivea' (Zone 4)

Aquilegia vulgaris var.
stellata 'Nora Barlow'
A.G.M. (Ranunculaceae)

Common name: European
columbine
Height: 3ft (90cm)
Spread: 2ft (60cm)
Aspect: Sun or half shade
Soil: Moist, well-drained
Hardiness: Zone 3
Propagation: Division,
in spring

Selected form with fully double, pompon
flowers. Tepals are red and green, spurless,
and quilted. Good proportion of seedlings
come true if plant is grown in isolation.

Aquilegia vulgaris
var. *stellata*
(Ranunculaceae)

Common name: European
columbine
Height: 3ft (90cm)
Spread: 2ft (60cm)
Aspect: Sun or half shade
Soil: Moist, well-drained
Hardiness: Zone 3
Propagation: Seed, in autumn
or spring

Variety with spurless flowers with tepals
that spread, resembling flowers of clematis
(*see pp.79–80*), in shades of blue or pink
Leaves 2-ternately lobed, midgreen.

Aquilegia vulgaris
'William Guiness'
(Ranunculaceae)

Common name: European
columbine
Height: 28in (70cm)
Spread: 24in (60cm)
Aspect: Sun or half shade
Soil: Moist, well-drained
Hardiness: Zone 3
Propagation: Division,
in spring

Selected form with dark purple to black
flowers, with sepals tipped white, in
terminal racemes. Leaves are midgreen and
2-ternately lobed.

Arabis blepharophylla 'Frühlingszauber' A.G.M. (Brassicaceae/Cruciferae)

Common names: None
Height: 4in (10cm)
Spread: 8in (20cm)
Aspect: Full sun
Soil: Well-drained
Hardiness: Zone 7
Propagation: Seed, in autumn

Arabis procurrens 'Variegata' A.G.M. (Brassicaceae/Cruciferae)

Common names: None
Height: 3in (8cm)
Spread: 16in (40cm)
Aspect: Full sun
Soil: Well-drained, sandy
Hardiness: Zone 5
Propagation: Seed, in autumn

Arctotheca calendula (Asteraceae/Compositae)

Common names: None
Height: 20in (50cm)
Spread: Indefinite
Aspect: Full sun
Soil: Well-drained
Hardiness: Zone 9
Propagation: Seed, in warmth in spring; division, in spring

Arctotis fastuosa 'Zulu Prince' (Asteraceae/Compositae)

Common name: African daisy
Height: 24in (60cm)
Spread: 16in (40cm)
Aspect: Full sun
Soil: Moist, well-drained, sandy
Hardiness: Zone 9
Propagation: Seed, in warmth in spring or summer

Compact, short-lived, evergreen perennial. Forms a rosette of toothed, obovate, dark green leaves. Racemes of dark pink-purple, fragrant flowers in spring to early summer.

Creeping evergreen. Rosettes of oblong- to lance-shaped leaves, glossy midgreen, edged cream, sometimes tinged pink. Racemes of white flowers, in spring. Superb wall plant.

Creeping, rhizomatous, spreading plant. Rosettes of pinnatifid, oblong, green leaves, white-woolly beneath. Flowers in spring or early summer, yellow, purple-tinted beneath.

Creeping perennial often treated as annual. Silvery white, elliptic, lobed leaves. Solitary flowers; cream ray florets, black triangles at the bases, midsummer to early autumn.

Arctotis x hybrida (Asteraceae/Compositae)

Common name: African daisy
Height: 2ft (60cm)
Spread: 1ft (30cm)
Aspect: Full sun
Soil: Moist, well-drained, sandy
Hardiness: Zone 9
Propagation: Seed, in warmth in spring or autumn

Arenaria montana A.G.M. (Caryophyllaceae)

Common name: Sandwort
Height: 2in (5cm)
Spread: 12in (30cm)
Aspect: Full sun
Soil: Moist, well-drained, gritty
Hardiness: Zone 4
Propagation: Seed, in autumn; division, in spring

Argyranthemum frutescens subsp. **canariae** A.G.M. (Asteraceae/Compositae)

Common name: Marguerite chrysanthemum
Height: 2ft (60cm)
Spread: 2ft (60cm)
Aspect: Full sun
Soil: Well-drained
Hardiness: Zone 9
Propagation: Seed, in warmth in spring

Argyranthemum 'Jamaica Primrose' A.G.M. (Asteraceae/Compositae)

Common name: Marguerite chrysanthemum
Height: 3ft (1m)
Spread: 3ft (1m)
Aspect: Full sun
Soil: Well-drained
Hardiness: Zone 9
Propagation: Greenwood cuttings, in spring

Range of hybrids. Flowers solitary, single, in red, yellow, pink, white, or orange; some with darker marks on ray florets. Leaves silvery, felted, elliptic, lobed, wavy-edged.

An evergreen, prostrate plant with gray-green, lance-shaped leaves. Flowers solitary or in cymes of a few flowers, white, in late spring. Good wall plant.

Free-flowering subshrub with pinnatisect, dissected, green leaves. Flowers in loose corymbs, white or very pale pink, spring to autumn. From the Canary Islands.

Hybrid, evergreen subshrub, often grown as an annual. Leaves pinnatisect, toothed, gray-green. Flowers solitary, single, pale yellow, with darker disc. Long-flowering.

Argyranthemum
'Vancouver' A.G.M.
(Asteraceae/Compositae)

Common name: Marguerite
chrysanthemum
Height: 3ft (1m)
Spread: 32in (80cm)
Aspect: Full sun
Soil: Well-drained
Hardiness: Zone 9
Propagation: Greenwood
cuttings, in spring

Handsome, evergreen, hybrid subshrub.
Leaves pinnatisect, grayish-green. Solitary,
double, anemone-centered flowers, spring to
autumn. Ray florets pink, disc florets rose.

**ADDITIONAL
ARGYRANTHEMUMS
with an A.G.M. (all Zone 9)**

A. 'Cornish Gold'

A. 'Donington Hero'

A. *foeniculaceum* 'Royal Haze'

A. *gracile* 'Chelsea Girl'

A. 'Levada Cream'

A. 'Mary Cheek'

A. 'Petite Pink'

A. 'Qinta White'

A. 'Snow Storm'

Arisaema amurense
(Araceae)

Common names: None
Height: 18in (45cm)
Spread: 6in (15cm)
Aspect: Half shade, cool
Soil: Moist, acidic,
humus-rich
Hardiness: Zone 6
Propagation: Seed, in autumn
or spring; offsets, in autumn

Tuberous. Large, solitary leaf, with 5 linear
to lance-shaped leaflets. Flowering spathe
green, striped white and purple, may be
followed by berries if both sexes grown.

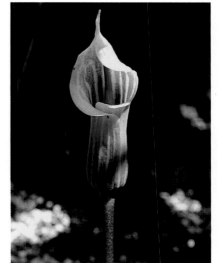

Arisaema candidissimum
A.G.M.
(Araceae)

Common names: None
Height: 12in (30cm)
Spread: 18in (45cm)
Aspect: Half shade, cool
Soil: Moist, humus-rich
Hardiness: Zone 6
Propagation: Seed, in autumn
or spring; offsets, in autumn

Tuberous plant. Spathe white striped pink,
scented; appears late, so mark position.
Large, 3-palmate leaves with ovate leaflets
follow. Will fruit if male and female grown.

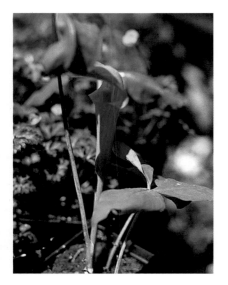

Arisaema triphyllum
(Araceae)

Common name: Jack-in-the-
pulpit
Height: 1ft (30cm)
Spread: 1ft (30cm)
Aspect: Half shade, cool
Soil: Moist, humus-rich
Hardiness: Zone 4
Propagation: Seed, in autumn
or spring; offsets, in autumn

A tuberous species. Leaves three-lobed,
green. Spathe hooded, green, striped purple
and white, may be followed by berries if
plants of both sexes are grown.

Arisarum proboscideum
(Araceae)

Common names: None
Height: 8in (20cm)
Spread: Indefinite
Aspect: Half shade,
woodland
Soil: Moist, humus-rich
Hardiness: Zone 7
Propagation: Seed, in spring;
division, in autumn

Rhizomatous, mat-forming perennial. Dark
green, glossy, arrow-shaped leaves. Hooded,
dark brown-purple spathe, with a long tip
like a mouse's tail. Can be invasive.

Aristea ecklonii
(Iridaceae)

Common names: None
Height: 24in (60cm)
Spread: 18in (45cm)
Aspect: Full sun
Soil: Moist, well-drained,
humus-rich
Hardiness: Zone 9
Propagation: Seed, in warmth
in spring

Rhizomatous evergreen, forming tangled
clumps. Lance-shaped, stem-clasping, and
linear basal leaves. Panicles of lilac or blue,
saucer-shaped flowers, lasting a day, summer.

Aristea major
(Iridaceae)

Common names: None
Height: 5ft (1.5m)
Spread: 18in (45cm)
Aspect: Full sun
Soil: Well-drained,
humus-rich
Hardiness: Zone 8
Propagation: Seed, in warmth
in spring

Handsome, rhizomatous evergreen. Leaves
both lance-shaped basal and long, linear
stem. Flowers in panicles in summer; purple
or blue, saucer-shaped, closing at night.

Armeria maritima
(Plumbaginaceae)

Common name: Sea pink
Height: 1ft (30cm)
Spread: 1ft (30cm)
Aspect: Full sun
Soil: Well-drained
Hardiness: Zone 4
Propagation: Seed or division,
both in spring

Clump-forming evergreen, with a cushion of linear, dark green leaves. Red, pink, or white, cup-shaped flowers, in spherical heads in spring and early summer.

Armeria maritima
'Alba'
(Plumbaginaceae)

Common name: White
sea thrift
Height: 1ft (30cm)
Spread: 1ft (30cm)
Aspect: Full sun
Soil: Well-drained
Hardiness: Zone 4
Propagation: Seed or division,
both in spring

White variant of the species. Leaves in a tight cushion, evergreen, linear, dark green. Small, spherical heads of cup-shaped, white flowers in early summer.

Armeria maritima
'Vindictive' A.G.M.
(Plumbaginaceae)

Common names: None
Height: 6in (15cm)
Spread: 4in (10cm)
Aspect: Full sun
Soil: Well-drained
Hardiness: Zone 4
Propagation: Division,
in spring

Compact, dwarf selected form; shorter stems than the species, bearing spherical heads of rose-pink, cup-shaped flowers. Leaves evergreen, linear, in a cushion.

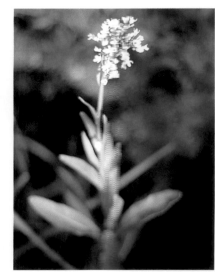

Armoracia rusticana
(Brassicaceae/Cruciferae)

Common name: Horseradish
Height: 3ft (1m)
Spread: 2ft (60cm)
Aspect: Full sun
Soil: Moist, well-drained,
fertile
Hardiness: Zone 5
Propagation: Division,
in winter

Clump-forming perennial cultivated for the culinary use of its roots. Leaves dark green, oblong-ovate, toothed. Flowers in terminal panicles, small, white. Sap may irritate.

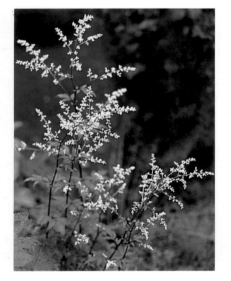

Artemisia lactiflora A.G.M.
(Asteraceae/Compositae)

Common name: White
mugwort
Height: 5ft (1.5m)
Spread: 2ft (60cm)
Aspect: Full sun
Soil: Moist, well-drained,
fertile
Hardiness: Zone 4
Propagation: Seed or division,
both in autumn or spring

Clump-forming culinary herb with deeply cut, pinnatisect, dark green leaves. Bears long-lasting white flowers, in panicles, from late summer to mid-autumn.

Artemisia schmidtiana
'Nana' A.G.M.
(Asteraceae/Compositae)

Common names: None
Height: 4in (10cm)
Spread: 12in (30cm)
Aspect: Full sun
Soil: Well-drained, fertile
Hardiness: Zone 4
Propagation: Seed or division,
both in spring or autumn

Dwarf, rhizomatous, evergreen culinary herb. Leaves pinnatisect, with linear lobes, silky-hairy, silver. Panicles of many small, yellow flowers, aging to cream, in summer.

**ADDITIONAL ARTEMISIAS
with an A.G.M.**

A. abrotanum (Zone 4)

A. absinthum 'Lambrook Mist'
(Zone 4)

A. absinthum 'Lambrook Silver'
(Zone 4)

A. alba 'Canescens' (Zone 6)

A. caucasica (Zone 5)

A. frigida (Zone 4)

A. ludoviciana 'Silver Queen'
(Zone 5)

A. ludoviciana 'Valerie Finnis'
(Zone 5)

A. pontica (Zone 4)

A. 'Powis Castle' (Zone 8)

Arthropodium candidum
'Maculatum'
(Anthericaceae/Liliaceae)

Common names: None
Height: 8in (20cm)
Spread: 4in (10cm)
Aspect: Full sun
Soil: Well-drained, sandy,
fertile
Hardiness: Zone 8
Propagation: Seed, in autumn
or spring; division, in spring

Tuberous perennial. Leaves linear, dull flesh-pink, mottled bronze. Flowers tiny, white, in racemes or panicles, in early to midsummer. Just big enough for a border.

An autumn show of Artemisia *backed by* Sedum.

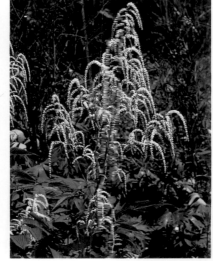

Arum italicum
(Araceae)

Common name: Italian arum
Height: 12in (30cm)
Spread: 6in (15cm)
Aspect: Sun or half shade
Soil: Well-drained,
humus-rich
Hardiness: Zone 6
Propagation: Seed, in
autumn; division, after
flowering

Woodlander with large, cream spathes in
early summer, then spikes of red berries.
Leaves spear- to arrow-shaped, green, in
late autumn. All parts toxic and irritant.

Arum italicum subsp.
italicum 'Marmoratum'
A.G.M. (Araceae)

Common name: Italian arum
Height: 12in (30cm)
Spread: 6in (15cm)
Aspect: Sun or half shade
Soil: Well-drained,
humus-rich
Hardiness: Zone 6
Propagation: Seed, in
autumn; division, after
flowering

Variegated form of the species, with green,
cream-veined, spear- to arrow-shaped
leaves. Cream spathes followed by spikes
of red berries. All parts toxic and irritant.

Aruncus dioicus
A.G.M.
(Rosaceae)

Common name: Goat's-beard
Height: 6ft (2m)
Spread: 4ft (1.2m)
Aspect: Full or half shade
Soil: Moist, fertile
Hardiness: Zone 7
Propagation: Seed or division,
both in spring or autumn

Rhizomatous woodlander. Leaves fernlike,
toothed, 2-pinnate; leaflets ovate. Dioecious:
female flowers greenish, males more upright,
creamy-white, in loose panicles in summer.

Aruncus dioicus
'Glasnevin'
(Rosaceae)

Common name: Sylvan
goat's-beard
Height: 6ft (2m)
Spread: 4ft (1.2m)
Aspect: Full or half shade
Soil: Moist, fertile
Hardiness: Zone 7
Propagation: Seed or division,
both in spring or autumn

Selected form with pendulous panicles,
better in male plants than female. Deadhead females to prevent seeding. Leaves
fernlike, toothed, 2-pinnate; leaflets ovate.

Asarina procumbens
(Scrophulariaceae)

Common name: Wild Ginger-
snapdragon
Height: 2in (5cm)
Spread: 24in (60cm)
Aspect: Half shade
Soil: Well-drained, sandy,
fertile
Hardiness: Zone 7
Propagation: Seed, in warmth
in spring

Evergreen, trailing, brittle-stemmed plant.
Leaves kidney-shaped, lobed, hairy, dark
green. Flowers snapdragonlike, cream with
yellow throats, in summer. Good on walls.

Asclepias incarnata
(Asclepiadaceae)

Common name: Swamp
milkweed
Height: 4ft (1.2m)
Spread: 2ft (60cm)
Aspect: Full sun
Soil: Moist, humus-rich
Hardiness: Zone 3
Propagation: Seed or division,
both in spring

Good marginal plant. Leaves elliptic-ovate,
midgreen. Clustered cymes of flowers with
pink-purple, reflexed petals and paler horns,
in summer to autumn. Silky seed heads.

Asclepias syriaca
(Asclepiadaceae)

Common names: Milkweed;
silkweed
Height: 6ft (2m)
Spread: Indefinite
Aspect: Full sun
Soil: Well-drained, fertile
Hardiness: Zone 3
Propagation: Seed or division,
both in spring

Rapidly spreading plant, not for the border.
Leaves softly hairy, ovate-oblong, midgreen,
blue-green beneath. Flowers in cymes, pink
and purple, scented; seed heads softly spiny.

Asclepias tuberosa
(Asclepiadaceae)

Common name:
Butterfly-weed
Height: 3ft (90cm)
Spread: 1ft (30cm)
Aspect: Full sun
Soil: Well-drained, fertile,
humus-rich
Hardiness: Zone 3
Propagation: Seed or division,
both in spring

Handsome but difficult, tuberous perennial.
Leaves lance-shaped to ovate-oblong, hairy,
midgreen. Flowers in cymes, orange, in
summer to autumn; seed heads nodding.

Asphodeline lutea
(Asphodelaceae/Liliaceae)

Common names: King's
spear; Jacob's-rod
Height: 5ft (1.5m)
Spread: 1ft (30cm)
Aspect: Full sun
Soil: Well-drained,
sandy, fertile
Hardiness: Zone 7
Propagation: Seed, in spring;
division, in autumn

Rhizomatous perennial. Leaves narrow,
grassy, gray-green. Dense racemes of yellow
flowers with large bracts, perfumed, in late
spring, followed by attractive seed heads.

Asphodelus albus
(Asphodelaceae/Liliaceae)

Common name: Asphodel
Height: 36in (90cm)
Spread: 12in (30cm)
Aspect: Full sun
Soil: Well-drained, sandy,
humus-rich
Hardiness: Zone 6
Propagation: Seed or division,
both in spring

Clump-forming perennial. Leaves linear,
grassy, keeled, midgreen. Flowers white,
brown-veined, star-shaped, with brownish
bracts, in few-branched racemes in spring.

Asphodelus ramosus
(Asphodelaceae/Liliaceae)

Common name: Asphodel
Height: 5ft (1.5m)
Spread: 1ft (30cm)
Aspect: Sun
Soil: Well-drained, sandy,
humus-rich
Hardiness: Zone 7
Propagation: Seed or division,
both in spring

Leaves grassy, flat, linear, keeled, green.
Flowers white with a rust midvein and
white bracts, in racemes in summer. From
southern Europe and North Africa.

Asplenium scolopendrium
A.G.M.
(Aspleniaceae)

Common name: Hart's-
tongue fern
Height: 28in (70cm)
Spread: 24in (60cm)
Aspect: Half shade
Soil: Moist, well-drained,
sandy
Hardiness: Zone 5
Propagation: Seed, in warmth
in spring; division, in spring

Evergreen terrestrial fern. Fronds strap-
shaped, fleshy, glossy, green. Remove old
fronds in spring to allow new to develop.
Good wall plant.

ASTER (Asteraceae)

Large genus of some 150 species, including annuals,
biennials, and a few subshrubs as well as perennials. They are
found chiefly in the northern hemisphere, and in North
America in particular, although some subshrubs originate in
South Africa. Asters grow in a wide range of habitats, from
woodland to mountain, and so come in all shapes and sizes;
they also vary in their degrees of hardiness. Their varying
cultural requirements mean that there are asters to suit a
range of garden situations, from scree beds to woodlands and
stream edges. They all have similar inflorescences: daisylike
flowerheads with ray florets usually of white, pink, purple, or
blue, and disc florets in shades of yellow. There are a few
exceptions to this, with yellow ray florets or pink disc florets.
All asters are prone to slug damage, and the many cultivars
of *A. novi-belgii*, the New York aster, are very prone to
powdery mildew; it may not be possible to grow them at all
in a wet garden, even with constant care. Taller species and
cultivars may need staking, and some will need to be lifted
and divided every few years to maintain their vigor.
Nonetheless, these are valuable late-season plants. Many of
them hold an Award of Garden Merit; some that have not
been profiled in detail are listed on p.58.

Aster alpinus
var. *albus*
(Asteraceae/Compositae)

Common name: White alpine
aster
Height: 25cm (10in)
Spread: 45cm (18in)
Aspect: Full sun
Soil: Well-drained, sandy
Hardiness: Zone 3
Propagation: Seed, in spring
or autumn

White form of a mostly violet species. Midgreen, narrow, lance-shaped leaves. Flowers
solitary, single, with white petals and yellow
disc florets, spring and early summer.

Aster amellus
'King George' A.G.M.
(Asteraceae/Compositae)

Common name: Italian aster
Height: 18in (45cm)
Spread: 18in (45cm)
Aspect: Sun
Soil: Well-drained, alkaline,
sandy
Hardiness: Zone 5
Propagation: Division,
in spring

Clump-forming, with lance-shaped leaves
of midgreen. Flowers in late summer to
autumn, large, violet-blue with a yellow
boss. One of a few cultivars with an A.G.M.

Aster divaricatus
(Asteraceae/Compositae)

Common names: None
Height: 2ft (60cm)
Spread: 2ft (60cm)
Aspect: Half shade
Soil: Moist
Hardiness: Zone 4
Propagation: Seed or division,
both in spring

Rhizomatous North American species.
Upper leaves ovate, lower leaves heart-shaped, midgreen. Lax corymbs of small white flowers, midsummer to autumn.

Aster ericoides
(Asteraceae/Compositae)

Common names: None
Height: 3ft (1m)
Spread: 16in (40cm)
Aspect: Half shade
Soil: Moist
Hardiness: Zone 3
Propagation: Seed or division,
both in spring

Lax, freely branching, slender-stemmed perennial. Leaves linear to lance-shaped, green. Loose panicles of small white flowers summer to autumn. From North America.

Aster x frikartii
(Asteraceae/Compositae)

Common names: None
Height: 32in (80cm)
Spread: 18in (45cm)
Aspect: Full sun
Soil: Well-drained, sandy
Hardiness: Zone 4
Propagation: Division,
in spring

Hybrid of garden origin. Leaves ovate, rough, green. Flowers in loose corymbs, light purple-blue, with orange discs, in late summer to autumn.

Aster x frikartii
'Mönch' A.G.M.
(Asteraceae/Compositae)

Common names: None
Height: 28in (70cm)
Spread: 16in (40cm)
Aspect: Full sun
Soil: Well-drained sandy
Hardiness: Zone 4
Propagation: Division,
in spring

Cloned selection, widely grown on account of its very long flowering season, from summer to early autumn. The flowers are of a more intense color than the type.

Aster lateriflorus
(Asteraceae/Compositae)

Common name: Calico aster
Height: 3ft (1m)
Spread: 1ft (30cm)
Aspect: Half shade
Soil: Moist, good drainage
Hardiness: Zone 3
Propagation: Seed, in spring

Clump-forming species. Leaves midgreen, linear-oblong. Flowers white, with pink disc florets, on spreading, branched stems from midsummer to autumn.

Aster macrophyllus
(Asteraceae/Compositae)

Common names: None
Height: 3ft (1m)
Spread: 28in (80cm)
Aspect: Half or full shade
Soil: Moist
Hardiness: Zone 3
Propagation: Seed, in spring

Invasive aster; good ground cover. Large leaves, heart-shaped, toothed, green. Flowers in corymbs, small, starry, pale violet fading to white, yellow disc florets, in autumn.

Aster novae-angliae 'Andenken
an Alma Pötschke' A.G.M.
(Asteraceae/Compositae)

Common name: New England
aster
Height: 4ft (1.2m)
Spread: 2ft (60cm)
Aspect: Sun or half shade
Soil: Moist, fertile
Hardiness: Zone 2
Propagation: Division,
in spring

Cloned selection of a rhizomatous aster. Leaves lance-shaped, midgreen. Flowers in sprays, bright salmon-pink with yellow disc florets, in autumn. Very desirable.

Aster novae-angliae
'Lye End Beauty'
(Asteraceae/Compositae)

Common name: New
England aster
Height: 5½ft (1.7m)
Spread: 32in (80cm)
Aspect: Sun or half shade
Soil: Moist, fertile
Hardiness: Zone 2
Propagation: Division,
in spring

Lovely clone of a rhizomatous species. Leaves lance-shaped, midgreen. Flowers in sprays, ray florets lilac, disc florets yellow, in autumn. One of many named varieties.

This large-flowered aster, Aster amellus 'King George', has soft blue-violet blooms borne on 2-ft (60-cm) stems.

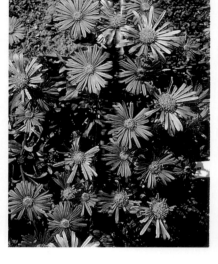

Aster novi-belgii
'Jenny'
(Asteraceae/Compositae)

Common name: New York
aster
Height: 4ft (1.2m)
Spread: 3ft (90cm)
Aspect: Full sun or half shade
Soil: Moist, fertile
Hardiness: Zone 2
Propagation: Division,
in spring

One of many cultivars of this rhizomatous
aster, very prone to powdery mildew. Leaves
lance-shaped, green. Double, purple-red
flowers with yellow disc florets in autumn.

Aster sedifolius
(Asteraceae/Compositae)

Common names: None
Height: 4ft (1.2m)
Spread: 2ft (60cm)
Aspect: Full sun
Soil: Well-drained, fertile
Hardiness: Zone 6
Propagation: Seed, in spring
or autumn

Leaves lance-shaped, green. Starry, lilac
flowers with yellow disc florets, on weak
stems. The form 'Nanus' is much more
compact, with flowers of a deeper blue.

Aster thomsonii
'Nanus'
(Asteraceae/Compositae)

Common names: None
Height: 18in (45cm)
Spread: 25cm (10in)
Aspect: Half shade
Soil: Moist, fertile
Hardiness: Zone 7
Propagation: Seed, in spring
or autumn

Dwarf cultivar. Leaves elliptic to ovate,
toothed, green. Flowers in terminal sprays,
blue-lilac, star-shaped, long-lasting, in
summer to early autumn.

Aster tongolensis
'Wartburgstern'
(Asteraceae/Compositae)

Common names: None
Height: 20in (50cm)
Spread: 20in (50cm)
Aspect: Full sun
Soil: Well-drained, fertile
Hardiness: Zone 8
Propagation: Division,
in spring

Selected form of a rhizomatous, mat-
forming species. Leaves hairy, elliptic, dark
green. Flowers solitary, single, in summer;
violet-blue ray florets, orange disc florets.

ADDITIONAL ASTERS
with an A.G.M.

A. 'Coombe Fishacre' (Zone 3)

A. cordifolius 'Chieftain' (Zone 3)

A. cordifolius 'Sweet Lavender'
(Zone 3)

A. ericoides 'Blue Star' (Zone 3)

A. ericoides 'Brimstone'(Zone 3)

A. ericoides 'Golden Spray'
(Zone 3)

A. ericoides 'Pink Cloud'
(Zone 3)

A. 'Kylie' (Zone 3)

A. 'Little Carlow' (Zone 3)

A. 'Ochtendgloren' (Zone 3)

A. 'Photograph' (Zone 3)

A. pilosus var. demotus (Zone 5)

A. pringlei 'Monte Cassino'
(Zone 4)

A. 'Ringdove' (Zone 3)

A. turbinellus (Zone 5)

Asteriscus maritimus
(Asteraceae)

Common names: None
Height: 10in (25cm)
Spread: 8in (20cm)
Aspect: Sun
Soil: Well-drained, sandy
Hardiness: Zone 8
Propagation: Seed, in warmth
in spring

Good wall plant from the Canary and
Cape Verde Islands. Leaves oblong to
spoon-shaped, hairy. Bears solitary, single,
orange-yellow flowers in autumn.

ASTILBE (Saxifragaceae)

There are only about a dozen species in this small genus; they
are rhizomatous and clump-forming, and found in the wild in
moist areas, on stream banks, and in the woodlands of North
America and southeast Asia. The vast majority of the astilbes
in cultivation are interspecific hybrids of complex parentage,
arising from crosses between A. x arendsii (Zone 6),
A. astilboides (Zone 6), A. chinensis (Zone 5), A. japonica
(Zone 5), A. simplicifolia (Zone 7), and A. thunbergii
(Zone 7). Many deservedly hold an Award of Garden Merit.
They are easy-to-please, being fairly hardy and tolerant of
sun or half shade and of boggy or dry soil. Their divided,
toothed foliage is handsome, and they make excellent ground
cover or bog or marginal plants. Astilbes are also long-
flowering, with tapering, usually open panicles of flowers, in
shades of white or cream through pinks to rich red, in
summer. These do not require staking, and are followed by
attractive seed heads, which will persist on the plants
throughout the winter. The flowers fade quickly when cut, but
the seed heads dry well. In all, they are almost exemplary
perennials. Their only drawback is that they do require
regular division and replanting if they are to stay at their best.

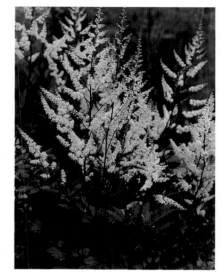

Astilbe chinensis var. pumila A.G.M. (Saxifragaceae)

Common names: None
Height: 10in (25cm)
Spread: 8in (20cm)
Aspect: Sun or half shade
Soil: Moist or boggy
Hardiness: Zone 5
Propagation: Division, in autumn or winter

Highly desirable astilbe from China, with 3-ternate, toothed, hairy leaves of red-green. Flowers in dense, conical panicles of reddish-pink in late summer.

Astilbe x arendsii 'Feuer' (Saxifragaceae)

Common name: Hybrid astilbe
Height: 24in (60cm)
Spread: 18in (45cm)
Aspect: Sun or half shade
Soil: Moist or boggy
Hardiness: Zone 6
Propagation: Division, in autumn or winter

A striking hybrid cultivar with flowers of a distinctive coral-red, in open panicles in summer. Handsome lobed, toothed, dark green leaves.

Astilbe x arendsii 'Glut' (Saxifragaceae)

Common name: Hybrid astilbe
Height: 24in (60cm)
Spread: 18in (45cm)
Aspect: Sun or half shade
Soil: Moist or boggy
Hardiness: Zone 6
Propagation: Division, in autumn or winter

A very desirable, compact hybrid astilbe. Foliage deep green, lobed, toothed. Crowded panicles of deep crimson-red flowers in summer.

Astilbe 'Jo Ophorst' (Saxifragaceae)

Common names: None
Height: 4ft (1.2m)
Spread: 2ft (60cm)
Aspect: Sun or half shade
Soil: Moist or boggy
Hardiness: Zone 6
Propagation: Division, in autumn or winter

An Astilbe x chinensis var. davidii hybrid, taller than most; it has panicles of pink flowers with a hint of lilac, in late summer. Leaves 3-ternate, toothed.

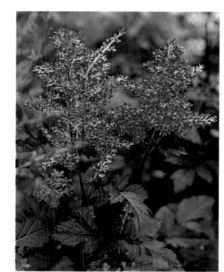

Astilbe chinensis var. taquetii 'Purpurlanze' (Saxifragaceae)

Common names: None
Height: 4ft (1.2m)
Spread: 3ft (90cm)
Aspect: Half shade or sun
Soil: Prefers moist or boggy
Hardiness: Zone 5
Propagation: Division, in autumn or winter

An astilbe for the dry garden, as it will tolerate this better than most. Tall, elegant panicles of purple-red in late summer to early autumn.

Astilbe 'Red Sentinel' (Saxifragaceae)

Common names: None
Height: 3ft (1m)
Spread: 20in (50cm)
Aspect: Sun or half shade
Soil: Moist or boggy
Hardiness: Zone 5
Propagation: Division, in autumn or winter

Clump-forming A. japonica hybrid, with dark green, toothed leaves. Erect panicles of dark crimson flowers are carried above the foliage in summer.

Astilbe 'Rheinland' A.G.M. (Saxifragaceae)

Common names: None
Height: 20in (50cm)
Spread: 18in (45cm)
Aspect: Sun or half shade
Soil: Moist or boggy
Hardiness: Zone 5
Propagation: Division, in autumn or winter

A. japonica hybrid, clump-forming, with midgreen foliage, and dense, upright panicles of deep pink flowers throughout the summer.

ADDITIONAL ASTILBES with an A.G.M.

A. x arendsii 'Brautschleier' (Zone 6)

A. x arendsii 'Fanal' (Zone 6)

A. 'Bronce Elegans' (Zone 7)

A. chinensis var. taquetii 'Superba' (Zone 5)

A. x crispa 'Perkeo' (Zone 6)

A. glaberrima var. saxatilis (Zone 6)

A. simplicifolia (Zone 7)

A. 'Straussenfeder' (Zone 7)

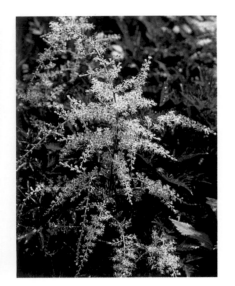

Astilbe
'Sprite' A.G.M.
(Saxifragaceae)

Common names: None
Height: 20in (50cm)
Spread: 3ft (1m)
Aspect: Sun or half shade
Soil: Moist or boggy
Hardiness: Zone 7
Propagation: Division, in
autumn or winter

A clump-forming *A. simplicifolia* hybrid.
Leaves midgreen, 2-ternate, leaflets
narrowly ovate. Flowers shell-pink, in open,
arching, feathery panicles in summer.

ASTRANTIA (Apiaceae/Umbelliferae)
Masterwort

This is a small genus of some ten clump-forming perennials,
found across Europe and into western Asia, of which just
two are in general cultivation. Their natural habitats are
mountain woodlands and stream margins; they are reliably
hardy, and they will grow in either sun or half shade. In the
garden they will also suit a mixed border as long as it
remains moist at all times. *Astrantia* form basal rosettes of
handsome, palmate green leaves, but with the exception of
A. major 'Sunningdale Variegated' they are primarily grown
for their airy sprays of small flowers. These have five petals,
and each is surrounded by a showy ruff of papery bracts in
shades of pink and red; they are carried above the foliage on
tall, wiry stems. They will self-seed freely about the garden,
so if this is not desired, plants should be scrupulously
deadheaded after flowering in summer: the flowers and their
bracts will dry well for winter, and they are extremely
popular for flower arrangements in either the fresh or the
dried state. *Astrantia* will attract both bees and butterflies
into the garden, but they are unfortunately also liked by
slugs. Another drawback of the genus is that they are
prone to powdery mildew.

Astrantia major
(Apiaceae/Umbelliferae)

Common name: Masterwort
Height: 36in (90cm)
Spread: 18in (45cm)
Aspect: Sun or half shade
Soil: Moist, fertile,
humus-rich
Hardiness: Zone 5
Propagation: Seed, when ripe

Clump-forming plant. Basal rosette of green
leaves with up to 7 lobes. Umbels of small,
white flowers backed by green-veined white
bracts, in summer, often again in autumn.

Astrantia major
'Hadspen Blood'
(Apiaceae/Umbelliferae)

Common name: Masterwort
Height: 36in (90cm)
Spread: 18in (45cm)
Aspect: Sun or half shade
Soil: Moist, fertile,
humus-rich
Hardiness: Zone 6
Propagation: Seed, when ripe

A handsome cultivar with dark red
flowers, surrounded by matching dark
red bracts, in summer. Species is from
Central and Eastern Europe.

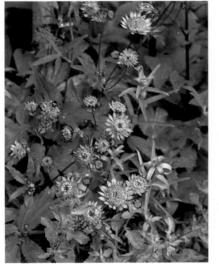

Astrantia major rubra
(Apiaceae/Umbelliferae)

Common name: Masterwort
Height: 36in (90cm)
Spread: 18in (45cm)
Aspect: Sun or half shade
Soil: Moist, fertile,
humus-rich
Hardiness: Zone 6
Propagation: Division,
in spring

Handsome cultivar with plum flowers
surrounded by pinkish bracts, in summer.
A favorite for flower-arranging. Basal
rosette of green leaves with up to 7 lobes.

Astrantia major
'Shaggy' A.G.M.
(Apiaceae/Umbelliferae)

Common name: Masterwort
Height: 36in (90cm)
Spread: 18in (45cm)
Aspect: Sun or half shade
Soil: Moist, fertile,
humus-rich
Hardiness: Zone 6
Propagation: Division,
in spring

Extremely attractive cultivar, sometimes
sold as 'Margery Fish'. Leaves very deeply
cut. Flowers in summer with very long and
sharp-pointed bracts, with green tips.

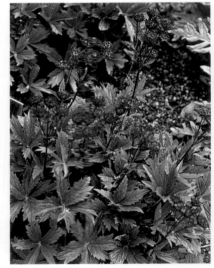

Astrantia major
'Ruby Wedding'
(Apiaceae/Umbelliferae)

Common name: Masterwort
Height: 36in (90cm)
Spread: 18in (45cm)
Aspect: Sun or half shade
Soil: Moist, fertile,
humus-rich
Hardiness: Zone 6
Propagation: Division,
in spring

Handsome cultivar with particularly
attractive toothed foliage. Flowers in
summer, with plum-colored petals and
bracts. A favorite for flower arranging.

Astrantia major
'Roma'
(Apiaceae/Umbelliferae)

Common name: Masterwort
Height: 36in (90cm)
Spread: 18in (45cm)
Aspect: Sun or half shade
Soil: Moist, fertile,
humus-rich
Hardiness: Zone 6
Propagation: Division,
in spring

Cultivar with deep pink flowers and bracts in summer. Very popular for fresh or dried flower arrangements. Leaves green, with up to 7 lobes, in basal rosettes.

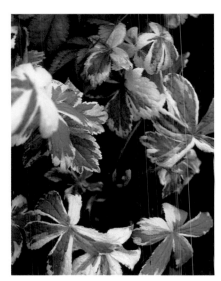

Astrantia major 'Sunningdale Variegated' A.G.M.
(Apiaceae/Umbelliferae)

Common name: Masterwort
Height: 36in (90cm)
Spread: 18in (45cm)
Aspect: Full sun
Soil: Moist, fertile,
humus-rich
Hardiness: Zone 6
Propagation: Division,
in spring

Cultivar grown for both flower and foliage. Leaves have either cream lobes or cream edges. Flowers have bracts of pale pink. Grow in full sun for maximum leaf color.

Astrantia maxima
A.G.M.
(Apiaceae/Umbelliferae)

Common name: Masterwort
Height: 2ft (60cm)
Spread: 1ft (30cm)
Aspect: Sun or half shade
Soil: Moist, fertile,
humus-rich
Hardiness: Zone 6
Propagation: Seed or division,
both in spring

Clump-forming perennial. Leaves green, with handsome, deeply divided lobes. Flowers small, pink, surrounded by sharp, pink bracts, in umbels, early to midsummer.

Athyrium filix-femina
A.G.M.
(Athyriaceae)

Common name: Lady fern
Height: 4ft (1.2m)
Spread: 3ft (90cm)
Aspect: Shade
Soil: Moist, acidic, fertile,
humus-rich
Hardiness: Zone 5
Propagation: Spores in heat
when ripe; division, in spring

Rhizomatous, deciduous, variable fern. Fronds light green, 2- or 3-pinnate, lance-shaped. Pinnae elliptic, segments oblong-to lance-shaped. Stalks sometimes reddish.

Aubrieta
'Red Carpet'
(Brassicaceae/Cruciferae)

Common name: Aubrietia
Height: 2in (5cm)
Spread: 24in (60cm) or more
Aspect: Full sun
Soil: Well-drained, neutral
or alkaline, sandy
Hardiness: Zone 7
Propagation: Softwood
cuttings, in early summer

One of several hybrid cultivars; good wall plant or ground cover. Leaves evergreen, oblong, hairy, midgreen. Flowers bright scarlet, 4-petalled. Trim after flowering.

Aurinia saxatilis
A.G.M.
(Brassicaceae/Cruciferae)

Common name: Golden-tuft
Height: 10in (25cm)
Spread: 16in (40cm)
Aspect: Full sun
Soil: Well-drained, sandy,
fertile
Hardiness: Zone 3
Propagation: Seed,
in autumn

Mound-forming evergreen. Leaves in rosettes, obovate, hairy, toothed, gray-green. Flowers in panicles, yellow, in spring and early summer. Good in a wall.

Bacopa monnieri
(Scrophulariaceae)

Common names: None
Height: 4in (10cm)
Spread: 16in (40cm)
Aspect: Sun
Soil: Aquatic or marginal
Hardiness: Zone 8
Propagation: Division,
in spring

Aquatic or semi-aquatic, mat-forming, creeping plant. Leaves spoon-shaped, apex dentate. Flowers small, 5-petalled, white or pale pink, summer. Worldwide distribution.

Ballota
'All Hallows Green'
(Labiatae/Lamiaceae)

Common names: None
Height: 24in (60cm)
Spread: 30in (75cm)
Aspect: Full sun
Soil: Well-drained, poor,
sandy
Hardiness: Zone 8
Propagation: Softwood
cuttings, in spring

Evergreen subshrub with lime-green, heart-shaped, aromatic, woolly leaves. Flowers small, two-lipped, pale green, with green calyces, in mid- to late summer.

Ballota pseudodictamnus
A.G.M.
(Labiatae/Lamiaceae)

Common names: None
Height: 20in (50cm)
Spread: 24in (60cm)
Aspect: Full sun
Soil: Well-drained, poor,
sandy
Hardiness: Zone 8
Propagation: Softwood
cuttings, in spring

Evergreen subshrub. Leaves ovate, grayish-
to yellowish-green. Flowers on white-
woolly stems, white or pinkish-white with
pale green calyces. Dislikes winter wet.

Baptisia australis
A.G.M.
(Leguminosae/Papilionaceae)

Common name: False or wild
indigo
Height: 5ft (1.5m)
Spread: 2ft (60cm)
Aspect: Full sun
Soil: Sharply drained, sandy
Hardiness: Zone 5
Propagation: Seed, when ripe;
division, in spring

Erect or spreading plant. Leaves palmate,
with inversely lance-shaped leaflets, deep
green. Flowers in racemes, pea-like, indigo-
blue, followed by inflated seed heads.

Begonia grandis
subsp. *evansiana*
(Begoniaceae)

Common names: None
Height: 32in (80cm)
Spread: 12in (30cm)
Aspect: Full sun or half shade
Soil: Moist, fertile,
humus-rich
Hardiness: Zone 8
Propagation: Bulbils,
in autumn

Tuberous begonia with ovate, olive-green
leaves. Pendent cymes of perfumed, bright
pink flowers on tallish, branched stems in
summer. Produces plenty of bulbils.

Belamcanda chinensis
(Iridaceae)

Common name: Blackberry-
lily
Height: 36in (90cm)
Spread: 8in (20cm)
Aspect: Sun or half shade
Soil: Moisture-retentive, but
well-drained
Hardiness: Zone 8
Propagation: Seed or division,
in spring

Rhizomatous, short-lived perennial. Leaves
sword-shaped, green. Flowers orange, with
maroon spots in summer, followed by
handsome, open seed heads; seeds black.

Bellis perennis
(Asteraceae/Compositae)

Common name: English daisy
Height: 8in (20cm)
Spread: 8in (20cm)
Aspect: Sun or half shade
Soil: Well-drained, fertile
Hardiness: Zone 4
Propagation: Seed or division,
both in spring

Well-known evergreen. Leaves obovate to
spoon-shaped, green. Flowers solitary, single
or double; disc florets yellow, ray florets
white, red, or pink. Good ground cover.

Bellis perennis
'Pomponette' A.G.M.
(Asteraceae/Compositae)

Common name: English daisy
Height: 8in (20cm)
Spread: 8in (20cm)
Aspect: Sun or half shade
Soil: Well-drained, fertile
Hardiness: Zone 4
Propagation: Seed or division,
both in spring

Cloned selection. Leaves spoon-shaped to
obovate, green. Flowerheads fully double,
with quilled petals. Evergreen ground
cover. Treat as a biennial in cold areas.

Bellium crassifolium
canescens
(Asteraceae/Compositae)

Common names: None
Height: 6in (15cm)
Spread: 8in (20cm)
Aspect: Half shade
Soil: Well-drained, fertile
Hardiness: Zone 8
Propagation: Seed, in spring

Mediterranean species, at home in coastal
gardens. Leaves elliptic to spoon-shaped,
fleshy, green. Flowers solitary, white, with
yellow discs, in summer.

Bergenia cordifolia
(Saxifragaceae)

Common name: Heartleaf
bergenia
Height: 24in (60cm)
Spread: 32in (80cm)
Aspect: Sun or half shade
Soil: Moist, well-drained,
humus-rich
Hardiness: Zone 3
Propagation: Division, in
spring or autumn

Evergreen from Siberia. Leaves round or
heart-shaped, midgreen, flushed purple in
winter. Panicles of pink flowers on long,
strong, red stems, late winter to early spring.

BERGENIA (Saxifragaceae)

This genus from the moorlands, woodlands, and meadows of Central and East Asia, contains only some half dozen or so species; however, these hybridize very readily and so have given rise to a large number of named-variety hybrids. They are all evergreen and rhizomatous, and generally hardy. Elephant's ears are extremely useful perennials, as they will grow in sun or shade and in dry or wet soil. The leaves are distinctive: large, round, glossy, and leathery, in rosettes, and coloring up well in winter, particularly in poor soil. They make excellent ground cover, and are good in a woodland situation. The flowering cymes are also handsome, and provide particularly welcome color when they appear in winter and early spring. The flowers last well in water, and the leaves will last for weeks, which gives them great appeal for flower-arrangers. They are suitable plants for those with allergies. They do benefit from regular lifting and dividing, but this is also the best way to propagate, as plants in gardens where more than one type is growing will produce hybrid seeds. Slugs can be a problem. Other cultivars with an Award of Garden Merit are 'Bressingham White' (Zone 4) and *B. cordifolia* 'Purpurea' (Zone 3).

Bergenia 'Silberlicht'
A.G.M.
(Saxifragaceae)

Common names: None
Height: 18in (45cm)
Spread: 24in (60cm)
Aspect: Sun or half shade
Soil: Moist, well-drained, humus-rich
Hardiness: Zone 6
Propagation: Division, in autumn or spring

Hybrid with large, broad, obovate green leaves with scalloped edges. White flowers in early and midspring age to pink, and have pink sepals.

Bergenia 'Sunningdale'
(Saxifragaceae)

Common names: None
Height: 18in (45cm)
Spread: 24in (60cm)
Aspect: Sun or half shade
Soil: Moist, well-drained, humus-rich
Hardiness: Zone 3
Propagation: Division, in autumn or spring

Clump-forming hybrid with large, round or obovate leaves, deep green turning red in winter. Flowers rich lilac-magenta, on long red stems in early and midwinter.

Blechnum spicant A.G.M.
(Blechnaceae)

Common name: Hard fern
Height: 20in (50cm)
Spread: 24in (60cm)
Aspect: Half or deep shade
Soil: Moist, acidic, humus-rich
Hardiness: Zone 5
Propagation: Spores, in late summer

Evergreen, rhizomatous fern. Lance-shaped, sterile, dark green fronds, pinnate and pinnatifid with oblong pinnae, surround taller, fertile fronds with linear pinnae.

Bletilla striata
(Orchidaceae)

Common names: None
Height: 2ft (60cm)
Spread: 2ft (60cm)
Aspect: Half shade
Soil: Moist, well-drained, humus-rich
Hardiness: Zone 7
Propagation: Division, in spring

Terrestrial, deciduous orchid. Pseudobulbs flattened, each producing 3 or 4 oblong to lance-shaped green leaves. Terminal racemes of magenta flowers, spring to early summer.

Bletilla striata
'Albostriata'
(Orchidaceae)

Common names: None
Height: 2ft (60cm)
Spread: 2ft (60cm)
Aspect: Half shade; protect from midday summer sun
Soil: Moist, well-drained, humus-rich
Hardiness: Zone 7
Propagation: Division, in spring

A selected form with white flowers, flushed pink, in spring to summer. Leaves oblong to lance-shaped, green. Grow in a peat bed or a woodland garden.

Brunnera macrophylla
A.G.M.
(Boraginaceae)

Common name: Heartleaf brunnera
Height: 2ft (60cm)
Spread: 2ft (60cm)
Aspect: Half or full shade
Soil: Moist, well-drained, humus-rich
Hardiness: Zone 3
Propagation: Seed or division, both in spring

Rhizomatous woodland or ground-cover plant. Leaves large and green; basal leaves heart-shaped, stem leaves elliptic. Flowers in panicles, bright blue, in spring.

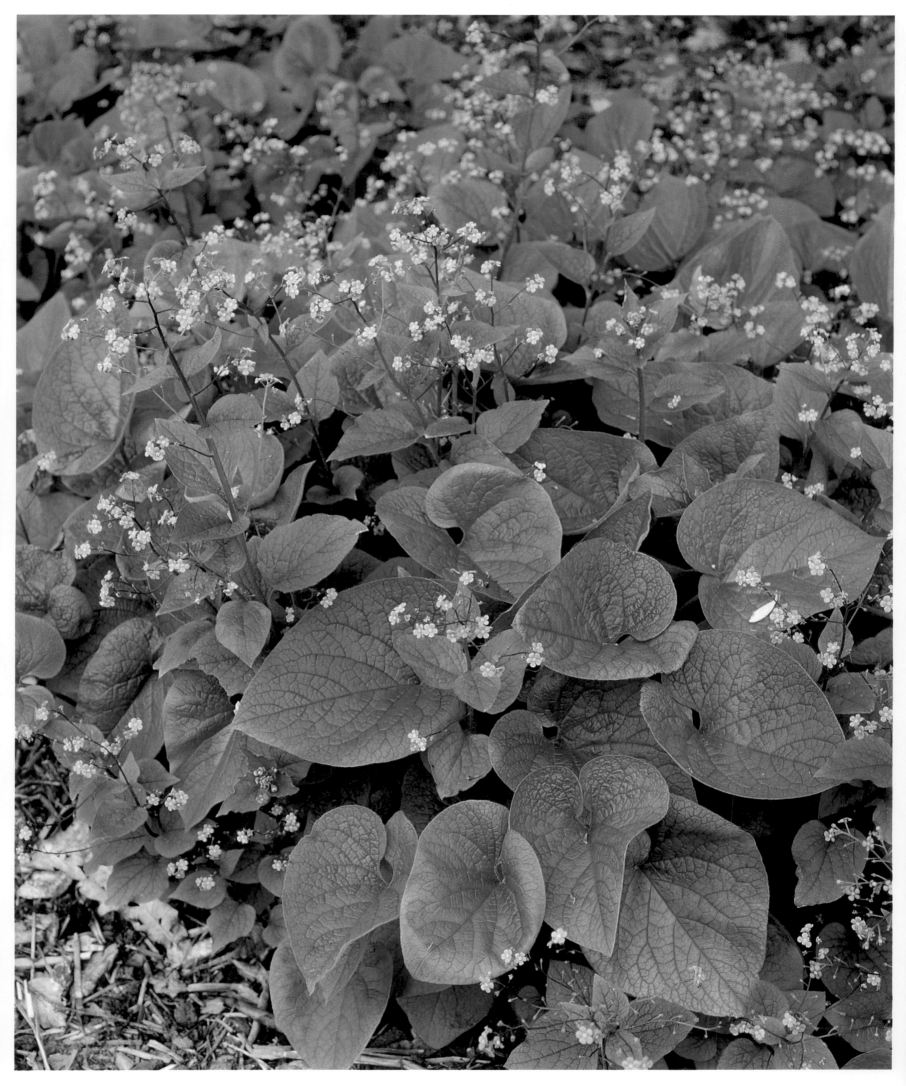

The delicate bright blue flowers of Brunnera macrophylla *appear above a bed of large heart-shaped leaves.*

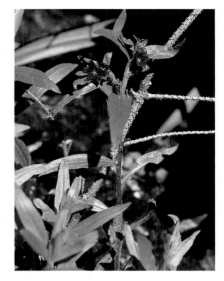

***Brunnera macrophylla*
'Dawson's White'
(Boraginaceae)**

Common name: Heartleaf
brunnera
Height: 2ft (60cm)
Spread: 2ft (60cm)
Aspect: Half or full shade
Soil: Moist, well-drained,
humus-rich
Hardiness: Zone 3
Propagation: Division,
in spring

Handsome variegated cultivar, good in
woodland. Leaves large, elliptic and heart-
shaped with wide cream margins. Flowers
blue. Will not come true from seed.

***Brunnera macrophylla*
'Hadspen Cream' A.G.M.
(Boraginaceae)**

Common name: Heartleaf
brunnera
Height: 2ft (60cm)
Spread: 2ft (60cm)
Aspect: Half or full shade
Soil: Moist, well-drained,
humus-rich
Hardiness: Zone 3
Propagation: Division,
in spring

Variegated clone, with large, cream-edged,
elliptic and heart-shaped leaves, contrasting
well with the bright blue flowers. Suits a
woodland setting, and good for cutting.

***Brunsvigia subacaulis*
(Amaryllidaceae/Liliaceae)**

Common names: None
Height: 18in (45cm)
Spread: 8in (20cm)
Aspect: Full sun
Soil: Sharply drained, sandy
Hardiness: Zone 9
Propagation: Seed, in warmth
in spring; offsets, in autumn

Bulbous perennial. Bright crimson flowers
should appear before leaves, but may not
do so for years. Leaves long, strap-shaped,
dark green. From South Africa.

***Buglossoides*
purpurocaerulea
(Boraginaceae)**

Common names: None
Height: 2ft (60cm)
Spread: Indefinite
Aspect: Full sun; protect from
midday sun
Soil: Well-drained, fertile
Hardiness: Zone 6
Propagation: Division,
in spring

Rhizomatous ground cover; nonflowering
shoots root as they run, spreading rapidly.
Leaves dark green, lance-shaped. Flowers
are small, purple, in erect cymes.

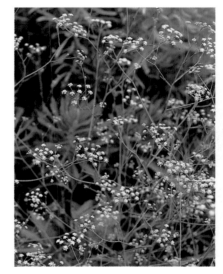

***Bulbine alooides*
(Asphodelaceae/Liliaceae)**

Common names: None
Height: 12in (30cm)
Spread: 6in (15cm)
Aspect: Full sun
Soil: Well-drained, sandy
Hardiness: Zone 9
Propagation: Seed, in warmth
in spring; division, in spring

Clump-forming perennial from South
Africa, with compact rosettes of green,
fleshy, lance-shaped leaves. Racemes of
yellow, star-shaped flowers in spring.

***Bulbinella hookeri*
(Asphodelaceae/Liliaceae)**

Common names: None
Height: 24in (60cm)
Spread: 18in (30cm)
Aspect: Sun or half shade
Soil: Well-drained, neutral
or acidic
Hardiness: Zone 8
Propagation: Seed, when ripe;
division, in autumn

Fleshy-rooted perennial from South Africa
with rosettes of grasslike, succulent leaves.
Flowers star-shaped, yellow, in dense
racemes, in spring to summer.

***Buphthalmum salicifolium*
(Asteraceae/Compositae)**

Common name: Willowleaf-
oxeye
Height: 24in (60cm)
Spread: 18in (45cm)
Aspect: Full sun
Soil: Dry, sandy, poor
Hardiness: Zone 4
Propagation: Seed or division,
both in spring

Leaves narrow, lance-shaped or obovate,
dark green. Flowers yellow, inulalike
daisies on erect stems all summer long,
especially if deadheaded regularly.

***Bupleurum falcatum*
(Apiaceae/Umbelliferae)**

Common names: None
Height: 3ft (90cm)
Spread: 2ft (60cm)
Aspect: Full sun
Soil: Well-drained
Hardiness: Zone 3
Propagation: Seed or division,
both in spring

Leaves narrow, linear, green. Yellow
flowers in umbels, similar to the familiar
Gypsophila paniculata (*see p.140*), not
spectacular, but lasting for many weeks.

65

Bupleurum fruticosum
(Apiaceae/Umbelliferae)

Common name: Shrubby
hare's ear
Height: 6ft (2m)
Spread: 9ft (3m)
Aspect: Full sun
Soil: Any, well-drained
Hardiness: Zone 7
Propagation: Seed or division,
both in spring

Dense, evergreen subshrub, too large for
the small garden. Leaves obovate, blue-
green. Flowers starry, yellow, in umbels,
summer to autumn. Good seaside plant.

Butomus umbellatus
A.G.M.
(Butomaceae)

Common name: Flowering-
rush
Height: 4ft (1.2m)
Spread: 18in (45cm)
Aspect: Full sun
Soil: Marginal, or aquatic to
35cm (10in) deep
Hardiness: Zone 5
Propagation: Seed, in mud in
spring; division, in spring

Rhizomatous aquatic perennial. Leaves
long, radical, green, turning bronze.
Flowers numerous, perfumed, pink,
in umbels in late summer.

Cacalia glabra
(Asteraceae)

Common names: None
Height: 32in (80cm)
Spread: 18in (45cm)
Aspect: Sun
Soil: Well-drained
Hardiness: Zone 6
Propagation: Seed, in spring

Leaves kidney-shaped, coarse, pale green,
with glabrous undersides. Flattish corymbs
of small, pink flowers in spring. European
member of a widely distributed genus.

Calamintha grandiflora
'Variegata'
(Labiatae/Lamiaceae)

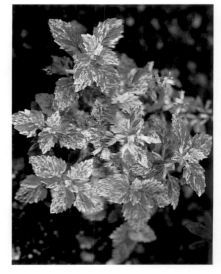

Common name: Calamint
Height: 18in (45cm)
Spread: 18in (45cm)
Aspect: Sun or half shade
Soil: Moist, well-drained
Hardiness: Zone 5
Propagation: Seed or division,
both in spring

Rhizomatous culinary herb; good ground
cover. Leaves aromatic, ovate, toothed,
variegated green and cream. Pink flowers
in lax cymes, in summer.

Calamintha nepeta
(Labiatae/Lamiaceae)

Common name: Lesser
calamint
Height: 18in (45cm)
Spread: 32in (80cm)
Aspect: Sun or half shade
Soil: Moist, well-drained
Hardiness: Zone 6
Propagation: Seed or division,
both in spring

Aromatic culinary herb; good ground
cover. Leaves ovate, hairy, green. Pink
flowers in branching cymes of up to 15,
in summer. From Eurasia and N. Africa.

Calamintha nepeta subsp.
glandulosa 'White Cloud'
(Labiatae/Lamiaceae)

Common name: Lesser
calamint
Height: 18in (45cm)
Spread: 32in (80cm)
Aspect: Sun or half shade
Soil: Moist, well-drained
Hardiness: Zone 6
Propagation: Seed or division,
both in spring

Long-flowering, cloned selection; good for
culinary use or ground cover. Flowers white,
in branching cymes, spring and summer.
Leaves aromatic, ovate, hairy, green.

Calandrinia grandiflora
(Portulacaceae)

Common names: None
Height: 36in (90cm)
Spread: 18in (45cm)
Aspect: Full sun
Soil: Sharply drained, acidic,
humus-rich
Hardiness: Zone 7
Propagation: Seed, in spring;
stem cuttings, in spring

An evergreen species from Chile, often
grown as an annual in cold areas. Leaves
fleshy, elliptic, green. Flowers in racemes,
cup-shaped, magenta, in summer.

Calanthe discolor
(Orchidaceae)

Common names: None
Height: 8in (20cm)
Spread: 8in (20cm)
Aspect: Half shade
Soil: Well-drained, sandy,
humus-rich
Hardiness: Zone 8
Propagation: Division, after
flowering

Evergreen terrestrial orchid from Korea,
Japan, and Taiwan. Leaves oblong, green.
Flowers in erect racemes of up to 10,
purplish with pink lips.

Calceolaria biflora
(Scrophulariaceae)

Common names: Slipper
flower; slipperwort
Height: 8in (20cm)
Spread: 8in (20cm)
Aspect: Sun or half shade
Soil: Porous, acidic, fertile
Hardiness: Zone 6
Propagation: Seed, in autumn
or spring; division, in spring

Rhizomatous evergreen from South America.
Leaves in rosettes, oblong, toothed, dark
green. Flowers yellow, 2-lipped, in loose
racemes of up to 8, all summer long.

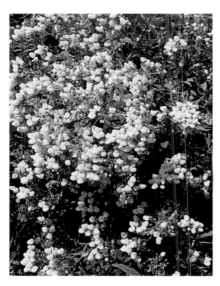

Calceolaria integrifolia
A.G.M.
(Scrophulariaceae)

Common names: Slipper
flower; slipperwort
Height: 3ft (1m)
Spread: 1ft (30cm)
Aspect: Sun or half shade
Soil: Porous, acidic, fertile
Hardiness: Zone 9
Propagation: Seed, in autumn
or spring; division, in spring

Lax subshrub. Leaves gray-green, ovate to
lance-shaped, toothed. Flowers in cymes of
as many as 35, yellow, all summer long.
Usually treated as an annual in cold areas.

Calceolaria polyrhiza
(Scrophulariaceae)

Common names: Slipper
flower; slipperwort
Height: 3in (8cm)
Spread: 8in (20cm)
Aspect: Sun or half shade
Soil: Sandy, acidic, fertile
Hardiness: Zone 9
Propagation: Seed, in autumn
or spring; division, in spring

Rhizomatous, dwarf evergeen from Chile
and Argentina. Leaves ovate, toothed, green.
Cymes of up to 6 yellow flowers, spotted
red, in summer. Good for an alpine house.

Calceolaria tenella
(Scrophulariaceae)

Common names: Slipper
flower; slipperwort
Height: 3in (8cm)
Spread: 18in (45cm)
Aspect: Sun or half shade
Soil: Sandy, acidic, fertile
Hardiness: Zone 9
Propagation: Seed, in autumn
or spring; division, in spring

An evergreen, creeping perennial from
Chile. Leaves ovate, toothed, light green.
Three-flowered cymes of pouched, yellow,
red-spotted blooms, in summer.

Caltha palustris
'Flore Pleno' A.G.M.
(Ranunculaceae)

Common names: Kingcup;
marsh marigold
Height: 10in (25cm)
Spread: 10in (25cm)
Aspect: Full sun
Soil: Marginal aquatic
Hardiness: Zone 3
Propagation: Division,
in autumn or spring

Rhizomatous marginal plant for temperate
climates. Leaves kidney-shaped, toothed,
deep green. Flowers in corymbs, yellow,
waxy, fully double.

Camassia leichtlinii
subsp. *leichtlinii* **A.G.M.**
(Hyacinthaceae/Liliaceae)

Common name: Quamash
Height: 4ft (1.2m)
Spread: 4in (10cm)
Aspect: Sun or half shade
Soil: Moist, well-drained,
humus-rich
Hardiness: Zone 3
Propagation: Seed, when ripe;
offsets, in summer

Bulbous perennial from the western U.S.A.
Leaves linear, green. Flowers in racemes,
star-shaped, off-white, in late spring. The
flowering season is very short.

Camassia leichtlinii
'Semiplena'
(Hyacinthaceae/Liliaceae)

Common name: Quamash
Height: 4ft (1.2m)
Spread: 4in (10cm)
Aspect: Sun or half shade
Soil: Moist, well-drained,
humus-rich
Hardiness: Zone 3
Propagation: Offsets,
in summer

Semidouble, sterile form (so cannot be
raised from seed). Flowers in dense racemes,
star-shaped, cream; short season in spring.
Bulbs become crowded very quickly.

Camassia quamash
(Hyacinthaceae/Liliaceae)

Common name: Quamash
Height: 36in (90cm)
Spread: 2in (5cm)
Aspect: Sun or half shade
Soil: Moist, well-drained,
humus-rich
Hardiness: Zone 5
Propagation: Seed, when ripe;
offsets, in summer

Edible, bulbous plant from North America.
Leaves linear, green. Flowers starry, cup-
shaped, blue, in racemes; short season in
late spring. Can be naturalized in grass.

CAMPANULA (Campanulaceae)
Bellflower

This is a very large genus, containing some 300 species, including annuals and biennials as well as perennials. They are found in very diverse habitats in temperate southern Europe, Turkey, and Asia. The species therefore have differing cultivation requirements, but as a whole they are fairly undemanding, and will grow in sun or dappled shade if given a soil that is well-drained and fertile. There is a campanula to suit most situations in a garden, from wall plants to borders, as the habits vary from trailing or spreading to clump-forming or upright; the taller varieties of the latter may require staking. Campanula flowers also show a wide variety of shapes, from tubular and bell-shaped to star-shaped, and intermediates between these. The flowering season is long, from late spring through the summer. Some species are rampant and invasive, and to be avoided unless you have plenty of room for them to spread or are willing to confine them to a container. Species that fall into this category are C. persicifolia, C. pulla, and C. takesimana; C. persicifolia will also self-seed liberally around the garden unless it is deadheaded. The only other disadvantage is that they are prone to attack by slugs and snails.

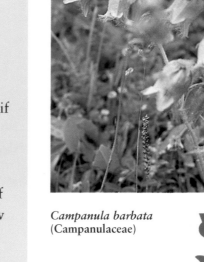

Campanula barbata
(Campanulaceae)

Common name: Bearded bellflower
Height: 12in (30cm)
Spread: 8in (20cm)
Aspect: Sun or half shade
Soil: Moist, well-drained
Hardiness: Zone 6
Propagation: Seed, in autumn

Short-lived perennial from the Alps and Norway. Leaves oblong, hairy, toothed, green. Flowers in one-sided racemes, pendent, blue, bell-shaped, in late spring.

Campanula
'Burghaltii' AG.M.
(Campanulaceae)

Common name: bellflower
Height: 2ft (60cm)
Spread: 1ft (30cm)
Aspect: Sun or half shade
Soil: Moist, well-drained, alkaline, fertile
Hardiness: Zone 7
Propagation: Division, in spring or autumn

Hybrid between C. punctata and C. latifolia. Basal leaves heart-shaped, stem leaves ovate, green. Pendent, tubular, lavender flowers, in racemes in summer.

Campanula carpatica
A.G.M.
(Campanulaceae)

Common name: Carpathian bellflower
Height: 8in (20cm)
Spread: 24in (60cm)
Aspect: Sun or half shade
Soil: Moist, well-drained
Hardiness: Zone 3
Propagation: Seed, in autumn

Clump-forming plant from the Carpathians. Leaves basal, ovate, toothed, green. Flowers solitary, upturned, open bells, blue, white, or violet, over a long period in summer.

Campanula carpatica
'Blaue Clips'
(Campanulaceae)

Common name: Carpathian bellflower
Height: 1ft (30cm)
Spread: 1ft (30cm)
Aspect: Sun or half shade
Soil: Moist, well-drained
Hardiness: Zone 3
Propagation: Division, in spring or autumn

Compact hybrid; comes almost true from seed. Very free-flowering; remontant if sheared after flowering. Flowers light sky blue, in summer. May need staking.

Campanula carpatica
'Weisse Clips'
(Campanulaceae)

Common name: Carpathian bellflower
Height: 1ft (30cm)
Spread: 1ft (30cm)
Aspect: Sun or half shade
Soil: Moist, well-drained
Hardiness: Zone 3
Propagation: Division, in spring or autumn

Compact hybrid, with flowers of pure white, over a long period; blooms again if sheared over after first flush. May need staking. Comes almost true from seed.

Campanula cochleariifolia
A.G.M.
(Campanulaceae)

Common names: None
Height: 4in (10cm)
Spread: 12in (30cm)
Aspect: Sun or half shade
Soil: Moist, well-drained
Hardiness: Zone 6
Propagation: Seed, in autumn

Rhizomatous, rosette-forming, miniature. Leaves round, toothed, green. Flowers solitary, blue, pendent, bells, in summer. Charming plant from the Alps.

**Campanula
'Elizabeth'**
(Campanulaceae)

Common name: Bellflower
Height: 16in (40cm)
Spread: 16in (40cm)
Aspect: Sun or half shade
Soil: Moist, well-drained
Hardiness: Zone 7
Propagation: Division,
in spring or autumn

A rhizomatous hybrid from *C. takesimana*.
Leaves in rosettes, heart-shaped. Flowers
in racemes, pendent bells, reddish, cream
inside; late summer. Good ground cover.

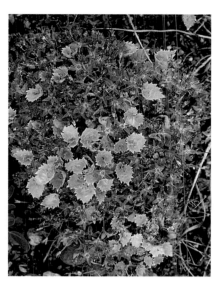

**Campanula garganica
'Dickson's Gold'**
(Campanulaceae)

Common name: Bellflower
Height: 2in (5cm)
Spread: 12in (30cm)
Aspect: Sun or half shade
Soil: Moist, well-drained
Hardiness: Zone 5
Propagation: Division,
in spring or autumn

Attractive *C. garganica* hybrid. Leaves
ovate to heart-shaped, toothed; the yellow
color is a striking contrast to the blue of
the upward-facing, starry flowers.

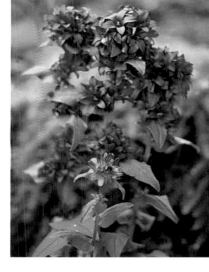

**Campanula glomerata
'Superba' A.G.M.**
(Campanulaceae)

Common name: Clustered
bellflower
Height: 2ft (60cm)
Spread: Indefinite
Aspect: Sun or half shade
Soil: Moist, well-drained,
alkaline
Hardiness: Zone 2
Propagation: Seed, in spring

Leaves ovate to lance-shaped, toothed, deep
green. Flowers in dense racemes, tubular,
violet-purple. Flowers again if sheared
after first flush. From Europe and Asia.

**Campanula glomerata
var. *alba***
(Campanulaceae)

Common names: Clustered
bellflower
Height: 2ft (60cm)
Spread: Indefinite
Aspect: Sun or half shade
Soil: Moist, well-drained,
alkaline
Hardiness: Zone 2
Propagation: Division,
in spring or autumn

Pure white sport of a purplish-flowered
species. Leaves ovate to lance-shaped,
round-toothed. May need staking. Will
flower twice if sheared after first flush.

**Campanula
'Kent Belle'**
(Campanulaceae)

Common name: Canterbury
bells
Height: 30in (75cm)
Spread: 12in (30cm)
Aspect: Sun or half shade
Soil: Moist, well-drained
Hardiness: Zone 3
Propagation: Division,
in spring or autumn

This very handsome hybrid is a recent
introduction. Tall stems bear large, silky,
shining bells, deep violet in color. Leaves
ovate, toothed, green.

**Campanula lactiflora
'Loddon Anna' A.G.M.**
(Campanulaceae)

Common name: Milky
bellflower
Height: 3ft (90cm)
Spread: 2ft (60cm)
Aspect: Sun or half shade
Soil: Moist, well-drained,
alkaline, fertile
Hardiness: Zone 5
Propagation: Division,
in spring or autumn

Cloned cultivar of an undemanding species.
Leaves ovate, toothed, green. Flowers lilac-
pink bells in conical panicles, early summer
to autumn. Flowers twice if deadheaded.

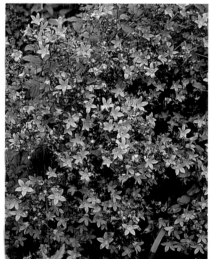

**Campanula lactiflora
'Pritchard's Variety.' A.G.M.**
(Campanulaceae)

Common name: Milky
bellflower
Height: 30in (75cm)
Spread: 24in (60cm)
Aspect: Sun or half shade
Soil: Moist, well-drained,
alkaline, fertile
Hardiness: Zone 5
Propagation: Division,
in spring or autumn

Handsome cloned cultivar. Flowers deep
purple, over a long period, early summer to
early autumn. Flowers twice if deadheaded.
Needs staking, but grows virtually anywhere.

**Campanula latifolia
'Alba'**
(Campanulaceae)

Common name: Great
bellflower
Height: 4ft (1.2m)
Spread: 2ft (60cm)
Aspect: Sun or half shade
Soil: Moist, well-drained,
alkaline, fertile
Hardiness: Zone 3
Propagation: Seed, in spring;
division, in spring or autumn

Vigorous perennial. Basal leaves toothed,
ovate-oblong, rough-surfaced, green; stem
leaves similar, pointed. Flowers in spiky
racemes, open, tubular, white, in summer.

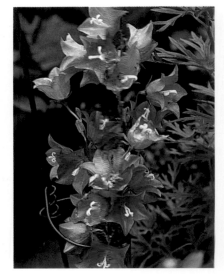

Campanula latiloba
'Hidcote Amethyst' A.G.M.
(Campanulaceae)

Common name: Bellflower
Height: 36in (90cm)
Spread: 18in (45cm)
Aspect: Sun or half shade
Soil: Moist, well-drained,
alkaline, fertile
Hardiness: Zone 3
Propagation: Division,
in spring or autumn

Handsome clone of a species from Turkey.
Leaves basal, lance-shaped, toothed, green.
Flowers cup-shaped, pale amethyst, shaded
purple, in racemes, in mid- and late summer.

Campanula persicifolia
'Alba'
(Campanulaceae)

Common name: Peach-leaved
bellflower
Height: 36in (90cm)
Spread: 18in (45cm)
Aspect: Sun or half shade
Soil: Moist, well-drained,
alkaline, fertile
Hardiness: Zone 3
Propagation: Seed, in spring;
division, in spring or autumn

Evergreen (rare in campanulas), rhizomatous
plant. Rosettes of basal, narrow, toothed,
green leaves. Racemes of cup-shaped, pure
white flowers in early and midsummer.

Campanula persicifolia
'Chettle Charm'
(Campanulaceae)

Common name: Peach-leaved
bellflower
Height: 3ft (90cm)
Spread: 1ft (30cm)
Aspect: Sun or half shade
Soil: Moist, well-drained,
alkaline, fertile
Hardiness: Zone 3
Propagation: Division,
in spring or autumn

Cloned cultivar of rhizomatous, unusual
evergreen species. Leaves lance-shaped to
oblong-ovate, toothed. Racemes of creamy-
white flowers, tinted blue, in summer.

Campanula persicifolia
'Telham Beauty'
(Campanulaceae)

Common name: Peach-leaved
bellflower
Height: 3ft (90cm)
Spread: 1ft (30cm)
Aspect: Sun or half shade
Soil: Moist, well-drained,
alkaline, fertile
Hardiness: Zone 3
Propagation: Division, spring
or autumn

Cloned cultivar; rhizomatous, evergreen.
Leaves basal, toothed, lance-shaped to
oblong-obovate. Flowers very large, blue,
in summer and again in autumn.

Campanula pulla
(Campanulaceae)

Common name: Bellflower
Height: 8in (20cm)
Spread: 12in (30cm)
Aspect: Sun or half shade
Soil: Moist, well-drained
Hardiness: Zone 6
Propagation: Seed in autumn

An invasive perennial from the Alps. Leaves
in basal rosettes, spoon-shaped, toothed,
green, shiny. Flowers solitary, bell-shaped,
pendent, deep purple, in spring to summer.

Campanula pyramidalis
(Campanulaceae)

Common name: Chimney
bellflower
Height: To 6ft (3m)
Spread: 2ft (60cm)
Aspect: Sun or half shade
Soil: Moist, well-drained,
alkaline, fertile
Hardiness: Zone 8
Propagation: Seed, in spring;
division, spring or autumn

A short-lived perennial often treated as a
biennial. Leaves in rosettes, ovate, toothed,
green. Flowers in racemes, cup-shaped,
fragrant, blue, from late spring to summer.

Campanula rotundifolia
(Campanulaceae)

Common names: Harebell;
Scottish bluebell
Height: 1ft (30cm)
Spread: 1ft (30cm)
Aspect: Sun or half shade
Soil: Moist, well-drained
Hardiness: Zone 3
Propagation: Seed in spring

Spreads by underground runners. Leaves
basal, round, toothed, green. Flowers
fragrant, cup-shaped, pale blue or white,
in racemes in late spring to summer.

Campanula takesimana
(Campanulaceae)

Common names: None
Height: 3ft (90cm)
Spread: Indefinite
Aspect: Sun or half shade
Soil: Well drained
Hardiness: Zone 7
Propagation: Seed, in spring;
division, in spring or autumn

Highly invasive rhizomatous species.
Leaves glossy, heart-shaped, green. Flowers
in arching sprays, off-white, flushed pink or
brown, pendent, bell-shaped, in summer.

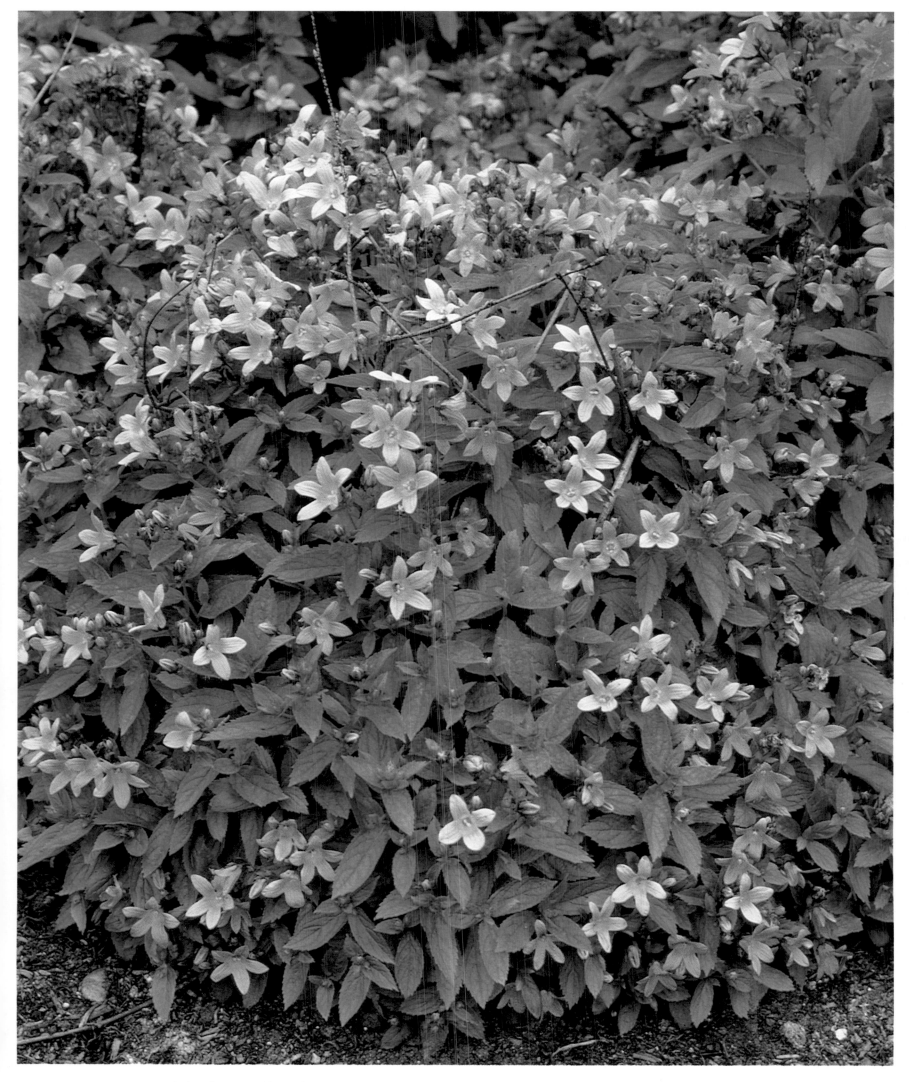

Campanula lactiflora 'Pouffe', a charming miniature campanula with small green hummocks covered in lavender-blue flowers.

Campanula trachelium
(Campanulaceae)

Common name: Coventry-bells
Height: 3ft (90cm)
Spread: 1ft (30cm)
Aspect: Sun or half shade
Soil: Well-drained, alkaline, fertile
Hardiness: Zone 3
Propagation: Seed, in spring; division, in spring or autumn

Woody-based Mediterranean species. Leaves nettlelike, ovate, toothed, mid-green. Flowers tubular, blue or white, in short racemes in mid- to late summer.

Canna indica
(Cannaceae)

Common name: Indian shot
Height: To 6ft (2m)
Spread: 2ft (60cm)
Aspect: Sun
Soil: Well-drained, fertile, humus-rich
Hardiness: Zone 8
Propagation: Seed, in warmth in spring; division, in spring

Rhizomatous South American plant. Leaves broad, elliptic, large, bronze-green. Flowers in racemes to panicles, irislike, orange or red, summer to autumn; best deadheaded.

Canna
'King Midas'
(Cannaceae)

Common names: None
Height: 5ft (1.5m)
Spread: 2ft (60cm)
Aspect: Sun
Soil: Well-drained, fertile, humus-rich
Hardiness: Zone 8
Propagation: Division, in spring

Rhizomatous hybrid of complex origin. Leaves, large, broad, dark green. Flowers in raceme, gladiolus-like, yellow with orange markings, midsummer to early autumn.

Canna
'Striata'
(Cannaceae)

Common names: None
Height: 5ft (1.5m)
Spread: 20in (50cm)
Aspect: Sun
Soil: Well-drained, fertile, humus-rich
Hardiness: Zone 8
Propagation: Division, in spring

Handsome perennial of uncertain origins. Leaves large, broad, pale green with bright yellow veins. Flowers gladioluslike, orange, in racemes, midsummer to early autumn.

Cardamine pentaphyllos
(Brassicaceae/Cruciferae)

Common name: Bittercress
Height: 2ft (60cm)
Spread: 1ft (30cm)
Aspect: Half or full shade
Soil: Moist, humus-rich
Hardiness: Zone 6
Propagation: Seed or division, both in spring

Clump-forming, rhizomatous perennial. Leaves 5-palmate, leaflets green, toothed, lance-shaped. Flowers in lax racemes, pink, white, or lilac, late spring and early summer.

Cardamine pratensis
'Flore Pleno' A.G.M.
(Brassicaceae/Cruciferae)

Common name: Cuckoo bittercress
Height: 8in (20cm)
Spread: 12in (30cm)
Aspect: Half or full shade
Soil: Moist, humus-rich
Hardiness: Zone 4
Propagation: Seed, in autumn or spring; division, in spring

Rhizomatous perennial. Leaves in rosettes, pinnate; leaflets ovate-round, deep green, glossy. Flowers in panicles, lilac-pink, double. Produces plantlets in leaf clusters.

Cardiocrinum giganteum
A.G.M.
(Liliaceae)

Common name: Giant-lily
Height: To 12ft (4m)
Spread: 18in (45cm)
Aspect: Half shade
Soil: Moist, well-drained, humus-rich
Hardiness: Zone 7
Propagation: Seed, when ripe; offsets, after flowering

Bulbous perennial, forming rosettes of large, broad, ovate, glossy leaves. Flowers large, trumpet-shaped, nodding, perfumed, white, in racemes of up to 20 in summer.

CAREX (Cyperaceae)
Sedge

This is an extremely large genus, containing some 1,500 or more rhizomatous or tufted species, most of which are evergreen, but some of which are herbaceous. Sedges are found naturally in a very wide range of habitats, and spread all over the world, so it is impossible to generalize about their cultural requirements as a genus; this also means that it is possible to find a sedge to suit every situation in every garden. They are generally hardy, but there are a few that are not. Large numbers of species and selections are in cultivation; however, many of these have little or no garden value. Out of all of them, two cultivars alone, C. *elata* 'Aurea' and C. *oshimensis* 'Evergold' (Zone 7); have achieved an Award of Garden Merit. For the most part, sedges are grown for their foliage, which is linear and grasslike, and may be flushed yellow or variegated. Flowers are grasslike, mostly in shades of brown and often inconspicuous, but a few sedges do also have attractive inflorescences. They are carried in panicles, generally short and spiked, sometimes longer or drooping, as in C. *pendula*. Without exception, sedges should be avoided by anyone who is seeking to create a low-allergen garden.

Carex comans
(Cyperaceae)

Common name: Sedge
Height: 16in (40cm)
Spread: 30in (75cm)
Aspect: Sun or half shade
Soil: Moist; dislikes extreme wet or dry conditions
Hardiness: Zone 7
Propagation: Seed, in warmth in spring; division, in early summer

An evergreen, rhizomatous, tufted sedge from New Zealand. Leaves 10in (25cm) long, arching, red-brown. Flowers, in summer, are inconspicuous.

Carex elata
'Aurea' A.G.M.
(Cyperaceae)

Common name: Tufted sedge
Height: 28in (70cm)
Spread: 18in (45cm)
Aspect: Sun or half shade
Soil: Moist to wet
Hardiness: Zone 7
Propagation: Division, in late spring

Deciduous, rhizomatous species. Leaves to 24in (60cm), golden-yellow, green-edged. Insignificant flowers in spring to summer; males are tall, above leaves, females shorter.

Carex pendula
(Cyperaceae)

Common names: Drooping, pendulous, or weeping sedge
Height: 5ft (1.5m)
Spread: 5ft (1.5m)
Aspect: Sun or half shade
Soil: Moist to wet, fertile
Hardiness: Zone 8
Propagation: Division, in late spring

Evergreen, tufted sedge. Leaves 3ft (90cm), keeled, shiny, green, blue-green beneath. Flowers in catkinlike cylinders, dark brown, spring to summer. Stems upright or arching.

Carex testacea
(Cyperaceae)

Common names: None
Height: 5ft (1.5m)
Spread: 5ft (1.5m)
Aspect: Sun or half shade
Soil: Moist; dislikes extreme wet or dry conditions
Hardiness: Zone 7
Propagation: Seed, in warmth in spring

Tufted evergreen species. Leaves arching, 2ft (60cm), pale green, orange-brown in full sun. Flower spikes brown, cylindrical, 2ft (60cm), in summer; seed heads longer.

Carlina acaulis
(Asteraceae/Compositae)

Common name: Smooth carlina
Height: 4in (10cm)
Spread: 10in (25cm)
Aspect: Sun
Soil: Very well-drained, poor
Hardiness: Zone 4
Propagation: Seed in autumn

Short-lived perennial from the Alps. Leaves in rosettes, pinnatisect, oblong, spiny. Flowers stemless, spiky, silvery, off-white bracts around a brown disc in summer.

Catananche caerulea 'Major' A.G.M. (Asteraceae/Compositae)

Common name: Blue Cupid's-dart
Height: 3ft (90cm)
Spread: 1ft (30cm)
Aspect: Full sun
Soil: Well-drained
Hardiness: Zone 7
Propagation: Seed or division, both in spring

Catananche caerulea 'Alba' (Asteraceae/Compositae)

Common name: White Cupid's-dart
Height: 3ft (90cm)
Spread: 1ft (30cm)
Aspect: Full sun
Soil: Well-drained
Hardiness: Zone 7
Propagation: Seed or division, both in spring

Cautleya gracilis (Zingiberaceae)

Common names: None
Height: 18in (45cm)
Spread: 10in (25cm)
Aspect: Half shade
Soil: Moist, humus-rich
Hardiness: Zone 8
Propagation: Seed, in warmth in spring; division, in spring

Cautleya spicata (Zingiberaceae)

Common names: None
Height: 24in (60cm)
Spread: 18in (45cm)
Aspect: Half shade
Soil: Moist, humus-rich
Hardiness: Zone 8
Propagation: Seed, in warmth in spring; division, in spring

Handsome cultivar of a plant from S.W. Europe. Leaves linear, grassy, hairy, gray-green. Flowers solitary, dark-centered, lilac-blue, surrounded by bracts to match.

White cultivar, often treated as a biennial. Solitary flowers have lilac-blue centers, pure white ray florets and bracts. Linear, grassy, hairy leaves are gray-green.

Woodlander; plant rhizomes 6in (15cm) deep. Leaves broad, lance-shaped, glossy, green, reddish-gray beneath. Flowers yellow, bracts red-brown, in spikes in late summer.

Rhizomatous Himalayan species. Leaves broad, lance-shaped, shiny, midgreen. Flowers yellow, two-lipped, with orange bracts, in stiff spikes in late summer.

Cedronella canariensis (Labiatae/Lamiaceae)

Common names: None
Height: 3ft (1m)
Spread: 2ft (60cm)
Aspect: Full sun
Soil: Well-drained, fertile
Hardiness: Zone 9
Propagation: Seed, in warmth in spring; softwood cuttings, in spring

Celmisia coriacea (Asteraceae/Compositae)

Common name: New Zealand daisy
Height: 24in (60cm)
Spread: 18in (30cm)
Aspect: Sun or half shade
Soil: Moist, well-drained, humus-rich
Hardiness: Zone 7
Propagation: Seed, when ripe; division, in spring

Celmisia hookeri (Asteraceae/Compositae)

Common name: New Zealand daisy
Height: 1ft (30cm)
Spread: 2ft (60cm)
Aspect: Sun or half shade
Soil: Moist, well-drained, acidic, humus-rich
Hardiness: Zone 7
Propagation: Seed, when ripe; division, in spring

Celmisia spectabilis (Asteraceae/Compositae)

Common name: New Zealand daisy
Height: 1ft (30cm)
Spread: 1ft (30cm)
Aspect: Sun or half shade
Soil: Moist, well-drained, acidic, humus-rich
Hardiness: Zone 7
Propagation: Seed, when ripe; division, in spring

Short-lived plant from the Canary Islands. Leaves aromatic, 3-palmate, green, used in herb teas and potpourri. Two-lipped, pink, white, or lilac flowers, in whorls in summer.

Rhizomatous evergreen; tricky in dry, warm areas. Leaves lance-shaped, gray-green, silky, hairy. Flowers late spring to summer, solitary; ray florets white, disc yellow.

Tufted evergreen from New Zealand. Good seaside plant; not for hot, dry areas. Leaves broad, oblong, glossy, deep green, felty white beneath. Solitary flowers; white, yellow disc.

Clump-forming, rhizomatous evergreen, not for hot, dry sites. Leaves glossy, silvery green above, felty white beneath, oblong. Flowers solitary, ray florets white, disc florets yellow.

Centaurea bella
(Asteraceae/Compositae)

Common name: Knapweed
Height: 12in (30cm)
Spread: 18in (45cm)
Aspect: Sun
Soil: Well-drained
Hardiness: Zone 6
Propagation: Seed, in spring;
division, in spring or autumn

Clump-forming plant from the Caucasus.
Leaves obovate, pinnatifid, feathery, green,
hairy beneath. Flowers solitary, florets
lobed, purple-pink, in summer.

Centaurea dealbata
'Steenbergii'
(Asteraceae/Compositae)

Common name: Persian
centaurea
Height: 2ft (60cm)
Spread: 2ft (60cm)
Aspect: Sun
Soil: Well-drained
Hardiness: Zone 3
Propagation: Seed, in spring;
division, in spring or autumn

Undemanding, clump-forming perennial
from the Caucasus. Leaves obovate,
pinnatisect, green, with gray-green
undersides. Flowers pink, in midsummer.

Centaurea hypoleuca
'John Coutts'
(Asteraceae/Compositae)

Common name: Knapweed
Height: 24in (60cm)
Spread: 18in (45cm)
Aspect: Sun
Soil: Well-drained
Hardiness: Zone 5
Propagation: Seed, in spring;
division, in spring or autumn

Cultivar of a species from the Caucasus.
Leaves lance-shaped, pinnatifid, wavy-edged,
green, white beneath. Flowers rose-pink,
solitary, fragrant, long-lasting, in summer.

Centaurea macrocephala
(Asteraceae/Compositae)

Common name: Globe
centaurea
Height: 6ft (1.5m)
Spread: 2ft (60cm)
Aspect: Sun
Soil: Well-drained
Hardiness: Zone 3
Propagation: Seed, in spring;
division, in spring or autumn

Vigorous perennial from the Caucasus and
Turkey. Leaves green, broad, lance-shaped,
pinnatifid. Flowers large, yellow, with a
basal support of brown, papery bracts.

Centaurea montana
(Asteraceae/Compositae)

Common name: Mountain
bluet
Height: 18in (45cm)
Spread: 24in (60cm)
Aspect: Sun
Soil: Well-drained
Hardiness: Zone 3
Propagation: Seed, in spring;
division, in spring or autumn

Rhizomatous perennial. Leaves ovate, green,
woolly beneath. Widely spaced florets give
red-violet flowers a lacy look. Deadhead
for more flowers and to prevent self-seeding.

Centaurea montana alba
(Asteraceae/Compositae)

Common name: White
mountain bluet
Height: 18in (45cm)
Spread: 24in (60cm)
Aspect: Sun
Soil: Well-drained
Hardiness: Zone 3
Propagation: Seed, in spring;
division, in spring or autumn

Rhizomatous perennial. Leaves lance-shaped
to ovate, pinnatifid, green, woolly beneath.
Flowers solitary, white, lacy. Deadhead for
more flowers and to prevent self-seeding.

Centaurium erythraea
(Gentianaceae)

Common name: Common
centaury
Height: 4in (10cm)
Spread: 2in (5cm)
Aspect: Sun or half shade
Soil: Moist, well-drained
Hardiness: Zone 8
Propagation: Seed, when ripe;
division, in spring

Short-lived perennial from Europe and
Weste Asia. Leaves basal, obovate, gray-
green, prominently veined. Flowers in flat-
topped cymes, pink, in summer.

Centranthus ruber
(Valerianaceae)

Common name: Red valerian
Height: 3ft (1m)
Spread: 3ft (1m)
Aspect: Sun
Soil: Well-drained, poor,
alkaline
Hardiness: Zone 7
Propagation: Seed, in spring

Woody, much-branched perennial. Leaves
fleshy, glaucous, ovate to lance-shaped.
Dense cymes, of small, pink or red, fragrant
flowers all summer; cut back after flowering.

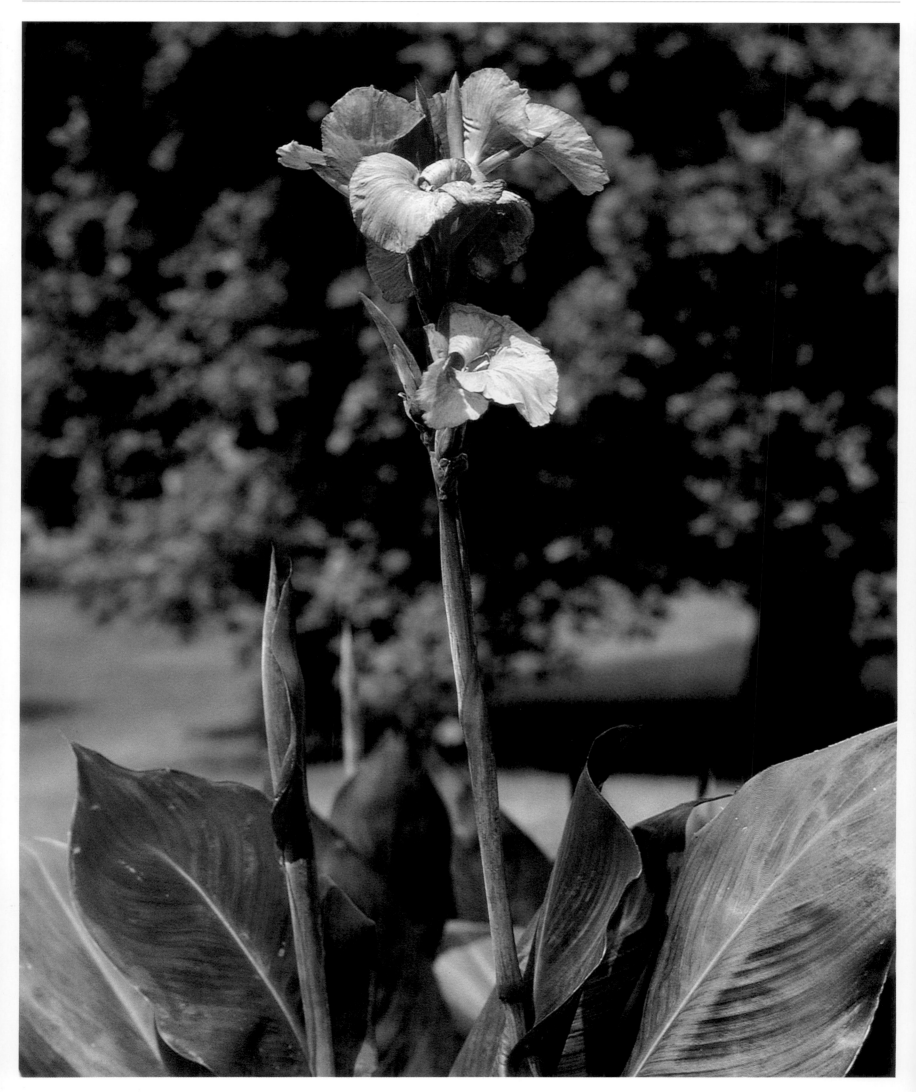

Popular for its large brownish leaves, Canna x *hybrida 'King Humbert' also boasts brilliant orange blooms.*

Centranthus ruber
'Albus'
(Valerianaceae)

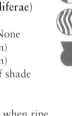

Common name: Red valerian
Height: 3ft (1m)
Spread: 3ft (1m)
Aspect: Sun
Soil: Well-drained, poor, alkaline
Hardiness: Zone 7
Propagation: Seed, in spring

Woody, branching plant. Leaves ovate to lance-shaped, fleshy, green, glaucous. White, fragrant, in dense cymes. Cut after flowering for more flowers and to prevent self-seeding.

Cephalaria gigantea
(Dipsacaceae)

Common name: Tatarian cephalaria
Height: 6ft (2m)
Spread: 32in (80cm)
Aspect: Sun or half shade
Soil: Moist, well-drained, fertile
Hardiness: Zone 6
Propagation: Seed or division, both in spring

Clump-forming perennial. Leaves toothed, pinnatifid-pinnatisect, lobes oblong, toothed, green. Flowers on branching stems, solitary, scabiouslike, primrose, in summer.

Cerastium tomentosum
(Caryophyllaceae)

Common name: Snow-in-summer
Height: 3in (8cm)
Spread: Indefinite
Aspect: Sun
Soil: Well-drained
Hardiness: Zone 4
Propagation: Seed, in autumn; division, in spring

Rampant, invasive perennial from Italy and Sicily. Leaves lance-shaped to linear, white-woolly. Flowers star-shaped, white, in cymes, all summer. Superb wall plant.

Chaerophyllum hirsutum
'Roseum'
(Apiaceae/Umbelliferae)

Common names: None
Height: 24in (60cm)
Spread: 18in (30cm)
Aspect: Sun or half shade
Soil: Moist, fertile
Hardiness: Zone 6
Propagation: Seed, when ripe

Tap-rooted perennial. Leaves aromatic, 2- or 3-pinnate; lobes ovate, toothed. Pink flowers in compound umbels, late spring to early summer. Flowers again if deadheaded.

Chamaemelum nobile
'Flore Pleno'
(Asteraceae/Compositae)

Common name: Double Roman camomile
Height: 12in (30cm)
Spread: 18in (45cm)
Aspect: Sun
Soil: Sandy, well-drained
Hardiness: Zone 4
Propagation: Seed, *in situ* in spring

Mat-forming, aromatic herb. Leaves fresh green, pinnate, feathery. Flowers double, ray florets cream, disc florets yellow, in summer. Highly allergenic, skin irritant.

Chelidonium majus
(Papaveraceae)

Common name: Greater celandine
Height: 24in (60cm)
Spread: 8in (20cm)
Aspect: Any, but best in half shade
Soil: Any
Hardiness: Zone 6
Propagation: Seed in spring

Clump-forming, woodland plant. Leaves lobed-pinnatisect, scalloped, green. Small, yellow, 4-petalled flowers in umbels, in summer. Highly allergenic and skin irritant.

Chelidonium majus
'Flore Pleno'
(Papaveraceae)

Common name: Double greater celandine
Height: 24in (60cm)
Spread: 8in (20cm)
Aspect: Any
Soil: Any
Hardiness: Zone 6
Propagation: Seed, in spring

Cultivar with double flowers, larger than in the species. Leaves green, lobed-pinnatisect, scalloped. Will grow anywhere, self-seeds freely. Skin irritant and very allergenic.

Chelone glabra
(Scrophulariaceae)

Common name: White turtle-head
Height: 3ft (1m)
Spread: 18in (45cm)
Aspect: Sun or half shade
Soil: Moist, fertile, deep
Hardiness: Zone 3
Propagation: Seed or division, both in spring

Sturdy perennial from the U.S.A. Leaves ovate to lance-shaped, green. White flowers, tinged pink, 2-lipped, very weather-resistant, in dense terminal racemes in autumn.

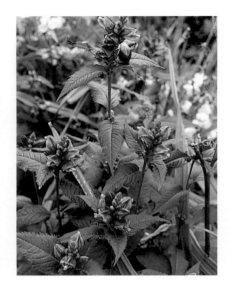

Chelone obliqua
(Scrophulariaceae)

Common name: Rose turtle-
head
Height: 2ft (60cm)
Spread: 1ft (30cm)
Aspect: Sun or half shade
Soil: Moist, fertile, deep
Hardiness: Zone 3
Propagation: Seed or division,
both in spring

Erect, sturdy plant from the U.S.A. Leaves
lance-shaped to elliptic, toothed, green,
boldly veined. Flowers in terminal racemes,
deep pink, resembling turtle heads, autumn.

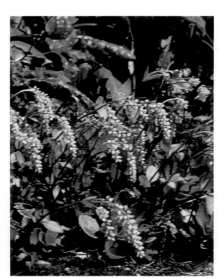

Chiastophyllum oppositifolium A.G.M.
(Crassulaceae)

Common names: None
Height: 8in (20cm)
Spread: 6in (15cm)
Aspect: Half shade
Soil: Moist, well-drained
Hardiness: Zone 7
Propagation: Seed, in
autumn; cuttings, in summer

Rhizomatous, mat-forming evergreen.
Leaves ovate-round, wavy-edged, fleshy,
green. Arching, branched racemes of bell-
shaped yellow flowers, spring to summer.

Chrysanthemum weyrichii
(Asteraceae/Compositae)

Common names: None
Height: 12in (30cm)
Spread: 18in (45cm)
Aspect: Sun
Soil: Moist, well-drained,
fertile
Hardiness: Zone 4
Propagation: Seed, in
autumn; division, in spring
or autumn

Rhizomatous, mat-forming perennial from
Russia. Leaves aromatic, 5-lobed, round,
green. Flowers daisylike, ray florets pink
and disc florets yellow, in autumn.

Chrysanthemum yezoense A.G.M.
(Asteraceae/Compositae)

Common names: None
Height: 12in (30cm)
Spread: 18in (45cm)
Aspect: Sun
Soil: Moist, well-drained
Hardiness: Zone 3
Propagation: Seed, in
autumn; division in spring
or autumn

Perennial from Japan. Leaves fleshy, ovate,
pinnate, lobes oblong. Flowers single, ray
florets white, disc florets yellow, weather-
resistant, in branching sprays, in autumn.

Chrysogonum virginianum
(Asteraceae/Compositae)

Common name: Golden star
Height: 10in (25cm)
Spread: 10in (25cm)
Aspect: Sun or half shade
Soil: Moist, well-drained,
humus-rich
Hardiness: Zone 5
Propagation: Seed, when ripe;
division, in spring or autumn

Rhizomatous, evergreen woodland ground
cover. Leaves ovate, hairy, green. Flowers
solitary, star-shaped, 5-petalled, yellow,
from early spring to late summer.

Cicerbita plumieri
(Asteraceae/Compositae)

Common names: None
Height: 4ft (1.2m)
Spread: 18in (45cm)
Aspect: Sun or half shade
Soil: Moist, acidic, fertile,
humus-rich
Hardiness: Zone 5
Propagation: Seed or division,
both in spring

Perennial from N. Europe. Leaves basal,
green, pinnatifid-pinnatisect. Flowers in
erect panicles, florets strap-shaped, lilac,
from summer to early autumn.

Cichorium intybus A.G.M.
(Asteraceae/Compositae)

Common name: Chicory
Height: 4ft (1.2m)
Spread: 2ft (60cm)
Aspect: Sun
Soil: Well-drained, fertile
Hardiness: Zone 3
Propagation: Seed, in autumn
or spring

Clump-forming, taprooted, culinary herb.
Leaves basal, inverse lance-shaped, toothed,
green. Flowers on branched stems, florets
strap-shaped, blue, closed by midday.

Cimicifuga racemosa A.G.M.
(Ranunculaceae)

Common names: Cohash
bugbane; snakeroot
Height: 6ft (2m)
Spread: 2ft (60cm)
Aspect: Half shade
Soil: Moist, fertile,
humus-rich
Hardiness: Zone 4
Propagation: Seed, when ripe;
division, in spring

Clump-forming perennial. Leaves basal,
green, 2- or 3-ternate; lobes oblong, toothed.
Racemes, sometimes arched, of offensive-
smelling white flowers, in summer.

Cimicifuga simplex
(Ranunculaceae)

Common name: Bugbane
Height: 4ft (1.2m)
Spread: 2ft (60cm)
Aspect: Half shade
Soil: Moist, well-drained,
fertile
Hardiness: Zone 5
Propagation: Seed, when ripe;
division, in spring

Clump-forming woodlander. Leaves basal,
3-ternate; leaflets ovate, purplish-green.
Malodorous white flowers in bottle-brush
racemes white, in autumn. No staking.

Cimicifuga simplex
var. *simplex* 'Atropurpurea'
(Ranunculaceae)

Common name: Bugbane
Height: 4ft (1.2m)
Spread: 2ft (60cm)
Aspect: Half shade
Soil: Moist, well-drained,
fertile
Hardiness: Zone 5
Propagation: Seed, when ripe;
division, in spring

Cloned form with purple foliage, stems,
and buds. Leaves basal, 3-ternate; leaflets
ovate. White, malodorous flowers in bottlebrush racemes in autumn. No staking

Cirsium rivulare
'Atropurpureum'
(Asteraceae/Compositae)

Common name: Plume
thistle
Height: 4ft (1.2m)
Spread: 2ft (60cm)
Aspect: Sun
Soil: Moist, well-drained
Hardiness: Zone 5
Propagation: Seed or division,
both in spring

Leaves prickly, green, elliptic to lance-
shaped, entire-pinnatifid. Flowers on erect
stems, spherical, crimson-purple, early and
midsummer. Deadhead to stop self-seeding.

Cirsium spinosissimum
(Asteraceae/Compositae)

Common names: None
Height: 4ft (1.2m)
Spread: 28in (70cm)
Aspect: Sun
Soil: Moist, sandy, humus-
rich
Hardiness: Zone 5
Propagation: Seed or division,
both in spring

Alpine species. Leaves whitish-green, oblong
to lance-shaped, pinnatifid; lobes ovate,
spiny. Flowerheads cream-white, backed by
narrow, prickly bracts, mid- to late summer.

Claytonia megarhiza
(Portulacaceae)

Common name: Spring
beauty
Height: 2in (5cm)
Spread: 6in (15cm)
Aspect: Sun
Soil: Well-drained, sandy,
humus-rich
Hardiness: Zone 4
Propagation: Seed, in autumn

Short-lived, tap-rooted evergreen from the
Rocky Mountains. Leaves fleshy, spoon-
shaped, deep green. Flowers cup-shaped,
white, in racemes on short stems in spring.

Claytonia virginica
(Portulacaceae)

Common name: Virginia
spring beauty
Height: 12in (30cm)
Spread: 8in (20cm)
Aspect: Half shade
Soil: Well-drained, sandy,
humus-rich
Hardiness: Zone 6
Propagation: Seed, in autumn

Cormous perennial from eastern North
America. Leaves basal, linear, fleshy, green.
Small flowers in racemes, pink with red
veins, in spring.

Clematis x eriostemon
'Hendersonii'
(Ranunculaceae)

Common names: None
Height: To 15ft (5m)
Spread: 3ft (1m)
Aspect: Sun or half shade
Soil: Well-drained, fertile,
humus-rich
Hardiness: Zone 4
Propagation: Division,
in spring

Hybrid herbaceous clematis; suits a mixed
border. Flowers solitary, bell-shaped, blue,
tinted indigo, with recurved tips and cream
anthers. Only for the large garden.

Clematis heracleifolia
(Ranunculaceae)

Common name: Tube
clematis
Height: 3ft (90cm)
Spread: 4ft (1.2m)
Aspect: Sun
Soil: Well-drained, fertile,
humus-rich
Hardiness: Zone 3
Propagation: Division,
in spring

Herbaceous clematis from China. Leaves
3-lobed, toothed, green. Flowers scented,
in racemes, blue, in summer, followed by
good seed heads. Not for the small garden.

Clematis heracleifolia
var. *davidiana*
(Ranunculaceae)

Common name: Tube
clematis
Height: 3ft (90cm)
Spread: 4ft (1.2m)
Aspect: Sun
Soil: Well-drained, fertile,
humus-rich
Hardiness: Zone 3
Propagation: Division,
in spring

A form of this late, large-flowered species
with rich blue flowers. The sepals are more
spreading and less reflexed than in the
species, giving a more substantial flower.

Clematis integrifolia
(Ranunculaceae)

Common name: Solitary
clematis
Height: 2ft (60cm)
Spread: 5ft (1.5m)
Aspect: Sun
Soil: Well-drained, fertile,
humus-rich
Hardiness: Zone 3
Propagation: Division in
spring

Herbaceous clematis from C. Europe.
Leaves inversely lance-shaped to elliptic,
downy. Flowers solitary, midblue bells,
in summer, followed by silvery seed heads.

Clematis integrifolia
'Rosea' A.G.M.
(Ranunculaceae)

Common name: Solitary
clematis
Height: 2ft (60cm)
Spread: 3ft (1m)
Aspect: Sun
Soil: Well-drained, fertile,
humus-rich
Hardiness: Zone 3
Propagation: Division,
in spring

Cloned cultivar with perfumed, sugar-pink
flowers with darker undersides, in summer.
Leaves inversely lance-shaped to elliptic,
downy. Suitable for the small garden.

Clintonia umbellulata
(Convallariaceae/Liliaceae)

Common name: Speckled
wood-lily
Height: 12in (30cm)
Spread: 6in (15cm)
Aspect: Half or full shade
Soil: Acid, moist, fertile,
humus-rich
Hardiness: Zone 4
Propagation: Seed or division,
both in autumn

Rhizomatous, hardy perennial. Bright green,
glossy, oblong-lanceolate leaves. White
flowers, spotted green and purple, in dense
umbels, late spring to summer. Seeds black.

Clivia nobilis
(Amaryllidaceae)

Common name: Green-tip
kafir-lily
Height 16in (40cm)
Spread: 12in (30cm)
Aspect: Half shade
Soil: Well-drained, fertile,
humus-rich
Hardiness: Zone 10
Propagation: Seed, in warmth
when ripe; division, in winter or spring

Bulbous evergreen from South Africa. Strap-
shaped, basal, bright green leaves. Flowers
narrow trumpets, scarlet with green mouths,
in pendent umbels, spring and summer.

Codonopsis clematidea
(Campanulaceae)

Common name: Clematis
Asia-bell
Height: 2ft (60cm)
Spread: 2ft (60cm)
Aspect: Sun or half shade
Soil: Moist, well-drained,
humus-rich
Hardiness: Zone 4
Propagation: Seed, in autumn
or spring

Branched, scrambling plant from C. Asia.
Leaves ovate-acuminate. Flowers solitary,
nodding, bell-shaped, pale blue; beautiful
black, yellow, and blue marks inside.

Colchicum autumnale
(Colchicaceae/Liliaceae)

Common names: Autumn
crocus; meadow saffron
Height: 6in (15cm)
Spread: 3in (8cm)
Aspect: Sun
Soil: Well-drained, fertile,
humus-rich
Hardiness: Zone 5
Propagation: Offsets,
in summer

European species of cormous perennial.
Flowers lavender-pink goblets, in autumn,
before erect, lance-shaped, green leaves.
All parts are poisonous and irritate skin.

Colchicum bivonae
(Colchicaceae/Liliaceae)

Common names: Autumn
crocus; meadow saffron
Height: 6in (15cm)
Spread: 4in (10cm)
Aspect: Sun
Soil: Well-drained, fertile,
humus-rich
Hardiness: Zone 6
Propagation: Seed, when ripe;
offsets, in summer

Cormous perennial from Italy and Turkey.
Flowers perfumed, tasselated, purplish-pink
goblets with cream centers, before strap-
shaped leaves, autumn. All parts poisonous.

Colchicum byzantinum
A.G.M.
(Colchicaceae/Liliaceae)

Common name: Byzantine
autumn crocus
Height: 5in (12cm)
Spread: 4in (10cm)
Aspect: Sun
Soil: Well-drained, fertile,
humus-rich
Hardiness: Zone 6
Propagation: Seed, when ripe;
offsets, in summer

Vigorous, probably hybrid, cormous plant.
Flowers open funnels, lilac, in autumn,
before elliptic to lance-shaped, ribbed
leaves. All parts poisonous and irritant.

Commelina coelestis
(Commelinaceae)

Common name: Mexican
dayflower
Height: 36in (90cm)
Spread: 18in (45cm)
Aspect: Sun or half shade
Soil: Well-drained, fertile
Hardiness: Zone 8
Propagation: Seed, in warmth
in spring; division, in spring

Clump-forming, erect tuberous plant from
Central and South America. Leaves lance-
shaped to oblong, midgreen. Flowers in
cymes, vivid blue, late summer to autumn.

Convallaria majalis
A.G.M.
(Convallariaceae/Liliaceae)

Common name: Lily-of-
the-valley
Height: 10in (25cm)
Spread: 18in (45cm)
Aspect: Half or full shade
Soil: Moist, fertile,
humus-rich
Hardiness: Zone 3
Propagation: Flesh-free seeds,
when ripe; division, in autumn

Rhizomatous, woodland ground cover.
Leaves basal, elliptic, smooth, midgreen.
Arching racemes of perfumed, spherical,
white bells, late spring. Seeds mildly toxic.

Convolvulus althaeoides
subsp. *tenuissimus*
(Convolvulaceae)

Common name: Bindweed
Height: 6in (15cm)
Spread: Indefinite
Aspect: Sun
Soil: Well-drained, sandy
Hardiness: Zone 8
Propagation: Seed, in warmth
in spring

Invasive, trailing or climbing perennial from
S. Europe. Leaves ovate, lobed, silver-green.
Flowers open funnels, clear pink, in mid-
to late summer. Best confined in a tub.

Convolvulus sabatius
A.G.M.
(Convolvulaceae)

Common name: Bindweed
Height: 6in (15cm)
Spread: 20in (50cm)
Aspect: Sun
Soil: Well-drained, sandy
Hardiness: Zone 8
Propagation: Seed, in warmth
in spring

Trailing perennial from Italy, Spain, and
N. Africa. Leaves oblong to broadly ovate,
midgreen. Flowers open cups, lavender-
blue, from summer to early autumn.

COREOPSIS (Asteraceae/Compositae)
Tickseed

The 100 or so annual and perennial species in this genus all
originate in Mexico and Central and North America. All the
perennials are fairly hardy, in spite of the generally southerly
bias in the distribution of the genus in the wild. *Coreopsis* are
found naturally in woodlands and open grasslands; in the
garden, their daisylike, usually bright yellow flowerheads
make an eye-catching addition to an annual or perennial
border. Many species, such as *C. grandiflora* (Zone 7) and
C. verticillata (Zone 6), can be short-lived; because of this
tendency, and the ability of most species to flower well in
their first year when grown from seed, some are more
commonly cultivated as annuals. Perennial *Coreopsis* are
easy-going spreaders, so if they are not grown as annuals,
they must be lifted and divided every few years to keep them
vigorous. Although they are upright in habit, *Coreopsis* do
not, as a rule, require staking; some of the taller cultivars
may, however, benefit from support. All will repeat-flower if
deadheaded. The flowerheads are attractive to both bees and
butterflies; they also make good cut flowers for arrangements,
as they last well in water. Unfotunately, they are without
exception highly allergenic.

Coreopsis grandiflora
(Asteraceae/Compositae)

Common name: Tickseed
Height: 36in (90cm)
Spread: 18in (45cm)
Aspect: Sun or half shade
Soil: Well-drained, fertile
Hardiness: Zone 7
Propagation: Seed, in spring;
division, in autumn

Clump-forming perennial from the U.S.A.
Leaves lance-shaped to palmately lobed.
Flowers solitary, single, yellow; ray florets
have jagged edges. Spring to late summer.

Coreopsis grandiflora 'Early Sunrise' (Asteraceae/Compositae)

Common name: Tickseed
Height: 18in (45cm)
Spread: 18in (45cm)
Aspect: Sun or half shade
Soil: Well-drained, fertile
Hardiness: Zone 7
Propagation: Division, in spring

Selected, double-flowered form, with jagged ray florets of golden yellow, flushed orange near the center, in late spring to summer. Leaves lance-shaped or palmately lobed.

Coreopsis grandiflora 'Sunray' (Asteraceae/Compositae)

Common name: Tickseed
Height: 30in (75cm)
Spread: 18in (45cm)
Aspect: Sun or half shade
Soil: Well-drained, fertile
Hardiness: Zone 7
Propagation: Division, in spring

A selected form, often treated as an annual, with semidouble, deep yellow flowers in late spring to summer. Leaves lance-shaped or palmately lobed.

Coreopsis rosea 'American Dream' (Asteraceae/Compositae)

Common name: Rose tickseed
Height: 24in (60cm)
Spread: 18in (30cm)
Aspect: Sun or half shade
Soil: Well-drained, fertile
Hardiness: Zone 4
Propagation: Division, in spring

A selected form of a species from North America. Leaves linear, bright green. Flowers solitary, single, in midsummer; ray florets deep pink, disc florets yellow.

Coreopsis verticillata 'Grandiflora' A.G.M. (Asteraceae/Compositae)

Common name: Threadleaf coreopsis
Height: 32in (80cm)
Spread: 18in (45cm)
Aspect: Sun or half shade
Soil: Well-drained, fertile
Hardiness: Zone 5
Propagation: Seed or division, both in spring

Bushy, rhizomatous perennial. Leaves are midgreen, deeply incised, 3-pinnate; lobes filamentous, linear. Yellow flowers in loose corymbs, early summer to early autumn.

Coreopsis verticillata 'Moonbeam' (Asteraceae/Compositae)

Common name: Threadleaf coreopsis
Height: 20in (50cm)
Spread: 18in (45cm)
Aspect: Sun or half shade
Soil: Well-drained, fertile
Hardiness: Zone 6
Propagation: Division, in spring

A selected form of the species with flowers of lemon-yellow, all summer long. Leaves are midgreen, deeply incised, 3-pinnate; lobes linear, filamentous.

Coreopsis verticillata 'Zagreb' (Asteraceae/Compositae)

Common name: Threadleaf coreopsis
Height: 1ft (30cm)
Spread: 1ft (30cm)
Aspect: Sun or half shade
Soil: Well-drained, fertile
Hardiness: Zone 6
Propagation: Division, in spring

Drought-resistant, cloned cultivar, with flowers of golden-yellow all summer. Midgreen leaves are deeply incised, 3-pinnate, with linear, filamentous lobes.

Coriaria terminalis (Coriariaceae)

Common names: None
Height: 3ft (1m)
Spread: 6ft (2m)
Aspect: Sun
Soil: Well-drained, fertile
Hardiness: Zone 8
Propagation: Seed, in warmth in spring; division, in spring

Rhizomatous, deciduous subshrub. Leaves alternate, lance-shaped, glossy-green. Insignificant flowers are followed by black berries with poisonous seeds.

Coriaria terminalis var. xanthocarpa (Coriariaceae

Common names: None
Height: 3ft (90cm)
Spread: 5ft (1.5m)
Aspect: Sun
Soil: Well-drained, fertile
Hardiness: Zone 8
Propagation: Seed, in warmth in spring; division, in spring

Rhizomatous, deciduous subshrub. Shoots arching, leaves lance-shaped, bright green. Insignificant flowers, followed by berries of translucent yellow with poisonous seeds.

The starry yellow flowers of Coreopsis verticillata *are borne from midsummer through to autumn.*

Cornus canadensis A.G.M.
(Cornaceae)

Common names: Bunchberry; dwarf cornel
Height: 6in (15cm)
Spread: Indefinite
Aspect: Sun or half shade
Soil: Moist, acidic
Hardiness: Zone 2
Propagation: Division, in spring or autumn

Highly invasive plant. Leaves lance-shaped to oval, midgreen. Flowers tiny, green, with large, white, pink-tinted bracts, spring and early summer, followed by red berries.

Cortaderia selloana 'Pumila' A.G.M.
(Poaceae/Bambusoideae)

Common name: Pampas grass
Height: To 5ft (1.5m)
Spread: 3ft (90cm)
Aspect: Sun
Soil: Well-drained, fertile
Hardiness: Zone 8
Propagation: Seed, in warmth in spring; division, in spring

Dwarf clone of a tall species; the only form for small gardens. Leaves long, razor-edged (wear gloves), arching, glaucous. Flowering panicles erect, silvery-yellow, in autumn.

Cortaderia selloana 'Rendatleri'
(Poaceae/Bambusoideae)

Common name: Pampas grass
Height: 8ft (2.5m)
Spread: 6ft (2m)
Aspect: Sun
Soil: Well-drained, fertile
Hardiness: Zone 8
Propagation: Seed, in warmth in spring; division, in spring

Pampas grass with most attractive pinkish-purple panicles. Place at the back of the border: razor-sharp leaf-blades will cut nearby plants in a wind. Wear gloves.

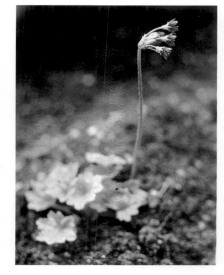

Cortusa matthioli
(Primulaceae)

Common names: None
Height: 12in (30cm)
Spread: 6in (15cm)
Aspect: Half shade
Soil: Moist, well-drained, fertile, humus-rich
Hardiness: Zone 7
Propagation: Seed, when ripe; division, in spring

European wood ander, for cool, moist sites. Leaves basal, round- or heart-shaped, midgreen. Flowers in one-sided umbels, bell-shaped, pink, late spring and early summer.

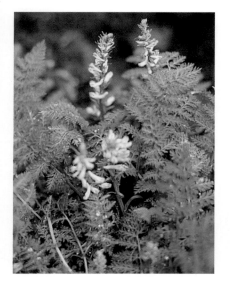

Corydalis cheilanthifolia
(Papaveraceae)

Common name: Fernleaved corydalis
Height: 12in (30cm)
Spread: 10in (25cm)
Aspect: Sun or half shade
Soil: Well-drained, fertile
Hardiness: Zone 6
Propagation: Seed, when ripe; division, in autumn

Fibrous-rooted evergreen. Leaves fern-like, 2- or 3-pinnate, leaflets lance-shaped to linear, tinted bronze. Deep yellow flowers in racemes, spring to summer. Good wall plant.

Corydalis flexuosa
(Papaveraceae)

Common names: None
Height: 12in (30cm)
Spread: 8in (20cm)
Aspect: Half shade
Soil: Moist, well-drained, humus-rich
Hardiness: Zone 7
Propagation: Seed, when ripe; division, in autumn

Woodlander from China. Leaves 2-ternate, leaflets ovate, glaucous green. Brilliant blue flowers in terminal and axillary racemes, late spring to summer. Summer dormant.

Corydalis lutea
(Papaveraceae)

Common name: Yellow corydalis
Height: 16in (40cm)
Spread: 12in (30cm)
Aspect: Sun or half shade
Soil: Moist, well-drained, fertile, humus-rich
Hardiness: Zone 6
Propagation: Seed, when ripe; division, in autumn

Rhizomatous, mound-forming, evergreen woodlander. Leaves midgreen, fernlike, 2- or 3-pinnate; leaflets obovate, 3-lobed. Flowers yellow, in racemes, all summer.

Corydalis ochroleuca
(Papaveraceae)

Common names: None
Height: 12in (30cm)
Spread: 12in (30cm)
Aspect: Sun or half shade
Soil: Moist, well-drained, fertile
Hardiness: Zone 5
Propagation: Seed, when ripe; division, in autumn

Evergreen fibrous-rooted woodlander. Leaves 2- or 3-pinnate, leaflets obovate. Flowers in small racemes, white, with yellow throats, late spring to early summer.

Corydalis ophiocarpa
(Papaveraceae)

Common names: None
Height: 30in (75cm)
Spread: 12in (30cm)
Aspect: Sun or half shade
Soil: Moist, well-drained,
fertile, humus-rich
Hardiness: Zone 6
Propagation: Seed, when ripe;
division, in autumn

Perennial from the E. Himalayas. Leaves in
a dense rosette, 2-pinnate, gray-green.
Flowers in a crowded terminal raceme,
ivory, the inner petals tipped red, in spring.

Corydalis solida
A.G.M.
(Papaveraceae)

Common names: None
Height: 12in (30cm)
Spread: 6in (15cm)
Aspect: Sun or half shade
Soil: Sharply drained, sandy
Hardiness: Zone 6
Propagation: Seed, when ripe;
division, in autumn

Tuberous perennial from N. Europe. Leaves
gray-green, 2- or 3-ternate; leaflets ovate,
deeply dissected. Flowers pale lilac-pink, red
or white, in dense spiky racemes, in spring.

Cosmos atrosanguineus
(Asteraceae/Compositae)

Common name: Chocolate
cosmos
Height: 30in (75cm)
Spread: 18in (45cm)
Aspect: Sun
Soil: Moist, well-drained,
fertile
Hardiness: Zone 8
Propagation: Seed, in warmth
in late spring

Spreading, with pinnate or 2-pinnate
leaves; lobes ovate to diamond-shaped.
Solitary, single, velvety, chocolate-scented,
maroon flowers, summer to autumn.

Crambe cordifolia
A.G.M.
(Brassicaceae/Cruciferae)

Common name: Greater
sea-kale
Height: 6ft (2m)
Spread: 5ft (1.5m)
Aspect: Sun
Soil: Well-drained, fertile
Hardiness: Zone 6
Propagation: Seed or division,
both in spring

Coastal plant. Leaves large, ovate to kidney-
shaped, toothed, deep green. Flowers tiny,
perfumed, cross-shaped, white, in branched
panicles, in late spring and early summer.

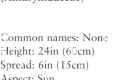

Crambe maritima
(Brassicaceae/Cruciferae)

Common name: Sea-kale
Height: 32in (80cm)
Spread: 24in (60cm)
Aspect: Sun
Soil: Well-drained, fertile
Hardiness: Zone 5
Propagation: Seed or division,
both in spring

Culinary herb from coastal Europe and the
Black Sea. Leaves glaucous green, large,
ovate, twisted. Flowers in dense racemes,
small, perfumed, white, from late spring.

Crepis incana
A.G.M.
(Asteraceae/Compositae)

Common name: Pink
dandelion
Height: 1ft (30cm)
Spread: 1ft (30cm)
Aspect: Full sun
Soil: Any well-drained
Hardiness: Zone 8
Propagation: Seed, when ripe

Perennial from Greece. Leaves dandelion-
like, inverse lance-shaped, pinnatifid, gray-
green. Corymbs of dandelion-like, bright
pink flowers. Flowers well if deadheaded.

Crinum macowanii
(Amaryllidaceae)

Common names: None
Height: 24in (60cm)
Spread: 6in (15cm)
Aspect: Sun
Soil: Moist, well-drained,
fertile, humus-rich
Hardiness: Zone 9
Propagation: Seed, in warmth
when ripe; offsets, in spring

Bulbous plant from South Africa. Leaves
basal straps, wavy-edged, green. Flowers in
umbels, perfumed, white or pink, with a
red stripe on each tepal. All parts toxic.

Crinum x powellii
A.G.M.
(Amaryllidaceae)

Common names: None
Height: 4ft (1.2m)
Spread: 1ft (30cm)
Aspect: Sun
Soil: Moist, well-drained,
fertile, humus-rich
Hardiness: Zone 6
Propagation: Seed or offsets,
both in spring

Deciduous, bulbous hybrid of garden origin.
Leaves long, arching, green straps. Flowers
perfumed, flared, pink trumpets, in umbels
late summer to autumn. All parts toxic.

Crinum x powellii
'Album' A.G.M.
(Amaryllidaceae)

Common names: None
Height: 4ft (1.2m)
Spread: 1ft (30cm)
Aspect: Sun
Soil: Moist, well-drained,
fertile, humus-rich
Hardiness: Zone 6
Propagation: Seed or offsets,
both in spring

White form of deciduous, bulbous hybrid.
Flared, scented trumpet flowers marginally
bigger than the pink form. Leaves long,
arching, green straps. All parts toxic.

CROCOSMIA (Iridaceae)
Montbretia

This genus of cormous perennials consists of some half a
dozen species from South Africa, which have been hybridized
extensively since the end of the 19th century. The original
cross was made in 1882, in France, between *C. pottsii* and
C. aurea, and given the unwieldy label *C.* x *crocosmiiflora*.
The terminology has become very complex, and is often given
only in part; here, they are dealt with in alphabetical order of
the cultivar name, as is common practice. The hybrids are
extremely handsome and useful plants, generally a great
improvement on the wild forms. Their degree of hardiness
varies, but most are fairly hardy. The corms form "chains" in
time, with new corms growing on old corms, and must be
lifted and divided when the clumps become too dense; the old
corms should not be detached in the process, as they are
stores of nourishment for the new ones. The leaves are erect,
linear to lance-shaped, pleated or ribbed, and green or
brownish-green. The flowers are in spikes, which may be
branched or unbranched, carried on wiry stems, and are
followed by attractive seed capsules. Both the leaves and the
flowering spikes last well in water, and montbretias are
popular for flower-arranging; they are low-allergen plants.

Crocosmia x crocosmiiflora
'Citronella'
(Iridaceae)

Common name: Montbretia
Height: 24in (60cm)
Spread: 4in (10cm)
Aspect: Sun or half shade
Soil: Moist, well-drained,
fertile, humus-rich
Hardiness: Zone 7
Propagation: Division,
in spring

A hybrid cultivar with flowers of pale
yellow in upright to slightly arched,
branching spikes, in late summer. Leaves
are pale green.

Crocosmia
'Emberglow'
(Iridaceae)

Common name: Montbretia
Height: 30in (75cm)
Spread: 4in (10cm)
Aspect: Sun or half shade
Soil: Moist, well-drained,
humus-rich, fertile
Hardiness: Zone 7
Propagation: Division in
spring

A hybrid with midgreen foliage and
flowers of dark red, arranged in 2 neat
rows along arching, branching spikes,
in late summer.

Crocosmia x crocosmiiflora
'Emily McKenzie'
(Iridaceae)

Common name: Montbretia
Height: 24in (60cm)
Spread: 4in (10cm)
Aspect: Sun or half shade
Soil: Moist, well-drained,
fertile, humus-rich
Hardiness: Zone 7
Propagation: Division,
in spring

A hybrid with midgreen foliage and large,
downward-facing flowers of bright orange,
with mahogany markings in the throat,
in late summer.

Crocosmia
'Firebird'
(Iridaceae)

Common name: Montbretia
Height: 32in (80cm)
Spread: 4in (10cm)
Aspect: Sun or half shade
Soil: Moist, well-drained,
fertile, humus-rich
Hardiness: Zone 7
Propagation: Division,
in spring

Robust hybrid bearing vibrant orange-red,
upward-facing flowers in late summer,
in generally unbranched spikes. Leaves
are midgreen.

Crocosmia x crocosmiiflora
'Jackanapes'
(Iridaceae)

Common name: Montbretia
Height: 24in (60cm)
Spread: 4in (10cm)
Aspect: Sun or half shade
Soil: Moist, well-drained,
fertile, humus-rich
Hardiness: Zone 7
Propagation: Division,
in spring

Striking hybrid with large, bicolored
flowers of red and orange in late summer,
on freely branching, arching stems above
midgreen foliage.

Crocosmia x *crocosmiiflora*
'Lady Hamilton'
(Iridaceae)

Common name: Montbretia
Height: 32in (80cm)
Spread: 4in (10cm)
Aspect: Sun or half shade
Soil: Moist, well-drained,
fertile, humus-rich
Hardiness: Zone 9
Propagation: Division,
in spring

A hybrid with leaves of mid-green and
flowers of rich yellow with apricot centers.
Flowers are borne on upright, branching
stems, in late summer.

Crocosmia
'Lucifer' A.G.M.
(Iridaceae)

Common name: Montbretia
Height: 3ft (1m)
Spread: 4in (10cm)
Aspect: Sun or half shade
Soil: Moist, well-drained,
fertile, humus-rich
Hardiness: Zone 7
Propagation: Division,
in spring

Very popular, dependable hybrid with
flowers of intense, deep tomato-red in late
summer, on branching, slightly arched
spikes. Leaves are pleated, midgreen.

Crocosmia masoniorum
AG.M.
(Iridaceae)

Common name: Montbretia
Height: 4ft (1.2m)
Spread: 4in (10cm)
Aspect: Sun or half shade
Soil: Moist, well-drained,
fertile, humus-rich
Hardiness: Zone 7
Propagation: Seed, when ripe;
division, in spring

Large, robust species from South Africa.
Leaves long, pleated, midgreen. Flowers
upward-facing, orange-red, in arching
spikes, in summer.

Crocosmia paniculata
(Iridaceae)

Common name: Montbretia
Height: 4ft (1.2m)
Spread: 4in (10cm)
Aspect: Sun or half shade
Soil: Moist, well-drained,
fertile, humus-rich
Hardiness: Zone 8
Propagation: Seed, when ripe;
division, in spring

Large species from South Africa, with
pleated leaves of olive-green. Flowering
spike branched, flowers orange-red,
downturned, in late summer.

Crocosmia
'Severn Sunrise'
(Iridaceae)

Common name: Montbretia
Height: 32in (80cm)
Spread: 4in (10cm)
Aspect: Sun or half shade
Soil: Moist, well-drained,
fertile, humus-rich
Hardiness: Zone 7
Propagation: Division,
in spring

A hybrid with flowers of glowing orange
with lighter throats, in generally upright,
branching spikes, above leaves of
midgreen, in late summer.

Crocosmia x *crocosmiiflora*
'Solfaterre' A.G.M.
(Iridaceae)

Common name: Montbretia
Height: 32in (80cm)
Spread: 4in (10cm)
Aspect: Sun or half shade
Soil: Moist, well-drained,
fertile, humus-rich
Hardiness: Zone 8
Propagation: Division,
in spring

Very old hybrid with unusual, bronze-
colored leaves. Bears flowers of apricot-
yellow in late summer. Excellent for
flower arrangements.

Crocosmia
'Vulcan'
(Iridaceae)

Common name: Montbretia
Height: 32in (80cm)
Spread: 4in (10cm)
Aspect: Sun or half shade
Soil: Moist, well-drained,
fertile, humus-rich
Hardiness: Zone 7
Propagation: Division,
in spring

A hybrid with midgreen leaves, and
spikes of plentiful, outward-facing flowers
of vibrant orange-red color, borne in
late summer.

Crocosmia
'Walburton Yellow'
(Iridaceae)

Common name: Montbretia
Height: 32in (80cm)
Spread: 4in (10cm)
Aspect: Sun or half shade
Soil: Moist, well-drained,
fertile, humus-rich
Hardiness: Zone
Propagation: Division,
in spring

Modern hybrid with typical large, upward-
facing flowers of clear yellow color, carried
in spikes above midgreen foliage, in late
summer.

CROCUS (Iridacae)
Crocus

These cormous perennials of varying hardiness are found naturally in Europe, North Africa, and through the Middle East to China. They are suitable for planting at the edges of beds or borders, and flower in spring or autumn. Their flowers are goblets, formed by six tepals, the outer three opening to reveal the inner three, which may be of a different color. Some are perfumed. The foliage is linear, semierect, midgreen, with a silver or pale green central stripe. In the spring-flowering types, the foliage appears with, or just after the flowers; in some of the autumn-flowering types it may appear before the flowers. Crocuses are universally deciduous. An Award of Garden Merit has been bestowed on no fewer than 39 crocuses, and it is for the specialist book to cover them in detail. The representatives of the genus here with one exception are all spring-flowering, and all but one hold an A.G.M. Those which require a dry summer dormancy are not covered here, since they need an alpine house or bulb frame; other types are easy to grow. All they ask is sun and good drainage, and they will increase and will require regular division. Wildlife can be a problem: sparrows pull the flowers apart, and garden rodents eat the corms.

Crocus chrysanthus 'Blue Pearl' A.G.M. (Iridaceae)

Common names: None
Height: 3in (7cm)
Spread: 2in (5cm)
Aspect: Sun
Soil: Well-drained, sandy, fertile
Hardiness: Zone 4
Propagation: Offsets, in summer

A hybrid cultivar of a species from S.E. Europe and Turkey. Flowers perfumed, white, with yellow throats, and outer tepals of lilac-blue, in spring.

Crocus chrysanthus 'Cream Beauty' A.G.M. (Iridaceae)

Common names: None
Height: 3in (7cm)
Spread: 2in (5cm)
Aspect: Sun
Soil: Moist, well-drained, sandy
Hardiness: Zone 4
Propagation: Offsets, in summer

A hybrid cultivar, with perfumed, cream flowers with brownish-green bases, and yellow throats, in spring. Leaves mid- to gray-green, appearing with or after

Crocus kotschyanus A.G.M. (Iridaceae)

Common names: None
Height: 4in (10cm)
Spread: 3in (6cm)
Aspect: Sun
Soil: Dry in summer, sandy
Hardiness: Zone 5
Propagation: Seed, when ripe; offsets, in summer

Vigorous crocus species found in Syria, Lebanon, and Turkey. Pale lilac flowers with cream stamens appear in autumn, before the leaves.

Crocus x luteus 'Golden Yellow' A.G.M. (Iridaceae)

Common names: None
Height: 4in (10cm)
Spread: 2in (5cm)
Aspect: Sun
Soil: Well-drained, sandy
Hardiness: Zone 4
Propagation: Offsets, in summer

Vigorous hybrid, with golden yellow flowers, the outer tepals marked with darker stripes on the back, in spring. Naturalizes well.

Crocus tomassinianus 'Ruby Giant' (Iridaceae)

Common names: None
Height: 4in (10cm)
Spread: 1in (3cm)
Aspect: Sun
Soil: Well-drained, sandy
Hardiness: Zone 5
Propagation: Offsets, in summer

Clump-forming, vigorous crocus that naturalizes well. Bears rich reddish-pink flowers in spring. A sterile hybrid cultivar, so does not set seed.

Crocus chrysanthus 'Snow Bunting' A.G.M. (Iridaceae)

Common names: None
Height: 3in (3cm)
Spread: 2in (5cm)
Aspect: Sun
Soil: Well-drained, sandy
Hardiness: Zone 4
Propagation: Offsets, in summer

A vigorous hybrid cultivar, flowering in spring. White flowers may have faint, feathery bluish markings. Mid- to gray-green leaves with or after the flowers.

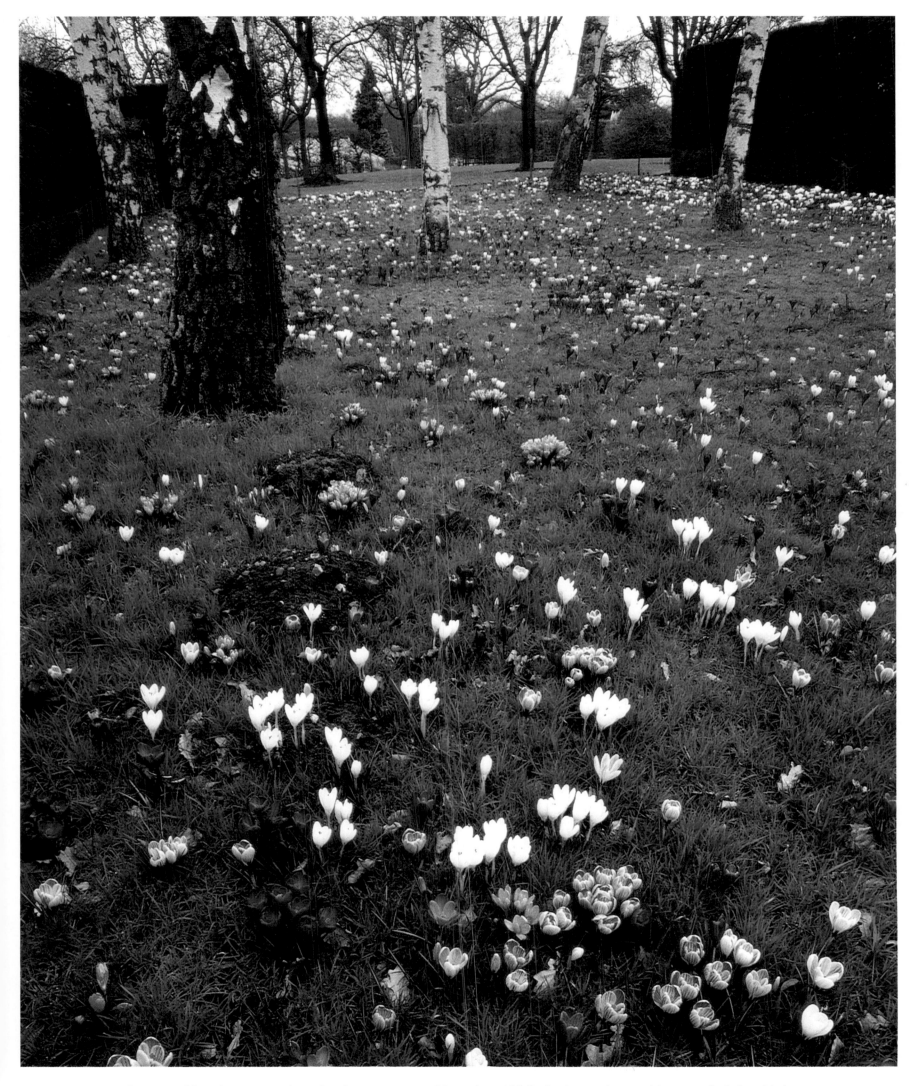

Spring would not be spring without the ubiquitous crocus. Here a beautiful display is complemented by a wood of silver birch.

Cuphea cyanea
(Lythraceae)

Common names: None
Height: 4ft (1.2m)
Spread: 3ft (1m)
Aspect: Sun or half shade
Soil: Well-drained, fertile
Hardiness: Zone 9
Propagation: Seed, in warmth
in spring; division, in spring

Evergreen subshrub from Mexico. Leaves
ovate; shoots sticky, glandular-hairy.
Flowers tubular, orange-red, tipped green,
with 2 violet petals, in racemes, summer.

Cuphea hyssopifolia
A.G.M.
(Lythraceae)

Common names: None
Height: 24in (60cm)
Spread: 32in (80cm)
Aspect: Sun or half shade
Soil: Well-drained, fertile
Hardiness: Zone 10
Propagation: Seed, in warmth
in spring; division, in spring

Evergreen subshrub. Leaves lance-shaped,
dark green. Flowers in short racemes on
downy stems, purple-pink, from summer
to autumn. From Mexico and Guatemala.

CYCLAMEN (Primulaceae)
Sowbread

This genus is found over a wide diversity of habitat and
terrain. Cyclamen grow in the Mediterranean region, Iran,
and Somalia; not surprisingly, they have varying degrees of
hardiness, from Zone 6 to Zone 9. The less hardy species are
not included here; they prefer a dry summer dormancy, and
are most suitable for alpine house or conservatory. There are
some 20 species, all tuberous, and ten have an Award of
Garden Merit. Cyclamen grow in any soil type. Mostly, they
are woodlanders, but some are found in dry areas, and so
their cultural requirements are not easy to summarize. They
are usually spring- or autumn-flowering, but may flower at
other times. The flowers are highly distinctive, with five
reflexed petals ranging in color from white through shades of
pink to red. Some are scented. After the flowers fade, the
stalks of many cyclamen coil down among the leaves to
release the seed as close to the ground as possible. The
foliage, often marked with silver, is handsome in all species,
and some are evergreen. The one constant rule when buying
cyclamen is to buy them while in growth, and not as dry
shrivelled tubers. Planting is best done in autumn, and the
tubers should be planted just below the soil surface.

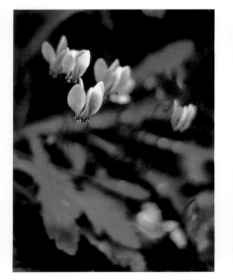

Cyclamen coum
A.G.M.
(Primulaceae)

Common name: Sowbread
Height: 3in (8cm)
Spread: 4in (10cm)
Aspect: Half shade
Soil: Well-drained, fertile,
humus-rich
Hardiness: Zone 6
Propagation: Seed, in
darkness when ripe

Tuberous plant from the Black Sea region.
Leaves round, shiny, plain green, or
marked silver. Flowers pink, red, or white,
in early autumn, with the leaves.

Cyclamen coum subsp.
coum f. **albissimum**
(Primulaceae)

Common name: Sowbread
Height: 3in (8cm)
Spread: 4in (10cm)
Aspect: Half shade
Soil: Well-drained, fertile,
humus-rich
Hardiness: Zone 6
Propagation: Seed, in
darkness when ripe

Charming, white-flowered form of the
species. The clear white flowers are
marked dark red at the mouth, appearing
in early autumn with the leaves.

Cyclamen repandum
(Primulaceae)

Common name: Sowbread
Height: 6in (15cm)
Spread: 5in (12cm)
Aspect: Half shade
Soil: Well-drained, fertile,
humus-rich
Hardiness: Zone 7
Propagation: Seed, in
darkness when ripe

Perennial from N. Mediterranean. Leaves
triangular, green, speckled, or marbled
silver. Flowers red, perfumed, appearing
with the leaves in mid- to late spring.

Cyclamen repandum
subsp. **peloponnesiacum**
A.G.M. (Primulaceae)

Common name: Sowbread
Height: 6in (15cm)
Spread: 5in (12cm)
Aspect: Half shade
Soil: Well-drained, fertile,
humus-rich
Hardiness: Zone 7
Propagation: Seed, in
darkness when ripe

A form of *C. repandum* from the
Peloponnese peninsula. Leaves scalloped,
more heavily marked silver than the type,
flowers pale pink; both in spring.

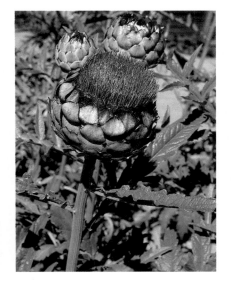

**Cynara cardunculus
A.G.M.
(Asteraceae/Compositae)**

Common name: Cardoon
Height: 5ft (1.5m)
Spread: 4ft (1.2m)
Aspect: Sun
Soil: Well-drained, fertile
Hardiness: Zone 6
Propagation: Seed or division,
both in spring

Clump-forming perennial from Morocco
and the S.W. Mediterranean. Leaves silver,
spiny, pinnatifid; blanched midribs edible.
Flowers huge thistles, on woolly stems.

Cynara baetica subsp.
maroccana
(Asteraceae/Compositae)

Common names: None
Height: 3ft (1m)
Spread: 2ft (60cm)
Aspect: Sun
Soil: Well-drained, sandy,
fertile
Hardiness: Zone 8
Propagation: Seed or division,
both in spring

Clump-forming perennial from Morocco.
Leaves pinnatisect; lobes linear, toothed,
spiny, with white woolly undersides.
Flower purple, thistlelike, good for drying.

Cynara scolymus
(Asteraceae/Compositae)

Common name: Globe
artichoke
Height: 6ft (2m)
Spread: 4ft (1.2m)
Aspect: Sun
Soil: Well-drained, fertile
Hardiness: Zone 6
Propagation: Seed or division,
both in spring

Culinary plant from the N. Mediterranean.
Leaves pinnatifid, gray-green, pointed,
white-woolly underneath. Flower purple,
with big bracts, in autumn, edible as a bud.

Cynoglossum nervosum
(Boraginaceae)

Common names: Chinese
forget-me-not; hound's
tongue
Height: 32in (80cm)
Spread: 24in (60cm)
Aspect: Sun or half shade
Soil: Well-drained, moist
Hardiness: Zone 5
Propagation: Seed or division,
both in spring

Perennial from N. India and W. Pakistan.
Leaves lance-shaped to oblong, hairy, bright
green. Cymes of intense blue, forget-me-not
flowers, spring to summer. Feed sparingly.

Cypella herbertii
(Iridaceae)

Common names: None
Height: 24in (60cm)
Spread: 4in (10cm)
Aspect: Sun
Soil: Well-drained, sandy,
humus-rich
Hardiness: Zone 9
Propagation: Seed, in warmth
when ripe

Bulbous perennial from South America.
Lance-shaped to linear, pleated leaves.
Outer tepals of flowers mustard, inner tepals
brown, spotted or streaked purple, summer.

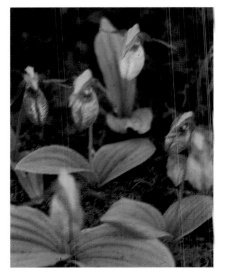

Cypripedium acaule
(Orchidaceae)

Common name: Pink
moccasin-flower
Height: 10in (25cm)
Spread: 10in (25cm)
Aspect: Half shade
Soil: Moist, acidic, fertile,
humus-rich
Hardiness: Zone 5
Propagation: Division,
in spring

Terrestrial, rhizomatous orchid from North
America. Leaves paired, elliptic. Flower
solitary, nodding, brown-green, with pink
lips, in summer. Extremely difficult to grow.

Cypripedium calceolus
(Orchidaceae)

Common name: Yellow
lady's-slipper
Height: 16in (40cm)
Spread: 16in (40cm)
Aspect: Half shade
Soil: Moist, acidic, fertile,
humus-rich
Hardiness: Zone 5
Propagation: Division,
in spring

Terrestrial rhizomatous orchid. Leaves
ovate-elliptic, dark green. Flower single or
paired, brown-purple, petals twisted, lips
large, yellow. Very difficult in cultivation.

Cypripedium reginae
(Orchidaceae)

Common name: Showy
lady's-slipper
Height: 30in (75cm)
Spread: 12in (30cm)
Aspect: Half shade
Soil: Moist, acidic, fertile,
humus-rich
Hardiness: Zone 4
Propagation: Division,
in spring

Terrestrial rhizomatous orchid from North
America. Leaves ovate to lance-shaped.
Flowers single or paired, white, with rose-
pink lips, in summer. Very difficult to grow.

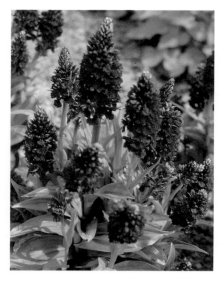

Cyrtanthus brachyscyphus
(Amaryllidaceae)

Common name: Fire lily
Height 12in (30cm)
Spread: 4in (10cm)
Aspect: Sun
Soil: Well-drained, fertile,
humus-rich
Hardiness: Zone 9
Propagation: Seed, in warmth
when ripe; offsets, in spring

Deciduous, bulbous perennial from South
Africa. Leaves lance-shaped, semierect,
green. Flowers in umbels, tubular, red, in
spring to summer.

Dactylis glomerata
'Variegata'
(Graminae/Poaceae)

Common names: None
Height: 18in (45cm)
Spread: 10in (25cm)
Aspect: Sun or half shade
Soil: Well-drained, fertile
Hardiness: Zone 5
Propagation: Division,
in spring

Clump-forming, evergreen, perennial grass
from Eurasia and North Africa. Leaves
linear, variegated cream. Flowering spike
one-sided, pale green.

Dactylorhiza elata
A.G.M.
(Orchidaceae)

Common name: Robust
marsh orchid
Height: 24in (60cm)
Spread: 6in (15cm)
Aspect: Half shade
Soil: Well-drained, moist,
humus-rich
Hardiness: Zone 6
Propagation: Division,
in spring

Tuberous, terrestrial orchid. Leaves linear to
lance-shaped, green, may be spotted brown.
Flowers in dense terminal racemes, purple,
with bracts, late spring. Easy in right place.

Dactylorhiza foliosa
A.G.M.
(Orchidaceae)

Common name: Madeiran
orchid
Height: 60cm (24in)
Spread: 15cm (6in)
Aspect: Half shade
Soil: Well-drained, moist,
humus-rich
Hardiness: Zone 7
Propagation: Division, in
spring

Terrestrial, tuberous orchid. Lance-shaped,
green leaves, can be spotted brown. Flowers
in racemes, pink or purple, with bracts, late
spring to early summer. Easy in right place.

Dactylorhiza fuchsii
(Orchidaceae)

Common name: Common
spotted orchid
Height: 24in (60cm)
Spread: 6in (15cm)
Aspect: Half shade
Soil: Moist, well-drained,
humus-rich
Hardiness: Zone 6
Propagation: Division,
in spring

Terrestrial, tuberous, deciduous orchid.
Leaves lance-shaped, spotted purple. Dense
terminal umbels of flowers, late spring and
early summer, mauve. Easy in right place.

Dactylorhiza praetermissa
(Orchidaceae)

Common name: Southern
marsh orchid
Height: 24in (60cm)
Spread: 6in (15cm)
Aspect: Half shade
Soil: Moist, well-drained,
humus-rich
Hardiness: Zone 6
Propagation: Division,
in spring

Tuberous, terrestrial, deciduous orchid from
N. Europe. Leaves lance-shaped, can be
spotted. Flowers in dense umbel, pale garnet,
with bracts. Easy in right conditions.

Dahlia
'Bishop of Llandaff' A.G.M.
(Asteraceae/Compositae)

Common names: None
Height: 4ft (1.2m)
Spread: 18in (45cm)
Aspect: Sun
Soil: Well-drained, fertile,
humus-rich
Hardiness: Zone 10
Propagation: Division,
in spring

Hybrid dahlia in the "miscellaneous"
classification. Leaves pinnate, lobes oval,
toothed, black-red. Peony-flowered,
blooms semidouble, bright red.

Dahlia merckii
(Asteraceae/Compositae)

Common names: None
Height: 6ft (2m)
Spread: 3ft (1m)
Aspect: Sun
Soil: Well-drained, fertile,
humus-rich
Hardiness: Zone 9
Propagation: Division,
in spring

Tuberous perennial from Mexico. Leaves
pinnate, green. Flowers on many-branched
stems, single pink, purple, or white, with
yellow disc florets.

Darmera peltata
A.G.M.
(Saxifragaceae)

Common name: Umbrella
plant
Height: 6ft (2m)
Spread: 5ft (1.5m)
Aspect: Sun or half shade
Soil: Marginal aquatic
Hardiness: Zone 6
Propagation: Seed or division,
both in spring

Rhizomatous marginal plant from the U.S.A.
Leaves large, peltate, round, deeply lobed,
toothed, veined, deep green. Flowers on tall
stems in large cymes, pink, in spring.

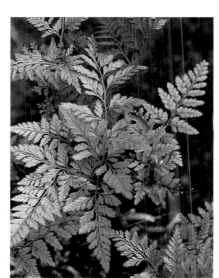

Davallia mariesii
A.G.M.
(Davalliaceae)

Common name: Hare's-foot
fern
Height: 6in (15cm)
Spread: Indefinite
Aspect: Half shade
Soil: Moist, sandy, humus-
rich
Hardiness: Zone 9
Propagation: Spores, in
warmth when ripe; division, in spring

Rhizomatous, deciduous, creeping fern
from East Asia. Fronds 3- to 4-pinnate,
finely cut, broad, midgreen. Segments
linear or triangular.

DELPHINIUM (Ranunculaceae)
Delphinium • Larkspur

Genus of some 250 species, from all parts of the world except
the Arctic, Australia, and Antarctica. Most are fibrous-rooted;
a few are tuberous. The best-known delphiniums are the tall
hybrids with dense spires of flowers, but some species are
small enough for the rock garden. The leaves are toothed and
3-, 5-, or 7-lobed. Tall hybrids almost always need staking.
They make excellent cut flowers, and are prized by flower-
arrangers. Delphiniums are low in allergens, but all parts are
poisonous and skin irritant. They are prone to powdery
mildew, slugs, and snails. They are classified in three groups.
Belladonna Group Upright, to 4ft (1.2m), branching, with
palmately lobed leaves and loose spikes of elfin-caplike single
flowers with spurs up to 1¼in (3cm), in early and late summer.
Elatum Group: Clump-forming, to over 5½ft (1.7m), with
tapering flower spikes and similar smaller, later-flowering
lateral shoots in late spring to early summer, again in autumn
if cut back; flowers single to double, with 5 large outer sepals
and an "eye" of 8 inner sepals. The most popular type.
Pacific Hybrids Short-lived, grown as annuals or biennials.
Over 5½ft (1.7m) tall, and bloom in spring and early summer.
Flowers are semidouble and short-lived.

Delphinium beesianum
'Cliveden Beauty'
(Ranunculaceae)

Common name: Larkspur
Height: 4ft (1.2m)
Spread: 18in (45cm)
Aspect: Sun
Soil: Well-drained, fertile
Hardiness: Zone 3
Propagation: Heeled basal
cuttings, in spring

Belladonna Group delphinium: upright,
suits a border. Branching stems bear
flowers of sky blue in very loose, open
spikes, early and late summer.

Delphinium beesianum
'Peace'
(Ranunculaceae)

Common name: Larkspur
Height: 4ft (1.2m)
Spread: 18in (45cm)
Aspect: Sun
Soil: Well-drained, fertile
Hardiness: Zone 3
Propagation: Heeled basal
cuttings, in spring

Belladonna Group delphinium with flowers
of intense blue, borne in open spikes in
early and late summer. Suits a border or
island bed.

Delphinium beesianum
'Volkerfrieden'
(Ranunculaceae)

Common name: Larkspur
Height: 4ft (1.2m)
Spread: 18in (45cm)
Aspect: Sun
Soil: Well-drained, fertile
Hardiness: Zone 3
Propagation: Heeled basal
cuttings, in spring

Vigorous Belladonna Group delphinium:
upright, suitable for a border or island
bed. Bears flowers of deep blue in early
and late summer.

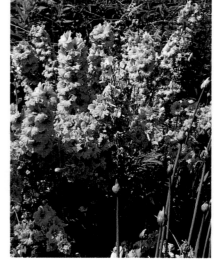

Delphinium
Blue Jade Group
(Ranunculaceae)

Common name: Larkspur
Height: 5ft (1.5m)
Spread: 2ft (60cm)
Aspect: Sun
Soil: Well-drained, fertile
Hardiness: Zone 3
Propagation: Heeled basal
cuttings, in spring

Clump-forming Elatum group delphinium,
with large flowers of mid-blue with darker
eyes, borne in dense spikes. Among the
shorter examples of this group.

Delphinium 'Dora Larkan' displays branched spikes of pretty blue flowers.

Delphinium cashmerianum
(Ranunculaceae)

Common name: Larkspur
Height: 16in (40cm)
Spread: 6in (15cm)
Aspect: Sun
Soil: Well-drained, fertile
Hardiness: Zone 5
Propagation: Seed, in spring

Perennial from the W. Himalayas. Leaves round, toothed, 5- to 7-lobed, green. Dark blue-purple, single flowers in open panicles, in early and again in late summer.

Delphinium
'Galahad'
(Ranunculaceae)

Common name: Larkspur
Height: 5½ft (1.7m)
Spread: 30in (75cm)
Aspect: Sun
Soil: Well-drained, fertile
Hardiness: Zone 3
Propagation: Seed, in spring

Pacific Hybrid delphinium, grown as an annual or biennial. Large, short-lived flowers of pure white. Suits a border or island bed.

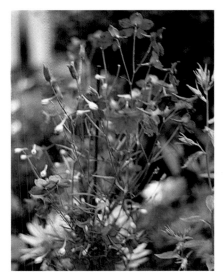

Delphinium grandiflorum
'Blue Butterfly'
(Ranunculaceae)

Common name: Siberian larkspur
Height: 16in (40cm)
Spread: 8in (20cm)
Aspect: Sun
Soil: Well-drained, fertile
Hardiness: Zone 3
Propagation: Seed, in spring

Selected form of a short-lived perennial from Japan and China to Siberia. Leaves 5-lobed, lobes narrowly divided. Flowers in open panicles, single, bright blue, early summer.

Delphinium
Magic Fountain Series
(Ranunculaceae)

Common name: Larkspur
Height: 5ft (1.5m)
Spread: 2ft (60cm)
Aspect: Sun
Soil: Well-drained, fertile
Hardiness: Zone 3
Propagation: Seed, in spring

Series with flowers in a range of colors, from the Elatum Group. One of the shorter examples of the group; suits a border or an island bed.

Delphinium nudicaule
(Ranunculaceae)

Common name: Orange larkspur
Height: 24in (60cm)
Spread: 8in (20cm)
Aspect: Sun
Soil: Well-drained, fertile
Hardiness: Zone 8
Propagation: Seed, in spring

Short-lived perennial from California. Leaves 3- to 5-lobed, fleshy, green. Flowers in open panicles, single, funnel-shaped, vermilion with yellow throats, in summer.

Delphinium speciosum
(Ranunculaceae)

Common name: Larkspur
Height: 30in (75cm)
Spread: 12in (30cm)
Aspect: Sun
Soil: Well-drained, fertile
Hardiness: Zone 6
Propagation: Seed, in spring

Perennial from the Caucasus and C. Asia. Leaves 3- to 5-lobed, segments broad, toothed, subdivided further. Flowers in racemes, intense blue, in summer.

ADDITIONAL HYBRID DELPHINIUMS with an A.G.M. (all Zone 5)

D. 'Blue Dawn'

D. 'Blue Nile'

D. 'Bruce'

D. 'Conspicuous'

D. 'Emily Hawkins'

D. 'Fanfare'

D. 'Faust'

D. 'Fenella'

D. 'Gillian Dallas'

D. 'Langdon's Royal Flush'

D. 'Loch Leven'

D. 'Lord Butler'

D. 'Mighty Atom'

D. 'Rosemary Brock'

D. 'Spindrift'

D. 'Summerfield Miranda'

D. 'Sungleam'

Desmodium elegans
(Leguminosae/Papilionaceae)

Common name: Beggarweed
Height: 5ft (1.5m)
Spread: 5ft (1.5m)
Aspect: Sun
Soil: Well-drained
Hardiness: Zone 6
Propagation: Seed, in autumn; softwood cuttings, in spring

Deciduous subshrub. Leaves long, 3-pinnate, leaflets obovate, green above, gray below. Flowers in terminal panicles, pealike, pink, from late summer to autumn.

Dianella nigra
(Liliaceae/Phormiaceae)

Common name: New Zealand
blueberry
Height: 24in (60cm)
Spread: 18in (45cm)
Aspect: Sun or half shade
Soil: Well-drained, acidic,
fertile, humus-rich
Hardiness: Zone 9
Propagation: Seed, in warmth
in spring; division, in spring

Evergreen woodlander from New Zealand.
Leaves grassy, linear to lance-shaped, dark
green. Loose panicles of small, off-white
flowers in summer, then black berries.

Dianella tasmanica
(Liliaceae/Phormiaceae)

Common name: Tasmanian
blueberry
Height: 4ft (1.2m)
Spread: 18in (45cm)
Aspect: Sun or half shade
Soil: Well-drained, acidic,
fertile, humus-rich
Hardiness: Zone 9
Propagation: Seed, in warmth
in spring; division, in spring

Rhizomatous evergreen from Tasmania and
S.E. Australia. Leaves stiff, rough-edged,
straplike. Lavender flowers in branching
panicles in summer, then blue berries.

DIANTHUS (Caryophyllaceae)
Carnation • Pink

Widely grown genus of some 300 species from Eurasia and
Africa, with one from arctic America. They are evergreen and
long-flowering, with perfumed flowers, excellent for cutting.
All *Dianthus* ask is a sandy, well-drained soil, in sun. They
may flower themselves to death, but are generally short-lived
and must be replaced on a regular basis, from cuttings in late
summer. They are also loved by pigeons and rabbits. All are
highly allergenic. There are four major categories, of which
only the last is included here.

Perpetual-flowering Carnations: Grown under glass for
exhibition or the cut-flower trade.

Malmaison Carnations: Grown under glass for exhibition or
the cut-flower trade.

Border Carnations: Summer-flowering, sometimes clove-
scented, fully double garden plants in a range of colors and
fancy or picotee-edged. They were derived initially from
D. plumarius, but lineage is now obscure.

Pinks: Summer-flowering garden plants, grouped into alpine,
old-fashioned, or modern. They may be single or double,
clove-scented or not. Sterile "mule" pinks are crosses between
border carnations and sweet william (*D. barbatus*).

Dianthus callizonus
(Caryophyllaceae)

Common name: Pink
Height: 8in (20cm)
Spread: 12in (30cm)
Aspect: Sun
Soil: Well-drained
Hardiness: Zone 5
Propagation: Cuttings of non-
flowering shoots, in summer

Mat-forming species from the Carpathians.
Leaves linear to lance-shaped, gray-green.
Flowers solitary, single, petals toothed,
lavender-pink with a purple eye, summer.

Dianthus
'Cranmere Pool' A.G.M.
(Caryophyllaceae)

Common name: Pink
Height: 18in (45cm)
Spread: 12in (30cm)
Aspect: Sun
Soil: Well-drained
Hardiness: Zone 3
Propagation: Cuttings of non-
flowering shoots, in summer

Hybrid garden pink cultivar, with double
flowers which are off-white with a rich
magenta center, slightly toothed, and
scented, in summer.

Dianthus
'Dainty Dame'
(Caryophyllaceae)

Common name: Pink
Height: 6in (15cm)
Spread: 8in (20cm)
Aspect: Sun
Soil: Well-drained
Hardiness: Zone 3
Propagation: Cuttings of non-
flowering shoots, in summer

A compact, hybrid pink cultivar with
perfumed, single, white flowers with a
deep maroon eye, the petals slightly
toothed, in summer.

Dianthus deltoides
A.G.M.
(Caryophyllaceae)

Common name:
Maiden pink
Height: 8in (20cm)
Spread: 12in (30cm)
Aspect: Sun
Soil: Well-drained
Hardiness: Zone 3
Propagation: Cuttings of non-
flowering shoots, in summer

Mat-forming pink species widespread in
Europe and Asia. Leaves dark green.
Flowers solitary, single, toothed, bearded,
white, pink, or red, in summer.

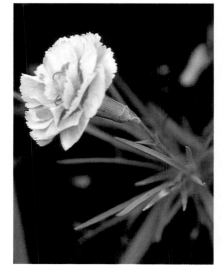

Dianthus deltoides
'Leuchtfunk'
(Caryophyllaceae)

Common name:
Maiden pink
Height: 8in (20cm)
Spread: 12in (30cm)
Aspect: Sun
Soil: Well-drained
Hardiness: Zone 3
Propagation: Cuttings of non-flowering shoots, in summer

Dianthus
'Devon Dove'® A.G.M.
(Caryophyllaceae)

Common name: Pink
Height: 18in (45cm)
Spread: 12in (30cm)
Aspect: Sun
Soil: Well-drained
Hardiness: Zone 3
Propagation: Cuttings of non-flowering shoots, in summer

Dianthus
'Dewdrop'
(Caryophyllaceae)

Common name: Pink
Height: 18in (45cm)
Spread: 12in (30cm)
Aspect: Sun
Soil: Well-drained
Hardiness: Zone 3
Propagation: Cuttings of non-flowering shoots, in summer

Dianthus
'Doris' A.G.M.
(Caryophyllaceae)

Common name: Pink
Height: 18in (45cm)
Spread: 12in (30cm)
Aspect: Sun
Soil: Any, well-drained
Hardiness: Zone 3
Propagation: Cuttings of non-flowering shoots, in summer

A cloned selection of the mat-forming maiden pink species, bearing abundant flowers of intense cerise, in summer. Leaves dark green.

A hybrid pink cultivar bearing double flowers of pure white, petals toothed, bearded, in summer. Leaves and stems a bloomy blue-green.

Hybrid pink cultivar with semidouble white flowers, with dark markings at the center, petals toothed, in summer. Leaves are linear.

Modern hybrid pink with perfumed, double, bicolored flowers of pale pink with a dark pink center, petals toothed, in summer.

Dianthus
'Gran's Favourite' A.G.M.
(Caryophyllaceae)

Common name: Laced pink
Height: 12in (30cm)
Spread: 8in (20cm)
Aspect: Sun
Soil: Well-drained
Hardiness: Zone 3
Propagation: Cuttings of non-flowering shoots, in summer

Dianthus gratianopolitanus
A.G.M.
(Caryophyllaceae)

Common name: Cheddar pink
Height: 6in (15cm)
Spread: 15in (35cm)
Aspect: Sun
Soil: Well-drained
Hardiness: Zone 3
Propagation: Cuttings of non-flowering shoots, in summer

Dianthus
'Haytor Rock' A.G.M.
(Caryophyllaceae)

Common name: Modern clove pink
Height: 18in (45cm)
Spread: 12in (30cm)
Aspect: Sun
Soil: Any, well-drained
Hardiness: Zone 3
Propagation: Cuttings of non-flowering shoots, in summer

Dianthus
'Houndspool Ruby' A.G.M.
(Caryophyllaceae)

Common name: Modern pink
Height: 18in (45cm)
Spread: 8in (20cm)
Aspect: Sun
Soil: Any well-drained
Hardiness: Zone 3
Propagation: Cuttings of non-flowering shoots, in summer

Popular, mound-forming, laced, modern pink with clove-scented, double white flowers, with pink centers and edges, in summer.

A mat-forming species from N.W. and C. Europe. Leaves gray-green. Flowers single, solitary, intensely perfumed, deep pink, in summer. Petals toothed, bearded.

Excellent modern hybrid pink bearing flushes of clove-scented, double, pink flowers, streaked red, in summer. Leaves gray-green.

Clump-forming modern pink with double, bicolored flowers of ruby-red with currant-red centers, in flushes through summer. Leaves gray-green.

Dianthus
'Inshriach Dazzler' A.G.M.
(Caryophyllaceae)

Common name: Alpine pink
Height: 4in (10cm)
Spread: 6in (15cm)
Aspect: Sun
Soil: Well-drained
Hardiness: Zone 3
Propagation: Cuttings of non-flowering shoots, in summer

An alpine pink with solitary, single flowers of deep carmine-red with fringed petals, carried on short stems, in summer. Good for border edge or rock garden.

Dianthus knappii
(Caryophyllaceae)

Common name: Pink
Height: 16in (40cm)
Spread: 12in (30cm)
Aspect: Sun
Soil: Well-drained
Hardiness: Zone 3
Propagation: Seed, in spring or autumn

The only yellow-flowered species. Flowers on long stems, in few-flowered clusters, yellow, with a purple spot near the base, in summer. From the W. Balkans.

Dianthus
'Mrs. Sinkins'
(Caryophyllaceae)

Common name: Old-fashioned pink
Height: 18in (45cm)
Spread: 12in (30cm)
Aspect: Sun
Soil: Well-drained
Hardiness: Zone 3
Propagation: Cuttings of non-flowering shoots, in summer

A popular, old-fashioned self with one flush of flowers, in summer. Flowers are shaggy, double, fringed, white, and strongly perfumed; calyces tend to split.

Dianthus myrtinervius
(Caryophyllaceae)

Common name: Pink
Height: 2in (5cm)
Spread: 8in (20cm)
Aspect: Sun
Soil: Well-drained
Hardiness: Zone 3
Propagation: Seed, in autumn or spring

Mat-forming species from the Balkans and Greece. Leaves lance, bright green. Flowers solitary, single, deep pink, with a pale eye, in summer.

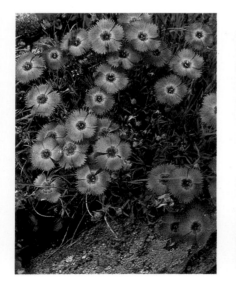

Dianthus pavonius
A.G.M.
(Caryophyllaceae)

Common name: Pink
Height: 3in (8cm)
Spread: 8in (20cm)
Aspect: Sun
Soil: Well-drained
Hardiness: Zone 4
Propagation: Seed, in autumn or spring

Mat-forming perennial from the Alps. Leaves linear, gray-green. Flowers solitary, single, toothed, bearded, deep pink in summer. Good for border or rock garden.

Dianthus
'Prince Charming'
(Caryophyllaceae)

Common name: Pink
Height: 4in (10cm)
Spread: 8in (20cm)
Aspect: Sun
Soil: Well-drained
Hardiness: Zone 3
Propagation: Seed, in autumn or spring

A small pink with single flowers, of a washed-out pink in color. Leaves are linear and green. Suitable for the edge of a border or for a rock garden.

Dianthus
'Queen of Henri'
(Caryophyllaceae)

Common name: Pink
Height: 18in (45cm)
Spread: 8in (20cm)
Aspect: Sun
Soil: Well-drained
Hardiness: Zone 3
Propagation: Cuttings of non-flowering shoots, in summer

Modern pink with patterned, perfumed flowers. The centers of the petals are white, their edges laced with pink. Leaves are gray-green.

Dianthus
'Rose Joy' A.G.M.
(Caryophyllaceae)

Common name: Pink
Height: 18in (45cm)
Spread: 8in (20cm)
Aspect: Sun
Soil: Well-drained
Hardiness: Zone 3
Propagation: Cuttings of non-flowering shoots, in summer

Dependable modern pink with double, toothed, pink-purple flowers, in clusters of 2–3, in flushes through summer. Foliage is gray-green.

The sweetly scented garden pink Dianthus pavonius has solitary flowers and gray-green leaves.

Dianthus
'Royal Velvet'
(Caryophyllaceae)

Common name: Pink
Height: 18in (45cm)
Spread: 8in (20cm)
Aspect: Sun
Soil: Well-drained
Hardiness: Zone 3
Propagation: Cuttings of
non-flowering shoots, in
summer

A modern hybrid pink, with single, laced, pink flowers, blotched white, in flushes through summer. Foliage is linear and gray-green.

Dianthus superbus
(Caryophyllaceae)

Common name: Superb pink
Height: 8in (20cm)
Spread: 8in (20cm)
Aspect: Sun
Soil: Well-drained
Hardiness: Zone 4
Propagation: Seed, in autumn
or spring

Species from the mountains of Eurasia. Leaves linear, green. Flowers single, solitary or in pairs, perfumed, purple-pink, with deeply fringed petals, in summer.

Dianthus
'Valda Wyatt' A.G.M.
(Caryophyllaceae)

Common name: Modern pink
Height: 1ft (30cm)
Spread: 1ft (30cm)
Aspect: Sun
Soil: Well-drained
Hardiness: Zone 3
Propagation: Cuttings of
nonflowering shoots, in
summer

Modern bicolored pink with double, clove-scented flowers of lavender-pink, with deeper pink centers, in flushes through summer.

Dianthus
'Waithman Beauty'
(Caryophyllaceae)

Common name: Modern pink
Height: 12in (30cm)
Spread: 8in (20cm)
Aspect: Sun
Soil: Well-drained
Hardiness: Zone 3
Propagation: Cuttings of
nonflowering shoots, in
summer

A modern hybrid pink with flowers of deep pink, blotched white and with white centers, in flushes in summer. Leaves are linear, gray-green.

Dianthus
'Whatfield Joy'
(Caryophyllaceae)

Common name: Modern pink
Height: 8in (20cm)
Spread: 4in (10cm)
Aspect: Sun
Soil: Well-drained
Hardiness: Zone 3
Propagation: Cuttings of
nonflowering shoots, in
summer

A modern hybrid pink with single, small flowers of rose pink, with a paler center, borne in flushes in summer. Leaves are linear and green.

Dianthus
'Widecombe Fair'
(Caryophyllaceae)

Common name: Modern pink
Height: 12in (30cm)
Spread: 8in (20cm)
Aspect: Sun
Soil: Well-drained
Hardiness: Zone 3
Propagation: Cuttings of
nonflowering shoots, in
summer

Modern hybrid pink with double, clove-scented, peach flowers, which open to blush pink, in flushes through summer. Leaves are linear, gray-green.

DIASCIA (Scrophulariaceae)
Twinspur

There are some 50 or so erect to creeping or trailing, annual and short-lived perennial species in this genus. They originate in the southern regions of the African continent, and consequentially they are for the most part not very hardy. They are, however, relatively recent arrivals, and some are proving hardier than at first thought, surviving in Zone 9 or even into Zone 8, provided they are given protection from excessive winter wet. They prefer moist soil, but do not tolerate waterlogged conditions. Diascias are chiefly valued for their long flowering season. The flowers are invariably pink or salmon-colored, and borne in racemes on stems that range from erect to prostrate. They are tubular and five-lobed; the two upper lobes are spurred and have curious sacs marked with yellow and purple patches, known as "windows," at the base. They should be deadheaded regularly to prolong flowering. The foliage is midgreen, linear to ovate, and toothed, and sometimes evergreen. Diascias also benefit from a shearing-over in late summer, and this provides a useful source of cuttings for propagation, either to safeguard in case of winter losses or to replace plants that have passed their best, every few years.

Diascia
'Coral Belle'®, syn. 'Hecbel'
(Scrophulariaceae)

Common name: Twinspur
Height: 12in (30cm)
Spread: 8in (20cm)
Aspect: Sun
Soil: Moist, well-drained,
fertile
Hardiness: Zone 8
Propagation: Cuttings, spring
or summer

A hybrid *Diascia*. Leaves ovate to lance-
shaped, midgreen. Racemes of flowers,
coral-pink in color, all summer long. Good
for the front of a border.

Diascia fetcaniensis
(Scrophulariaceae)

Common name: Twinspur
Height: 10in (25cm)
Spread: 12in (30cm)
Aspect: Sun
Soil: Moist, well-drained,
fertile
Hardiness: Zone 8
Propagation: Seed, in warmth
in spring; cuttings, in spring

Species from the Drakensberg mountains of
southern Africa. Leaves ovate, hairy, green.
Flowers in loose racemes, rose-pink, spurs
downturned, summer and early autumn.

Diascia
'Joyce's Choice' A.G.M.
(Scrophulariaceae)

Common name: Twinspur
Height: 12in (30cm)
Spread: 8in (20cm)
Aspect: Sun
Soil: Moist, well-drained,
fertile
Hardiness: Zone 8
Propagation: Cuttings,
in spring or summer

Reliable hybrid *Diascia*. Leaves ovate-
linear, midgreen. Flowers in loose racemes,
bicolored light and dark yellowish-pink, all
summer.

Diascia
'Lady Valerie' A.G.M.
(Scrophulariaceae)

Common name: Twinspur
Height: 12in (30cm)
Spread: 8in (20cm)
Aspect: Sun
Soil: Moist, well-drained,
fertile
Hardiness: Zone 8
Propagation: Cuttings,
in spring or summer

A hybrid *Diascia*. Leaves ovate to heart-
shaped, midgreen. Flowers of a strong
yellowish-pink are carried in loose
racemes all summer.

Diascia rigescens
A.G.M.
(Scrophulariaceae)

Common name: Twinspur
Height: 12in (30cm)
Spread: 16in (40cm)
Aspect: Sun
Soil: Moist, well-drained,
fertile
Hardiness: Zone 8
Propagation: Seed or cuttings,
both in spring

Trailing species from South Africa. Leaves
heart-shaped, toothed, midgreen. Flowers
in dense racemes, deep pink, in summer.
Flops over if not staked.

Diascia
'Rose Queen'
(Scrophulariaceae)

Common name: Twinspur
Height: 18in (45cm)
Spread: 12in (30cm)
Aspect: Sun
Soil: Moist, well-drained,
fertile
Hardiness: Zone 8
Propagation: Cuttings,
in spring or summer

A very floriferous and handsome hybrid
Diascia cultivar with flowers of a most
intense pink, borne in loose racemes all
summer long.

Diascia
'Ruby Field' A.G.M.
(Scrophulariaceae)

Common name: Twinspur
Height: 10in (25cm)
Spread: 18in (45cm)
Aspect: Sun
Soil: Moist, well-drained,
fertile
Hardiness: Zone 8
Propagation: Cuttings,
in spring or summer

An early hybrid *Diascia* cultivar. Leaves
heart-shaped, midgreen. Very prolific in
flowering, bearing masses of salmon-pink
flowers all summer.

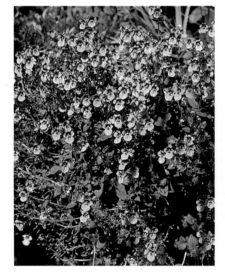

Diascia vigilis
A.G.M.
(Scrophulariaceae)

Common name: Twinspur
Height: 12in (30cm)
Spread: 18in (45cm)
Aspect: Sun
Soil: Moist, well-drained,
fertile
Hardiness: Zone 8
Propagation: Seed or cuttings,
both in spring

Species from the Drakensberg mountains
of southern Africa. Leaves ovate to lance-
shaped, toothed, fleshy. Flowers in loose
racemes, clear pink, all summer.

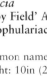

DICENTRA (Fumariaceae/Papaveraceae)
Bleeding-heart

A genus of some 20 or so annuals and perennials found in both Asia and North America, originating for the most part in moist woodland habitats. They may be rhizomatous, tuberous, or have fleshy tap roots. All are reliably hardy. The foliage is much-divided, fernlike, and silver-gray; some species are evergreen, but most are deciduous. The flowers are pendent, carried in arching panicles or racemes. They are highly distinctive: the two outer petals are pouched, giving a generally heart-shaped outline, while the two inner petals form a hood over the anthers. This curious appearance has earned the plants in the genus a variety of common names, from bleeding-heart (most often used for *D. spectabilis*) to Dutchman's breeches. They last well in water, and make excellent and unusual cut flowers; they and the foliage are valuable for flower arrangements. Most of the perennials in the genus make good border plants, but one or two are simply too invasive and better placed in a woodland garden. *D. spectabilis* is not long-lived. *Dicentra* are low in allergens, but all parts of the plants are poisonous and skin irritant. Their preferred conditions are half shade and moist, fertile soil, but they are drought-tolerant.

Dicentra
'Adrian Bloom'
(Fumariaceae/Papaveraceae)

Common name: Bleeding-heart
Height: 16in (40cm)
Spread: 18in (45cm)
Aspect: Half shade
Soil: Moist, well-drained, fertile
Hardiness: Zone 5
Propagation: Division, in spring or just after the leaves die down

Clump-forming, rhizomatous hybrid. Leaves pinnate, lobes long, gray-green. Flowers in narrow racemes, carmine, in late spring and sporadically to autumn.

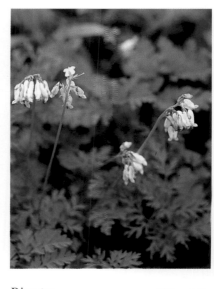

Dicentra
'Pearl Drops'
(Fumariaceae/Papaveraceae)

Common name: Bleeding-heart
Height: 12in (30cm)
Spread: 18in (45cm)
Aspect: Half shade
Soil: Moist, well-drained, fertile
Hardiness: Zone 5
Propagation: Division, in spring or just after the leaves die down

Rhizomatous, invasive, hybrid cultivar. Leaves lobed, glaucous blue-green. Flowers white, tinted pink, in racemes from mid-spring to summer.

Dicentra scandens
(Fumariaceae/Papaveraceae)

Common name: Bleeding-heart
Height: 5ft (1.5m)
Spread: 18in (45cm)
Aspect: Half shade
Soil: Moist, well-drained, fertile
Hardiness: Zone 6
Propagation: Seed, when ripe or in spring

Scrambling or climbing species. Leaves deeply lobed, segments ovate to lance-shaped, midgreen. Long racemes of yellow flowers, on leafy, wiry stems, in summer.

Dicentra spectabilis
A.G.M.
(Fumariaceae/Papaveraceae)

Common name: Bleeding-heart
Height: 3ft (1m)
Spread: 18in (45cm)
Aspect: Half shade
Soil: Moist, well-drained, fertile
Hardiness: Zone 6
Propagation: Seed, when ripe or in spring

Clump-forming species. Leaves 2-ternate, lobes ovate to cut, midgreen. Flowers in arching racemes, outer petals rose-pink, inner ones white, spring to early summer.

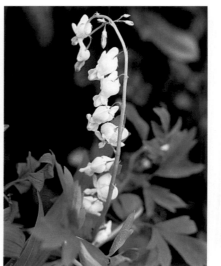

Dicentra spectabilis
'Alba' A.G.M.
(Papaveraceae)

Common name: Bleeding-heart
Height: 4ft (1.2m)
Spread: 18in (45cm)
Aspect: Half shade
Soil: Moist, well-drained, fertile
Hardiness: Zone 6
Propagation: Seed, when ripe or in spring

Pure white form of the species, and more robust and longer-lived. Late spring to midsummer. Woodlander from Siberia, China, and Korea.

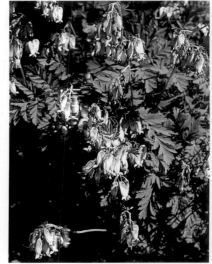

Dicentra
'Spring Morning'
(Fumariaceae/Papaveraceae)

Common name: Bleeding-heart
Height: 18in (45cm)
Spread: 18in (45cm)
Aspect: Half shade
Soil: Moist, well-drained, fertile
Hardiness: Zone 5
Propagation: Division, in spring or just after the leaves die down

Clump-forming, rhizomatous hybrid, with finely divided, dark green leaves, which contrast well with the racemes of pale pink, nodding flowers.

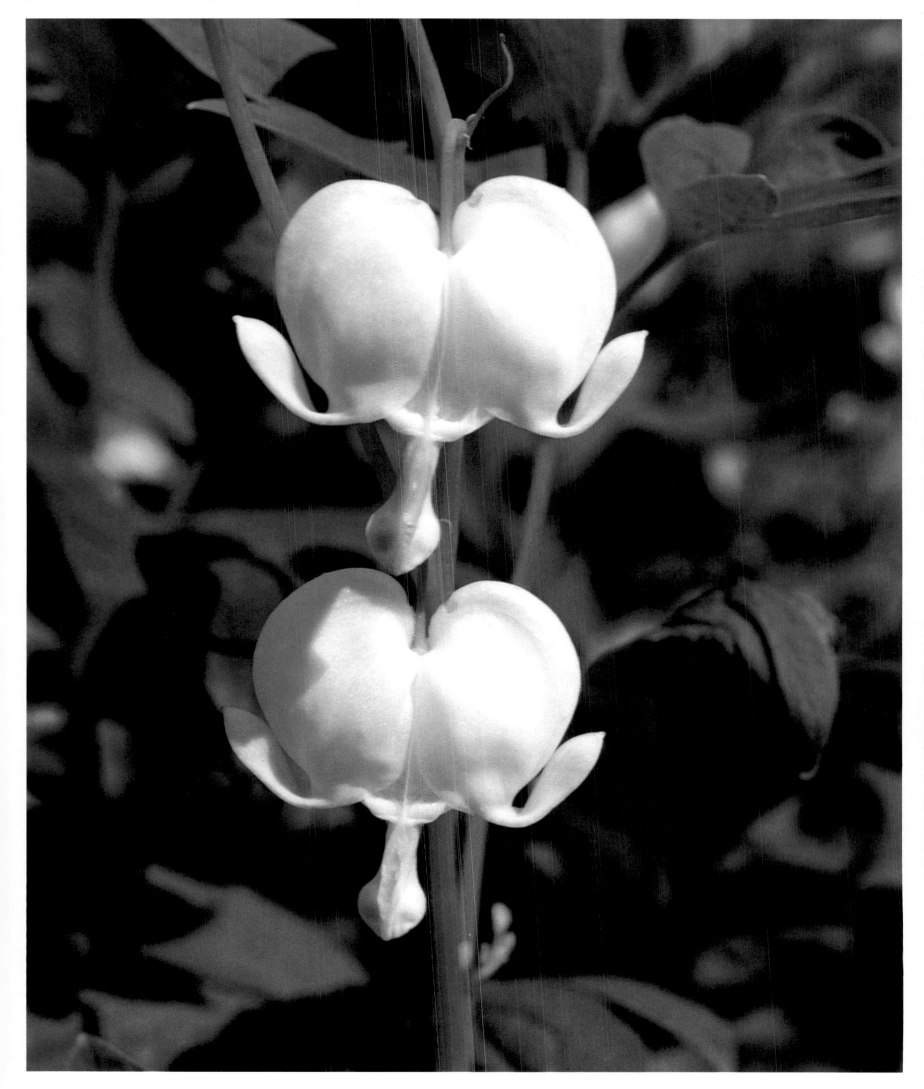

This form of bleeding-heart Dicentra spectabilis *'Alba' has arching racemes of pure white flowers.*

Dicksonia antarctica
A.G.M.
(Cyathaceae/Dicksoniaceae)

Common name: Tree fern
Height: To 15ft (5m)
Spread: To 12ft (4m)
Aspect: Half or full shade
Soil: Acidic, humus-rich
Hardiness: Zone 8
Propagation: Spores,
when ripe

Dictamnus albus
A.G.M.
(Rutaceae)

Common names: Dittany;
gasplant
Height: 36in (90cm)
Spread: 24in (60cm)
Aspect: Sun or half shade
Soil: Dry, well-drained
Hardiness: Zone 3
Propagation: Seed, when ripe;
division, in spring or autumn

Dictamnus albus
var. purpureus A.G.M.
(Rutaceae)

Common name: Dittany;
gasplant
Height: 36in (90cm)
Spread: 24in (60cm)
Aspect: Sun or half shade
Soil: Dry, well-drained
Hardiness: Zone 3
Propagation: Seed, when ripe;
division, in spring or autumn

Dierama pendulum
(Iridaceae)

Common names: None
Height: 6ft (2m)
Spread: 2ft (60cm)
Aspect: Sun
Soil: Well-drained, humus-
rich
Hardiness: Zone 7
Propagation: Seed, when ripe;
division, in spring

Rhizomatous, treelike fern from Australia and Tasmania. Fronds 2- to 3-pinnate, pale green, darkening with age, evergreen in mild climates. Trunk up to 2ft (60cm) across.

Leaves pinnate, spiny, lemon-scented, green. Flowers in long, open racemes, white. Oil in flowers and fruit aromatic; can be ignited on hot days. Toxic, skin irritant, allergenic.

Purple-flowered form. Leaves pinnate, spiny, lemon-scented, green. Flowers in long, open racemes. On hot days oil in flowers and fruit can be ignited. Toxic, irritant, allergenic.

Cormous evergreen from South Africa. Leaves basal, arching, grasslike, gray-green. Flowers bell-shaped, pendent, pink, on arching stems in summer. Seed heads good.

Dierama pulcherrimum
(Iridaceae)

Common names: None
Height: 5ft (1.5m)
Spread: 2ft (60cm)
Aspect: Sun
Soil: Well-drained,
humus-rich
Hardiness: Zone 7
Propagation: Seed, when
ripe; division, in spring

Dietes bicolor
(Iridaceae)

Common name: Wild iris
Height: 3ft (1m)
Spread: 1ft (30cm)
Aspect: Sun or half shade
Soil: Moist, well-drained
Hardiness: Zone 9
Propagation: Seed, in autumn
or spring

Dietes grandiflora
(Iridaceae)

Common name: Wild iris
Height: 3ft (1m)
Spread: 1ft (30cm)
Aspect: Sun or half shade
Soil: Moist, well-drained
Hardiness: Zone 9
Propagation: Seed, in autumn
or spring

Digitalis ferruginea
(Scrophulariaceae)

Common name: Rusty
foxglove
Height: 4ft (1.2m)
Spread: 18in (45cm)
Aspect: Half shade
Soil: Moist avoiding
extremes of wet or dry,
humus-rich
Hardiness: Zone 7
Propagation: Seed, in spring

Cormous evergreen from South Africa and Zimbabwe. Leaves basal, grassy, green. Flowers tubular to bell-shaped, white or pink, pendent, on arching stems, summer.

Rhizomatous evergreen from Africa. Leaves basal, erect, leathery, sword-shaped, pale green. Flowers flat; 3 cream tepals have a brown spot at the base, spring to summer.

Rhizomatous plant from South Africa. Erect, linear, leathery, pale green, basal leaves. Flat, evanescent flowers; 3 white tepals marked mauve and yellow, spring and early summer.

Tall woodlander. Dark green, oblong, entire leaves in rosettes. Flowers in long narrow spikes, golden-brown, veined red-brown inside, in summer. Toxic and skin irritant.

DIGITALIS (Scrophulariaceae)
Foxglove

There are 20 or so biennial and short-lived perennial species from Eurasia and North Africa in this genus. They are tall, architectural plants which do not require staking except in very exposed situations. They are fine woodland plants. Most are perennial, but in Britain they all tend to be thought of as biennial because the native *D. purpurea* is that; this species, too, can be perennial, but the flowers deteriorate markedly in later years. Foxgloves self-seed, so the fact that they are short-lived is not really a problem. Their self-seeding is not invasive, with the seedlings appearing around the base of the parent plant, but if it is a problem, deadheading will cure it. They are very drought-tolerant, but they are prone to powdery mildew. The foliage is handsome, oblong to obovate, toothed or entire, midgreen, growing in basal rosettes. The flowers are in upright racemes, which are usually one-sided, and are open bells or tubules in a range of golden or purple shades, often marked with spots or veins inside. They are very attractive to bees, and an imposing addition to flower arrangements. They are low in allergens, so suitable for the gardener with allergies, but all parts of the plant are poisonous and contact can irritate skin.

Digitalis
'Glory of Roundway'
(Scrophulariaceae)

Common name: Foxglove
Height: 36in (90cm)
Spread: 12in (30cm)
Aspect: Half shade
Soil: Moist, avoiding wet or dry extremes, humus-rich
Hardiness: Zone 5
Propagation: Division, in spring

Hybrid foxglove cultivar with tall racemes of funnel-shaped, flowers of pale yellow, tinted pink, in summer. Good woodland plant. All parts toxic and skin irritant.

Digitalis grandiflora
A.G.M.
(Scrophulariaceae)

Common name: Yellow foxglove
Height: 3ft (1m)
Spread: 18in (45cm)
Aspect: Half shade
Soil: Humus-rich
Hardiness: Zone 4
Propagation: Seed, in spring

Woodlander from Europe to Siberia. Leaves ovate-oblong, toothed, veined, midgreen. Raceme of pale yellow tubular flowers in early to mid-summer. Toxic and irritant.

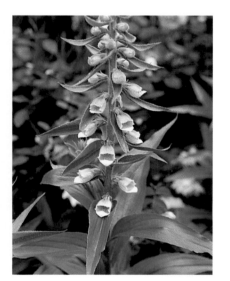

Digitalis
'John Innes Tetra'
(Scrophulariaceae)

Common name: Foxglove
Height: 36in (90cm)
Spread: 12in (30cm)
Aspect: Half shade
Soil: Humus-rich
Hardiness: Zone 6
Propagation: Division, in spring

A hybrid foxglove cultivar with racemes of tubular, orange, yellow-lipped flowers in summer. Good for a woodland garden. All parts toxic and skin irritant.

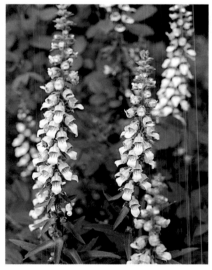

Digitalis lanata
A.G.M.
(Scrophulariaceae)

Common name: Grecian foxglove
Height: 24in (60cm)
Spread: 12in (30cm)
Aspect: Half shade
Soil: Humus-rich
Hardiness: Zone 7
Propagation: Seed, in spring

Woodland species. Leaves oblong to lance-shaped, midgreen. Dense raceme of cream to fawn flowers, veined brown, pale lower lip, in midsummer. Toxic and skin irritant.

Digitalis lutea
(Scrophulariaceae)

Common name: Straw foxglove
Height: 24in (60cm)
Spread: 12in (30cm)
Aspect: Half shade
Soil: Humus-rich
Hardiness: Zone 4
Propagation: Seed, in spring

Woodland species. Leaves glossy, green, inverse-lance-shaped to oblong, toothed. Slim raceme of pale yellow flowers, early-to midsummer. Toxic and skin irritant.

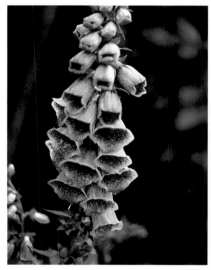

Digitalis x *mertonensis*
A.G.M.
(Scrophulariaceae)

Common names: None
Height: 36in (90cm)
Spread: 12in (30cm)
Aspect: Half shade
Soil: Humus-rich
Hardiness: Zone 5
Propagation: Division, in spring

Tetraploid hybrid; comes true from seed. Leaves toothed, veined, glossy, lance-shaped to ovate. Racemes of pinkish-buff flowers, spring to early summer. Toxic and irritant.

Digitalis purpurea
(Scrophulariaceae)

Common name: Biennial
foxglove
Height: To 6ft (2m)
Spread: 2ft (60cm)
Aspect: Half shade
Soil: Humus-rich
Hardiness: Zone 6
Propagation: Seed, in spring

Biennial or short-lived perennial European
species. Leaves lance-shaped, toothed, deep
green. Flowers in one-sided racemes, pink,
purple, or white. Toxic and skin irritant.

Dionaea muscipula
(Droseraceae)

Common name: Venus
flytrap
Height: 12in (30cm)
Spread: 6in (15cm)
Aspect: Sun
Soil: Moist, acidic
Hardiness: Zone 8
Propagation: Seed, in warmth
in spring

Rosette-forming, insectivorous species from
North America. Leaves yellow-green, stalks
winged, spiny-edged. Flowers in umbels on
bare stalks, white, early to midsummer.

Diphylleia cymosa
(Berberidaceae)

Common names: None
Height: 3ft (1m)
Spread: 1ft (30cm)
Aspect: Full or half shade
Soil: Moist, humus-rich
Hardiness: Zone 7
Propagation: Seed or division,
both in spring

Rhizomatous woodlander. Leaves large,
peltate, toothed, dark green. Flowers in
terminal cymes, white, bowl-shaped, in late
spring to early summer; blue berries follow.

Diplarrhena moraea
(Iridaceae)

Common names: None
Height: 24in (60cm)
Spread: 10in (25cm)
Aspect: Sun or half shade
Soil: Moist, well-drained,
sandy, acidic
Hardiness: Zone 7
Propagation: Seed or division,
both in spring

Rhizomatous plant from Australia. Leaves
basal, long, linear, dark green. Flowers
scented, white; purple and yellow marks on
inner tepals, in late spring to early summer.

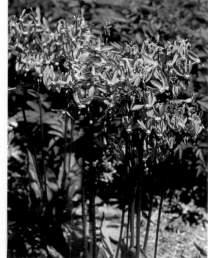

Disa uniflora
(Orchidaceae)

Common names: None
Height: 24in (60cm)
Spread: 8in (20cm)
Aspect: Half shade
Soil: Peaty, mossy, sandy
Hardiness: Zone 10
Propagation: Division, after
growth starts

Terrestrial orchid from South Africa. Leaves
lance-shaped, green. Short raceme of up to
10 flowers in summer, red with gold veins.
Not easy; keep cool and shaded in summer.

Disporum smithii
(Convallariaceae/Liliaceae)

Common names: None
Height: 2ft (60cm)
Spread: 1ft (30cm)
Aspect: Half shade
Soil: Moist, well-drained,
humus-rich
Hardiness: Zone 6
Propagation: Seed, in
autumn; division, in spring

Rhizomatous woodlander. Leaves ovate to
lance-shaped, scalloped, green. Flowers in
umbels, pendent, tubular, greenish-white,
in spring; orange berries in late summer.

Dodecatheon meadia
A.G.M.
(Primulaceae)

Common name: Common
shooting-star
Height: 16in (40cm)
Spread: 10in (25cm)
Aspect: Sun or half shade
Soil: Moist, well-drained,
acidic, humus-rich
Hardiness: Zone 3
Propagation: Seed, when ripe,
after cold exposure; division, in spring

Clump-forming woodlander from the U.S.A.
Leaves ovate to spoon-shaped, midgreen.
Flowers in umbels, magenta, in spring.
D. meadia f. *album* also has an A.G.M.

Dodecatheon pulchellum
A.G.M.
(Primulaceae)

Common name: Southern
shooting-star
Height: 14in (35cm)
Spread: 6in (15cm)
Aspect: Sun or half shade
Soil: Moist, well-drained,
acidic, humus-rich
Hardiness: Zone 5
Propagation: Seed, when ripe,
after cold exposure; division, in spring

Clump-forming woodlander from western
North America. Leaves spoon-shaped to
ovate, midgreen. Flowers in umbels of up
to 20, cerise, in spring.

Doronicum orientale 'Magnificum' (Asteraceae/Compositae)

Common name: Oriental
leopard's-bane
Height: 20in (50cm)
Spread: 36in (90cm)
Aspect: Half shade
Soil: Moist, humus-rich
Hardiness: Zone 5
Propagation: Seed, in spring;
division, in autumn

Spreading, rhizomatous woodlander from
Europe and the near East. Leaves basal,
ovate, scalloped, midgreen. Flowers large,
solitary, yellow daisies, mid- to late spring.

Doronicum pardalianches (Asteraceae Compositae)

Common names: None
Height: 36in (90cm)
Spread: 36in (90cm)
Aspect: Half shade
Soil: Moist, humus-rich
Hardiness: Zone 6
Propagation: Seed, in spring;
division, in autumn

Spreading, rhizomatous woodlander from
Europe. Leaves basal, ovate, toothed, hairy,
midgreen. Flowers yellow, daisylike, in
corymbs, spring to midsummer.

Doronicum plantagineum (Asteraceae/Compositae)

Common name: Plantain
leopard's-bane
Height: 32in (30cm)
Spread: 18in (45cm)
Aspect: Half shade
Soil: Moist, humus-rich
Hardiness: Zone 6
Propagation: Seed, in spring;
division, in autumn

Rhizomatous woodlander from W. Europe.
Leaves basal, ovate, hairy, midgreen; die
down soon after flowering. Flowers on
branching stems, yellow, in late spring.

Draba longisiliqua A.G.M. (Brassicaceae/Cruciferae)

Common names: None
Height: 4in (10cm)
Spread: 8in (20cm)
Aspect: Sun; protect against
winter wet
Soil: Sharply drained, gritty
Hardiness: Zone 6
Propagation: Seed, after cold
exposure, in autumn

Cushion-forming evergreen. Rosettes of
leaves, obovate, gray-hairy. Flowers yellow,
in dense, short racemes, in spring. Grow in
alpine house or cover with glass in winter.

Dracunculus vulgaris (Araceae)

Common name: Dragon
arum
Height: 5ft (1.5m)
Spread: 2ft (60cm)
Aspect: Sun, but tolerates
half shade
Soil: Well-drained, dry in
summer, humus-rich
Hardiness: Zone 9
Propagation: Offsets, in autumn or spring

Tuberous Mediterranean woodlander. Basal,
pedate, deep green leaves; brownish marks.
Flowers spring to summer; maroon spathe,
black spadix, malodorous. May bear berries.

Dryas octopetala A.G.M. (Rosaceae)

Common name: Mt.
Washington dryad
Height: 4in (10cm)
Spread: 3ft (1m)
Aspect: Sun or half shade
Soil: Well-drained, gritty,
humus-rich
Hardiness: Zone 2
Propagation: Seed, when ripe;
softwood cuttings, in summer

Subshrub from Europe. Leaves ovate,
scalloped, green. Flowers almost stemless,
upward-facing, white with yellow stamens,
in late spring to early summer.

Dryopteris affinis A.G.M. (Aspidiaceae/ Dryopteridaceae)

Common name: Golden male
fern
Height: 3ft (90cm)
Spread: 3ft (90cm)
Aspect: Half shade
Soil: Moist, humus-rich
Hardiness: Zone 6
Propagation: Spores, in
warmth when ripe

Evergreen, rhizomatous, terrestrial fern.
Fronds lance-shaped, 2-pinnate, pale green,
turning dark green, with a dark spot where
each pinna joins the brown midrib.

Echinacea pallida (Asteraceae/Compositae)

Common name: Pink
coneflower
Height: 4ft (1.2m)
Spread: 18in (45cm)
Aspect: Sun
Soil: Well-drained,
humus-rich
Hardiness: Zone 5
Propagation: Seed, in spring;
division, in autumn or spring

Rhizomatous perennial from the U.S.A.
Leaves linear to lance-shaped, bristly, dark
green. Flowers daisylike, disc florets brown,
ray florets drooping, pale pink, late summer.

Echinacea purpurea
(Asteraceae/Compositae)

Common name: Purple
coneflower
Height: 5ft (1.5m)
Spread: 18in (45cm)
Aspect: Sun
Soil: Well-drained,
humus-rich
Hardiness: Zone 3
Propagation: Seed, in spring;
division, in spring or autumn

Rhizomatous perennial from the U.S.A.
Leaves ovate, toothed, smooth, green.
Flowers solitary, single, ray florets reflexed,
purple, disc florets golden-brown.

Echinacea purpurea
'Robert Bloom'
(Asteraceae/Compositae)

Common name: Purple
coneflower
Height: 5ft (1.5m)
Spread: 18in (45cm)
Aspect: Sun
Soil: Well-drained,
humus-rich
Hardiness: Zone 3
Propagation: Seed, in spring;
division, in spring or autumn

A selected form of *E. purpurea*. Flowers
mauve-crimson, reflexed ray florets, with
prominent discs of orange-brown. Leaves
ovate, toothed, smooth, green.

Echinacea purpurea
'Magnus'
(Asteraceae/Compositae)

Common name: Great purple
coneflower
Height: 5ft (1.5m)
Spread: 18in (45cm)
Aspect: Sun
Soil: Well-drained,
humus-rich
Hardiness: Zone 3
Propagation: Seed, in spring;
division, in spring or autumn

Large-flowered form of *E. purpurea*, in
which the flowerheads are 7in (18cm)
across. Ray florets held almost horizontal.
Leaves ovate, toothed, smooth, green.

Echinacea purpurea
'White Lustre'
(Asteraceae/Compositae)

Common name: White
coneflower
Height: 5ft (1.5m)
Spread: 18in (45cm)
Aspect: Sun
Soil: Well-drained,
humus-rich
Hardiness: Zone 3
Propagation: Seed, in spring;
division, in spring or autumn

White form of *E. purpurea*. Flowers have
creamy-white, reflexed ray florets, and
orange-brown disc florets. Leaves ovate,
toothed, smooth, green.

Echinacea purpurea
'White Swan'
(Asteraceae/Compositae)

Common name: White
coneflower
Height: 5ft (1.5m)
Spread: 18in (45cm)
Aspect: Sun
Soil: Well-drained,
humus-rich
Hardiness: Zone 3
Propagation: Seed, in spring;
division, in spring or autumn

Selected white form of *E. purpurea*.
Flowers are large, with white ray florets
and orange-brown disc florets. Leaves are
ovate, toothed, smooth, green.

Echinops bannaticus
(Asteraceae/Compositae)

Common name: Globe-
thistle
Height: 4ft (1.2m)
Spread: 2ft (60cm)
Aspect: Sun
Soil: Well-drained, poor
Hardiness: Zone 3
Propagation: Seed, in
midspring; division, in spring
or autumn

Clump-forming perennial from S.E. Europe.
Leaves ovate, spiny, hairy, pinnatisect,
gray-green. Flowers terminal, spherical,
blue-gray, with bristly bracts, late summer.

Echinops ritro
A.G.M.
(Asteraceae/Compositae)

Common name: Small globe-
thistle
Height: 24in (60cm)
Spread: 18in (45cm)
Aspect: Sun
Soil: Well-drained, poor
Hardiness: Zone 3
Propagation: Seed, in
midspring; division, in spring
or autumn

Clump-forming plant. Leaves oblong,
pinnatisect, spiny, dark green, cobwebby
above, white-downy beneath. Flowerhead
spherical, bright blue, in late summer.

Echium pininana
(Boraginaceae)

Common name: Bugloss
Height: 12ft (4m)
Spread: 3ft (1m)
Aspect: Sun
Soil: Well-drained, fertile
Hardiness: Zone 9
Propagation: Seed, in warmth
in summer

Leaves in rosettes, lance-shaped, silver-
hairy. Flowers in huge paniclelike cyme,
blue, funnel-shaped, with big bracts. Toxic
and skin irritant. From the Canary Islands.

Echium wildpretii
(Boraginaceae)

Common names: Bugloss
Height: 6ft (2m)
Spread: 2ft (60cm)
Aspect: Sun
Soil: Well-drained, fertile
Hardiness: Zone 9
Propagation: Seed, in warmth
in summer

Perennial from the Canary Islands. Leaves
in a basal rosette, narrow, lance-shaped,
hairy, pale green. Flowers in dense cymes,
funnel-shaped, red, late spring to summer.

Earaianthus pumilio
A.G.M.
(Campanulaceae)

Common names: None
Height: 1in (3cm)
Spread: 6in (15cm)
Aspect: Sun
Soil: Sharply drained, sandy,
chalky
Hardiness: Zone 6
Propagation: Seed, in
autumn; softwood cuttings,
in summer

Dwarf, cushion-forming perennial from
Dalmatia. Leaves linear, hairy, silver-green.
Flowers solitary, stemless, upturned bells,
deep purple-blue, in early summer.

Elsholtzia stauntonii
(Labiatae/Lamiaceae)

Common name: Staunton
elsholtzia
Height: 4ft (1.2m)
Spread: 3ft (1m)
Aspect: Sun
Soil: Well-drained, fertile
Hardiness: Zone 4
Propagation: Seed, in warmth
when ripe; softwood cuttings,
in summer

Deciduous subshrub with toothed, lance-
shaped, midgreen leaves, aging red, mint-
scented. Flowers small, purple-pink; dense
panicles or racemes, late summer to autumn.

Elymus hispidus
(Graminae/Poaceae)

Common name: Blue wild
rye
Height: 30in (75cm)
Spread: 16in (40cm)
Aspect: Sun
Soil: Moist, well-drained,
fertile
Hardiness: Zone 5
Propagation: Seed, in situ
in autumn or spring

Noninvasive evergreen grass from Eurasia.
Leaves silvery blue, ridged below, upright,
then arching. Dense, wheatlike flower
panicle in summer, silver-blue turning beige.

Elymus magellanicus
(Graminae/Poaceae)

Common name: Wild rye
Height: 6in (15cm)
Spread: 12in (30cm)
Aspect: Sun
Soil: Moist, well-drained,
fertile
Hardiness: Zone 5
Propagation: Seed, in situ
in autumn or spring

Mound-forming, tufted grass from South
America. Leaves linear, folded, blue.
Flower spike lax or prostrate, bearing up
to 7 flowers, all summer long.

Eomecon chionantha
(Papaveraceae)

Common names: None
Height: 16in (40 cm)
Spread: Indefinite
Aspect: Half shade
Soil: Moist, well-drained,
humus-rich
Hardiness: Zone 7
Propagation: Seed or division,
both in spring

Invasive woodlander from eastern China.
Leaves handsome, leathery, kidney-shaped,
green. Flowers like white poppies, in loose
panicles, from late spring to midsummer.

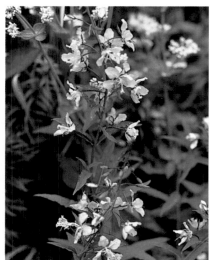

Epilobium angustifolium
(Onagraceae)

Common name: Fireweed;
rosebay
Height: 5ft (1.5m)
Spread: 3ft (1m)
Aspect: Sun or half shade
Soil: Moist, well-drained,
humus-rich
Hardiness: Zone 3
Propagation: Seed, when ripe;
division, in spring or autumn

Highly invasive, rhizomatous plant. Leaves
lance-shaped, midgreen. Flowers in
racemes, pink saucers, from summer to
early autumn. Self-seeds very prolifically.

Epilobium angustifolium
var. album
(Onagraceae)

Common name: White
rosebay
Height: 5ft (1.5m)
Spread: 3ft (1m)
Aspect: Sun or half shade
Soil: Moist, well-drained,
humus-rich
Hardiness: Zone 3
Propagation: Seed, when ripe;
division, in spring or autumn

White-flowered form; flowers in racemes
from summer to early autumn. Claimed to
be less invasive than the usual form of the
species, but still a liberal self-seeder.

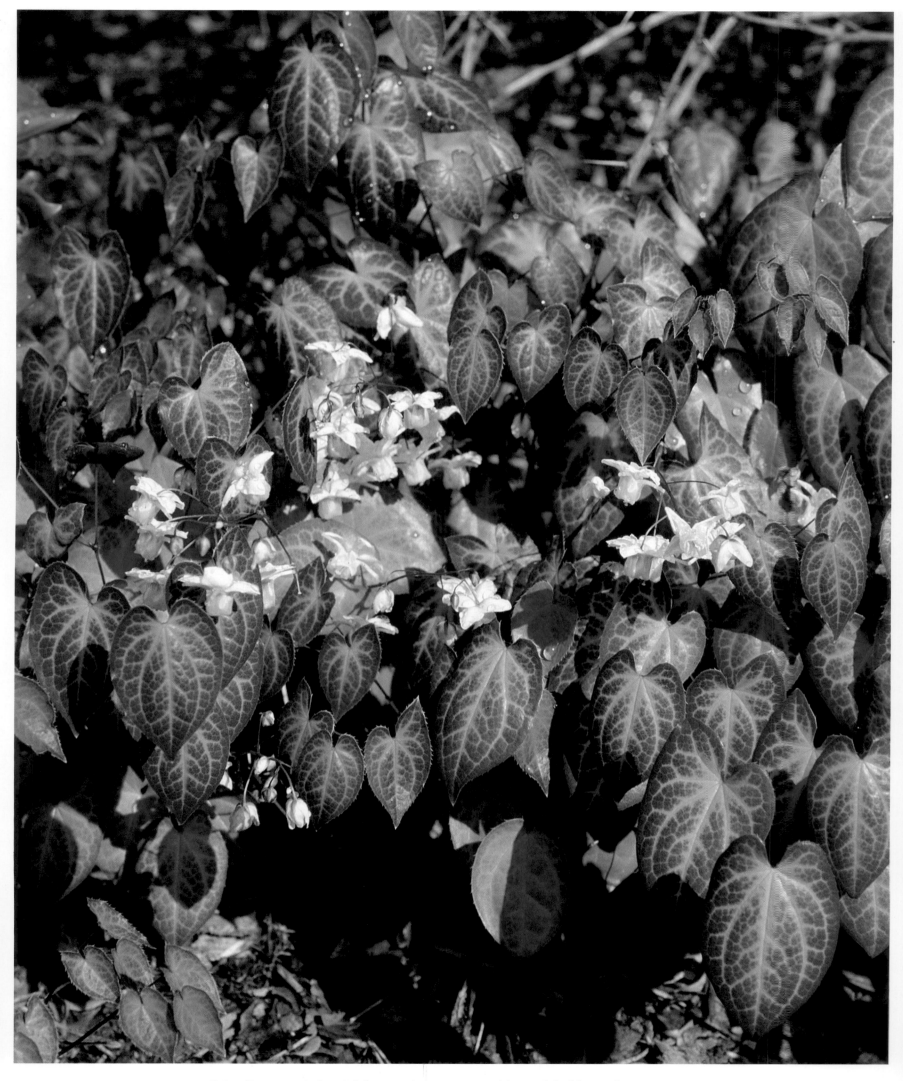

Epimedium × versicolor 'Sulphureum' has attractive red-brown lobed leaves that turn green.

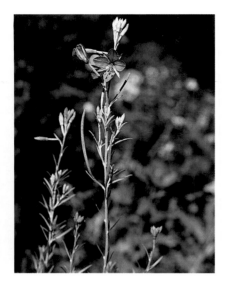

Epilobium dodonaei
(Onagraceae)

Common name: Willow-weed
Height: 36in (90cm)
Spread: 8in (20cm)
Aspect: Sun or half shade
Soil: Moist, well-drained, humus-rich
Hardiness: Zone 6
Propagation: Seed, when ripe; division, in spring or autumn

An invasive perennial from C. Europe to W. Asia. Leaves linear, toothed, hairy, midgreen. Flowers in loose terminal racemes, dark pink-purple, all summer.

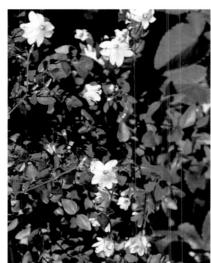

Epilobium glabellum
(Onagraceae)

Common name: Willow-weed
Height: 8in (20cm)
Spread: 8in (20cm)
Aspect: Half shade
Soil: Moist, well-drained, humus-rich
Hardiness: Zone 8
Propagation: Seed, when ripe; division, in spring or autumn

Clump-forming woodland ground cover. Leaves elliptic-ovate, toothed, dark green. Flowers solitary, on branching stems, white or pink, summer. Evergreen in milc areas.

EPIMEDIUM (Berberidaceae)
Bishop's-hat

A genus of some 40 rhizomatous, clump-forming, perennial species, of varying hardiness, found from the Mediterranean across to temperate regions of East Asia. Their natural habitat is woodland or shady scrub, and they all prefer a sheltered and partly shaded site. Some species are evergreen, others semievergreen, yet others deciduous. All have handsome, mainly basal foliage, and will make excellent ground cover, especially in a woodland or other partly shaded situation; smaller types are suitable for a rock garden. New growth in spring may be tinted bronze, and the leaves of many deciduous species color attractively in autumn. The foliage of the semi-evergreen and deciduous types should be sheared over in late winter before new growth begins, to show the flowers to their best. Although *Epimedium* are not spectacular when in bloom, they have a quiet charm. The individual flowers are delicate in appearance. They are mainly cup- or saucer-shaped and composed of two sets of four tepals surrounding four petals; these often have elongated spurs. They are nodding, in shades of pink, purple, buff, white, or yellow, and carried in erect to arching racemes or panicles on slender stems. *Epimedium* are low in allergens.

Epimedium davidii
(Berberidaceae)

Common names: None
Height: 12in (30cm)
Spread: 18in (45cm)
Aspect: Half shade
Soil: Moist, well-drained, fertile, humus-rich
Hardiness: Zone 7
Propagation: Seed, when ripe; division, in autumn

Clump-forming evergreen from W China. Leaves bronze aging to green, 3-palmate, lobes ovate to lance-shaped. Flowers yellow, with curved spurs, spring to early summer.

Epimedium grandiflorum
A.G.M.
(Berberidaceae)

Common name: Bishop's-hat
Height: 1ft (30cm)
Spread: 1ft (30cm)
Aspect: Half shade,
Soil: Moist, well-drained, fertile, humus-rich
Hardiness: Zone 5
Propagation: Seed, when ripe; division, in autumn

Rhizomatous, deciduous plant. Leaves lobed, leaflets ovate to heart-shaped. spiny-edged, bronze turning green. Flowers pink, white, purple, or yellow, spurred, in spring.

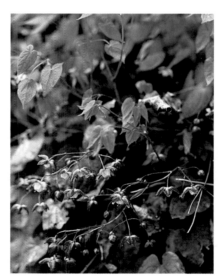

Epimedium × rubrum
A.G.M.
(Berberidaceae)

Common names None
Height: 1ft (30cm)
Spread: 1ft (30cm)
Aspect: Half shade
Soil Moist, well-drained, fertile, humus-rich
Hardiness: Zone 5
Propagation: Seed, when ripe; division, in autumn

Rhizomatous, semievergreen perennial of garden origin. Leaves 2-ternate, lobes spiny, ovate, pointed, red turning brown, lasting over winter. Flowers red and cream, spring.

Epimedium × versicolor
'Sulphureum' A.G.M.
(Berberidaceae)

Common names: None
Height: 1ft (30cm)
Spread: 3ft (1m)
Aspect: Half shade
Soil: Moist, well-drained, fertile, humus-rich
Hardiness: Zone 5
Propagation: Seed, when ripe; division, in autumn

Rhizomatous, evergreen perennial of garden origin. Leaves lobed, 5-11 ovate, spiny leaflets, red-brown turning green. Flowers deep yellow, spurs long, in spring.

Epimedium × *youngianum*
'Roseum'
(Berberidaceae)

Common names: None
Height: 1ft (30cm)
Spread: 1ft (30cm)
Aspect: Half shade
Soil: Moist, well-drained,
humus-rich, fertile
Hardiness: Zone 5
Propagation: Seed, when ripe;
division, in autumn

Deciduous rhizomatous perennial with
ovate leaves, sometimes spotted or with
pale green centers and dark green edges.
Flowers dusky pink, in spring.

Epipactis gigantea
(Orchidaceae)

Common name: Giant
helleborine
Height: 16in (40cm)
Spread: To 3ft (1m)
Aspect: Half or full shade
Soil: Moist, well-drained,
humus-rich
Hardiness: Zone 6
Propagation: Division, such
that each piece has an eye, in spring

Rhizomatous terrestrial orchid. Ovate to
lance-shaped, green leaves. Flowers nodding,
in spikes, greenish-yellow, veined maroon
and brown. Spreads rapidly in ideal sites.

Eranthis hyemalis
A.G.M
(Ranunculaceae)

Common name: Winter
aconite
Height: 3in (8cm)
Spread: 2in (5cm)
Aspect: Sun or half shade
Soil: Reliably moist through
summer, fertile, humus-rich
Hardiness: Zone 5
Propagation: Seed or division,
both in spring

Tuberous perennial from S. Europe. Basal
leaves lobed-pinnate, green. Stem leaves in
a ruff below flower, dissected, bright green.
Flowers yellow cups. All parts poisonous.

Eremurus himalaicus
(Asphodelaceae/Liliaceae)

Common name: Himalayan
desert-candle
Height: 6ft (2m)
Spread: 2ft (60cm)
Aspect: Sun
Soil: Sandy, well-drained,
fertile
Hardiness: Zone 3
Propagation: Seed, in autumn;
division, after flowering

Fleshy-rooted perennial. Leaves in rosettes,
linear, green. Flowers in tall racemes,
white, spring to early summer. Must have
winter cold to flower. Do not dig near base.

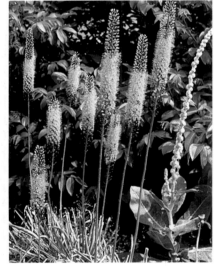

Eremurus robustus
(Asphodelaceae/Liliaceae)

Common name: Giant desert-
candle
Height: 10ft (3m)
Spread: 3ft (1m)
Aspect: Sun
Soil: Well-drained, sandy,
fertile
Hardiness: Zone 6
Propagation: Seed, in
autumn; division, after flowering

Perennial from C. Asia. Leaves blue-green,
strap-shaped, rough-edged. Flowers pink,
in racemes, in early to midsummer. Needs
winter cold to flower. Do not dig near base.

Eremurus stenophyllus
(Asphodelaceae/Liliaceae)

Common name: Bunge
Desert-candle
Height: 3ft (1m)
Spread: 2ft (60cm)
Aspect: Sun
Soil: Well-drained, sandy,
fertile
Hardiness: Zone 5
Propagation: Seed, in
autumn; division, after flowering

Perennial from W. Asia, Iran, and Pakistan.
Leaves linear, hairy, gray-green. Flowers in
racemes, yellow, fading to orange, early to
midsummer. Do not dig or hoe near base.

ERIGERON (Asteraceae/Compositae)
Fleabane

There are over 200 species in this genus, most of them
perennials; their main distribution in the wilds in North
America. They range from mat- or mound-forming alpines to
taller, clump-forming border types. They are invaluable
border perennials, with several excellent characteristics. They
have a long flowering season: *Erigeron karvinskianus* is the
longest-flowering of all hardy perennials, blooming nonstop
for up to six months; few gardeners could ask for more.
They are easy-going, requiring only sun and reasonably
fertile, well-drained soil; some of the alpines benefit from
protection against excessive winter wet. Almost all are
reliably hardy, and they are excellent for coastal gardens,
E. glaucus especially so. They are much appreciated by bees
and butterflies in the garden, and also by flower arrangers, as
they last very well in water if picked when open. There have
to be disadvantages, and as a genus they need to be lifted and
divided every few years. Some of the taller hybrids do require
staking, and slugs are fond of the new growth in spring. All
Erigeron are unfortunately highly allergenic, and so should be
avoided by allergic gardeners (note that this is not the only
genus commonly called fleabane).

Erigeron aurantiacus
(Asteraceae/Compositae)

Common name: Daisy
fleabane
Height: 1ft (30cm)
Spread: 1ft (30cm)
Aspect: Sun
Soil: Well-drained, fertile,
humus-rich
Hardiness: Zone 6
Propagation: Seed or division,
both in spring

Clump-forming perennial from Turkestan.
Leaves spoon-shaped to elliptic, velvety,
green. Flowerheads solitary, single, bright
orange with yellow discs, in summer.

Erigeron
'Charity'
(Asteraceae/Compositae)

Common name: Fleabane
Height: 24in (60cm)
Spread: 18in (45cm)
Aspect: Sun
Soil: Well-drained, fertile,
humus-rich
Hardiness: Zone 5
Propagation: Division,
in spring

Clump-forming hybrid cultivar. Leaves
midgreen, lance-shaped. Flowerheads lilac-
pink with yellow discs, semidouble, in
early and midsummer.

Erigeron compositus
(Asteraceae/Compositae)

Common name: Fernleaf
fleabane
Height: 6in (15cm)
Spread: 4in (10cm)
Aspect: Sun
Soil: Well-drained, fertile,
humus-rich
Hardiness: Zone 5
Propagation: Seed or division,
both in spring

Cushion-forming perennial. Leaves 3- or
4-ternate, lobed, hairy, gray-green. Yellow-
centered, pale blue, white, or pink, solitary,
single flowerheads, in summer. Self-seeds.

Erigeron
'Dignity'
(Asteraceae/Compositae)

Common name: Fleabane
Height: 20in (50cm)
Spread: 18in (45cm)
Aspect: Sun
Soil: Well-drained, fertile,
humus-rich
Hardiness: Zone 5
Propagation: Division,
in spring

Hybrid fleabane cultivar with lance- to
spoon-shaped leaves, and violet-mauve
flowerheads with yellow centers in early
and midsummer.

Erigeron
'Four Winds'
(Asteraceae/Compositae)

Common name: Fleabane
Height: 20in (50cm)
Spread: 18in (45cm)
Aspect: Sun
Soil: Well-drained, fertile,
humus-rich
Hardiness: Zone 5
Propagation: Division,
in spring

Hybrid cultivar with lance-shaped,
midgreen leaves, and solitary, single
flowerheads of strong pink with yellow
centers, in early and midsummer.

Erigeron glaucus
(Asteraceae/Compositae)

Common name: Beach
fleabane
Height: 12in (30cm)
Spread: 18in (45cm)
Aspect: Sun
Soil: Well-drained, fertile,
humus-rich
Hardiness: Zone 3
Propagation: Seed or division,
both in spring

Coastal species. Leaves lance-shaped to
obovate, glaucous green. Flowerheads
solitary, semidouble, pale mauve with
yellow discs, late spring to midsummer.

Erigeron karvinskianus
A.G.M.
(Asteraceae/Compositae)

Common name: Bonytip
fleabane
Height: 1ft (30cm)
Spread: 3ft (1m)
Aspect: Sun
Soil: Well-drained, fertile,
humus-rich
Hardiness: Zone 7
Propagation: Seed or division,
both in spring

Vigorous, spreading; excellent wall plant.
Leaves hairy, gray-green, lance-shaped.
Flowerheads single, small, white turning
pink, summer to early winter in mild areas.

Erigeron philadelphicus
(Asteraceae/Compositae)

Common name: Philadelphia
fleabane
Height: 2ft (60cm)
Spread: 1ft (30cm)
Aspect: Sun
Soil: Well-drained, moist
Hardiness: Zone 2
Propagation: Seed or division,
both in spring

Species from northern U.S.A. and Canada.
Leaves obovate, hairy, scalloped, green.
Flowerheads solitary, single, rose-lilac,
with a yellow disc.

Erigeron
'Rotes Meer'
(Asteraceae/Compositae)

Common name: Fleabane
Height: 2ft (60cm)
Spread: 2ft (60cm)
Aspect: Sun
Soil: Well-drained, fertile,
humus-rich
Hardiness: Zone 5
Propagation: Division,
in autumn

Hybrid fleabane cultivar with semidouble
flowerheads of a deep red with yellow
centers, borne in summer. Leaves are
spoon-shaped.

Erigeron
'Schneewitschen'
(Asteraceae/Compositae)

Common name: Fleabane
Height: 28in (70cm)
Spread: 24in (60cm)
Aspect: Sun
Soil: Well-drained, fertile,
humus-rich
Hardiness: Zone 3
Propagation: Division,
in spring

A hybrid garden cultivar bearing single
flowerheads of purest white, with yellow
centers, in summer. Good in a herbaceous
or a mixed border.

Erigeron
'Serenity'
(Asteraceae/Compositae)

Common name: Fleabane
Height: 30in (75cm)
Spread: 18in (45cm)
Aspect: Sun
Soil: Well-drained, fertile,
humus-rich
Hardiness: Zone 5
Propagation: Division,
in spring

Hybrid cultivar of lax habit, bearing
semidouble flowerheads of violet-mauve, in
corymbs, in early and midsummer. Leaves
are lance-shaped.

Erinus alpinus
A.G.M.
(Scrophulariaceae)

Common name: Alpine
liverbalsam
Height: 4in (10cm)
Spread: 4in (10cm)
Aspect: Sun or half shade
Soil: Well-drained
Hardiness: Zone 6
Propagation: Seed, in autumn

Semievergreen. Inverse-lance-shaped, sticky
leaves. Flowers 2-lipped, pink, purple, or
white in short racemes, late spring to early
summer. May repeat-flower if deadheaded.

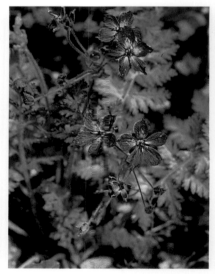

Eriogonum umbellatum
(Polygonaceae)

Common name:
Sulfur-flower
Height: 1ft (30cm)
Spread: 1m (3ft)
Aspect: Sun
Soil: Well-drained, sandy
Hardiness: Zone 7
Propagation: Seed, in
autumn; cuttings, in spring

Leaves in rosettes, ovate, midgreen, white
undersides. Yellow flowers turning red, in
umbels, in summer. Hates winter wet. Not
always free-flowering. Trim after flowering.

Eriogonum umbellatum
var. *torreyanum*
(Polygonaceae)

Common name:
Sulfur-flower
Height: 1ft (30cm)
Spread: 3ft (1m)
Aspect: Sun
Soil: Well-drained, sandy
Hardiness: Zone 7
Propagation: Seed, in
autumn; cuttings, in spring

Subshrub from U.S.A. Leaves ovate, shiny,
dark green. Flowers in umbels, yellow,
with pronounced bracts, in summer. Free-
flowering, in contrast to the species.

Eriophyllum lanatum
(Asteraceae/Compositae)

Common name: Woolly
eriophyllum
Height: 2ft (60 cm)
Spread: 2ft (60cm)
Aspect: Sun
Soil: Well-drained, sandy
Hardiness: Zone 5
Propagation: Seed, in
autumn; division, in spring

Perennial from W. North America. Leaves
divided, white-woolly, silver-gray. Flowers
solitary or in corymbs, yellow, spring to
summer. Can be invasive.

Erodium carvifolium
(Geraniaceae)

Common name: Heronbill
Height: 14in (35cm)
Spread: 8in (20cm)
Aspect: Sun
Soil: Well-drained, sandy,
humus-rich
Hardiness: Zone 7
Propagation: Seed, when ripe;
division, in spring

Long-flowering plant from Spain. Leaves
basal, 2-pinnate, green with white midrib.
Flowers in umbels of up to 10, deep pink,
over a long period in spring and summer.

ERODIUM (Geraniaceae)
Heronbill

A genus of some 60 species distributed across Europe, Asia, North Africa, North and South America, and Australia. Most are perennials, but the genus also includes annuals and both deciduous and evergreen subshrubs. Most are reliably hardy, but one or two are less so; all are drought-tolerant. *Erodium* are invaluable garden plants, on account of their long flowering season, which stretches from spring to late summer, and their handsome foliage. The leaves may be lobed, pinnatisect, or pinnate. The flowers are usually borne in umbels, but sometimes singly, and range in color from pink to purple, often with darker veins or markings, as well as some yellow or white examples. They are five-petalled and geraniumlike, but can be distinguished by their stamens: *Erodium* have five stamens, whereas geraniums have ten. Some types are too small for a border and are best grown in a rock garden, but others are excellent plants for the front of the border. All make good plants for coastal gardens. They are easy to cultivate, provided they have a sunny position and good drainage, and they do not require staking. They do have a tendency to self-seed, so should be cut back after flowering if this is not desired.

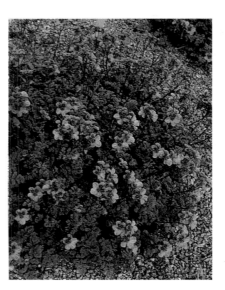

**Erodium
'Fran's Choice'
(Geraniaceae)**

Common name: Heronbill
Height: 8in (20cm)
Spread: 8in (20cm)
Aspect: Sun
Soil: Well-drained, sandy,
humus-rich
Hardiness: Zone 7
Propagation: Seed, when ripe;
division, in spring

Hybrid, clump-forming cultivar. Leaves pinnatisect, toothed, midgreen. Flowers borne in short terminal umbels, pink, in summer.

**Erodium manescaui
(Geraniaceae)**

Common name: Pyrenees
heronbill
Height: 18in (45cm)
Spread: 8in (20cm)
Aspect: Sun
Soil: Well-drained, sandy,
humus-rich
Hardiness: Zone 6
Propagation: Seed, when ripe;
division, in spring

Clump-forming. Leaves toothed, hairy, midgreen, pinnate; lobes ovate. Flowers in long-stemmed umbels, magenta, upper two petals spotted, spring to summer.

**Erodium
'Merstham Pink'
(Geraniaceae)**

Common name: Heronbill
Height: 9in (22cm)
Spread: 10in (25cm)
Aspect: Sun
Soil: Well-drained, sandy,
humus-rich
Hardiness: Zone 6
Propagation: Division,
in spring

Hybrid cultivar; superb wall plant. Leaves fernlike or carrotlike, dark green. Flowers in umbels, pink, over a long period, in summer to autumn.

**Erodium pelargoniiflorum
(Geraniaceae)**

Common name: Geranium
heronbill
Height: 1ft (30cm)
Spread: 1ft (30cm)
Aspect: Sun
Soil: Well-drained, sandy,
humus-rich
Hardiness: Zone 6
Propagation: Seed, when ripe;
division, in spring

Species from Anatolia. Leaves midgreen, geraniumlike, ovate-cordate, lobed. Flowers in umbels, white, upper two petals spotted purple, over a long period, summer.

ERYNGIUM (Apiaceae/Umbelliferae)
Sea holly

A genus of over 200 species, which can be split into "old-world" and "new-world." The species from dry regions of North Africa, Turkey, Asia, China, and Korea are usually taprooted, and have rounded leaves and congested, white or blue flowerheads with conspicuous bracts. Those from wet regions of South America and warm regions of Central and North America are usually fibrous-rooted and evergreen, with long, narrow leaves and flowers of greenish-white or purple. They are excellent border plants, especially for coastal gardens, and can be long-flowering. Eryngiums usually have spiny, silver-veined leaves in basal rosettes; wear gloves when handling. The flowerhead is a rounded, crowded head of small, stalkless flowers, like that of a thistle. Flowers dry well, and are useful for flower-arranging, either fresh or dry. Eryngiums like a position in sun and well-drained soil, which should not be too rich, or they will make soft growth and suffer from powdery mildew. They attract bees and butterflies, and are low in allergens. They dislike transplantation, so should be sited carefully in the first instance. Some will self-seed, especially *E. giganteum*, and some require staking.

115

Eryngium agavifolium
(Apiaceae/Umbelliferae)

Common name: Sea holly
Height: 5ft (1.5m)
Spread: 2ft (60cm)
Aspect: Sun
Soil: Moist, well-drained,
fertile
Hardiness: Zone 7
Propagation: Seed, when ripe;
division, in spring

Rosette-forming evergreen from Argentina.
Leaves sword-shaped, toothed, glossy.
Flowers in cylindrical umbels, greenish-
white, bracts spiny or entire, late summer.

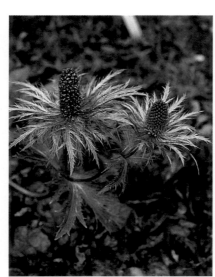

Eryngium alpinum
A.G.M.
(Apiaceae/Umbelliferae)

Common name: Sea holly
Height: 28in (70cm)
Spread: 18in (45cm)
Aspect: Sun
Soil: Well-drained to dry,
poor, humus-rich
Hardiness: Zone 5
Propagation: Seed, when ripe;
division, in spring

Tap-rooted European species. Basal leaves
spiny and heart-shaped; stem, 3-lobed.
Flowers in cylindrical umbels, steely-blue
or white, with bracts, summer to autumn.

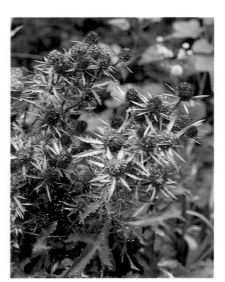

Eryngium alpinum
'Amethyst'
(Apiaceae/Umbelliferae)

Common name: Sea holly
Height: 28in (70cm)
Spread: 18in (45cm)
Aspect: Sun
Soil: Well-drained to dry,
poor, humus-rich
Hardiness: Zone 5
Propagation: Seed, when ripe;
division, in spring

Cloned selection of *E. alpinum*, in which
the flowers are smaller and violet-blue. Is
tap-rooted, so resents disturbance. Basal
leaves spiny, heart-shaped; stem, 3-lobed.

Eryngium alpinum
'Slieve Donard'
(Apiaceae/Umbelliferae)

Common name: Sea holly
Height: 28in (70cm)
Spread: 18in (45cm)
Aspect: Sun
Soil: Well-drained to dry,
poor, humus-rich
Hardiness: Zone 5
Propagation: Seed, when ripe;
division, in spring

Cloned selection of *E. alpinum*, with
flowers and bracts of creamy-green, in
summer to autumn. Basal leaves spiny,
heart-shaped; stem leaves, 3-lobed.

Eryngium bourgatii
(Apiaceae/Umbelliferae)

Common name: Sea holly
Height: 18in (45cm)
Spread: 12in (30cm)
Aspect: Sun
Soil: Well-drained to dry,
poor, humus-rich
Hardiness: Zone 5
Propagation: Seed, when ripe;
division, in spring

Tap-rooted species from the Pyrenees. Dark
green, silver-veined, rounded, pinnatifid,
spiny leaves. Flowers in cylindrical umbels,
blue with silver bracts, mid- to late summer.

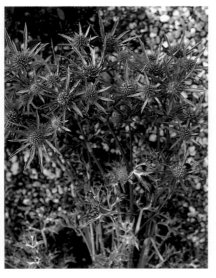

Eryngium bourgatii
'Picos'
(Apiaceae/Umbelliferae)

Common name: Sea holly
Height: 18in (45cm)
Spread: 12in (30cm)
Aspect: Sun
Soil: Well-drained to dry,
poor, humus-rich
Hardiness: Zone 5
Propagation: Division,
in spring

Cloned selection of *E. bourgatii*, with
bright blue flowers and silver bracts in
summer. Rounded, pinnatifid, spiny, dark
green, silver-veined leaves. Very desirable.

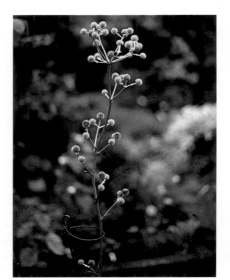

Eryngium eburneum
(Apiaceae/Umbelliferae)

Common name: Sea holly
Height: 4ft (1.2m)
Spread: 1ft (30cm)
Aspect: Sun
Soil: Moist but well-drained,
humus-rich, fertile
Hardiness: Zone 5
Propagation: Seed, when ripe;
division, in spring

Evergreen from South America. Leaves in
a rosette, narrow, linear, spiny, midgreen.
Spherical umbels of gray-green flowers and
bracts on branched stems, late summer.

Eryngium giganteum
A.G.M.
(Apiaceae/Umbelliferae)

Common name: Sea holly
Height: 3ft (90cm)
Spread: 1ft (30cm)
Aspect: Sun
Soil: Well-drained to dry,
poor, humus-rich
Hardiness: Zone 5
Propagation: Seed, when ripe

Short-lived or monocarpic species. Leaves
heart-shaped, basal and stem, ovate, spiny,
silver-veined, midgreen. Branched umbels
of steel-blue flowers with silver-gray bracts.

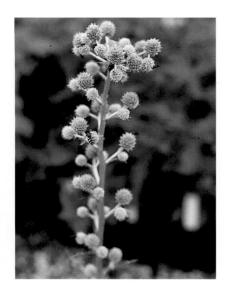

Eryngium horridum
(Apiaceae/Umbelliferae)

Common name: Sea holly
Height: 10ft (3m)
Spread: 3ft (1m)
Aspect: Sun
Soil: Moist but well-drained, fertile
Hardiness: Zone 5
Propagation: Seed, when ripe; division, in spring

Species from Brazil and Argentina. Leaves linear, arched, midgreen. Flowerheads spherical, on branching stems, in summer. Unspectacular, but unusual.

Eryngium × oliverianum
A.G.M.
(Apiaceae/Umbelliferae)

Common name: Sea holly
Height: 36in (90cm)
Spread: 18in (45cm)
Aspect: Sun
Soil: Well-drained to dry, poor
Hardiness: Zone 5
Propagation: Division, in autumn

Tap-rooted, deciduous garden hybrid. Basal leaves ovate, 3-lobed, spiny, dark green; stem leaves 4- to 5-palmately lobed. Flowers and bracts silver-blue, summer to autumn.

Eryngium pandanifolium
(Apiaceae/Umbelliferae)

Common name: Sea holly
Height: 12ft (4m)
Spread: 6ft (2m)
Aspect: Sun
Soil: Moist, well-drained, fertile
Hardiness: Zone 8
Propagation: Seed when ripe; division in spring

Clump-forming species from Argentina and Brazil. Leaves linear, spiny, silver-green. Flowers brown-purple with dark bracts, in cylindrical umbels, late summer to autumn.

Eryngium proteiflorum
(Apiaceae/Umbelliferae)

Common name: Sea holly
Height: 3ft (90cm)
Spread: 2ft (60cm)
Aspect: Sun
Soil: Well-drained to dry, poor
Hardiness: Zone 8
Propagation: Seed, when ripe; division, in autumn

Tap-rooted evergreen from Mexico. Leaves in rosettes, linear, spiny-edged, silvery green. Flowers in cylindrical umbels, gray-blue, with spiny bracts, in spring.

Eryngium × tripartitum
A.G.M.
(Apiaceae/Umbelliferae)

Common name: Sea holly
Height: 36in (90cm)
Spread: 20in (50cm)
Aspect: Sun
Soil: Well-drained, poor
Hardiness: Zone 5
Propagation: Seed, when ripe; division, in spring

Tap-rooted Mediterranean species. Leaves ovate, 3-lobed, toothed, dark green. Violet-blue flowers with blue-gray bracts, in spherical umbels, in summer to autumn.

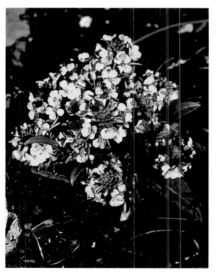

Erysimum alpinum syn.
E. heiraciifolium
(Brassicaceae/Cruciferae)

Common name: Alpine wallflower
Height: 6in (15cm)
Spread: 6in (15cm)
Aspect: Sun
Soil: Well-drained, fertile
Hardiness: Zone 6
Propagation: Seed, in spring

Dwarf wallflower from Scandinavia, with lance-shaped, midgreen leaves and perfumed, sulfur-yellow flowers, borne in racemes in summer.

Erysimum
'Bowles Mauve' A.G.M.
(Brassicaceae/Cruciferae)

Common name: Wallflower
Height: 30in (75cm)
Spread: 24in (60cm)
Aspect: Sun
Soil: Well-drained, fertile
Hardiness: Zone 7
Propagation: Heeled softwood cuttings, in spring or summer

Strong, evergreen, hybrid, woody subshrub. Leaves lance-shaped, gray-green. Mauve flowers in racemes on long stems, over a long period from early spring to summer.

Erysimum linifolium
'Variegatum'
(Brassicaceae/Cruciferae)

Common name: Alpine wallflower
Height: 28in (70cm)
Spread: 10in (25cm)
Aspect: Sun
Soil: Well-drained, fertile
Hardiness: Zone 6
Propagation: Heeled softwood cuttings, in spring or summer

Mat-forming, woody evergreen with gray-green, white-variegated, narrow, linear to lance-shaped leaves. Lilac flowers in long racemes on long stems, spring to autumn.

Erysimum
'Orange Flame'
(Brassicaceae/Cruciferae)

Common name: Wallflower
Height: 4in (10cm)
Spread: 12in (30cm)
Aspect: Sun
Soil: Well-drained, fertile
Hardiness: Zone 7
Propagation: Heeled
softwood cuttings, in
spring or summer

Mat-forming, creeping, evergreen, hybrid
perennial. Leaves inverse lance-shaped,
dark green. Flowers in lax racemes,
orange, from spring to autumn.

ERYTHRONIUM (Liliaceae)
Dogtooth fawn-lily

There are some 22 clump-forming, bulbous species in this genus. They are found in open meadow and deciduous woodland habitats, distributed across Eurasia and North America, and as a consequence they are suited to a range of garden situations, from a rock garden or mixed border to a woodland planting. They are hardy, and grow well in acidic, moisture-retentive but well-drained conditions, in dappled half shade. The bulbs are toothlike, with long points, and should be planted vertically in the autumn, quite deeply; there should be 5in (12cm) of soil above the top of the bulb. Bulbs should never be bought in the dry state, nor allowed to dry out when dividing established clumps, as they will give you only limited success at best, and they may not recover at all. The leaves are basal and invariably handsome, being glossy, green, and often mottled, marbled, or otherwise marked with bronze, maroon, or white. The nodding, bell- to hat-shaped flowers are borne singly or in clusters of up to ten, at the tops of erect, leafless stems. They have a delicate, charming appearance, with recurved tepals in shades of white, yellow, pink, or purple, and prominent stamens. The only significant problem is attack by slugs and snails.

Erythronium californicum
'White Beauty' A.G.M.
(Liliaceae)

Common name: California
fawn-lily
Height: 35cm (14in)
Spread: 10cm (4in)
Aspect: Half shade
Soil: Well-drained, acidic,
humus-rich
Hardiness: Zone 5
Propagation: Division, after
flowering

Cloned selection of a bulbous woodlander.
Leaves elliptic, deep green, mottled cream.
Flowers 1–3 per stem, pendent, cream,
with white anthers and prominent stamens.

Erythronium dens-canis
A.G.M.
(Liliaceae)

Common name: Dogtooth
fawn-lily
Height: 6in (15cm)
Spread: 4in (10cm)
Aspect: Sun or half shade
Soil: Well-drained, acidic,
humus-rich
Hardiness: Zone 3
Propagation: Division, after
flowering

Eurasian species. Leaves elliptic-oblong,
midgreen, marbled brown. Flowers
downturned, solitary, pink, white, or lilac
with purple anthers, in spring.

Erythronium grandiflorum
(Liliaceae)

Common name: Avalanche
fawn-lily
Height: 12in (30cm)
Spread: 4in (10cm)
Aspect: Half shade
Soil: Well-drained, acidic,
humus-rich
Hardiness: Zone 3
Propagation: Division, after
flowering

Species from the western U.S.A. Leaves
elliptic, bright green. Flowers 1–3 per
stem, golden-yellow, with distinctive
stigmas and anthers, in spring.

Erythronium helenae
(Liliaceae)

Common names: None
Height: 14in (35cm)
Spread: 6in (15cm)
Aspect: Half shade
Soil: Well-drained, acidic,
humus-rich
Hardiness: Zone 5
Propagation: Division, after
flowering

A species from California, closely related
to *E. oregonum* and *E. californicum*.
Leaves elliptic, bright green. Flowers
cream, with yellow centers, in spring.

Erythronium
'Pagoda' A.G.M.
(Liliaceae)

Common names: None
Height: 14in (35cm)
Spread: 4in (10cm)
Aspect: Half shade
Soil: Well-drained, acidic,
humus-rich
Hardiness: Zone 5
Propagation: Division, after
flowering

A vigorous hybrid cultivar. Leaves elliptic,
deep green, mottled. Flowers, up to 10 per
stem, are yellow, with dark yellow anthers,
in spring.

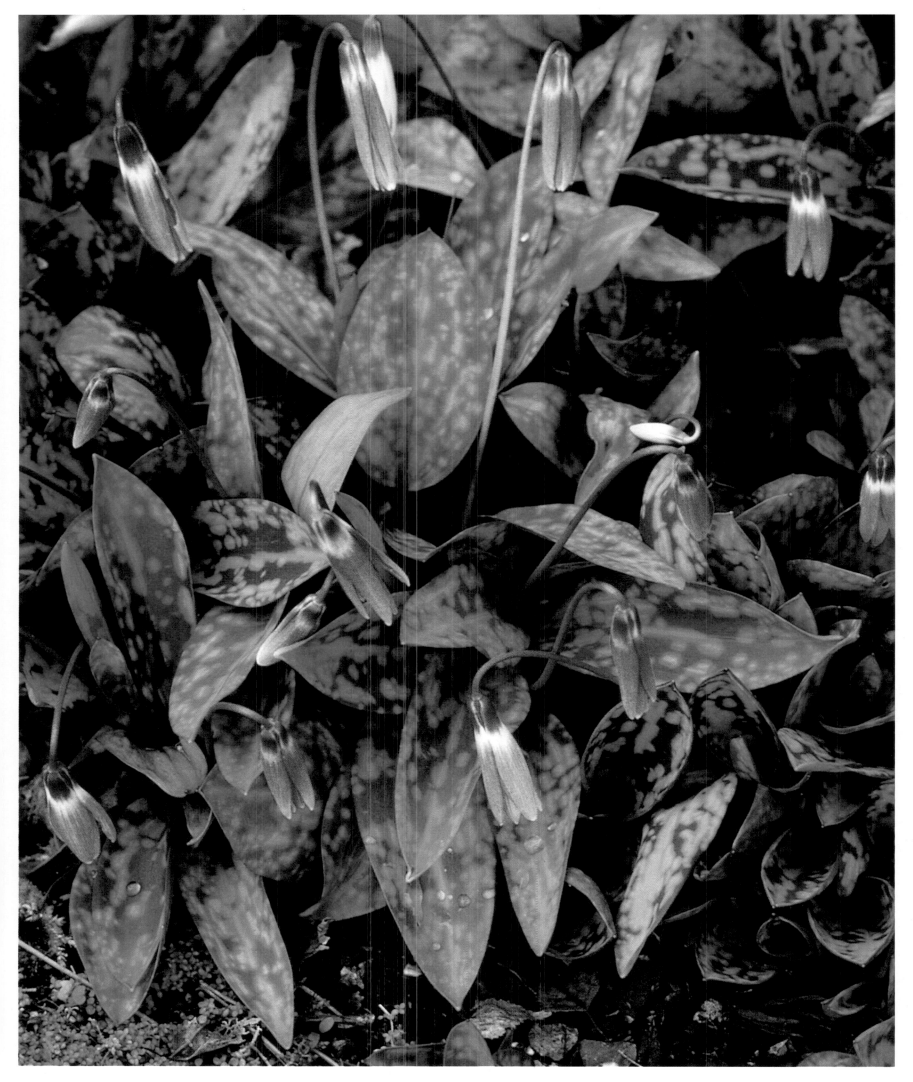

Dogtooth fawn-lily, Erythronium dens-canis, *is a low-growing plant with beautifully marked leaves and delicate blooms.*

Erythronium tuolumnense
A.G.M.
(Liliaceae)

Common name: Tuolumne
fawn-lily
Height: 14in (35cm)
Spread: 3in (8cm)
Aspect: Half shade
Soil: Well-drained, acidic,
humus-rich
Hardiness: Zone 5
Propagation: Division, after
flowering

Vigorous species from C. California.
Leaves elliptic, pale green. Flowers bright
yellow, strongly recurved, with yellow
anthers, up to 7 on a stem, in spring.

Eucomis autumnalis
(Hyacinthaceae/Liliaceae)

Common names: None
Height: 12in (30cm)
Spread: 8in (20cm)
Aspect: Sun
Soil: Well-drained, dry in
winter, fertile
Hardiness: Zone 8
Propagation: Offsets in spring

Bulbous, with a basal rosette of straplike,
broad, wavy-edged leaves. Small, starry,
greenish-white flowers in racemes topped
by spiky bracts, late summer to autumn.

Eucomis bicolor
(Hyacinthaceae/Liliaceae)

Common names: None
Height: 24in (60cm)
Spread: 8in (20cm)
Aspect: Sun
Soil: Well-drained, fertile
Hardiness: Zone 8
Propagation: Offsets in spring

Bulbous plant. Leaves broad straps, wavy-
edged, bright green. Flowers in racemes,
topped by pineapplelike, pink-edged green
bracts, in late summer and autumn.

Eucomis pallidiflora
(Hyacithaceae/Liliaceae)

Common names: None
Height: 28in (70cm)
Spread: 8in (20cm)
Aspect: Sun
Soil: Well-drained, fertile
Hardiness: Zone 8
Propagation: Offsets in spring

Vigorous, bulbous plant from South
Africa. Leaves semierect, strap-shaped,
wavy-edged, green. Flowers in racemes,
greenish-white, in late summer.

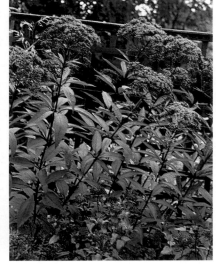

Eupatorium album
(Asteraceae/Compositae)

Common name: Hemp
agrimony
Height: 3ft (1m)
Spread: 1ft (30cm)
Aspect: Sun or half shade
Soil: Moist
Hardiness: Zone 4
Propagation: Seed or division,
both in spring

Coarse woodland or waterside plant from
the eastern U.S.A. Leaves oblong to lance-
shaped, toothed, midgreen. Tubular, white
flowers in corymbs.

Eupatorium purpureum
(Asteraceae/Compositae)

Common name: Bluestem
Joe-Pye-weed
Height: 6ft (2m)
Spread: 3ft (1m)
Aspect: Sun or half shade
Soil: Moist
Hardiness: Zone 4
Propagation: Seed or division,
both in spring

Clump-forming plant. Leaves lance-shaped,
toothed, midgreen tinged purple. Tubular
flowers in terminal panicles, pink, from
midsummer to early autumn.

EUPHORBIA (Euphorbiaceae)
Spurge

A vast genus containing over 2,000 species, from annuals and
perennials to succulents and shrubs, from many habitats in
many parts of the world. As a consequence, their cultural
requirements differ widely. They range from extremely hardy
to tender, and may be evergreen, semievergreen, or deciduous.
Nearly all bear highly characteristic "cyathia," small cups of
long-lasting bracts that may be green, yellow, red, brown, or
purple, cupping nectaries and insignificant flowers with
much-reduced parts. In the perennial and shrubby species,
these are carried in dense clusters. The leaves are very varied,
and often ephemeral. Gardeners tend to be polarized into
enthusiasm or antipathy toward this genus. Some species are
too invasive to be included in the garden, especially
E. cyparissias (Zone 4) and *E. pseudovirgata* (Zone 6).
Others, such as *E. lathyris* (Zone 6), *E. hyberna* (Zone 9),
E. coralloides (Zone 8), and *E. wallichii* (Zone 7) will self-
seed prolifically. All euphorbias resent disturbance, so site
them carefully at the outset. All are useful for flower-
arranging, in the fresh and the dry state, but it must be noted
that all parts of euphorbias are poisonous and bleed a skin-
irritant milky sap, and the flowers are also highly allergenic.

Euphorbia amygdaloides
(Euphorbiaceae)

Common name: Wood
spurge
Height: 32in (80cm)
Spread: 12in (30cm)
Aspect: Half shade
Soil: Moist, humus-rich
Hardiness: Zone 7
Propagation: Seed or division,
both in spring

Evergreen from Europe, Turkey, and the
Caucasus. Leaves obovate, matt, green.
Cymes of green-yellow involucres and
cyathia from midspring to early summer.

Euphorbia amygdaloides
'Purpurea'
(Euphorbiaceae)

Common name: Wood
spurge
Height: 32in (80cm)
Spread: 12in (30cm)
Aspect: Half shade
Soil: Moist, humus-rich
Hardiness: Zone 7
Propagation: Seed or division,
both in spring

A variant of the species with obovate,
purple leaves. Involucres and cyathia are
acid yellow, in cymes from midspring to
early summer.

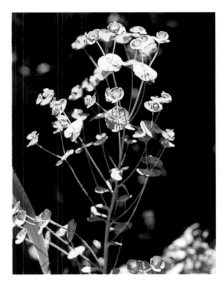

Euphorbia amygdaloides
var. robbiae A.G.M.
(Euphorbiaceae)

Common name: Wood
spurge
Height: 32in (80cm)
Spread: 12in (30cm)
Aspect: Sun or half shade
Soil: Moist
Hardiness: Zone 7
Propagation: Division,
in spring

A select form of E. amygdaloides. Spreads
by rhizomes, and may be invasive. Leaves
broad, leathery, shiny green. Cymes to 7in
(18cm) tall, less dense than in the species.

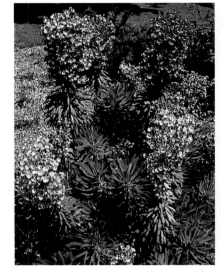

Euphorbia characias
(Euphorbiaceae)

Common name: Wood
spurge
Height: 4ft (1.2m)
Spread: 3ft (1m)
Aspect: Sun
Soil: Well-drained, sandy
Hardiness: Zone 8
Propagation: Seed or division,
both in spring

Evergreen Mediterranean subshrub. Leaves
linear, gray-green. Cyathia yellow-green,
cupped by green involucres, in dense
terminal cymes in spring and summer.

Euphorbia characias
subsp. characias A.G.M.
(Euphorbiaceae)

Common name: Wood
spurge
Height: 4ft (1.2m)
Spread: 3ft (1m)
Aspect: Sun
Soil: Well-drained, sandy
Hardiness: Zone 8
Propagation: Division,
in spring

A variant of E. characias in which the
nectaries in the cyathia are dark reddish-
brown, with notched or short horns.
Leaves are linear, gray-green.

Euphorbia characias
subsp. wulfenii A.G.M.
(Euphorbiaceae)

Common names: None
Height: 4ft (1.2m)
Spread: 3ft (1m)
Aspect: Sun
Soil: Well-drained, sandy
Hardiness: Zone 7
Propagation: Division,
in spring

Popular variant of E. characias in which
the cyathia and nectaries are yellow-green.
The leaves are linear and gray-green, as in
the species.

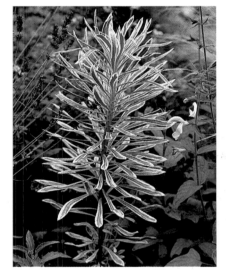

Euphorbia characias
subsp. wulfenii 'Variegata'
(Euphorbiaceae)

Common names: None
Height: 4ft (1.2m)
Spread: 3ft (1m)
Aspect: Sun
Soil: Well-drained, sandy
Hardiness: Zone 7
Propagation: Division,
in spring

Cultivar of E. characias subsp. wulfenii,
in which the leaves are edged with cream.
The cyathia and nectaries are yellow-green,
the involucres green.

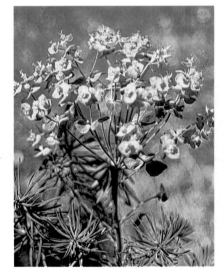

Euphorbia cyparissias
'Fens Ruby'
(Euphorbiaceae)

Common name: Cypress
spurge
Height: 16in (40cm)
Spread: 16in (40cm)
Aspect: Sun
Soil: Well-drained
Hardiness: Zone 4
Propagation: Division,
in spring

Selected form of a rhizomatous, invasive
species from Europe. Leaves feathery,
linear, blue-green. Cyathia and involucres
yellow-green, in terminal cymes.

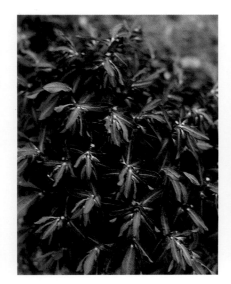

Euphorbia dulcis
'Chameleon'
(Euphorbiaceae)

Common name: Spurge
Height: 1ft (30cm)
Spread: 1ft (30cm)
Aspect: Shade
Soil: Moist, humus-rich
Hardiness: Zone 5
Propagation: Division,
in spring

Form of a rhizomatous species from
Europe. Leaves inverse lance-shaped,
purple. Cyathia and involucres yellow-
green, tinted purple.

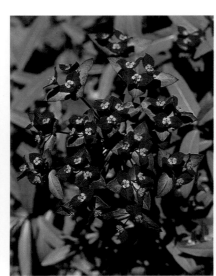

Euphorbia griffithii
'Fireglow'
(Euphorbiaceae)

Common name: Spurge
Height: 3ft (90cm)
Spread: 2ft (60cm)
Aspect: Half shade
Soil: Moist, humus-rich
Hardiness: Zone 5
Propagation: Division,
in spring

Selected form of a rhizomatous species.
Leaves lance-shaped, dark green, midribs
red; good in autumn. Flowers, early summer
in cymes; involucres red, cyathia yellow.

Euphorbia polychroma
A.G.M.
(Euphorbiaceae)

Common name: Cushion
euphorbia
Height: 16in (40cm)
Spread: 24in (60cm)
Aspect: Sun or half shade
Soil: Well-drained,
humus-rich
Hardiness: Zone 6
Propagation: Seed or division,
both in spring

Herbaceous species from Europe to Turkey.
Leaves obovate, dark green. Flowers in
terminal cymes, cyathia yellow, involucres
yellow-green, midspring to midsummer.

Euphorbia polychroma
'Candy'
(Euphorbiaceae)

Common name: Cushion
euphorbia
Height: 16in (40cm)
Spread: 24in (60cm)
Aspect: Sun or half shade
Soil: Well-drained,
humus-rich
Hardiness: Zone 6
Propagation: Seed or division,
both in spring

A variant of the species with stems and
obovate leaves of dark purple. Cyathia and
involucres a paler yellow. Flowers in
terminal cymes, midspring to midsummer.

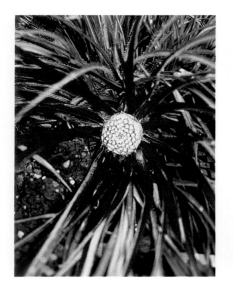

Fascicularia bicolor
(Bromeliaceae)

Common names: None
Height: 18in (45cm)
Spread: 24in (60cm)
Aspect: Sun
Soil: Sharply drained, poor
Hardiness: Zone 8
Propagation: Seed or division,
both in spring

Rosetted, evergreen, terrestrial bromeliad.
Leaves arching, long, tough, spiny, green;
inner leaves turn red as corymb of blue
flowers and white bracts appears in summer.

Felicia petiolata
(Asteraceae/Compositae)

Common name: Blue daisy
Height: 3ft (1m)
Spread: 3ft (1m)
Aspect: Sun
Soil: Sharply drained, fertile
Hardiness: Zone 9
Propagation: Stem-tip
cuttings, in autumn

Prostrate plant from South Africa. Leaves
lanceolate, green. Flowers daisylike, pink
or white, with yellow centers, over long
periods in summer. Not for damp climates.

Ferula communis
(Apiaceae/Umbelliferae)

Common name: Common
giant fennel
Height: To 10ft (3m)
Spread: 2ft (60cm)
Aspect: Sun
Soil: Well-drained, fertile
Hardiness: Zone 8
Propagation: Seed, when ripe

Tap-rooted, inedible plant. Leaves green,
malodorous, finely divided. Slow to flower;
umbels of yellow, white, or purple in
summer. *(See also Foeniculum p.123.)*

Festuca glauca
'Elijah Blue'
(Graminae/Poaceae)

Common name: Blue fescue
Height: 12in (30cm)
Spread: 10in (25cm)
Aspect: Sun
Soil: Well-drained to dry
Hardiness: Zone 5
Propagation: Division,
in spring

Evergreen grass. Leaves blue-green, narrow,
linear. Flowers brownish-green, in dense
panicles, in early and midsummer. Regular
division keeps foliage color good.

Festuca ovina
'Tetra Gold'
(Graminae/Poaceae)

Common name: Sheep's
fescue
Height: 12in (30cm)
Spread: 10in (25cm)
Aspect: Sun
Soil: Dry, well-drained
Hardiness: Zone 5
Propagation: Division,
in spring

Hybrid evergreen grass. Leaves narrow,
linear, yellow-green. Dense panicle of
brown flowers, in early and midsummer.
Regular division keeps leaf color brilliant.

Filipendula purpurea
A.G.M.
(Rosaceae)

Common name: Japanese
meadowsweet
Height: 4ft (1.2m)
Spread: 2ft (60cm)
Aspect: Sun or half shade
Soil: Moist, well-drained,
fertile, humus-rich
Hardiness: Zone 6
Propagation: Seed or division,
both in autumn or spring

Perennial from Japan. Leaves toothed,
pinnate, leaflets 5- to 7-lobed, green.
Flowers perfumed, red fading to pink, in
crowded corymbs, in mid- to late summer.

Filipendula ulmaria
'Variegata'
(Rosaceae)

Common name: Queen-of-
the-meadow
Height: 3ft (90cm)
Spread: 2ft (60cm)
Aspect: Sun or half shade
Soil: Moist, well-drained,
fertile, humus-rich
Hardiness: Zone 2
Propagation: Seed or division,
both in autumn or spring

Species from Europe and W. Asia. Leaves
pinnate, veined, inverse lance-shaped, green,
striped or marked yellow. Flowers in dense,
branching corymbs, creamy-white, summer.

Filipendula vulgaris
(Rosaceae)

Common name: Double
dropwort
Height: 24in (60cm)
Spread: 18in (45cm)
Aspect: Sun
Soil: Dry, well-drained
Hardiness: Zone 3
Propagation: Seed or division,
both in autumn or spring

Rhizomatous species from Eurasia. Leaves
pinnate, fernlike, toothed, dark green.
Flowers perfumed, in loose corymbs,
white, in early and midsummer.

Foeniculum vulgare
'Purpureum'
(Apiaceae/Umbelliferae)

Common name: Fennel
(edible)
Height: 6ft (1.8m)
Spread: 2ft (60cm)
Aspect: Sun
Soil: Moist, well-drained,
fertile
Hardiness: Zone 5
Propagation: Seed, in warmth
or *in situ*, in spring

Deep-rooting herb from S. Europe. Leaves
aromatic, bronze-purple, hairlike, finely cut.
Flowers tiny, yellow, on branching stems,
in compound umbels, mid- to late summer.

Fragaria
'Lipstick'
(Rosaceae)

Common name: Strawberry
Height: 6in (15cm)
Spread: Indefinite
Aspect: Sun or half shade
Soil: Moist, well-drained,
fertile
Hardiness: Zone 5
Propagation: Plantlets from
runners, at any time

Sterile, stoloniferous ground cover. Leaves
3-palmate, lobes toothed, broad, ovate.
Flowers single, in cymes, cerise, spring to
autumn. Evergreen in mild areas.

Fragaria
'Pink Panda'®
(Rosaceae)

Common name: Strawberry
Height: 6in (15cm)
Spread: Indefinite
Aspect: Sun or half shade
Soil: Moist, well-drained,
fertile
Hardiness: Zone 5
Propagation: Plantlets from
runners, at any time

Stoloniferous, sterile ground cover. Leaves
3-palmate, lobes broad, ovate, toothed,
bright green, evergreen in mild areas. Pink,
single flowers in cymes, spring to autumn.

Fragaria vesca
(Rosaceae)

Common name: European
strawberry
Height: 8in (20cm)
Spread: Indefinite
Aspect: Sun or half shade
Soil: Moist, well-drained,
fertile
Hardiness: Zone 5
Propagation: Plantlets from
runners, at any time

Stoloniferous ground cover species. Leaves
3-palmate, lobes ovate, toothed, bright
green. Flowers in cymes, white, followed
by small, red, edible fruits.

An unusual and impressive plant, Fritillaria imperialis *bears drooping flowers and a crown of leaves on a tall stem.*

Francoa sonchifolia
(Saxifragaceae)

Common names: None
Height: 3ft (1m)
Spread: 18in (45cm)
Aspect: Sun or half shade
Soil: Moist, well-drained, humus-rich
Hardiness: Zone 7
Propagation: Seed or division, both in spring

Evergreen perennial from Chile. Leaves in a basal rosette, hairy, broad, deeply lobed, green. Flowers in tall, compact racemes, pink, with deep pink marks, in summer.

Francoa sonchifolia
Rodgerson's form
(Saxifragaceae)

Common names: None
Height: 3ft (1m)
Spread: 18in (45cm)
Aspect: Sun or half shade
Soil: Moist, well-drained, humus-rich
Hardiness: Zone 7
Propagation: Seed or division, both in spring

Selected form of this evergreen woodlander from Chile. Basal rosette of hairy, broad, deeply lobed leaves. Tall flowering raceme of dark pink flowers.

FRITILLARIA (Liliaceae)
Fritillary

A genus of some 100 species, all of which are bulbous perennials, distributed across temperate regions of the northern hemisphere. They are found especially in southwestern Asia, the Mediterranean area, and western North America, and come from a wide range of habitats, and consequently vary in their cultural requirements, but all are hardy. Fritillaries range in size from diminutive species, suitable only for the rock garden, to tall plants, eminently suitable for beds or borders, and woodland species. However, some species require more particular conditions, which in wet regions can be met only by growing them in a bulb frame or alpine house; the smaller species are for the dedicated exhibitor. The fragile bulbs require careful handling. The leaves are for the greater part lance-shaped or linear. The flowers are usually pendulous, and tubular to bell- or saucer-shaped, with 6 tepals. They are often marked with a distinctive checked, or "tessellated," pattern. Flowers are borne singly or in terminal racemes or umbels; in some types, most notably *F. imperialis*, there is a cluster of leaflike bracts above the flowers. Unfortunately, nearly all fritillaries have a distinctly unpleasant smell.

Fritillaria acmopetala
A.G.M.
(Liliaceae)

Common name: Fritillary
Height: 16in (40cm)
Spread: 3in (8cm)
Aspect: Sun
Soil: Well-drained, fertile
Hardiness: Zone 7
Propagation: Offsets, in summer; seed, gathered in autumn, kept cold until spring, then sown in warmth

Bulbous perennial from E. Mediterranean. Leaves linear, blue-green. Flowers bell-shaped, pendent, pale green to brown, in late spring.

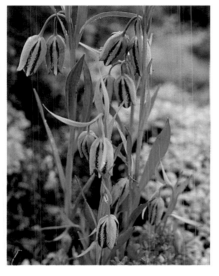

Fritillaria hermonis
subsp. *amana*
(Liliaceae)

Common name: Fritillary
Height: 12in (30cm)
Spread: 3in (7cm)
Aspect: Sun
Soil: Sharply drained, fertile
Hardiness: Zone 8
Propagation: Offsets, in summer; seed, gathered in autumn, kept cold until spring, then sown in warmth

Bulbous plant from the Lebanon to Turkey. Leaves lance-shaped, glaucous gray-green. Flowers single or paired, pendent bells, green, tessellated brown, or purple, spring.

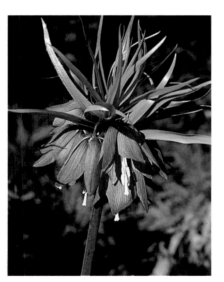

Fritillaria imperialis
(Liliaceae)

Common name: Crown imperial
Height: 4ft (1.2m)
Spread: 1ft (30cm)
Aspect: Sun
Soil: Well-drained, dry in summer, limy, fertile
Hardiness: Zone 4
Propagation: Offsets, after foliage dies down

Handsome, bulbous species. Leaves lance-shaped, in whorls. Flowers in umbels, pendent, orange, crowned by leaflike bracts, late spring. Plant 8in (20cm) deep.

Fritillaria imperialis
'Maxima Lutea' A.G.M.
(Liliaceae)

Common name: Yellow crown imperial
Height: 4ft (1.2m)
Spread: 1ft (30cm)
Aspect: Sun
Soil: Well-drained, dry in summer, limy, fertile
Hardiness: Zone 4
Propagation: Offsets, after foliage dies down

Variant of the species with yellow flowers, pendent, in umbels, crowned by leaflike bracts, late spring. Leaves lance-shaped, in whorls. Plant 8in (20cm) deep.

Fritillaria imperialis 'Rubra'
(Liliaceae)

Common name: Crown imperial
Height: 4ft (1.2m)
Spread: 1ft (30cm)
Aspect: Sun
Soil: Well-drained, limy, fertile
Hardiness: Zone 4
Propagation: Offsets, after foliage dies down

Very handsome, a crown of leaflike bracts on top of the red flower, but demanding; given sun, lime, potash, and deep planting, it may flower. Leaves lance-shaped.

Fritillaria meleagris A.G.M.
(Liliaceae)

Common name: Guinea-hen fritillary
Height: 12in (30cm)
Spread: 4in (10cm)
Aspect: Sun or half shade
Soil: Humus-rich
Hardiness: Zone 4
Propagation: Offsets, after foliage dies down

Bulbous Eurasian species. Leaves gray-green, linear. Flowers pendent, solitary or paired bells, white or purple, with bold tessellation, spring. Also shown is F. alba, A.G.M.

Fritillaria michailovskyi A.G.M.
(Liliaceae)

Common name: Fritillary
Height: 6in (15cm)
Spread: 2in (5cm)
Aspect: Sun
Soil: Sharply drained, dry during dormancy, fertile
Hardiness: Zone 7
Propagation: Offsets, after foliage dies down

Handsome species from Turkey. Leaves lance-shaped, midgreen. Flowers pendent bells, purple-brown, yellow-edged tepals, in umbels in late spring.

Fritillaria persica
(Liliaceae)

Common name: Persian fritillary
Height: 3ft (1m)
Spread: 4in (10cm)
Aspect: Sun
Soil: Well-drained, sandy, fertile
Hardiness: Zone 5
Propagation: Offsets, after foliage dies down

Robust bulbous species from Turkey, best in hot, dry areas. Leaves lance-shaped, glaucous green. Flowers purple or brown-green, pendent bells, in racemes, in spring.

Fritillaria pudica
(Liliaceae)

Common name: Yellow fritillary
Height: 6in (15cm)
Spread: 2in (5cm)
Aspect: Sun
Soil: Well-drained, dry during dormancy, fertile
Hardiness: Zone 6
Propagation: Offsets, after foliage has died down

Bulbous species from North America. Mid-green, lance-shaped leaves. Flowers solitary or paired, pendent bells, yellow or orange-yellow, in early spring. Dislikes wet.

FUCHSIA (Onagraceae)
Fuchsia

A genus of subshrubs from Central and South America and New Zealand, of only 100 or so species, but with over 8,000 hybrids in cultivation. They are mostly deciduous and mostly tender, but some are hardy, and some are evergreen, especially in warm regions. They are happy in any soil that is reliably moist, and have a flowering season from midsummer to autumn. The flowers are handsome, and unique. They are pendent, in terminal clusters, and tubular or bell-shaped, with long tubes, widely spread sepals, and below these a skirt of petals; these may be of a similar color, or of different colors. The number of petals varies; 4 in single-flowered types, between 5 and 7 in semidouble varieties, and more than 8 in fully double varieties. The group derived from *Fuchsia triphylla* is single-flowered, with very long tubes. Fuchsias in cold areas need the warmest corner of the garden; even then, frost will kill off much of the top growth in winter. In very cold areas, give them a winter mulch to protect from frost. They are excellent plants for mixed beds or borders, or hanging baskets, but will not grow under trees. Trailing types are good for baskets. A few are grown for their foliage value, rather than their flowers; all have berries after flowering.

Fuchsia 'Bicentennial'
(Onagraceae)

Common names: None
Height: 18in (45cm)
Spread: 24in (60cm)
Aspect: Sun or half shade
Soil: Moist, well-drained
Hardiness: Zone 9
Propagation: Softwood cuttings, in spring

Hybrid fuchsia, with arching stems bearing an abundance of fully double flowers with sepals of pale orange-pink and petals of magenta-pink.

Fuchsia
'Genii' A.G.M.
(Onagraceae)

Common names: None
Height: 36in (90cm)
Spread: 36in (90cm)
Aspect: Sun or half shade
Soil: Moist, well-drained
Hardiness: Zone 9
Propagation: Softwood
cuttings, in spring

Hybrid fuchsia grown principally for its foliage value. Leaves broadly ovate, lime-green. Flowers small, single, tubes and sepals red, corolla purple.

Fuchsia
'Coralle' A.G.M.
(Onagraceae)

Common names: None
Height: 36in (90cm)
Spread: 24in (60cm)
Aspect: Sun or half shade
Soil: Well-drained, moist
Hardiness: Zone 9
Propagation: Softwood
cuttings, in spring

Upright Triphylla group hybrid. Olive-green leaves. Flowers in terminal clusters on strong stems; long, tapering orange tubes, salmon-pink sepals and corolla.

Fuchsia
'Madame Cornélissen'
A.G.M. (Onagraceae)

Common names: None
Height: 36in (90cm)
Spread: 12in (30cm)
Aspect: Sun or half shade
Soil: Moist, well-drained
Hardiness: Zone6
Propagation: Softwood
cuttings, in spring

Strong, upright hybrid fuchsia. Medium-sized, semidouble or double flowers have red tubes, recurved red sepals, and a white corolla, from midsummer to late autumn.

Fuchsia magellanica
'Versicolor' A.G.M.
(Onagraceae)

Common name: Magellan fuchsia
Height: 3ft (1m)
Spread: 5ft (1.5m)
Aspect: Sun or half shade
Soil: Moist, well-drained
Hardiness: Zone 6
Propagation: Softwood
cuttings, in spring

Species fuchsia. Leaves copper in the early season, gray-green with pink tips later. Flowers small, with red tubes, red, wide-spreading sepals, and purple corollas.

Fuchsia
'Phénoménal'
(Onagraceae)

Common names: None
Height: 1ft (30cm)
Spread: 1ft (30cm)
Aspect: Sun or half shade
Soil: Moist, well-drained
Hardiness: Zone 8
Propagation: Softwood
cuttings, in spring

Hybrid fuchsia with very large, double flowers. Tube and sepals red, corolla mauve-purple. Long flowering, from summer to late autumn.

Fuchsia
'Reading Show'
(Onagraceae)

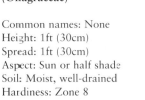

Common names: None
Height: 1ft (30cm)
Spread: 1ft (30cm)
Aspect: Sun or half shade
Soil: Moist, well-drained
Hardiness: Zone 8
Propagation: Softwood
cuttings, in spring

Long-flowering hybrid fuchsia. Very large, double flowers, with red tube and sepals and a deep blue corolla with a red base, from summer to late autumn.

Fuchsia splendens
A.G.M.
(Onagraceae)

Common names: None
Height: 6ft (2m)
Spread: 3ft (1m)
Aspect: Sun or half shade
Soil: Moist, well-drained
Hardiness: Zone 9
Propagation: Seed, in warmth
in spring; softwood cuttings,
in spring

Species from Mexico and Costa Rica. Ovate, toothed, hairy, green leaves. Small, solitary flowers; tubes broad and orange, sepals green with a red base, petals green.

Fuchsia
'Thalia' A.G.M.
(Onagraceae)

Common names: None
Height: 36in (90cm)
Spread: 36in (90cm)
Aspect: Sun
Soil: Moist, well-drained
Hardiness: Zone 9
Propagation: Softwood
cuttings, in spring

Triphylla group fuchsia. Leaves deep olive-green, velvety. Flowers in terminal clusters, long, slim, red; tubes and sepals red, petals orange-red, in summer.

Fuchsia
'Thornley's Hardy'
(Onagraceae)

Common names: None
Height: 12in (30cm)
Spread: 8in (20cm)
Aspect: Sun or half shade
Soil: Moist, well-drained
Hardiness: Zone 5
Propagation: Softwood
cuttings, in spring

Hybrid fuchsia, with a sprawling habit.
Flowers pendent, small. Tube creamy-
white, sepals spreading and creamy-white,
corolla deep rose-pink.

Fuchsia
'Tom West'
(Onagraceae)

Common names: None
Height: 2ft (60cm)
Spread: 2ft (60cm)
Aspect: Sun or half shade
Soil: Moist, well-drained
Hardiness: Zone 9
Propagation: Softwood
cuttings, in spring

Hybrid fuchsia, grown principally for its
foliage. Leaves variegated green and cream,
and veined pink. Flowers small, single;
tubes and sepals red, corolla purple.

Gaillardia
'Burgunder'
(Asteraceae/Compositae)

Common name: Blanket-
flower
Height: 24in (60cm)
Spread: 18in (45cm)
Aspect: Sun
Soil: Well-drained,
sandy, poor
Hardiness: Zone 4
Propagation: Softwood
cuttings, in spring

Hybrid of garden origin. Leaves basal, in
rosettes, inverse lance-shaped, gray or
green. Flowers daisylike, single, dark wine-
red, from summer to early autumn.

Gaillardia
'Kobold'
(Asteraceae/Compositae)

Common name: Blanket-
flower
Height: 12in (30cm)
Spread: 18in (45cm)
Aspect: Sun
Soil: Well-drained sandy,
poor
Hardiness: Zone 4
Propagation: Softwood
cuttings, in spring

Hybrid, known also as 'Goblin'. Leaves
basal, in rosettes, green. Flowers single, ray
florets red with yellow tips, disc florets
deep red, summer to early autumn.

Galanthus nivalis
A.G.M.
(Amaryllidaceae)

Common name: Snowdrop
Height: 4in (10cm)
Spread: 4in (10cm)
Aspect: Half shade
Soil: Moist, well-drained,
humus-rich
Hardiness: Zone 4
Propagation: Division, after
flowering

Bulbous woodlander from N. Europe.
Leaves narrow, glaucous. Flowers solitary,
scented, white; inner tepals marked green at
tip, late winter. All parts toxic and irritant.

Galega x *hartlandii*
'Alba' A.G.M.
(Leguminosae/Papilionaceae)

Common name: Goat's-rue
Height: 5ft (1.5m)
Spread: 3ft (90cm)
Aspect: Sun or half shade
Soil: Moist
Hardiness: Zone 4
Propagation: Seed, in spring;
division, in autumn or spring

Clump-forming perennial. Leaves pinnate,
leaflets oval, green. Flowers in erect
axillary racemes, pealike, white, from early
summer to early autumn.

Galega officinalis
(Leguminosae/Papilionaceae)

Common name: Common
goat's-rue
Height: 1.5m (5ft)
Spread: 90cm (3ft)
Aspect: Sun or half shade
Soil: Moist
Hardiness: Zone 4
Propagation: Seed, in spring;
division in early or
late winter

Species from S.E. Europe to Pakistan. Soft
green, pinnate leaves, leaflets lance-shaped.
Flowers in racemes, white, mauve, or
bicolored, early summer to early autumn.

Galium odoratum
(Rubiaceae)

Common name: Sweet
woodruff
Height: 18in (45cm)
Spread: Indefinite
Aspect: Sun or half shade
Soil: Moist, humus-rich
Hardiness: Zone 5
Propagation: Seed, when ripe;
division, in spring or autumn

Rhizomatous plant from N. Africa, Europe,
and Siberia. Leaves lance-shaped, emerald
green, whorled. Small, starry, scented, white
flowers in cymes, late spring to midsummer.

Galtonia candicans
(Hyacinthaceae/Liliaceae)

Common name: Giant
summer hyacinth
Height: 4ft (1.2m)
Spread: 4in (10cm)
Aspect: Sun
Soil: Moist, well-drained,
fertile
Hardiness: Zone 6
Propagation: Seed or offsets,
both in spring

Bulbous, moist-grassland plant from South
Africa. Leaves lance-shaped, gray-green.
Flowers in tall slim racemes, pendent,
scented, tubular, white, in late summer.

Galtonia princeps
(Hyacinthaceae/Liliaceae)

Common name: Summer
hyacinth
Height: 36in (90cm)
Spread: 4in (10cm)
Aspect: Sun
Soil: Moist, well-drained,
fertile
Hardiness: Zone 8
Propagation: Seed or offsets,
both in spring

Bulbous species from southern Africa.
Flowers rather smaller than those of
G. candicans, and tinted green, in late
summer. Leaves lance-shaped, green.

Galtonia viridiflora
A.G.M.
(Hyacinthaceae/Liliaceae)

Common name: Summer
hyacinth
Height: 36in (1m)
Spread: 4in (10cm)
Aspect: Sun
Soil: Moist, well-drained,
fertile
Hardiness: Zone 8
Propagation: Seed or offsets,
both in spring

Bulbous perennial from southern Africa.
Leaves lance-shaped, gray-green. Flowers
in tallish, compact racemes of up to 30,
trumpet-shaped, pendent, pale green.

Gaura lindheimeri
A.G.M.
(Onagraceae)

Common name: White gaura
Height: 5ft (1.5m)
Spread: 3ft (1m)
Aspect: Sun
Soil: Well-drained, sandy
Hardiness: Zone 4
Propagation: Seed or division,
both in spring

Clump-forming plant from Louisiana and
Texas. Flowers in loose panicles, white,
summer to autumn. Graceful in a wind.
Leaves lance- to spoon-shaped, toothed.

Gaura lindheimeri
'Siskiyou Pink'
(Onagraceae)

Common name: Pink gaura
Height: 5ft (1.5m)
Spread: 3ft (1m)
Aspect: Sun
Soil: Well-drained, sandy
Hardiness: Zone 4
Propagation: Seed or division,
both in spring

Delightful form of the species. Flowers in
loose panicles, pale and deep pink, over a
long period from summer to autumn.
Leaves lance- to spoon-shaped, toothed.

Gazania
Chansonette Series A.G.M.
(Asteraceae/Compositae)

Common name: Treasure
flower
Height: 8in (20cm)
Spread: 8in (20cm)
Aspect: Sun
Soil: Well-drained, sandy
Hardiness: Zone 9
Propagation: Seed, in warmth
in spring; cuttings, in autumn

Selected hybrids of evergreens from tropical
Africa. Leaves basal, lance-shaped, glossy
green above, gray-felted below. Single pink,
yellow, orange, or bronze flowers, summer.

Gazania
Daybreak Series A.G.M.
(Asteraceae /Compositae)

Common name: Treasure
flower
Height: 8in (20cm)
Spread: 8in (20cm)
Aspect: Sun
Soil: Well-drained, sandy
Hardiness: Zone 9
Propagation: Seed, in warmth
in spring; cuttings, in autumn

Hybrids of evergreens from tropical Africa.
Leaves lance-shaped, green above, white-
felted below. Flowers single, solitary, white,
orange, yellow, or pink, spring and summer.

Gazania
Talent Series A.G.M.
(Asteraceae/Compositae)

Common name: Treasure
flower
Height: 8in (20cm)
Spread: 8in (20cm)
Aspect: Sun
Soil: Well-drained, sandy
Hardiness: Zone 9
Propagation: Seed, in warmth
in spring; cuttings, in autumn

Selected hybrids of evergreens from tropical
Africa. Leaves lance-shaped, gray-felted
above and below. Flowers single, solitary,
yellow, brown, orange, or pink, in summer.

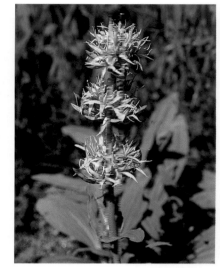

Gentiana angustifolia
(Gentianaceae)

Common names: Gentian
Height: 4in (10cm)
Spread: 12in (30cm)
Aspect: Sun
Soil: Well-drained, light,
humus-rich
Hardiness: Zone 7
Propagation: Seed or division,
both in spring

Evergreen perennial from the Pyrenees, Alps,
and Jura mountains. Leaves lance-shaped,
in rosettes. Flowers on short stems, deep
blue, single, trumpet-shaped, early summer.

Gentiana asclepiadea
A.G.M.
(Gentianaceae)

Common name: Willow
gentian
Height: 36in (90cm)
Spread: 18in (45cm)
Aspect: Half shade
Soil: Moist, well-drained,
acidic, humus-rich
Hardiness: Zone 6
Propagation: Seed, when ripe;
division, in spring

Clump-forming herbaceous species from C.
and S. Europe. Leaves willowlike, lance-
shaped to ovate, pointed. Axillary clusters
of flowers on arching stems, blue trumpets.

Gentiana asclepiadea
var. alba
(Gentianaceae)

Common name: White
willow gentian
Height: 36in (90cm)
Spread: 18in (45cm)
Aspect: Sun
Soil: Well-drained, light,
humus-rich
Hardiness: Zone 6
Propagation: Seed or division,
both in spring

Naturally occuring form of the species,
bearing white flowers on more upright
stems. Leaves lance-shaped to ovate,
pointed, willowlike.

Gentiana lutea
(Gentianaceae)

Common name: Yellow
gentian
Height: 6ft (2m)
Spread: 2ft (60cm)
Aspect: Sun
Soil: Well-drained,
humus-rich
Hardiness: Zone 4
Propagation: Seed or division,
both in spring

Robust, fleshy-rooted mountain species.
Basal leaves blue-green, ovate, ribbed; stem
leaves paired, ovate, green. Flowers yellow,
star-shaped, in clusters of up to 10, summer.

Gentiana septemfida
A.G.M.
(Gentianaceae)

Common names: None
Height: 8in (20cm)
Spread: 12in (30cm)
Aspect: Sun
Soil: Moist, well-drained,
humus-rich
Hardiness: Zone 3
Propagation: Seed or division,
both in spring

Spreading, herbaceous species from Turkey
to C. Asia. Leaves ovate, pointed, paired.
Flowers in terminal clusters, narrow bells,
bright blue, white throats, in summer.

Gentiana tibetica
(Gentianaceae)

Common name: Tibetan
gentian
Height: 24in (60cm)
Spread: 8in (20cm)
Aspect: Sun
Soil: Well-drained,
humus-rich
Hardiness: Zone 6
Propagation: Seed or division,
both in spring

Species from Tibet. Basal leaves broad,
lance, green; stem leaves linear. Flowers in
dense terminal racemes, white, surrounded
by apical leaves, in summer.

GERANIUM (Geraniaceae)
Cranesbill

A genus of over 300 species from temperate regions of both
hemispheres. The perennial species are indispensable for beds
and borders: they have beautiful flowers, make excellent
ground cover, and are easy to grow and long-lived. They
dislike waterlogged soil: this is reflected in their distribution
in the wild, where they are found in all habitats except boggy
ones. They are a diverse group, and vary in both their degree
of hardiness and their cultural requirements. G. malviflorum
(Zone 8) is unusual in that it makes top-growth over winter,
flowers in spring, and disappears till winter. Geranium
flowers are mostly saucer-shaped, but may be flat or stellate;
they may be borne in umbels, panicles, or cymes. The leaves
are basal and stem, palmately lobed, and often deeply divided
and toothed; some species are evergreen. Many geranium
species are floppy or scramble, and most need support of
some kind to make them look reasonable. All should be
sheared over in the autumn to encourage new basal growth.
All are low-allergen plants, and most are drought-tolerant.
G. nodosum (Zone 6) and G. procurrens (Zone 7) root as
they touch the soil, and G. thunbergii (Zone 7) self-seeds to
an unacceptable degree, so must be deadheaded.

Geranium
'Ann Folkard' A.G.M.
(Geraniaceae)

Common names: None
Height: 2ft (60cm)
Spread: 5ft (1.5m)
Aspect: Sun or half shade
Soil: Well-drained
Hardiness: Zone 7
Propagation: Division,
in spring

Geranium cinereum
'Ballerina' A.G.M.
(Geraniaceae)

Common names: None
Height: 6in (15cm)
Spread: 12in (30cm)
Aspect: Sun or half shade
Soil: Well-drained
Hardiness: Zone 5
Propagation: Division,
in spring

Geranium cinereum
var. *subcaulescens* A.G.M.
(Geraniaceae)

Common names: None
Height: 6in (15cm)
Spread: 12in (30cm)
Aspect: Sun or half shade
Soil: Well-drained
Hardiness: Zone 5
Propagation: Seed or division,
both in spring

Geranium himalayense
(Geraniaceae)

Common names: None
Height: 18in (45cm)
Spread: 24in (60cm)
Aspect: Any
Soil: Well-drained
Hardiness: Zone 4
Propagation: Seed or division,
both in spring

Hybrid, scrambling ground cover. Leaves 5-lobed, toothed, yellow at first, turning green. Flowers saucer-shaped, magenta with dark centers and veining, all summer.

Long-flowering hybrid evergreen. Leaves 5- to 7-lobed, divisions 3-lobed, gray-green. Flowers cup-shaped, upward-facing, pale pink veined dark pink, spring to summer.

Species from Italy, the Balkans, and Turkey. Leaves deeply lobed, deep green. Flowers on longish stems, brilliant magenta with black centers, in summer.

Rhizomatous species. Leaves basal, 7-lobed, veined, green, colorful in autumn. Loose cymes of flowers, saucer-shaped, deep blue, in flushes from early summer to autumn.

Geranium himalayense
'Plenum'
(Geraniaceae)

Common names: None
Height: 10in (25cm)
Spread: 24in (60cm)
Aspect: Any
Soil: Well-drained
Hardiness: Zone 4
Propagation: Seed or division,
both in spring

Geranium ibericum
subsp. *jubatum*
(Geraniaceae)

Common name: Caucasus
geranium
Height: 20in (50cm)
Spread: 24in (60cm)
Aspect: Sun or half shade
Soil: Well-drained
Hardiness: Zone 6
Propagation: Seed or division,
both in spring

Geranium incanum
(Geraniaceae)

Common names: None
Height: 16in (40cm)
Spread: 24in (60cm)
Aspect: Sun
Soil: Well-drained
Hardiness: Zone 9
Propagation: Seed or division,
both in spring

Geranium
'Johnson's Blue' A.G.M.
(Geraniaceae)

Common names: None
Height: 18in (45cm)
Spread: 30in (75cm)
Aspect: Sun or half shade
Soil: Well-drained
Hardiness: Zone 4
Propagation: Division,
in spring

Fully double form of *G. himalayense*. More compact than the single form, and with smaller leaves. Flowers purplish-pink, shaded blue, darkly veined.

Clump-forming; 9- to 11-lobed, basal, hairy, leaves. Cymes of violet-blue, cup-shaped, upward-facing flowers in flushes from early summer. From Turkey, Iran, the Caucasus.

Evergreen from South Africa. Leaves basal, filigree, aromatic, deeply cut into 5-toothed, lobed, gray-green segments. Loose cymes of dark pink flowers, summer to autumn.

Rhizomatous hybrid. Leaves 7-lobed, basal; leaflets further lobed, toothed, mid-green. Flowers in loose cymes, blue saucers with pink centers, in summer.

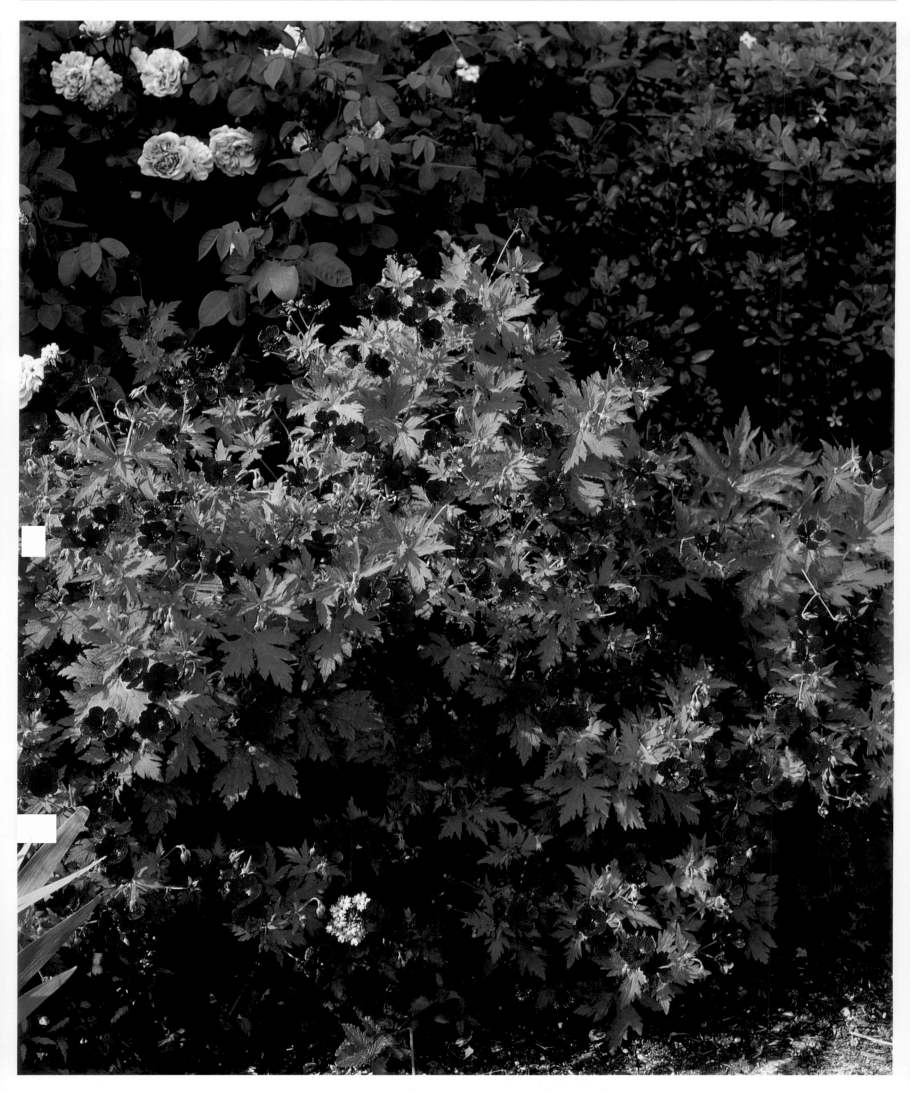

The clump-forming Geranium psilostemon *bears cymes of deep-purple flowers in late summer.*

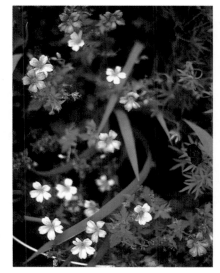

Geranium macrorrhizum 'Ingwersen's Variety' A.G.M. (Geraniaceae)

Common names: None
Height: 1ft (30cm)
Spread: 2ft (60cm)
Aspect: Sun or half shade
Soil: Well-drained
Hardiness: Zone 4
Propagation: Division, in spring

Cloned selection of a rhizomatous species. Leaves 7-lobed, toothed, aromatic, sticky, light green. Flowers flat, pale pink, calyx inflated, stamens prominent, early summer.

Geranium maculatum (Geraniaceae)

Common names: Cranesbill; wild geranium
Height: 24in (60cm)
Spread: 18in (45cm)
Aspect: Sun
Soil: Moist, well-drained
Hardiness: Zone 4
Propagation: Seed or division, both in spring

Tuberous species from eastern North America. Leaves basal, 5- to 7-lobed, glossy, green. Flowers in loose cymes, lilac saucers, from late spring for many weeks.

Geranium maderense A.G.M. (Geraniaceae)

Common names: None
Height: 5ft (1.5m)
Spread: 5ft (1.5m)
Aspect: Sun
Soil: Well-drained
Hardiness: Zone 9
Propagation: Seed or division, both in spring

Species from Madeira. Bright green, basal, 5- to 7-lobed, toothed leaves. Panicles of flat, pale-veined magenta flowers on purple-hairy stems, spring to late summer.

Geranium x *oxonianum* 'Rose Clair' (Geraniaceae)

Common names: None
Height: 3ft (90cm)
Spread: 2ft (60cm)
Aspect: Sun or half shade
Soil: Well-drained
Hardiness: Zone 5
Propagation: Division, in spring

Clump-forming, robust hybrid. Leaves basal, 5-lobed, each with 5 leaflets, green, toothed, veined. Flowers in loose cymes, pink, fading to white, spring to autumn.

Geranium phaeum (Geraniaceae)

Common names: None
Height: 2ft (60cm)
Spread: 18in (45cm)
Aspect: Half or full shade
Soil: Moist, well-drained
Hardiness: Zone 5
Propagation: Seed or division, both in spring

Herbaceous species from the mountains of Eurasia. Leaves basal, 7- to 9-lobed, green. Flowers in cymes, violet-blue, black, white, or maroon in late spring and early summer.

Geranium 'Phillippe Vapelle' (Geraniaceae)

Common names: None
Height: 16in (40cm)
Spread: 12in (30cm)
Aspect: Sun or half shade
Soil: Well-drained
Hardiness: Zone 7
Propagation: Division, in spring

A hybrid of *G. renardii* x *G. platypetalum*. Leaves basal, lobed, softly hairy, blue-gray. Flowers large, blue-purple, with bold, dark veins, long period from spring to summer.

Geranium pratense (Geraniaceae)

Common name: Meadow geranium
Height: 3ft (90cm)
Spread: 2ft (60cm)
Aspect: Sun or half shade
Soil: Well-drained
Hardiness: Zone 5
Propagation: Seed or division, both in spring

Herbaceous species from Europe to China. Leaves basal, 7 to 9 deeply divided lobes, toothed, green. Flowers in dense cymes, blue, violet, or white saucers, in summer.

Geranium pratense 'Mrs. Kendall Clark' A.G.M. (Geraniaceae)

Common name: Meadow geranium
Height: 3ft (90cm)
Spread: 2ft (60cm)
Aspect: Sun or half shade
Soil: Well-drained
Hardiness: Zone 5
Propagation: Division, in spring

Cloned selection of the species. Leaves basal, 7- to 9-lobed, toothed, midgreen. Flowers in umbels, saucer-shaped, pearl-gray, over a long period in summer.

Geranium pratense 'Plenum Violaceum' A.G.M. (Geraniaceae)

Common name: Meadow geranium
Height: 3ft (90cm)
Spread: 2ft (60cm)
Aspect: Sun or half shade
Soil: Well-drained
Hardiness: Zone 5
Propagation: Division, in spring

Double-flowered form. Leaves basal, lobed, toothed, midgreen. Flowers in dense cymes, rich, deep violet-blue saucers, tinged purple in the center, over a long period in summer.

Geranium psilostemon A.G.M. (Geraniaceae)

Common names: None
Height: 4ft (1.2m)
Spread: 4ft (1.2m)
Aspect: Sun or half shade
Soil: Well-drained
Hardiness: Zone 6
Propagation: Seed or division, both in spring

Clump-forming; leaves basal, lobed, toothed, green, red in spring and autumn. Flowers large, deep purple, black centers and veins, in loose cymes; very long period in summer.

Geranium pyrenaicum 'Bill Wallis' (Geraniaceae)

Common names: None
Height: 2ft (60cm)
Spread: 1ft (30cm)
Aspect: Sun or half shade
Soil: Well-drained
Hardiness: Zone 7
Propagation: Seed, in spring

Cultivar of an evergreen species. Leaves small, lobed, midgreen. Flowers small, in loose cymes, rich purple; long period in summer. Self-seeds; comes true from seed.

Geranium x riversleaianum 'Mavis Simpson' (Geraniaceae)

Common names: None
Height: 1ft (30cm)
Spread: 4ft (1.2m)
Aspect: Sun or half shade
Soil: Well-drained
Hardiness: Zone 7
Propagation: Division, in spring

Cultivar of a hybrid of garden origin. Leaves basal, 7-lobed blunt-toothed, gray-green. Flowers in loose cymes, clear pink, nonstop all summer. Superb ground cover.

Geranium x riversleaianum 'Russell Pritchard' A.G.M. (Geraniaceae)

Common names: None
Height: 1ft (30cm)
Spread: 3ft (1m)
Aspect: Sun or half shade
Soil: Well-drained
Hardiness: Zone 7
Propagation: Division, in spring

Cultivar of a garden hybrid. Leaves basal, 7-lobed, toothed, gray-green. Flowers in loose cymes, dark magenta, over long periods in summer. Excellent ground cover.

Geranium sanguineum 'Elsbeth' (Geraniaceae)

Common name: Blood-red geranium
Height: 8in (20cm)
Spread: 12in (30cm)
Aspect: Sun or half shade
Soil: Well-drained
Hardiness: Zone 5
Propagation: Division, in spring

Cloned selection of a rhizomatous European species. Leaves stem, 5- to 7-lobed, toothed, mid-green. Flowers in loose cymes, large, bright purple saucers, spring to summer.

Geranium sanguineum 'Shepherd's Warning' A.G.M. (Geraniaceae)

Common name: Blood-red geranium
Height: 6in (15cm)
Spread: 6in (15cm)
Aspect: Sun or half shade
Soil: Well-drained
Hardiness: Zone 5
Propagation: Division, in spring

Cultivar of a rhizomatous species, low-growing, mat-forming, and with flowers of deep pink which fade to white, in summer. Excellent ground cover.

Geranium sanguineum var. striatum A.G.M. (Geraniaceae)

Common name: Blood-red geranium
Height: 4in (10cm)
Spread: 6in (15cm)
Aspect: Sun or half shade
Soil: Well-drained
Hardiness: Zone 5
Propagation: Seed or division, both in spring

Form from Walney Island, off the coast of Cumbria. Leaves stem, 5- to 7-lobed. Large flowers in loose cymes, pale pink with dark pink veins, for many weeks in summer.

Hardy geraniums will spread to make attractive ground cover; some, such as Geranium himalayense, *will even flourish in deep shade.*

Geranium sanguineum var. *striatum* 'Splendens' (Geraniaceae)

Common name: Blood-red geranium
Height: 18in (45cm)
Spread: 12in (30cm)
Aspect: Sun or half shade
Soil: Well-drained
Hardiness: Zone 5
Propagation: Seed or division, both in spring

One of the taller cultivars of the species. Leaves stem, 5- to 7-lobed, midgreen. Flowers large, deep pink with darker veins, in summer.

Geranium 'Stanhoe' (Geraniaceae)

Common names: None
Height: 8in (20cm)
Spread: 8in (20cm)
Aspect: Sun or half shade
Soil: Well-drained
Hardiness: Zone 7
Propagation: Division, in spring

A hybrid of garden origin, between *G. sessiliflorum* and *G. traversii*. Leaves small, round, hairy, gray-green. Flowers delicate pink, from midsummer to autumn.

Geranium sylvaticum 'Album' A.G.M. (Geraniaceae)

Common name: Forest-loving cranesbill
Height: 30in (75cm)
Spread: 24in (60cm)
Aspect: Sun or half shade
Soil: Moist, well-drained
Hardiness: Zone 4
Propagation: Seed or division, both in spring

Clump-forming geranium. Leaves basal, 7-lobed, lobes deeply cut, toothed. Flowers in dense cymes, white, blue or pink saucers, in spring and early summer.

Geranium sylvaticum 'Amy Doncaster' (Geraniaceae)

Common names: Forest-loving cranesbill
Height: 30in (75cm)
Spread: 24in (60cm)
Aspect: Sun or half shade
Soil: Moist, well-drained
Hardiness: Zone 4
Propagation: Division, in spring

Cloned cultivar of the woodland geranium, with flowers of deep blue with white eyes, in spring and summer. Leaves basal, 7-lobed, lobes deeply cut, toothed.

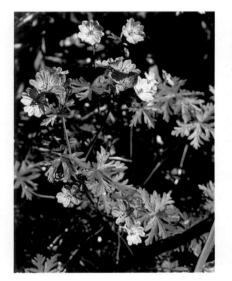

Geranium tuberosum (Geraniaceae)

Common names: None
Height: 12in (30cm)
Spread: 10in (25cm)
Aspect: Sun or half shade
Soil: Well-drained
Hardiness: Zone 8
Propagation: Seed or division, both in spring

Mediterranean species. Summer-dormant; makes deeply cut, toothed, midgreen leaves over winter and bears loose cymes of bright pink flowers with dark veins in spring.

Geranium wallichianum 'Buxton's Variety' A.G.M. (Geraniaceae)

Common name: Wallich geranium
Height: 1ft (30cm)
Spread: 1m (3ft)
Aspect: Sun or half shade
Soil: Well-drained
Hardiness: Zone 7
Propagation: Division, in spring

Cultivar of a trailing species from Kashmir and Afghanistan. Leaves 3- to 5-lobed, toothed. Flowers in loose cymes, large, sky-blue saucers, from midsummer to autumn.

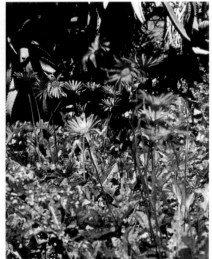

Gerbera jamesonii (Asteraceae/Compositae)

Common name: Transvaal daisy
Height: 18in (45cm)
Spread: 24in (60cm)
Aspect: Sun
Soil: Well-drained, fertile
Hardiness: Zone 8
Propagation: Seed in warmth or division, both in spring

From Indonesia, Madagascar and South Africa. Leaves inverse lance-shaped, lobed, woolly below. Flowers solitary, single, red with yellow centers, spring to late summer.

Geum 'Dolly North' (Rosaceae)

Common name: Avens
Height: 2ft (60cm)
Spread: 2ft (60cm)
Aspect: Sun or half shade
Soil: Well-drained, fertile
Hardiness: Zone 5
Propagation: Seed or division, both in autumn or spring

A *Geum chiloense* hybrid. Leaves basal, in rosettes, pinnate, leaflets heart- to kidney-shaped, wrinkled. Flowers glowing orange, in cymes on branched stems, early summer.

GEUM (Rosaceae)
Avens

A genus of some 50 species, all perennial and hardy, from temperate and polar regions of both hemispheres, with the exception of Australia. Their natural habitats range from mountainsides to woodlands and damp meadows, and they will grow in just about any soil as long as it is not waterlogged. They prefer full sun, but will tolerate light or dappled shade. Avens have handsome, evergreen foliage, mainly borne in basal rosettes. They are very useful border plants, since they bloom in early summer before the main summer flowering season, and can be persuaded to repeat-flower by deadheading. The flowers, in pink, red, orange, yellow or cream, are open and bowl- to saucer-shaped. In the garden they are much appreciated by bees, and they are also excellent for cutting and low in allergens. One drawback of this genus is that they do begin to flower less well after a few years, and will become free-flowering again only if they are lifted and divided, with the old, woody growth being discarded, and only the soft, new growth replanted. By far the best time to do this is in late spring; division at other times will mean losing a year's flowering. They can be grown from seed, but tend to hybridize readily.

Geum coccineum
(Rosaceae)

Common name: Avens
Height: 20in (50cm)
Spread: 12in (30cm)
Aspect: Sun or half shade
Soil: Well-drained, fertile
Hardiness: Zone 4
Propagation: Seed or division, both in spring or autumn

An evergreen perennial from the Balkans. Leaves basal, pinnate, hairy, and stem, entire. toothed. Flowers in cymes, brick-red with yellow stamens, in early summer.

Geum
'Lady Stratheden' A.G.M.
(Rosaceae)

Common name: Avens
Height: 2ft (60cm)
Spread: 2ft (60cm)
Aspect: Sun or half shade
Soil: Well-drained, fertile
Hardiness: Zone 6
Propagation: Seed or division, both in spring or autumn

A *Geum chiloense* hybrid. Leaves pinnate, hairy, lobes kidney-shaped to ovate. Flowers semi-double, in cymes of up to 5, yellow, all summer.

Geum
'Mrs J. Bradshaw' A.G.M.
(Rosaceae)

Common name: Avens
Height: 2ft (60cm)
Spread: 2ft (60cm)
Aspect: Sun or half shade
Soil: Well-drained, fertile
Hardiness: Zone 6
Propagation: Seed or division, both in spring or autumn

A *Geum chiloense* hybrid. Leaves pinnate, hairy, lobes ovate to heart-shaped, mid-green. Flowers in cymes of up to 5, semi-double, red, from early to late summer.

Geum
'Princess Juliana'
(Rosaceae)

Common name: Avens
Height: 2ft (60cm)
Spread: 2ft (60cm)
Aspect: Sun or half shade
Soil: Well-drained, fertile
Hardiness: Zone 5
Propagation: Seed or division, both in spring or autumn

A *Geum chiloense* hybrid. Leaves pinnate, hairy, lobes ovate to heart-shaped, mid-green. Flowers in cymes of up to 5, semi-double, strong yellow, early and midsummer.

Geum rivale
(Rosaceae)

Common name: Water avens
Height: 2ft (60cm)
Spread: 18in (45cm)
Aspect: Sun or half shade
Soil: Wet or marginal aquatic, humus-rich
Hardiness: Zone 3
Propagation: Seed or division, both in spring or autumn

European species. Leaves in basal rosettes, pinnate, obovate, veined, scalloped. Cymes of flowers, pendent, orange-yellow or pink bells, from late spring to midsummer.

Geum
'Tangerine'
(Rosaceae)

Common name: Avens
Height: 1ft (30cm)
Spread: 1ft (30cm)
Aspect: Sun or half shade
Soil: Moist, fertile
Hardiness: Zone 3
Propagation: Division, in spring or autumn

Geum rivale hybrid. Leaves in basal rosettes, pinnate, obovate to wedge-shaped, dark green, scalloped. Flowers in cymes, orange, pendent saucers, late spring to midsummer.

Gillenia trifoliata
A.G.M.
(Rosaceae)

Common name: Bowman's-root
Height: 3ft (1m)
Spread: 2ft (60cm)
Aspect: Half shade
Soil: Moist, well-drained, acidic
Hardiness: Zone 4
Propagation: Seed or division, both in spring or autumn

Rhizomatous woodlander. Leaves 3-palmate, toothed, veined, leaflets ovoid, bronze-green. Flowers asymmetric, starry, white; long period from spring to late summer.

GLADIOLUS (Iridaceae)
Gladiolus

A genus of almost 200 species of cormous perennials from many countries, especially Africa, and South Africa in particular, Madagascar, the Arabian peninsula and western Asia. Some are hardy, but others are half-hardy or tender. All like sun and well-drained, fertile soil. The genus has been hybridized extensively for the flower trade and exhibition: over 10,000 cultivars and hybrids exist, and new ones are produced continually. There are different ways of classifying them; of most use to the gardener is the grouping of most into Grandiflorus, Nanus and Primulinus. Grandiflorus are tall, with a single, long, dense spike of many large flowers. Nanus are shorter, with 2 or 3 dense spikes of small flowers. Both of these groups are tender and need lifting each year. Primulinus, with a single loose spike of many flowers, contain some that can be left in the ground all year round in warmer areas. For the greater part, they do not need staking. Some species, *G. papilio* and *G. communis* subsp. *byzantinus* for example, are invasive; in transplanting them, make sure that all the tiny cormlets are moved as well, or they will make plants of flowering size by the next season. They make excellent cut flowers, and are low in allergens.

Gladiolus callianthus
A.G.M.
(Iridaceae)

Classification: Species
Height: 3ft (1m)
Spread: 4in (10cm)
Aspect: Sun
Soil: Well-drained, fertile
Hardiness: Zone 9
Propagation: Seed, in warmth in spring; offsets when dormant

Tender species, formerly *Acidanthera*. Leaves basal, erect, linear, green. Flowers in arching spikes, scented, white with a purple throat, in late summer and early autumn.

Gladiolus cardinalis
(Iridaceae)

Classification: Species
Height: 3ft (90cm)
Spread: 4in (10cm)
Aspect: Sun
Soil: Well-drained, fertile
Hardiness: Zone 9
Propagation: Seed, in warmth in spring; offsets, when dormant

A tender, cormous perennial from South Africa. Leaves basal, erect, linear, green. Flowers in spikes of up to 12, funnel-shaped, bright red with white flash on each tepal.

Gladiolus communis subsp. **byzantinus** A.G.M.
(Iridaceae)

Classification: Species
Height: 1m (3ft)
Spread: 4in (10cm)
Aspect: Sun
Soil: Well-drained, fertile
Hardiness: Zone 6
Propagation: Seed, in spring; offsets, when dormant

Invasive type. Leaves basal, erect, linear, green. Flowers in spikes of up to 20, funnel-shaped, magenta with pale streaks on the lower tepal. Divide regularly.

Gladiolus 'Green Woodpecker'
A.G.M. (Iridaceae)

Classification: Grandiflorus
Height: 5ft (1.5m)
Spread: 5in (12cm)
Aspect: Sun
Soil: Well-drained, fertile
Hardiness: Zone 9
Propagation: Offsets, when dormant

Leaves basal, erect, linear, green. Flowers in spikes of up to 25, ruffled, green-yellow with red marks on the throat, in mid- and late summer.

Gladiolus papilio
(Iridaceae)

Classification: Species
Height: 3ft (90cm)
Spread: 3in (8cm)
Aspect: Sun
Soil: Well-drained, fertile
Hardiness: Zone 8
Propagation: Offsets, when dormant

Highly invasive species from South Africa. Leaves basal, erect to arching, linear, mid-green. Flowers in spikes of up to 5, hooded, gray-green with red internal marks.

Gladiolus 'The Bride' A.G.M. (Iridaceae)

Classification: Cardinalis hybrid
Height: 2ft (60cm)
Spread: 2in (5cm)
Aspect: Sun
Soil: Well-drained, fertile
Hardiness: Zone 8
Propagation: Offsets, when dormant

Hybrid cultivar. Leaves basal, erect, linear, midgreen. Flowering spike of up to 6 white flowers, marked pink on the lower tepal, from early spring to early summer.

Gladiolus tristis (Iridaceae)

Classification: Species
Height: 5ft (1.5m)
Spread: 2in (5cm)
Aspect: Sun
Soil: Well-drained, fertile
Hardiness: Zone 7
Propagation: Seed, in spring; offsets, when dormant

South African species. Leaves basal, erect, linear. Tall spike of up to 20 open funnel-shaped, scented flowers, creamy-white, with dark flushing or dots, in spring

Glaucium flavum (Papaveraceae)

Common name: Yellow horned poppy
Height: 3ft (90cm)
Spread: 18in (45cm)
Aspect: Sun
Soil: Well-drained, fertile
Hardiness: Zone 7
Propagation: Seed, sown in situ in spring or autumn

Rosette-forming, short-lived, coastal plant. Leaves pinnatifid, lobes toothed, rough, glaucous blue-green. Flowers single, yellow, in summer, followed by good seed heads.

Glaucium flavum f. fulvum (Papaveraceae)

Common name: Horned poppy
Height: 36in (90cm)
Spread: 18in (45cm)
Aspect: Sun
Soil: Well-drained, fertile
Hardiness: Zone 7
Propagation: Seed, sown in situ in spring or autumn

Form of the species with flowers of bright orange, in summer, followed by long, curved seed pods. Short-lived, but self-seeds; resents disturbance.

Glyceria maxima var. variegata (Graminae/Poaceae)

Common names: None
Height: 28in (70cm)
Spread: Indefinite
Aspect: Sun
Soil: Water to 15cm (6in) deep
Hardiness: Zone 5
Propagation: Division, in spring

Rhizomatous, aquatic grass from Europe and Asia. Leaves narrow straps, striped cream, white and green. Flowers in panicles, purplish-green, in mid- to late summer.

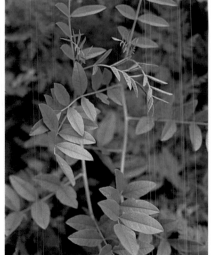

Glycyrrhiza glabra (Leguminosae/Papilionaceae)

Common name: Licorice
Height: 3ft (1m)
Spread: 18in (45cm)
Aspect: Sun
Soil: Moist, deep, fertile
Hardiness: Zone 8
Propagation: Seed or division, both in spring

Tap-rooted plant from the Mediterranean to SW Asia. Leaves pinnate, leaflets ovate, sticky, glandular, pale green. Flowers in racemes, pale blue and white, late summer.

Goniolimon tataricum (Plumbaginaceae)

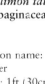

Common name: Tatarian sea-lavender
Height: 1ft (30cm)
Spread: 1ft (30cm)
Aspect: Sun
Soil: Well-drained, gritty
Hardiness: Zone 4
Propagation: Seed, in spring

Rosette-forming plant. Leaves inverse lance-shaped, smooth, leathery, pale green. Wide panicles of tubular flowers, white sepals and red petals. Excellent for cutting and drying.

Grindelia chiloensis (Asteraceae/Compositae)

Common name: Gumweed
Height: 3ft (1m)
Spread: 3ft (1m)
Aspect: Sun
Soil: Well-drained
Hardiness: Zone 6
Propagation: Seed, in spring; semi-ripe cuttings, in summer

Evergreen subshrub from Argentina and Chile. Leaves basal, inverse lance-shaped, gray-green. Flowers solitary, semi-double, yellow, on long stalks, over summer.

Gypsophila paniculata
(Caryophyllaceae)

Common name: Baby's-
breath
Height: 4ft (1.2m)
Spread: 4ft (1.2m)
Aspect: Sun
Soil: Well-drained, sandy
Hardiness: Zone 4
Propagation: Seed, in warmth
in winter to spring

Taprooted plant. Leaves lance-shaped to
linear, glaucous-green. Loose panicles of
many small, white, trumpet flowers, over a
long period in mid- to late summer.

Gypsophila repens
A.G.M.
(Caryophyllaceae)

Common name: Creeping
gypsophila
Height: 8in (20cm)
Spread: 12in (30cm)
Aspect: Sun
Soil: Well-drained, sandy
Hardiness: Zone 4
Propagation: Seed, in warmth
in winter to spring

Mat-forming perennial from the mountains
of S Europe. Leaves linear, midgreen.
Flowers in loose panicles, white or pink,
over a long period in summer.

Gypsophila
'Rosenschleier' A.G.M.
(Caryophyllaceae)

Common name: Baby's-
breath
Height: 18in (45cm)
Spread: 18in (45cm)
Aspect: Sun
Soil: Well-drained, sandy
Hardiness: Zone 4
Propagation: Seed, in warmth
in winter to spring

A robust, semi-evergreen hybrid. Leaves
lance-shaped to linear, blue-green. Flowers
in loose, many-flowered panicles, double,
white, turning pink, mid- to late summer.

Hacquetia epipactis
A.G.M.
(Apiaceae/Umbelliferae)

Common names: None
Height: 2in (5cm
Spread: 8in (20cm
Aspect: Half shade
Soil: Moist, well-drained,
acidic, humus-rich
Hardiness: Zone 7
Propagation: Seed when ripe;
division, in spring

Rhizomatous; sole species in genus. Tiny,
yellow flowers with large, green bracts in
late winter, followed by round, lime green,
3-lobed leaves, each lobe wedge-shaped.

Hakonechloa macra
'Mediovariegata'
(Graminae/Poaceae)

Common names: None
Height: 18in (45cm)
Spread: 18in (45cm)
Aspect: Sun or half shade
Soil: Moist, well-drained,
humus-rich
Hardiness: Zone 5
Propagation: Division,
in spring

Leaves arching, linear, green, with median
stripes and asymmetric narrow margins
of pale yellow. Panicles of pale green
spikelets, late summer to midautumn.

Haplopappus glutinosus
(Asteraceae/Compositae)

Common names: None
Height: 6in (15cm)
Spread: 12in (30cm)
Aspect: Sun
Soil: Sharply drained, fertile,
protected from winter wet
Hardiness: Zone 9
Propagation: Seed, when ripe
or in spring

An evergreen, tender perennial from Chile
and Argentina. Leaves in dense cushions,
oblong, lobed or pinnatisect, sticky, green.
Flowers solitary, single, yellow, in summer.

Hedychium densiflorum
(Zingiberaceae)

Common name: Ginger-lily
Height: 15ft (5m)
Spread: 6ft (2m)
Aspect: Sun or half shade
Soil: Moist, well-drained,
humus-rich
Hardiness: Zone 8
Propagation: Seed, in warmth
when ripe; division, in spring

Rhizomatous Himalayan plant. Leaves
oblong, pointed, shiny green. Flowers in
dense, cylindrical racemes, tubular, scented,
orange or yellow, in late summer.

Hedychium forrestii
(Zingiberaceae)

Common name: Ginger-lily
Height: 5ft (1.5m)
Spread: 2ft (60cm)
Aspect: Sun or half shade
Soil: Moist, well-drained,
humus-rich
Hardiness: Zone 9
Propagation: Seed, in warmth
when ripe; division, in spring

Tender, rhizomatous perennial from China.
Leaves narrow, lance-shaped, veined, green.
Flowers in racemes, white, in late summer
and early autumn. Excellent for cutting.

Hedychium yunnanense
(Zingiberaceae)

Common name: Ginger-lily
Height: 3ft (1m)
Spread: 2ft (60cm)
Aspect: Sun or half shade
Soil: Moist, well-drained,
humus-rich
Hardiness: Zone 9
Propagation: Seed, in warmth
when ripe; division, in spring

Tender, rhizomatous species from Yunnan.
Leaves broad obovate, shiny green.
Raceme of white, deeply divided flowers
with orange bracts; attractive seed heads.

Hedysarum coronarium
(Leguminosae/Papilionaceae)

Common name: Sulla
sweetvetch
Height: 3ft (1m)
Spread: 2ft (60cm)
Aspect: Sun
Soil: Well-drained, gritty
Hardiness: Zone 3
Propagation: Seed, when ripe
or in spring

Perennial from the Mediterranean. Leaves
pinnate, with up to 15 obovate leaflets,
midgreen. Flowers in racemes, perfumed,
deep red, pealike, on erect stems in spring.

HELENIUM (Asteraceae/Compositae)
Sneezeweed

A genus of 40 or so species of generally clump-forming
annuals, biennials and perennials from Central and North
America. Their natural habitats are woodland edges or
grasslands and are usually damp, and they will do well in a
sunny position. The genus has been much hybridized, such
that there is a large number of hybrids of uncertain
parentage, but of great value in the garden. Sneezeweeds
flower over long periods in late summer and autumn, and the
earlier-flowering types can be persuaded to flower again if
deadheaded. The flowers are daisylike, with prominent discs
of yellow or brown, and ray florets of yellow, orange, and
red, bringing rich autumn tints in the border. They are much-
visited by bees and butterflies, providing valuable late food.
The foliage is midgreen, lance-shaped, and unspectacular. The
taller species and cultivars usually need to be staked, and all
become congested fairly rapidly, so it is necessary to lift and
divide them every few years or so. The flowers are excellent
for cutting, and are popular for flower-arranging, but they are
named sneezeweed for a reason, being highly allergenic. The
plants are also poisonous, and contact with the foliage can
cause skin irritation.

Helenium autumnale
(Asteraceae/Compositae)

Common name: Common
sneezeweed
Height: 5ft (1.5m)
Spread: 18in (45cm)
Aspect: Sun
Soil: Moist, well-drained,
fertile
Hardiness: Zone 3
Propagation: Seed, in spring;
division, in spring or autumn

A perennial from North America. Leaves
lance-shaped, toothed, midgreen. Flowers
solitary, ray florets yellow, disc florets
brown, from late summer to midautumn.

**Helenium
'Crimson Beauty'**
(Asteraceae/Compositae)

Common name: Common
sneezeweed
Height: 4ft (1.2m)
Spread: 2ft (60cm)
Aspect: Sun
Soil: Moist, well-drained,
humus-rich
Hardiness: Zone 3
Propagation: Seed, in spring;
division, in spring or autumn

Very hardy hybrid cultivar. Leaves ovate,
midgreen. Flowers solitary, ray florets
bright red, disc florets brown, from late
summer to midautumn.

**Helenium
'Goldene Jugend'**
(Asteraceae/Compositae)

Common name: Common
sneezeweed
Height: 32in (80cm)
Spread: 24in (60cm)
Aspect: Sun
Soil: Moist, well-drained,
humus-rich
Hardiness: Zone 5
Propagation: Seed, in spring;
division, in spring or autumn

A hybrid cultivar. Leaves ovate, midgreen.
Flowers solitary, ray florets yellow, disc
florets pale brown, over a long period in
early and midsummer.

**Helenium
'Moerheim Beauty'**
(Asteraceae/Compositae)

Common name: Common
sneezeweed
Height: 3ft (90cm)
Spread: 2ft (60cm)
Aspect: Sun
Soil: Moist, well-drained,
humus-rich
Hardiness: Zone 3
Propagation: Seed, in spring;
division, in spring or autumn

Very hardy hybrid Helenium. Leaves ovate,
midgreen. Flowers solitary, ray florets
dark, coppery-red, disc florets brown, over
a long period from early to late summer.

Helenium
'Sahin's Early Flowerer'
(Asteraceae/Compositae)

Common name: Common
sneezeweed
Height: 3ft (90cm)
Spread: 2ft (60cm)
Aspect: Sun
Soil: Moist, well-drained,
humus-rich
Hardiness: Zone 5
Propagation: Seed, in spring;
division, in spring or autumn

A hybrid *Helenium*. Leaves ovate,
midgreen. Flowers single, ray florets bright
red, disc florets dark brown, in late spring
to midsummer.

Helenium
'Waldtraut'
(Asteraceae/Compositae)

Common name: Common
sneezeweed
Height: 3ft (90cm)
Spread: 2ft (60cm)
Aspect: Sun
Soil: Moist, well-drained,
humus-rich
Hardiness: Zone 3
Propagation: Seed, in spring;
division, in spring or autumn

Very hardy hybrid *Helenium*. Leaves ovate,
midgreen. Flowers single, ray florets
orange, disc florets brown, over a long
period in late summer and early autumn.

Helianthemum
'Ben Fhada'
(Cistaceae)

Common name: Sunrose
Height: 8in (20cm)
Spread: 8in (20cm)
Aspect: Sun
Soil: Well-drained, fertile
Hardiness: Zone 6
Propagation: Softwood
cuttings, in spring to
early summer

Subshrub, evergreen in mild areas. Leaves
oblong to linear, gray-green. Flowers yellow
with an orange center, 5-petalled saucers, in
cymes; long period in late spring to summer.

Helianthemum
'Fireball'
(Cistaceae)

Common name: Sunrose
Height: 8in (20cm)
Spread: 12in (30cm)
Aspect: Sun
Soil: Well-drained, fertile
Hardiness: Zone 6
Propagation: Softwood
cuttings, in spring to
early summer

Hybrid, evergreen or semi-evergreen
subshrub. Leaves oblong, gray-green.
Flowers in cymes, double, bright scarlet,
over a long period in late spring to summer.

Helianthemum
'Laurenson's Pink'
(Cistaceae)

Common name: Sunrose
Height: 8in (20cm)
Spread: 12in (30cm)
Aspect: Sun
Soil: Well-drained, fertile
Hardiness: Zone 6
Propagation: Softwood
cuttings, in spring to summer

A hybrid subshrub. Leaves linear, midgreen. Flowers in cymes, single, pale pink
with an orange center, over a long period
in spring to midsummer.

Helianthemum
nummularium
(Cistaceae)

Common name: Sunrose
Height: 8in (20cm)
Spread: 12in (30cm)
Aspect: Sun
Soil: Well-drained, fertile
Hardiness: Zone 6
Propagation: Seed, when ripe
or in spring

Subshrub from mainland Europe. Leaves
ovate to lance-shaped, gray-green. Flowers
in cymes, single, petals deep pink, paler at
base; long period from spring to summer.

HELIANTHUS (Asteraceae/Compositae)
Sunflower

A genus of some 80 species, annual and perennial, from
North, Central and South America. They are generally tall,
coarse plants demanding quite a bit of space. The taller,
spreading types are best in a wild garden. They require full
sun and good drainage, and should not be overfed, as this
will result in more foliage than flowers. There are many
cultivars and hybrids, and the nomenclature of these is highly
confused and liable to change frequently. Sunflowers are
grown for their large, daisylike flowers with usually yellow
ray florets and brown, purple or yellow disc florets; these are
borne over lengthy periods in summer, and long, hot summers
are needed for good flowering. The flowers of perennial
species are generally smaller than those of the annuals. They
attract bees and are excellent for cutting; unfortunately they
are also highly allergic. Sunflowers are prone to powdery
mildew, and so should not be allowed to dry out in summer.
Slugs are fond of their new growth in spring. Some will
spread aggressively, and it is necessary to dig around them
annually to sever the spreading roots. They need to be staked,
and they must be lifted and divided every few years. Contact
with the foliage may cause skin irritation.

Helianthus decapetalus
(Asteraceae/Compositae)

Common name: Thinleaf
sunflower
Height: 4ft (1.2m)
Spread: Indefinite
Aspect: Sun
Soil: Moist, well-drained,
humus-rich
Hardiness: Zone 5
Propagation: Division, in
spring or autumn

Rampant, rhizomatous species. Leaves ovate
to lance-shaped, smooth above, hairy-rough
below. Flowers single, daisylike, yellow
with brown centers, late summer to autumn.

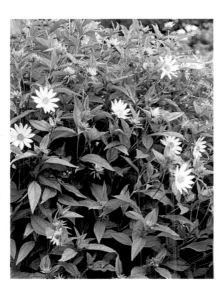

Helianthus doronicoides
(Asteraceae/Compositae)

Common name: Sunflower
Height: 5ft (1.5m)
Spread: 2ft (60cm)
Aspect: Sun
Soil: Moist, well-drained,
humus-rich
Hardiness: Zone 4
Propagation: Division, in
spring or autumn

Invasive herbaceous species from the U.S.A.
Leaves ovate to lance-shaped, large, bristly.
Flowers single, daisylike, lemon, over a
long period from summer to autumn.

Helianthus
'Lemon Queen'
(Asteraceae/Compositae)

Common name: Sunflower
Height: 6ft (1.8m)
Spread: 4ft (1.2)
Aspect: Sun
Soil: Moist, well-drained,
humus-rich
Hardiness: Zone 5
Propagation: Division, in
spring or autumn

Hybrid sunflower. Leaves ovate, veined,
dark green. Flowers pale yellow, daisylike,
with darker yellow centers, over a long
period in late summer to autumn.

Helianthus x *multiflorus*
(Asteraceae/Compositae)

Common name: Sunflower
Height: 6ft (2m)
Spread: 3ft (1m)
Aspect: Sun
Soil: Moist, well-drained,
humus-rich
Hardiness: Zone 5
Propagation: Division, in
spring or autumn

Clump-forming garden hybrid. Leaves ovate
to lance-shaped, hairy, deep green. Flowers
with yellow ray florets and brown disc
florets, over a long period from late summer.

Helianthus x *multiflorus*
'Loddon Gold' A.G.M.
(Asteraceae/Compositae)

Common name: Sunflower
Height: 5ft (1.5m)
Spread: 3ft (90cm)
Aspect: Sun
Soil: Moist, well-drained
humus-rich
Hardiness: Zone 5
Propagation: Division, in
spring or autumn

Hybrid, also called *Helianthus* 'Loddon
Gold'. Leaves lance-shaped to ovate, hairy,
dark green. Flowers double, rich yellow;
long period from late summer onward.

Helianthus x *multiflorus*
'Triomphe de Gand'
(Asteraceae/Compositae)

Common name: Sunflower
Height: 4ft (1.2m)
Spread: 3ft (90cm)
Aspect: Sun
Soil: Moist, well-drained,
humus-rich
Hardiness: Zone 5
Propagation: Division, in
spring or autumn

Hybrid, also called *Helianthus* 'Triomphe de
Gand'. Leaves ovate to lance-shaped, hairy,
dark green. Flowers large, single, yellow,
disc florets quilled, in late summer.

Helianthus salicifolius
(Asteraceae/Compositae)

Common name:
Willowleaved sunflower
Height: 8ft (2.5m)
Spread: 3ft (90cm)
Aspect: Sun
Soil: Moist, well-drained,
humus-rich
Hardiness: Zone 4
Propagation: Division, in
spring or autumn

Rhizomatous species from the U.S.A. Very
handsome foliage, arching, linear to lance-
shaped, bright green. Flowers single, yellow,
over a long period from early autumn.

Helichrysum italicum
A.G.M.
(Asteraceae/Compositae)

Common name: Straw-flower
Height: 2ft (60cm)
Spread: 3ft (90cm)
Aspect: Sun
Soil: Well-drained, protected
from winter wet
Hardiness: Zone 8
Propagation: Seed or division,
both in spring

Evergreen subshrub from S Europe. Leaves
linear, aromatic, silver-gray. Flowers dark
yellow, "everlasting" in corymbs on long
stems; long period from summer to autumn.

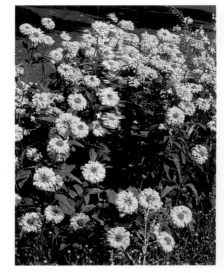

Helichrysum 'Schwefellicht'
(Asteraceae/Compositae)

Common name: Straw-flower
Height: 16in (40cm)
Spread: 12in (30cm)
Aspect: Sun
Soil: Well-drained, protected
from winter wet
Hardiness: Zone 6
Propagation: Seed or division,
both in spring

A hybrid herbaceous perennial. Leaves
lance-shaped, woolly, silver-white. Flowers
"everlasting," fluffy, yellow, in tight
corymbs, in late summer.

Helictotrichon sempervirens
A.G.M.
(Graminae/Poaceae)

Common names: None
Height: 4ft (1.2m)
Spread: 2ft (60cm)
Aspect: Sun
Soil: Well-drained
Hardiness: Zone 5
Propagation: Seed or division,
both in spring

Evergreen perennial grass from Europe.
Leaves linear, flat or rolled, blue-gray.
Flowers in stiff spikelets, straw-colored,
shiny, in panicles in early to midsummer.

Heliopsis helianthoides
'Ballerina'
(Asteraceae/Compositae)

Common name: Sunflower
heliopsis
Height: 3ft (1m)
Spread: 2ft (60cm)
Aspect: Sun
Soil: Moist, well-drained,
fertile, humus-rich
Hardiness: Zone 4
Propagation: Division, in
spring or autumn

Hybrid cultivar. Leaves ovate to lance-
shaped, toothed, midgreen. Flowers semidouble, yellow with orange discs, on
branching stems, summer to early autumn.

Heliopsis helianthoides
'Canary Bird'
(Asteraceae/Compositae)

Common name: Sunflower
heliopsis
Height: 1m (3ft)
Spread: 60cm (2ft)
Aspect: Sun
Soil: Moist, well-drained,
fertile, humus-rich
Hardiness: Zone 4
Propagation: Division, in
spring or autumn

Hybrid cultivar. Leaves ovate to lance-
shaped, toothed, midgreen. Flowers semidouble, yellow with dark centers, from
midsummer to early autumn.

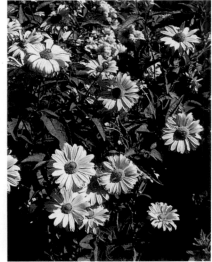

Heliopsis helianthoides
'Gigantea'
(Asteraceae/Compositae)

Common name: Sunflower
heliopsis
Height: 4ft (1.2m)
Spread: 2ft (60cm)
Aspect: Sun
Soil: Well-drained, fertile,
humus-rich
Hardiness: Zone 4
Propagation: Division, in
spring or autumn

Hardy cultivar. Leaves ovate to lance-
shaped, toothed, midgreen. Flowers semidouble, yellow with dark centers, from
midsummer to early autumn.

Heliopsis helianthoides var.
scabra 'Light of Loddon'
(Asteraceae/Compositae)

Common name: Sunflower
heliopsis
Height: 4ft (1.2m)
Spread: 2ft (60cm)
Aspect: Sun
Soil: Well-drained, fertile,
humus-rich
Hardiness: Zone 4
Propagation: Division, in
spring or autumn

Hardy cultivar. Leaves lance-shaped to
ovate, toothed, dark green. Flowers semidouble, with yellow ray florets and brown
disc florets, midsummer to early autumn.

HELLEBORUS (Ranunculaceae)
Hellebore

A small genus of only 15 or so rhizomatous species, but one
that gives the gardener some handsome weather-resistant
winter flowers of excellent quality and form. They are native
to central and eastern Europe and western Asia. Their natural
habitats vary quite considerably, from rocky scrub and
grassland to woodland, and so their cultural requirements
also vary; some do well in full sun, and are good in a sunny
border, while others enjoy dappled shade, and are excellent
for naturalizing in a woodland garden. Some species perform
best if their soil is acidic, but others prefer alkaline
conditions; what they all have in common is a dislike of soils
with extremes of wetness or dryness. All hellebores are
reliably hardy. The flowers appear in late winter and spring
and vary from open saucer-shaped to bell-shaped and
tubular; each has 5 tepals, numerous stamens, and leafy
bracts. They range in color from pure white through to deep
purple, with some spotted and green types. The foliage may
be evergreen or deciduous, and is leathery, toothed, and dark
green. Hellebores are high-allergen plants, and all parts are
poisonous and may also cause skin irritation on contact, so
they are best avoided by the allergic gardener.

Helleborus argutifolius
A.G.M.
(Ranunculaceae)

Common names: None
Height: 4ft (1.2m)
Spread: 3ft (90cm)
Aspect: Sun or half shade
Soil: Alkaline, humus-rich
Hardiness: Zone 7
Propagation: Seed, when ripe;
division, in spring or autumn

Species from Corsica and Sardinia. Leaves 3-lobed, leaflets elliptic, spiny-toothed, dark green, leathery. Pendent, pale green flowers in dense cymes, late winter to early spring.

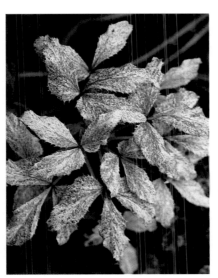

Helleborus argutifolius
'Pacific Frost'
(Ranunculaceae)

Common names: None
Height: 4ft (1.2m)
Spread: 3ft (90cm)
Aspect: Half shade
Soil: Alkaline, humus-rich
Hardiness: Zone 7
Propagation: Division, in spring or autumn

Grown for its outstanding leaves, blotched pale green and silver, ovate. Flowers in many-flowered cymes, pendent, pale green, in late winter to early spring.

Helleborus niger
A.G.M.
(Ranunculaceae)

Common name: Christmas-rose
Height: 12in (30cm)
Spread: 18in (45cm)
Aspect: Half shade
Soil: Alkaline, humus-rich
Hardiness: Zone 3
Propagation: Seed, when ripe;
division, in spring or autumn

Species from central Europe. Leaves dark green, oblong to lance-shaped, apex toothed. Flowers solitary or paired, white saucers, pink-flushed, in late winter to early spring.

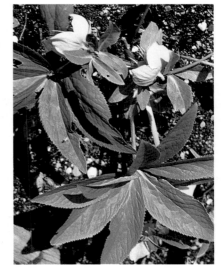

Helleborus odorus
(Ranunculaceae)

Common name: Hellebore
Height: 20in (50cm)
Spread: 20in (50cm)
Aspect: Sun or half shade
Soil: Alkaline, humus-rich
Hardiness: Zone 6
Propagation: Seed, when ripe;
division, in spring or autumn

Leaves dark green, basal, pedate, 3 lateral leaflets, each divided into 3–5 toothed lobes. Cymes of up to 5 green, fragrant, saucer-shaped flowers, late winter to early spring.

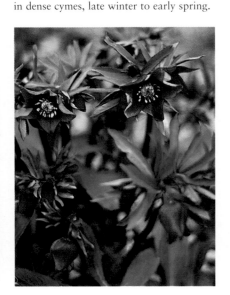

Helleborus orientalis
hybrid
(Ranunculaceae)

Common name: Lenten-rose
Height: 20in (50cm)
Spread: 18in (45cm)
Aspect: Sun or half shade
Soil: Alkaline, humus-rich
Hardiness: Zone 6
Propagation: Division, in spring or autumn

Leaves leathery, basal, pedate, deep green, with 7 to 9 elliptic leaflets. Flowers deep pink, outward-facing saucers, midwinter to midspring. One of many cultivars.

Helleborus orientalis
hybrid
(Ranunculaceae)

Common name: Lenten-rose
Height: 20in (50cm)
Spread: 18in (45cm)
Aspect: Sun or half shade
Soil: Alkaline, humus-rich
Hardiness: Zone 6
Propagation: Division, in spring or autumn

Leaves basal, leathery, pedate, deep green, with 7 to 9 elliptic leaflets. Flowers pale pink, downward-facing saucers, midwinter to midspring. One of many cultivars.

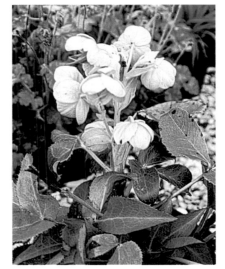

Helleborus x sternyii
Blackthorn Group A.G.M.
(Ranunculaceae)

Common name: Hellebore
Height: 14in (35cm)
Spread: 12in (30cm)
Aspect: Sun or half shade
Soil: Alkaline, humus-rich
Hardiness: Zone 7
Propagation: Seed, when ripe;
division, in spring or autumn

Hybrid evergreen hellebore. Leaves with 3 elliptic leaflets, boldly veined, grayish-green. Flowers in many-flowered cymes, green, suffused pink, from midwinter to spring.

Helleborus viridis
(Ranunculaceae)

Common name: Green hellebore
Height: 16in (40cm)
Spread: 18in (45cm)
Aspect: Sun or half shade
Soil: Alkaline, humus-rich
Hardiness: Zone 6
Propagation: Seed, when ripe;
division, in spring or autumn

Evergreen species. Leaves basal, with up to 13 oblong leaflets, midgreen. Flowers in cymes of up to 4, pendent, green, in winter or early spring.

The flowers of day-lilies, such as the star-shaped Hemerocallis *'Burford', can light up a border all summer.*

Heloniopsis orientalis
(Liliaceae/Melanthiaceae)

Common names: None
Height: 8in (20cm)
Spread: 8in (20cm)
Aspect: Half shade
Soil: Moist, well-drained,
acidic, humus-rich
Hardiness: Zone 7
Propagation: Seed, in spring
or autumn; division, in spring

Rhizomatous, evergreen woodlander.
Leaves broad, lance-shaped, leathery, pale
green. Flowers pink, nodding funnels, in
racemes of up to 10.

HEMEROCALLIS (Hemerocallidaceae/Liliaceae)
Day-lily

A genus of about 15 perennials from Japan, China, and
Korea. They have been extensively hybridized, however, to
the extent that 30,000 hybrids are in cultivation. They are
clump-forming, and need to be lifted and divided every few
years. *Hemerocallis fulva* and *H. lilio-asphodelus* are as
invasive as weeds, however, and should not be admitted to
the small garden. They will thrive in sun or light shade, and
are not demanding as to soil type, so long as it is not too dry.
The foliage is grassy, arching, and bright green; it may be
evergreen or semievergreen, and disguises the fading leaves of
spring-flowering bulbs well. The flowering stems are stout,
and staking is not usually required. The flowers may be
circular, triangular, stellate, or spider-shaped in outline, and
may be single or double. They are summer-flowering. Each
flower lasts for just one day (or one night in the case of the
nocturnal varieties, which open in the late afternoon), but is
usually followed by a succession of others. Some are
perfumed. Day-lilies are indispensable plants for the mixed
border, and are good for ground cover. They make excellent
cut flowers, and are cherished by flower-arrangers. They are
low in allergens, and suitable for allergic gardeners.

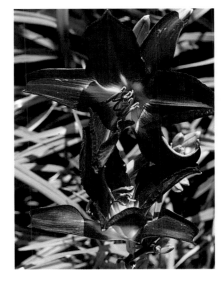

Hemerocallis
'Amersham'
(Hemerocallidaceae/Liliaceae)

Common name: Day-lily
Height: 28in (70 cm)
Spread: 26in (65cm)
Aspect: Sun
Soil: Moist, well-drained,
fertile
Hardiness: Zone 4
Propagation: Division, in
spring or autumn

A deciduous, hybrid day-lily bearing a
succession of single, star-shaped flowers
of striking dark red with a contrasting
yellow throat.

Hemerocallis
'Bette Davis Eyes'
(Hemerocallidaceae/Liliaceae)

Common name: Day-lily
Height: 26in (65cm)
Spread: 26in (65cm)
Aspect: Sun
Soil: Moist, well-drained,
fertile
Hardiness: Zone 4
Propagation: Division, in
spring or autumn

A hardy, hybrid *Hemerocallis* cultivar with
a succession of circular flowers of a
delicate, peach-pink color, with a dark
magenta throat.

Hemerocallis
'Black Magic'
(Hemerocallidaceae/Liliacea)

Common name: Day-lily
Height: 2ft (60cm)
Spread: 2ft (60cm)
Aspect: Sun
Soil: Moist, well-drained,
fertile
Hardiness: Zone 4
Propagation: Division, in
spring or autumn

A hardy, hybrid *Hemerocallis* with star-
shaped flowers of rich maroon, with a
central pale stripe on each petal, and
a yellow throat.

Hemerocallis
'Cartwheels' A.G.M.
(Hemerocallidaceae/Liliaceae)

Common name: Day-lily
Height: 30in (75cm)
Spread: 30in (75cm)
Aspect: Sun
Soil: Moist, well-drained,
fertile
Hardiness: Zone 4
Propagation: Division, in
spring

A hardy, evergreen, nocturnal-flowering
hybrid day-lily. A free-flowering cultivar,
with star-shaped flowers of clear,
unmarked yellow.

Hemerocallis
'Chemistry'
(Hemerocallidaceae/Liliaceae)

Common name: Day-lily
Height: 28in (70cm)
Spread: 28in (70cm)
Aspect: Sun
Soil: Moist, well-drained,
fertile
Hardiness: Zone 4
Propagation: Division, in
spring or autumn

A hardy, hybrid dayilily with a succession
of star-shaped flowers of amber, marked
with a brown ring near the center and an
orange throat.

Hemerocallis
'Chicago Royal Robe'
(Hemerocallidaceae/Liliaceae)

Common name: Day-lily
Height: 24in (60cm)
Spread: 6in (15cm)
Aspect: Sun
Soil: Moist, well-drained,
humus-rich
Hardiness: Zone 4
Propagation: Division, in
spring or autumn

A hardy, semievergreen, hybrid day-lily
with a succession of large, perfumed,
circular flowers of dark purple with a
yellow-green throat.

Hemerocallis
'Chicago Sunrise'
(Hemerocallidaceae/Liliaceae)

Common name: Day-lily
Height: 28in (70cm)
Spread: 6in (15cm)
Aspect: Sun
Soil: Moist, well-drained,
humus-rich
Hardiness: Zone 4
Propagation: Division, in
spring or autumn

Freeflowering, hardy, semievergreen hybrid
day-lily, with a succession of circular, clear
yellow flowers with a darker throat, from
midsummer.

Hemerocallis
'Corky' A.G.M.
(Hemerocallidaceae/Liliaceae)

Common name: Daylily
Height: 32in (80cm)
Spread: 3½in (9cm)
Aspect: Sun
Soil: Moist, well-drained,
humus-rich
Hardiness: Zone 4
Propagation: Division, in
spring

Very freeflowering, evergreen, hardy hybrid
day-lily, with black stems, mahogany buds,
and small, star-shaped flowers of lemon-
yellow, in midsummer.

Hemerocallis.
'Golden Scroll'
(Hemerocallidaceae/Liliaceae)

Common name: Daylily
Height: 19in (48cm)
Spread: 6in (15cm)
Aspect: Sun
Soil: Moist, well-drained,
humus-rich
Hardiness: Zone 4
Propagation: Division, in
spring or autumn

A hybrid day-lily with lush foliage and
ruffled, circular, mixed tangerine-orange to
deep peach flowers, with a green throat, in
late summer.

Hemerocallis
'King Haiglar'
(Hemerocallidaceae/Liliaceae)

Common name: Day-lily
Height: 28in (70cm)
Spread: 5in (13cm)
Aspect: Sun
Soil: Moist, well-drained,
humus-rich
Hardiness: Zone 4
Propagation: Division, in
spring or autumn

A very freeflowering, hybrid day-lily
cultivar bearing large flowers of rich
scarlet, with a small yellow throat,
in midsummer.

Hemerocallis
'Lady Neva'
(Hemerocallidaceae/Liliaceae)

Common name: Day-lily
Height: 36in (90cm)
Spread: 9in (22cm)
Aspect: Sun
Soil: Moist, well-drained,
humus-rich
Hardiness: Zone 4
Propagation: Division, in
spring or autumn

A hybrid day-lily with ruffled flowers of
buff to bright yellow, marked maroon;
throat flared, yellow, filaments yellow,
anthers gray.

Hemerocallis
'Little Grapette'
(Hemerocallidaceae/Liliaceae)

Common name: Day-lily
Height: 12in (30cm)
Spread: 18in (45cm)
Aspect: Sun
Soil: Moist, well-drained,
fertile
Hardiness: Zone 4
Propagation: Division, in
spring or autumn

A hybrid day-lily with star-shaped flowers
of deep purple with a green throat, in
midsummer. Shorter daylilies such as this
are excellent for containers.

Hemerocallis
'Mighty Mogul'
(Hemerocallidaceae/Liliaceae)

Common name: Day-lily
Height: 36in (90cm)
Spread: 18in (45cm)
Aspect: Sun
Soil: Moist, well-drained,
humus-rich
Hardiness: Zone 4
Propagation: Division, in
spring

A hybrid day-lily with a succession of
bright scarlet flowers with a yellow throat.
The petals are reflexed and have slightly
ruffled edges.

Hemerocallis
'Stella de Oro' A.G.M.
(Hemerocallidaceae/Liliaceae)

Common name: Day-lily
Height: 12in (30cm)
Spread: 18in (45cm)
Aspect: Sun
Soil: Moist, well-drained,
humus-rich
Hardiness: Zone 4
Propagation: Division, in
spring

A vigorous, freeflowering, hybrid evergreen day-lily, with a succession of circular, bright yellow flowers on slender stems in early summer.

Hesperis matronalis
(Brassicaceae/Cruciferae)

Common name: Dame's
rocket
Height: 36in (90cm)
Spread: 18in (45cm)
Aspect: Sun or half shade
Soil: Moist, well-drained,
fertile
Hardiness: Zone 3
Propagation: Seed, sown
in situ in spring

Short-lived, rosette-forming plant from Asia and Europe. Leaves dark green, ovate, toothed, hairy. Flowers perfumed, lilac-purple, in panicles, spring to midsummer.

Heuchera cylindrica
'Greenfinch'
(Saxifragaceae)

Common name: Coral-bells
Height: 3ft (90cm)
Spread: 2ft (60cm)
Aspect: Any
Soil: Moist, well-drained,
fertile
Hardiness: Zone 4
Propagation: Division, in
autumn

Cloned cultivar. Leaves round, scalloped, dark green, mottled pale green. Flowers in panicles or tall spikes, green, from mid-spring to midsummer. Good ground cover.

Heuchera micrantha
var. *diversifolia*
'Palace Purple' A.G.M.

Common name: Coral-bells
Height: 2ft (60cm)
Spread: 2ft (60cm)
Aspect: Any
Soil: Moist, well-drained,
fertile
Hardiness: Zone 5
Propagation: Division, in
autumn

Leaves large, shiny, jagged, metallic bronze. Flowers in very tall, loose panicles, cream, anthers red, followed by good seed heads in early summer. Good ground cover.

Heuchera
'Persian Carpet'
(Saxifragaceae)

Common name: Coral-bells
Height: 14in (35cm)
Spread: 24in (60cm)
Aspect: Any
Soil: Moist, well-drained,
fertile
Hardiness: Zone 7
Propagation: Division, in
autumn

Hybrid with large, round, metallic, silvery red-purple leaves. Flowers on tall spikes in panicles, greenish, in early summer. Handsome ground cover. Liked by bees.

Heuchera
'Pewter Moon'
(Saxifragaceae)

Common name: Coral-bells
Height: 16in (40cm)
Spread: 12in (30cm)
Aspect: Any
Soil: Moist, well-drained,
fertile
Hardiness: Zone 7
Propagation: Division, in
autumn

Hybrid with ovate to heart-shaped leaves, bronze-purple, marbled gray. Flowers in panicles, ice-pink, in early summer. A good evergreen ground cover for shade.

Heuchera
'Rachel'
(Saxifragaceae)

Common name: Coral-bells
Height: 1ft (30cm)
Spread: 1ft (30cm)
Aspect: Any
Soil: Moist, well-drained,
fertile
Hardiness: Zone 7
Propagation: Division, in
autumn

Hybrid with rounded, lobed, toothed leaves of dark green with bronzed edges. Flowers in erect panicles, pale pink, in early summer. Evergreen ground cover for shade.

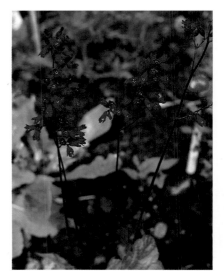

Heuchera
'Red Spangles' A.G.M.
(Saxifragaceae)

Common name: Coral-bells
Height: 20in (50cm)
Spread: 10in (25cm)
Aspect: Any
Soil: Moist, well-drained,
fertile
Hardiness: Zone 4
Propagation: Division, in
autumn

Hybrid with round, lobed, toothed leaves of dark green, marbled pale green. Flowers in short, open panicles, scarlet, all summer. Evergreen ground cover for shade.

**x *Heucherella alba*
'Bridget Bloom'**
(Saxifragaceae)

Common names: None
Height: 16in (40cm)
Spread: 12in (30cm)
Aspect: Any
Soil: Moist, well-drained,
fertile, acidic
Hardiness: Zone 5
Propagation: Division, in
autumn or spring

**x *Heucherella alba*
'Rosalie'**
(Saxifragaceae)

Common names: None
Height: 16in (40cm)
Spread: 8in (20cm)
Aspect: Any
Soil: Moist, well-drained,
fertile, acidic
Hardiness: Zone 5
Propagation: Division, in
spring or autumn

ature *Hieracium lanatum*
(Asteraceae/Compositae)

Common name: Hawkweed
Height: 18in (45cm)
Spread: 8in (20cm)
Aspect: Sun
Soil: Well-drained, poor
Hardiness: Zone 7
Propagation: Seed, in autumn
or spring; division, in spring

Hieracium maculatum
(Asteraceae/Compositae)

Common name: Hawkweed
Height: 32in (80cm)
Spread: 8in (20cm)
Aspect: Sun
Soil: Well-drained poor
Hardiness: Zone 6
Propagation: Seed, in autumn
or spring; division, in spring

Evergreen hybrid of *Heuchera* and *Tiarella*.
Leaves ovate, 7- to 9-lobed, toothed, green.
Panicles of tiny, pink flowers in late spring
and again in autumn. Ground cover.

Hybrid of *Heuchera* and *Tiarella*. Leaves
ovate, 7- to 9-lobed, toothed, green, veined
brown. Flowers in panicles, tiny, pale pink,
in spring and again in autumn.

Clump-forming. Leaves linear to lance-
shaped, densely white-hairy, gray-green,
margined white. Loose panicles of semidouble, chrome-yellow flowers, in summer.

Leaves ovate to lance-shaped, toothed,
dark green, spotted brown-purple. Flowers
in corymbs, yellow daisies. Seeds
everywhere, so deadhead after flowering.

Hordeum jubatum
(Graminae/Poaceae)

Common name: Squirrel-tail
grass
Height: 20in (50cm)
Spread: 12in (30cm)
Aspect: Sun
Soil: Well-drained, fertile
Hardiness: Zone 5
Propagation: Seed, sown
in situ in spring or autumn

Grass from Asia and North America.
Leaves erect to arching, linear, pale green.
Dense, broad panicles of arched, silky,
bristled spikelets in early and midsummer.

HOSTA (Hostaceae/Liliaceae)
Plantain-lily

A genus of some 70 species from eastern Russia, China,
Japan, and Korea. They are soundly perennial, and are grown
principally for their foliage value. Some of them have very
nice flowers, and therefore qualify on both accounts. Some
give a second, albeit brief, display in autumn. The leaves may
be round, ovate, or lance- or heart-shaped, 5–20in (12–50cm)
in length, and come in all shades of green, solid or with
margins or centers marked with variegation in shades from
white to rich yellow. The flowers are in one-sided racemes,
and may be bell- or trumpet-shaped. Hostas will grow in sun
or full shade, but flower better in sun; the yellow-foliaged
types do best in sun. They demand moisture at the roots, and
more so when in full sun, so must be watered in dry spells;
the foliage will wilt as a warning. They respond readily to
division at almost any time of year. The great scourge of the
genus is the attention of the slug and snail families; should
they nibble the emergent shoots, the leaves will be scarred for
the rest of the season, so take preventative measures early in
spring. Hostas are good plants for the allergic gardener, since
they are low in allergens. The foliage and flowers are very
useful in flower-arranging.

Hosta crispula
A.G.M.
(Hostaceae/Liliaceae)

Common name: Plantain-lily
Height: 3ft (90cm)
Spread: 3ft (90cm)
Aspect: Full shade
Soil: Moist, well-drained,
fertile
Hardiness: Zone 5
Propagation: Division, in
autumn or spring

Leaves lance- to heart-shaped, edges
scalloped, deep green margined irregularly
in white. Flowers lavender-white, funnel-
shaped, on scapes in summer.

Hosta
'Eric Smith'
(Hostaceae/Liliaceae)

Common name: Plantain-lily
Height: 4ft (1.2m)
Spread: 2ft (60cm)
Aspect: Any
Soil: Moist, well-drained, fertile
Hardiness: Zone 5
Propagation: Division, in autumn or spring

A hardy hybrid in the Tardiana Group. Leaves large, rounded, bluish-green. Flowers lilac-pink funnels on tall scapes, in midsummer.

Hosta
'Frances Williams' A.G.M.
(Hostaceae/Liliaceae)

Common name: Plantain-lily
Height: 26in (65cm)
Spread: 36in (1m)
Aspect: Full or half shade
Soil: Moist, well-drained, fertile
Hardiness: Zone 5
Propagation: Division, in spring or autumn

Clump-forming hybrid. Leaves glaucous blue-green, margined yellow-green, heart-shaped. Flowers gray-white bells on scapes, in early summer. Relatively slug-resistant.

Hosta
'Ground Master'
(Hostaceae/Liliaceae)

Common name: Plantain-lily
Height: 20in (50cm)
Spread: 22in (55cm)
Aspect: Full or half shade
Soil: Moist, well-drained, fertile
Hardiness: Zone 5
Propagation: Division, in autumn or spring

Hybrid cultivar. Leaves ovate to lance-shaped, matt green, with irregular wavy margins of cream, fading to white. Flowers on scapes, purple funnels, in summer.

Hosta
'Honeybells' A.G.M.
(Hostaceae/Liliaceae)

Common name: Plantain-lily
Height: 3ft (90cm)
Spread: 4ft (1.2m)
Aspect: Half shade or sun
Soil: Moist, well-drained, fertile
Hardiness: Zone 5
Propagation: Division, in autumn or spring

A robust hybrid. Leaves ovate or heart-shaped, wavy-edged, strongly veined, luminous pale green. Flowers perfumed, white bells, on scapes in late summer.

Hosta plantaginea
(Hostaceae/Liliaceae)

Common name: Fragrant plantain-lily
Height: 75cm (30in)
Spread: 1m (3ft)
Aspect: Half shade or sun
Soil: Moist, well-drained, fertile
Hardiness: Zone 5
Propagation: Division, in autumn or spring

Leaves glossy pale green, ovate to heart-shaped, veins prominent. Flowers scented, white trumpets, on scapes, late summer to autumn. Shy-flowering in cold areas.

Hosta rohdeifolia
(Hostaceae/Liliaceae)

Common name: Plantain-lily
Height: 3ft (1m)
Spread: 18in (45cm)
Aspect: Full or half shade
Soil: Moist, well-drained, fertile
Hardiness: Zone 5
Propagation: Division, in autumn or spring

A species from Japan. Leaves lance- to inverse-lance-shaped, olive-green. Flowers on leafy scapes, purple funnels, with dark purple stripes, in summer.

Hosta
'Royal Standard' A.G.M.
(Hostaceae/Liliaceae)

Common name: Plantain-lily
Height: 3ft (1m)
Spread: 4ft (1.2m)
Aspect: Any
Soil: Moist, well-drained, fertile
Hardiness: Zone 5
Propagation: Division, in autumn or spring

Robust, hybrid perennial. Leaves ovate to heart-shaped, ribbed, shiny pale green. Flowers white, perfumed funnels on scapes in late summer.

Hosta sieboldiana
(Hostaceae/Liliaceae)

Common name: Siebold plantain-lily
Height: 3ft (1m)
Spread: 4ft (1.2m)
Aspect: Half shade or sun
Soil: Moist, well-drained, fertile
Hardiness: Zone 5
Propagation: Division, in autumn or spring

Species from Japan. Leaves large, ovate to heart-shaped, thick, gray-green, green, or blue. Flowers in scapes, pale lilac-gray bells, in early summer.

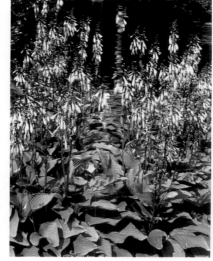

Hosta
'So Sweet'
(Hostaceae/Liliaceae)

Common name: Plantain-lily
Height: 24in (60cm)
Spread: 22in (55cm)
Aspect: Half shade or sun
Soil: Moist, well-drained,
fertile
Hardiness: Zone 5
Propagation: Division, in
autumn or spring

Hybrid with ovate to lance-shaped, glossy,
midgreen leaves, margined creamy-white.
Flowers white, purple-striped, fragrant,
funnel-shaped, in mid- and late summer.

Hosta
'Sun Power'
(Hostaceae/Liliaceae)

Common name: Plantain-lily
Height: 4ft (1.2m)
Spread: 3ft (1m)
Aspect: Full or half shade
Soil: Moist, well-drained,
fertile
Hardiness: Zone 5
Propagation: Division, in
autumn or spring

A hybrid perennial. Leaves ovate to heart-
shaped, bright yellow or yellow-green.
Flowers pale lavender or white, on scapes
in summer.

Hosta
'Sweet Susan'
(Hostaceae/Liliaceae)

Common name: Plantain-lily
Height: 18in (45cm)
Spread: 28in (70cm)
Aspect: Half shade or sun
Soil: Moist, well-drained
Hardiness: Zone 5
Propagation: Division, in
autumn or spring

Hybrid with large, heart-shaped, midgreen
leaves. Flowers funnel-shaped, perfumed,
white, edged purple, on scapes in early and
again in late summer.

Hosta
'Tall Boy'
(Hostaceae/Liliaceae)

Common name: Plantain-lily
Height: 3ft (1m)
Spread: 3ft (1m)
Aspect: Any
Soil: Moist, well-drained,
fertile
Hardiness: Zone 5
Propagation: Division, in
autumn or spring

A hybrid perennial. Leaves ovate, green.
Flowers funnel-shaped, purple, in dense
racemes on scapes well above the leaves, in
late summer.

Hosta undulata
var. *undulata* A.G.M.
(Hostaceae/Liliaceae)

Common name: Wavy-leaved
plantain-lily
Height: 32in (80cm)
Spread: 18in (45cm)
Aspect: Any
Soil: Moist, well-drained,
fertile
Hardiness: Zone 5
Propagation: Division, in
autumn or spring

Leaves lance-shaped to elliptic, twisted,
green with pronounced central white band.
Flowers on arching scapes, mauve, funnel-
shaped, in early and midsummer.

Hosta
'Wide Brim' A.G.M.
(Hostaceae/Liliaceae)

Common name: Plantain-lily
Height: 22in (55cm)
Spread: 3ft (1m)
Aspect: Any
Soil: Moist, well-drained,
fertile
Hardiness: Zone 5
Propagation: Division, in
autumn or spring

Clump-forming hybrid. Leaves relatively
small, heart-shaped, puckered, dark green,
margined cream. Flowers pale lavender
funnels, in summer.

Houttuynia cordata
'Chameleon'
(Saururaceae)

Common names: None
Height: 1ft (30cm)
Spread: Indefinite
Aspect: Sun
Soil: Moist, humus-rich,
fertile
Hardiness: Zone 5
Propagation: Division in
spring

Rampant ground cover. Leaves aromatic,
ovate or heart-shaped, heavily variegated
in red, yellow, and green. Flowers tiny,
green-yellow, with white bracts, in spring.

Houttuynia cordata
'Flore Pleno'
(Saururaceae)

Common names: None
Height: 1ft (30cm)
Spread: Indefinite
Aspect: Sun or half shade
Soil: Moist, humus-rich,
fertile
Hardiness: Zone 5
Propagation: Division, in
spring

Highly invasive, rhizomatous woodlander.
Leaves aromatic, ovate or heart-shaped,
gray-green. Flowers tiny, green-yellow, with
pure white bracts. Ground cover in shade.

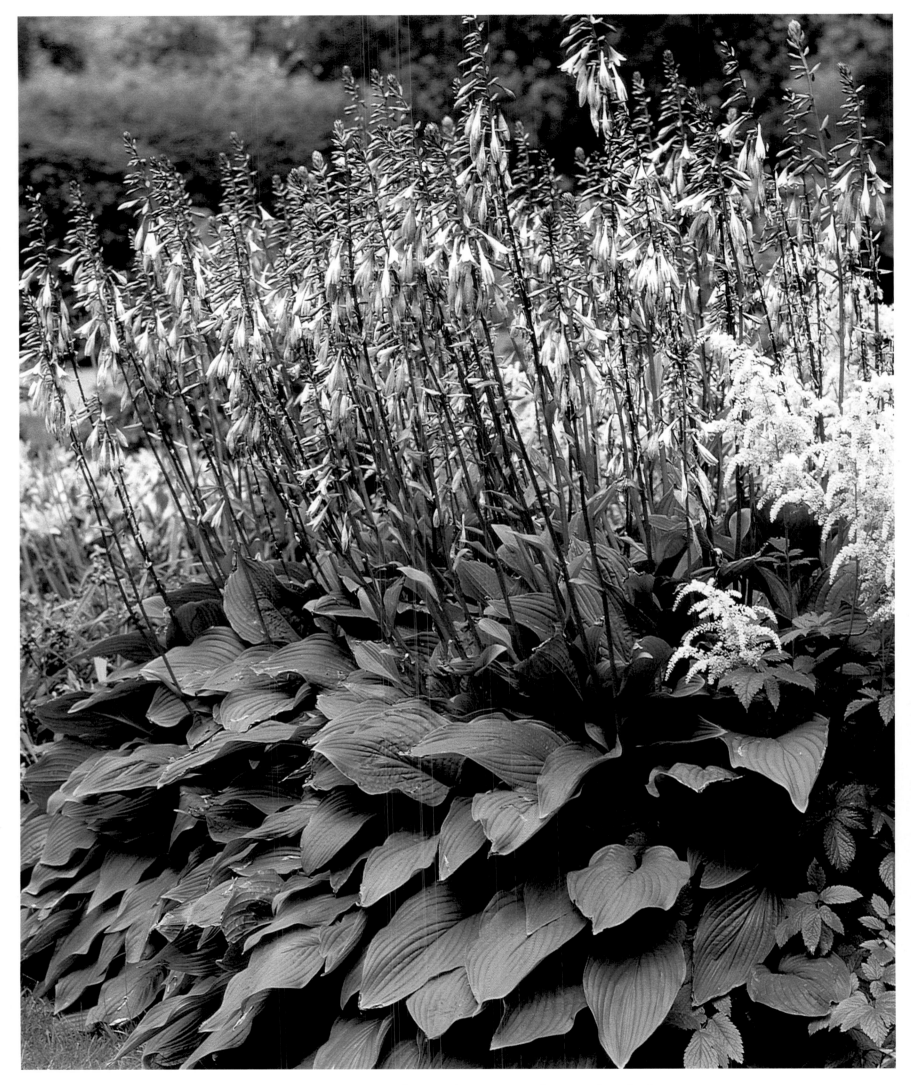

One of the taller hostas, 'Tall Boy' makes an impact when massed in a border.

Hyacinthoides non-scripta var. *alba* (Hyacinthaceae/Liliaceae)

Common names: None
Height: 16in (40cm)
Spread: 4in (10cm)
Aspect: Half shade
Soil: Moist, well-drained, fertile, humus-rich
Hardiness: Zone 5
Propagation: Offsets, in summer

Vigorous, bulbous, woodlander. Leaves linear, glossy, dark green. Flowers in one-sided, arched racemes, pendent, perfumed, bell-shaped, white. Spreads rapidly.

Hyacinthoides non-scripta var. *rosea* (Hyacinthaceae/Liliaceae)

Common names: None
Height: 16in (40cm)
Spread: 4in (10cm)
Aspect: Half shade
Soil: Moist, well-drained, fertile, humus-rich
Hardiness: Zone 5
Propagation: Offsets, in summer

Vigorous, bulbous woodlander. Leaves linear, glossy-green. Flowers in one-sided, arching racemes, lilac-pink, perfumed, bell-shaped. Excellent in half shade.

Hyacinthus orientalis 'Blue Jacket' A.G.M. (Hyacinthaceae/Liliaceae)

Common name: Common hyacinth
Height: 12in (30cm)
Spread: 3in (8cm)
Aspect: Sun or half shade
Soil: Well-drained, fertile
Hardiness: Zone 5
Propagation: Offsets, in summer

Hybrid of a bulbous plant from the Middle East. Leaves linear, channelled, green. Flowers in dense, erect racemes, perfumed, single, tubular, navy blue, in early spring.

Hyacinthus orientalis 'City of Haarlem' A.G.M. (Hyacinthaceae/Liliaceae)

Common name: Common hyacinth
Height: 12in (30cm)
Spread: 3in (8cm)
Aspect: Sun or half shade
Soil: Well-drained, fertile
Hardiness: Zone 5
Propagation: Offsets, in summer

Hybrid cultivar. Leaves linear, channelled, green. Flowers in erect, dense racemes of up to 40, perfumed, tubular, primrose, in early spring.

Hyacinthus orientalis 'Gipsy Queen' A.G.M. (Hyacinthaceae/Liliaceae)

Common name: Common hyacinth
Height: 12in (30cm)
Spread: 3in (8cm)
Aspect: Sun or half shade
Soil: Well-drained, fertile
Hardiness: Zone 5
Propagation: Offsets, in summer

Hybrid cultivar. Leaves linear, channelled, green. Flowers in erect racemes of up to 40, perfumed, tubular, single, salmon-pink, in early spring.

Hyacinthus orientalis 'L'Innocence' A.G.M. (Hyacinthaceae/Liliaceae)

Common name: Common hyacinth
Height: 12in (30cm)
Spread: 3in (8cm)
Aspect: Sun or half shade
Soil: Well-drained, fertile
Hardiness: Zone 5
Propagation: Offsets, in summer

Hybrid cultivar. Leaves linear, channelled, green. Flowers in erect racemes of up to 40, single, perfumed, tubular, pure white, in early spring.

Hylomecon japonica (Papaveraceae)

Common names: None
Height: 8in (20cm)
Spread: 18in (45cm)
Aspect: Half or full shade
Soil: Moist, well-drained, acidic, humus-rich
Hardiness: Zone 7
Propagation: Seed, when ripe; division, in spring

Rhizomatous woodlander. Leaves pinnate, lobes ovate, toothed, pale green. Flowers solitary, single, 4-petalled cups, chrome yellow, from spring to summer.

Hymenocallis × festalis (Amaryllidaceae)

Common name: Spider-lily
Height: 32in (80cm)
Spread: 12in (30cm)
Aspect: Sun or half shade
Soil: Moist, well-drained, fertile
Hardiness: Zone 8
Propagation: Seed, in warmth when ripe; offsets in summer

Evergreen, tender bulbous garden hybrid. Leaves basal, oblong, shiny, green. Flowers in umbels on erect stems, white, perfumed, central cup, petals long and twisted.

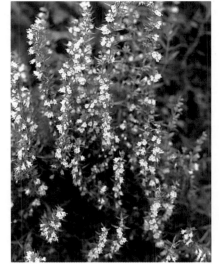

Hypericum cerastioides
(Clusiaceae/Guttiferae)

Common name: Rhodope St.
John's-wort
Height: 8in (20cm)
Spread: 18in (45cm)
Aspect: Sun
Soil: Well-drained, sandy
Hardiness: Zone 7
Propagation: Division,
in spring or autumn

A herb from Greece, Turkey and Bulgaria.
Leaves ovate, downy gray-green. Flowers
in cymes of up to 5, star-shaped, golden
yellow, late spring and early summer.

Hypericum olympicum
A.G.M.
(Clusiaceae/Guttiferae)

Common name: Olympia St.
John's-wort
Height: 1ft (30cm)
Spread: 1ft (30cm)
Aspect: Sun
Soil: Well-drained, sandy
Hardiness: Zone 6
Propagation: Greenwood
cuttings, in summer

A subshrub from Greece and Turkey.
Leaves oblong, pointed, gray-green.
Flowers in cymes of up to 5, star-shaped,
deep yellow, in summer.

Hypericum perforatum
(Clusiaceae/Guttiferae)

Common name: Common St.
John's-wort
Height: 4ft (1.2m)
Spread: 2ft (60cm)
Aspect: Sun
Soil: Well-drained, sandy
Hardiness: Zone 3
Propagation: Division,
in spring or autumn

A hardy perennial from Europe and Asia.
Leaves ovate, midgreen, with large, opaque
spots. Flowers in cymes, star-shaped,
bright yellow, in summer.

Hyssopus officinalis
f. **albus**
(Labiatae/Lamiaceae)

Common name: Hyssop
Height: 2ft (60cm)
Spread: 3ft (90cm)
Aspect: Sun
Soil: Well-drained, fertile
Hardiness: Zone 3
Propagation: Seed, in autumn

Hardy, aromatic subshrub. Leaves linear,
midgreen. Flowers funnel-shaped, scented,
whorled, white (deep blue in the species),
in spikes, from midsummer to autumn.

Iberis sempervirens
'Pinky Perpetual'
(Brassicaceae/Cruciferae)

Common name: Evergreen
candytuft
Height: 12in (30cm)
Spread: 16in (40cm)
Aspect: Sun
Soil: Moist, well-drained,
fertile
Hardiness: Zone 4
Propagation: Softwood
cuttings, in late spring

Hardy, evergreen subshrub from Europe.
Leaves linear, short, dark green. Flowers
pink, in racemes, in late spring and early
summer. The species has white flowers.

Iberis sempervirens
'Weisser Zwerg'
(Brassicaceae/Cruciferae)

Common name: Evergreen
candytuft
Height: 4in (10cm)
Spread: 8in (20cm)
Aspect: Sun
Soil: Moist, well-drained,
fertile
Hardiness: Zone 4
Propagation: Softwood
cuttings, in late spring

A very compact cloned selection. Leaves
are short, linear, dark green. Bears a
profusion of white, stemless flowers
in spring.

Impatiens tinctoria
(Balsaminaceae)

Common name: Balsam
Height: 7ft (2.2m)
Spread: 3ft (1m)
Aspect: Half shade
Soil: Moist, well-drained,
humus-rich
Hardiness: Zone 10
Propagation: Seed, in warmth
in early spring

Robust, tuberous plant. Leaves oblong to
lance-shaped, toothed, spirally arranged,
green. Flowers in racemes, white, scented,
with a violet throat, summer to autumn.

Imperata cylindrica
'Rubra'
(Graminae/Poaceae)

Common names: None
Height: 2ft (60cm)
Spread: 1ft (30cm)
Aspect: Sun or half shade
Soil: Moist, well-drained,
humus-rich
Hardiness: Zone 8
Propagation: Division,
in spring

Half-hardy grass from Japan. Leaves linear,
flat, pale green, turning bright red from the
tips downward. Panicles of fluffy, silvery
spikelets in late summer in warm areas.

INCARVILLEA (Bignoniaceae)

A genus of some 15 or so annuals and taprooted perennials from rocky mountains and high-altitude grasslands of central and eastern Asia. The flowers are held high, singly or in panicles or racemes, on stiff stems, and are tubular to trumpet-shaped, with 5 petals. They are mostly purple or pink in color, but white forms exist; flowering time is early or midsummer. The foliage is dark green, and the alternate leaves pinnate or pinnatisect. *Incarvillea* would be worth taking some time over, but in fact they are easy and accommodating plants; the delicate, exotic look of the flowers belies the fact that these plants are hardy or half-hardy. They are suitable for either a rock garden or a mixed border. They have carrot-like roots, and so resent disturbance once they have become established. They should be planted with their crowns 3–4in (8–10cm) below the soil surface, and damage to the fleshy roots should be avoided at all costs. Some protection should be given from very high levels of wet in winter, and a mulch protection used in prolonged frosts. *Incarvillea* are easy to grow from seed, but they will take three years to flower, except for *I. arguta*, which may well flower in its first season.

Incarvillea arguta
(Bignoniaceae)

Common names: None
Height: 3ft (90cm)
Spread: 1ft (30cm)
Aspect: Sun, shade in summer
Soil: Moist, well-drained, fertile
Hardiness: Zone 8
Propagation: Seed, in spring or autumn

Leaves pinnate, deep green, leaflets lance-shaped, toothed. Flowers in racemes of up to 20, pendent, tubular, pink or white, in early and midsummer.

Incarvillea delavayi
(Bignoniaceae)

Common names: None
Height: 2ft (60cm)
Spread: 1ft (30cm)
Aspect: Sun, shade in summer
Soil: Moist, well-drained, fertile
Hardiness: Zone 6
Propagation: Seed, in spring or autumn

Taprooted plant from China. Leaves dark green, pinnate, leaflets lance-shaped, toothed. Flowers in racemes of up to 10, purple-pink, in early and midsummer.

Incarvillea delavayi f. alba
(Bignoniaceae)

Common names: None
Height: 2ft (60cm)
Spread: 1ft (30cm)
Aspect: Sun, shade in summer
Soil: Moist, well-drained, fertile
Hardiness: Zone 6
Propagation: Seed, in spring or autumn

Leaves dark green, pinnate, leaflets lance-shaped, toothed, terminal segment large. Flowers in racemes of up to 10, white with a yellow throat, in early and midsummer.

Incarvillea delavayi 'Bees Pink'
(Bignoniaceae)

Common names: None
Height: 2ft (60cm)
Spread: 1ft (30cm)
Aspect: Sun, shade in summer
Soil: Moist, well-drained, fertile
Hardiness: Zone 6
Propagation: Division, in spring

Selected form of the species. Leaves dark green, pinnate, leaflets lance-shaped, toothed. Flowers in racemes of up to 10, pink trumpets, in early and midsummer.

Incarvillea mairei
(Bignoniaceae)

Common names: None
Height: 20in (50cm)
Spread: 12in (30cm)
Aspect: Sun, shade in summer
Soil: Moist, well-drained, fertile
Hardiness: Zone 4
Propagation: Seed, in spring or autumn

Leaves dark green, pinnate, leaflets ovate, toothed. Few-flowered racemes of purple-crimson trumpets with a yellow throat, in early summer.

Incarvillea sinensis 'Alba'
(Bignoniaceae)

Common names: None
Height: 34in (85cm)
Spread: 12in (30cm)
Aspect: Sun
Soil: Moist, well-drained, fertile
Hardiness: Zone 4
Propagation: Seed, in spring or autumn

Taprooted plant from China and Nepal. Leaves dark green, pinnatisect, pinnae linear to lance-shaped. Tall, few-flowered racemes of white trumpets, in late summer.

Incarvillea
'Snowtop'
(Bignoniaceae)

Common names: None
Height: 2ft (60cm)
Spread: 1ft (30cm)
Aspect: Sun
Soil: Moist, well-drained,
fertile
Hardiness: Zone 6
Propagation: Division, in
spring, with care

Hardy hybrid. Pure white flowers in
summer. Dies down very early, so mark the
position well, to prevent damaging the
roots of the dormant plant.

Incarvillea zhongdianensis
(Bignoniaceae)

Common names: None
Height: 16in (40cm)
Spread: 8in (20cm)
Aspect: Sun
Soil: Moist, well-drained,
fertile
Hardiness: Zone 7
Propagation: Seed, in autumn
or spring

Recent introduction (as *I. compacta*) from
China. Foliage dark glossy-green. Flowers
of a glorious purplish-pink, with a yellow
throat. Should become very popular.

INULA (Asteraceae/Compositae)

A genus of some 100 species, mostly perennial, but including
some annuals and biennials; all the perennial species are
hardy, easy to grow, and some (for example, *Inula hookeri*
and *I. racemosa*) are frankly invasive. Their native habitats,
ranging across temperate and tropical regions of Asia, Africa,
and Europe, range from moist, shady lowlands to sunny and
mountainous areas. They will grow in any soil, but prefer a
moisture-retentive one; if they become too dry, they are prone
to powdery mildew. *I magnifica* will even grow in boggy soil.
All species suit a sunny position, but *I. ensifolia* will tolerate
light shade, and *I. hookeri* prefers half shade. In general, the
robust, taller species naturalize well in wildflower gardens,
although some need to be staked if they are not supported by
other plants, and the smaller types are a good choice for
growing in rock gardens. *I. helenium* has been cultivated as a
medicinal herb; its roots were once used to produce an
expectorant. The flowers, borne singly or in corymbs in
summer, are yellow or orange and daisylike, and are much
visited by bees and butterflies. Some are good for cutting.
The foliage is unremarkable; the basal leaves are large,
sometimes toothed or hairy, and the stem leaves are
progressively smaller as they ascend.

Inula acaulis
(Asteraceae/Compositae)

Common name: Stemless
inula
Height: 4in (10cm)
Spread: 1ft (30cm)
Aspect: Sun
Soil: Moist, well-drained,
Hardiness: Zone 6
Propagation: Seed or division,
both in spring or autumn

Choice, compact, rhizomatous species from
Asia. Leaves inversely lance-shaped, midgreen. Flowers solitary, single, ray florets
yellow, disc florets brown, in summer.

Inula ensifolia
(Asteraceae/Compositae)

Common name: Swordleaf
inula
Height: 2ft (60cm)
Spread: 1ft (30cm)
Aspect: Sun or half shade
Soil: Moist, well-drained,
fertile
Hardiness: Zone 5
Propagation: Seed or division,
both in spring or autumn

Rhizomatous, free-flowering species.
Leaves stemless, linear, midgreen. Flowers
in corymbs or solitary, single, daisylike,
golden-yellow, in mid- to late summer.

Inula helenium
(Asteraceae/Compositae)

Common name: Elecampane
Height: 5ft (1.5m)
Spread: 3ft (90cm)
Aspect: Sun
Soil: Moist, well-drained,
fertile
Hardiness: Zone 5
Propagation: Seed or division,
both in spring or autumn

A medicinal rhizomatous plant. Leaves in
basal rosette, ovate, toothed, midgreen.
Flowers in corymbs or solitary, single,
daisylike, yellow, in mid- and late summer.

Inula hookeri
(Asteraceae/Compositae)

Common names: None
Height: 32in (80cm)
Spread: Indefinite
Aspect: Half shade
Soil: Moist, well-drained,
fertile
Hardiness: Zone 6
Propagation: Seed or division,
both in spring or autumn

Invasive species. Leaves ovate, toothed,
hairy, green. Flowers solitary or in heads of
2 or 3, single, ray florets thin, pale yellow,
in late summer to midautumn.

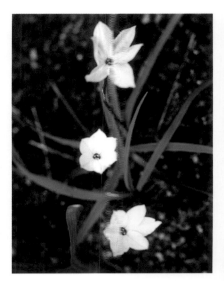

Inula magnifica
(Asteraceae/Compositae)

Common names: None
Height: 6ft (1.8m)
Spread: 3ft (90cm)
Aspect: Sun
Soil: Moist, well-drained, fertile
Hardiness: Zone 6
Propagation: Seed or division, both in spring or autumn

Species from the Caucasus. Leaves very large, elliptic-ovate, dark green. Single, daisylike flowers in corymbs of up to 20, golden-yellow, in late summer.

Inula orientalis
(Asteraceae/Compositae)

Common name: Caucasian inula
Height: 3ft (1m)
Spread: 2ft (60cm)
Aspect: Sun
Soil: Moist, well-drained, fertile
Hardiness: Zone 6
Propagation: Seed or division, both in spring or autumn

Rhizomatous species. Leaves ovate-elliptic, toothed, hairy, midgreen. Solitary, yellow daisylike flowers, with reflexed and incurved ray florets, in summer.

Inula royleana
(Asteraceae/Compositae)

Common name: Himalayan elecampene
Height: 32in (80cm)
Spread: 18in (45cm)
Aspect: Sun
Soil: Moist, well-drained, fertile
Hardiness: Zone 6
Propagation: Seed or division, both in spring or autumn

A hardy species from the Himalayas. Leaves ovate, hairy, toothed, veined, green. Flowers solitary, single, yellow, daisylike, from midsummer to autumn.

Ipheion
'Alberto Castillo'
(Alliaceae/Liliaceae)

Common names: None
Height: 8in (20cm)
Spread: 2in (5cm)
Aspect: Sun
Soil: Moist, well-drained, humus-rich
Hardiness: Zone 6
Propagation: Offsets, in summer

Selected form of a bulbous Argentinian plant. Leaves straplike, narrow, blue-green. Flowers upward-facing, larger than the type, solitary, scented, white, in spring.

Ipheion uniflorum
(Alliaceae/Liliaceae)

Common names: None
Height: 8in (20cm)
Spread: 2in (5cm)
Aspect: Sun
Soil: Moist, well-drained, humus-rich
Hardiness: Zone 6
Propagation: Offsets, in summer

A hardy bulbous perennial from Argentina. Leaves narrow, straplike, blue-green. Flowers solitary, upward-facing, perfumed, pale silvery blue stars, in spring.

Ipheion uniflorum
'Froyle Mill' A.G.M.
(Alliaceae/Liliaceae)

Common names: None
Height: 12in (30cm)
Spread: 2in (5cm)
Aspect: Sun
Soil: Moist, well-drained, humus-rich
Hardiness: Zone 6
Propagation: Offsets, in summer

Selected form of a bulbous hardy perennial from Argentina. Leaves narrow, straplike, blue-green. Flowers solitary, perfumed, dusky violet stars, in spring.

IRIS (Iridaceae)
Flag • Fleur de Lis • Sword lily

A genus of some 300 species from very diverse and scattered habitats in the northern hemisphere. They can be bulbous, rhizomatous, or fleshy-rooted, evergreen or deciduous, and vary widely in their cultural requirements. The classification by the American Iris Society (*see right*) will be used here. An iris flower has three outer and three inner tepals. The outer three bend back, and may also hang down, and so are called "falls"; they are usually the most colorfully marked part of the flower. The falls are especially large and colorful in the bearded irises, which have white or colored hairs, like a beard, in the center of each fall. Crested irises have a ridge, or crest, on each fall. The three inner tepals are called "standards," since they generally stand upright in the center of the flower, but they may lie horizontal, as in *I. tectorum*; droop, as in *I. bucharica*; or be much reduced, as in *I. danfordiae*. Three modified styles called stigma flaps reach out over the falls from the middle of the flower and can form an important element. All parts of the plant are poisonous, and contact with the sap may cause skin irritation. Iris are low-allergen plants, however. The flowers and foliage are much used by flower-arrangers.

Iris
'Brighteyes'
(Iridaceae)

Classification: Bearded iris
Height: 16in (40cm)
Spread: Indefinite
Aspect: Sun
Soil: Well-drained, fertile, acidic
Hardiness: Zone 6
Propagation: Division, in summer to autumn

An intermediate, rhizomatous iris. Leaves narrow, green. Pale yellow flowers with distinctive brown markings on the falls, hence its name.

Iris bucharica
A.G.M.
(Iridaceae)

Classification: Bulbous iris
Height: 16in (40cm)
Spread: 4in (10cm)
Aspect: Sun
Soil: Well-drained, neutral to alkaline
Hardiness: Zone 5
Propagation: Seed, in autumn or spring; division, in summer or autumn

A Juno iris from Central Asia. Leaves glossy, green. Flowers have standards below falls; standards yellow, falls white with a yellow spot.

Iris chrysographes
(Iridaceae)

Classification: Beardless iris
Height: 20in (50cm)
Spread: Indefinite
Aspect: Sun or half shade
Soil: Well-drained, acidic
Hardiness: Zone 5
Propagation: Seed, in autumn or spring; division, in summer or autumn

A rhizomatous Siberian iris from China. Leaves linear, grey-green. Flowers perfumed, dark violet-red, with silver stripes on the falls.

Iris cristata
(Iridaceae)

Classification: Crested iris
Height: 4in (10cm)
Spread: Indefinite
Aspect: Sun or half shade
Soil: Moist, humus-rich
Hardiness: Zone 4
Propagation: Seed, in autumn or spring; division, in summer or autumn

A crested iris species from eastern United States. Leaves lance-shaped, green. Flowers lilac-blue, with an orange patch on each fall, in late spring.

CLASSIFICATION of IRIS by the R.H.S.

Bearded species and cultivars, in various sizes from miniature dwarf to tall, form the most widely cultivated group of irises. They are rhizomatous, and prefer well-drained conditions.

Aril irises are a group of bearded irises that includes the Oncocyclus, Regelia, Regeliocyclus, and Arilbred types. These become dormant in summer after flowering, and should be kept dry while dormant.

Beardless irises generally have more flowers per stem than bearded types. They include Pacific Coast Native, Siberian, Spuria, Laevigatae, Louisiana and Unguiculares, and are rhizomatous. They prefer well-drained conditions, apart from the Laevigatae, which need damp soil.

Crested irises are rhizomatous and spread freely. They prefer moist soil.

Bulbous irises, grouped as Juno, Reticulata, or Xiphium, are beardless and summer dormant. They prefer well-drained soil.

Iris danfordiae
(Iridaceae)

Classification: Bulbous iris
Height: 6in (15cm)
Spread: 2in (5cm)
Aspect: Sun
Soil: Well-drained, alkaline
Hardiness: Zone 5
Propagation: Seed, in autumn or spring; division, in summer or autumn

A Reticulata species from Turkey. Leaves paired, narrow, green. Flowers have much-reduced standards. Falls bright yellow, speckled green.

Iris douglasiana
A.G.M.
(Iridaceae)

Classification: Beardless iris
Height: 28in (70cm)
Spread: Indefinite
Aspect: Sun or half shade
Soil: Well-drained, acidic
Hardiness: Zone 7
Propagation: Seed, in autumn or spring; division, in summer or autumn

An evergreen Pacific Coast iris. Leaves stiff, glossy, green. Flowers lavender-blue, white, or cream on branched stems, in late spring and early summer.

Iris ensata
A.G.M. (Iridaceae)

Classification: Beardless iris
Height: 3ft (90cm)
Spread: Indefinite
Aspect: Sun
Soil: Moist to wet, deep, acidic, humus-rich
Hardiness: Zone 5
Propagation: Seed, in autumn or spring; division, in summer or autumn

A Laevigatae beardless iris. Leaves long straps, green. Flowers lilac, purple, or red on branching stems, in midsummer. Marginal aquatic.

A beautiful display of Iris ensata *at Koichikawa Garden, in Tokyo.*

Iris ensata
'Freckled Geisha'
(Iridaceae)

Classification: Beardless iris
Height: 3ft (90cm)
Spread: Indefinite
Aspect: Sun
Soil: Moist to wet, deep,
acidic, humus-rich
Hardiness: Zone 5
Propagation: Division, in
summer or autumn

A hybrid, rhizomatous Laevigatae iris with
very large flowers of lilac and white, with
yellow bases on the falls. Marginal
aquatic plant.

Iris ensata
'Galatea Marx'
(Iridaceae)

Classification: Beardless iris
Height: 3ft (90cm)
Spread: Indefinite
Aspect: Sun
Soil: Moist to wet, deep,
acidic, humus-rich
Hardiness: Zone 5
Propagation: Division, in
summer or autumn

A hybrid Laevigatae iris cultivar. Single,
sometimes branched stems bear flowers
with pale blue falls and purple standards.
Marginal aquatic.

Iris ensata
'Moonlight Waves'
(Iridaceae)

Classification: Beardless iris
Height: 3ft (90cm)
Spread: Indefinite
Aspect: Sun
Soil: Moist to wet, deep,
acidic, humus-rich
Hardiness: Zone 5
Propagation: Division, in
summer or autumn

A hybrid Laevigatae iris cultivar, each
stem bearing 3 or 4 large flowers of a rich,
deep, purple-blue in midsummer.
Marginal aquatic

Iris graminea
A.G.M. (Iridaceae)

Classification: Beardless iris
Common name: Plum tart iris
Height: 16in (40cm)
Spread: Indefinite
Aspect: Sun or half shade
Soil: Well-drained, acidic
Hardiness: Zone 5
Propagation: Seed, in autumn
or spring; division, in summer
or autumn

A Spuria iris from Spain and across Europe
to Russia. Leaves linear, flat, bright green.
Flowers perfumed, of purple or violet
color, falls have white tips, veined violet.

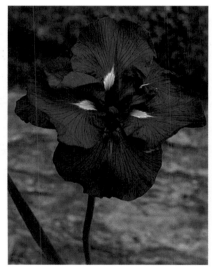

Iris
'Holden Clough' A.G.M.
(Iridaceae)

Classification: Beardless iris
Height: 3ft (90cm)
Spread: Indefinite
Aspect: Sun or half shade
Soil: Moist, deep, acidic,
humus-rich
Hardiness: Zone 6
Propagation: Division, in
summer or autumn

A hybrid Laevigatae iris. Leaves angled
outward, so plant takes up a lot of room;
evergreen in warm areas. Flowers pale
brown, veined purple. Marginal aquatic.

Iris innominata
(Iridaceae)

Classification: Beardless iris
Height: 8in (20cm)
Spread: Indefinite
Aspect: Sun or half shade
Soil: Well-drained, acidic
Hardiness: Zone 7
Propagation: Seed, in autumn
or spring; division, in summer
or autumn

An evergreen Pacific Coast iris, from the
southwestern U.S.A. Leaves narrow, green.
Flowers pale lavender-blue, purple, yellow,
or cream, in early summer.

Iris japonica
A.G.M. (Iridaceae)

Classification: Crested iris
Height: 18in (45cm)
Spread: Indefinite
Aspect: Sun or half shade
Soil: Moist, humus-rich
Hardiness: Zone 7
Propagation: Seed, in autumn
or spring; division, in summer
or autumn

Leaves glossy, straplike. Flowers white or
lavender, frilly; falls have orange crests and
purple patches. Long-flowering. Rhizomes
lie on soil surface and spread slowly.

Iris laevigata
A.G.M.
(Iridaceae)

Classification: Beardless iris
Height: 2ft (60cm)
Spread: Indefinite
Aspect: Sun or half shade
Soil: Moist to wet, deep,
acidic, humus-rich
Hardiness: Zone 4
Propagation: Seed, in autumn
or spring; division, in summer
or autumn

A Laevigatae iris from Russia and the Far
East. Leaves broad, green straps. Flowers
purple-blue, with a yellow patch on the
falls. Marginal aquatic.

Iris latifolia
A.G.M.
(Iridaceae)

Classification: Bulbous iris
Height: 2ft (60cm)
Spread: 8in (20cm)
Aspect: Sun
Soil: Well-drained, alkaline
Hardiness: Zone 5
Propagation: Seed, in autumn
or spring; division, in summer
or autumn

A Xiphium iris from Spain. Leaves narrow,
green, lance-shaped. Flowers white, blue,
or violet, with a yellow spot on the falls, in
early summer.

Iris missouriensis
(Iridaceae)

Classification: Beardless iris
Height: 20in (50cm)
Spread: Indefinite
Aspect: Sun or half shade
Soil: Well-drained, acidic
Hardiness: Zone 9
Propagation: Seed, in autumn
or spring

Tender iris from western and central North
America. Leaves narrow, taller than flowers,
which have short, blue standards and
larger blue falls, veined purple, in summer.

Iris pallida
'Argentea Variegata'
(Iridaceae)

Classification: Bearded iris
Height: 3ft (90cm)
Spread: Indefinite
Aspect: Sun
Soil: Well-drained, fertile,
acidic
Hardiness: Zone 6
Propagation: Division, in
summer or autumn

From Croatia. Leaves short, bright green,
silver-striped, straplike, evergreen. Tall
spikes of scented flowers, blue with yellow
beards, in late spring and early summer.

Iris pseudacorus
(Iridaceae)

Classification: Beardless iris
Height: 4ft (1.2m)
Spread: Indefinite
Aspect: Sun
Soil: Moist to wet, deep,
acidic, humus-rich
Hardiness: Zone 6
Propagation: Seed, in autumn
or spring; division, in summer
or autumn

A robust Laevigatae iris from Europe, Asia,
and North Africa. Leaves ribbed, straplike,
gray-green. Flowers yellow, with brown
markings on standards. Marginal aquatic.

Iris pumila
(Iridaceae)

Classification: Miniature
dwarf bearded iris
Height: 4in (15cm)
Spread: Indefinite
Aspect: Sun
Soil: Well-drained, fertile,
acidic
Hardiness: Zone 4
Propagation: Seed, in autumn
or spring; division, in summer or autumn

A miniature dwarf bearded iris from
Europe and the Urals. Leaves straplike,
green. Flowers solitary, perfumed, purple,
blue or yellow, in spring.

Iris reticulata
A.G.M.
(Iridaceae)

Classification: Bulbous iris
Height: 6in (15cm)
Spread: 2in (5cm)
Aspect: Sun
Soil: Moist, well-drained,
alkaline
Hardiness: Zone 5
Propagation: Seed, in autumn
or spring; division, in summer
or autumn

Reticulata from Turkey and the Caucasus.
Leaves linear. Flowers solitary, scented, deep
purple with yellow ridge on falls. Bulb may
split into tiny, slow-to-flower bulbils.

Iris sibirica
A.G.M.
(Iridaceae)

Classification: Beardless iris
Height: 3ft (1m)
Spread: Indefinite
Aspect: Sun or half shade
Soil: Acid, moist
Hardiness: Zone 4
Propagation: Seed in autumn
or spring; division in summer
or autumn

From East Europe, Turkey, and Russia.
Leaves grasslike, green. Flowers violet-
blue, falls white next to the hafts, and
darkly veined.

Iris sibirica
'Limeheart'
(Iridaceae)

Classification: Beardless iris
Height: 4ft (1.2m)
Spread: Indefinite
Aspect: Sun or half shade
Soil: Moist, acid
Hardiness: Zone 4
Propagation: Division, in
summer or autumn

A hybrid Siberian iris, one of a large
number of cultivars from this species.
Leaves are grasslike, flowers are white
with greenish hafts.

Iris sibirica
'Wisley White' A.G.M.
(Iridaceae)

Classification: Beardless iris
Height: 4ft (1.2m)
Spread: Indefinite
Aspect: Sun or half shade
Soil: Moist, acidic
Hardiness: Zone 4
Propagation: Division, in
summer or autumn

A handsome and hardy hybrid cultivar of
the Siberian iris. Leaves narrow, grasslike.
Flowers white, with yellow markings on
the falls.

Iris spuria
'Destination'
(Iridaceae)

Classification: Beardless iris
Height: 3ft (1m)
Spread: Indefinite
Aspect: Sun or half shade
Soil: Well-drained, acidic
Hardiness: Zone 5
Propagation: Division, in
summer or autumn

A rhizomatous, hybrid Spuria iris cultivar.
The species originates in Eurasia. Leaves
broad, tough, green. Flowers clear
golden-yellow.

Iris
'Tinkerbell'
(Iridaceae)

Classification: Bearded iris
Height: 8in (20cm)
Spread: Indefinite
Aspect: Sun
Soil: Well-drained, fertile,
acidic
Hardiness: Zone 6
Propagation: Division, in
autumn or spring

A rhizomatous, standard dwarf bearded
hybrid iris cultivar. Leaves lance-shaped,
green. Flowers pale blue, with a darker
blue center.

Iris tenax
(Iridaceae)

Classification: Beardless iris
Height: 14in (35cm)
Spread: Indefinite
Aspect: Sun or half shade
Soil: Well-drained, acidic
Hardiness: Zone 7
Propagation: Seed, in autumn
or spring; division, in summer
or autumn

A Pacific Coast iris from the northwestern
U.S.A. Leaves narrow, dark green. Flowers
blue, white, cream, or yellow, from midspring to early summer.

Iris
'Three Cherries'
(Iridaceae)

Classification: Bearded iris
Height: 8in (20cm)
Spread: Indefinite
Aspect: Sun
Soil: Acid, well-drained
Hardiness: Zone 6
Propagation: Division, in
summer or autumn

A rhizomatous, hybrid, miniature dwarf
bearded iris with yellow flowers. The falls
have bands of brown and cream toward
the tip.

Iris tridentata
(Iridaceae)

Classification: Beardless iris
Height: 28in (70cm)
Spread: Indefinite
Aspect: Half shade
Soil: Moist, acidic
Hardiness: Zone 5
Propagation: Seed, in autumn
or spring; division, in summer
or autumn

A rhizomatous species from the eastern
U.S.A. Leaves linear, dull green. Flowers
purple-blue, with white basal spots, in
early summer. Tricky to cultivate

Iris uromovii
(Iridaceae)

Classification: Beardless iris
Height: 1ft (30cm)
Spread: Indefinite
Aspect: Sun or half shade
Soil: Well-drained, acidic
Hardiness: Zone 6
Propagation: Seed, in autumn
or spring; division, in summer
or autumn

A rhizomatous Spuria iris originating in
Bulgaria. Leaves linear, sharp, green.
Flowers strong violet-blue, with white falls
veined violet-blue.

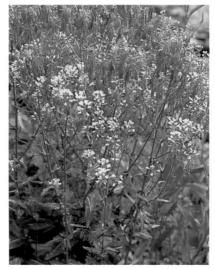

Isatis tinctoria
(Brassicaceae/Cruciferae)

Common name: Woad
Height: 4ft (1.2m)
Spread: 18in (45cm)
Aspect: Sun
Soil: Moist, well-drained
Hardiness: Zone 7
Propagation: Seed or division,
both in spring

Short-lived, taprooted plant from Europe.
Leaves in basal rosettes, oblong to lance-
shaped, gray-green. Flowers on branched
stems, in panicles, yellow, in early summer.

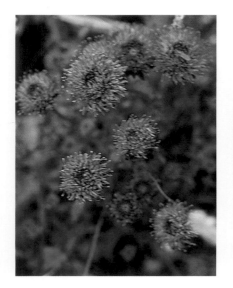

Jasione laevis
(Campanulaceae)

Common names: None
Height: 12in (30cm)
Spread: 8in (20cm)
Aspect: Sun
Soil: Well-drained, sandy
Hardiness: Zone 5
Propagation: Seed, when ripe;
division, in spring or autumn

A perennial from Europe, including
Britain. Leaves in basal rosettes, narrow,
oblong, green. Solitary, spherical heads of
blue flowers, in summer.

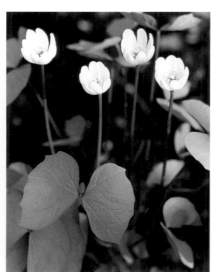

Jeffersonia diphylla
(Berberidaceae)

Common name: American
twinleaf
Height: 8in (20cm)
Spread: 6in (15cm)
Aspect: Full or half shade
Soil: Moist, humus-rich
Hardiness: Zone 5
Propagation: Seed, when ripe;
division, in spring

Choice woodlander from the U.S.A. Leaves
kidney-shaped, cleft, gray-green, with
glaucous undersides. Flowers cup-shaped,
starry, white in late spring.

Juncus effusus
'Spiralis'
(Juncaceae)

Common names: Corkscrew
rush, spiral rush
Height: 1ft (30cm)
Spread: Indefinite
Aspect: Sun or half shade
Soil: Moist, acidic
Hardiness: Zone 4
Propagation: Seed or division,
both in spring

Invasive, leafless, marginal aquatic. Stems
shiny, spiraled, dark green, forming a
tangle. Flowers small, brown, on short
stalks in cymes, all summer.

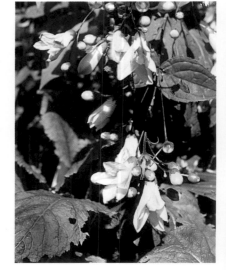

Kirengeshoma palmata
A.G.M. (Hydrangeaceae)

Common names: None
Height: 4ft (1.2m)
Spread: 6ft (2m)
Aspect: Half shade
Soil: Moist, acidic,
humus-rich
Hardiness: Zone 5
Propagation: Seed or division,
both in spring

Distinctive rhizomatous woodlander. Leaves
very large, broad, ovate, pale gray-green.
Terminal cymes of 3 nodding flowers, broad
yellow tubes, late summer to early autumn.

Knautia arvensis
(Dipsacaceae)

Common names: None
Height: 5ft (1.5m)
Spread: 18in (45cm)
Aspect: Sun
Soil: Well-drained, fertile
Hardiness: Zone 6
Propagation: Seed or basal
cuttings, both in spring

Taprooted perennial from Eurasia. Leaves
pinnatifid or simple, dull green. Flowers
flat, lilac-blue, with involucral bracts, from
midsummer to autumn.

Knautia macedonica
(Dipsacaceae)

Common names: None
Height: 32in (80cm)
Spread: 18in (45cm)
Aspect: Sun
Soil: Well-drained, fertile
Hardiness: Zone 6
Propagation: Seed or basal
cuttings, both in spring

Clump-forming perennial from Macedonia.
Leaves basal and stem, pinnatifid, midgreen. Flowers purple-red, with involucral
bracts, in mid- and late summer.

KNIPHOFIA (Asphodelaceae/Liliaceae)
Red hot poker

This genus contains some 70 or so species of rhizomatous
perennials from central and southern Africa. Their native
habitats are usually moist places, often along the banks of
rivers or in grasslands on mountainsides. They will thrive in
any soil as long as it is moisture-retentive, and they prefer sun
but will take light shade; they vary from tender to fully
hardy. Many will tolerate coastal conditions. Red hot pokers
are mostly clump-forming, with arching, linear to strap-
shaped leaves, and may be evergreen or deciduous; leaves of
the deciduous types tend to be narrow, those of the
evergreens both longer and broader. The flowers are
cylindrical or tubular and usually pendent, but upright in
some types. They are borne well above the leaves in spikelike
racemes, usually dense. There are various colors, including
green and toffee, but the most commonly seen are those that
open red and then turn yellow, giving a characteristic,
bicolored inflorescence. Red hot pokers make good cut
flowers, and are popular with flower-arrangers. Bees and
butterflies are attracted to them, and they are low-allergen
plants. Cultivars ranging in height from 20in (50cm) to 6ft
(2m) are available; the taller varieties may require staking.

Kniphofia
'Atlanta'
(Asphodelaceae/Liliaceae)

Common name: Red hot
poker
Height: 4ft (1.2m)
Spread: 32in (80cm)
Aspect: Sun or half shade
Soil: Moist, well-drained,
humus-rich
Hardiness: Zone 5
Propagation: Division, in
spring

Rhizomatous, evergreen hybrid. Leaves
strap-shaped, gray-green. Flowers orange-
red, in racemes, fading to yellow from base
of spike, in late spring to early summer.

Kniphofia
'Bees Sunset' A.G.M.
(Asphodelaceae/Liliaceae)

Common name: Red hot
poker
Height: 3ft (90cm)
Spread: 2ft (60cm)
Aspect: Sun or half shade
Soil: Moist, well-drained,
humus-rich
Hardiness: Zone 5
Propagation: Division, in
spring

A hardy, deciduous red hot poker. Leaves
linear, toothed, midgreen. Flowers in
racemes, yellow-orange, borne from early
to late summer.

Kniphofia caulescens
A.G.M.
(Asphodelaceae/Liliaceae)

Common name: Red hot
poker
Height: 4ft (1.2m)
Spread: 2ft (60cm)
Aspect: Sun or half shade
Soil: Moist, well-drained,
humus-rich
Hardiness: Zone 7
Propagation: Seed or division,
both in spring

Evergreen hardy species. Leaves linear,
arched, glaucous, toothed, keeled. Flowers
in short racemes, coral-red fading to
cream, from late summer to midautumn.

Kniphofia
'Fiery Fred'
(Asphodelaceae/Liliaceae)

Common name: Red hot
poker
Height: 4ft (1.2m)
Spread: 2ft (60cm)
Aspect: Sun or half shade
Soil: Moist, well-drained,
humus-rich, fertile
Hardiness: Zone 6
Propagation: Division, in
spring

A hardy herbaceous perennial. Leaves
linear, midgreen. Flowers in racemes,
orange-red fading to light brown, from
early to late summer.

Kniphofia
'Green Jade'
(Asphodelaceae/Liliaceae)

Common name: Red hot
poker
Height: 5ft (1.5m)
Spread: 30in (75cm)
Aspect: Sun or half shade
Soil: Moist, well-drained,
humus-rich, fertile
Hardiness: Zone 5
Propagation: Division, in
spring

A hardy, evergreen perennial. Leaves linear,
keeled, green. Flowers green fading to
cream, in dense racemes in late summer
and early autumn.

Kniphofia
'Shining Sceptre'
(Asphodelaceae/Liliaceae)

Common name: Red hot
poker
Height: 4ft (1.2m)
Spread: 2ft (60cm)
Aspect: Sun or half shade
Soil: Moist, well-drained,
humus-rich, fertile
Hardiness: Zone 5
Propagation: Division, in
spring

A hardy, deciduous perennial. Leaves
linear, midgreen. Flowers in racemes,
opening clear yellow and fading to ivory,
in summer.

Kniphofia 'Sunningdale
Yellow' A.G.M.
(Asphodelaceae/Liliaceae)

Common name: Red hot
poker
Height: 4ft (1.2m)
Spread: 2ft (60cm)
Aspect: Sun or half shade
Soil: Moist, well-drained,
humus-rich, fertile
Hardiness: Zone 5
Propagation: Division, in
spring

A hardy, deciduous perennial cultivar.
Leaves linear, midgreen. Long-lasting
flowers in racemes, clear yellow, in mid-
and late summer.

Kniphofia thompsonii
var. *snowdenii*
(Asphodelaceae/Liliaceae)

Common name: Red hot
poker
Height: 36in (90cm)
Spread: 18in (45cm)
Aspect: Sun or half shade
Soil: Moist, well-drained,
humus-rich, fertile
Hardiness: Zone 8
Propagation: Seed or division,
both in spring

Rhizomatous species from Kenya and
Uganda. Leaves linear, upright, midgreen.
Flowers in very open few-flowered racemes,
coral-pink, midsummer to late autumn.

Single-colored Kniphofia, *such as 'Queen Victoria', make an elegant alternative to the bolder red and yellow types.*

**Kniphofia triangularis
A.G.M.**
(Asphodelaceae/Liliaceae)

Common name: Red hot
poker
Height: 36in (90cm)
Spread: 18in (45cm)
Aspect: Sun or half shade
Soil: Moist, well-drained,
humus-rich, fertile
Hardiness: Zone 6
Propagation: Seed or division,
both in spring

A hardy species, known also as *K. galpinii*.
Leaves grassy, arching, linear, green.
Flowers in dense racemes, reddish-orange,
in early and midsummer.

Lamium galeobdolon
(Labiatae/Lamiaceae)

Common names: Golden
dead nettle; jellow archangel
Height: 2ft (60cm)
Spread: Indefinite
Aspect: Half or full shade
Soil: Moist, well-drained
Hardiness: Zone 6
Propagation: Division, in
spring or autumn

Highly invasive rhizomatous plant. Leaves
ovate to heart-shaped, toothed, midgreen,
may be silver-marked. Flowers 2-lipped,
yellow, spotted brown, in spikes in summer.

**Lamium galeobdolon
'Hermann's Pride'**
(Labiatae/Lamiaceae)

Common name: Golden dead
nettle
Height: 18in (45cm)
Spread: Indefinite
Aspect: Full or half shade
Soil: Moist, well-drained
Hardiness: Zone 6
Propagation: Division, in
spring or autumn

More compact and marginally less invasive
form of the species. Grown primarily for
its small, ovate leaves, heavily streaked
silver. Good ground cover in shade.

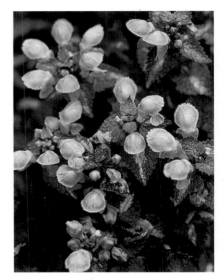

Lamium maculatum
(Labiatae/Lamiaceae)

Common name: Spotted dead
nettle
Height: 8in (20cm)
Spread: 4ft (1.2m)
Aspect: Half or full shade
Soil: Moist, well-drained
Hardiness: Zone 4
Propagation: Division, in
spring or autumn

Rhizomatous, creeping plant. Leaves ovate,
toothed, matt-green, often marked silver.
Flowers in spikes, pink, purple, or white,
in early summer. Good ground cover.

**Lamium maculatum
f. *album***
(Labiatae/Lamiaceae)

Common name: Dead nettle
Height: 8in (20cm)
Spread: 4ft (1.2m)
Aspect: Full or half shade
Soil: Moist, well-drained
Hardiness: Zone 4
Propagation: Division, in
spring or autumn

White form of the species. Ovate, toothed
leaves silver-gray, flowers pure white; a
pleasing combination. A good ground
cover plant for shady areas.

**Lamium maculatum
'Aureum'**
(Labiatae/Lamiaceae)

Common name: Dead nettle
Height: 8in (20cm)
Spread: 36in (90cm)
Aspect: Full or half shade
Soil: Moist, well-drained
Hardiness: Zone 4
Propagation: Division, in
spring or autumn

A cultivar of the species with pink flowers
that contrast with the yellow of the
toothed, ovate leaves. Makes a colorful
ground cover.

**Lamium maculatum
'Ickwell Beauty'**
(Labiatae/Lamiaceae)

Common name: Dead nettle
Height: 8in (20cm)
Spread: 36in (90cm)
Aspect: Full or half shade
Soil: Moist, well-drained
Hardiness: Zone 4
Propagation: Division, in
spring or autumn

A form with toothed, ovate leaves that all
have some variegation, but in differing
degrees and in different colors. Unique
ground cover.

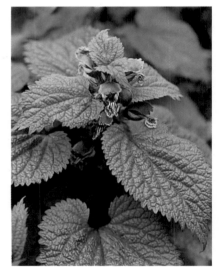

Lamium orvala
(Labiatae/Lamiaceae)

Common name: Dead nettle
Height: 2ft (60cm)
Spread: 1ft (30cm)
Aspect: Full or half shade
Soil: Moist, well-drained
Hardiness: Zone 6
Propagation: Seed or division,
spring or autumn.

A hardy perennial from Europe. Leaves
large, broad, ovate, toothed, hairy, green.
Flowers in spikes, purplish-pink, from late
spring to summer. Non-invasive.

Lathyrus vernus
A.G.M.
(Leguminosae/Papilionaceae)

Common name: Spring
vetchling
Height: 18in (45cm)
Spread: 18in (45cm)
Aspect: Sun or half shade
Soil: Well-drained, humus-
rich, fertile
Hardiness: Zone 4
Propagation: Seed (after
soaking) in spring

A hardy herbaceous plant. Leaves paired,
ovate, pointed, midgreen. Flowers pea-like,
in one-sided racemes, blue-purple, in
spring, followed by purple seed pods.

Lavandula stoechas
A.G.M
(Labiatae/Lamiaceae)

Common name: Lavender
Height: 2ft (60cm)
Spread: 2ft (60cm)
Aspect: Sun
Soil: Well-drained, fertile
Hardiness: Zone 8
Propagation: Seed, in spring;
semiripe cuttings, in summer

Evergreen Mediterranean subshrub. Leaves
linear, aromatic, gray-green. Flowers purple,
perfumed, in dense spikes topped by
purple bracts, from late spring to summer.

Lavatera
'Barnsley' A.G.M.
(Malvaceae)

Common name: Herb tree-
mallow
Height: 6ft (2m)
Spread: 4ft (1.2m)
Aspect: Sun
Soil: Well-drained, fertile
Hardiness: Zone 7
Propagation: Softwood
cuttings, in early summer

Robust, architectural, hybrid subshrub.
Leaves palmate, gray-green. Flowers open
funnels, white with a red eye, in racemes
all summer long.

Lavatera
'Bredon Springs'
(Malvaceae)

Common name: Herb tree-
mallow
Height: 6ft (2m)
Spread: 4ft (1.2m)
Aspect: Sun
Soil: Well-drained, fertile
Hardiness: Zone 8
Propagation: Softwood
cuttings, in early summer

Architectural, hybrid subshrub. Leaves
palmate, 3- to 5-lobed, gray-green. Flowers
in racemes, open funnels, dusky pink
flushed mauve, all summer.

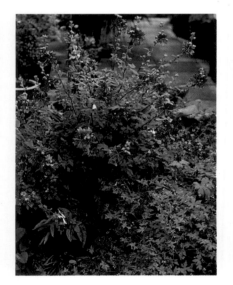

Lavatera
'Burgundy Wine'
(Malvaceae)

Common name: Herb tree-
mallow
Height: 4ft (1.2m)
Spread: 3ft (90cm)
Aspect: Sun
Soil: Well-drained, fertile
Hardiness: Zone 7
Propagation: Softwood
cuttings, in summer

Robust, hybrid subshrub. Leaves palmate,
3- to 5-lobed, gray-green. Flowers deep
pink, darker-veined, in racemes all summer.
The best mallow for the small garden.

Lavatera
'Candy Floss'
(Malvaceae)

Common name: Herb tree-
mallow
Height: 6ft (2m)
Spread: 4ft (1.2m)
Aspect: Sun
Soil: Well-drained, fertile
Hardiness: Zone 8
Propagation: Softwood
cuttings, in summer

Robust, architectural, hybrid subshrub.
Leaves palmate, 3- to 5-lobed, gray-green.
Flowers in racemes, open, pale pink
funnels, all summer.

Leontopodium alpinum
(Asteraceae/Compositae)

Common name: Edelweiss
Height: 6in (15cm)
Spread: 6in (15cm)
Aspect: Sun
Soil: Sharply drained, alkaline
Hardiness: Zone 4
Propagation: Seed, in spring

Clump-forming alpine for a scree bed.
Leaves linear to lance-shaped, basal, gray-
green. Flowers white, surrounded by gray-
white, woolly bracts, in spring.

Leonotis dysophylla
(Labiatae/Lamiaceae)

Common names: None
Height: 10ft (3m)
Spread: 3ft (1m)
Aspect: Sun
Soil: Well-drained, fertile
Hardiness: Zone 9
Propagation: Seed, in warmth
in spring

A tall, tender, architectural perennial from
South Africa. Leaves inversely lance-
shaped, midgreen. Flowers in whorls,
tubular, brilliant orange, in autumn.

The intense color of a drift of lavender is echoed by Eryngium in the foreground at Hestercombe, in Somerset, England

Leonotis leonurus
(Labiatae/Lamiaceae)

Common name: Lion's-ear
Height: 8ft (2.5m)
Spread: 3ft (1m)
Aspect: Sun
Soil: Well-drained, fertile
Hardiness: Zone 9
Propagation: Seed, in warmth
in spring

Leptinella dendyi
(Asteraceae/Compositae)

Common names: None
Height: 16in (40cm)
Spread: 4in (10cm)
Aspect: Sun
Soil: Sharply drained, gritty
Hardiness: Zone 8
Propagation: Seed, when ripe;
division, in spring

Leucanthemopsis alpina
(Asteraceae/Compositae)

Common names: None
Height: 4in (10cm)
Spread: 6in (15cm)
Aspect: Sun
Soil: Sharply drained
Hardiness: Zone 6
Propagation: Seed, when ripe

Leucanthemum x *superbum*
'Aglaia' A.G.M.
(Asteraceae/Compositae)

Common name: Shasta daisy
Height: 2ft (60cm)
Spread: 2ft (60cm)
Aspect: Sun or half shade
Soil: Moist, well-drained,
fertile
Hardiness: Zone 5
Propagation: Division, in
spring or autumn

A tall, unusual, tender perennial from South Africa. Leaves are inversely lance-shaped, midgreen. Flowers in whorls, tubular, two-lipped, scarlet, in late autumn.

Compact, cushion-forming scree plant from New Zealand. Leaves 2-pinnatifid, leathery, aromatic, gray-green. Flowers solitary, semi-double, cream, from late spring to summer.

Mat-forming, rhizomatous plant. Silver-gray leaves, from ovate- to spoon-shaped to pinnatisect or pinnatifid. Flowers solitary, ray florets white, disc florets yellow.

One of the very best shasta daisies, with inversely lance-shaped, glossy, dark green leaves. Flowers semidouble, white, shaggy, all summer.

LEUCANTHEMUM (Asteraceae/Compositae)
Shasta daisy

A genus of about 26 annual and perennial species from a range of habitats in temperate Asia and Europe, and previously included under *Chrysanthemum*. The plants in the genus that are of prime importance for perennial beds are *Leucanthemum* x *superbum*, the shasta daisy, a hybrid strain of garden origin, still also known as *Chrysanthemum maximum*. This group provides us with an invaluable set of robust, soundly perennial, easy-going plants, which will grow in sun or half shade in any good soil; in heavy clay soils they have a reputation for giving up the fight. They are inclined to be lax plants, and some form of support is required. The foliage is handsome, but it will be attacked by slugs as the plants break ground in spring, and will not reappear unless the plants are protected. The flowers are solitary and may be single or double. Although other species in the genus have yellow flowers, the flowers of these hybrids had been exclusively white, with yellow discs (which tend to be paler in double-flowered types), until the cultivar 'Sonnenschein' made its appearance; it has yellow buds that open to cream flowers. The flowers are excellent for cutting, and are liked by flower-arrangers.

Leucanthemum x *superbum*
'Beauté Nivelloise'
(Asteraceae/Compositae)

Common name: Shasta daisy
Height: 34in (85cm)
Spread: 2ft (60cm)
Aspect: Sun or half shade
Soil: Moist, well-drained,
fertile
Hardiness: Zone 5
Propagation: Division, in
spring or autumn

Leucanthemum x *superbum*
'Droitwich Beauty'
(Asteraceae/Compositae)

Common name: Shasta daisy
Height: 3ft (90cm)
Spread: 2ft (60cm)
Aspect: Sun or half shade
Soil: Moist, well-drained,
fertile
Hardiness: Zone 5
Propagation: Division, in
spring or autumn

Leaves inversely lance-shaped, glossy, dark green. Flowers single, ray florets twisted and irregularly incurved or reflexed, white, disc florets yellow, all summer.

Leaves inversely lance-shaped, shiny, dark green. Flowers semidouble, shaggy, with white ray florets and pale yellow disc florets, all summer.

Leucanthemum × *superbum* 'Phyllis Smith' (Asteraceae/Compositae)

Common name: Shasta daisy
Height: 3ft (90cm)
Spread: 2ft (60cm)
Aspect: Sun or half shade
Soil: Moist, well-drained, fertile
Hardiness: Zone 5
Propagation: Division, in spring or autumn

Leaves inversely lance-shaped, glossy, dark green. Flowers single, ray florets white, twisted, reflexed, and incurved, disc florets yellow, all summer.

Leucanthemum × *superbum* 'Snowcap' (Asteraceae/Compositae)

Common name: Shasta daisy
Height: 18in (45cm)
Spread: 18in (45cm)
Aspect: Sun or half shade
Soil: Moist, well-drained, fertile
Hardiness: Zone 5
Propagation: Division, in spring or autumn

Leaves inversely lance-shaped, glossy, dark green. Flowers single, ray florets white, disc florets yellow, all summer. The best dwarf form may not need staking.

Leucanthemum × *superbum* 'Sonnenschein' (Asteraceae/Compositae)

Common name: Shasta daisy
Height: 3ft (90cm)
Spread: 2ft (60cm)
Aspect: Sun or half shade
Soil: Moist, well-drained, fertile
Hardiness: Zone 5
Propagation: Division, in spring or autumn

Very desirable shasta daisy. Leaves inversely lance-shaped, glossy, dark green. Flowers single, ray florets cream, disc florets yellow, all summer.

Leucanthemum × *superbum* 'White Iceberg' (Asteraceae/Compositae)

Common name: Shasta daisy
Height: 3ft (90cm)
Spread: 2ft (60cm)
Aspect: Sun or half shade
Soil: Moist, well-drained, fertile
Hardiness: Zone 5
Propagation: Division, in spring or autumn

Leaves inversely lance-shaped, glossy dark green. Flowers single, ray florets white, incurved and reflexed, disc florets yellow, all summer.

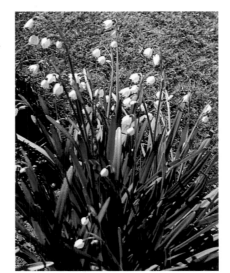

Leucanthemum × *superbum* 'Wirral Supreme' A.G.M. (Asteraceae/Compositae)

Common name: Shasta daisy
Height: 32in (80cm)
Spread: 24in (60cm)
Aspect: Sun or half shade
Soil: Moist, well-drained
Hardiness: Zone 5
Propagation: Division, in spring or autumn

Leaves inversely lance-shaped, glossy, dark green. Flowers double, ray florets white, long on the periphery, short in the center, disc florets yellow, all summer.

Leucojum aestivum (Amaryllidaceae)

Common name: Summer snowflake
Height: 24in (60cm)
Spread: 4in (10cm)
Aspect: Sun
Soil: Moist to wet, humus-rich
Hardiness: Zone 4
Propagation: Offsets, after foliage dies down

Bulbous plant from Eurasia and the Near East. Leaves strap-shaped, dark glossy green. Up to 8 flowers per leafless stem, white bells with green tips, chocolate-scented, in spring.

Leucojum vernum A.G.M. (Amaryllidaceae)

Common name: Spring snowflake
Height: 12in (30cm)
Spread: 3in (8cm)
Aspect: Sun
Soil: Moist to wet, humus-rich
Hardiness: Zone 5
Propagation: Offsets, after foliage dies down

Bulbous plant from Europe. Leaves strap-shaped, glossy-green. Flowers 1 or 2 on each stem, white bells with green tips, in early spring.

Levisticum officinale (Apiaceae/Umbelliferae)

Common name: Lovage
Height: 6ft (2m)
Spread: 3ft (1m)
Aspect: Sun
Soil: Moist, well-drained, fertile
Hardiness: Zone 4
Propagation: Seed, when ripe; division, in spring

Vigorous Mediterranean herb. Dark green leaves in rosettes, 2- or 3-pinnate, lobes ovate, toothed. Flowers starry, in umbels, yellow, in summer; good seed heads.

171

Lewisia
Cotyledon Hybrids
(Portulacaceae)

Common names: None
Height: 1ft (30cm)
Spread: 16in (40cm)
Aspect: Half shade
Soil: Sharply drained, acidic, humus-rich, fertile
Hardiness: Zone 6
Propagation: Seed, in autumn; division, in early summer

Hybrid evergreen. Leaves in rosettes, dark green, fleshy. Flowers in compact panicles, funnel-shaped, pink, orange, yellow, or magenta, spring to summer. Keep neck dry.

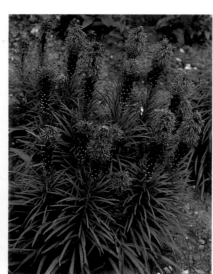

Liatris spicata
(Asteraceae/Compositae)

Common name: Spike
Height: 4ft (1.2m)
Spread: 18in (45cm)
Aspect: Sun
Soil: Moist, well-drained, fertile
Hardiness: Zone 3
Propagation: Seed in autumn; division in spring

Tuberous or cormous plant. Leaves basal, linear to lance-shaped, and stem, green. Flowers pink in dense spikes open from the top down, late summer and early autumn.

Liatris spicata 'Alba'
(Asteraceae/Compositae)

Common name: Spike
Height: 4ft (1.2m)
Spread: 18in (45cm)
Aspect: Sun
Soil: Moist, well-drained, fertile
Hardiness: Zone 3
Propagation: Seed, in autumn; division, in spring

White-flowered form of the species. Flowers in dense spikes, opening from the top downward, white, in late summer to early autumn. Attracts bees.

Libertia formosa
(Iridaceae)

Common name: Showy libertia
Height: 3ft (90cm)
Spread: 2ft (60cm)
Aspect: Sun
Soil: Moist, well-drained, humus-rich, fertile
Hardiness: Zone 8
Propagation: Seed, when ripe; division, in spring

Rhizomatous evergreen from Chile. Leaves linear, rigid, leathery, midgreen. Flowers in clustered panicles, white or cream from late spring to midsummer; good seed heads.

Libertia grandiflora
(Iridaceae)

Common names: None
Height: 3ft (90cm)
Spread: 2ft (60cm)
Aspect: Sun
Soil: Moist, well-drained, humus-rich, fertile
Hardiness: Zone 8
Propagation: Seed, when ripe; division, in spring

Rhizomatous evergreen from New Zealand. Leaves linear, leathery, dark green. Flowers in panicles, in clusters of up to 6, white, in late spring and early summer.

LIGULARIA (Asteraceae/Compositae)

A genus of some 150 species of perennials, mostly from Asia, with a few examples from Europe. Their natural habitats are moist areas, from the banks of mountain streams to damp grasslands and woodlands. As a consequence, they like a moisture-retaining or even a wet soil in the garden, and are not happy in dry climates unless the soil is kept reliably moist; their leaves droop obviously when they need to be watered. They prefer light shade, or at least shade from the midday sun, and are hardy. *Ligularia* are universally large and fairly coarse in appearance, and so are not for the very small garden; if you have the room for them, they will naturalize well in a moist wildflower garden, and make an impressive picture beside water. Despite being tall, they have stiff stems and do not need to be staked except in exposed areas. As with so many plants with daisylike flowers, they are highly allergenic, and should be avoided by the allergic gardener; aside from this consideration, some of them do make good cut flowers. All are visited by bees. Unfortunately, the plants are also liked by slugs, which eat the emergent shoots in spring; the leaves will never recover fully from this, so as ever with slug control, take preventative measures early in the season, before growth begins.

Ligularia dentata
(Asteraceae/Compositae)

Common name: Bigleaf golden-ray
Height: 5ft (1.5m)
Spread: 3ft (1m)
Aspect: Half shade
Soil: Moist, deep, fertile, humus-rich
Hardiness: Zone 4
Propagation: Seed, in autumn or spring; division, in spring

Clump-forming plant. Leaves rounded, toothed, midgreen. Flowers orange-yellow with brown centers, in flat corymbs, from midsummer to early autumn.

Liatris spicata, *seen here in the dwarf cultivar 'Kobold', is unusual in opening from the top of the flowering spike downward.*

Ligularia dentata
'Othello'
(Asteraceae/Compositae)

Common name: Bigleaf
golden-ray
Height: 3ft (1m)
Spread: 2ft (60cm)
Aspect: Half shade
Soil: Moist, deep, fertile,
humus-rich
Hardiness: Zone 4
Propagation: Division, in
spring or autumn

A selected form of *L. dentata* with leaves
of dark brownish color, and corymbs of
deep orange flowers. A striking plant, one
of the best forms.

Ligularia × hessei
(Asteraceae/Compositae)

Common names: None
Height: 6ft (2m)
Spread: 3ft (1m)
Aspect: Half shade
Soil: Moist, humus-rich,
deep, fertile
Hardiness: Zone 5
Propagation: Division, in
spring or autumn

An interspecific hybrid plant of garden
origin. Leaves oblong to heart-shaped,
midgreen. Flowers in upright panicles,
orange-yellow.

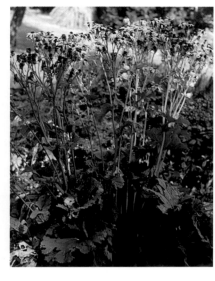

Ligularia hodgsonii
(Asteraceae/Compositae)

Common names: None
Height: 3ft (90cm)
Spread: 2ft (60cm)
Aspect: Half shade
Soil: Moist, humus-rich,
deep, fertile
Hardiness: Zone 5
Propagation: Seed, in autumn
or spring; division, in spring

Clump-forming species from Japan. Leaves
kidney-shaped, toothed, midgreen. Flowers
in many-flowered corymbs, yellow-orange,
disc brown, in summer to early autumn.

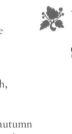

Ligularia japonica
(Asteraceae/Compositae)

Common names: None
Height: 6ft (2m)
Spread: 3ft (1m)
Aspect: Half shade
Soil: Moist, humus-rich,
deep, fertile
Hardiness: Zone 5
Propagation: Seed in autumn
or spring; division in spring

Clump-forming species. Leaves basal,
heart-shaped, lobed, toothed, midgreen.
Flowers in racemes of 8 or more, orange-
yellow, in early summer.

Ligularia przewalskii
(Asteraceae/Compositae)

Common names: None
Height: 6ft (2m)
Spread: 3ft (1m)
Aspect: Half shade
Soil: Moist, deep, humus-
rich, fertile
Hardiness: Zone 5
Propagation: Seed, in spring;
division, in spring or autumn

Species from China. Leaves palmate, lobed,
deeply cut, toothed, midgreen. Flowers in
dense, slender racemes, on purple stems,
yellow, in mid- to late summer.

Ligularia
'The Rocket' A.G.M.
(Asteraceae/Compositae)

Common names: None
Height: 6ft (1.8m)
Spread: 3ft (1m)
Aspect: Half shade
Soil: Moist, deep, humus-
rich, fertile
Hardiness: Zone 4
Propagation: Division, in
spring or autumn

Hybrid cultivar, and the best of all. Leaves
triangular, deep-cut, toothed, midgreen.
Flowers on branched black stems, in
compact panicles, yellow.

Ligularia
'Wiehenstephan'
(Asteraceae/Compositae)

Common names: None
Height: 6ft (1.8m)
Spread: 3ft (1m)
Aspect: Half shade
Soil: Moist, humus-rich,
deep, fertile
Hardiness: Zone 5
Propagation: Division, in
spring or autumn

A chance seedling in the Weihenstephan
garden in Germany. Leaves triangular,
deep-cut, toothed, midgreen. Flowers in
dense racemes, bright yellow.

Lilium
'African Queen' (Div. 6)
(Liliaceae)

Common names: None
Height: 6ft (2m)
Spread: Nil
Aspect: Sun or half shade
Soil: Sharply drained,
moisture-retentive
Hardiness: Zone 3
Propagation: Scales, offsets,
or bulbils in late summer

Hybrid strain. Leaves lance-shaped, glossy
green. Flowers perfumed, large, in racemes
of up to 12, outward-facing, outside purple-
brown, inside apricot, mid- and late summer.

LILIUM (Liliaceae)
Lily

Genus of some 100 mostly bulbous species from the northern hemisphere, mostly Eurasia and North America, with a few from the Philippines. Many are beautiful and easily grown; as with most popular garden plants, there are many cultivars. The habitats of the genus vary, and so cultural requirements vary, but the great majority have one basic need: drainage. Most lilies will not thrive in heavy clay soil; raised beds or planters are the simple answer in such circumstances. Some, however, like moist soil, and some also prefer the soil to be slightly acidic. Moving and division are best done while the plants are still in active growth after flowering in summer, so that they have a spell of warm weather to settle before winter. Most lilies do not spread; plant the bulbs 3 times their own width apart. They may require staking. The flowers have six tepals, and may be bell-, bowl-, star-, trumpet-, Turk's-cap- or funnel-shaped; are classified as being small, medium or large; and may be upward- or outward-facing or pendent. They may be hardy or tender, fragrant or not, and of any color except blue. They make excellent cut flowers, and are prized by flower-arrangers, but are highly allergenic, with sticky, staining pollen: florists often remove anthers as buds open.

Lilium bulbiferum
(Div. 9)
(Liliaceae)

Common name: Bulbil lily
Height: 5ft (1.5m)
Spread: Indefinite
Aspect: Sun or half shade
Soil: Sharply drained, moisture-retentive
Hardiness: Zone 7
Propagation: Scales, offsets or bulbils, all in late summer

Invasive species once satisfied. Leaves lance-shaped, hairy-edged, green. Flowers in umbels, of up to 5, bright orange-red bowls, in early to midsummer.

Lilium candidum
A.G.M. (Div. 9)
(Liliaceae)

Common name: Madonna lily
Height: 6ft (1.8m)
Spread: Nil
Aspect: Sun or half shade
Soil: Sharply drained, moisture-retentive
Hardiness: Zone 6
Propagation: Scales, offsets or bulbils, all in late summer

Leaves spirally-arranged, lance-shaped, midgreen. Flowers in racemes of up to 20, perfumed, trumpet-shaped, white with yellow bases, in summer.

Lilium formosanum
(Div. 9)
(Liliaceae)

Common name: Formosa lily
Height: 5ft (1.5m)
Spread: Nil
Aspect: Sun or half shade
Soil: Moist, acidic
Hardiness: Zone 5
Propagation: Scales, in late summer

Rhizomatous species. Leaves linear, dark green. Flowers scented, paired or solitary trumpets in umbels of up to 10, white flushed red-purple outside, in late summer.

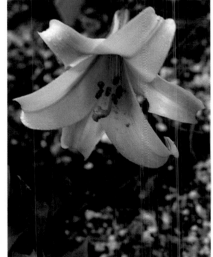

Lilium formosanum
var. *pricei* A.G.M. (Div. 9)
(Liliaceae)

Common name: Formosa lily
Height: 1ft (30cm)
Spread: Nil
Aspect: Sun or half shade
Soil: Moist, acidic
Hardiness: Zone
Propagation: Scales, in late summer

A very dwarf form of *Lilium formosanum*, making it suitable for rock gardens, the front of the border or containers. Flowers earlier and deeper flushed than the species.

Lilium grayi
(Div. 9)
(Liliaceae)

Common name: Gray's lily
Height: 5ft (1.5m)
Spread: Nil
Aspect: Sun or half shade
Soil: Moist, acidic
Hardiness: Zone 5
Propagation: Scales, offsets, or bulbils, all in late summer

A species from the eastern U.S.A. Leaves lance-shaped, whorled, green. Flowers in umbels of up to 10, perfumed, funnel-shaped to tubular, red.

Classification according to the International Lily register, 1982, with amendments by the Royal Horticultural Society, 1992

Division 1 Asiatic hybrids, with racemes or umbels of usually unscented flowers.

Division 2 Martagon hybrids, with racemes of Turk's-cap, sometimes scented flowers.

Division 3 Candidum hybrids, with usually Turk's-cap, sometimes scented flowers, solitary or in umbels or racemes.

Division 4 American hybrids, with racemes of mostly Turk's-cap, sometimes scented flowers.

Division 5 Longiflorum hybrids, with umbels of large, often scented, trumpet- or funnel-shaped flowers.

Division 6 Trumpet and Aurelian hybrids, with racemes or umbels of usually scented flowers of various shapes.

Division 7 Oriental hybrids, with racemes or panicles of often scented flowers of various shapes.

Division 8 Other hybrids

Division 9 All true species

Lilium henryi
A.G.M. (Div. 9)
(Liliaceae)

Common name: Henry lily
Height: 10ft (3m)
Spread: Indefinite
Aspect: Sun or half shade
Soil: Well-drained, alkaline,
humus-rich
Hardiness: Zone 5
Propagation: Scales, offsets or
bulbils, all in late summer

Vigorous, easy species. Leaves lance-shaped
to ovate. Flowers perfumed, Turk's-cap,
orange, spotted black, in racemes of up to
10, in late summer. Good beginner's lily.

Lilium lancifolium
(Div. 9)
(Liliaceae)

Common names: None
Height: 5ft (1.5m)
Spread: Nil
Aspect: Sun or half shade
Soil: Moist, acidic
Hardiness: Zone 4
Propagation: Scales, offsets or
bulbils, all in late summer

Species from the Far East. Leaves narrow,
lance-shaped, green. Flowers in racemes of
up to 40, nodding, Turk's-cap, orange, in
late summer and early autumn.

Lilium martagon
(Div. 9)
(Liliaceae)

Common name: Martagon
lily; Turk's-cap lily
Height: 6ft (2m)
Spread: Nil
Aspect: Sun or half shade
Soil: Any, well-drained
Hardiness: Zone 4
Propagation: Scales, offsets
or bulbils, all in late summer

A species from Europe across to Mongolia.
Leaves stem, inversely lance-shaped, green.
Flowers unpleasantly scented, in racemes
of up to 50, nodding, Turk's-cap, pink.

Lilium martagon
var. *album* A.G.M. (Div. 9)
(Liliaceae)

Common name: White
martagon lily
Height: 6ft (2m)
Spread: Nil
Aspect: Sun or half shade
Soil: Well-drained
Hardiness: Zone 4
Propagation: Scales, offsets
or bulbils, all in late summer

White-flowered form of the species.
Flowers smaller than the species, pure
white, downturned Turk's-caps, with the
same offensive smell.

Lilium monadelphum
A.G.M. (Div. 9)
(Liliaceae)

Common name:
Caucasian lily
Height: 5ft (1.5m)
Spread: Nil
Aspect: Sun
Soil: Fertile
Hardiness: Zone 5
Propagation: Scales, offsets
or bulbils, all in late summer

Leaves inverse-lance-shaped, bright green.
Flowers in racemes of up to 30, perfumed,
nodding trumpets, yellow, flushed brown
outside. From Turkey and the Caucasus.

Lilium
Pink Perfection Group
A.G.M. (Div. 6) (Liliaceae)

Common names: None
Height: 6ft (2m)
Spread: Nil
Aspect: Sun or half shade
Soil: Well-drained, moisture-
retentive
Hardiness: Zone 7
Propagation: Seed, in warmth
when ripe

A hybrid group derived from Asiatic
species. Leaves linear, green. Flowers in
racemes or umbels, perfumed, nodding
trumpets, purple-pink, in summer.

Lilium pumilum
A.G.M. (Div. 9)
(Liliaceae)

Common name: Coral lily
Height: 18in (45cm)
Spread: Nil
Aspect: Sun or half shade
Soil: Well-drained, acidic
Hardiness: Zone 5
Propagation: Scales, offsets
or bulbils, all in late summer

A species from Russia and the Far East.
Leaves linear, scattered, green. Flowers in
racemes of up to 30, perfumed, nodding,
Turk's-cap, scarlet, in early summer.

Lilium regale
A.G.M. (Div. 9)
(Liliaceae)

Common name: Regal lily
Height: 6ft (2m)
Spread: Nil
Aspect: Sun
Soil: Moist, well-drained
Hardiness: Zone 5
Propagation: Scales, offsets
or bulbils, all in late summer

A species from China. Leaves linear, glossy,
dark green. Flowers in umbels of up to 25,
perfumed trumpets, white with yellow
throats, in summer.

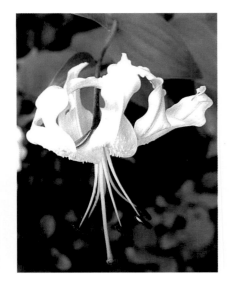

**Lilium speciosum
var. album** (Div. 9)
(Liliaceae)

Common names: Speciosum
lily
Height: 5ft (1.5m)
Spread: Nil
Aspect: Half shade
Soil: Moist, acidic
Hardiness: Zone 8
Propagation: Scales, offsets
or bulbils, all in late summer

A species from the Far East. Leaves lance-
shaped, scattered, green. Racemes of up to
12, large, perfumed, pendent, white
flowers, in late summer to early autumn.

Limonium latifolium
(Plumbaginaceae)

Common name: Wide-leaf sea
lavender
Height: 36in (90cm)
Spread: 18in (45cm)
Aspect: Sun
Soil: Sandy, well-drained
Hardiness: Zone 5
Propagation: Seed, in spring

Evergreen seaside plant. Leaves in rosettes,
dark green spoons. Flowers in open
panicles, dense spikes of minute, blue-
violet trumpets, in early summer.

Linaria purpurea
(Scrophulariaceae)

Common name: Purple
toadflax
Height: 3ft (90cm)
Spread: 1ft (30cm)
Aspect: Sun
Soil: Well-drained, sandy
Hardiness: Zone 6
Propagation: Seed or division,
both in spring

Leaves linear, midgreen. Flowers in dense,
slender racemes, pink, violet, or purple,
snapdragonlike, with curved spurs, from
early summer to early autumn.

Linaria purpurea
'Canon Went'
(Scrophulariaceae)

Common name: Purple
toadflax
Height: 3ft (90cm)
Spread: 1ft (30cm)
Aspect: Sun
Soil: Well-drained, sandy
Hardiness: Zone 6
Propagation: Seed or division,
both in spring

Selected form that comes true from seed.
Leaves linear, midgreen. Slender, dense
racemes of pink, snapdragonlike flowers,
from early summer to early autumn.

Linaria purpurea
'Springside White'
(Scrophulariaceae)

Common name: Purple
toadflax
Height: 3ft (90cm)
Spread: 1ft (30cm)
Aspect: Sun
Soil: Well-drained, sandy
Hardiness: Zone 6
Propagation: Seed or division,
both in spring

A selected form of the species that comes
true from seed, with white flowers
appearing over a long period from early
summer to early autumn.

Linaria triornithophora
(Scrophulariaceae)

Common name: Three birds
flying
Height: 4ft (1.2m)
Spread: 2ft (60cm)
Aspect: Sun
Soil: Well-drained, sandy
Hardiness: Zone 7
Propagation: Seed or division,
both in spring

Invasive species. Leaves lance-shaped, midgreen, in whorls. Flowers in loose racemes,
purple and yellow, snapdragonlike, in
whorls of 3, from summer to autumn.

Linum flavum
'Compactum'
(Linaceae)

Common name: Golden flax
Height: 6in (15cm)
Spread: 8in (20cm)
Aspect: Sun
Soil: Sharply drained, humus-
rich, with protection from
winter wet
Hardiness: Zone 5
Propagation: Seed, in spring
or autumn

Compact form of a European plant. Leaves
lance-shaped, deep green. Flowers many-
branched cymes of upward-facing, golden
cups, opening only in sun, in summer.

Linum monogynum
(Linaceae)

Common name: Flax
Height: 2ft (60cm)
Spread: 1ft (30cm)
Aspect: Sun
Soil: Well-drained, sandy
Hardiness: Zone 8
Propagation: Seed, in spring
or autumn

A perennial flax from New Zealand.
Leaves narrow, gray-green. Flowers in
corymbs, white, upward-facing, in
terminal clusters.

In many of the red-flowered lobelias, such as this L. fulgens (syn. L. splendens), *the stems and leaves are purple-flushed, making a powerful impact in a border.*

Linum narbonense
(Linaceae)

Common name: Narbonne
flax
Height: 24in (60cm)
Spread: 18in (45cm)
Aspect: Sun
Soil: Well-drained, sandy
Hardiness: Zone 5
Propagation: Seed, in spring
or autumn

Short-lived Mediterranean species. Leaves
narrow, lance-shaped, glaucous green.
Few-flowered cymes of rich blue saucers
with white eyes, in early to midsummer.

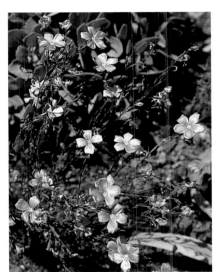

Linum perenne
(Linaceae)

Common name:
Perennial flax
Height: 2ft (60cm)
Spread: 1ft (30cm)
Aspect: Sun
Soil: Well-drained, sandy
Hardiness: Zone 5
Propagation: Seed, in spring
or autumn

Lax, straggly species. Leaves narrow, lance-
shaped, glaucous. Flowers in terminal
panicles, blue cups, fading over the day,
over a long period in early to midsummer.

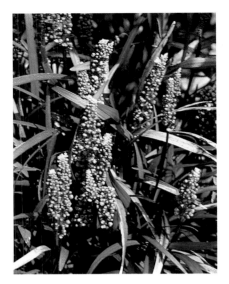

Liriope muscari
A.G.M.
(Convallariaceae/Liliaceae)

Common name: Big blue lily-
turf
Height: 12in (30cm)
Spread: 18in (45cm)
Aspect: Full or half shade
Soil: Moist, well-drained,
sandy, fertile
Hardiness: Zone 6
Propagation: Seed or division,
both in spring

An evergreen, robust perennial from
China. Leaves linear to straplike, dark
green. Flowers in dense spikes, violet-
mauve, from early to late autumn.

Lithodora diffusa
'Heavenly Blue' A.G.M.
(Boraginaceae)

Common names: None
Height: 6in (15cm)
Spread: 32in (80cm)
Aspect: Sun
Soil: Acidic, humus-rich
Hardiness: Zone 7
Propagation: Semiripe
cuttings, in summer

Selected form of an evergreen subshrub
from Europe. Leaves elliptic, deep green.
Flowers in terminal cymes, blue, over a
long period in late spring and early summer.

LOBELIA (Campanulaceae/Lobeliaceae)
Lobelia

A genus of some 370 species of annuals, perennials, and
shrubs with a worldwide distribution, but from South,
Central, and North America in particular. They are found in
a wide variety of habitats from marshlands to mountainsides,
and range from hardy through half-hardy to tender. In
general lobelias prefer a sunny position, but will tolerate light
shade, and like moisture at the roots; some, indeed, are
happiest as marginal aquatics, particularly if the soil is acid.
The species vary widely in appearance, but all have alternate,
simple leaves, and two-lipped, tubular flowers. The lips are
divided into lobes: the upper lip into a pair of usually upright
lobes, and the lower lip into three spreading lobes. The calyx
tubes are sometimes swollen. In most species, the flowers are
borne in terminal panicles or racemes, but in others they may
be solitary. The foliage is handsome, and darkly colored in
some types. Their main drawback is that they are short-lived
in the garden, and some need to be lifted and divided
regularly to keep them at their best. Lobelias make good cut
flowers, and are much used by flower-arrangers, but care
should be taken in handling them, as contact with the sap
may cause skin irritation.

Lobelia
'Butterfly Rose'
(Campanulaceae/Lobeliaceae)

Common names: None
Height: 36in (90cm)
Spread: 12in (30cm)
Aspect: Sun or half shade
Soil: Moist, deep, humus-rich
Hardiness: Zone 7
Propagation: Seed, when ripe;
division, in spring

A hybrid, clump-forming perennial. Leaves
inversely lance-shaped, shiny, green.
Flowers in racemes, pale pink, some dark
pink appearing in them, in summer.

Lobelia cardinalis
A.G.M.
(Campanulaceae/Lobeliaceae)

Common name: Cardinal-
flower
Height: 36in (90cm)
Spread: 12in (30cm)
Aspect: Sun or half shade
Soil: Moist, humus rich,
fertile
Hardiness: Zone 3
Propagation: Seed, when ripe;
bud cuttings, in summer

Short-lived, rhizomatous species. Leaves
ovate, toothed, bronze-green. Flowers in
racemes, tubular, scarlet; purplish bracts.
Will grow in a bog or marginal aquatic site.

**Lobelia
'Eulalia Berrige'**
(Campanulaceae/Lobeliaceae)

Common names: None
Height: 30in (75cm)
Spread: 12in (30cm)
Aspect: Sun or half shade
Soil: Moist, deep, humus-rich
Hardiness: Zone 8
Propagation: Division, in
spring

A hybrid perennial lobelia. Leaves ovate,
midgreen. Flowers in open, upright
racemes, cerise-mauve. Good for growing
in a border.

**Lobelia
'Fan Zinnoberrosa' A.G.M.**
(Campanulaceae/Lobeliaceae)

Common names: None
Height: 24in (60cm)
Spread: 10in (25cm)
Aspect: Sun or half shade
Soil: Moist, deep, humus-rich
Hardiness: Zone 8
Propagation: Division, in
spring

A reliable hybrid perennial lobelia. Leaves
ovate, bronze-green. Flowers borne in
dense, upright racemes, cinnabar rose,
in summer.

**Lobelia x gerardii
'Vedrariensis'**
(Campanulaceae/Lobeliaceae)

Common names: None
Height: 4ft (1.2m)
Spread: 1ft (30cm)
Aspect: Sun or half shade
Soil: Moist, deep, humus-rich
Hardiness: Zone 7
Propagation: Division, in
spring

A rhizomatous hybrid lobelia. Leaves
basal, in rosettes, lance-shaped to elliptic,
dark green. Flowers in racemes, tubular,
violet, all summer.

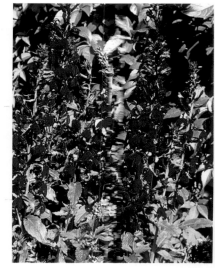

**Lobelia 'Kompliment
Scharlach' A.G.M.**
(Campanulaceae/Lobeliaceae)

Common names: None
Height: 36in (90cm)
Spread: 12in (30cm)
Aspect: Sun or half shade
Soil: Moist, deep, humus-rich
Hardiness: Zone 7
Propagation: Division in
spring

A clump-forming, hybrid perennial lobelia.
Leaves elliptic, dark green. Flowers in
loose racemes, tubular, scarlet, borne
in summer.

Lobelia siphilitica
(Campanulaceae/Lobeliaceae)

Common name: Big blue
lobelia
Height: 4ft (1.2m)
Spread: 1ft (30cm)
Aspect: Sun or half shade
Soil: Moist, deep, humus-rich
Hardiness: Zone 5
Propagation: Seed, when ripe;
division, in spring

A hardy, clump-forming species. Leaves
ovate, toothed, hairy, pale green. Flowers
in dense racemes, bright blue, with leafy
bracts, in late summer to autumn.

**Lobelia siphilitica
'Alba'**
(Campanulaceae/Lobeliaceae)

Common name: Big white
lobelia
Height: 4ft (1.2m)
Spread: 1ft (30cm)
Aspect: Sun or half shade
Soil: Moist, deep, humus-rich
Hardiness: Zone 5
Propagation: Seed, when ripe;
division, in spring

The white form of the species. Leaves
ovate, toothed, hairy, light green. Flowers
in dense racemes, white, from late summer
to midautumn.

Lobelia tupa
(Campanulaceae/Lobeliaceae)

Common names: None
Height: 36in (90cm)
Spread: 12in (30cm)
Aspect: Sun or half shade
Soil: Moist, deep, humus-rich
Hardiness: Zone 8
Propagation: Seed, when ripe;
division, in spring

A clump-forming perennial from Chile.
Leaves ovate, downy green. Flowers in
racemes, brick-red, with reddish-purple
calyces, in late summer.

Lobelia 'Will Scarlet'
(Campanulaceae/Lobeliaceae)

Common names: None
Height: 36in (90cm)
Spread: 12in (30cm)
Aspect: Sun or half shade
Soil: Moist, deep, humus-rich
Hardiness: Zone 7
Propagation: Division, in
spring

A hybrid lobelia. Leaves ovate, greenish-
blue or greenish-maroon. Flowers in
racemes, bright red, from midsummer to
early autumn.

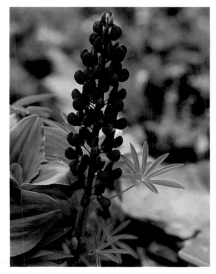

Lotus corniculatus
(Leguminosae/Papilionaceae)

Common name: Bird's-foot
trefoil
Height: 12in (30cm)
Spread: 18in (45cm)
Aspect: Sun
Soil: Well-drained, fertile
Hardiness: Zone 5
Propagation: Seed, in autumn
or spring

A spreading perennial of worldwide
distribution. Leaves pinnate, leaflets
obovate, blue-green. Flowers in racemes,
clear yellow.

Lotus maculatus
A.G.M.
(Leguminosae/papilionaceae)

Common names: None
Height: 8in (20cm)
Spread: Indefinite
Aspect: Sun
Soil: Well-drained, fertile
Hardiness: Zone 10
Propagation: Seed, in warmth
in spring

Creeping plant. Leaves palmate, leaflets
linear, midgreen. "Lobster-claw" flowers,
solitary or in small clusters, yellow, tipped
orange or red, in spring and early summer.

Lunaria rediviva
(Cruciferae)

Common name: Perennial
honesty
Height: 3ft (90cm)
Spread: 1ft (30cm)
Aspect: Sun or half shade
Soil: Moist, well-drained,
fertile
Hardiness: Zone 8
Propagation: Seed, in spring

Perennial from Eurasia. Leaves dark green,
large, triangular, toothed. Flowers scented,
lilac-white, in racemes in late spring and
early summer, followed by flat seed pods.

Lupinus 'Band of Nobles'
Series A.G.M.
(Leguminosae/Papilionaceae)

Common name: Lupine
Height: 5ft (1.5m)
Spread: 30in (75cm)
Aspect: Sun or half shade
Soil: Well-drained, sandy,
acidic, fertile
Hardiness: Zone 5
Propagation: Seed, after
soaking, in spring or autumn

Strain of hybrid lupines. Leaves basal,
hairy, palmate, midgreen. Flowers in
racemes, perfumed, in colors from red,
pink, yellow, white, or blue to bicolored.

LUPINUS (Leguminosae/Papilionaceae)
Lupine

A genus of some 200 species, including annuals, perennials,
and both semievergreen and evergreen subshrubs or shrubs,
from North Africa, southern Europe, and the Americas. Their
native habitats range from dry uplands to woodlands,
riverbanks, and coastal situations. Lupines are an invaluable
genus of repeat-flowering, handsome plants with attractive
leaves for the border. The flowers are pealike, and are borne
in long, upright terminal racemes or spikes; they are scented,
and attract bees. They are also, unfortunately, highly
allergenic. There is a very large number of hybrids in
cultivation, and many are derived from crosses with *Lupinus
polyphyllus*, from western North America, as one parent;
many hybrids have bicolored flowers. Lupines will grow in
sun or half shade, and tolerate a range of soils except alkaline
or waterlogged ones. Their drawbacks are that they are prey
to slugs and prone to powdery mildew. They are also short-
lived, and resent disturbance, but they are easy to propagate.
The seeds of lupines are poisonous, so children should be
warned. The flowers last well in water provided that they are
inverted and the hollow stem is filled with water and plugged
with cotton wool before they are put in the vase.

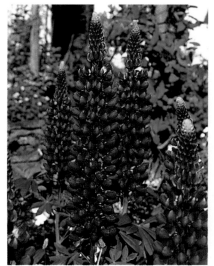

Lupinus
'Chandelier'
(Leguminosae/Papilionaceae)

Common name: Lupine
Height: 36in (90cm)
Spread: 30in (75cm)
Aspect: Sun or half shade
Soil: Well-drained, sandy,
acidic, fertile
Hardiness: Zone 5
Propagation: Basal cuttings,
in midspring

A hybrid perennial lupine. Leaves basal,
palmate, hairy, midgreen. Scented flowers
in racemes, bright yellow, in early and
midsummer.

Lupinus
'My Castle'
(Leguminosae/Papilionaceae)

Common name: Lupine
Height: 36in (90cm)
Spread: 30in (75cm)
Aspect: Sun or half shade
Soil: Well-drained, sandy,
acidic, fertile
Hardiness: Zone 5
Propagation: Basal cuttings,
in midspring

A hybrid, clump-forming perennial lupine.
Leaves basal, palmate, hairy, midgreen.
Flowers in racemes, deep pink, in early and
midsummer.

**Lupinus
'Noble Maiden'
(Leguminosae/Papilionaceae)**

Common name: Lupine
Height: 36in (90cm)
Spread: 30in (75cm)
Aspect: Sun or half shade
Soil: Well-drained, sandy,
acidic, fertile
Hardiness: Zone 5
Propagation: Basal cuttings,
in midspring

A clump-forming, hybrid lupine cultivar.
Leaves basal, palmate, hairy, midgreen.
Flowers in racemes, creamy-white, in early
and midsummer.

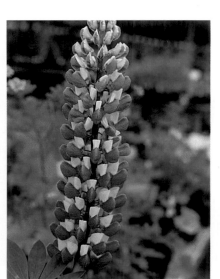

**Lupinus
'The Chatelaine'
(Leguminosae/Papilionaceae)**

Common name: Lupine
Height: 36in (90cm)
Spread: 30in (75cm)
Aspect: Sun or half shade
Soil: Well-drained, sandy
acidic, fertile
Hardiness: Zone 5
Propagation: Basal cuttings,
in midspring

A clump-forming, hybrid lupine. Leaves
basal, palmate, hairy, midgreen. Flowers in
racemes, bicolored, pink and white, in
early and midsummer.

Lupinus
'The Governor'
(Leguminosae/Papilionaceae)

Common name: Lupine
Height: 36in (90cm)
Spread: 30in (75cm)
Aspect: Sun or half shade
Soil: Well-drained, sandy,
fertile
Hardiness: Zone 5
Propagation: Basal cuttings,
in midspring

A hybrid, clump-forming cultivar. Leaves
basal, palmate, hairy, midgreen. Flowers in
racemes, bicolored, blue and white, in
early and midsummer.

**Lupinus
'The Page'
(Leguminosae/Papilionaceae)**

Common name: Lupine
Height: 36in (90cm)
Spread: 30in (75cm)
Aspect: Sun or half shade
Soil: Well-drained, sandy,
fertile
Hardiness: Zone 5
Propagation: Basal cuttings,
in midspring

A hybrid, clump-forming lupine cultivar.
Leaves basal, palmate, hairy, midgreen.
Flowers in panicles, carmine red, in early
and midsummer.

**Luzula sylvatica
'Aurea'
(Juncaceae)**

Common names: None
Height: 32in (80cm)
Spread: 18in (45cm)
Aspect: Full or half shade
Soil: Moist, well-drained,
humus-rich, fertile
Hardiness: Zone 6
Propagation: Seed, in spring
or autumn; division, in spring

A tufted, evergreen grass. Leaves linear,
channelled, shiny yellow. Flowers in open
panicles, small, chestnut-brown, from midspring to early summer.

LYCHNIS (Caryophyllaceae)
Campion • Catchfly

A genus of some 20 species of biennials and perennials from
arctic and northern temperate regions; they are reliably hardy.
Their natural habitats range from alpine conditions to damp
woodlands and grasslands, and they will grow in sun or
partial shade, and in any soil as long as it is well-drained and
fertile. *Lychnis flos-cuculi* is even happy in bog conditions.
Lychnis are upright, generally with branching stems, and bear
tubular to salverform or star-shaped flowers in terminal
cymes or panicles. The flowers come in a range of colors
from purple through scarlet to pink or white, and some types
make good cut flowers. The smaller, alpine types are most
suitable for a rock or alpine garden, while the taller forms
will do well in a sunny border or naturalized in a wildflower
garden. Some species, most notably *L.* x *arkwrightii*,
L. coronaria, and *L.* x *haageana*, are short-lived, but the
others are soundly perennial. The taller varieties need to be
staked. *L. flos-jovis* and *L. chalcedonica* attract both bees and
butterflies, while *L. flos-cuculi* is loved by bees. All are prone
to damage by slugs in spring, so preventative action must be
taken early. All seem to self-seed prolifically; deadhead after
flowering to avoid this if it is not wanted.

**Lychnis alpina
(Caryophyllaceae)**

Common names: Alpine
campion; alpine catchfly
Height: 6in (15cm)
Spread: 6in (15cm)
Aspect: Sun or half shade
Soil: Well-drained, fertile
Hardiness: Zone 5
Propagation: Seed, when ripe
or in spring

A mountain perennial. Leaves in rosettes,
lance-shaped, dark green. Flowers in
terminal cymes of up to 20, pink, petals
2-lobed, frilled, in summer.

**Lychnis x arkwrightii
'Vesuvius'**
(Caryophyllaceae)

Common name: Arkwright
campion
Height: 18in (45cm)
Spread: 12in (30cm)
Aspect: Sun or half shade
Soil: Well-drained, fertile
Hardiness: Zone 5
Propagation: Basal cuttings
or division, both in spring

Short-lived, hybrid, clump-forming plant.
Leaves lance-shaped, hairy, dark green-
brown. Flowers in terminal cymes of up to
10, star-shaped, scarlet-orange, in summer.

**Lychnis chalcedonica
'Flore Pleno'**
(Caryophyllacae)

Common name: Maltese
cross
Height: 4ft (1.2m)
Spread: 1ft (30cm)
Aspect: Sun or half shade
Soil: Moist, fertile
Hardiness: Zone 4
Propagation: Seed or division,
both in spring

Leaves basal, ovate, midgreen. Flowers in
terminal, rounded cymes, vermilion, petals
deeply notched, double, in early and
midsummer. From European Russia.

**Lychnis chalcedonica
'Rosea'**
(Caryophyllaceae)

Common name: Pink Maltese
cross
Height: 4ft (1.2m)
Spread: 30cm (1ft)
Aspect: Sun or half shade
Soil: Moist, fertile
Hardiness: Zone 5
Propagation: Seed or division,
both in spring

Single-flowered, pink form of the species.
Leaves basal, ovate, midgreen. Flowers in
terminal cymes, single, star-shaped, pink,
in early and midsummer.

Lychnis coronaria
(Caryophyllaceae)

Common name: Rose
campion
Height: 32in (80cm)
Spread: 18in (45cm)
Aspect: Sun
Soil: Dry, well-drained, fertile
Hardiness: Zone 4
Propagation: Seed or division,
both in spring

Short-lived species. Leaves ovate to lance-
shaped, woolly silver-gray. Flowers in few-
flowered, terminal racemes, single, scarlet
or purple, over a long period in late summer.

**Lychnis coronaria
'Alba' A.G.M.**
(Caryophyllaceae)

Common name: White rose
campion
Height: 32in (80cm)
Spread: 18in (45cm)
Aspect: Sun
Soil: Dry, well-drained
Hardiness: Zone 4
Propagation: Seed or division,
both in spring

White form of the species. Leaves ovate to
lance-shaped, silver-gray, woolly. Flowers
in few-flowered terminal cymes, single,
white, over a long period in late summer.

**Lychnis coronaria
Oculata Group**
(Caryophyllaceae)

Common name: Rose
campion
Height: 32in (80cm)
Spread: 18in (45cm)
Aspect: Sun
Soil: Dry, well-drained, fertile
Hardiness: Zone 4
Propagation: Seed or division,
both in spring

A free-flowering cultivar. Leaves ovate to
lance-shaped, silver-gray, woolly. Flowers
in terminal cymes, white with a cherry-pink
eye, over a long period in late summer.

**Lychnis flos-cuculi
var. albiflora**
(Caryophyllaceae)

Common name: White
ragged robin
Height: 30in (75cm)
Spread: 36in (90cm)
Aspect: Sun or half shade
Soil: Moist, well-drained,
fertile
Hardiness: Zone 6
Propagation: Seed or division,
both in spring

White form of a rampant species. Leaves
basal, inversely lance-shaped; stem, oblong,
bluish-green. Flowers in terminal cymes,
star-shaped, in late spring and early summer.

Lychnis flos-jovis
(Caryophyllaceae)

Common name: Flower-of-
love
Height: 24in (60cm)
Spread: 18in (45cm)
Aspect: Sun
Soil: Dry, well-drained, fertile
Hardiness: Zone 5
Propagation: Seed or division,
both in spring

Mat-forming species from the Alps. Leaves
basal and stem, spoon- to lance-shaped,
gray-green. Flowers in cymes, single, pink,
white, or scarlet, early to late summer.

Lychnis miqueliana
(Caryophyllaceae)

Common names: None
Height: 2ft (60cm)
Spread: 1ft (30cm)
Aspect: Sun or half shade
Soil: Well-drained, fertile
Hardiness: Zone 6
Propagation: Seed or division, both in spring

A hardy species from Japan. Leaves oblong to ovate, midgreen. Flowers single, large, petals toothed, vermilion, in few-flowered cymes, in summer.

LYSIMACHIA (Primulaceae)
Loosestrife

A genus of some 150 species of evergreen and herbaceous perennials and shrubs from northern temperate and southern subtropical regions; they vary from hardy to half-hardy, as a consequence. Their natural habitats are damp woodlands and grasslands, often near water; in the garden, they prefer a soil which is moist, and moisture-retentive, especially in summer, but also like good drainage. If they are given the moist root run they enjoy, they can be invasive (except *Lysimachia ephemerum*), so they are best used as water marginals, or in a bog garden or wild or woodland garden. Many make large plants, and some of the taller types may require staking. Slugs also enjoy the moist conditions preferred by these plants, and measures to protect the foliage from attack should be taken early. Some species, however, are low-growing, and make good ground cover. They will grow in sun or part-shade. Leaf shapes and arrangements vary, although the leaves are generally simple. All bear 5-petalled flowers, ranging from cup- or saucer-shaped to star-shaped, which are either solitary and axillary or carried in terminal panicles or racemes. The flowers are usually yellow in color, but there are also white-, pink-, or purple-flowered types.

Lysimachia ciliata
(Primulaceae)

Common name: Fringed loosestrife
Height: 4ft (1.2m)
Spread: 2ft (60cm)
Aspect: Sun or half shade
Soil: Moist, humus-rich
Hardiness: Zone 4
Propagation: Seed or division, both in spring

Invasive, rhizomatous species from North America. Leaves ovate to lance-shaped, midgreen. Flowers on slim stems, single or paired, pendent, yellow stars, in summer.

Lysimachia ciliata
'Firecracker' A.G.M.
(Primulaceae)

Common name: Fringed loosestrife
Height: 4ft (1.2m)
Spread: 2ft (60cm)
Aspect: Sun or half shade
Soil: Moist, humus-rich
Hardiness: Zone 4
Propagation: Division, in spring

A form of the species with purple foliage, which contrasts well with the yellow flowers. This is also known as *Lysimachia ciliata* 'Purpurea'.

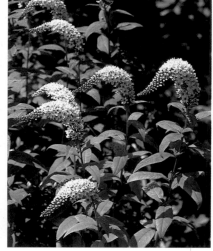

Lysimachia clethroides
A.G.M.
(Primulaceae)

Common name: Japanese loosestrife
Height: 3ft (90cm)
Spread: 2ft (60cm)
Aspect: Sun or half shade
Soil: Moist, humus-rich
Hardiness: Zone 4
Propagation: Seed or division, both in spring

Invasive rhizomatous species. Leaves lance-shaped, pointed, midgreen, paler beneath. Flowers in dense, tapering, arching racemes, white, single, starry, mid- and late summer.

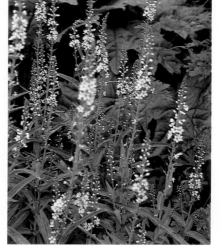

Lysimachia ephemerum
(Primulaceae)

Common name: Loosestrife
Height: 3ft (90cm)
Spread: 1ft (30cm)
Aspect: Sun or half shade
Soil: Moist, humus-rich
Hardiness: Zone 7
Propagation: Seed or division, both in spring

Non-spreading species. Leaves linear to lance-shaped, glaucous gray-green. Flowers white saucers, in dense, upright, terminal racemes, in early and midsummer.

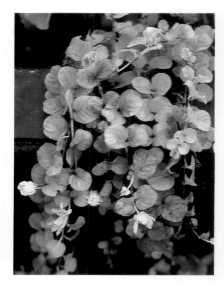

Lysimachia nummularia
'Aurea' A.G.M.
(Primulaceae)

Common names: Creeping Jenny; moneywort; creeping Charlie
Height: 2in (5cm)
Spread: Indefinite
Aspect: Sun or half shade
Soil: Moist, humus-rich
Hardiness: Zone 5
Propagation: Seed or division, both in spring

Golden form of a rampant, evergreen species from Europe. Leaves ovate to round, golden-yellow. Flowers solitary, single, cup-shaped, upturned, yellow.

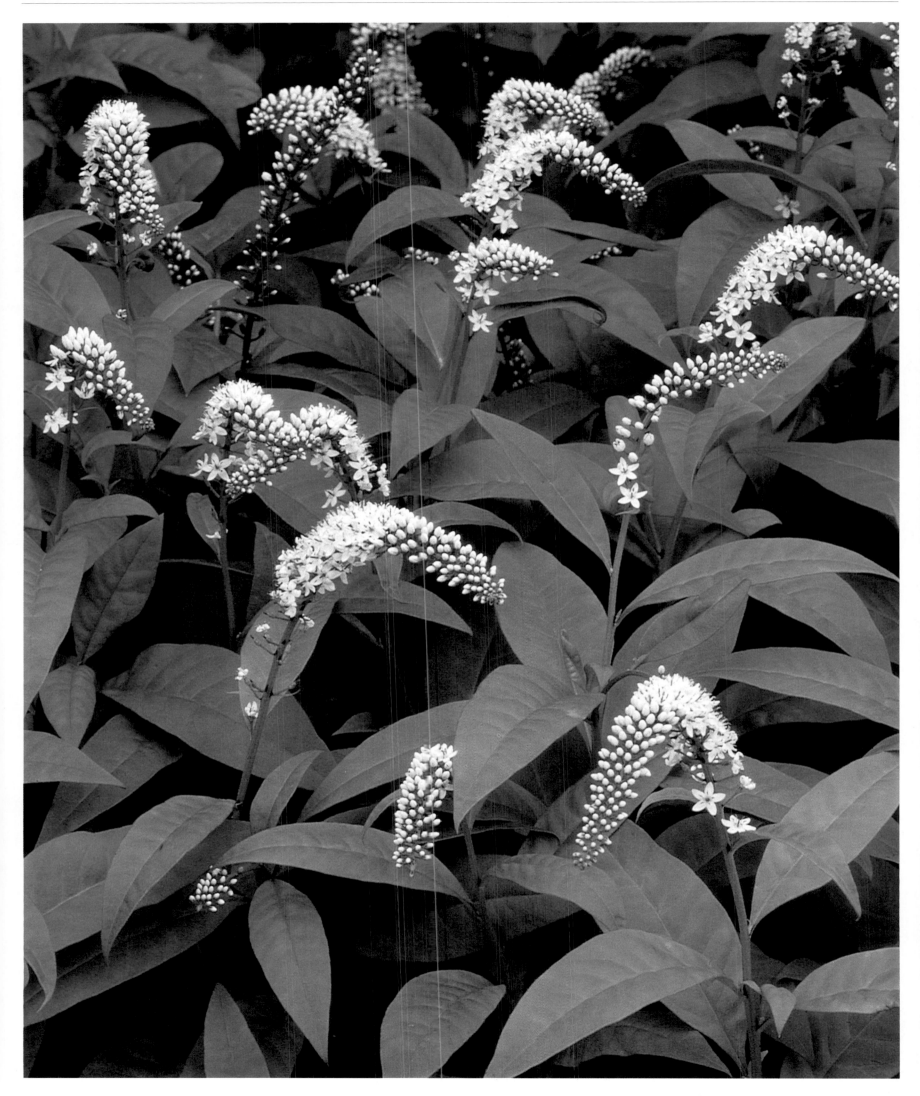

A white-flowered loosestrife, such as this Lysimachia clethroides, *makes a cool statement on a pond margin.*

185

Lysimachia punctata
(Primulaceae)

Common name: Yellow
loosestrife
Height: 3ft (90cm)
Spread: 2ft (60cm)
Aspect: Sun or half shade
Soil: Moist, humus-rich
Hardiness: Zone 5
Propagation: Seed or division,
both in spring

An invasive, rhizomatous species. Leaves
elliptic- to lance-shaped, dark green. Yellow
flowers in whorls from the leaf axils, in
mid- and late summer.

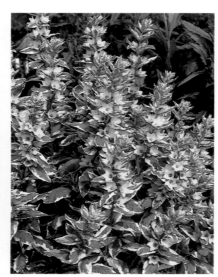

Lysimachia punctata
'Alexander'
(Primulaceae)

Common name: Yellow
loosestrife
Height: 3ft (90cm)
Spread: 2ft (60cm)
Aspect: Sun or half shade
Soil: Moist, humus-rich
Hardiness: Zone 5
Propagation: Division, in
spring

A selected cultivar of the species. Leaves
elliptic- to lance-shaped, dark green edged
cream or white. Flowers yellow, in whorls
in the leaf axils, mid- and late summer.

Lythrum salicaria
(Lythraceae)

Common name: Purple
loosestrife
Height: 4ft (1.2m)
Spread: 18in (45cm)
Aspect: Sun
Soil: Wet to marginal aquatic,
fertile
Hardiness: Zone 3
Propagation: Seed, in warmth
in spring; division, in spring

Clump-forming plant. Leaves lance-shaped,
downy, green. Flowers bright purple-red
stars in spiky racemes, midsummer to early
autumn. Deadhead to prevent self-seeding.

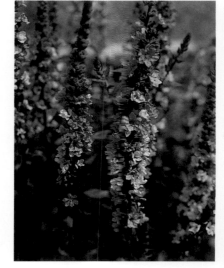

Lythrum salicaria
'Blush'
(Lythraceae)

Common name: Pink
loosestrife
Height: 4ft (1.2m)
Spread: 18in (45cm)
Aspect: Sun
Soil: Wet to marginal aquatic,
fertile
Hardiness: Zone 3
Propagation: Division, in
spring

Selected form of the species. Leaves lance-
shaped, downy, green. Flowers blush-pink
stars in spiky racemes, midsummer to early
autumn. Deadhead to prevent self-seeding.

Lythrum salicaria
'Robert'
(Lythraceae)

Common name: Pink
loosestrife
Height: 4ft (1.2m)
Spread: 18in (45cm)
Aspect: Sun
Soil: Wet to marginal aquatic,
fertile
Hardiness: Zone 3
Propagation: Division, in
spring

A selected form with bright pink, starry
flowers in spiky racemes, midsummer to
early autumn. Leaves lance-shaped, downy,
green. Deadhead to prevent self-seeding.

Lythrum virgatum
'The Rocket'
(Lythraceae)

Common name: Pink
loosestrife
Height: 36in (90cm)
Spread: 18in (45cm)
Aspect: Sun
Soil: Moist, fertile
Hardiness: Zone 4
Propagation: Seed or division,
both in spring

A clump-forming perennial from Europe,
Asia, and China. Leaves linearly lance-
shaped, midgreen. Flowers in slim, spiky
racemes, deep pink, all summer.

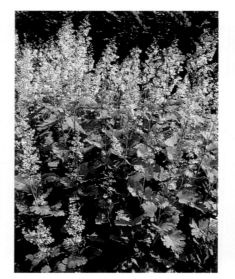

Macleaya cordata
A.G.M.
(Papaveraceae)

Common name: Plume-poppy
Height: 8ft (2.5m)
Spread: 3ft (90cm)
Aspect: Sun or half shade
Soil: Moist, well-drained,
fertile
Hardiness: Zone 3
Propagation: Seed, in spring;
division, in spring or autumn

Rhizomatous plant from the Far East.
Leaves handsome, 5- to 7-lobed, gray-green,
white-downy below. Flowers creamy-white,
tubular, in panicles, mid- and late summer.

Maianthemum bifolium
(Convallariaceae/Liliaceae)

Common name: Wild
lily-of-the-valley
Height: 6in (15cm)
Spread: Indefinite
Aspect: Full or half shade
Soil: Moist, well-drained,
acidic, humus rich
Hardiness: Zone 3
Propagation: Seed, when ripe;
division of runners, in spring

Invasive ground cover. Leaves ovate to
heart-shaped, glossy deep green. Flowers in
racemes of up to 20, perfumed, white, in
early summer, followed by small, red berries.

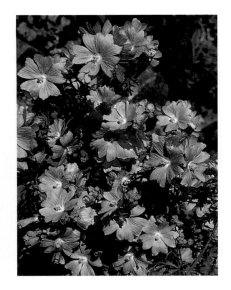

Malva moschata
(Malvaceae)

Common name: Musk
mallow
Height: 3ft (90cm)
Spread: 2ft (60cm)
Aspect: Sun
Soil: Moist, well-drained,
fertile
Hardiness: Zone 3
Propagation: Seed or basal
cuttings, both in spring

A short-lived perennial from Africa. Leaves
heart-shaped and pinnatisect, midgreen.
Flowers in axillary clusters, pink saucers,
early summer to early autumn.

Malva moschata
f. alba A.G.M.
(Malvaceae)

Common name: White musk
mallow
Height: 3ft (90cm)
Spread: 2ft (60cm)
Aspect: Sun
Soil: Moist, well-drained,
fertile
Hardiness: Zone 3
Propagation: Seed or basal
cuttings, both in spring

A white form of the species. Leaves heart-
shaped and pinnatisect, midgreen, musk-
scented. Flowers in axillary clusters, white
saucers, early summer to early autumn.

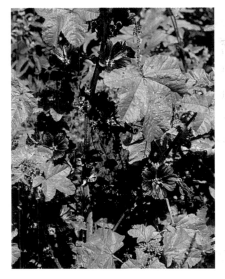

Malva sylvestris
(Malvaceae)

Common name: Mallow
Height: 4ft (1.2m)
Spread: 2ft (60cm)
Aspect: Sun
Soil: Moist, well-drained,
fertile
Hardiness: Zone 5
Propagation: Seed or basal
cuttings, both in spring

Leaves round to heart-shaped, light green.
Flowers in axillary clusters, purplish-pink,
with dark veins, from late spring to midautumn. From Eurasia and North Africa.

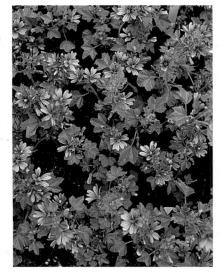

Malva sylvestris
'Primley Blue'
(Malvaceae)

Common name: Mallow
Height: 8in (20cm)
Spread: 24in (60cm)
Aspect: Sun
Soil: Moist, well-drained,
fertile
Hardiness: Zone 5
Propagation: Basal cuttings,
in spring

Desirable, prostrate, hybrid. Leaves heart-
shaped, midgreen. Flowers pale blue, with
darker blue veining, in axillary clusters,
from late spring to midautumn.

Malvastrum lateritium
(Malvaceae)

Common name: False mallow
Height: 6in (15cm)
Spread: Indefinite
Aspect: Sun
Soil: Well-drained
Hardiness: Zone 8
Propagation: Seed or
softwood cuttings, both
in spring

A prostrate perennial from South America.
Leaves rounded, lobed, rough, dark green.
Flowers solitary, peach-colored, yellow-
centered, sporadically throughout summer.

Marrubium peregrinum
(Labiatae/Lamiaceae)

Common name: Horehound
Height: 2ft (60cm)
Spread: 1ft (30cm)
Aspect: Sun
Soil: Well-drained, poor
Hardiness: Zone 8
Propagation: Seed or
softwood cuttings, both
in spring

Leaves aromatic, obovate, hairy, crenate,
dark green. Flowers tubular, 2-lipped, pale
pink, in whorls, in early summer. Deadhead
to prevent self-seeding. From Eurasia.

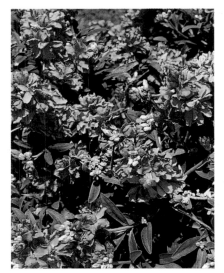

Matthiola
pink perennial
(Brassicaceae/Cruciferae)

Common name: Perennial
common stock
Height: 18in (45cm)
Spread: 12in (30cm)
Aspect: Sun
Soil: Moist, well-drained,
fertile
Hardiness: Zone 7
Propagation: Seed, in spring
or autumn

Short-lived plant, probably of garden origin.
Leaves linear-ovate, gray-green. Flowers in
terminal spikes, cruciform, pink, double,
scented, over a long period in summer.

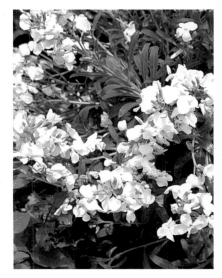

Matthiola
white perennial
(Brassicaceae/Cruciferae)

Common name: Perennial
common stock
Height: 18in (45cm)
Spread: 12in (30cm)
Aspect: Sun
Soil: Moist, well-drained,
fertile
Hardiness: Zone 7
Propagation: Seed, in spring
or autumn

Short-lived plant, of garden origin. Leaves
linear-ovate, gray-green. Flowers in
terminal spikes, perfumed, cruciform,
white, over a long period in summer.

Mazus reptans
'Albus'
(Scrophulariaceae)

Common names: None
Height: 2in (5cm)
Spread: 18in (45cm)
Aspect: Sun
Soil: Moist, well-drained,
fertile
Hardiness: Zone 3
Propagation: Seed or division,
both in spring

Woodlander ground cover. Leaves lance-shaped, toothed, midgreen. Flowers in short racemes of up to 5, white, narrow, tubular, in late spring to summer.

MECONOPSIS (Papaveraceae)
Poppy

A genus of some 45 species of annuals, biennials, and deciduous or evergreen, often monocarpic or short-lived perennials. Most originate in the Himalayas, Burma, and China. One, *Meconopsis cambrica*, is native to western Europe; this species will grow anywhere, and is exempt from the cultural guidance below, which applies to species from the Far East. *Meconopsis* have handsome foliage in basal rosettes, and striking seed heads, but it is for quality of flower that they are best loved. The flowers are single, open cups, usually pendent, and may be solitary (usually on leafless stems) or in short panicles or racemes (usually on leafy stems), which open from above. *M. cambrica* is yellow or orange, but the coloring of the blue species is quite exquisite, and worth any effort. These come from a range of habitats, from moist, shady woodlands to mountain screes and meadows; some are very hardy, others much less so. They like some degree of shade, and the soil should be acid, humus-rich to a degree, moist, but well-drained and never waterlogged; in dry summers they must be watered. They do best in cooler climates, especially those with cool, damp summers. They may need staking in exposed areas.

Meconopsis betonicifolia
A.G.M.
(Papaveraceae)

Common name: Blue-poppy
Height: 4ft (1.2m)
Spread: 18in (45cm)
Aspect: Half shade
Soil: Moist, well-drained,
acidic, humus-rich
Hardiness: Zone 7
Propagation: Seed, when ripe

Deciduous, short-lived species. Leaves in basal rosettes, ovate, toothed, light blue-green. Flowers solitary, pendent or horizontal, blue saucers, in early summer.

Meconopsis betonicifolia
var. *alba*
(Papaveraceae)

Common name: White-poppy
Height: 4ft (1.2m)
Spread: 18in (45cm)
Aspect: Half shade
Soil: Moist, well-drained,
acidic, humus-rich
Hardiness: Zone 7
Propagation: Seed, when ripe

Leaves in basal rosettes, blue-green, rusty-hairy, ovate, toothed. Flowers single, white, pendent, in early summer. Prevent flowering for a year or two to improve longevity.

Meconopsis cambrica
(Papaveraceae)

Common name: Welsh-poppy
Height: 18in (45cm)
Spread: 12in (30cm)
Aspect: Any
Soil: Any
Hardiness: Zone 6
Propagation: Seed, when ripe

Taprooted perennial from Europe. Leaves stem and basal, pinnatisect, fernlike, fresh green. Flowers solitary, single, yellow cups, from spring to autumn. Seeds prolifically.

Meconopsis cambrica
var. *aurantiaca* 'Flore
Pleno' (Papaveraceae)

Common name: Orange
Welsh-poppy
Height: 18in (45cm)
Spread: 12in (30cm)
Aspect: Any
Soil: Any
Hardiness: Zone 6
Propagation: Seed, when ripe

A double-flowered form of the orange variety of Welsh poppy. It does not self-seed prolifically, and so is not the nuisance that the single form can represent.

Meconopsis cambrica
'Flore Pleno'
(Papaveraceae)

Common name: Double
Welsh-poppy
Height: 18in (45cm)
Spread: 12in (30cm)
Aspect: Any
Soil: Any
Hardiness: Zone 5
Propagation: Division, in
spring

The double yellow form of the Welsh poppy, perhaps less graceful than the single form, but having the virtue of not self-seeding everywhere.

Meconopsis chelidoniifolia
(Papaveraceae)

Common names: None
Height: 3ft (1m)
Spread: 2ft (60cm)
Aspect: Half shade
Soil: Moist, well-drained,
acidic, humus-rich
Hardiness: Zone 8
Propagation: Seed, when ripe

Meconopsis grandis
A.G.M.
(Papaveraceae)

Common names: None
Height: 4ft (1.2m)
Spread: 2ft (60cm)
Aspect: Half shade
Soil: Moist, well-drained,
acidic, humus-rich
Hardiness: Zone 5
Propagation: Seed, when ripe

Meconopsis napaulensis
(Papaveraceae)

Common names: None
Height: 8ft (2.5m)
Spread: 3ft (90cm)
Aspect: Half shade
Soil: Moist, well-drained,
acidic, humus-rich
Hardiness: Zone 8
Propagation: Seed, when ripe

Meconopsis paniculata
(Papaveraceae)

Common names: None
Height: 6ft (2m)
Spread: 2ft (60cm)
Aspect: Half shade
Soil: Moist, well-drained,
acidic, humus-rich
Hardiness: Zone 8
Propagation: Seed, when ripe

A species from China. Leaves pinnatisect, lobes pinnatifid, hairy, pale green. Flowers on upper leaf stalks, single, pendent or horizontal, yellow.

Clump-forming species; monocarpic in dry conditions. Leaves basal rosette and stem, elliptic, toothed, brown-hairy. Flowers blue, solitary, single, shallow cups, early summer.

Monocarpic species. Leaves in rosettes, pinnatisect, yellow-green, red-hairy, lobes oblong. Flowers in racemes of up to 17, pendent bowls, late spring to midsummer.

Monocarpic evergreen. Leaves in rosettes, pinnatisect, yellow-hairy, gray-green. Flowers in racemes, cup-shaped, pendent pale yellow, late spring to summer.

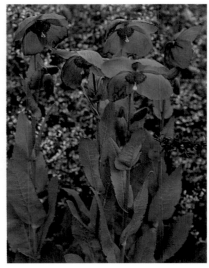

Meconopsis punicea
(Papaveraceae)

Common names: None
Height: 30in (75cm)
Spread: 12in (30cm)
Aspect: Half shade
Soil: Moist, well-drained,
acidic, humus-rich
Hardiness: Zone 7
Propagation: Seed, when ripe

Meconopsis
quintuplinervia A.G.M.
(Papaveraceae)

Common names: None
Height: 18in (45cm)
Spread: 12in (30cm)
Aspect: Half shade
Soil: Moist, well-drained,
acidic, humus-rich
Hardiness: Zone 8
Propagation: Seed, when ripe

Meconopsis regia
(Papaveraceae)

Common names: None
Height: 6ft (2m)
Spread: 3ft (1m)
Aspect: Half shade
Soil: Moist, well-drained,
acidic, humus-rich
Hardiness: Zone 8
Propagation: Seed, when ripe

Meconopsis x *sheldonii*
A.G.M.
(Papaveraceae)

Common names: None
Height: 5ft (1.5m)
Spread: 2ft (60cm)
Aspect: Half shade
Soil: Moist, well-drained,
acidic, humus-rich
Hardiness: Zone 6
Propagation: Division, after
flowering

Taprooted species. Leaves in rosettes, inversely lance-shaped, gray-hairy, mid-green. Flowers on scapes, pendent, crimson, petals flared, summer to autumn.

Clump-forming species. Leaves in rosettes, lance-shaped, golden-hairy, midgreen. Flowers solitary, pendent, lavender cups, from early to late summer.

Monocarpic evergreen from Nepal. Leaves in rosettes, elliptic, silver-hairy, midgreen. Flowers outward-facing on branched stems, red cups, from late spring to midsummer.

Hybrid perennial of garden origin. Leaves in rosettes, lance-shaped, hairy, dark green. Flowers solitary, cup-shaped, deep rich blue, in late spring and early summer.

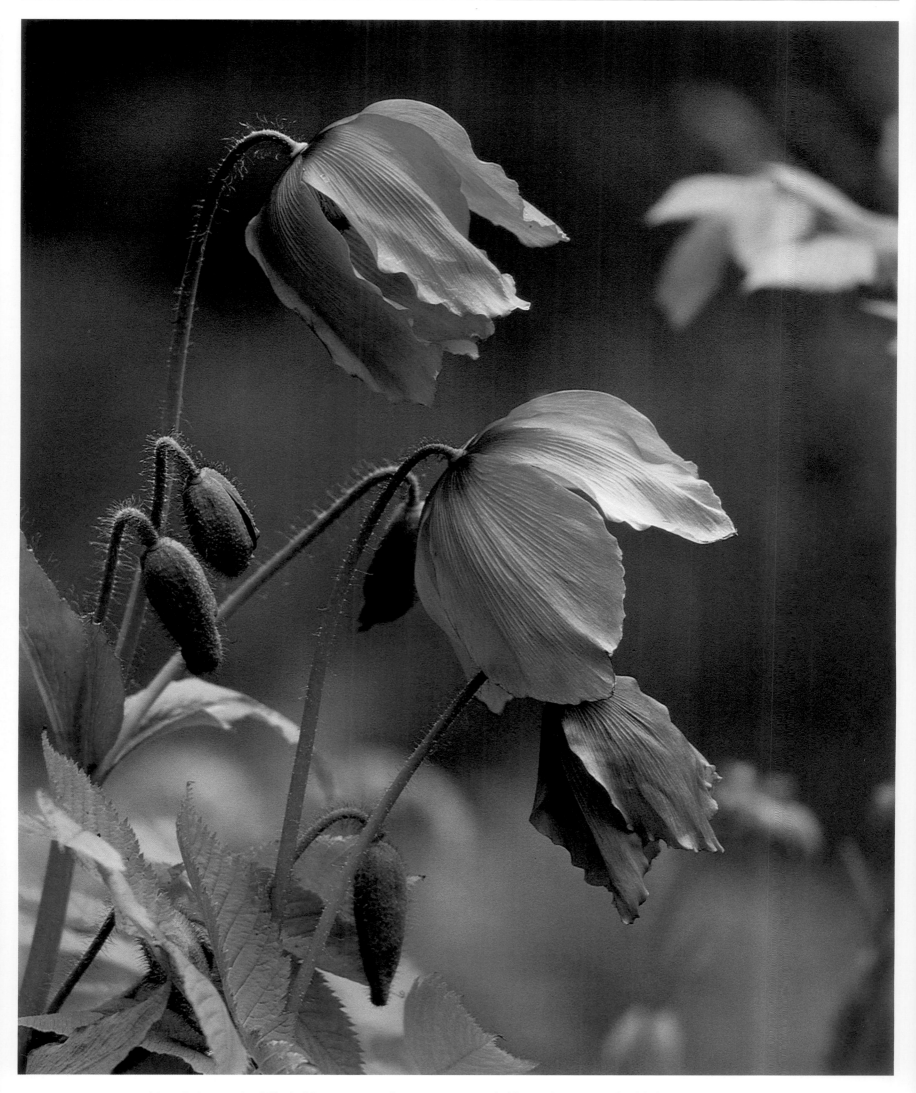

Although they can be difficult, blue poppies such as Meconopsis × sheldonii *'Slieve Donard' add glamour to any garden*

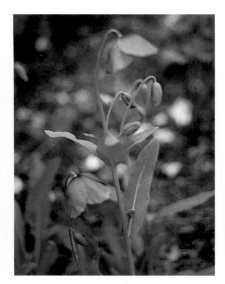

**Meconopsis × sheldonii
'Slieve Donard' A.G.M.
(Papaveraceae)**

Common names: None
Height: 5ft (1.5m)
Spread: 2ft (60cm)
Aspect: Half shade
Soil: Moist, well-drained,
acidic, humus-rich
Hardiness: Zone 6
Propagation: Division, after
flowering

A selected form of this garden hybrid, with
flowers of brilliant, rich blue in late spring
and early summer. Leaves in rosettes, dark
green, lance-shaped, hairy.

**Megacarpaea polyandra
(Brassicaceae/Cruciferae)**

Common names: None
Height: 6ft (2m)
Spread: 2ft (60cm)
Aspect: Sun
Soil: Well-drained, fertile
Hardiness: Zone 7
Propagation: Seed, when ripe

Taprooted perennial from the Himalayas.
Leaves pinnate, lobes ovate, toothed, midgreen. Flowers in dense racemes, off-white,
in spring and summer.

**Melianthus major
A.G.M.
(Melianthaceae)**

Common name: Large honey-
bush
Height: 10ft (3m)
Spread: 10ft (3m)
Aspect: Sun
Soil: Well-drained, fertile
Hardiness: Zone 9
Propagation: Seed in warmth,
suckers or softwood cuttings,
all in spring

Tender perennial, evergreen in warm areas,
from South Africa. Leaves pinnate, leaflets
ovate, toothed, gray-green. Flowers in
racemes, red, from late spring to summer.

**Melissa officinalis
'Aurea'
(Labiatae/Lamiaceae)**

Common name: Lemon balm
Height: 4ft (1.2m)
Spread: 18in (45cm)
Aspect: Sun
Soil: Poor, well-drained
Hardiness: Zone 4
Propagation: Seed or division,
both in spring

Bushy perennial. Leaves aromatic, ovate,
wrinkled, dark green, splashed gold.
Flowers small, in spikes, pale yellow, all
summer. Liked by bees and butterflies.

**Mellitis melissophyllum
(Labiatae/Lamiaceae)**

Common names: None
Height: 28in (70cm)
Spread: 20in (50cm)
Aspect: Half shade
Soil: Moist, well-drained,
fertile
Hardiness: Zone 6
Propagation: Seed, when ripe;
division, in spring

Woodlander. Leaves honey-scented, oval,
scalloped, veined, hairy, wrinkled, green.
Flowers in whorls, 2-lipped, tubular, white,
pink-lipped, in spring and early summer.

**Mentha × gracilis
'Variegata'
(Labiatae/Lamiaceae)**

Common name: Ginger mint
Height: 18in (45cm)
Spread: Indefinite
Aspect: Sun
Soil: Moist, poor
Hardiness: Zone 7
Propagation: Division, in
spring or autumn

A very invasive perennial from Europe.
Leaves aromatic, ginger-flavored, ovate,
flecked or striped yellow. Flowers in
whorls, lilac, in summer. Ground cover.

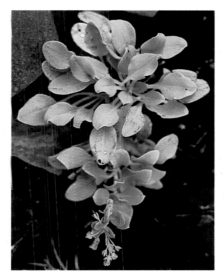

**Mertensia pulmonarioides
A.G.M.
(Boraginaceae)**

Common name: Bluebells
Height: 18in (45cm)
Spread: 10in (25cm)
Aspect: Half shade
Soil: Sharply drained, poor
Hardiness: Zone 3
Propagation: Seed or root
cuttings, both in autumn;
division, in spring

A clump-forming woodlander from North
America. Leaves ovate, blue-green. Flowers
in terminal cymes, tubular, blue, in mid-
and late spring.

**Mertensia simplicissima
(Boraginaceae)**

Common names: None
Height: 3ft (90cm)
Spread: 1ft (30cm)
Aspect: Half shade
Soil: Sharply drained, poor
Hardiness: Zone 6
Propagation: Seed or root
cuttings, both in autumn;
division, in spring

Prostrate plant from Russia to the Far East.
Leaves ovate, glaucous, blue-green. Flowers
tubular, turquoise, in terminal cymes on
prostrate stems, spring to early autumn.

Microseris ringens
(Asteraceae/Compositae)

Common names: None
Height: 2ft (60cm)
Spread: 1ft (30cm)
Aspect: Sun
Soil: Well-drained, humus-rich
Hardiness: Zone 8
Propagation: Seed, in spring or autumn

Australian perennial. Leaves ovate, hairy, rough, soft green. Flowers single, yellow, daisylike, in large, flat-topped racemes in early summer and again in late summer.

Milium effusum
'Aureum'
(Graminae/Poaceae)

Common names: None
Height: 2ft (60cm)
Spread: 1ft (30cm)
Aspect: Half shade or sun
Soil: Moist, well-drained, humus-rich
Hardiness: Zone 6
Propagation: Seed, *in situ* in spring; division, in spring

A spreading grass from Eurasia and North America. Leaves flat, linear, yellow-green. Flowers in open panicles, single-flowered spikes from late spring to midsummer.

Mimulus
'Andean Nymph' A.G.M.
(Scrophulariaceae)

Common name: Monkey-flower
Height: 8in (20cm)
Spread: 12in (30cm)
Aspect: Wet, humus-rich, fertile
Soil: Sun or half shade
Hardiness: Zone 6
Propagation: Division, in spring; softwood cuttings, in early summer

Short-lived, rhizomatous hybrid aquatic marginal. Leaves ovate, hairy, toothed, light green. Flowers in racemes, white with pink throats, over a long period in summer.

Mimulus aurantiacus
A.G.M.
(Scrophulariaceae)

Common name: Monkey-flower
Height: 3ft (1m)
Spread: 3ft (1m)
Aspect: Sun or half shade
Soil: Moist, humus-rich, fertile
Hardiness: Zone 8
Propagation: Seed in autumn or spring; division in spring

Subshrub from the U.S.A. Leaves oblong, toothed, sticky, glossy green. Flowers in leafy racemes, red, orange, or yellow trumpets, in late summer to autumn.

Mimulus cardinalis
A.G.M.
(Scrophulariaceae)

Common name: Scarlet monkey-flower
Height: 36in (90cm)
Spread: 24in (60cm)
Aspect: Sun or half shade
Soil: Wet, humus-rich, fertile
Hardiness: Zone 7
Propagation: Seed, in autumn or spring; division, in spring

A creeping perennial from the western U.S.A. and Mexico. Leaves ovate, toothed, downy, green. Flowers on erect stems, solitary, tubular, scarlet, all summer long.

Mimulus luteus
(Scrophulariaceae)

Common name: Yellow monkey-flower
Height: 1ft (30cm)
Spread: 2ft (60cm)
Aspect: Sun or half shade
Soil: Wet, humus-rich, fertile
Hardiness: Zone 7
Propagation: Seed, in spring or autumn; division, in spring

Invasive species from Chile. Leaves ovate-oblong, midgreen. Flowers on upright or decumbent stems, yellow, spotted red-purple, from late spring to summer.

Mirabilis jalapa
(Nyctaginaceae)

Common name: Common four-o'clock flower
Height: 2ft (60cm)
Spread: 2ft (60cm)
Aspect: Sun
Soil: Well-drained, fertile, protected from winter wet
Hardiness: Zone 8
Propagation: Seed, in warmth in spring; division, in spring

Tuberous perennial. Leaves ovate, midgreen. Flowers perfumed, pink, red, yellow, white, or magenta open in late afternoon, and die next morning. Blooms all summer.

Mitchella repens
(Rubiaceae)

Common names: Creeping-box; partridge-berry
Height: 2in (5cm)
Spread: 12in (30cm)
Aspect: Half shade
Soil: Moist, well-drained, acidic, humus-rich
Hardiness: Zone 3
Propagation: Seed, in autumn; division of runners, in spring

A creeping, evergreen perennial from the U.S.A. Leaves ovate, green. Flowers white, perfumed, in summer, followed by red berries.

MONARDA (Labiatae/Lamiaceae)
Bee-balm • Bergamot

A genus of only some 15 species of annuals and rhizomatous, clump-forming, herbaceous perennials from North America, but one which has been hybridized extensively to produce many very garden-worthy, hardy herbaceous perennials. Most hybrids derive from *Monarda didyma* or *M. fistulosa*. They like sun, but will grow in dappled shade. Their natural habitats include both dry prairie and woodlands, so they vary in that some like drier soils while others prefer them moist, but the soil must be moisture-retentive for all; in dry spells they are very prone to mildew. The flowers are in whorls, sagelike, tubular, 2-lipped, with a hooded upper lip and a spreading lower lip, and often have colored bracts. Bergamots are long-flowering, make excellent cut flowers, and are often used for flower arrangements, in both the fresh and dried state. Bees also like the flowers, but only bumblebees can gain direct access; honey bees can reach the pollen only after other insects have made holes. The stems are distinctive in that they are square; in the taller varieties they require staking. The foliage is unspectacular, but aromatic. Slugs attack the young growth in spring. Bergamots are low-allergen plants, so suit the allergic gardener.

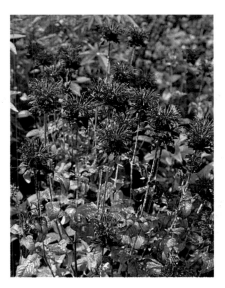

Monarda
'Aquarius'
(Labiatae/Lamiaceae)

Common name: Bergamot
Height: 36in (1m)
Spread: 18in (45cm)
Aspect: Sun or half shade
Soil: Moist, well-drained, humus-rich, fertile
Hardiness: Zone 4
Propagation: Division or basal cuttings, both in spring

Rhizomatous hybrid. Leaves aromatic, ovate, toothed, dark green. Flowers 2-lipped, deep lilac-purple with purple-green bracts, from summer to autumn.

Monarda
'Balance'
(Labiatae/Lamiaceae)

Common name: Bergamot
Height: 36in (1m)
Spread: 18in (45cm)
Aspect: Sun or half shade
Soil: Moist, humus-rich, well-drained, fertile
Hardiness: Zone 4
Propagation: Division basal or cuttings in spring

A rhizomatous hybrid cultivar. Leaves aromatic, ovate, toothed, dark green. Flowers 2-lipped, brick-red, from summer to autumn.

Monarda
'Cambridge Scarlet'
(Labiatae/Lamiaceae)

Common name: Bergamot
Height: 36in (1m)
Spread: 18in (45cm)
Aspect: Sun or half shade
Soil: Moist, well-drained, humus-rich, fertile
Hardiness: Zone 4
Propagation: Division or basal cuttings, both in spring

Hybrid, rhizomatous cultivar. Leaves aromatic, ovate, toothed, dark green. Flowers 2-lipped, scarlet with brown bracts, from summer to autumn.

Monarda
'Croftway Pink'
(Labiatae/Lamiaceae)

Common name: Bergamot
Height: 36in (1m)
Spread: 18in (45cm)
Aspect: Sun or half shade
Soil: Moist, well-drained, humus-rich, fertile
Hardiness: Zone 4
Propagation: Division or basal cuttings, both in spring

Rhizomatous, hybrid cultivar. Leaves aromatic, ovate, toothed, dark green. Flowers 2-lipped, pink with pink-tinged bracts, from summer to autumn.

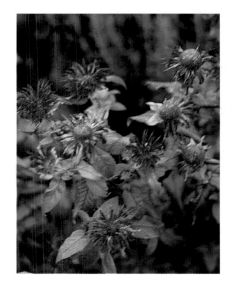

Monarda didyma
(Labiatae/Lamiaceae)

Common names: Bee-balm; Oswego-tea
Height: 36in (1m)
Spread: 18in (45cm)
Aspect: Sun or half shade
Soil: Moist, well-drained, humus-rich, fertile
Hardiness: Zone 4
Propagation: Seed, in spring or autumn; division, in spring

Rhizomatous species from the eastern U.S.A. Leaves aromatic, ovate, toothed, dull green. Flowers pink with red-tinted bracts, from mid- to late summer.

Monarda fistulosa
(Labiatae/Lamiaceae)

Common name: Wild bergamot
Height: 4ft (1.2m)
Spread: 18in (45cm)
Aspect: Sun
Soil: Moist, well-drained, humus-rich, fertile
Hardiness: Zone 4
Propagation: Seed, in spring or autumn; division, in spring

A rhizomatous perennial. Leaves aromatic, ovate, toothed, dull green. Flowers sage-like, 2-lipped, pale pink with purple bracts, from summer to autumn.

Monarda
'Gardenview Scarlet'
(Labiatae/Lamiaceae)

Common name: Bergamot
Height: 3ft (1m)
Spread: 18in (45cm)
Aspect: Sun or half shade
Soil: Moist, well-drained,
humus-rich, fertile
Hardiness: Zone 4
Propagation: Division or
basal cuttings, both in spring

A hybrid, rhizomatous bergamot. Leaves aromatic, ovate, toothed, dark green. Flowers 2-lipped, scarlet with dark bracts, from summer to autumn.

Monarda
'Isla'
(Labiatae/Lamiaceae)

Common name: Bergamot
Height: 3ft (1m)
Spread: 18in (45cm)
Aspect: Sun or half shade
Soil: Moist, well-drained,
humus-rich, fertile
Hardiness: Zone 4
Propagation: Division or
basal cuttings, both in spring

A rhizomatous, hybrid cultivar. Leaves aromatic, ovate, toothed, dark green. Flowers sagelike, 2-lipped, pink with pinkish bracts, from summer to autumn.

Monarda
'Prärienacht'
(Labiatae/Lamiaceae)

Common name: Bergamot
Height: 3ft (1m)
Spread: 18in (45cm)
Aspect: Sun or half shade
Soil: Moist, well-drained,
humus-rich, fertile
Hardiness: Zone 4
Propagation: Division or
basal cuttings, both in spring

A rhizomatous, hybrid bergamot. Leaves aromatic, ovate, toothed, dark green. Flowers 2-lipped, purple-lilac with red-green bracts, from midsummer to autumn.

Monarda punctata
(Labiatae/Lamiaceae)

Common name: Horse-mint
Height: 3ft (1m)
Spread: 18in (45cm)
Aspect: Sun or half shade
Soil: Moist, well-drained,
humus-rich, fertile
Hardiness: Zone 4
Propagation: Division or
basal cuttings, both in spring; seed, in autumn

A species from the U.S.A. Leaves aromatic, toothed, pale green. Flowers in whorls, sagelike, 2-lipped, pink, spotted purple, bracts green, tinged pink, in summer.

Monarda
'Scorpion'
(Labiatae/Lamiaceae)

Common name: Bergamot
Height: 3ft (1m)
Spread: 18in (45cm)
Aspect: Sun or half shade
Soil: Moist, well-drained,
humus-rich, fertile
Hardiness: Zone 4
Propagation: Division or
basal cuttings, both in spring

A hybrid, rhizomatous cultivar. Leaves aromatic, ovate, toothed, dark green, Flowers in whorls, 2-lipped, hooded, deep pink, from summer to autumn.

Monarda
'Squaw'
(Labiatae/Lamiaceae)

Common name: Bergamot
Height: 3ft (1m)
Spread: 18in (45cm)
Aspect: Sun or half shade
Soil: Moist, well-drained,
humus-rich, fertile
Hardiness: Zone 4
Propagation: Division or
basal cuttings, both in spring

A rhizomatous, hybrid bergamot. Leaves aromatic, ovate, toothed, dark green. Flowers in whorls, sagelike, hooded, bright crimson, from summer to autumn.

Monarda
'Twins'
(Labiatae/Lamiaceae)

Common name: Bergamot
Height: 3ft (1m)
Spread: 18in (45cm)
Aspect: Sun or half shade
Soil: Moist, well-drained,
humus-rich, fertile
Hardiness: Zone 4
Propagation: Division or
basal cuttings, both in spring

A hybrid, rhizomatous bergamot. Leaves aromatic, toothed, dark green. Flowers in whorls, sagelike, hooded, lilac-pink, from summer to autumn.

Moraea spathulata
(Iridaceae)

Common names: None
Height: 3ft (90cm)
Spread: 3in (8cm)
Aspect: Sun
Soil: Well-drained, humus-rich, fertile
Hardiness: Zone 5
Propagation: Seed, in warmth in autumn; offsets, when dormant

A cormous perennial from Africa. Leaves basal, narrowly linear, flat, green. Flowers in succession, in clusters, each short-lived, irislike, from spring to summer.

Morina longifolia
(Morinaceae)

Common name: Whorlflower
Height: 3ft (90cm)
Spread: 1ft (30cm)
Aspect: Sun
Soil: Sharply drained,
humus-rich, protected from
winter wet
Hardiness: Zone 6
Propagation: Seed, when ripe;
root cuttings, in winter

Evergreen with leaves in a basal rosette,
lance-shaped, spiny, dark green. Flowers in
tiered whorls, with spiny bracts, white,
becoming pink, then red, in summer.

Muscari armeniacum
A.G.M.
(Hyacinthaceae/Liliaceae)

Common name: American
grape-hyacinth
Height: 8in (20cm)
Spread: 2in (5cm)
Aspect: Sun
Soil: Moist, well-drained,
fertile
Hardiness: Zone 4
Propagation: Offsets, in
summer

A vigorous, bulbous perennial from the
Caucasus. Leaves linear, midgreen, after
the flowers. Flowers in dense racemes,
bright blue with white mouths, in spring.

Muscari azureum
A.G.M.
(Hyacinthaceae/Liliaceae)

Common name: Grape-
hyacinth
Height: 4in (10cm)
Spread: 2in (5cm)
Aspect: Sun
Soil: Moist, well-drained,
fertile
Hardiness: Zone 8
Propagation: Offsets, in
summer

A bulbous perennial from Turkey. Leaves
inverse lance-shaped, gray-green. Flowers
in dense racemes, sky-blue bells with a
dark stripe on each lobe, in spring.

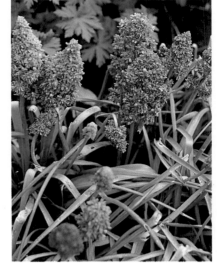

Muscari comosum
'Plumosum'
(Hyacinthaceae/Liliaceae)

Common name: Feather-
hyacinth
Height: 24in (60cm)
Spread: 2in (5cm)
Aspect: Sun
Soil: Moist, well-drained,
fertile
Hardiness: Zone 4
Propagation: Offsets, in
summer

Bulbous perennial from Europe and Turkey.
Leaves linear, spreading, midgreen. Flowers
are absent; heads are composed of sterile,
purple threads.

Muscari latifolium
(Hyacinthaceae/Liliaceae)

Common name: Grape-
hyacinth
Height: 8in (20cm)
Spread: 2in (5cm)
Aspect: Sun
Soil: Moist, well-drained,
fertile
Hardiness: Zone 4
Propagation: Offsets, in
summer

Bulbous perennial. Leaves midgreen, semierect, inverse lance-shaped. Dense racemes
of purple-black, urn-shaped flowers are
crowned by sterile, blue flowers.

Myosotidium hortensia
(Boraginaceae)

Common names: None
Height: 2ft (60cm)
Spread: 3ft (90cm)
Aspect: Half shade
Soil: Moist, well-drained,
sandy
Hardiness: Zone 8
Propagation: Seed, when ripe;
division, in spring

Leaves large, ovate to heart-shaped, with
conspicuous veins, glossy green. Flowers in
cymes, blue bells with white margins in
early summer. Not for a hot, dry garden.

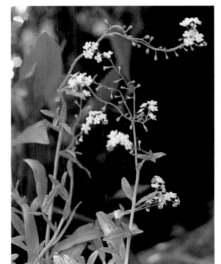

Myosotis scorpioides
(Boraginaceae)

Common names: True forget-
me-not
Height: 1ft (30cm)
Spread: 1ft (30cm)
Aspect: Sun or half shade
Soil: Marginal aquatic
Hardiness: Zone 5
Propagation: Seed or division,
both in spring

A rampant, rhizomatous perennial from
Eurasia and North America. Leaves ovate,
midgreen. Flowers in open cymes, small,
blue, salverform, in early summer.

Myrrhis odorata
(Apiaceae/Umbelliferae)

Common names: Myrrh;
sweet Cicely
Height: 6ft (2m)
Spread: 5ft (1.5m)
Aspect: Half shade
Soil: Moist, well-drained,
fertile
Hardiness: Zone 5
Propagation: Seed, in spring;
division, in spring or autumn

Aniseed-flavored culinary herb. Leaves 2-
or 3-pinnate, lobes lance-shaped, toothed,
bright green. Flowers in compound umbels,
small, star-shaped, white; fruits brown.

NARCISSUS (Amaryllidaceae)
Daffodil

A genus of some 50 species of bulbous perennials from varied habitats in Europe and North Africa; the genus has been hybridized extensively, and several thousand cultivars have been developed. Daffodils are an excellent garden plant, suitable for naturalizing, growing in a border, or planting in containers. They will grow in sun or half-shade, although the former is preferred. They like the soil to be moist during the growing season but dry during the dormant period, and so a humus-rich but sharply drained soil is best. The flowers are borne on leafless stems, which may carry anything from one to 20 blooms. The flower has a perianth and a corona: the perianth is made up of six petals, spreading or reflexed, and the corona may be any shape between a shallow cup and a long trumpet. The leaves are basal, and usually strap-shaped, sometimes cylindrical; they should be left to die down, not cut back, or flowering will be poorer the following year. Daffodils benefit from lifting and dividing every few years, and as this is best done during the summer dormancy, it is advisable to mark the positions of the clumps while the foliage is there to guide you. The bulbs are poisonous, and contact with the sap may cause skin irritation.

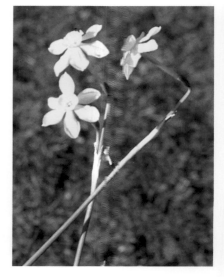

Narcissus
'Actaea' A.G.M. (Div. 9)
(Amaryllidaceae)

Common name: Daffodil
Height: 18in (45cm)
Spread: 6in (15cm)
Aspect: Sun or half shade
Soil: Well-drained, fertile, humus-rich
Hardiness: Zone 4
Propagation: Offsets, in summer or autumn

A reliable hybrid with perfumed flowers. Flowers with white, wavy, open perianth and low, bowl-shaped, red-rimmed, yellow corona, in late spring.

Narcissus
'Baby Moon' (Div. 7)
(Amaryllidaceae)

Common name: Daffodil
Height: 10in (25cm)
Spread: 3in (8cm)
Aspect: Sun or half shade
Soil: Well-drained, alkaline, humus-rich, fertile
Hardiness: Zone 4
Propagation: Offsets, in summer or autumn

A hybrid Jonquilla narcissus. Flowers small, perfumed, with the perianth and small-cupped corona both yellow, in midspring.

Narcissus
'Bantam' A.G.M. (Div. 2)
(Amaryllidaceae)

Common name: Daffodil
Height: 10in (25cm)
Spread: 6in (15cm)
Aspect: Sun or half shade
Soil: Well-drained, fertile, humus-rich
Hardiness: Zone 4
Propagation: Offsets, in summer or autumn

A good hybrid narcissus. Flowers with short, golden yellow perianth segments and short, flared, orange, cup-shaped, red-rimmed corona, in midspring.

Narcissus
'Bravoure' A.G.M. (Div. 1)
(Amaryllidaceae)

Common name: Daffodil
Height: 18in (45cm)
Spread: 6in (15cm)
Aspect: Sun or half shade
Soil: Moist, well-drained, humus-rich
Hardiness: Zone 4
Propagation: Offsets, in summer or autumn

A robust Trumpet daffodil. Flowers with pointed, overlapping, white perianth segments and a long, yellow, trumpet-shaped corona, in midspring.

Narcissus bulbocodium
(Div. 10)
(Amaryllidaceae)

Common name: Petticoat daffodil
Height: 6in (15cm)
Spread: 3in (8cm)
Aspect: Sun or half shade
Soil: Well-drained, acidic, humus-rich
Hardiness: Zone 6
Propagation: Seed, when ripe; offsets, in summer or autumn

A species from Europe and North Africa. Flowers small, yellow, with reduced, pointed perianth segments and an expanded, megaphone-shaped corona, in midspring.

Narcissus
'Canaliculatus' (Div. 8)
(Amaryllidaceae)

Common name: Daffodil
Height: 5in (12cm)
Spread: 6in (15cm)
Aspect: Sun or half shade
Soil: Well-drained, alkaline, humus-rich
Hardiness: Zone 8
Propagation: Offsets, in summer or autumn

A perfumed, cluster-headed, Tazetta narcissus. Flower with reflexed, white perianth and a yellow, barrel-shaped corona, in midspring.

Narcissus cyclamineus
A.G.M. (Div. 10)
(Amaryllidaceae)

Common name: Daffodil
Height: 8in (20cm)
Spread: 3in (8cm)
Aspect: Sun or half shade
Soil: Well-drained, acidic,
humus-rich
Hardiness: Zone 5
Propagation: Seed, when ripe;
offsets, in summer or autumn

Species from Spain and Portugal. Leaves
narrow, keeled, spreading. Flowers small,
nodding, yellow. Perianth totally reflexed,
corona long and narrow, in early spring.

Narcissus
'February Gold' A.G.M.
(Div. 6) (Amaryllidaceae)

Common name: Daffodil
Height: 12in (30cm)
Spread: 3in (8cm)
Aspect: Sun or half shade
Soil: Well-drained, acidic,
humus-rich, fertile
Hardiness: Zone 6
Propagation: Offsets, in
summer or autumn

A robust, hybrid, Cyclamineus narcissus.
Flowers with golden-yellow, reflexed
perianth and long, trumpet-shaped corona
of deeper yellow, in early spring.

Narcissus
'Hawera' A.G.M. (Div. 5)
(Amaryllidaceae)

Common name: Daffodil
Height: 7in (18cm)
Spread: 3in (8cm)
Aspect: Sun or half shade
Soil: Well-drained, acidic,
humus-rich, fertile
Hardiness: Zone 4
Propagation: Offsets, in
summer or autumn

A Triandrus hybrid with many flowers on
each stem. Perianth segments reflexed,
canary yellow; corona a shallow cup of
paler yellow. Flowers in late spring.

Narcissus
'Ice Follies' A.G.M. (Div. 2)
(Amaryllidaceae)

Common name: Daffodil
Height: 16in (40cm)
Spread: 6in (16cm)
Aspect: Sun or half shade
Soil: Well-drained, fertile,
humus-rich
Hardiness: Zone 6
Propagation: Offsets, in
summer or autumn

A prolific daffodil, with large, cream
perianth segments and a wide, frilly-edged,
cup-shaped corona, lemon fading to almost
white, in midspring.

DIVISIONS OF NARCISSUS by the American Daffodil Society

1) Trumpet

2) Large-cupped

3) Small-cupped

4) Double

5) Triandrus

6) Cyclamineus

7) Jonquilla

8) Tazetta

9) Poeticus

10) Species, wild forms, and hybrids

11) Miscellaneous

Each daffodil illustrated will have a
division number.

Narcissus
'Jack Snipe' A.G.M. (Div. 6)
(Amaryllidaceae)

Common name: Daffodil
Height: 8in (20cm)
Spread: 3in (8cm)
Aspect: Sun or half shade
Soil: Well-drained, acidic,
humus-rich
Hardiness: Zone 6
Propagation: Offsets, in
summer or autumn

A robust, hybrid, Cyclamineus daffodil.
Flowers with reflexed, white perianth
segments and a yellow, trumpet-shaped
corona, in early to midspring.

Narcissus
'Jetfire' A.G.M. (Div. 6)
(Amaryllidacae)

Common name: Daffodil
Height: 8in (20cm)
Spread: 6in (15cm)
Aspect: Sun or half shade
Soil: Well-drained, acidic,
humus-rich, fertile
Hardiness: Zone 6
Propagation: Offsets, in
summer or autumn

A robust, hybrid, Cyclamineus daffodil.
Flowers with reflexed, golden-yellow
perianth and a long, orange, trumpet-
shaped corona in early spring.

Narcissus jonquilla
A.G.M. (Div. 10)
(Amaryllidaceae)

Common name: Jonquil
Height: 12in (30cm)
Spread: 3in (8cm)
Aspect: Sun or half shade
Soil: Well-drained, acidic,
humus-rich, fertile
Hardiness: Zone 4
Propagation: Seed, when ripe;
offsets, in summer or autumn

A species from Spain. Leaves narrow, erect
to spreading, midgreen. Flowers strongly
scented, yellow; perianth segments pointed,
corona a small, flat cup, in late spring.

Daffodils can range from robust, yellow trumpets to the cool grace of Narcissus triandrus *var.* albus, *the white form of the Angel's-tears daffodil.*

Narcissus
'Minnow' A.G.M. (Div. 8)
(Amaryllidaceae)

Common name: Daffodil
Height: 7in (18cm)
Spread: 3in (8cm)
Aspect: Sun or half shade
Soil: Well-drained, acidic,
humus-rich, fertile
Hardiness: Zone 8
Propagation: Offsets, in
summer or autumn

A robust, hybrid Tazetta daffodil. Flowers
with cream perianth segments fading to
white and a yellow, cup-shaped corona,
in midspring.

Narcissus obvallaris
A.G.M. (Div. 10)
(Amaryllidaceae)

Common name: Daffodil
Height: 12in (30cm)
Spread: 6in (16cm)
Aspect: Sun or half shade
Soil: Well-drained, humus-
rich, fertile
Hardiness: Zone 4
Propagation: Seed, when ripe;
offsets, in summer or autumn

A species found in South Wales and across
W Europe. Leaves erect, glaucous green.
Flowers golden-yellow, with spreading
perianth segments and a long corona.

Narcissus
'Peeping Tom' A.G.M.
(Div. 6) (Amaryllidaceae)

Common name: Daffodil
Height: 8in (20cm)
Spread: 3in (8cm)
Aspect: Sun or half shade
Soil: Well-drained, acidic,
humus-rich, fertile
Hardiness: Zone 6
Propagation: Offsets, in
summer or autumn

A robust, hybrid, Cyclamineus daffodil.
Flowers yellow, with strongly reflexed
perianth segments, and a long, trumpet-
shaped corona, in midspring.

Narcissus
'Pipit' (Div. 7)
(Amaryllidaceae)

Common name: Daffodil
Height: 10in (25cm)
Spread: 3in (8cm)
Aspect: Sun or half shade
Soil: Well-drained, acidic,
humus-rich, fertile
Hardiness: Zone 4
Propagation: Offsets, in
summer or autumn

A perfumed, hybrid, Jonquilla daffodil.
Flowers with recurved, lemon perianth
segments and a yellow, cup-shaped corona,
in mid- to late spring.

Narcissus
'Rippling Waters' A.G.M.
(Div. 5) (Amaryllidaceae)

Common name: Daffodil
Height: 8in (20cm)
Spread: 3in (8cm)
Aspect: Sun or half shade
Soil: Well-drained, acidic,
humus-rich, fertile
Hardiness: Zone 4
Propagation: Offsets, in
summer or autumn

Hybrid with multiflowered stems. Flowers
with large, reflexed, white perianth
segments and a pale yellow, cup-shaped,
shallow corona, in mid- and late spring.

Narcissus
'Rip van Winkle' (Div. 4)
(Amaryllidaceae)

Common name: Daffodil
Height: 6in (15cm)
Spread: 6in (15cm)
Aspect: Sun or half shade
Soil: Well-drained, humus-
rich, fertile
Hardiness: Zone 4
Propagation: Offsets, in
summer or autumn

A hybrid with double flowers. Perianth
segments narrow, pointed, cream. Corona
divided, segments doubled into irregular
central mass, yellow, in early spring

Narcissus
'Salomé' (Div. 2)
(Amaryllidaceae)

Common name: Daffodil
Height: 18in (45cm)
Spread: 6in (15cm)
Aspect: Sun or half shade
Soil: Well-drained, humus-
rich, fertile
Hardiness: Zone 4
Propagation: Offsets, in
summer or autumn

Large-cupped, hybrid daffodil. Flowers
with pale cream perianth segments and a
large, peach, cup-shaped, almost trumpet-
shaped corona, in midspring.

Narcissus
'Sundial' (Div. 7)
(Amaryllidaceae)

Common name: Daffodil
Height: 8in (20cm)
Spread: 3in (8cm)
Aspect: Sun or half shade
Soil: Well-drained, acidic,
humus-rich, fertile
Hardiness: Zone 4
Propagation: Offsets, in
summer or autumn

A small, hybrid Jonquilla daffodil. Flowers
with perianth segments of cream, and a
small, golden-yellow, cup-shaped corona,
in midspring.

Narcissus
'Tête-à-tête' A.G.M.
(Div. 11) (Amaryllidaceae)

Common name: Daffodil
Height: 6in (15cm)
Spread: 6in (15cm)
Aspect: Sun or half shade
Soil: Well-drained, humus-
rich, fertile
Hardiness: Zone 4
Propagation: Offsets, in
summer or autumn

A vigorous, Miscellaneous section daffodil.
Flowers with golden-yellow, reflexed
perianth segments and a yellow, cup-
shaped corona, in early spring.

Narcissus
'Thalia' (Div. 5)
(Amaryllidaceae)

Common name: Daffodil
Height: 14in (35cm)
Spread: 3in (8cm)
Aspect: Sun or half shade
Soil: Well-drained, acidic,
humus-rich, fertile
Hardiness: Zone 4
Propagation: Offsets, in
summer or autumn

A Triandrus daffodil. Flowers milk-white,
in pairs, with twisted, reflexed, narrow
perianth segments and an open, cup-
shaped corona, in midspring.

Nectaroscordum siculum
(Alliaceae/Liliaceae)

Common names: None
Height: 5ft (1.5m)
Spread: 4in (10cm)
Aspect: Sun or half shade
Soil: Well-drained, fertile
Hardiness: Zone 6
Propagation: Seed, in autumn
or spring; offsets, in summer

A vigorous, bulbous plant from Italy and
France. Leaves basal, linear, keeled, midgreen. Flowers in umbels of up to 30, open,
pendulous, plum-colored bells, in summer.

Nemesia denticulata
(Scrophulariaceae)

Common names: None
Height: 16in (40cm)
Spread: 8in (20cm)
Aspect: Sun
Soil: Moist, well-drained,
acidic, fertile
Hardiness: Zone 8
Propagation: Seed in warmth
in spring or autumn

A neat, compact, mound-forming perennial
from South Africa. Leaves lance-shaped,
toothed. Flowers large, flattish, lilac, from
spring to autumn.

Nepeta govaniana
(Labiatae/Lamiaceae)

Common name: Catmint
Height: 36in (90cm)
Spread: 24in (60cm)
Aspect: Sun or half shade
Soil: Well-drained
Hardiness: Zone 5
Propagation: Division, in
spring or autumn; seed, in
autumn

A clump-forming Himalayan plant. Leaves
aromatic, ovate, hairy, pointed, scalloped,
midgreen. Flowers in panicles, pale yellow,
from midsummer to early autumn.

Nepeta sibirica
(Labiatae/Lamiceae)

Common names: Catmint;
catnip
Height: 36in (90cm)
Spread: 18in (45cm)
Aspect: Sun
Soil: Well-drained
Hardiness: Zone 3
Propagation: Division, in
spring or autumn; seed, in
autumn

Species from Russia and Asia. Leaves
aromatic, lance-shaped, toothed, dark
green. Flowers in whorled cymes, blue,
in mid- and late summer.

Nepeta subsessilis
(Labiatae/Lamiaceae)

Common names: Catmints;
catnip
Height: 36in (90cm)
Spread: 12in (30cm)
Aspect: Sun
Soil: Well-drained
Hardiness: Zone 7
Propagation: Division, in
spring or autumn; seed, in
autumn

A clump-forming perennial from Japan.
Leaves aromatic, ovate, toothed, dark
green. Flowers in upright, whorled cymes,
from midsummer to early autumn.

Nerine bowdenii
A.G.M.
(Amaryllidaceae)

Common name: Cape Colony
nerine
Height: 18in (45cm)
Spread: 3in (8cm)
Aspect: Sun
Soil: Well-drained
Hardiness: Zone 8
Propagation: Seed, in warmth
when ripe; division, after
flowering

A bulbous perennial from Africa. Leaves
broad straps midgreen. Flowers in open
umbels of up to 7, perfumed, pink funnels
with recurved tepals, in late autumn.

Nierembergia repens
(Solanaceae)

Common name: White
cupflower
Height: 2in (5cm)
Spread: 18in (45cm)
Aspect: Sun
Soil: Moist, well-drained
Hardiness: Zone 8
Propagation: Seed or division,
both in spring

A prostrate perennial from the Andes.
Leaves spoon-shaped, bright green.
Flowers open, upward-facing cups, white,
over long periods in summer.

Nomocharis pardanthina
(Liliaceae)

Common names: None
Height: 36in (90cm)
Spread: 4in (10cm)
Aspect: Half shade, or sun in
cool areas
Soil: Moist in summer, acidic,
humus-rich
Hardiness: Zone 7
Propagation: Seed, in warmth
in autumn or spring

A woodlander from China. Leaves lance-
shaped, midgreen. Flowers in racemes of
up to 6, nodding, saucer-shaped, pink,
spotted purple, in early summer.

Nymphaea alba
(Nymphaeaceae)

Common name: European
white water-lily
Height: Surface
Spread: 5ft (1.5m)
Aspect: Sun
Soil: Undisturbed water
Hardiness: Zone 5
Propagation: Seed, covered
by an inch of water, in
warmth when ripe

A rhizomatous, aquatic perennial from
Eurasia and North Africa. Leaves round,
deep green. Flowers perfumed, star-shaped,
yellow-centered, in summer.

Nymphaea
'James Brydon' A.G.M.
(Nymphaeaceae)

Common name: Water-lily
Height: Surface
Spread: 4ft (1.2m)
Aspect: Sun
Soil: Still water
Hardiness: Zone 4
Propagation: Division of
rhizomes or separated offsets,
both in summer

A rhizomatous, hybrid, aquatic perennial.
Leaves rounded, bronze-green. Flowers
cup-shaped, vivid rose-red with yellow
stamens, in summer.

Nymphoides peltata
(Menyanthaceae)

Common name: Floating-
heart
Height: 3in (8cm)
Spread: Indefinite
Aspect: Sun
Soil: Still water
Hardiness: Zone 6
Propagation: Separated
runners, in summer

A rhizomatous, herbaceous perennial from
Eurasia. Leaves ovate, mottled, green.
Flowers on long stems, yellow, funnel-
shaped, in summer.

OENOTHERA (Onagraceae)
Evening-primrose • Sundrops

A genus of some 125 species of annuals, biennials, and
perennials from North America in particular, but also
distributed in Central and South America. The perennial
members of the genus are mostly short-lived. Their natural
habitats are often on mountainsides, and in the garden they
prefer a position in sun in a well-drained soil; small types
such as *Oenothera macrocarpa* are suitable for a rock garden.
Some evening-primroses are taprooted, and resent
disturbance, so these should be sited carefully when they are
first planted. The individual flowers are often short-lived, but
they are borne in succession over a long period throughout
the summer. The flowers are cup- or saucer-shaped,
sometimes trumpet-shaped, white, yellow, or pink, and often
perfumed. They are borne either singly in the axils or in
terminal racemes. All are attractive to bees. The taller forms
of evening-primrose require staking. Many of them seed
around to an unacceptable degree; deadheading to prevent
self-seeding is not easy in this genus, since ripened seed pods
and unopened flower buds are found on the same stem, so
naturalizing them in a wild garden may be a preferred
option for these types.

Oenothera deltoides
(Onagraceae)

Common name: Desert
evening-primrose
Height: 12in (30cm)
Spread: 8in (20cm)
Aspect: Sun
Soil: Sharply drained
Hardiness: Zone 9
Propagation: Seed, in early
spring

A perennial from Arizona; Baja California,
and Mexico. Leaves ovate, midgreen.
Flowers solitary, white bowls, on erect and
decumbent stems, in summer.

Oenothera fruticosa
(Onagraceae)

Common name: Common
sundrops
Height: 3ft (90cm)
Spread: 1ft (30cm)
Aspect: Sun
Soil: Sharply drained, fertile
Hardiness: Zone 4
Propagation: Seed, in early
spring

A short-lived species from North America.
Leaves ovate, toothed, midgreen. Flowers
in racemes of up to 10, deep yellow cups,
from late spring to late summer.

Oenothera fruticosa
'Fyrverkeri' A.G.M.
(Onagraceae)

Common name: Common
sundrops
Height: 3ft (90cm)
Spread: 1ft (30cm)
Aspect: Sun
Soil: Sharply drained, fertile
Hardiness: Zone 4
Propagation: Division, in
early spring

A selected form of the species, with purple-
brown-flushed leaves, and red buds
opening to chrome-yellow flowers, from
late spring for many weeks.

Oenothera macrocarpa
A.G.M.
(Onagraceae)

Common name: Ozark
sundrops
Height: 6in (15cm)
Spread: 18in (45cm)
Aspect: Sun
Soil: Sharply drained
Hardiness: Zone 5
Propagation: Seed, in early
spring

A robust perennial from the southern
U.S.A. Leaves lance-shaped, toothed, midgreen. Flowers solitary, golden cups, over a
long period from spring to autumn.

Oenothera nuttallii
(Onagraceae)

Common name: Suncrops
Height: 3ft (90cm)
Spread: 2ft (60cm)
Aspect: Sun
Soil: Sharply drained
Hardiness: Zone 5
Propagation: Seed, in early
spring

North American species. Leaves oblong,
dull green. Flowers on straggly stems, large,
creamy-white, in summer. Long-lived. Very
late to reappear, so mark position.

Oenothera rosea
(Onagraceae)

Common name: Rose
sundrops
Height: 2ft (60cm)
Spread: 1ft (30cm)
Aspect: Sun
Soil: Sharply drained
Hardiness: Zone 6
Propagation: Seed, in early
spring

A species from the Americas. Leaves
oblong, midgreen. Flowers small, pink,
diurnal cups. Not to be confused with
O. speciosa 'Rosea', a superior plant.

Oenothera speciosa
(Onagraceae)

Common name: Showy
evening-primrose
Height: 1ft (30cm)
Spread: 1ft (30cm)
Aspect: Sun
Soil: Sharply drained
Hardiness: Zone 5
Propagation: Seed, in early
spring

Species from the southwest U.S.A. Leaves
basal, in rosettes, oblong, midgreen.
Flowers solitary, single white cups, aging
to pink, over a long period in summer.

Oenothera speciosa
'Rosea'
(Onagraceae)

Common name: Showy
evening-primrose
Height: 1ft (30cm)
Spread: 1ft (30cm)
Aspect: Sun
Soil: Sharply drained
Hardiness: Zone 5
Propagation: Seed, in early
spring

A form of the species with yellow-centered
flowers that have white petals suffused
pink towards the periphery. Long-
flowering, but can be invasive.

Oenothera speciosa
'Siskiyou'
(Onagraceae)

Common name: Showy
evening-primrose
Height: 1ft (30cm)
Spread: 1ft (30cm)
Aspect: Sun
Soil: Sharply drained
Hardiness: Zone 5
Propagation: Division, in
early spring

A selected form of the species with yellow-
centered flowers that have white petals
suffused pink around the perimeter.
Can be invasive.

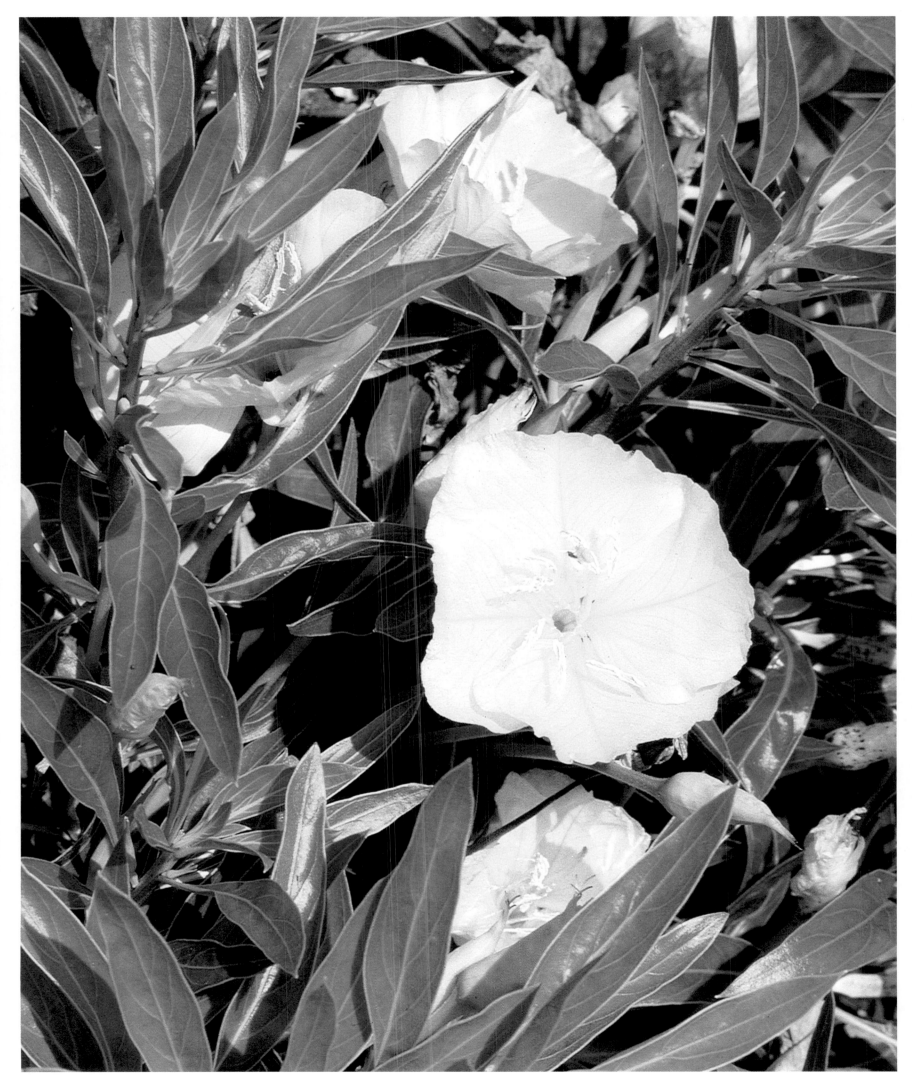

Oenothera macrocarpa *makes a long-flowering candidate for a scree bed similar to its natural habitat.*

Oenothera stubbei
(Onagraceae)

Common name: Evening-primrose
Height: 4ft (1.2m)
Spread: 1ft (30cm)
Aspect: Sun
Soil: Sharply drained
Hardiness: Zone 8
Propagation: Seed, in early spring

A perennial from Mexico. Leaves in a basal rosette, and stem, elliptic to lance-shaped, midgreen. Flowers yellow aging to orange, then red, in summer.

Olsynium douglasii album
(Iridaceae)

Common names: None
Height: 12in (30cm)
Spread: 4in (10cm)
Aspect: Half shade
Soil: Moist, humus-rich, fertile
Hardiness: Zone 9
Propagation: Seed, in autumn

A tender, clump-forming perennial from North America. Leaves linear, gray-green. Flowers nodding, bell-shaped, in spathes of up to 4, white, in early spring.

Omphalodes cappadocica
'Cherry Ingram' A.G.M.
(Boraginaceae)

Common name: Navel-seed
Height: 1ft (30cm)
Spread: 1ft (30cm)
Aspect: Half shade
Soil: Moist, humus-rich, fertile
Hardiness: Zone 6
Propagation: Division, in early spring

An evergreen, clump-forming, woodland ground cover. Leaves basal, ovate, veined, pointed, dull green. Flowers deep blue, in racemes, in spring, intermittently thereafter.

Omphalodes cappadocica
'Starry Eyes'
(Boraginaceae)

Common name: Navel-seed
Height: 12in (30cm)
Spread: 18in (45cm)
Aspect: Half shade
Soil: Moist, humus-rich, fertile
Hardiness: Zone 6
Propagation: Division, in early spring

Evergreen woodland ground cover. Leaves ovate, green. Flowers pale blue with a central white stripe on each petal, in loose racemes in spring, intermittently thereafter.

Onoclea sensibilis
A.G.M.
(Aspidiaceae)

Common name: Sensitive fern
Height: 2ft (60cm)
Spread: Indefinite
Aspect: Half shade
Soil: Moist, acidic, fertile, humus-rich
Hardiness: Zone 4
Propagation: Spores, in warmth when ripe; division, in spring

A deciduous fern from North America and Asia. Spring fronds sterile, pinnate, lobes lance-shaped, pale green. Autumn fronds fertile, erect, 2-pinnate; pinnate black lobes.

Onosma alborosea
(Boraginaceae)

Common names: None
Height: 10in (25cm)
Spread: 10in (25cm)
Aspect: Sun
Soil: Dry, sharply drained
Hardiness: Zone 7
Propagation: Seed in autumn

Clump-forming evergreen from Asia. Leaves obovate, white-hairy, gray-green. Flowers in terminal, congested cymes, narrow, white, tubular, tips turning pink with age.

Ophiopogon planiscapus
'Nigrescens' A.G.M.
(Convallariaceae/Liliaceae)

Common name: Lily-turf
Height: 8in (20cm)
Spread: 12in (30cm)
Aspect: Sun or half shade
Soil: Acidic, humus-rich, fertile
Hardiness: Zone 6
Propagation: Seed, when ripe; division, in spring

A stoloniferous, evergreen ground cover from Japan. Leaves near-black straps. Flowers in racemes, pinkish-white, in summer, followed by black berries.

Orchis mascula
(Orchidaceae)

Common name: Early purple orchid
Height: 12in (30cm)
Spread: 6in (15cm)
Aspect: Half shade
Soil: Sharply drained, humus-rich, fertile
Hardiness: Zone 5
Propagation: Offsets, in spring

A terrestrial orchid from Europe. Leaves long, pointed, purple-spotted, midgreen. Flowers in erect racemes, pale or dark purple, in spring and summer.

Origanum amanum
A.G.M.
(Labiatae/Lamiaceae)

Common names: Marjoram;
oregano
Height: 8in (20cm)
Spread: 12in (30cm)
Aspect: Sun
Soil: Well-drained, alkaline,
fertile
Hardiness: Zone 8
Propagation: Seed, division or
basal cuttings, all in spring

Evergreen subshrub from Turkey. Leaves
aromatic, ovate, bright green. Flowers in
terminal whorls, pink surrounded by green
bracts, in summer and autumn.

Origanum
'Buckland'
(Labiatae/Laamiaceae)

Common names: Marjoram;
oregano
Height: 8in (20cm)
Spread: 6in (15cm)
Aspect: Sun
Soil: Well-drained, alkaline,
fertile
Hardiness: Zone 7
Propagation: Division or
basal cuttings, both in spring

A hybrid marjoram. Leaves aromatic,
rounded, hairy, gray-green. Flowers in
whorls, pink, tubular, surrounded by pink
bracts, in summer and autumn.

Origanum laevigatum
A.G.M.
(Labiatae/Lamiaceae)

Common names: Marjoram;
oregano
Height: 24in (60cm)
Spread: 18in (45cm)
Aspect: Sun
Soil: Well-drained, alkaline,
fertile
Hardiness: Zone 3
Propagation: Seed, division or
basal cuttings, all in spring

A perennial from Turkey and Cyprus.
Leaves aromatic, ovate, dark green.
Flowers in whorls, tubular, purple-pink,
from spring to autumn.

Origanum laevigatum
'Herrenhausen' A.G.M.
(Labiatae/Lamiaceae)

Common names: Marjoram;
oregano
Height: 18in (45cm)
Spread: 18in (45cm)
Aspect: Sun
Soil: Well-drained, alkaline,
fertile
Hardiness: Zone 8
Propagation: Division or
basal cuttings, both in spring

A hybrid evergreen perennial. Leaves
aromatic, ovate, purple-green. Flowers in
whorls, denser form than the species, deep
pink, from spring to autumn.

Origanum vulgare
'Aureum' A.G.M.
(Labiatae/Lamiaceae)

Common name: Wild
marjoram
Height: 2ft (60cm)
Spread: 1ft (30cm)
Aspect: Sun
Soil: Well-drained, alkaline,
fertile
Hardiness: Zone 5
Propagation: Division or
basal cuttings, both in spring

A rhizomatous perennial from Europe.
Leaves aromatic, ovate, golden. Flowers in
whorls, tubular, pink, midsummer to early
autumn. Less invasive than the species.

Ornithogalum arabicum
(Hyacinthaceae/Liliaceae)

Common name: Arabian star-
of-Bethlehem
Height: 32in (80cm)
Spread: 4in (10cm)
Aspect: Sun
Soil: Well-drained, fertile
Hardiness: Zone 9
Propagation: Seed, in autumn
or spring; offsets, when
dormant

Bulbous Mediterranean plant. Leaves dark
green, linear, broad, arching. Flowers cup-
shaped, in corymbs of up to 25, perfumed,
white with a black ovary, in early summer.

Ornithogalum narbonense
(Hyacinthaceae/Liliaceae)

Common name: Star-of-
Bethlehem
Height: 36in (90cm)
Spread: 8in (20cm)
Aspect: Sun
Soil: Well-drained, fertile
Hardiness: Zone 7
Propagation: Seed, in autumn
or spring; offsets, when
dormant

A bulbous perennial from Turkey and Iran.
Leaves basal, linear, arching, gray-green.
Flowers starry, white, in narrow, tapering
racemes, in late spring and early summer.

Ornithogalum nutans
A.G.M.
(Hyacinthaceae/Liliaceae)

Common name: Nodding
star-of-Bethlehem
Height: 24in (60cm)
Spread: 2in (5cm)
Aspect: Sun
Soil: Well-drained, fertile
Hardiness: Zone 6
Propagation: Seed, autumn or
spring; offsets, when dormant

Bulbous plant from Eurasia. Leaves semierect, strap-shaped, green with a central
silver stripe. Flowers in one-sided racemes
of up to 20, silver-white funnels, in spring.

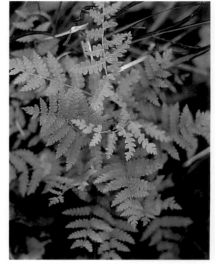

Ornithogalum thyrsoides
(Hyacinthaceae/Liliaceae)

Common name: Cape
chinkerichee
Height: 32in (80cm)
Spread: 4in (10cm)
Aspect: Sun
Soil: Well-drained, fertile
Hardiness: Zone 9
Propagation: Seed, in autumn
or spring; offsets, when
dormant

A bulbous plant from South Africa. Leaves
basal, narrow, lance-shaped, midgreen,
before the many-flowered, dense racemes
of white cups, in spring and early summer.

Ornithogalum umbellatum
(Hyacinthaceae/Liliaceae)

Common name: Star-of-
Bethlehem
Height: 12in (30cm)
Spread: 4in (10cm)
Aspect: Sun
Soil: Well-drained, fertile
Hardiness: Zone 5
Propagation: Seed, in autumn
or spring; offsets, when
dormant

A robust, bulbous perennial from Europe
to the Middle East. Leaves basal, linear,
veined silver, green. Flowers in racemes of
up to 20, starry, white, in early summer.

Orthrosanthus
chimboracensis
(Iridaceae)

Common names: None
Height: 24in (60cm)
Spread: 8in (20cm)
Aspect: Sun
Soil: Well-drained, fertile,
humus-rich
Hardiness: Zone 9
Propagation: Seed, in warmth
in spring; division, in spring

A tender, rhizomatous, evergreen perennial
from Mexico to Peru. Leaves basal, linear,
rough, green. Flowers in loose panicles,
lavender bowls, in summer.

Osmunda cinnamomea
(Osmundaceae)

Common name:
Cinnamon fern
Height: 3ft (90cm)
Spread: 2ft (60cm)
Aspect: Half shade
Soil: Moist, acidic, fertile,
humus-rich
Hardiness: Zone 3
Propagation: Spores, in
summer; division, in autumn or spring

Deciduous fern. Sterile, blue-green, ovate
to lance-shaped, pinnate fronds, segments
pinnatifid, surround erect, narrow, fertile
fronds topped by cinnamon sporangia.

OSTEOSPERMUM (Asteraceae/Compositae)
Veldt daisy

A genus of some 70 species of annuals, perennials, and
evergreen subshrubs from mountainous, forest edge, or
grassland habitats in southern Africa and the Arabian
Peninsula. They are mostly tender or half-hardy, but a few
are reliably hardy, and hybrids are being produced from these
which are also hardy. In frost-prone areas the more tender
types can be treated as annuals. *Osteospermum* have three
features that commend them to the gardener: they have a
very long flowering season, stretching from late spring to
autumn, they are evergreen, and they make excellent ground
cover, so are worth taking some trouble over. Their daisylike
flowerheads have ray florets of pink, white, or yellow, with a
wider range of shades available in the cultivars, and often
contrasting, darker disc florets. They require little more than
a position in full sun (the flowers of many will close in shade
or dull weather) and well-drained soil; a sunny bank is an
ideal situation. Deadheading will improve and prolong
flowering. They make good cut flowers. Regrettably, like
most daisylike flowers, they are highly allergenic, so best
avoided by the allergic gardener. They are prone to downy
mildew in wet areas.

Osteospermum
'Buttermilk' A.G.M.
(Asteraceae/Compositae)

Common name: Veldt daisy
Height: 2ft (60cm)
Spread: 2ft (60cm)
Aspect: Sun
Soil: Well-drained, fertile
Hardiness: Zone 9
Propagation: Softwood
cuttings, in spring; semiripe
cuttings, in summer

Evergreen subshrub. Leaves inverse lance-
shaped, midgreen. Flowers solitary, single,
daisylike, ray florets primrose, disc florets
mauve, from late spring to autumn.

Osteospermum caulescens
syn. O. 'White Pim' A.G.M.
(Asteraceae/Compositae)

Common name: Veldt daisy
Height: 4in (10cm)
Spread: 24in (60cm)
Aspect: Sun
Soil: Well-drained, fertile
Hardiness: Zone 8
Propagation: Seed, in warmth
in spring

Subshrub from South Africa. Leaves inverse
lance-shaped, toothed, midgreen. Flowers
solitary, single, ray florets white, disc
florets blue, from late spring to autumn.

Osteospermum jucundum A.G.M.
(Asteraceae/Compositae)

Common name: Veldt daisy
Height: 20in (50cm)
Spread: 36in (90cm)
Aspect: Sun
Soil: Well-drained, fertile
Hardiness: Zone 7
Propagation: Seed, in warmth in spring

Rhizomatous subshrub. Leaves inverse lance-shaped, grayish-green. Flowers single, solitary, ray florets mauve, disc florets purple, from late spring to autumn.

Osteospermum 'Nairobi Purple'
(Asteraceae/Compositae)

Common name: Veldt daisy
Height: 6in (15cm)
Spread: 36in (90cm)
Aspect: Sun
Soil: Well-drained, fertile
Hardiness: Zone 9
Propagation: Softwood cuttings, in spring; semiripe cuttings, in summer

Tender, evergreen hybrid subshrub. Leaves ovate to spoon-shaped, bright green. Flowers solitary, single, ray florets purple, disc florets black, from late spring to autumn.

Osteospermum 'Silver Sparkler' A.G.M.
(Asteraceae/Compositae)

Common names: Veldt daisy
Height: 18in (45cm)
Spread: 36in (90cm)
Aspect: Sun
Soil: Well-drained, fertile
Hardiness: Zone 8
Propagation: Softwood cuttings, in spring; semiripe cuttings, in summer

Evergreen subshrub. Leaves inverse lance-shaped, gray-green, edged white. Flowers solitary, single, ray florets steely-white, disc florets brown, late spring to autumn.

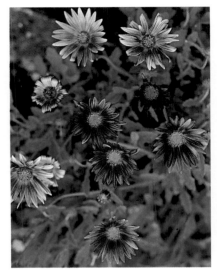

Osteospermum 'Sirius'
(Asteraceae/Compositae)

Common name: Veldt daisy
Height: 1ft (30cm)
Spread: 1ft (30cm)
Aspect: Sun
Soil: Well-drained, fertile
Hardiness: Zone 8
Propagation: Softwood cuttings, in spring; semiripe cuttings, in summer

Hybrid, evergreen subshrub. Leaves ovate to spoon-shaped, dull green. Flowers single, solitary, ray florets cerise, aging to pink, disc florets green, late spring to autumn.

Osteospermum 'Sunny Alex'
(Asteraceae/Compositae)

Common name: Veldt daisy
Height: 1ft (30cm)
Spread: 1ft (30cm)
Aspect: Sun
Soil: Well-drained, fertile
Hardiness: Zone 8
Propagation: Softwood cuttings, in spring; semiripe cuttings, in summer

Evergreen subshrub. Leaves inverse lance-shaped, toothed, dull green. Flowers single, solitary, ray florets bright yellow, disc florets orange, from late spring to autumn.

Ostrowskia magnifica
(Campanulaceae)

Common names: None
Height: 5ft (1.5m)
Spread: 18in (45cm)
Aspect: Sun
Soil: Moist, well-drained, deep, fertile
Hardiness: Zone 7
Propagation: Seed, when ripe

Leaves in whorls, ovate, toothed. Flowers in racemes, outward-facing, milky-blue or white, open bells, in early and midsummer. Taproot is easily damaged; avoid moving it.

Othonna cheirifolia
(Asteraceae/Compositae)

Common names: None
Height: 12in (30cm)
Spread: 18in (45cm)
Aspect: Sun
Soil: Sharply drained, fertile
Hardiness: Zone 8
Propagation: Seed, in warmth in spring; basal cuttings, in summer

An evergreen, spreading subshrub from North Africa. Leaves spoon-shaped, fleshy, gray-green. Flowers in corymbs, daisylike, yellow, in late autumn and early winter.

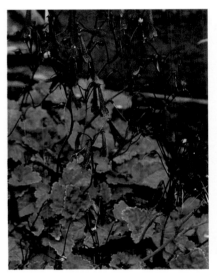

Ourisia coccinea
(Scrophulariaceae)

Common names: None
Height: 8in (20cm)
Spread: 16in (40cm)
Aspect: Half shade
Soil: Moist, humus-rich, fertile
Hardiness: Zone 7
Propagation: Seed, when ripe or in spring

Mat-forming evergreen from the Andes. Leaves in rosettes, oblong, veined, toothed, pale green. Flowers tubular, 2-lipped, pendent, scarlet, in racemes, all summer.

Oxalis acetosella
(Oxalidaceae)

Common names: Shamrock; sorrel
Height: 2in (5cm)
Spread: Indefinite
Aspect: Full or half shade
Soil: Moist, humus-rich, fertile
Hardiness: Zone 3
Propagation: Division, in spring

Hardy, highly invasive woodland plant. Leaves 3-lobed, leaflets inverse heart-shaped, pale green. Flowers solitary, dark-veined pink cups, in spring.

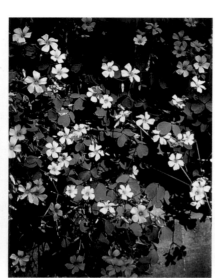

Oxalis hedysarioides
(Oxalidaceae)

Common names: Shamrock; sorrel
Height: 36in (1m)
Spread: 18in (45cm)
Aspect: Full or half shade
Soil: Sharply drained, fertile
Hardiness: Zone 9
Propagation: Seed, in warmth in late winter to spring

A tender subshrub from Central America. Leaves 3-lobed, leaflets ovate, light green. Flowers in axillary cymes, funnel-shaped, yellow, in summer.

Oxalis pes-caprae
(Oxalidaceae)

Common name: Buttercup oxalis
Height: 5in (12cm)
Spread: Indefinite
Aspect: Shade
Soil: Moist, humus-rich
Hardiness: Zone 9
Propagation: Seed, in warmth in late winter to spring

Rampant, bulbous plant. Leaves 3-lobed, leaflets inverse heart-shaped, bright green. Flowers in umbellate cymes, solitary, deep golden-yellow, in spring and early summer.

Oxalis tetraphylla
'Iron Cross'
(Oxalidaceae)

Common name: Four-leaf oxalis
Height: 6in (15cm)
Spread: 6in (15cm)
Aspect: Full or half shade
Soil: Moist, humus-rich, fertile
Hardiness: Zone 8
Propagation: Seed or offsets, both in spring

Invasive, bulbous plant. Leaves 4-lobed, each leaflet inversely triangular, midgreen, with a purple basal band. Flowers in cymes of up to 12, funnel-shaped, pink, in summer.

Pachyphragma macrophyllum
(Brassicaceae/Cruciferae)

Common names: None
Height: 16in (40cm)
Spread: 90cm (36in)
Aspect: Half shade
Soil: Humus-rich, fertile
Hardiness: Zone 7
Propagation: Seed, in autumn; division, in spring

Woodland plant. Leaves large, basal, rounded, scalloped, some overwintering. Flowers in flat corymbs, cruciform, white, malodorous, in spring, followed by berries.

PAEONIA (Paeoniaceae)
Peony

A genus of some 30 or so species from rocky scrubland and meadows across Eurasia and western North America. There are two types of plant in the genus: the herbaceous, tuberous perennials, and the shrubs that are known as tree peonies; only one of the latter will be included here. The perennial peonies are long-lived and easy to grow in sun or part-shade, and in any soil provided that it is not waterlogged. They do not take kindly to root disturbance, so site them carefully when first planting them; they can become large in time, so leave them plenty of room. Most peonies flower in early summer. The flowers are large, often brightly colored, showy, and sometimes perfumed; they may be single, semi-double, double, or anemone-form, and are followed by attractive, lobed seed pods containing red or black seeds. The foliage is dissected and handsome. Some species are invasive, notably *P. mascula* subsp. *arietiana* (Zone 8), *P. mollis* (Zone 6), *P. officinalis*, *P. peregrina* (Zone 8), and *P. tenuifolia*, but the rest are well-behaved. They may require staking in exposed areas, especially those with large and double flowers. They are low-allergen, and suit the allergic gardener. All parts of the plants are poisonous, however.

Paeonia lactiflora
'Bowl of Beauty' A.G.M.
(Paeoniaceae)

Common name: Chinese peony
Height: 3ft (1m)
Spread: 3ft (1m)
Aspect: Sun or half shade
Soil: Moist, well-drained, fertile, humus-rich
Hardiness: Zone 6
Propagation: Division, in spring or autumn

A herbaceous perennial. Leaves 2-ternate, lobes obovate, midgreen. Flowers large, anemone-form, carmine red with a cream center, in early summer.

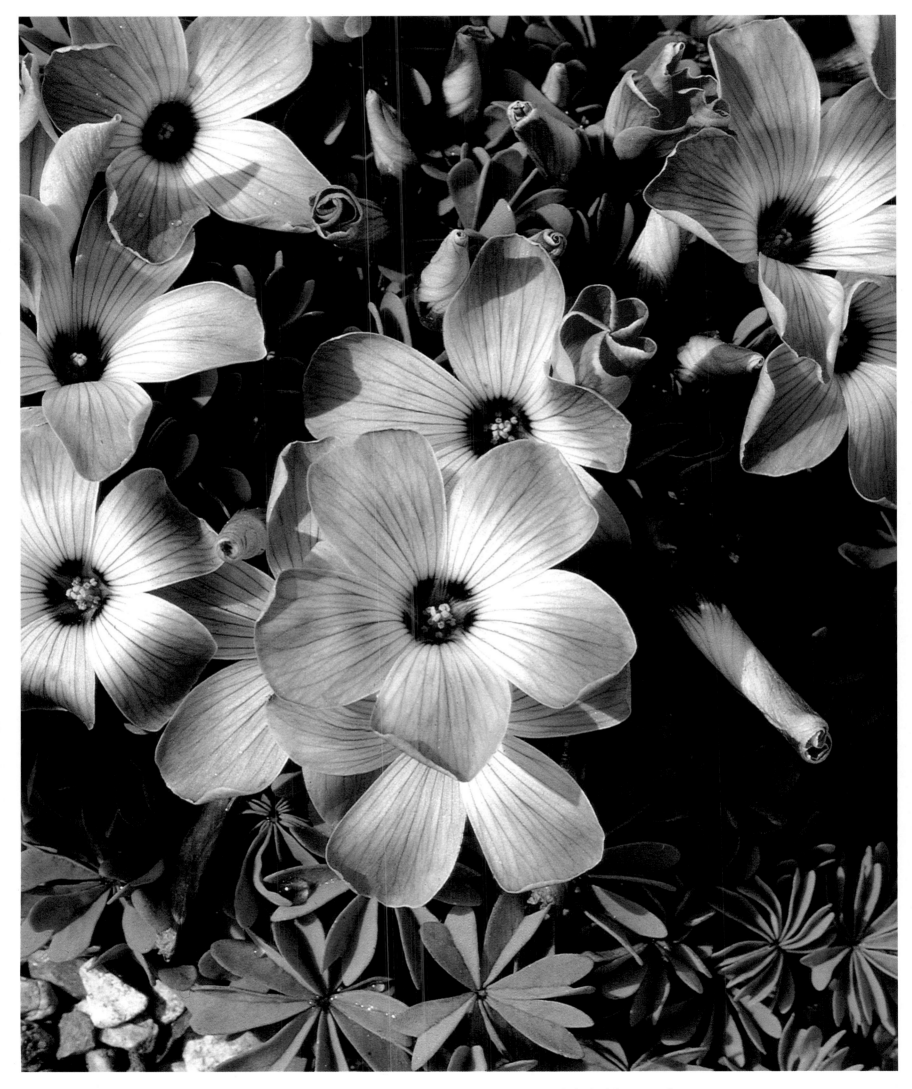

The clump-forming Oxalis adenophylla *covers itself with purplish-pink flushed flowers in late spring.*

Paeonia broteroi
(Paeoniaceae)

Common name: Peony
Height: 20in (50cm)
Spread: 20in (50cm)
Aspect: Sun or half shade
Soil: Moist, well-drained,
fertile, humus-rich
Hardiness: Zone 7
Propagation: Seed, in autumn
to early winter

A herbaceous perennial from Spain and
Portugal. Leaves divided, glossy, midgreen. Flowers single, pink cups, in late
spring and early summer.

Paeonia delavayi
A.G.M.
(Paeoniaceae)

Common name: Tree peony
Height: 6ft (2m)
Spread: 4ft (1.2m)
Aspect: Sun or half shade
Soil: Moist, well-drained,
fertile, humus-rich
Hardiness: Zone 6
Propagation: Seed, in autumn
or spring; semiripe cuttings,
in summer

A robust tree peony from China. Leaves
2-pinnate, lobes deeply cut, dark green.
Flowers single, cup-shaped, rich, dark red,
in early summer.

Paeonia lactiflora
'Lady Alexandra Duff'
A.G.M. (Paeoniaceae)

Common name: Chinese
peony
Height: 28in (70cm)
Spread: 28in (70cm)
Aspect: Sun or half shade
Soil: Moist, well-drained,
fertile, humus-rich
Hardiness: Zone 6
Propagation: Division, in
spring or autumn

One of many cultivars of this species.
Leaves divided, leaflets elliptic to lance-
shaped. Flowers double, pale pink, in
midsummer.

Paeonia mascula
subsp. *arietina*
(Paeoniaceae)

Common name: Peony
Height: 3ft (1m)
Spread: 3ft (1m)
Aspect: Sun or half shade
Soil: Moist, well-drained,
fertile, humus-rich
Hardiness: Zone 8
Propagation: Seed in autumn
or winter; division, in spring
or autumn

A herbaceous perennial. Leaves divided
into 9 ovate leaflets, bluish-green. Flowers
single, rose-pink cups with yellow stamens,
in early summer.

Paeonia mascula
subsp. *russii*
(Paeoniaceae)

Common name: Peony
Height: 18in (45cm)
Spread: 18in (45cm)
Aspect: Sun or half shade
Soil: Moist, well-drained,
fertile, humus-rich
Hardiness: Zone 8
Propagation: Seed, in autumn
or winter; division, in spring
or autumn

A very compact form of the species, found
in Greece, Corsica, Sicily, and Sardinia.
Leaves tinged purple. Flowers single, rose-
pink with yellow stamens, in early summer.

Paeonia mascula
subsp. *triternata*
(Paeoniaceae)

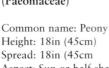

Common name: Peony
Height: 18in (45cm)
Spread: 18in (45cm
Aspect: Sun or half shade
Soil: Moist, well-drained,
fertile, humus-rich
Hardiness: Zone 8
Propagation: Seed, in autumn
or winter; division, in spring
or autumn

A form of the species from Asia Minor and
the Balkans. Flowers single, pink; the
bright red seed heads found in this and
many other peonies are shown here.

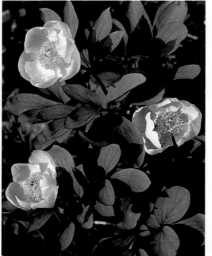

Paeonia mlokosewitschii
A.G.M.
(Paeoniaceae)

Common name: Peony
Height: 3ft (90cm)
Spread: 3ft (90cm)
Aspect: Sun or half shade
Soil: Moist, well-drained,
fertile, humus-rich
Hardiness: Zone 6
Propagation: Seed, in autumn
or early winter; division, in
spring or autumn

Leaves divided into 9 ovate leaflets, bluish-
green. Flowers short-lived, single, bowl-
shaped, petals broad, lemon-yellow, in late
spring and early summer.

Paeonia obovata
var. *alba* A.G.M.
(Paeoniaceae)

Common name: Peony
Height: 28in (70cm)
Spread: 28in (70cm)
Aspect: Sun or half shade
Soil: Moist, well-drained,
fertile, humus-rich
Hardiness: Zone 7
Propagation: Seed, in autumn
or early winter; division, in
spring or autumn

Peony from China. Leaves divided into
9 leaflets, with elliptic lobes, dark green.
Flowers single, cup-shaped, white, with
yellow anthers and purple filaments.

Paeonia officinalis
(Paeoniaceae)

Common name: Common peony
Height: 28in (70cm)
Spread: 28in (70cm)
Aspect: Sun or half shade
Soil: Moist, well-drained, humus-rich, fertile
Hardiness: Zone 8
Propagation: Seed, in autumn or early winter; division, in spring or autumn

A species from Europe. Leaves divided into 9 leaflets, with oblong lobes, dark green. Flowers single, cup-shaped, rose-pink with yellow stamens, in early to midsummer.

Paeonia officinalis
'Anemoniflora Rosea'
A.G.M. (Paeoniaceae)

Common name: Anemone-flowered peony
Height: 28in (70cm)
Spread: 28in (70cm)
Aspect: Sun or half shade
Soil: Moist, well-drained, humus-rich, fertile
Hardiness: Zone 8
Propagation: Seed, in autumn or early winter; division, in spring or autumn

A form of the European common peony with anemone-centered flowers of pale pink. Leaves dark green, divided into 9 leaflets with oblong lobes.

Paeonia tenuifolia
(Paeoniaceae)

Common name: Fern-leaved peony
Height: 28in (70cm)
Spread: 28in (70cm)
Aspect: Sun or half shade
Soil: Moist, well-drained, humus-rich, fertile
Hardiness: Zone 8
Propagation: Seed, in autumn or early winter; division, in spring or autumn

Leaves many-segmented, segments linear, dark green. Flowers single, cup-shaped, deep red with yellow stamens, late spring to early summer. From Europe and Russia.

Paeonia lactiflora
'White Wings'
(Paeoniaceae)

Common name: Chinese peony
Height: 35in (85cm)
Spread: 35in (85cm)
Aspect: Sun or half shade
Soil: Moist, well-drained, humus-rich, fertile
Hardiness: Zone 7
Propagation: Seed, in autumn or early winter; division, in spring or autumn

A hardy perennial cultivar. Leaves dark, glossy green. Flowers single, cup-shaped, perfumed, white, with ruffled petals, in early summer.

PAPAVER (Papaveraceae)
Poppy

A genus of some 70 species of annuals, biennials, and perennials from many parts of the world, including Europe, Asia, South Africa, North America, Australia, and some subarctic areas. The perennial members of the genus are easy to grow. All are sun-lovers, and will grow well so long as they are in sun and their soil is not waterlogged; they do best in poor but deeply cultivated, well-drained soil, or even sharply drained in the case of the *Papaver alpinum* and its forms. Poppies are taprooted and do not transplant well, so should be sited carefully when they are first planted. The flowers are short-lived but beautiful, being brightly colored and silky, and are followed by decorative, distinctively shaped "pepper-pot" seed capsules. These are best removed if abundant self-seeding is not desired, but if seed is wanted they must ripen on the plant. The flowers are low-allergen. They are good for arrangements, but they need to be picked at night before the bud opens, and the bottom of the stem dipped in very hot water, kept cool overnight, then arranged in the morning. The seed pods are also good, either fresh or dried. The only drawbacks of poppies are that they often need to be staked, and they are prone to downy mildew.

Papaver anomalum album
(Papaveraceae)

Common names: None
Height: 16in (40cm)
Spread: 5in (15cm)
Aspect: Sun
Soil: Well-drained, deep, fertile
Hardiness: Zone 7
Propagation: Seed, in spring

A perennial poppy from China. Leaves basal, 2-pinnatisect, glabrous, blue-green. Flowers solitary, single, white (yellow in type) with yellow centers, in late spring.

Papaver atlanticum
(Papaveraceae)

Common names: None
Height: 12in (30cm)
Spread: 6in (15cm)
Aspect: Sun
Soil: Well-drained, deep, fertile
Hardiness: Zone 6
Propagation: Seed, in spring

A short-lived, clump-forming perennial from Morocco. Leaves oblong, toothed, midgreen. Flowers solitary, single, orange saucers, in summer.

Papaver nudicaule
(Papaveraceae)

Common name: Iceland
poppy
Height: 12in (30cm)
Spread: 6in (15cm)
Aspect: Sun
Soil: Well-drained, deep,
fertile
Hardiness: Zone 3
Propagation: Seed, in spring

A hardy plant derived from the sub-arctic
P. croceum. Dense tuft of oval, pinnatisect,
hairy, gray-green leaves. Flowers scented, in
all colors, solitary, single bowls, summer.

Papaver fauriei
(Papaveraceae)

Common names: None
Height: 4in (10cm)
Spread: 4in (10cm)
Aspect: Sun
Soil: Well-drained, deep,
fertile
Hardiness: Zone 2
Propagation: Seed, in spring

A hardy, mound-forming, short-lived plant
from Japan and Russia. Leaves pinnate,
lobes lance-shaped, deep-cut, gray-green.
Flowers solitary, single yellow in summer.

Papaver
'Fireball'
(Papaveraceae)

Common names: None
Height: 1ft (30cm)
Spread: Indefinite
Aspect: Sun
Soil: Well-drained, deep,
fertile
Hardiness: Zone 7
Propagation: Seed, in spring

An invasive perennial of uncertain origin.
Leaves lance-shaped, toothed, midgreen.
Flowers semidouble, solitary, scarlet-
orange, from late spring to summer.

Papaver orientale
'Allegro'
(Papaveraceae)

Common name: Oriental
poppy
Height: 36in (90cm)
Spread: 75cm (30in)
Aspect: Sun
Soil: Well-drained
Hardiness: Zone 3
Propagation: Division, in
spring

Spreading, clump-forming cultivar. Leaves
pinnatisect, leaflets lance-shaped, toothed.
Flowers solitary cups, scarlet-orange with
black basal spots, late spring to midsummer.

Papaver orientale
'Beauty of Livermere'
A.G.M. (Papaveraceae)

Common name: Oriental
poppy
Height: 4ft (1.2m)
Spread: 3ft (90cm)
Aspect: Sun
Soil: Well-drained, deep,
fertile
Hardiness: Zone 3
Propagation: Division, in
spring

Clump-forming, spreading cultivar. Leaves
pinnatisect, leaflets lance-shaped, toothed.
Flowers solitary, single cups, scarlet with
black basal marks, spring to midsummer.

Papaver orientale
'Black and White' A.G.M.
(Papaveraceae)

Common name: Oriental
poppy
Height: 3ft (90cm)
Spread: 3ft (90cm)
Aspect: Sun
Soil: Well-drained, deep,
fertile
Hardiness: Zone 3
Propagation: Division, in
spring

Clump-forming cultivar. Leaves pinnatisect,
leaflets lance-shaped, toothed, midgreen.
Flowers solitary, single cups, white with red
or black basal marks, spring to midsummer.

Papaver orientale
'Charming'
(Papaveraceae)

Common name: Oriental
poppy
Height: 3ft (90cm)
Spread: 3ft (90cm)
Aspect: Sun
Soil: Well-drained, deep,
fertile
Hardiness: Zone 3
Propagation: Division, in
spring

Leaves pinnatisect, leaflets lance-shaped,
toothed, midgreen. Flowers solitary, single
cups, blush pink with plum-colored basal
marks, late spring to midsummer.

Papaver orientale
'Harvest Moon'
(Papaveraceae)

Common name: Oriental
poppy
Height: 3ft (90cm)
Spread: 3ft (90cm)
Aspect: Sun
Soil: Well-drained, deep,
fertile
Hardiness: Zone 3
Propagation: Division, in
spring

Hybrid oriental poppy. Leaves pinnatisect,
leaflets lance-shaped, toothed, midgreen.
Flowers solitary, single cups, burnt orange,
from late spring to midsummer.

Papaver orientale 'Patty's Plum' (Papaveraceae)

Common name: Oriental poppy
Height: 3ft (90cm)
Spread: 3ft (90cm)
Aspect: Sun
Soil: Well-drained, deep, fertile
Hardiness: Zone 3
Propagation: Division, in spring

Hybrid oriental poppy. Leaves pinnatisect, leaflets lance-shaped, toothed, midgreen. Flowers solitary, single, plum-colored cups, from late spring to midsummer.

Papaver rupifragum (Papaveraceae)

Common name: Spanish poppy
Height: 18in (45cm)
Spread: 8in (20cm)
Aspect: Sun
Soil: Well-drained, deep, fertile
Hardiness: Zone 7
Propagation: Seed, in spring

A short-lived perennial species from Spain. Leaves obovate, toothed, midgreen. Flowers solitary, single, dark orange bowls, in summer.

Papaver spicatum (Papaveraceae)

Common names: None
Height: 24in (60cm)
Spread: 6in (15cm)
Aspect: Sun
Soil: Well-drained, deep, fertile
Hardiness: Zone 8
Propagation: Seed, in spring

A species from Turkey. Leaves in a basal rosette, oblong-elliptic, toothed, pale green. Flowers pale orange, outward-facing, in a slender raceme, in succession, in summer.

Paradisea liliastrum A.G.M. (Asphodelaceae/Liliaceae)

Common name: St-Bruno-lily
Height: 2ft (60cm)
Spread: 1ft (30cm)
Aspect: Sun or half shade
Soil: Moist, well-drained, fertile
Hardiness: Zone 7
Propagation: Seed, when ripe or in spring; division, in spring

A rhizomatous, clump-forming perennial. Leaves grassy. Flowers white with large yellow anthers, strongly scented, in one-sided racemes, late spring or early summer.

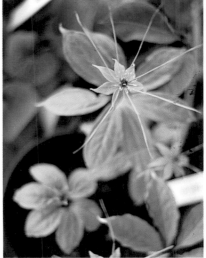

Paradisea lusitanicum (Asphodelaceae/Liliaceae)

Common names: None
Height: 4ft (1.2m)
Spread: 16in (40cm)
Aspect: Sun or half shade
Soil: Moist, well-drained, fertile
Hardiness: Zone 8
Propagation: Seed, when ripe or in spring; division, in spring

A rhizomatous perennial from Spain and Portugal. Leaves in basal rosettes, linear, green. Flowers in racemes of up to 25, white, perfumed trumpets, in summer.

Parahebe perfoliata A.G.M. (Scrophulariaceae)

Common names: None
Height: 32in (80cm)
Spread: 18in (45cm)
Aspect: Sun
Soil: Well-drained, fertile
Hardiness: Zone 9
Propagation: Seed, when ripe or in spring

Tender, evergreen perennial from Australia. Leaves in perfoliate pairs, toothed, leathery, glaucous, blue-green. Flowers in racemes, blue saucers, in late summer.

Paraquilegia anemonoides (Scrophulariaceae)

Common names: None
Height: 4in (10cm)
Spread: 4in (10cm)
Aspect: Sun
Soil: Sharply drained, alkaline, poor, protected from winter wet
Hardiness: Zone 5
Propagation: Seed, when ripe

A perennial from Asia. Leaves ferny, 2- or 3-ternate, segments blue-green, deeply lobed. Flowers nodding, lilac, in late spring. For cool summers; best in a raised bed.

Paris polyphylla (Trilliaceae)

Common names: None
Height: 3ft (90cm)
Spread: 1ft (30cm)
Aspect: Full or half shade
Soil: Moist, humus-rich
Hardiness: Zone 7
Propagation: Seed, in autumn; division, after foliage dies down

Rhizomatous woodlander. Bare stems topped with whorls of oval, green leaves, then of greenish sepals, then of greenish-yellow petals. Violet stigma.

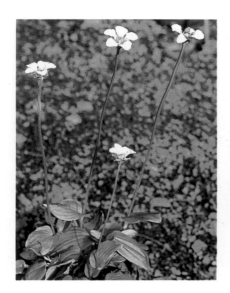

Parnassia nubicola
(Parnassiaceae/Saxifragaceae)

Common name: Grass of
Parnassus
Height: 12in (30cm)
Spread: 6in (15cm)
Aspect: Sun
Soil: Wet, humus-rich, fertile
Hardiness: Zone 4
Propagation: Seed, in autumn;
division, in spring or autumn

A hardy, waterside perennial from the
Himalayas. Leaves elliptic, matt green.
Flowers open saucers, white with yellow
staminodes, in late summer.

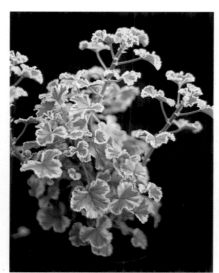

Pelargonium crispum
'Variegatum' A.G.M.
(Geraniaceae)

Common name: Finger
pelargonium
Height: 18in (45cm)
Spread: 6in (15cm)
Aspect: Sun
Soil: Well-drained, fertile
Hardiness: Zone 10
Propagation: Softwood
cuttings, in spring, summer,
or autumn

An upright, tender perennial subshrub
from South Africa. Leaves pale green,
margined cream, aromatic. Flowers pale
mauve, in spring and summer.

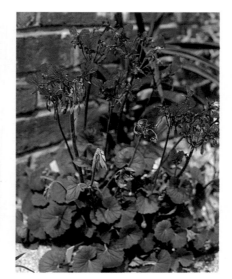

**Pelargonium
endlicherianum**
(Geraniaceae)

Common names: None
Height: 10in (25cm)
Spread: 6in (15cm)
Aspect: Sun
Soil: Sharply drained,
alkaline, fertile, protected
from winter wet
Hardiness: Zone 7
Propagation: Seed, in spring

A hardy perennial from Asia Minor, Syria,
and Armenia. Leaves basal, rounded,
crenate, hairy, dark green. Flowers deep
pink, veined purple, in scapes, in summer.

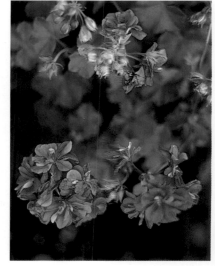

Pelargonium peltatum
hybrids
(Geraniaceae)

Common name: Ivy-leaved
geraniums
Height: 8in (20cm)
Spread: 18in (45cm)
Aspect: Sun
Soil: Well-drained, fertile
Hardiness: Zone 10
Propagation: Softwood
cuttings, in spring, summer,
or autumn

Tender, trailing evergreens. Leaves peltate,
fleshy, bright green. Flowers purple, pink,
red, white, or mauve, single or double,
over a long period in spring and summer.

Pelargonium zonale
hybrids
(Geraniaceae)

Common name: Zonal
geraniums
Height: 2ft (60cm)
Spread: 1ft (30cm)
Aspect: Sun or half shade
Soil: Well-drained, fertile
Hardiness: Zone 10
Propagation: Softwood
cuttings, in spring, summer,
or autumn

Bushy evergreens. Leaves rounded, green,
edged or zoned maroon or bronze. Flowers
single or double, red, purple, pink, or
orange, in spring and summer.

PENSTEMON (Scrophulariaceae)
Penstemon

A genus of about 250 species of evergreen to deciduous
perennials and subshrubs from North and Central America,
and one which has been hybridized comprehensively. They
come from a wide range of habitats, from mountain areas to
plains, and as a result the genus varies in hardiness. The
majority of species are half-hardy, with just a few tender or
reliably hardy types. They are most likely to remain evergreen
in mild areas. Penstemons prefer a sunny position, but they
will tolerate light shade. The soil should be well-drained, and
not too fertile; otherwise they become lush, flower less freely,
and are less likely to survive the winter. A dry winter mulch is
advisable in frost-prone areas. They are long-flowering, with
a season lasting from early summer until well into autumn if
deadheaded. The flowers are tubular, funnel-shaped, or bell-
shaped, and 2-lipped, the upper lip usually 2-lobed and the
lower lip usually 3-lobed. They are borne in upright panicles
or racemes, and the colors range from deep purple through
reds and pinks to white, with rare yellows. Penstemons are
low-allergen plants. Their drawbacks are that they are prey to
slugs and susceptible to powdery mildew. Some of the taller
varieties need to be staked.

Penstemon 'Andenken an
Friedrich Hahn' A.G.M.
(Scrophulariaceae)

Common names: None
Height: 30in (75cm)
Spread: 24in (60cm)
Aspect: Sun or half shade
Soil: Well-drained, fertile
Hardiness: Zone 7
Propagation: Division, in
spring

Hybrid cultivar. Leaves linear to lance-
shaped, midgreen. Flowers tubular, deep
wine red, in racemes, from midsummer to
midautumn. Has also been called 'Garnet'.

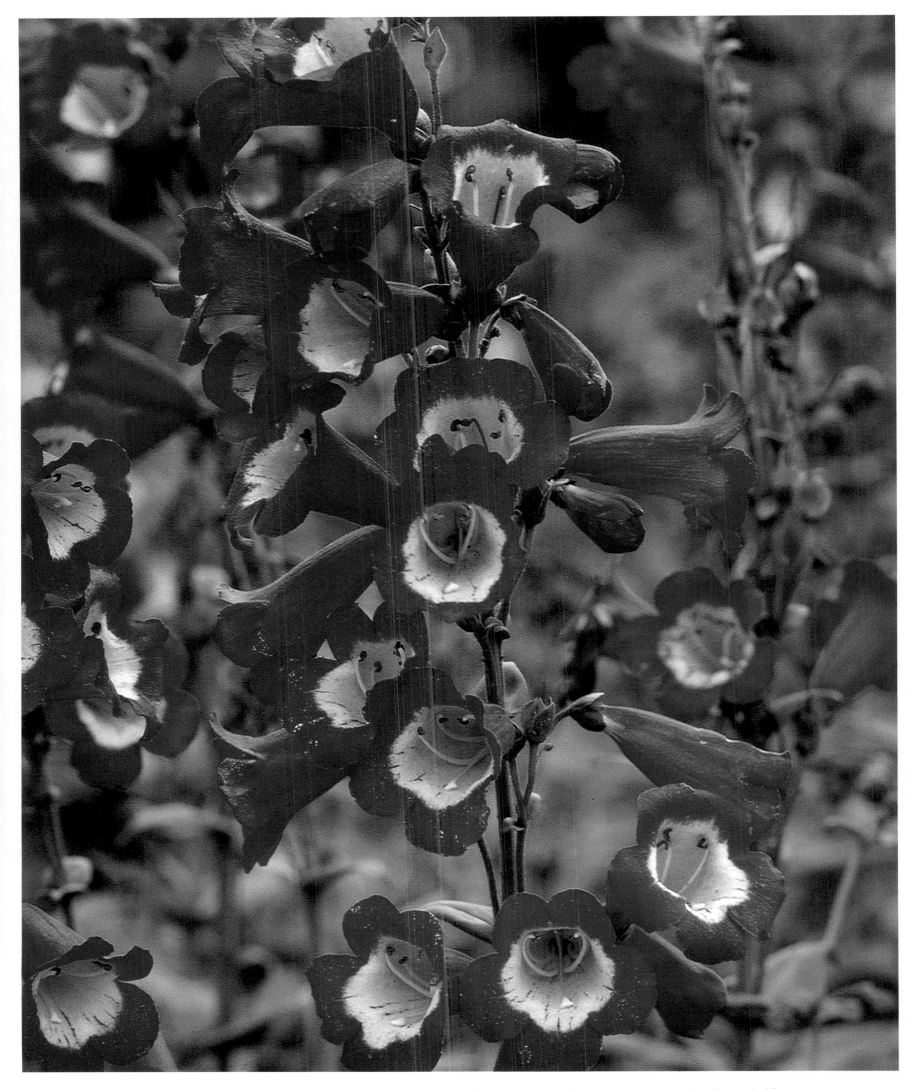

The open spires of flowers on Penstemon hartwegii *'Scarlet and White' make a long-lasting contribution to borders or bedding.*

Penstemon barbatus
(Scrophulariaceae)

Common name: Bearlip
penstemon
Height: 6ft (1.8m)
Spread: 20in (50cm)
Aspect: Sun or half shade
Soil: Well-drained, fertile
Hardiness: Zone 3
Propagation: Seed, in late
winter or spring; division, in
spring

A tall penstemon species. Leaves in basal
rosettes, lance-shaped, midgreen. Flowers
in panicles, pendent, tubular, red, from
early summer to early autumn.

Penstemon cardwellii
f. albus
(Scrophulariaceae)

Common names: None
Height: 8in (20cm)
Spread: 12in (30cm)
Aspect: Sun or half shade
Soil: Well-drained, fertile
Hardiness: Zone 8
Propagation: Seed, in late
winter or spring; division, in
spring

A dwarf, evergreen subshrub. Leaves
elliptic, toothed, midgreen. Flowers in few-
flowered panicles, tubular, white, (deep
purple in type) in early summer.

Penstemon
'Charles Rudd'
(Scrophulariaceae)

Common names: None
Height: 24in (60cm)
Spread: 18in (45cm)
Aspect: Sun or half shade
Soil: Well-drained, fertile
Hardiness: Zone 7
Propagation: Division, in
spring

A hybrid penstemon. Leaves lance-shaped
to linear, midgreen. Flowers in racemes,
small, tubular, magenta with a white
throat, from midsummer to midautumn.

Penstemon
'Cherry Ripe' A.G.M.
(Scrophulariaceae)

Common names: None
Height: 3ft (1m)
Spread: 18in (45cm)
Aspect: Sun or half shade
Soil: Well-drained, fertile
Hardiness: Zone 7
Propagation: Division, in
spring

Short-lived cultivar. Leaves linear to lance-
shaped, bluish-green. Flowers rose-pink
with a white throat, nodding, tubular, in
open panicles, midsummer to autumn.

Penstemon
'Chester Scarlet' A.G.M.
(Scrophulariaceae)

Common names: None
Height: 24in (60cm)
Spread: 18in (45cm)
Aspect: Sun or half shade
Soil: Well-drained, fertile
Hardiness: Zone 7
Propagation: Division, in
spring

A hybrid penstemon. Leaves elliptic, midgreen. Flowers in panicles, large, tubular to
bell-shaped, scarlet, with a white throat,
from midsummer to midautumn.

Penstemon digitalis
(Scrophulariaceae)

Common name: White
penstemon
Height: 36in (1m)
Spread: 18in (45cm)
Aspect: Sun or half shade
Soil: Well-drained, fertile
Hardiness: Zone 3
Propagation: Seed, in late
winter or spring; division, in
spring

Hardy species. Leaves in basal rosettes,
inverse lance-shaped, midgreen. Flowers in
panicles, tubular to bell-shaped, white,
interior striped purple, all summer.

Penstemon digitalis
'Husker's Red'
(Scrophulariaceae)

Common names: None
Height: 30in (75cm)
Spread: 12in (30cm)
Aspect: Sun or half shade
Soil: Well-drained, fertile
Hardiness: Zone 3
Propagation: Division, in
spring

A selected form of the species. Leaves in
basal rosettes, inverse lance-shaped,
maroon-red. Flowers white, tinted pink,
from early to late summer.

Penstemon
'Drinkstone'
(Scrophulariaceae)

Common names: None
Height: 32in (80cm)
Spread: 18in (45cm)
Aspect: Sun or half shade
Soil: Well-drained, fertile
Hardiness: Zone 7
Propagation: Division, in
spring

Also called 'Drinkstone Red'. Leaves
ovate-elliptic, midgreen. Flowers tubular to
bell-shaped, scarlet-vermilion, streaked
magenta inside, early to late summer.

Penstemon heterophyllus
(Scrophulariaceae)

Common name: Chaparral
penstemon
Height: 20in (50cm)
Spread: 20in (50cm)
Aspect: Sun or half shade
Soil: Well-drained, fertile
Hardiness: Zone 8
Propagation: Seed, in late
winter to early spring;
division, in spring

An evergreen subshrub from California.
Leaves linear to lance-shaped, midgreen.
Flowers in racemes, tubular to bell-shaped,
blue, lobes lilac, in summer.

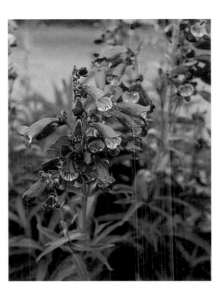

Penstemon
'Modesty'
(Scrophulariaceae)

Common names: None
Height: 32in (80cm)
Spread: 18in (45cm)
Aspect: Sun or half shade
Soil: Well-drained, fertile
Hardiness: Zone 7
Propagation: Division, in
spring

A hybrid penstemon. Leaves lance-shaped
to linear, midgreen. Flowers in racemes,
tubular to bell-shaped, pink with a white
throat, from summer to autumn.

Penstemon
'Osprey' A.G.M.
(Scrophulariaceae)

Common names: None
Height: 36in (1m)
Spread: 18in (45cm)
Aspect: Sun or half shade
Soil: Well-drained, fertile
Hardiness: Zone 7
Propagation: Division, in
spring

Tall hybrid. Leaves linear to lance-shaped,
midgreen. Flowers in racemes, tubular to
bell-shaped, rose-carmine, throat white, in
summer to autumn.

Penstemon
'Peace'
(Scrophulariaceae)

Common names: None
Height: 24in (60cm)
Spread: 18in (45cm)
Aspect: Sun or half shade
Soil: Moist, well-drained
Hardiness: Zone 7
Propagation: Division, in
spring

A hybrid cultivar. Leaves linear to lance-
shaped, midgreen. Flowers in racemes,
tubular to bell-shaped, white with pink
margins to the lobes, summer to autumn.

Penstemon
'Pennington Gem' A.G.M.
(Scrophulariaceae)

Common names: None
Height: 30in (75cm)
Spread: 18in (45cm)
Aspect: Sun or half shade
Soil: Well-drained, fertile
Hardiness: Zone 7
Propagation: Division, in
spring

A hybrid penstemon. Leaves lance-shaped
to linear, midgreen. Flowers in racemes,
tubular to bell-shaped, pink with white
throats, from midsummer to midautumn.

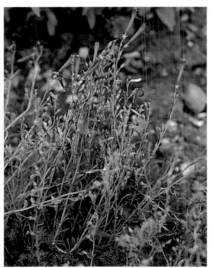

Penstemon pinifolius
A.G.M.
(Scrophulariaceae)

Common names: None
Height: 16in (40cm)
Spread: 10in (25cm)
Aspect: Sun or half shade
Soil: Moist, well-drained
Hardiness: Zone 8
Propagation: Seed, in late
winter to spring; division,
in spring

An evergreen species from Mexico and the
southern U.S.A. Leaves needlelike, midgreen. Flowers in terminal racemes,
tubular, scarlet, in summer.

Penstemon pinifolius
'Mersea Yellow'
(Scrophulariaceae)

Common names: None
Height: 16in (40cm)
Spread: 10in (25cm)
Aspect: Sun or half shade
Soil: Well-drained, fertile
Hardiness: Zone 8
Propagation: Seed, in late
winter to spring; division,
in spring

A yellow-flowered form of the species.
Leaves needlelike, pale green. Flowers in
racemes, tubular, yellow, in summer. The
best of the yellow penstemons.

Penstemon
'Pershore Pink Necklace'
(Scrophulariaceae)

Common names: None
Height: 3ft (1m)
Spread: 18in (45cm)
Aspect: Sun or half shade
Soil: Moist, well-drained
Hardiness: Zone 7
Propagation: Division, in
spring

Leaves lance-shaped to linear, midgreen.
Flowers in racemes, pink with white throat
and carmine band at base of lower lobes,
tubular to bell-shaped, in summer.

Penstemon
'Port Wine' A.G.M.
(Scrophulariaceae)

Common names: None
Height: 36in (90cm)
Spread: 18in (45cm)
Aspect: Sun or half shade
Soil: Well-drained, fertile
Hardiness: Zone 7
Propagation: Division, in
spring

A hybrid penstemon. Leaves linear to lance-shaped, midgreen. Flowers in racemes, tubular to bell-shaped, claret with white throat, from early to late summer.

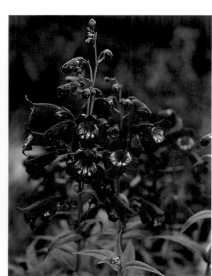

Penstemon
'Red Emperor'
(Scrophulariaceae)

Common names: None
Height: 36in (90cm)
Spread: 18in (45cm)
Aspect: Sun or half shade
Soil: Well-drained, fertile
Hardiness: Zone 7
Propagation: Division, in
spring

A hybrid cultivar. Leaves linear to lance-shaped, midgreen. Flowers in racemes, tubular to bell-shaped, deep red with a white ring around mouth, in summer.

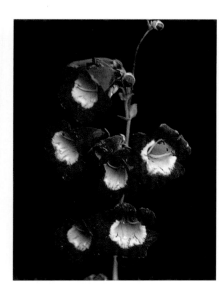

Penstemon
'Rubicundus' A.G.M.
(Scrophulariaceae)

Common names: None
Height: 4ft (1.2m)
Spread: 18in (45cm)
Aspect: Sun or half shade
Soil: Well-drained, fertile
Hardiness: Zone 7
Propagation: Division, in
spring

Short-lived hybrid. Leaves lance-shaped to linear, light green. Flowers in racemes, tubular to bell-shaped, red, mouth white, streaked red, in summer to autumn.

Penstemon rupicola
'Diamond Lake'
(Scrophulariaceae

Common names: None
Height: 8in (20cm)
Spread: 18in (45cm)
Aspect: Sun or half shade
Soil: Moist, well-drained
Hardiness: Zone 8
Propagation: Division in
spring

Selected form of evergreen species. Leaves elliptic-round, toothed, thick, blue-green. Flowers pink with white mouths, tubular to funnel-shaped, in racemes, early summer.

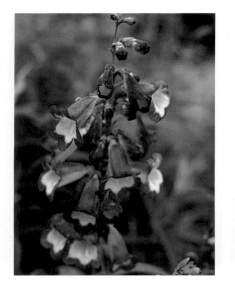

Penstemon
'Sour Grapes'
(Scrophulariaceae)

Common names: None
Height: 24in (60cm)
Spread: 18in (45cm)
Aspect: Sun or half shade
Soil: Well-drained, fertile
Hardiness: Zone 8
Propagation: Division, in
spring

A hybrid penstemon. Leaves elliptic-ovate, midgreen. Flowers in racemes, tubular to bell-shaped, dull lilac-blue, with white throats, from midsummer to midautumn.

Penstemon
'White Bedder' A.G.M.
(Scrophulariaceae)

Common names: None
Height: 28in (70cm)
Spread: 12in (30cm)
Aspect: Sun or half shade
Soil: Well-drained, fertile
Hardiness: Zone 7
Propagation: Division, in
spring

A hybrid penstemon. Leaves elliptic-ovate, bright green. Flowers tubular to bell-shaped, pure white, in racemes, from midsummer to early autumn.

Penstemon
'Whitethroat'
(Scrophulariaceae)

Common names: None
Height: 36in (90cm)
Spread: 18in (45cm)
Aspect: Sun or half shade
Soil: Well-drained, fertile
Hardiness: Zone 7
Propagation: Division, in
spring

A hybrid penstemon. Leaves lance-shaped to linear, midgreen. Flowers in racemes, tubular to bell-shaped, cerise, throat pure white, from summer to autumn.

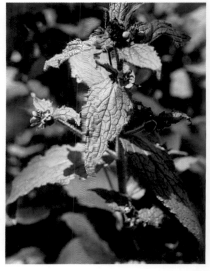

Pentaglottis sempervirens
(Boraginaceae

Common names: None
Height: 3ft (1m)
Spread: 3ft (1m)
Aspect: Full or half shade
Soil: Moist, humus-rich
Hardiness: Zone 7
Propagation: Seed, when ripe
or in spring; division, in
spring

Taprooted perennial. Basal leaves in rosette, large, ovate; stem leaves smaller, midgreen. Flowers in leafy cymes, small, bright blue, from spring to early summer.

Pentas lanceolata
(Rubiaceae)

Common name: Egyptian
star-clusters
Height: 6ft (2m)
Spread: 3ft (1m)
Aspect: Sun
Soil: Well-drained, fertile
Hardiness: Zone 10
Propagation: Seed, in warmth
in spring; softwood cuttings,
at any time

Evergreen from the Arabian Peninsula and
Africa. Leaves hairy, midgreen, ovate to
lance-shaped. Flowers in domed corymbs,
long-tubed, starry, pink, spring to autumn.

Perovskia atriplicifolia
(Labiatae/Lamiaceae)

Common names: None
Height: 4ft (1.2m)
Spread: 3ft (1m)
Aspect: Sun
Soil: Well-drained, fertile
Hardiness: Zone 6
Propagation: Softwood
cuttings, in late spring; semi-
ripe cuttings, in summer

A subshrub from Afghanistan. Leaves
ovate, deeply cut, gray-green. Flowers in
tall panicles, small, tubular, lilac-blue, from
late summer to early autumn.

Perovskia
'Blue Spire' A.G.M.
(Labiatae/Lamiaceae)

Common names: None
Height: 4ft (1.2m)
Spread: 3ft (1m)
Aspect: Sun
Soil: Well-drained, fertile
Hardiness: Zone 6
Propagation: Softwood
cuttings, in late spring; semi-
ripe cuttings, in summer

An upright subshrub, with ovate, deeply
divided, silver-gray leaves. Flowers in
panicles, tubular, violet-blue, in late
summer and early autumn.

Persicaria affinis
(Polygonaceae)

Common name: Himalayan
fleece-flower
Height: 10in (25cm)
Spread: Indefinite
Aspect: Sun or half shade
Soil: Moist
Hardiness: Zone 3
Propagation: Division, in
spring or autumn

A vigorous, evergreen ground cover. Leaves
dark green, lance-shaped to elliptic. Flowers
in spikes, bright rose-red cups, fading to
pink, then brown, midsummer to autumn.

PERSICARIA (Polygonaceae)
Mountain fleece • Snakeweed

A genus of around 80 species of annuals, stoloniferous or
rhizomatous perennials, and a few subshrubs, from very
varied habitats worldwide. They may be hardy or half-hardy,
and deciduous to evergreen. *Persicaria* like growing in sun, as
long as they are in a moisture-retentive soil, but tolerate light
shade; some species, such as *P. bistorta,* will even tolerate dry
soil. Some members of the genus, most notably *P. affinis,*
P. cuspidatum (Zone 4), and *P. sachalinense* (Zone 4), are
rampant invaders, and best avoided in a small garden. Most
species are undemanding, easy-going plants, however, and
make excellent ground cover, or can be naturalized in a wild
garden. Some have a long flowering season. They bear small,
cup-, bell-, or funnel-shaped flowers, in densely packed spikes
or racemes. The flowers are usually long-lasting and may be
red, pink, or white; they are followed by distinctive, ovoid or
3-angled fruits, usually brownish in color. Many of the
members of the genus were, until very recently, classified
under *Polygonum,* and may still be found under that name in
old catalogs and books. The main drawbacks of these plants
are that all members of the genus are highly allergenic,
poisonous, and skin-irritant.

Persicaria amplexicaulis
(Polygonaceae)

Common name: Mountain
fleece
Height: 4ft (1.2m)
Spread: 1.2m (4ft)
Aspect: Sun or half shade
Soil: Moist
Hardiness: Zone 5
Propagation: Division, in
spring or autumn

Vigorous, clump-forming perennial. Leaves
lance-shaped to ovate, pointed, midgreen.
Flowers in narrow spikes, bright red bells,
from midsummer to early autumn.

Persicaria amplexicaulis
'Firetail' A.G.M.
(Polygonaceae)

Common name: Mountain
fleece
Height: 4ft (1.2m)
Spread: 4ft (1.2m)
Aspect: Sun or half shade
Soil: Moist
Hardiness: Zone 5
Propagation: Division, in
spring or autumn

A selected form of the species, with flowers
of larger size and brighter red, from
midsummer to early autumn. Leaves ovate
to lance-shaped, pointed, midgreen.

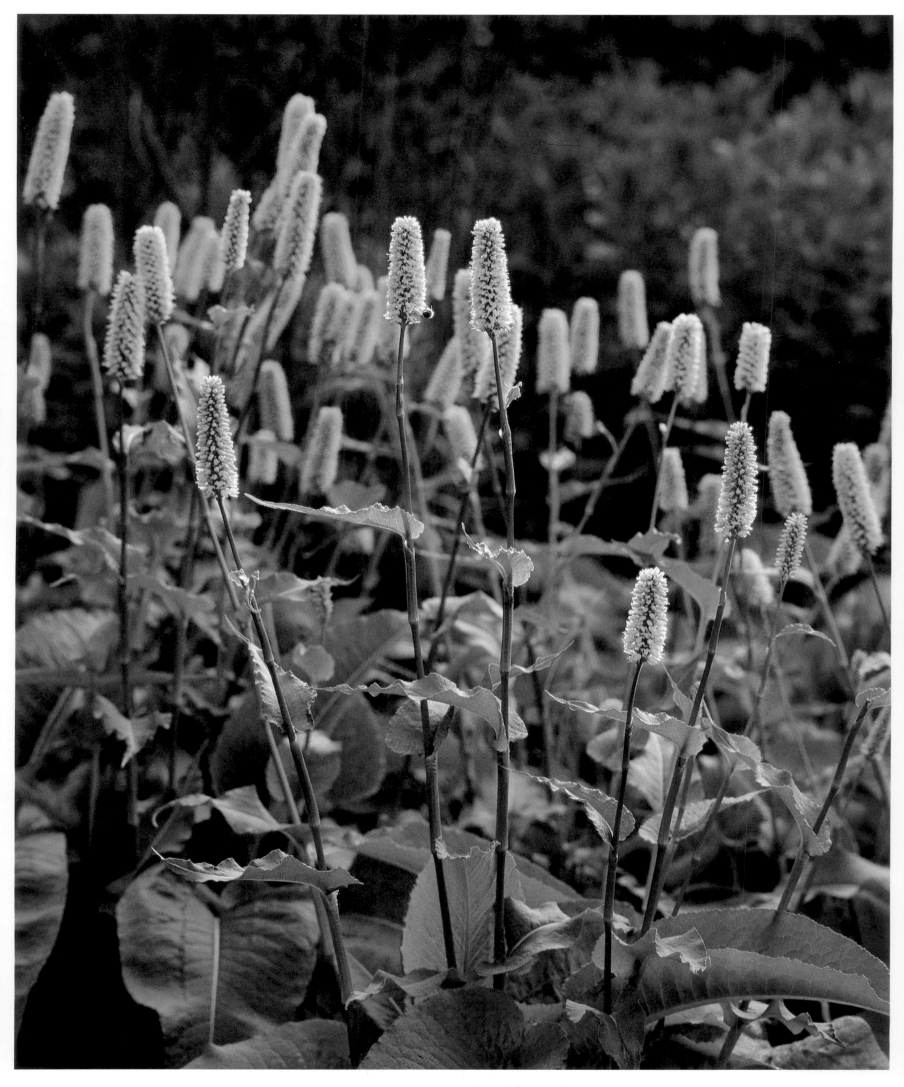

Persicaria bistorta 'Superba' gives excellent value in a garden, with abundant pink flowers throughout summer and attractive fruits in autumn.

Persicaria amplexicaulis var. pendula (Polygonaceae)

Common names: None
Height: 4ft (1.2m)
Spread: 4ft (1.2m)
Aspect: Sun or half shade
Soil: Moist
Hardiness: Zone 6
Propagation: Division, in spring or autumn

A form of this vigorous, clump-forming species, with narrow, arching spikes of red flowers, and pale green, ovate to lance-shaped, pointed leaves.

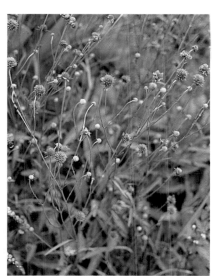

Persicaria bistorta subsp. carnea (Polygonaceae)

Common name: Snakeweed
Height: 28in (70cm)
Spread: 18in (45cm)
Aspect: Sun or half shade
Soil: Moist
Hardiness: Zone 4
Propagation: Division, in spring or autumn

A robust, clump-forming perennial. Leaves broad, ovate, pointed, veined, midgreen. Flowers in spherical spikes, deep pink, from early summer to midautumn.

Persicaria bistorta 'Superba' A.G.M. (Polygonaceae)

Common name: Snakeweed
Height: 3ft (90cm)
Spread: 3ft (90cm)
Aspect: Sun or half shade
Soil: Moist
Hardiness: Zone 4
Propagation: Division, in spring or autumn

A robust perennial from Eurasia. Leaves broad, ovate, pointed, veined, midgreen. Flowers in dense, cylindrical spikes, pink bells, over a long period in summer.

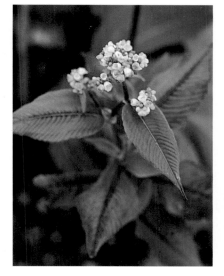

Persicaria campanulata (Polygonaceae)

Common names: None
Height: 3ft (90cm)
Spread: 3ft (90cm)
Aspect: Sun or half shade
Soil: Moist
Hardiness: Zone 8
Propagation: Division, in spring or autumn

Stoloniferous perennial. Leaves basal and stem, elliptic, hairy, veined, midgreen, white below. Flowers scented, pink bells, in loose panicles, midsummer to autumn.

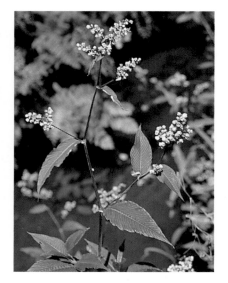

Persicaria campanulata 'Rosenrot' (Polygonaceae)

Common names: None
Height: 3ft (90cm)
Spread: 3ft (90cm)
Aspect: Sun or half shade
Soil: Moist
Hardiness: Zone 8
Propagation: Division, in spring

Selected form of the species with rosy red flowers, in loose panicles, midsummer to autumn. Leaves basal and stem, elliptic, hairy, veined, midgreen, white below.

Persicaria capitata (Polygonaceae)

Common name: Pinkhead knotweed
Height: 3in (8cm)
Spread: Indefinite
Aspect: Sun or half shade
Soil: Moist
Hardiness: Zone 8
Propagation: Division, in spring or autumn

Creeping, stem-rooting ground cover from the Himalayas. Leaves ovate, dark green, with a purple "V." Flowers pink bells, in short-stemmed, dense panicles, in summer.

Persicaria virginiana 'Painter's Palette' (Polygonaceae)

Common names: None
Height: 4ft (1.2m)
Spread: 4ft (1.2m)
Aspect: Sun or half shade
Soil: Moist
Hardiness: Zone 5
Propagation: Division, in spring or autumn

A selected form of a herbaceous species. Leaves ovate-elliptic, with a central "V," and variegated red, yellow, and green. Flowers insignificant.

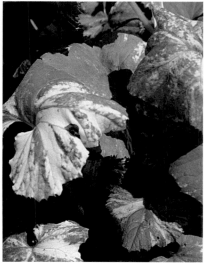

Petasites japonicus var. giganteus 'Variegatus' (Asteraceae/Compositae)

Common name: Japanese butterbur
Height: 4ft (1.2m)
Spread: 5ft (1.5m)
Aspect: Full or half shade
Soil: Moist, humus-rich, fertile, deep
Hardiness: Zone 5
Propagation: Division, in spring or autumn

Rhizomatous perennial. Leaves basal, huge, reniform, toothed, green and cream. Flowers scented, in dense corymbs, yellowish-white, in late winter to spring.

Phaenosperma globosa
(Poaceae)

Common names: None
Height: 5ft (1.5m)
Spread: 2ft (60cm)
Aspect: Sun
Soil: Well-drained
Hardiness: Zone 7
Propagation: Seed, in autumn
or spring

A deciduous grass. Leaves broad, linear, long, light green with darker ribs. Flower stems tall, with pyramidal panicles of pale brown flowers.

Phlomis fruticosa
AG.M.
(Labiatae/Lamiaceae)

Common names: None
Height: 3ft (1m)
Spread: 5ft (1.5m)
Aspect: Sun
Soil: Well-drained, fertile
Hardiness: Zone 7
Propagation: Seed, in warmth
in spring; softwood cuttings,
in summer

Evergreen, Mediterranean subshrub. Leaves ovate to lance-shaped, sagelike, gray-green, wrinkled. Flowers in whorls, dead-nettle-like, yellow, in early and midsummer.

Phlomis italica
(Labiatae/Lamiaceae)

Common names: None
Height: 1ft (30cm)
Spread: 2ft (60cm)
Aspect: Sun
Soil: Well-drained, fertile
Hardiness: Zone 8
Propagation: Seed, in warmth
in spring; softwood cuttings,
in summer

An evergreen subshrub from the Balearic islands. Leaves lance-shaped to oblong, gray-woolly. Flowers in whorls, tubular, dead-nettlelike, lilac, in summer.

Phlox adsurgens
'Wagon Wheel'
(Polemoniaceae)

Common name: Periwinkle
phlox
Height: 1ft (30cm)
Spread: 1ft (30cm)
Aspect: Half shade
Soil: Moist, well-drained,
fertile, humus-rich
Hardiness: Zone 6
Propagation: Softwood
cuttings of blind shoots, in spring

A prostrate woodlander from the U.S.A. Leaves ovate, midgreen. Flowers salmon-pink, salverform, narrow-petalled, in open cymes, in late spring and early summer.

PHLOX (Polemoniaceae)
Phlox

A genus of over 60 species, all North American except one from Siberia. They come from three types of habitat: alpine phloxes need a sharply drained soil and sun; woodlanders, represented by *Phlox divaricata* and its cultivars, require a humus-rich soil in part shade; waterside species, most notably *P. paniculata*, have given us the modern, hybrid, border phloxes, which need a moist, fertile soil, in sun or half shade. This group has been hybridized extensively; some of the hybrids have large, colorful flowers, but are shorter-lived than one might hope, given that *P. paniculata* is soundly perennial; their survival depends on their having moisture and nutrients at the roots at all times, so they require annual top-dressing, but they dislike waterlogged soil. They have a rich fragrance and attract bees and butterflies. Phlox are low-allergen plants. They benefit from being lifted and divided every few years, keeping the young growths and discarding the woody center. Some taller varieties may need staking. All can be devoured by slugs in spring, especially the woodland types, so one must take action early. All are also prone to powdery mildew in some degree; border phloxes must never be allowed to dry out, or be enclosed closely by other plants.

Phlox
'Chattahoochee' A.G.M.
(Polemoniaceae)

Common names: None
Height: 6in (15cm)
Spread: 12in (30cm)
Aspect: Half shade
Soil: Moist, well-drained,
fertile, humus-rich
Hardiness: Zone 4
Propagation: Softwood
cuttings of blind shoots,
in spring

Short-lived, prostrate hybrid. Leaves lance-shaped, purple becoming midgreen. Flowers in cymes, salverform, lavender-blue with a red eye, long periods in summer to autumn.

Phlox divaricata
'Blue Dreams'
(Polemoniaceae)

Common name: Wild blue
phlox
Height: 14in (35cm)
Spread: 20in (50cm)
Aspect: Half shade
Soil: Moist, well-drained,
humus-rich, fertile
Hardiness: Zone 4
Propagation: Softwood
cuttings of blind shoots, in spring

A spreading, hybrid perennial. Leaves ovate, hairy, midgreen. Flowers in open cymes salverform, lavender-blue with a dark eye, in early summer.

Phlox maculata
(Polemoniaceae)

Common name: Wild sweet
William
Height: 36in (1m)
Spread: 18in (45cm)
Aspect: Sun or half shade
Soil: Moist, fertile
Hardiness: Zone 5
Propagation: Division, in
spring or autumn

A herbaceous perennial from the eastern
U.S.A. Leaves linear, midgreen. Flowers in
cymes, perfumed, salverform, violet, white,
or pink, in early and midsummer.

Phlox paniculata
'Fujiyama' A.G.M.
(Polemoniaceae)

Common name: Garden
phlox
Height: 30in (75cm)
Spread: 36in (90cm)
Aspect: Sun or half shade
Soil: Moist, fertile
Hardiness: Zone 4
Propagation: Division, in
spring or autumn

A hybrid perennial. Leaves thin, ovate,
toothed, midgreen. Flowers white,
perfumed, salverform, in cymes, from
summer to midautumn.

Phlox paniculata
'Harlequin'
(Polemoniaceae)

Common name: Garden
phlox
Height: 3ft (1m)
Spread: 3ft (1m)
Aspect: Sun or half shade
Soil: Moist, fertile
Hardiness: Zone 4
Propagation: Division, in
spring or autumn

A hybrid perennial. Leaves thin, ovate,
toothed, pale green, margined ivory.
Flowers in cymes, perfumed, red-purple,
from summer to early autumn.

Phlox paniculata
'Magnificence'
(Polemoniaceae)

Common name: Garden
phlox
Height: 3ft (1m)
Spread: 3ft (1m)
Aspect: Sun or half shade
Soil: Moist, fertile
Hardiness: Zone 4
Propagation: Division, in
spring or autumn

A hybrid perennial. Leaves thin, ovate,
toothed, midgreen. Flowers in cymes,
scented, salverform, bright, clear pink,
from summer to autumn.

Phlox paniculata
'Norah Leigh'
(Polemoniaceae)

Common name: Garden
phlox
Height: 3ft (1m)
Spread: 3ft (1m)
Aspect: Sun or half shade
Soil: Moist, fertile
Hardiness: Zone 4
Propagation: Division, in
spring or autumn

A hybrid perennial. Leaves thin, ovate,
toothed, variegated pale green and cream.
Flowers in small cymes, perfumed, pale
lilac, from summer to autumn.

Phlox paniculata
'Otley Choice'
(Polemoniaceae)

Common name: Garden
phlox
Height: 3ft (1m)
Spread: 3ft (1m)
Aspect: Sun or half shade
Soil: Moist, fertile
Hardiness: Zone 4
Propagation: Division, in
spring or autumn

A hybrid perennial. Leaves thin, ovate,
toothed, midgreen. Flowers in cymes,
scented, salverform, cerise, from
midsummer to autumn.

Phlox paniculata
'Starfire'
(Polygonaceae)

Common name: Garden
phlox
Height: 4ft (1.2m)
Spread: 3ft (90cm)
Aspect: Sun or half shade
Soil: Moist, fertile
Hardiness: Zone 4
Propagation: Division in
spring or autumn

A hybrid perennial. Leaves ovate, toothed,
dark green. Flowers in cymes, perfumed,
salverform, deep crimson-red, from
midsummer to early autumn.

Phormium cookianum
'Jester'
(Agavaceae/Phormiaceae)

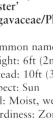

Common name: Fiber-lily
Height: 6ft (2m)
Spread: 10ft (3m)
Aspect: Sun
Soil: Moist, well-drained
Hardiness: Zone 8
Propagation: Division, in
spring

Hybrid evergreen. Leaves linear, keeled,
arching to erect, bronze and green. Flowers
in panicles, tubular, green, in summer.
Foliage very good for flower arrangements.

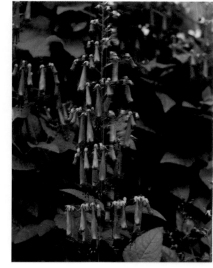

Phormium
'Sundowner' A.G.M.
(Agavaceae/Phormiaceae)

Common name:
Fiber-lily
Height: 6ft (2m)
Spread: 10ft (3m)
Aspect: Sun
Soil: Moist, well-drained
Hardiness: Zone 8
Propagation: Division, in
spring

Evergreen hybrid. Leaves linear, keeled,
arching to erect, long, bronze-green with
pink margins. Flowers green-yellow, in tall
panicles, in summer; good seed heads.

Phormium tenax
A.G.M.
(Agavaceae/Phormiaceae)

Common name: New
Zealand fiber-lily
Height: 12ft (4m)
Spread: 6ft (2m)
Aspect: Sun
Soil: Moist, well-drained
Hardiness: Zone 8
Propagation: Seed or division,
both in spring

A tall, evergreen perennial from New
Zealand. Leaves stiff, linear, dark green
above, blue-green below. Flowers in tall
panicles, dull red, in summer.

Phuopsis stylosa
(Rubiaceae)

Common names: None
Height: 6in (15cm)
Spread: 30in (75cm)
Aspect: Sun or half shade
Soil: Moist, sharply drained,
fertile
Hardiness: Zone 7
Propagation: Seed, in
autumn; division, in spring

Trailing, mat-forming perennial. Leaves in
whorls, musk-scented, pale green, elliptic,
pointed. Flowers in globular heads, tubular,
small, pink, over a long period in summer.

Phygelius aequalis
(Scrophulariaceae)

Common names: None
Height: 3ft (1m)
Spread: 3ft (1m)
Aspect: Sun
Soil: Moist, well-drained,
fertile
Hardiness: Zone 8
Propagation: Seed, softwood
cuttings or separated suckers,
all in spring

A subshrub from South Africa. Leaves
ovate, dark green. Flowers in panicles,
long, pendent, dusky pink with yellow
throats, in summer.

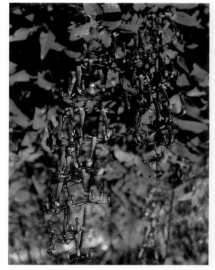

Phygelius aequalis
'Yellow Trumpet' A.G.M.
(Scrophulariaceae)

Common names: None
Height: 3ft (1m)
Spread: 3ft (1m)
Aspect: Sun
Soil: Moist, well-drained,
fertile
Hardiness: Zone 8
Propagation: Softwood
cuttings or separated suckers,
both in spring

A yellow sport of the species; suckering
subshrub with a long flowering season in
summer. Flowers creamy-yellow, leaves
pale green.

Phygelius x *rectus*
'Moonraker'
(Scrophulariaceae)

Common names: None
Height: 5ft (1.5m)
Spread: 5ft (1.5m)
Aspect: Sun
Soil: Moist, well-drained,
fertile
Hardiness: Zone 8
Propagation: Softwood
cuttings or separated suckers,
both in spring

An evergreen, suckering subshrub of
garden origin. Leaves ovate, dark green.
Flowers in panicles, tubular, curved, pale
yellow, over a long period in summer.

Phygelius x *rectus*
'Salmon Leap'
(Scrophulariaceae)

Common names: None
Height: 4ft (1.2m)
Spread: 5ft (1.5m)
Aspect: Sun
Soil: Moist, well-drained,
fertile
Hardiness: Zone 8
Propagation: Softwood
cuttings or separated suckers,
both in spring

Evergreen, suckering subshrub of garden
origin. Leaves ovate, dark green. Flowers
in panicles, tubular, curved, deeply lobed,
orange, over a long period in summer.

Phygelius x *rectus*
'Winchester Fanfare'
(Scrophulariaceae)

Common names: None
Height: 5ft (1.5m)
Spread: 5ft (1.5m)
Aspect: Sun
Soil: Moist, well-drained,
fertile
Hardiness: Zone 8
Propagation: Softwood
cuttings or separated suckers,
both in spring

An evergreen, suckering subshrub of
garden origin. Leaves ovate, dark green.
Flowers in panicles, pendent, tubular,
dusky pink, over a long period in summer.

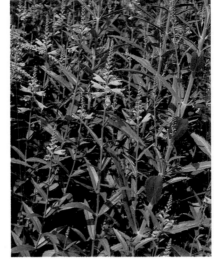

Physalis alkekengi var. franchettii (Solanaceae)

Common names: Chinese-lantern; strawberry ground-cherry
Height: 30in (75cm)
Spread: Indefinite
Aspect: Sun or half shade
Soil: Well-drained
Hardiness: Zone 6
Propagation: Seed or division, both in spring

Rhizomatous perennial from Europe and Asia. Leaves broad, ovate, bright green. Flowers solitary, white, in summer, then orange berries inside papery, red calyces.

Physostegia virginiana (Labiatae/Lamiaceae)

Common name: Virginia lion's-heart
Height: 4ft (1.2m)
Spread: Indefinite
Aspect: Sun or half shade
Soil: Moist, humus-rich, fertile
Hardiness: Zone 4
Propagation: Seed, in autumn; division, in early spring

Invasive rhizomatous ground cover. Leaves ovate to lance-shaped, toothed, midgreen. Flowers in racemes, bright pink, from midsummer to early autumn.

Physostegia virginiana 'Alba' (Labiatae/Lamiaceae)

Common names: Virginia lion's-heart
Height: 4ft (1.2m)
Spread: Indefinite
Aspect: Sun or half shade
Soil: Moist, humus-rich, fertile
Hardiness: Zone 4
Propagation: Seed, in autumn; division, in early spring

White-flowered form of the species; invasive ground cover. Leaves ovate, toothed, midgreen. Flowers in racemes, white, from midsummer to early autumn.

Physostegia virginiana subsp. speciosa 'Bouquet Rose' (Labiatae/Lamiaceae)

Common name: Virginia lion's-heart
Height: 4ft (1.2m)
Spread: Indefinite
Aspect: Sun or half shade
Soil: Moist, humus-rich, fertile
Hardiness: Zone 4
Propagation: Division, in early spring

A selected form of the species, with racemes of pale lilac-pink flowers from midsummer to early autumn. Leaves ovate, toothed, midgreen. Good ground cover.

Physostegia virginiana 'Summer Snow' (Labiatae/Lamiaceae)

Common name: Virginia lion's-heart
Height: 4ft (1.2m)
Spread: Indefinite
Aspect: Sun or half shade
Soil: Moist, well-drained, fertile
Hardiness: Zone 4
Propagation: Division, in early spring

A selected form; invasive ground cover. Leaves ovate, toothed, midgreen. Flowers white with green calyces, in racemes, midsummer to early autumn.

Physostegia virginiana subsp. speciosa 'Variegata' (Labiatae/Lamiaceae)

Common name: Virginia lion's-heart
Height: 4ft (1.2m)
Spread: Indefinite
Aspect: Sun or half shade
Soil: Moist, well-drained, fertile
Hardiness: Zone 4
Propagation: Division, in early spring

Invasive ground cover. Grown for its ovate, toothed, grayish-green, white-margined leaves. Racemes of purple flowers from midsummer to early autumn.

Phyteuma orbiculare (Campanulaceae)

Common name: Ballhead rampion
Height: 20in (50cm)
Spread: 18in (45cm)
Aspect: Sun
Soil: Well-drained, fertile
Hardiness: Zone 6
Propagation: Seed, in autumn

A perennial from Eurasia. Leaves elliptic to lance-shaped, toothed, midgreen. Flowers in terminal dense spherical clusters, blue, with acuminate bracts, in summer.

Phytolacca americana (Phytolaccaceae)

Common name: Common poke-berry
Height: 12ft (4m)
Spread: 3ft (1m)
Aspect: Sun or half shade
Soil: Moist, fertile
Hardiness: Zone 4
Propagation: Seed, in warmth in early spring

A foul-smelling North American perennial. Leaves ovate, midgreen. Flowers white or pink, in racemes, from midsummer to early autumn; maroon berries extremely toxic.

Phytolacca polyandra
(Phytolaccaceae)

Common names: None
Height: 6ft (2m)
Spread: 2ft (60cm)
Aspect: Sun or half shade
Soil: Moist, fertile
Hardiness: Zone 6
Propagation: Seed, in warmth
in early spring

Perennial from China. Leaves elliptic-ovate,
midgreen, yellow in autumn. Pink flowers
in compact racemes on red stems in late
summer, followed by toxic, black berries.

Pilosella aurantiaca
(Asteraceae/Compositae)

Common names: None
Height: 12in (30cm)
Spread: 30in (75cm)
Aspect: Sun or half shade
Soil: Sharply drained, fertile
Hardiness: Zone 5
Propagation: Seed or division,
in autumn or spring

A stoloniferous perennial. Leaves in basal
rosettes, lance-shaped to elliptic, bluish-
green. Flowers in clusters of up to 10,
orange-red, daisylike, in summer.

Pimpinella major
'Rosea'
(Apiaceae/Umbelliferae)

Common names: None
Height: 3ft (90cm)
Spread: 2ft (60cm)
Aspect: Sun or half shade
Soil: Moist, fertile
Hardiness: Zone 5
Propagation: Seed, when ripe

A taprooted perennial from Eurasia.
Leaves basal and stem, pinnate, leaflets
ovate, midgreen. Flowers small, pink, in
compound, flat umbels, in spring.

Plantago major
'Rosularis'
(Plantaginaceae)

Common name: Broad-leaved
plantain
Height: 1ft (30cm)
Spread: 1ft (30cm)
Aspect: Sun
Soil: Sharply drained, acidic,
fertile
Hardiness: Zone 5
Propagation: Division, in
spring

Invasive perennial from Europe. Leaves in
basal rosettes, ovate, light green. Flowering
spike a scape reduced to a rosette of green
leaves, said to resemble a rose flower.

Plantago major
'Rubrifolia'
(Plantaginaceae)

Common name: Broad-leaved
plantain
Height: 1ft (30cm)
Spread: 1ft (30cm)
Aspect: Sun
Soil: Sharply drained, acidic,
fertile
Hardiness: Zone 5
Propagation: Seed, in
autumn; division, in spring

A hardy European perennial, a weed of
lawns. Leaves in basal rosettes, ovate,
purple and green. Flowers in slender
spikes, brownish-green, in summer.

Platycodon grandiflorus
A.G.M.
(Campanulaceae)

Common name: Balloon-
flower
Height: 2ft (60cm)
Spread: 1ft (30cm)
Aspect: Sun or half shade
Soil: Moist, well-drained,
humus-rich, fertile
Hardiness: Zone 4
Propagation: Seed, *in situ* in
spring; division or separation, in summer

Perennial from Asia. Leaves ovate, toothed,
bluish-green. Flowers in clusters, open,
purple-blue, 5-petalled saucers, in late
summer. Late to appear, so mark position.

Platycodon grandiflorus
f. *albus*
(Campanulaceae)

Common name: Balloon-
flower
Height: 2ft (60cm)
Spread: 1ft (30cm)
Aspect: Sun or half shade
Soil: Moist, well-drained,
humus-rich, fertile
Hardiness: Zone 4
Propagation: Seed, *in situ* in
spring; division or separation, in summer

White-flowered form. Leaves ovate,
toothed, bluish-green. Flowers pure white
saucers, in late summer. Late to reappear
in spring, so mark its position.

Platycodon grandiflorus
'Fuji Pink'
(Campanulaceae)

Common name: Balloon-
flower
Height: 2ft (60cm)
Spread: 1ft (30cm)
Aspect: Sun or half shade
Soil: Moist, well-drained,
humus-rich, fertile
Hardiness: Zone 4
Propagation: Division or separation of
rooted basal shoots, both in summer

A form of the species with flowers of lilac-
pink, in late summer. Leaves ovate, toothed,
bluish-green. Is late to emerge in spring, so
mark its position.

The sole species in the genus, Platycodon grandiflorus *has given rise to many garden-worthy cultivars.*

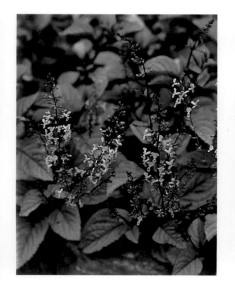

Plectranthus ciliatus
(Labiatae/Lamiaceae)

Common names: None
Height: 18in (45cm)
Spread: Indefinite
Aspect: Full or half shade
Soil: Any
Hardiness: Zone 9
Propagation: Seed, when ripe;
division, in spring

A tender, invasive, evergreen ground cover
from South Africa. Leaves ovate, toothed,
bright green. Flowers in short sprays,
starry, mauve, in summer to autumn.

Pleione formosana
A.G.M.
(Orchidaceae)

Common names: None
Height: 6in (15cm)
Spread: 12in (30cm)
Aspect: Half shade
Soil: Sharply drained, humus-
rich, fertile
Hardiness: Zone 8
Propagation: Division, in
spring

Terrestrial or lithophytic orchid. Single, midgreen, lance-shaped to elliptic, folded leaf
from each pseudobulb. Flowers pale pink,
white lips spotted brown, solitary, spring.

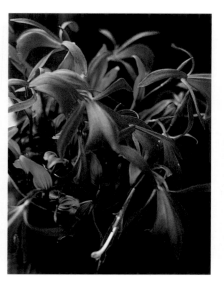

Pleione speciosa
(Orchidaceae)

Common names: None
Height: 3in (7cm)
Spread: 4in (10cm)
Aspect: Half shade
Soil: Sharply drained, humus-
rich, fertile
Hardiness: Zone 8
Propagation: Division, in
spring

Terrestrial or lithophytic orchid. Single leaf
from each pseudobulb, lance-shaped, midgreen. Flowers solitary, bright magenta
with peach-blotched lip, in spring.

Podophyllumm hexandrum
(Berberidaceae)

Common names: None
Height: 18in (45cm)
Spread: 12in (30cm)
Aspect: Full or half shade
Soil: Moist, humus-rich,
fertile
Hardiness: Zone 6
Propagation: Seed, when ripe;
division, in spring or autumn

Leaves 3- to 5-lobed, purple-blotched,
toothed. Flower solitary, single, open cups,
white with yellow anthers, in spring to
summer; edible red fruit. Plant poisonous.

Polemonium caeruleum
(Polemoniaceae)

Common name: Jacob's-
ladder
Height: 3ft (90cm)
Spread: 1ft (30cm)
Aspect: Sun or half shade
Soil: Moist, well-drained,
fertile
Hardiness: Zone 2
Propagation: Seed or division,
both in spring

A clump-forming perennial from Eurasia
and North America. Leaves 2-pinnate, with
up to 27 oblong leaflets, midgreen. Flowers
in cymes, open, blue bells, in early summer.

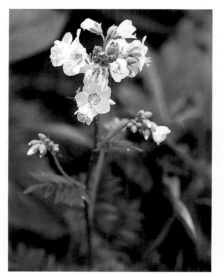

Polemonium caeruleum
subsp. **caeruleaum**
var. **album** (Polemoniaceae)

Common name: Jacob's-
ladder
Height: 3ft (90cm)
Spread: 1ft (30cm)
Aspect: Sun or half shade
Soil: Moist, well-drained,
fertile
Hardiness: Zone 2
Propagation: Seed or division,
both in spring

White form of a good low-allergen plant.
Flowers in cymes, open white bells in early
summer. Leaves 2-pinnate, with up to 27
oblong leaflets, midgreen.

Polemonium caeruleum
'Brise d'Anjou'
(Polemoniaceae)

Common name: Jacob's-
ladder
Height: 30in (75cm)
Spread: 12in (30cm)
Aspect: Sun or half shade
Soil: Moist, well-drained,
fertile
Hardiness: Zone 2
Propagation: Division, in
spring or autumn

A form of Jacob's ladder with midgreen,
cream-margined, 2-pinnate leaves with up
to 27 oblong leaflets. Flowers pink, in
cymes, in early summer.

Polemonium carneum
(Polemoniaceae)

Common name: Salmon
polemonium
Height: 16in (40cm)
Spread: 8in (20cm)
Aspect: Sun or half shade
Soil: Moist, well-drained,
fertile
Hardiness: Zone 6
Propagation: Seed, in autumn
or spring; division, in spring

A hardy, clump-forming perennial from the
western U.S.A. Leaves pinnate, leaflets
ovate-elliptic, midgreen. Flowers in cymes,
pale pink saucers, in early summer.

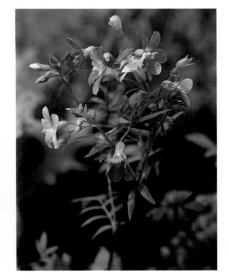

Polemonium carneum
'Apricot Delight'
(Polemoniaceae)

Common name: Salmon
polemonium
Height: 16in (40cm)
Spread: 8in (20cm)
Aspect: Sun or half shade
Soil: Moist, well-drained,
fertile
Hardiness: Zone 6
Propagation: Division, in
spring

A selected form of the species. Leaves
pinnate, leaflets elliptic-ovate. Flowers
large, apricot, borne over a rather longer
season than the type.

Polygala chamaebuxus
A.G.M.
(Polygalaceae)

Common names: Groundbox
polygala
Height: 6in (15cm)
Spread: 12in (30cm)
Aspect: Sun or half shade
Soil: Sharply drained, fertile,
humus-rich
Hardiness: Zone 6
Propagation: Seed, in autumn; softwood
cuttings, in early summer

Dwarf, evergreen subshrub. Leaves leathery,
lance-shaped, dark green. Flowers with
yellow lips and wings, yellow keel aging to
purple, in late spring and early summer.

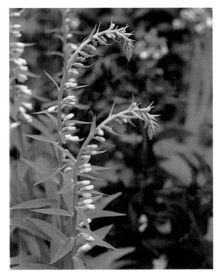

Polygonatum × hybridum
A.G.M.
(Convallariaceae/Liliaceae)

Common name: Common
Solomon's seal
Height: 5ft (1.5m)
Spread: 1ft (30cm)
Aspect: Sun or half shade
Soil: Moist, well-drained,
fertile, humus-rich
Hardiness: Zone 6
Propagation: Seed, in
autumn; division, in spring

Rhizomatous woodlander. Leaves ovate to
lance-shaped, midgreen. Flowers pendent,
tubular, creamy-white, axillary, in late
spring. May bear berries. All parts toxic.

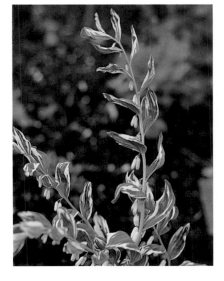

Polygonatum × hybridum
'Striatum'
(Convallariaceae/Liliaceae)

Common name: Common
Solomon's seal
Height: 5ft (1.5m)
Spread: 1ft (30cm)
Aspect: Sun or half shade
Soil: Moist, well-drained,
fertile, humus-rich
Hardiness: Zone 6
Propagation: Division, in
spring

Form of Solomon's seal with leaves striped
green and creamy-white. Flowers pendent,
tubular, creamy-white, axillary, in late
spring. May bear berries. All parts toxic.

Polygonatum stewartianum
(Convallariaceae/Liliaceae)

Common names: None
Height: 36in (90cm)
Spread: 10in (25cm)
Aspect: Sun or half shade
Soil: Moist, well-drained,
humus-rich, fertile
Hardiness: Zone 6
Propagation: Seed, in
autumn; division, in spring

A rhizomatous perennial. Leaves in whorls,
linear to lance-shaped, midgreen. Flowers
in clusters, pendent, tubular, pink, spring
to midsummer. May have red berries.

POLYPODIUM (Polypodaceae)
Polypody

A genus of some 75 species of evergreen and deciduous ferns.
They originate mainly in the tropical areas of North, Central,
and South America, with a few distributed in more temperate
regions, in Africa and in western Europe, including Britain
with *P. cambricum*, the Welsh polypody. The majority of the
species are evergreen. They vary from tender to hardy; the
hardier types are terrestrial, but the more numerous tropical
types are epiphytic. In moist, frost-free areas, they can be
found growing on trees and damp walls, and at the other
extreme on sand dunes. Terrestrial types are good colonizers,
spreading by creeping rhizomes, often on the surface of the
soil. This makes them excellent ground cover plants,
especially in dry positions in sun or dappled shade, where
they will provide greenery through the winter; they are also
suitable for growing in mixed borders or rock gardens.
Polypody ferns like a sharply drained but moisture-retentive
soil. They are good architectural plants, with simple to
pinnatifid or pinnate, occasionally more divided, fronds, with
the sori arranged in rows either side of the midrib of each
frond or pinna. They are borne along the rhizomes in double
rows, seemingly at random.

Polypodium cambricum
'Omnilacerum Oxford'
(Polypodiaceae)

Common names: None
Height: 2ft (60cm)
Spread: Indefinite
Aspect: Sun or half shade
Soil: Sharply drained,
alkaline, humus-rich, fertile
Hardiness: Zone 6
Propagation: Spores, in
warmth when ripe; division, in spring or
autumn

A deciduous, terrestrial fern from Europe.
Fronds tall, erect, lance-shaped to oblong,
pinnate, pinnae lance-shaped, deeply cut,
midgreen. Sori yellow in winter.

229

Polypodium vulgare
'Cornubiense'
(Polypodiaceae)

Common name: Common
polypody
Height: 16in (40cm)
Spread: Indefinite
Aspect: Sun or half shade
Soil: Sharply drained, humus-
rich, fertile
Hardiness: Zone 3
Propagation: Spores, in warmth
when ripe; division, in autumn or spring

An evergreen, terrestrial or epiphytic fern
from Eurasia and Africa. Fronds thin,
leathery, 3-pinnate, pinnae oblong to
linear, dark green.

POLYSTICHUM (Dryopteridaceae)
Holly fern • Shield fern

A genus of some 200 or so terrestrial, usually evergreen,
rhizomatous ferns from many and varied habitats all over the
world. Shield ferns are generally regarded as some of the
most desirable and garden-worthy ferns in cultivation. They
are easy to grow and remarkably trouble-free plants,
provided that their simple needs are met; they require good
drainage and a moisture-retentive, fertile soil that is
preferably neutral or acid, although they will tolerate slightly
alkaline conditions. Due to their diverse natural ranges, they
vary from hardy to tender. They are mostly shade-lovers
(although *P. setiferum* 'Acutilobum' will grow in sun, and
almost anywhere); they are even tolerant of dry conditions,
making them a good choice for the notoriously difficult areas
of dry shade under trees. Shield ferns are excellent subjects
for a fernery, and also suit a mixed border. They bear
handsome, often lance-shaped fronds, which are pinnate to
3-pinnate. The pinnae are hollylike, often with pointed lobes,
giving rise to one of the common names. The old foliage
should be removed in late spring as the new growth
is about to unfold, to give the fronds space to develop when
they appear in early summer.

Polystichum setiferum
A.G.M.
(Aspidaceae/Dryopteridaceae)

Common name: Soft shield
fern
Height: 4ft (1.2m)
Spread: 3ft (90cm)
Aspect: Full or half shade
Soil: Well-drained, humus-
rich, fertile
Hardiness: Zone 7
Propagation: Spores, when
ripe; division, in spring; offsets, in autumn

A rhizomatous, terrestrial European fern.
Fronds in "shuttlecocks," 2-pinnate, lance-
shaped, midgreen. Lobes of pinnae ovate,
toothed, angled obtusely from midrib.

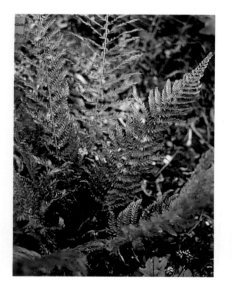

Polystichum setiferum
'Pulcherrimum Bevis' A.G.M.
(Aspidaceae/Dryopteridaceae)

Common name: Soft shield
fern
Height: 18in (45cm)
Spread: 3ft (90cm)
Aspect: Full or half shade
Soil: Well-drained, humus-
rich, fertile
Hardiness: Zone 4
Propagation: Spores, when
ripe; division, in spring; offsets, in autumn

Rhizomatous fern from North America.
Fronds in a "shuttlecock," narrow, lance-
shaped, pinnate, pinnae like holly, dark
green. Fertile fronds narrow sharply to tip.

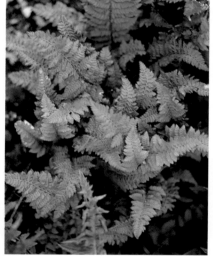

Polystichum setiferum
'Congestum'
(Aspidaceae/Dryopteridaceae)

Common name: Soft shield
fern
Height: 20in (50cm)
Spread: 2ft (60cm)
Aspect: Full or half shade
Soil: Well-drained, humus-
rich, fertile
Hardiness: Zone 7
Propagation: Spores, when
ripe; division, in spring; offsets, in autumn

Evergreen, rhizomatous, hardy fern. A very
compact, congested form of the species; the
congestion of the fronds is often combined
with cresting.

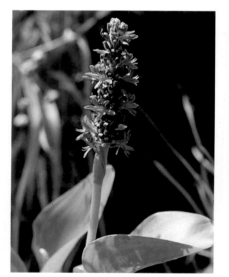

Pontederia cordata
A.G.M.
(Pontederiaceae)

Common name: Pickerel-
weed
Height: 4ft (1.2m)
Spread: 32in (80cm)
Aspect: Sun
Soil: Marginal aquatic
Hardiness: Zone 3
Propagation: Seed, when ripe;
division, in late spring

A marginal aquatic from the Americas.
Leaves broadly ovate, erect, floating and
submerged, glossy-green. Flowers in closely
packed spikes, tubular, blue, late summer.

Potentilla
'Blazeaway'
(Rosaceae)

Common name: Cinquefoil
Height: 18in (45cm)
Spread: 2ft (60cm)
Aspect: Sun
Soil: Well-drained, poor
Hardiness: Zone 5
Propagation: Division, in
autumn or spring

Hybrid cultivar. Leaves pinnate; 5 to 7 midgreen, oblong leaflets. Flowers large, single,
orange with a red band around a dark
center, in cymes, early to late summer.

POTENTILLA (Rosaceae)
Cinquefoil

A genus of some 500 species of shrubs and clump-forming subshrubs, as well as a few annuals and biennials. They come from habitats across the northern hemisphere, ranging from mountain to grassland. Cinquefoils have 3- to 7-palmate or pinnate leaves, and saucer- or cup-shaped flowers in colors from yellow to red, as well as some in white or pink. The shrubby types, derived from *Potentilla fruticosa*, make good low hedging. The clump-forming subshrubs are used extensively in beds and borders because of their long flowering season, and are hybrids derived from *P. nepalensis* and *P. atrosanguinea* (Zone 5). They have attractive, 5-palmate leaves, which closely resemble the leaves of strawberry plants. The flowers are the typical saucer- or cup-shape, and are borne in panicles or cymes over a long period from spring to autumn, in a range of colors. They like a position in sun. The soil should be well-drained, and poor to moderately fertile; if it is too rich, the plants will produce foliage at the expense of flowers. They benefit from being cut back hard in autumn. *P. anserina* is very invasive, and should be avoided in the garden. Cinquefoils are low-allergen plants; the flowers attract bees and are good for cutting.

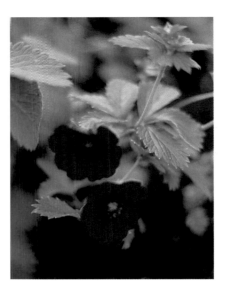

Potentilla 'Flamenco' (Rosaceae)

Common name: Cinquefoil
Height: 18in (45cm)
Spread: 24in (60cm)
Aspect: Sun
Soil: Well-drained, poor
Hardiness: Zone 5
Propagation: Division, in spring or autumn

A clump-forming hybrid. Leaves palmate, leaflets narrow, elliptic, midgreen. Flowers in cymes, single, bright scarlet with a black center, from late spring to midsummer.

Potentilla fruticosa (Rosaceae)

Common name: Bush cinquefoil
Height: 3ft (1m)
Spread: 5ft (1.5m)
Aspect: Sun
Soil: Well-drained, poor
Hardiness: Zone 2
Propagation: Seed, in spring or autumn; greenwood cuttings, in early summer

A deciduous subshrub. Leaves pinnate; 5 to 7 narrow, oblong, dark green leaflets. Flowers in cymes of up to 3, yellow saucers, from spring to autumn.

Potentilla fruticosa 'Abbotswood Silver' (Rosaceae)

Common name: Bush cinquefoil
Height: 3ft (1m)
Spread: 5ft (1.5m)
Aspect: Sun
Soil: Well-drained, poor
Hardiness: Zone 2
Propagation: Greenwood cuttings, in early summer

A selected form of shrubby cinquefoil, with pinnate leaves of dark blue-green, and saucer-shaped, white flowers from late spring to midautumn.

Potentilla nepalensis 'Miss Willmott' A.G.M. (Rosaceae)

Common name: Nepal cinquefoil
Height: 18in (45cm)
Spread: 2ft (60cm)
Aspect: Sun
Soil: Well-drained, poor
Hardiness: Zone 5
Propagation: Division, in autumn or spring

Hybrid cultivar. Leaves 5-palmate leaflets obovate, hairy, toothed, midgreen. Flowers in loose cymes, cherry with darker pink center, all summer.

Potentilla recta 'Warrenii' (Rosaceae)

Common name: Sulfur cinquefoil
Height: 2ft (60cm)
Spread: 18in (45cm)
Aspect: Sun
Soil: Well-drained, poor
Hardiness: Zone 4
Propagation: Division, in spring or autumn

A selected form of the species. Leaves 5- to 7-palmate, leaflets oblong, toothed, midgreen. Flowers in loose cymes, canary yellow, from early to late summer.

Potentilla x tonguei (Rosaceae)

Common name: Tormentilla cinquefoil
Height: 4in (10cm)
Spread: 12in (30cm)
Aspect: Sun
Soil: Well-drained, poor
Hardiness: Zone 5
Propagation: Division, in spring or autumn

Clump-forming garden hybrid. Leaves 3- to 5-palmate, leaflets obovate, dark green. Flowers solitary or in cymes, flat, apricot saucers with a red eye, in summer.

Pratia pedunculata
'County Park'
(Campanulaceae)

Common names: None
Height: 1in (3cm)
Spread: Indefinite
Aspect: Full or deep shade
Soil: Humus-rich, fertile
Hardiness: Zone 7
Propagation: Division, at
any time

Creeping, mat-forming perennial from
Australia. Leaves ovate, midgreen. Flowers
almost stemless, small, deep blue stars, in
summer. Excellent ground cover.

PRIMULA (Primulaceae)
Primrose • Primula

A large genus of over 400 species of perennials, mostly
herbaceous, but some evergreen and woody. A few species are
from the southern hemisphere, but the majority of them
originate in the northern hemisphere; nearly half of those
from the northern hemisphere are native to the Himalayas.
Their range of habitats is very wide, from mountains to
marshes, and their botanical classification is complex: the
species have given rise to an abundance of cultivars. Of the
large number of botanical groups, some are good rock-garden
plants and a few have value as border plants; others require
alpine house conditions, or a warm greenhouse or
conservatory, and some are so difficult to cultivate that they
are for the enthusiast only. All have basal rosettes of leaves
that range from linear to ovate in shape. The flowers are
usually salverform, but may be bell- or funnel-shaped or even
tubular, and may be borne among the leaves or in whorls,
umbels, or racemes on upright stalks. The color range in
species includes yellow, orange, white, and shades of pink
and purple; cultivars are often intensely colored or boldly
patterned. Many members of the genus are highly allergenic,
and contact with the foliage may cause skin irritation.

Primula auricula hort.
(B) A.G.M.
(Primulaceae)

Common name: Auricula
primrose
Height: 8in (20cm)
Spread: 8in (20cm)
Aspect: Sun or half shade
Soil: Moist, well-drained,
humus-rich, fertile
Hardiness: Zone 3
Propagation: Seed, when ripe
or in spring; division, over winter

Evergreen hybrid. Leaves obovate, shiny,
gray-green, white-mealy sometimes. Flowers
in arched umbels, large, salverform, purple
with a cream center, in spring.

Primula bulleyana
(4) A.G.M.
(Primulaceae)

Common name: Bulleys
primrose
Height: 2ft (60cm)
Spread: 2ft (60cm)
Aspect: Half shade
Soil: Moist, acidic, deep,
humus-rich
Hardiness: Zone 6
Propagation: Seed, when ripe or late winter
to spring; division, in autumn or spring

Candelabra primula from China. Leaves
ovate, toothed, midgreen. Flowers in
whorls, salverform, red, aging quickly to
orange, in summer.

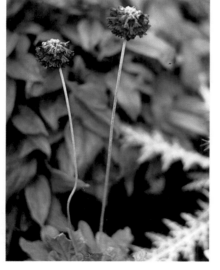

Primula capitata
(5)
(Primulaceae)

Common names: Purplehead
primrose
Height: 16in (40cm)
Spread: 8in (20cm)
Aspect: Half shade
Soil: Moist, acidic, deep,
humus-rich
Hardiness: Zone 5
Propagation: Seed, when ripe or late winter
to spring; division, in autumn or spring

Short-lived perennial from India, Tibet,
and Bhutan. Leaves lance-shaped, toothed,
mealy, pale green. Flowers in flat racemes,
tubular, dark purple, early to late summer.

Primula denticulata
(9) A.G.M.
(Primulaceae)

Common name: Himalayan
primrose
Height: 18in (45cm)
Spread: 18in (45cm)
Aspect: Sun or half shade
Soil: Moist, acidic, deep,
humus-rich
Hardiness: Zone 5
Propagation: Seed, when ripe or late winter
to spring; division, in autumn or spring

Vigorous primula from the Himalayas.
Leaves spoon-shaped, white-mealy below.
Flowers open bells, purple, yellow-eyed, in
tight, globular umbels, in early summer.

Primula denticulata
var. *alba* (9)
(Primulaceae)

Common name: White
Himalayan primrose
Height: 18in (45cm)
Spread: 18in (45cm)
Aspect: Sun or half shade
Soil: Moist, well-drained,
acidic, deep, humus-rich
Hardiness: Zone 5
Propagation: Seed, when ripe or late winter
to spring; division, in autumn or spring

Pure white-flowered form of the species.
Tight, globular umbels of flowers in early
summer. An excellent plant for lighting up
a semishady corner.

Primula
'Inverewe' (4) A.G.M.
(Primulaceae)

Common name: Candelabra
primrose
Height: 30in (75cm)
Spread: 24in (60cm)
Aspect: Half shade
Soil: Moist, acidic, deep,
humus-rich
Hardiness: Zone 6
Propagation: Division, in
autumn or spring

A hybrid candelabra primula. Leaves oval
to lance-shaped, toothed, coarse, midgreen.
Flowers in whorls, salverform, scarlet, in
summer.

Primula japonica
(4) A.G.M.
(Primulaceae)

Common name: Japanese
primrose
Height: 18in (45cm)
Spread: 18in (45cm)
Aspect: Half shade
Soil: Moist, acidic, deep,
humus-rich
Hardiness: Zone 5
Propagation: Seed, when ripe or late winter
to early spring; division, in autumn or spring

Vigorous perennial from Japan. Leaves
obovate, toothed, midgreen. Flowers in
whorls of up to 25, salverform, pink and
purple, in late spring and early summer.

Primula japonica
'Alba' (4)
(Primulaceae)

Common name: White
Japanese primrose
Height: 18in (45cm)
Spread: 18in (45cm)
Aspect: Half shade
Soil: Moist, acidic, deep,
humus-rich
Hardiness: Zone 5
Propagation: Seed, when ripe or late winter
to early spring; division, in autumn or spring

Flowers in whorls of up to 25, salverform,
white, in late spring and early summer.
Excellent for lighting up a semishady
corner, but must have moisture at all times.

Primula juliae
(30)
(Primulaceae)

Common names: None
Height: 4in (10cm)
Spread: 10in (25cm)
Aspect: Sun or half shade
Soil: Moist, well-drained,
acidic, deep, humus-rich,
fertile
Hardiness: Zone 5
Propagation: Seed, when ripe or late winter
to early spring; division, in autumn or spring

A primula from the Caucasus. Leaves in
basal rosettes, round, scalloped, dark
green. Flowers solitary, magenta saucers,
on long stems, in spring and summer.

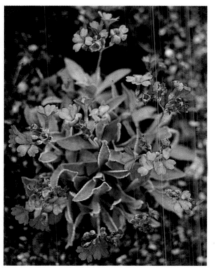

Primula marginata
(2) A.G.M.
(Primulaceae)

Common name: Silveredge
primrose
Height: 6in (15cm)
Spread: 12in (30cm)
Aspect: Sun or half shade,
shaded from midday sun
Soil: Moist, sharply drained,
alkaline
Hardiness: Zone 7
Propagation: Seed, when ripe or in late
winter to early spring

An auricula primula from the Alps. Leaves
obovate, toothed, midgreen. Flowers in
umbels, of up to 20, perfumed, lavender-
blue cups, with white-mealy eyes.

Primula prolifera
(4) A.G.M.
(Primulaceae)

Common name: Candelabra
primrose
Height: 2ft (60cm)
Spread: 2ft (60cm)
Aspect: Half shade
Soil: Moist, acidic, deep,
humus-rich
Hardiness: Zone 6
Propagation: Seed, when ripe or late winter
to early spring; division, in autumn or spring

Primula from India, Myanmar, China and
Indonesia. Leaves dark green, toothed,
spoon-shaped. Flowers in whorls, scented,
white-mealy, yellow, in early summer.

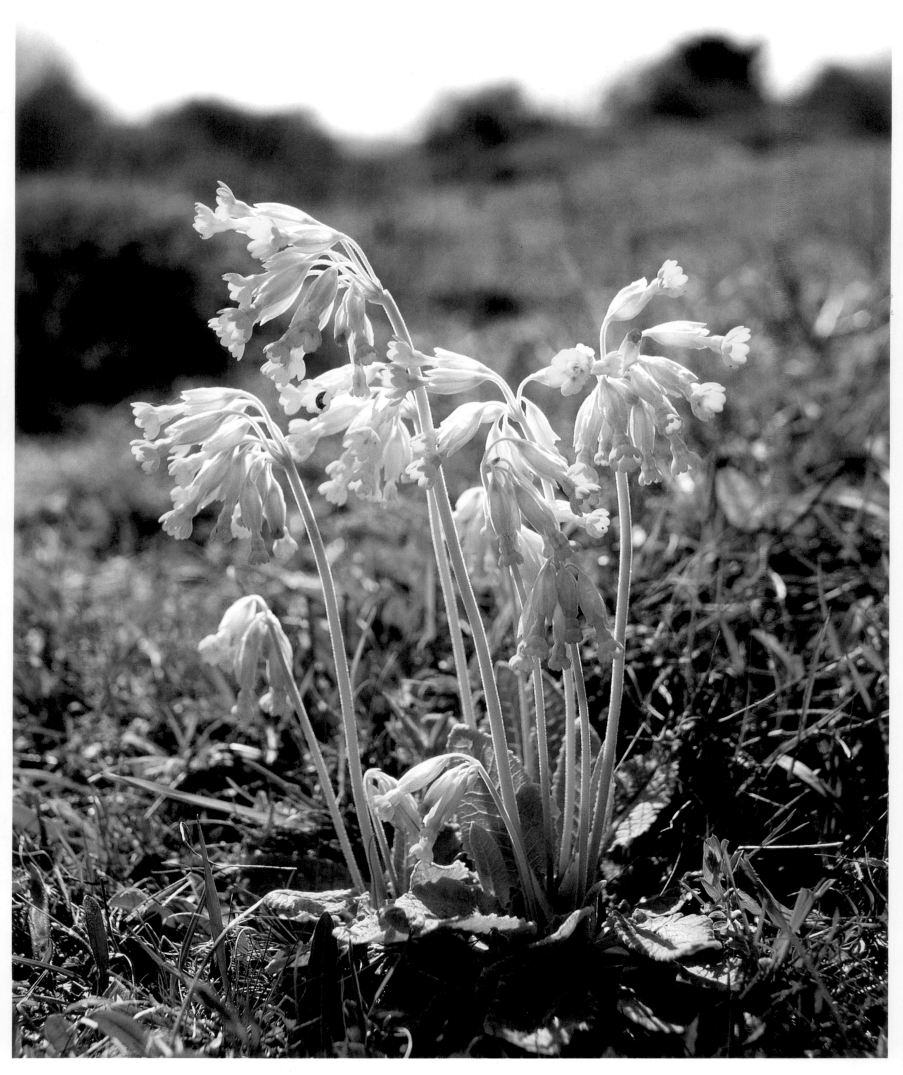

Once a common flower in meadows, Primula veris *can be naturalized in a reliably moist, fertile soil.*

Primula pulverulenta
(4) A.G.M.
(Primulaceae)

Common name: Silverdust
primrose
Height: 3ft (90cm)
Spread: 2ft (60cm)
Aspect: Half shade
Soil: Moist, acidic, humus-
rich, deep
Hardiness: Zone 6
Propagation: Seed, when ripe or late winter
to early spring; division, in autumn or spring

A primula from wet areas of China. Leaves
obovate, toothed, midgreen. Flowers in
whorls, tubular, deep red with dark eyes,
in late spring and early summer.

Primula rosea
(11) A.G.M.
(Primulaceae)

Common names: None
Height: 8in (20cm)
Spread: 8in (20cm)
Aspect: Half shade
Soil: Moist, acidic, deep,
humus-rich
Hardiness: Zone 6
Propagation: Seed, when ripe
or in late winter to early spring; division,
in autumn or spring

Perennial from wet Himalayan meadows.
Leaves obovate, toothed, bronze turning
midgreen. Flowers in umbels of up to 12,
pinkish-red with a yellow eye, in spring.

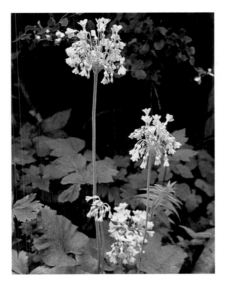

Primula sikkimensis
(26)
(Primulaceae)

Common name: Sikkim
primrose
Height: 3ft (90cm)
Spread: 2ft (60cm)
Aspect: Half shade
Soil: Moist, acidic, deep,
humus-rich
Hardiness: Zone 6
Propagation: Seed, when ripe or late winter
to early spring; division, in autumn or spring

Perennial from wet Himalayan meadows.
Leaves oblong, toothed, shiny green. Flowers
in umbels, pendent, funnel-shaped, yellow,
white-mealy, late spring and early summer.

Primula veris
(30) A.G.M.
(Primulaceae)

Common name: Cowslip
primrose
Height: 10in (25cm)
Spread: 10in (25cm)
Aspect: Sun or half shade
Soil: Moist, well-drained,
acidic, humus-rich
Hardiness: Zone 5
Propagation: Seed, when ripe or late winter
to early spring; division, in autumn or spring

A perennial from Eurasia, including
Britain. Leaves ovate, midgreen. Flowers in
umbels, perfumed, pendent, salverform,
deep yellow, in mid- to late spring.

Primula vialii
(17) A.G.M.
(Primulaceae)

Common name: Littons
primrose
Height: 2ft (60cm)
Spread: 1ft (30cm)
Aspect: Half shade
Soil: Moist, acidic, deep,
humus-rich
Hardiness: Zone 7
Propagation: Seed, in late winter to early
spring; division, in autumn or spring

Perennial from wetlands in China. Leaves
broad, lance-shaped, toothed, midgreen.
Spikes of many, pendent, tubular flowers,
violet opening from red buds, in summer.

Primula vulgaris
(30)
(Primulaceae)

Common name: English
primrose
Height: 8in (20cm)
Spread: 12in (30cm)
Aspect: Half shade
Soil: Moist, acidic, deep,
humus-rich
Hardiness: Zone 6
Propagation: Seed, in early
spring; division, in autumn or spring

Perennial from Europe and Turkey. Leaves
evergreen in mild areas, obovate, toothed,
veined, bright green. Clusters of pale yellow,
scented, saucer flowers, early to late spring.

Prunella grandiflora
(Labiatae/Lamiaceae)

Common name: Bigflower
self-heal
Height: 6in (15cm)
Spread: 4ft (1.2m)
Aspect: Sun or half shade
Soil: Any
Hardiness: Zone 5
Propagation: Seed, in spring;
division, in spring or autumn

An invasive, ground-covering perennial
from Europe. Leaves ovate, toothed, dark
green. Flowers in whorls, on upright leafy
spikes, purple, in summer.

Prunella grandiflora
'Pink Loveliness'
(Labiatae/Lamiaceae)

Common name: Bigflower
self-heal
Height: 6in (15cm)
Spread: 4ft (1.2m)
Aspect: Sun or half shade
Soil: Any
Hardiness: Zone 5
Propagation: Seed, in spring;
division, in spring or autumn

Form of the species with clear pink flowers
in whorls on upright leafy spikes, in
summer. Invasive ground cover, only for a
wild or woodland garden.

Pulmonaria angustifolia
A.G.M.
(Boraginaceae)

Common name: Cowslip
bungwort
Height: 12in (30cm)
Spread: 18in (45cm)
Aspect: Full or half shade
Soil: Moist, humus-rich,
fertile
Hardiness: Zone 3
Propagation: Seed, when ripe;
division, after flowering or in autumn

Rhizomatous European perennial; excellent
ground cover in shade. Leaves lance-shaped,
midgreen. Flowers on erect stems, blue,
funnel-shaped, from early to late spring.

Pulmonaria officinalis
(Boraginaceae)

Common name: Common
lungwort
Height: 10in (25cm)
Spread: 2ft (60cm)
Aspect: Full or half shade
Soil: Moist, humus-rich,
fertile
Hardiness: Zone 6
Propagation: Seed, when ripe;
division, after flowering or in autumn

Rhizomatous, evergreen ground cover.
Leaves ovate, midgreen, spotted white.
Flowers tubular, pink, turning violet, then
blue, in terminal cymes, early to late spring.

Pulmonaria rubra
'Bowles' Red'
(Boraginaceae)

Common name: Red
lungwort
Height: 16in (40cm)
Spread: 36in (90cm)
Aspect: Full or partial shade
Soil: Moist, humus-rich,
fertile
Hardiness: Zone 5
Propagation: Seed, when ripe;
division, after flowering or in autumn

Rhizomatous, evergreen ground cover.
Leaves elliptic, bright green with pale green
spots. Flowers in cymes, coral-red, funnel-
shaped, from late winter to midspring.

Pulmonaria saccharata
(Boraginaceae)

Common name: Bethlehem
sage
Height: 1ft (30cm)
Spread: 2ft (60cm)
Aspect: Full or half shade
Soil: Moist, humus-rich,
fertile
Hardiness: Zone 3
Propagation: Seed, when ripe;
division, after flowering or in autumn

Rhizomatous, evergreen ground cover from
Italy and France. Leaves elliptic, spotted
white. Flowers pink, turning blue, funnel-
shaped, in cymes, late winter to late spring.

Pulsatilla alpina
subsp. *apiifolia* A.G.M.
(Ranunculaceae)

Common name: Alpine
anemone
Height: 12in (30cm)
Spread: 8in (20cm)
Aspect: Sun
Soil: Sharply drained, acidic,
humus-rich,
Hardiness: Zone 5
Propagation: Seed, as soon as
ripe; root cuttings, in winter

A clump-forming perennial. Leaves
2-pinnate, hairy, midgreen. Flowers pale
yellow cups, petals silky-hairy, in spring,
followed by attractive seed heads.

Pulsatilla vulgaris
A.G.M.
(Ranunculaceae)

Common name: Pasqueflower
Height: 8in (20cm)
Spread: 8in (20cm)
Aspect: Sun
Soil: Sharply drained, fertile
Hardiness: Zone 5
Propagation: Seed, as soon as
ripe; root cuttings, in winter

A clump-forming perennial. Leaves pinnate,
leaflets pinnatisect, lobes linear, light green.
Flowers solitary, cup-shaped, silky-hairy,
purple, in spring. Dislikes transplantation.

Pulsatilla vulgaris
'Alba' A.G.M.
(Ranunculaceae)

Common name: White
pasqueflower
Height: 8in (20cm)
Spread: 8in (20cm)
Aspect: Sun
Soil: Sharply drained, fertile
Hardiness: Zone 5
Propagation: Seed, as soon
as ripe

Differs from the species in its white, silky-
hairy, cup-shaped flowers. Leaves pinnate,
leaflets pinnatisect, lobes linear, light green.
Dislikes transplantation.

Pulsatilla vulgaris rosea
(Ranunculaceae)

Common name: Pink
pasqueflower
Height: 8in (20cm)
Spread: 8in (20cm)
Aspect: Sun
Soil: Sharply drained, fertile
Hardiness: Zone 5
Propagation: Seed, as soon as
ripe; root cuttings, in winter

Pink form of the pasque flower with silky-
hairy, cup-shaped flowers. Very handsome
leaves, pinnate, leaflets pinnatisect, lobes
linear, light green. Dislikes transplantation.

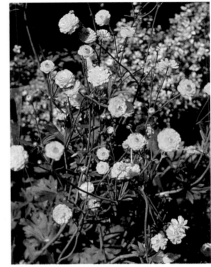

Pulsatilla vulgaris var. *rubra* (Ranunculaceae)

Common name: Red pasqueflower
Height: 8in (20cm)
Spread: 8in (20cm)
Aspect: Sun
Soil: Sharply drained, fertile
Hardiness: Zone 5
Propagation: Seed, as soon as ripe; root cuttings, in winter

Red form of the species. Leaves pinnate, leaflets pinnatisect, lobes linear, light green. Flowers solitary, cup-shaped, silky-hairy, in spring. Dislikes transplantation.

Puschkinia scilloides var. *libanotica* (Hyacinthaceae/Liliaceae)

Common name: Striped squill
Height: 8in (20cm)
Spread: 2in (5cm)
Aspect: Sun or half shade
Soil: Well-drained
Hardiness: Zone 5
Propagation: Offsets, in summer after foliage dies down

Bulbous plant from the Lebanon and Turkey. Leaves basal, paired, semierect, linear, midgreen. Flowers open bell-shaped, in dense racemes of up to 10, white, spring.

Ramonda myconi A.G.M. (Gesneriaceae)

Common name: Rosette-mullein
Height: 4in (10cm)
Spread: 6in (15cm)
Aspect: Half shade
Soil: Moist, well-drained, humus-rich, fertile
Hardiness: Zone 6
Propagation: Seed, as soon as ripe; leaf cuttings, in autumn

Slow-growing, rosette-forming evergreen. Leaves spoon-shaped, crinkled, hairy, dark green. Flowers in cymes or solitary, lilac-blue, in late spring and early summer.

Ranunculus acris 'Flore Pleno' (Ranunculaceae)

Common name: Tall buttercup
Height: 3ft (90cm)
Spread: 10in (25cm)
Aspect: Sun
Soil: Moist, well-drained, humus-rich
Hardiness: Zone 5
Propagation: Seed, when ripe; division, in spring or autumn

Leaves ovate, palmately 3- to 7-lobed, toothed. Flowers in panicles, double, dazzling yellow, in early and midsummer. Unlike the single form, this is not invasive.

RANUNCULUS (Ranunculaceae)
Buttercup

A genus of some 400 species of annuals, biennials, and perennials from temperate regions of both hemispheres. They come from very varied habitats, such that it is not possible to generalize about their cultural requirements. They are variably hardy, and may be evergreen or deciduous. The root system can be fibrous, tuberous, rhizomatous, or fleshy and suckering. Some are bog plants, some originate in high alpine conditions, some are woodlanders, and some can be kept only in an alpine house in wet countries because they need a dry summer dormancy. A good number, however, are reliably hardy, easy to cultivate, and suitable for a mixed border. Their foliage may be basal or stem, and the leaf shape varies widely. They are grown for their 5-petalled, cup-, bowl-, or saucer-shaped flowers, which are usually yellow, but also orange, red, pink, or white, and borne in spring or summer, or sometimes in autumn. *R. acris* (Zone 5), *R. ficaria*, and *R. repens* are invasive weeds, and best kept out of beds or borders, and reserved for the wild or woodland garden. Some species are skin-irritant, whilst others are poisonous, and all appear to be highly allergenic, so allergic gardeners should treat them with caution.

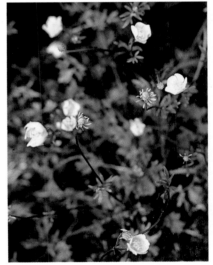

Ranunculus aquatilis (Ranunculaceae)

Common name: Water buttercup
Height: Nil
Spread: Indefinite
Aspect: Sun
Soil: Marginal aquatic
Hardiness: Zone 5
Propagation: Seed, when ripe; division, in spring or autumn

Spreading, evergreen, aquatic plant. Leaves floating and submerged, round to reniform, deeply divided, midgreen. Flowers solitary white saucers, surface-borne, in summer.

Ranunculus bulbosus 'F.M. Burton' (Ranunculaceae)

Common name: Bulbous buttercup
Height: 30in (75cm)
Spread: 12in (30cm)
Aspect: Sun or half shade
Soil: Moist, well-drained, fertile
Hardiness: Zone 7
Propagation: Offsets, in spring or autumn

Selected form of a bulbous species. Leaves basal and stem, ovate, trilobed, dark green. Flowers in panicles of a few glossy, pale cream saucers, late spring and early summer.

Ranunculus cortusifolius
(Ranunculaceae)

Common names: None
Height: 4ft (1.2m)
Spread: 2ft (60cm)
Aspect: Sun
Soil: Moist, well-drained, fertile
Hardiness: Zone 9
Propagation: Seed, when ripe; division, in spring or autumn

Tender perennial from the Canary Islands, the Azores, and Madeira. Leaves basal, leathery, rounded, toothed, midgreen. Flowers in corymbs, scented, yellow.

Ranunculus creticus
(Ranunculaceae)

Common name: Crete buttercup
Height: 12in (30cm)
Spread: 6in (15cm)
Aspect: Half shade
Soil: Moist, well-drained, fertile
Hardiness: Zone 8
Propagation: Seed, when ripe; division, in spring or autumn

Pubescent perennial from Crete. Basal leaves rounded, hairy, 5-lobed, stem leaves midgreen. Flowers large, several to a stem, yellow, in spring.

Ranunculus ficaria
(Ranunculaceae)

Common name: Lesser-celandine
Height: 2in (5cm)
Spread: 18in (45cm)
Aspect: Full or half shade
Soil: Moist, humus-rich
Hardiness: Zone 5
Propagation: Seed, when ripe; division, in spring or autumn

A tuberous perennial with axillary bulbils; highly invasive. Leaves broad, heart-shaped, scalloped, dark green. Flowers solitary, yellow or orange cups, in spring.

Ranunculus gramineus
A.G.M.
(Ranunculaceae)

Common name: Grassy buttercup
Height: 12in (30cm)
Spread: 8in (20cm)
Aspect: Sun or half shade
Soil: Moist, well-drained, fertile
Hardiness: Zone 7
Propagation: Seed, when ripe; division, in spring or autumn

A clump-forming perennial. Leaves basal, grassy, linear, glaucous green. Flowers on branched stems, up to 3 on a stem, lemon-yellow, in late spring and early summer.

Ranunculus lingua
(Ranunculaceae)

Common names: None
Height: 4ft (1.2m)
Spread: 6ft (2m)
Aspect: Sun
Soil: Marginal aquatic
Hardiness: Zone 4
Propagation: Seed, when ripe; division, in spring or autumn

A large aquatic marginal. Leaves on non-flowering stems heart-shaped, on flowering stems linear. Flowers yellow, solitary or in few-flowered panicles, in early summer.

Ranunculus lyalii
(Ranunculaceae)

Common name: Lyall buttercup
Height: 36in (1m)
Spread: 14in (35cm)
Aspect: Sun or half shade
Soil: Moist, well-drained, fertile
Hardiness: Zone 6
Propagation: Seed, when ripe; division, in spring or autumn

Rhizomatous perennial from New Zealand. Leaves basal, rounded, leathery, peltate, dark green, evergreen in mild areas. Flowers in panicles, white cups, in summer.

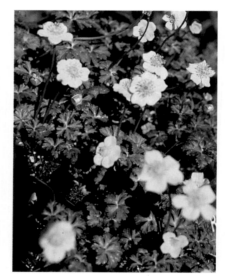

Ranunculus psilostachys
(Ranunculaceae)

Common names: None
Height: 12in (30cm)
Spread: 8in (20cm)
Aspect: Sun
Soil: Moist, well-drained, fertile
Hardiness: Zone 6
Propagation: Seed, when ripe; division, after flowering

Tuberous, spreading plant from Turkey and the Balkans. Leaves basal, 3-lobed, segments obovate, toothed, hairy below. Flowers upward-facing, yellow, early summer.

Ratibida columnifera
(Asteraceae/Compositae)

Common name: Prairie cone-flower
Height: 3ft (90cm)
Spread: 1ft (30cm)
Aspect: Sun
Soil: Dry, well-drained, fertile
Hardiness: Zone 3
Propagation: Seed, in early spring; division, in spring, when young

Perennial from North America and Mexico. Leaves pinnate, hairy, gray-green. Flowers daisylike, rays reflexed, yellow, disc brown, columnar, early summer to early autumn.

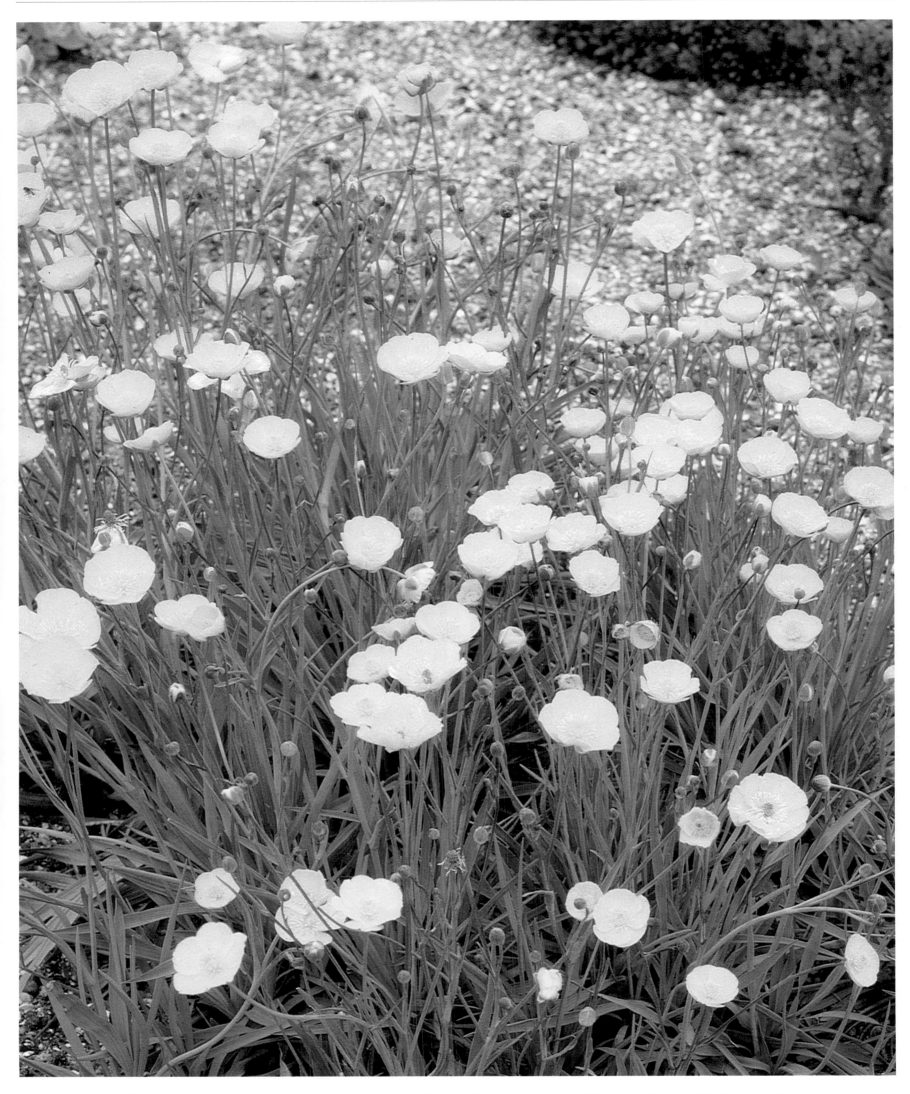

There are many non-invasive buttercups, such as Ranunculus gramineus, *that make a miniature meadow possible in any garden.*

Rehmannia elata
(Scrophulariaceae)

Common name: Beverly-bells
rehmannia
Height: 4ft (1.2m)
Spread: 20in (50cm)
Aspect: Sun
Soil: Well-drained, humus-
rich, fertile
Hardiness: Zone 9
Propagation: Seed, in warmth in late
winter; separated runners, in spring

Rosette-forming perennial. Leaves obovate,
toothed, veined, hairy. Flowers in leafy
racemes, tubular, semipendent, pink with
spotted throats, from summer to autumn.

Rehmannia glutinosa
A.G.M.
(Scrophulariaceae)

Common names: None
Height: 1ft (30cm)
Spread: 1ft (30cm)
Aspect: Sun
Soil: Well-drained, humus-
rich, fertile
Hardiness: Zone 9
Propagation: Seed, in warmth
in late winter; separated
runners, in spring

Leaves in rosettes, obovate, scalloped,
veined. Flowers pendent, tubular, reddish-
brown with purple veins and pale brown
lips, in racemes, midspring to summer.

Reineckea carnea
(Convallariaceae/Liliaceae)

Common names: None
Height: 8in (20cm)
Spread: 2ft (60cm)
Aspect: Half shade
Soil: Moist, well-drained,
acidic, humus-rich
Hardiness: Zone 7
Propagation: Seed, when ripe;
division, in spring

Rhizomatous evergreen. Leaves arching,
linear, glossy, bright green. Flowers shallow
pink cups fading to white, in dense spikes,
in late spring. Red berries in warm areas.

Rheum
'Ace of Hearts'
(Polygonaceae)

Common name: Rhubarb
Height: 4ft (1.2m)
Spread: 4ft (1.2m)
Aspect: Sun or half shade
Soil: Moist, deep, humus-rich
Hardiness: Zone 7
Propagation: Seed, in
autumn; division, in early
spring

A rhizomatous, hybrid perennial. Leaves
large, heart-shaped, dark green, veined red.
Flowers in panicles, tiny, pink stars, in
mid- and late summer.

Rheum palmatum
var. *tanguticum*
(Polygonaceae)

Common name: Rhubarb
Height: 6ft (2m)
Spread: 6ft (2m)
Aspect: Sun or half shade
Soil: Moist, humus-rich,
fertile
Hardiness: Zone 7
Propagation: Seed, in
autumn; division, in early
spring

Rhizomatous perennial. Leaves large, jagged,
reddish-green turning dark green and purple.
Flowers in huge many-flowered panicles,
white, red, or pink, in early summer.

Rhodanthemum gayanum
(Asteraceae/Compositae)

Common names: None
Height: 1ft (30cm)
Spread: 1ft (30cm)
Aspect: Sun
Soil: Sharply drained, fertile
Hardiness: Zone 8
Propagation: Seed, in spring;
softwood cuttings, in early
summer

Leaves deeply 3-lobed, hairy, gray-green.
Flowers solitary, daisylike, ray florets pale
pink or white, disc florets brown, in
summer. From Algeria and Morocco.

Rhodanthemum
hosmariense A.G.M.
(Asteraceae/Compositae)

Common names: None
Height: 1ft (30cm)
Spread: 1ft (30cm)
Aspect: Sun
Soil: Sharply drained, fertile
Hardiness: Zone 8
Propagation: Seed, in spring;
softwood cuttings, in early
summer

Spreading subshrub from Morocco. Leaves
deeply 3-lobed, hairy, silver. Flowers single,
solitary, white, daisylike with yellow
centers, and surrounded by silver bracts.

Rhodiola wallichiana
(Crassulaceae)

Common names: None
Height: 16in (40cm)
Spread: 12in (30cm)
Aspect: Sun
Soil: Fertile
Hardiness: Zone 6
Propagation: Seed, in spring
or autumn division, in spring
or early summer

Rhizomatous Himalayan perennial. Leaves
linear to lance-shaped, toothed, midgreen.
Flowers in dense terminal corymbs, pale or
greenish-yellow stars, in early summer.

Rhodohypoxis baurii
A.G.M.
(Hypoxidaceae)

Common names: None
Height: 4in (10cm)
Spread: 4in (10cm)
Aspect: Sun
Soil: Well-drained, humus-rich, fertile
Hardiness: Zone 8
Propagation: Seed, in warmth when ripe; offsets, in late autumn

A cormous perennial from South Africa. Leaves narrow, lance-shaped, keeled, grayish-green. Flowers solitary, flat, reddish-pink or white, all summer.

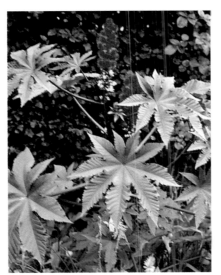

Ricinus communis
'Impala'
(Euphorbiaceae)

Common name: Castor-bean
Height: 4ft (1.2m)
Spread: 12ft (4m)
Aspect: Sun
Soil: Well-drained, humus-rich, fertile
Hardiness: Zone 9
Propagation: Seed, after soaking in late spring

Tender subshrub, good in mixed plantings. Leaves large, broad, ovate, toothed, glossy, reddish-purple. Flowers in spikes, females with red stigma, males yellow, in summer.

RODGERSIA (Saxifragaceae)

A genus of only some half-dozen species from the Far East, but one which gives us very hardy and handsome architectural plants for our gardens. They originate in the mountains of Burma, Korea, China, and Japan, growing along streams in scrub and woodlands. They are naturally moisture-lovers, but do not do well in waterlogged soil, and will grow in sun or half shade; they will tolerate drier soil in a partially shaded position better than they will in a sunny site. *Rodgersia* are large plants, and not really suitable for the very small garden, but do not usually require staking. Their large, palmate or pinnate leaves are handsome, although deciduous; some species have good autumn color. The flowers are petalless and star-shaped, borne in summer in upright, pyramidal panicles on tall stems, and are followed by attractive, dark red or brown seed capsules. *Rodgersia* will build up into quite large clumps requiring lots of room, and to prevent this, the roots should be divided in a circle around the plant. They are low-allergen plants and suit the allergic gardener. The young leaves may be damaged by slugs, and since they are grown as much for their foliage as their flowers, preventative measures must be taken early or the plant will look untidy all season.

Rodgersia aesculifolia
A.G.M.
(Saxifragaceae)

Common names: None
Height: 6ft (2m)
Spread: 3ft (1m)
Aspect: Sun or half shade
Soil: Moist, humus-rich
Hardiness: Zone 5
Propagation: Seed or division, both in spring

Rhizomatous plant. Leaves basal, palmate, 5- to 9-lobed, leaflets obovate, toothed, midgreen, red-veined. Tall panicles of many small, starry, pink or white flowers, summer.

Rodgersia pinnata
'Alba'
(Saxifragaceae)

Common names: None
Height: 3ft (90cm)
Spread: 4ft (1.2m)
Aspect: Sun or half shade
Soil: Moist, humus-rich
Hardiness: Zone 5
Propagation: Seed or division, both in spring

Clump-forming, rhizomatous plant. Leaves large, palmate, 5- to 9-lobed, obovate, glossy leaflets. Flowers small, starry, white, in fluffy panicles, in mid- and late summer

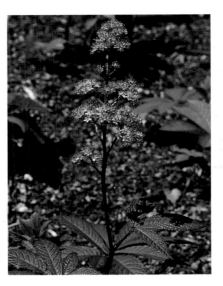

Rodgersia pinnata
'Elegans'
(Saxifragaceae)

Common names: None
Height: 3ft (90cm)
Spread: 4ft (1.2m)
Aspect: Sun or half shade
Soil: Moist, humus-rich
Hardiness: Zone 5
Propagation: Seed or division, both in spring

Cultivar with starry, pink flowers, tinted cream. Leaves large, palmate, 5- to 9-lobed, obovate, glossy leaflets. Lovely seed heads after flowering.

Rodgersia pinnata
'Superba' A.G.M.
(Saxifragaceae)

Common names: None
Height: 4ft (1.2m)
Spread: 30in (75cm)
Aspect: Sun or half shade
Soil: Moist, humus-rich
Hardiness: Zone 5
Propagation: Seed or division, both in spring

Tall selected form; may be a separate species. Leaves very large, palmate, lobes fewer than in type, glossy, veined, bronze-tinted. Large panicle of salmon-pink flowers.

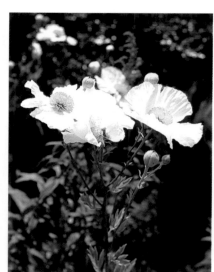

Rodgersia podophylla
A.G.M.
(Saxifragaceae)

Common name: Bronzeleaf
Rodger's-flower
Height: 5ft (1.5m)
Spread: 6ft (1.8m)
Aspect: Sun or half shade
Soil: Moist, humus-rich
Hardiness: Zone 5
Propagation: Seed or division,
both in spring

Rhizomatous plant from Japan and Korea.
Leaves huge, palmate, with 5 jagged, glossy
midgreen, obovate leaflets. Creamy-green
flowers (*not open here*) in panicles, summer.

Romneya coulteri
A.G.M.
(Papaveraceae)

Common name: Matilija-
poppy
Height: 8ft (2.5m)
Spread: Indefinite
Aspect: Sun
Soil: Well-drained, fertile
Hardiness: Zone 7
Propagation: Seed or basal
cuttings, both in spring; root
cuttings, in winter

Suckering subshrub. Leaves glaucous gray-
green, rounded-pinnatifid, lobes ovate to
lance-shaped. Flowers solitary, scented,
large, yellow-centered white cups, summer.

Romulea bulbocodium
(Iridaceae)

Common names: None
Height: 4in (10cm)
Spread: 2in (5cm)
Aspect: Sun
Soil: Well-drained, fertile
Hardiness: Zone 7
Propagation: Seed, in
autumn; offsets, when
dormant

Cormous perennial from the Mediterranean
and Africa. Leaves basal, linear, channelled,
arched. Up to 5 flowers per stem, lilac
funnels with white centers, in spring.

Roscoea auriculata
(Zingiberaceae)

Common names: None
Height: 2ft (60cm)
Spread: 8in (20cm)
Aspect: Half shade
Soil: Moist, well-drained,
humus-rich, fertile
Hardiness: Zone 6
Propagation: Seed, when ripe;
division, in spring

Tuberous perennial from Nepal and India.
Leaves linear to lance-shaped, dark green.
Flowers axillary, hooded, lips large, bracts
overlapping, purple, late summer to autumn.

Roscoea
'Beesiana'
(Zingiberaceae)

Common names: None
Height: 18in (45cm)
Spread: 12in (30cm)
Aspect: Half shade
Soil: Moist, well-drained,
humus-rich, fertile
Hardiness: Zone 6
Propagation: Seed, when ripe;
division, in spring

Hybrid perennial. Leaves lance-shaped,
arching, dark green. Flowers hooded, with
overlapping bracts, yellow, striped mauve
sometimes, in late summer to autumn.

Roscoea cautleyoides
A.G.M.
(Zingiberaceae)

Common names: None
Height: 2ft (60cm)
Spread: 8in (20cm)
Aspect: Half shade
Soil: Moist, well-drained,
humus-rich, fertile
Hardiness: Zone 6
Propagation: Seed, when ripe;
division, in spring

Tuberous perennial from China. Leaves
linear, midgreen. Flowers hooded, with
overlapping bracts, on leafy stalks, yellow,
purple, or white, late summer to autumn.

Roscoea purpurea
(Zingiberaceae)

Common names: None
Height: 2ft (60cm)
Spread: 1ft (30cm)
Aspect: Half shade
Soil: Moist, well-drained,
humus-rich, fertile
Hardiness: Zone 6
Propagation: Seed, when ripe;
division, in spring

A tuberous perennial from the Himalayas.
Leaves lance-shaped, dark green. Flowers
hooded, purple, in late summer to early
autumn. Appears late, so mark position.

Rosmarinus officinalis
'Severn Sea' A.G.M.
(Labiatae/Lamiaceae)

Common names: Rosemary
Height: 3ft (90cm)
Spread: 5ft (1.5m)
Aspect: Sun
Soil: Well-drained, fertile
Hardiness: Zone 6
Propagation: Semiripe
cuttings in summer

An aromatic evergreen subshrub from the
Mediterranean. Leaves linear, dark green,
white-woolly below. Flowers in axillary
whorls, blue, in late spring to summer.

Rosularia sedoides
(Crassulaceae)

Common name: Himalayan
houseleek
Height: 2in (5cm)
Spread: 8in (20cm)
Aspect: Sun
Soil: Sharply drained,
humus-rich
Hardiness: Zone 7
Propagation: Separated
offsets, in spring

Succulent, stoloniferous evergreen from the
Himalayas. Leaves ovoid, hairy, green, red
in sun, in rosettes like a houseleek. Flowers
star-shaped, white, late summer to autumn.

Rudbeckia fulgida var.
***sullivantii* 'Goldsturm' A.G.M.**
(Asteraceae/Compositae)

Common name: Showy
coneflower
Height: 2ft (60cm)
Spread: 18in (45cm)
Aspect: Sun or half shade
Soil: Well-drained, humus-
rich, fertile
Hardiness: Zone 4
Propagation: Division, in
autumn or spring

Cultivar of a rhizomatous plant from the
U.S.A. Leaves basal and stem, lance-shaped,
midgreen. Flowers solitary, single, golden-
yellow, daisylike, late summer to autumn.

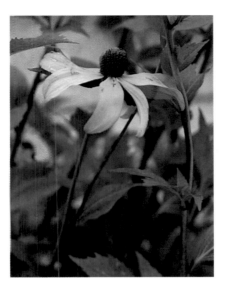

Rudbeckia
'Herbstonne'
(Asteraceae/Compositae)

Common name: Coneflower
Height: 1.8m (6ft)
Spread: 3ft (90cm)
Aspect: Sun or half shade
Soil: Well-drained, humus-
rich, fertile
Hardiness: Zone 3
Propagation: Division, in
spring or autumn

Hardy, rhizomatous, clump-forming, short-
lived hybrid. Leaves ovate, toothed, glossy
green. Flowers solitary, yellow, with a high,
green boss, summer to early autumn.

Rudbeckia hirta
(Asteraceae/Compositae)

Common name: Black-eyed
Susan
Height: 36in (90cm)
Spread: 18in (45cm)
Aspect: Sun or half shade
Soil: Well-drained, humus-
rich, fertile
Hardiness: Zone 4
Propagation: Seed, in spring;
division, in spring or autumn

Rhizomatous, short-lived perennial. Leaves
basal and stem, ovate, midgreen. Solitary,
large, yellow, daisylike flowers with black,
domed centers, summer to early autumn.

Rudbeckia subtomentosa
(Asteraceae/Compositae)

Common name: Sweet
coneflower
Height: 28in (70cm)
Spread: 2ft (60cm)
Aspect: Sun or half shade
Soil: Well-drained, humus-
rich, fertile
Hardiness: Zone 5
Propagation: Seed, in spring;
division, in spring or autumn

A short-lived perennial from the central
U.S.A. Leaves ovate, midgreen. Flowers
solitary, single, daisylike, yellow with dark
purple-brown centers, in autumn.

Rumex sanguineus
(Polygonaceae)

Common names: Bloody
dock; red-veined dock
Height: 32in (80cm)
Spread: 12in (30cm)
Aspect: Sun
Soil: Well-drained, fertile
Hardiness: Zone 6
Propagation: Seed, sown
in situ in spring

Taprooted perennial. Leaves in rosettes,
oblong, dark green, boldly red-veined.
Flowers in panicles, minute stars, green,
turning brown, in early to midsummer.

Ruta graveolens
(Rutaceae)

Common name: Common rue
Height: 3ft (90cm)
Spread: 32in (80cm)
Aspect: Sun or half shade
Soil: Sharply drained, fertile
Hardiness: Zone 5
Propagation: Seed, in spring;
semiripe cuttings, in summer

Evergreen subshrub. Leaves 2-pinnatisect,
ovate, lobes obovate, glaucous blue-green,
aromatic. Flowers in cymes, yellow cups,
in summer. Irritant; poisonous in quantity.

Sagittaria latifolia
(Alismataceae)

Common name: Common
arrowhead
Height: 4ft (1.2m)
Spread: 3ft (90cm)
Aspect: Sun
Soil: Marginal aquatic
Hardiness: Zone 7
Propagation: Seed, as soon as
ripe; division or separated
runners, both in spring

A tuberous, aquatic marginal perennial
from the U.S.A. Leaves aerial, arrow-
shaped. Flowers in whorled racemes,
white, in summer.

Sagittaria sagittifolia
(Alismataceae)

Common name: Double
Oldworld arrowhead
Height: 3ft (90cm)
Spread: Indefinite
Aspect: Sun
Soil: Marginal aquatic
Hardiness: Zone 7
Propagation: Seed, as soon as
ripe; division or separated
runners, both in spring

Spreading, tuberous plant from Eurasia.
Leaves arrow-shaped, midgreen, aerial.
Flowers in racemes, white with a purple
spot at the base of each petal, in summer.

SALVIA (Labiatae/Lamiaceae)
Sage

A very large and varied genus of about 900 species of
annuals, biennials, perennials, and shrubs from grassland,
scrub, or woodland habitats in tropical and temperate regions
the world over. The perennials may be rhizomatous, tuberous,
or fibrous-rooted, and evergreen or herbaceous, and they vary
widely in hardiness from fully hardy to tender. The foliage is
aromatic in many, hairy in some, and silvery in others. *Salvia*
species all prefer light, alkaline soils that are well drained and
moisture retentive. Almost all require full sun, especially the
low-growing types with woolly or densely hairy leaves, but a
few will tolerate light shade. The leaves are both basal and
stem, and the two types often differ in form. The flowers are
two-lipped; the upper petal arches forward to form a hood,
and the lower petal is two-toothed. They are borne in
panicles or in axillary whorls on upright stems. Many types
attract bees, and some have culinary or medicinal use:
S. officinalis is the common culinary sage. All sages are low-
allergen, and suitable for the allergic gardener. Some of the
taller varieties may need to be staked. The silvery-woolly
types dislike winter wet and cold, drying winds, so should be
either lifted and brought in or covered with a cloche.

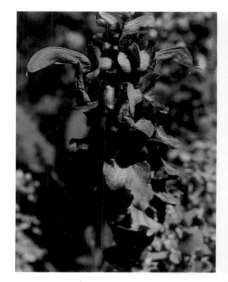

Salvia africana-lutea
(Labiatae/Lamiaceae)

Common names: None
Height: 3ft (90cm)
Spread: 3ft (90cm)
Aspect: Sun
Soil: Moist, well-drained,
humus-rich, fertile
Hardiness: Zone 9
Propagation: Basal or
softwood cuttings, both in
spring; semiripe cuttings, in autumn

A tender, evergreen subshrub from Africa.
Leaves rounded, aromatic, hairy, white-
woolly. Flowers in terminal racemes, red-
brown, from summer to late autumn.

Salvia argentea
A.G.M.
(Labiatae/Lamiaceae)

Common name: Silver sage
Height: 3ft (90cm)
Spread: 2ft (60cm)
Aspect: Sun
Soil: Moist, well-drained,
humus-rich, fertile
Hardiness: Zone 5
Propagation: Seed or division,
both in spring

Short-lived perennial. Leaves large, in basal
rosette, silky, silver-hairy. Flowers white or
pale pink, in branched panicles, in summer;
if cut down, will flower again in autumn.

Salvia azurea
(Labiatae/Lamiaceae)

Common name: Blue sage
Height: 4ft (1.2m)
Spread: 3ft (90cm)
Aspect: Sun or half shade
Soil: Moist, well-drained,
humus-rich, fertile
Hardiness: Zone 4
Propagation: Basal or
softwood cuttings, both in
spring; semiripe cuttings, in late summer

A straggly perennial from the U.S.A.
Leaves lance-shaped, softly hairy, midgreen. Flowers in dense terminal racemes,
blue or white, from autumn to winter.

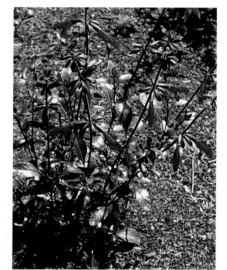

Salvia buchananii
A.G.M.
(Labiatae/Lamiaceae)

Common names: None
Height: 1ft (30cm)
Spread: 1ft (30cm)
Aspect: Sun or half shade
Soil: Moist, well-drained,
humus-rich, fertile
Hardiness: Zone 9
Propagation: Basal or
softwood cuttings, both in
spring; semiripe cuttings, in late summer

Spreading evergreen. Leaves ovate,
toothed, leathery, glossy green. Flowers in
terminal racemes, red with brown-purple
calyces, from midsummer to midautumn.

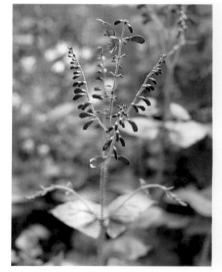

Salvia cacaliifolia
A.G.M.
(Labiatae/Lamiaceae)

Common names: None
Height: 4ft (1.2m)
Spread: 1ft (30cm)
Aspect: Sun or half shade
Soil: Moist, well-drained,
humus-rich, fertile
Hardiness: Zone 9
Propagation: Basal or
softwood cuttings, both in
spring; semiripe cuttings, in late summer

A tender perennial from Mexico and
Guatemala. Leaves triangular, midgreen.
Flowers in terminal panicles, in pairs, deep
blue, all summer and into autumn.

Salvia farinacea 'Victoria' is a particularly densely branching cultivar; it is tender, and usually treated as an annual.

Salvia coccinea
(Labiatae/Lamiaceae)

Common name: Red Texas
sage
Height: 30in (75cm)
Spread: 12in (30cm)
Aspect: Sun or half shade
Soil: Moist, well-drained,
humus-rich, fertile
Hardiness: Zone 8
Propagation: Seed, in spring

A short-lived perennial from the Americas.
Leaves oval, hairy, toothed, dark green.
Flowers cherry-red, in open spikes, from
summer to autumn.

Salvia coccinea
'Coral Nymph'
(Labiatae/Lamiaceae)

Common names: None
Height: 30in (75cm)
Spread: 12in (30cm)
Aspect: Sun or half shade
Soil: Moist, well-drained,
humus-rich, fertile
Hardiness: Zone 8
Propagation: Division, in
spring

A selected form of the species, with flowers
having an upper lip of salmon-pink, and a
lower lip of pale pink. Leaves oval, hairy,
toothed, dark green.

Salvia confertiflora
(Labiatae/Lamiaceae)

Common names: None
Height: 4ft (1.2m)
Spread: 2ft (60cm)
Aspect: Sun or half shade
Soil: Moist, well-drained,
humus-rich, fertile
Hardiness: Zone 9
Propagation: Basal or
softwood cuttings, both in
spring; semiripe cuttings, in late summer

Leaves ovate, scalloped, green-yellow,
woolly below, pungent. Flowers in terminal
spikes, indigo-black with hairy, brown
calyces, in late summer to midautumn.

Salvia darcyi
(Labiatae/Lamiaceae)

Common names: None
Height: 1m (3ft)
Spread: 2ft (60cm)
Aspect: Sun or half shade
Soil: Moist, well-drained,
humus-rich, fertile
Hardiness: Zone 8
Propagation: Basal or
softwood cuttings, both in
spring; semiripe cuttings, in late summer

Subshrub from Mexico. Leaves triangular,
hairy, crenate, midgreen. Flowers in whorls
of up to 6 on unbranched spikes, red, from
summer to late autumn.

Salvia farinacea
(Labiatae/Lamiaceae)

Common name: Mealycup
sage
Height: 2ft (60cm)
Spread: 1ft (30cm)
Aspect: Sun or half shade
Soil: Moist, well-drained,
humus-rich, fertile
Hardiness: Zone 9
Propagation: Seed, in spring

Bushy perennial from Mexico and the U.S.A.
Leaves ovate, thin, glossy, midgreen, white
below. Flowers in whorls of up to 16, in
spikes, lavender-blue, summer to autumn.

Salvia forsskaolii
(Labiatae/Lamiaceae)

Common names: None
Height: 3ft (90cm)
Spread: 18in (45cm)
Aspect: Sun or half shade
Soil: Moist, well-drained,
humus-rich, fertile
Hardiness: Zone 7
Propagation: Seed, in spring

Perennial from the Black Sea coast. Leaves
basal, broad, ovate, toothed, midgreen.
Flowers in spikes, tubes white, lips violet,
lower lip marked yellow, all summer.

Salvia fulgens
A.G.M.
(Labiatae/Lamiaceae)

Common names: None
Height: 1m (3ft)
Spread: 1m (3ft)
Aspect: Sun or half shade
Soil: Moist, well-drained,
humus-rich, fertile
Hardiness: Zone 9
Propagation: Basal or
softwood cuttings, both in
spring; semiripe cuttings, in late summer

Tender, evergreen perennial from Mexico.
Leaves ovate, toothed, bright green, white-
woolly below. Flowers in terminal racemes,
red, lower lip downy, in summer.

Salvia glutinosa
(Labiatae/Lamiaceae)

Common name: Jupiter's
distaff
Height: 3ft (90cm)
Spread: 2ft (60cm)
Aspect: Half shade
Soil: Moist, humus-rich,
fertile
Hardiness: Zone 5
Propagation: Seed, in spring

Eurasian perennial. Leaves heart-shaped,
hairy, toothed. Flowers sticky, in loose
terminal racemes, pale yellow, spotted
maroon, from midsummer to midautumn.

Salvia greggii
(Labiatae/Lamiaceae)

Common name: Autumn sage
Height: 30in (75cm)
Spread: 30in (75cm)
Aspect: Sun or half shade
Soil: Moist, well-drained,
humus-rich, fertile
Hardiness: Zone 9
Propagation: Basal or
softwood cuttings, both in spring; semi-
ripe cuttings, in late summer

Evergreen from Texas and Mexico. Leaves
elliptic, small, leathery. Flowers in pairs in
terminal racemes, mauvish-red, pink,
yellow, or violet, late summer to autumn

Salvia greggii
'Peach' A.G.M.
(Labiatae/Lamiaceae)

Common name: Autumn sage
Height: 30in (75cm)
Spread: 30in (75cm)
Aspect: Sun or half shade
Soil: Moist, well-drained,
humus-rich, fertile
Hardiness: Zone 9
Propagation: Basal or
softwood cuttings, both in
spring; semiripe cuttings, in late summer

A selected form of the species, with flowers
in pairs, of a strong peach color, from late
summer to autumn. Leaves elliptic, small,
leathery, midgreen.

Salvia hians
(Labiatae/Lamiaceae)

Common names: None
Height: 2ft (60cm)
Spread: 2ft (60cm)
Aspect: Sun or half shade
Soil: Moist, well-drained,
humus-rich, fertile
Hardiness: Zone 6
Propagation: Seed or division,
both in spring

Short-lived perennial from the Himalayas.
Leaves ovate, toothed, veined, wrinkled,
dark green. Flowers in terminal spikes,
purplish-blue, lower lip white, all summer.

Salvia involucrata
'Bethellii'
(Labiatae/Lamiaceae)

Common names: None
Height: 5ft (1.5m)
Spread: 3ft (90cm)
Aspect: Sun or half shade
Soil: Moist, well-drained,
humus-rich, fertile
Hardiness: Zone 9
Propagation: Basal or
softwood cuttings, both in
spring; semiripe cuttings, in late summer

Selected form of a perennial from Mexico.
Leaves ovate, hairy, bright green. Flowers in
dense, terminal racemes, purplish-crimson,
bracts pink, late summer to midautumn.

Salvia involucrata
'Boutin' A.G.M.
(Labiatae/Lamiaceae)

Common names: None
Height: 5ft (1.5m)
Spread: 3ft (90cm)
Aspect: Sun or half shade
Soil: Moist, well-drained,
humus-rich, fertile
Hardiness: Zone 9
Propagation: Basal or
softwood cuttings, both in
spring; semiripe cuttings, in late summer

Selected form of the species with flowers in
dense, terminal racemes, dark pink with
dark pink bracts, from late summer to
midautumn. Leaves ovate, hairy.

Salvia leucantha
A.G.M.
(Labiatae/Lamiaceae)

Common name: Mexican bush
Height: 3ft (90cm)
Spread: 3ft (90cm)
Aspect: Sun or half shade
Soil: Moist, well-drained,
humus-rich, fertile
Hardiness: Zone 10
Propagation: Basal or
softwood cuttings, both in spring;
semiripe cuttings, in late summer

Evergreen subshrub. Leaves ovate, hairy,
gray, white-tomentose below. Flowers in
terminal racemes, white with bell-shaped,
lavender calyces, in autumn to winter.

Salvia microphylla
(Labiatae/Lamiaceae)

Common name: Myrtle sage
Height: 4ft (1.2m)
Spread: 4ft (1.2m)
Aspect: Sun or half shade
Soil: Moist, well-drained,
humus-rich, fertile
Hardiness: Zone 9
Propagation: Basal or
softwood cuttings, both in
spring; semiripe cuttings, in late summer

Evergreen perennial. Leaves small, ovate,
hairy, toothed, midgreen. Flowers paired or
whorled in terminal racemes, crimson, in
late summer and autumn.

Salvia microphylla
var. neurepia
(Labiatae/Lamiaceae)

Common names: Myrtle sage
Height: 4ft (1.2m)
Spread: 4ft (1.2m)
Aspect: Sun or half shade
Soil: Moist, well-drained,
humus-rich, fertile
Hardiness: Zone 9
Propagation: Basal or
softwood cuttings, both in
spring; semiripe cuttings, in late summer

A form of the species with shiny, glabrous
leaves of pale green, and red flowers paired
or whorled in terminal racemes, from late
summer to autumn.

Salvia nemorosa 'Ostfriesland' A.G.M. (Labiatae/Lamiaceae)

Common names: None
Height: 3ft (1m)
Spread: 2ft (60cm)
Aspect: Sun or half shade
Soil: Moist, well-drained, humus-rich, fertile
Hardiness: Zone 5
Propagation: Basal or softwood cuttings, both in spring; semiripe cuttings, in late summer

A selected form of a species from Eurasia. Leaves ovate, crenulate, midgreen. Flowers in very dense, terminal racemes, deep violet-blue, from summer to autumn.

Salvia officinalis (Labiatae/Lamiaceae)

Common name: Garden sage
Height: 18in (45cm)
Spread: 18in (45cm)
Aspect: Sun or half shade
Soil: Moist, well-drained, humus-rich, fertile
Hardiness: Zone 5
Propagation: Seed or cuttings, both in spring

An evergreen, Mediterranean culinary herb. Leaves aromatic, oblong, woolly, gray-green. Flowers in racemes, lilac, in early to midsummer.

Salvia officinalis 'Kew Gold' A.G.M. (Labiatae/Lamiaceae)

Common name: Garden sage
Height: 1ft (30cm)
Spread: 1ft (30cm)
Aspect: Sun or half shade
Soil: Moist, well-drained, humus-rich, fertile
Hardiness: Zone 5
Propagation: Division, in spring

A form of the common sage with oblong, woolly, aromatic leaves of pale green splashed with gold. Flowers in racemes, lilac, in early to midsummer.

Salvia officinalis 'Tricolor' A.G.M. (Labiatae/Lamiaceae)

Common name: Garden sage
Height: 12in (30cm)
Spread: 18in (45cm)
Aspect: Sun or half shade
Soil: Moist, well-drained, humus-rich, fertile
Hardiness: Zone 5
Propagation: Division, in spring

Form of the common sage with gray-green leaves margined cream and pink; young leaves have more pink than cream. Flowers in racemes, lilac, in early to midsummer.

Salvia patens A.G.M. (Labiatae/Lamiaceae)

Common name: Gentian salvia
Height: 2ft (60cm)
Spread: 18in (45cm)
Aspect: Sun or half shade
Soil: Moist, well-drained, humus-rich, fertile
Hardiness: Zone 8
Propagation: Seed or division, both in spring

A tuberous perennial from Mexico. Leaves ovate, hairy, toothed, midgreen. Flowers in few-flowered racemes, deep blue, from midsummer to midautumn.

Salvia patens 'Cambridge Blue' A.G.M. (Labiatae/Lamiaceae)

Common name: Gentian salvia
Height: 2ft (60cm)
Spread: 18in (45cm)
Aspect: Sun or half shade
Soil: Moist, well-drained, humus-rich, fertile
Hardiness: Zone 8
Propagation: Division, in spring

A form of the species with flowers of pale blue in few-flowered racemes, from midsummer to midautumn. Leaves ovate, hairy, toothed, midgreen.

Salvia patens 'White Trophy' (Labiatae/Lamiaceae)

Common name: Gentian salvia
Height: 2ft (60cm)
Spread: 18in (45cm)
Aspect: Sun or half shade
Soil: Moist, well-drained, fertile, humus-rich
Hardiness: Zone 8
Propagation: Division, in spring

A white-flowered form of the species, bearing few-flowered racemes from midsummer to midautumn. Leaves ovate, hairy, toothed, midgreen.

Salvia pratensis Haematodes Group A.G.M. (Labiatae/Lamiaceae)

Common name: Meadow sage
Height: 1m (3ft
Spread: 1ft (30cm)
Aspect: Sun or half shade
Soil: Moist, well-drained, humus-rich, fertile
Hardiness: Zone 5
Propagation: Seed, in spring

Also called S. haematodes. Leaves in basal rosettes, large, ovate, dark green. Flowers in panicles, bluish-violet with pale throats, from early to midsummer. Short-lived.

Salvia purpurea
(Labiatae/Lamiaceae)

Common names: None
Height: 6ft (1.8m)
Spread: 3ft (90cm)
Aspect: Sun
Soil: Moist, well-drained,
humus-rich, fertile
Hardiness: Zone 9
Propagation: Basal or
softwood cuttings, both in
spring; semiripe cuttings, in late summer

A tender perennial from Central America.
Leaves ovate, toothed, midgreen. Flowers
in short racemes, pinkish-lilac, upper lip
densely hairy, from winter to spring.

Salvia roemeriana
A.G.M.
(Labiatae/Lamiaceae)

Common names: None
Height: 1ft (30cm)
Spread: 1ft (30cm)
Aspect: Sun or half shade
Soil: Moist, well-drained,
humus-rich, fertile
Hardiness: Zone 8
Propagation: Seed or basal
or softwood cuttings, all in
spring

A small perennial from Texas, Arizona,
and Mexico. Leaves rounded, toothed,
bright green. Flowers in loose racemes,
scarlet, from midsummer to midautumn.

Salvia sclarea var.
turkestanica hort.
(Labiatae/Lamiaceae)

Common names: Clary; clary
sage
Height: 1m (3ft)
Spread: 1ft (30cm)
Aspect: Sun or half shade
Soil: Moist, well-drained,
humus-rich, fertile
Hardiness: Zone 5
Propagation: Softwood cuttings, in spring;
semiripe cuttings, in late summer

Unpleasant-smelling perennial. Leaves in
basal rosette, ovate, toothed, wrinkled,
midgreen. Flowers in terminal panicles,
white, edged pink, from spring to summer.

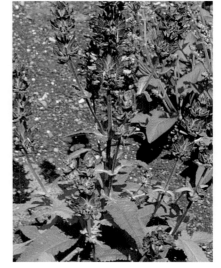

Salvia spathacea
A.G.M.
(Labiatae/Lamiaceae)

Common names: None
Height: 1ft (30cm)
Spread: 3ft (90cm)
Aspect: Half shade
Soil: Moist, well-drained,
humus-rich, fertile
Hardiness: Zone 8
Propagation: Seed or basal
cuttings, both in spring

A rhizomatous, spreading perennial from
California. Leaves oblong, sticky-hairy,
light green. Flowers in whorls, deep pink,
surrounded by bracts, in summer.

Salvia uliginosa
A.G.M.
(Labiatae/Lamiaceae)

Common names: None
Height: 5ft (1.5m)
Spread: 3ft (1m)
Aspect: Sun
Soil: Wet, humus-rich, fertile
Hardiness: Zone 9
Propagation: Basal or
softwood cuttings, both in
spring; semiripe cuttings, in
late summer

Rhizomatous perennial from swampy areas
of South America. Leaves oblong, toothed,
midgreen. Flowers in terminal racemes,
clear blue, late summer to midautumn.

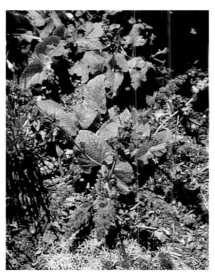

Salvia verticillata
(Labiatae/Lamiaceae)

Common names: None
Height: 32in (80cm)
Spread: 20in (50cm)
Aspect: Sun or half shade
Soil: Moist, well-drained,
humus-rich, fertile
Hardiness: Zone 6
Propagation: Basal or
softwood cuttings, both in
spring; semiripe cuttings, in late summer

A herbaceous perennial from Europe.
Leaves ovate, hairy, midgreen. Flowers on
branched stems, whorled, in racemes, lilac,
all summer.

Salvia verticillata
'Alba'
(Labiatae/Lamiaceae)

Common names: None
Height: 32in (80cm)
Spread: 20in (50cm)
Aspect: Sun or half shade
Soil: Moist, well-drained,
humus-rich, fertile
Hardiness: Zone 6
Propagation: Basal or
softwood cuttings, both in
spring; semiripe cuttings, in late summer

The white-flowered form of the species.
Flowers borne in whorled racemes, on
branched stems, all summer. Leaves ovate,
hairy, midgreen.

Sanguinaria canadensis
'Plena' A.G.M.
(Papaveraceae)

Common name: Bloodroot
Height: 6in (15cm)
Spread: 12in (30cm)
Aspect: Full or deep shade
Soil: Moist, well-drained,
humus-rich, fertile
Hardiness: Zone 3
Propagation: Seed, in
autumn; division, just after
flowering

Hardy rhizomatous woodlander. Leaves
heart- or kidney-shaped, blue-green. Flowers
solitary, white, double, very brief period in
spring. Leaves also vanish; mark position.

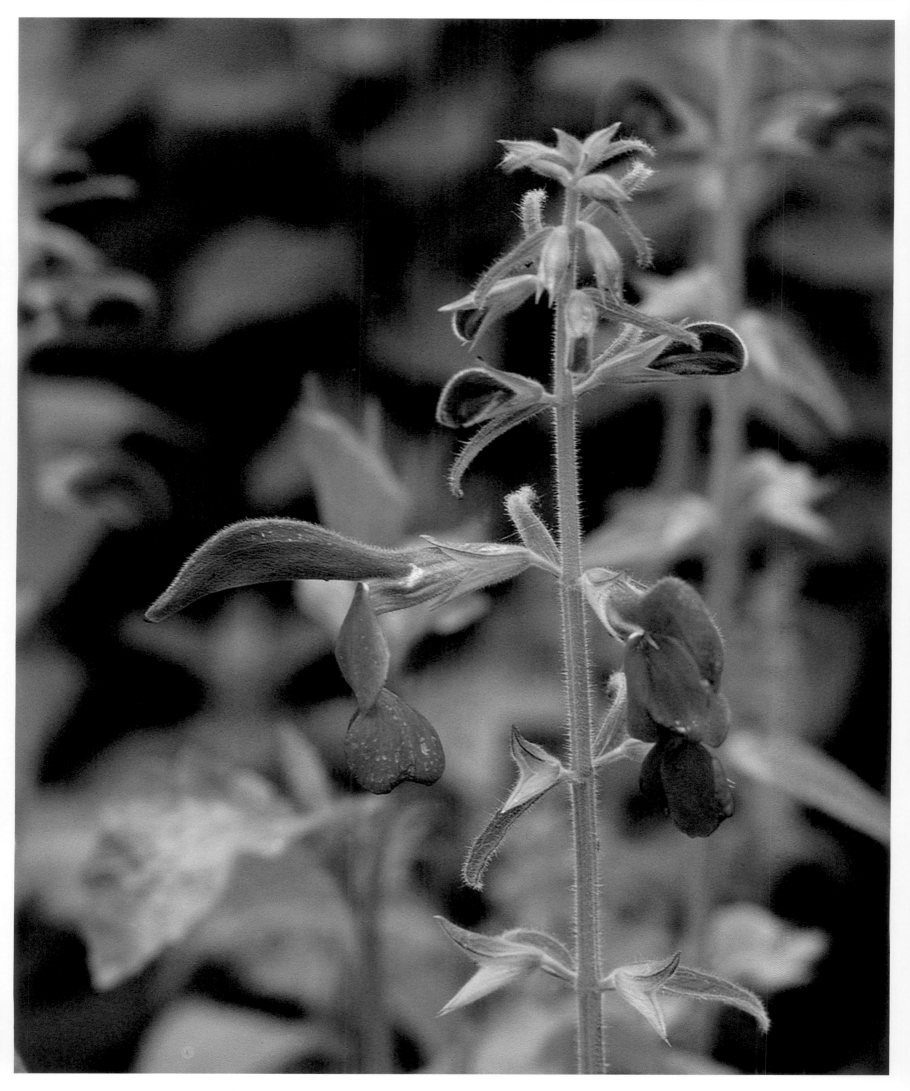

The robust, reliable Salvia patens is one of the best blue-flowered forms for the garden.

Sanguisorba albiflora
(Rosaceae)

Common name: Burnet
Height: 2ft (60cm)
Spread: 2ft (60cm)
Aspect: Sun or half shade
Soil: Moist, well-drained, humus-rich, fertile
Hardiness: Zone 5
Propagation: Seed or division, both in spring or autumn

Short-lived, rhizomatous perennial. Leaves pinnate, leaflets ovate, gray-green. Flowers in arching, bottlebrush spikes, small, fluffy, white, summer to early autumn.

Sanguisorba canadensis
(Rosaceae)

Common name: American burnet
Height: 6ft (2m)
Spread: 3ft (1m)
Aspect: Sun or half shade
Soil: Moist, well-drained, humus-rich, fertile
Hardiness: Zone 4
Propagation: Seed or division, both in spring or autumn

Rhizomatous, invasive perennial. Leaves pinnate, leaflets oblong, gray-green. Flowers in bottlebrush spikes, small, white, fluffy, from midsummer to midautumn.

Sanguisorba menziesii
(Rosaceae)

Common name: Burnet
Height: 2ft (60cm)
Spread: 1ft (30cm)
Aspect: Sun
Soil: Moist, well-drained, humus-rich, fertile
Hardiness: Zone 5
Propagation: Seed or division, both in spring or autumn

A dwarf perennial. Leaves pinnate, leaflets obovate, toothed, light green. Flowers in bottlebrush spikes, small, maroon, over a few weeks in summer.

Sanguisorba obtusa
(Rosaceae)

Common name: Burnet
Height: 2ft (60cm)
Spread: 2ft (60cm)
Aspect: Sun or half shade
Soil: Moist, well-drained, humus-rich, fertile
Hardiness: Zone 5
Propagation: Seed or division, both in spring or autumn

Rhizomatous, spreading perennial from Japan. Leaves pinnate, leaflets oblong, gray-green. Flowers in bottlebrush spikes, small, fluffy, pink, summer to early autumn.

Sanguisorba officinalis 'Tanna'
(Rosaceae)

Common name: Burnet
Height: 10in (25cm)
Spread: 2ft (60cm)
Aspect: Sun or half shade
Soil: Moist, well-drained, humus-rich, fertile
Hardiness: Zone 4
Propagation: Division, in spring or autumn

Form of a rhizomatous, dwarf plant. Leaves basal, pinnate, leaflets elliptic, midgreen. Flowers maroon-purple, in short, bottlebrush spikes, late summer to early autumn.

Sanguisorba tenuifolia 'Rosea'
(Rosaceae)

Common name: Burnet
Height: 4ft (1.2m)
Spread: 2ft (60cm)
Aspect: Sun or half shade
Soil: Wet, humus-rich, fertile
Hardiness: Zone 4
Propagation: Seed or division, both in spring or autumn

Rhizomatous perennial from the Far East. Leaves basal, large, pinnate, leaflets deeply divided, feathery. Flowers pink, in arching bottlebrushes, late summer to early autumn.

Santolina chamaecyparissus A.G.M.
(Asteraceae/Compositae)

Common name: Lavender-cotton
Height: 18in (45cm)
Spread: 36in (1m)
Aspect: Sun
Soil: Well-drained, fertile
Hardiness: Zone 7
Propagation: Seed, in autumn or spring

Evergreen Mediterrenean subshrub. Leaves aromatic, pinnatisect, leaflets toothed, gray-white, deeply dissected. Flowers bright yellow buttons, in mid- to late summer.

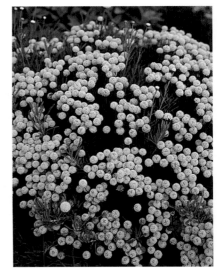

Santolina pinnata subsp. neapolitana 'Edward Bowles'
(Asteraceae/Compositae)

Common name: Lavender-cotton
Height: 30in (75cm)
Spread: 36in (1m)
Aspect: Sun
Soil: Well-drained, fertile
Hardiness: Zone 7
Propagation: Seed, in autumn or spring

An evergreen subshrub from Italy. Leaves aromatic, pinnate, leaflets cylindrical, gray-green. Flowers on long stems, creamy-white buttons, in summer.

Santolina rosmarinifolia subsp. rosmarinifolia
(Asteraceae/Compositae)

Common names: None
Height: 2ft (60cm)
Spread: 3ft (1m)
Aspect: Sun
Soil: Well-drained, fertile
Hardiness: Zone 7
Propagation: Seed, in spring
or autumn

Evergreen subshrub from Europe. Leaves aromatic, pinnate, leaflets narrowly linear, toothed, bright green. Flowers on slim stems, pale yellow buttons, in midsummer.

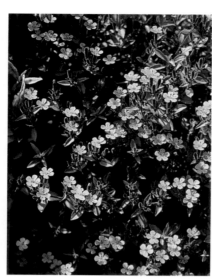

Saponaria ocymoides
A.G.M.
(Caryophyllaceae)

Common name: Rock
soapwort
Height: 4in (10cm)
Spread: 18in (45cm)
Aspect: Sun
Soil: Well-drained, fertile,
alkaline
Hardiness: Zone 4
Propagation: Seed, in autumn
or spring

A creeping, mat-forming perennial. Leaves ovate, hairy, bright green. Flowers in loose cymes, pink, in summer. Cut to the ground after flowering to keep compact.

Saponaria officinalis
(Caryophyllaceae)

Common names: Bouncing
Bet
Height: 2ft (60cm)
Spread: 18in (45cm)
Aspect: Sun
Soil: Well-drained, fertile
Hardiness: Zone 4
Propagation: Seed or division,
both in autumn or spring

Untidy, extremely invasive, rhizomatous perennial. Leaves ovate, veined, rough, midgreen. Flowers in cymes, scented, pink, white, or red from summer to autumn.

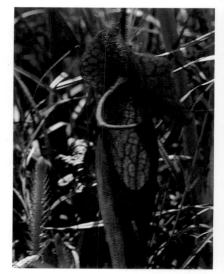

Sarracenia × catesbyi
A.G.M.
(Sarraceniaceae)

Common name: Pitcher-plant
Height: 30in (75cm)
Spread: 36in (1m)
Aspect: Sun
Soil: Moist, sharply-drained,
acidic, humus-rich
Hardiness: Zone 5
Propagation: Seed or division,
both in spring

Carnivorous, natural hybrid. Leaves form vases, or "pitchers," which secrete nectar and trap insects. Pitcher erect, red. Flowers (*not shown*) large red, in spring.

Sarracenia flava
A.G.M.
(Sarraceniaceae)

Common name: Trumpet
pitcher-plant
Height: 3ft (1m)
Spread: 3ft (1m)
Aspect: Sun
Soil: Moist, well-drained,
acidic, humus-rich
Hardiness: Zone 7
Propagation: Seed or division,
both in spring

Carnivorous perennial. Leaves form vases, or "pitchers," which secrete nectar and trap insects. Pitchers yellow-green. Flowers (*not shown*) yellow, in spring.

Sauromatum venosum
(Araceae)

Common name: Monarch-of-
the-East
Height: 18in (45cm)
Spread: 8in (20cm)
Aspect: Half shade
Soil: Well-drained, acidic,
humus-rich, fertile
Hardiness: Zone 10
Propagation: Offsets, in
winter when dormant

Tuberous perennial. Spathe green, spotted black, spadix long, arched, foul-smelling, in spring to summer, then a single leaf stem with a crown of lance-shaped segments.

Saururus cernuus
(Saururaceae)

Common name: Swamp lily
Height: 4ft (1.2m)
Spread: 2ft (60cm)
Aspect: Sun
Soil: Wet
Hardiness: Zone 5
Propagation: Seed, when ripe

A rhizomatous perennial from the U.S.A. Leaves heart-shaped, pointed, midgreen. Flowers small, in arching spikes, white, in early summer.

Saxifraga fortunei
A.G.M. (4)
(Saxifragaceae

Common name: Saxifrage
Height: 1ft (30cm)
Spread: 1ft (30cm)
Aspect: Full or half shade
Soil: Moist, well-drained,
humus-rich
Hardiness: Zone 7
Propagation: Seed, in
autumn; division, in spring

Clump-forming perennial. Leaves rounded, scalloped, 7-lobed, midgreen, red beneath. Flowers in large, wide panicles, small, starry, white, from early autumn to early winter.

SAXIFRAGA (Saxifragaceae)
Saxifrage

A genus of over 400 species of perennials, biennials, and a few annuals, found in mountain habitats, principally in the northern hemisphere. The great majority of species are cushion-forming or mat-forming alpine plants that are more suited to the rock garden than the herbaceous border, but some make good ground cover; *Saxifraga* x *urbium* is excellent for this, even in the poorest of soils. The genus is a complex one botanically, subdivided into sections as outlined below. The species vary greatly in both their habit and their leaf form, but the leaves of all are in rosettes, and many are evergreen. In a monocarpic saxifrage, only the flowering rosette dies, not the plant; new rosettes will replace the old. The flowers are small, cup-shaped or star-shaped, and may be borne singly or in racemes, cymes, or panicles; they are generally pink, white, or yellow. Saxifrages are low-allergen plants. Many species are difficult to cultivate in the open garden, as they must be completely protected from winter wet, so must be given overhead cover. These types are really only suitable for growing in an alpine house, and are therefore not covered here. Slugs are the most common problem with the saxifrages that can be grown outside.

Saxifraga 'Flore Pleno' (*granulata*) (11) (Saxifragaceae)

Common name: Meadow saxifrage
Height: 14in (35cm)
Spread: 12in (30cm)
Aspect: Sun or light shade
Soil: Moist, sharply drained, humus-rich
Hardiness: Zone 5
Propagation: Seed, in autumn; division, in spring

Bulbous perennial. Leaves in loose rosettes, kidney-shaped, toothed, midgreen. Flowers in panicles, on sticky stems, double white, in late spring; summer dormant.

Saxifraga 'Southside Seedling' A.G.M. (7) (Saxifragaceae)

Common name: Saxifrage
Height: 1ft (30cm)
Spread: 1ft (30cm)
Aspect: Sun or half shade; shaded from midday sun
Soil: Moist, sharply drained, humus-rich
Hardiness: Zone 7
Propagation: Division, in spring

A hybrid saxifrage. Leaves in rosettes, spoon-shaped, light green. Flowers in arched panicles, cup-shaped, white, spotted red, in late spring and early summer.

Saxifraga stolonifera A.G.M. (4) (Saxifragaceae)

Common name: Strawberry saxifrage
Height: 1ft (30cm)
Spread: 1ft (30cm)
Aspect: Full or half shade
Soil: Moist, well-drained, humus-rich
Hardiness: Zone 6
Propagation: Seed, in autumn; division, in spring

A stoloniferous perennial from Japan and China. Leaves in rosettes or tufts, rounded, midgreen. Flowers in loose panicles, tiny, white, spotted red or yellow, in summer.

Saxifraga 'Tumbling Waters' A.G.M. (7) (Saxifragaceae)

Common name: Saxifrage
Height: 18in (45cm)
Spread: 12in (30cm)
Aspect: Sun
Soil: Sharply drained, fertile
Hardiness: Zone 7
Propagation: Division, in spring

Hybrid perennial. Leaves in large, tight rosettes, linear, silver-green, lime-encrusted. Flowers only after a few years, small, white cups, in dense, arched panicles, in spring.

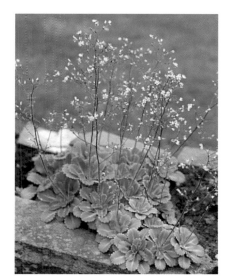

Saxifraga x *urbium* A.G.M. (3) (Saxifragaceae)

Common names: None
Height: 1ft (30cm)
Spread: Indefinite
Aspect: Full or half shade
Soil: Moist, well-drained, humus-rich
Hardiness: Zone 6
Propagation: Seed, in autumn; division, in spring

Rampant ground cover. Leaves in large rosettes, leathery, toothed, midgreen spoons. Flowers in upright, loose panicles, small, white stars, flushed pink, in summer.

CLASSIFICATION of SAXIFRAGE by G. Hegi, 1975

Classes 3, 4, 7, 8, 11, and 12 are of general horticultural interest.

Class 1 Micranthes

Class 2 Hirculus

Class 3 Gymnopera

Class 4 Diptera

Class 5 Trachyphyllum

Class 6 Xanthizoon

Class 7 Aizoonia

Class 8 Porophyllum

Class 9 Porophyrion

Class 10 Miscopetalum

Class 11 Saxifraga

Class 12 Trachyphylloides

Class 13 Cymbalaria

Class 14 Discogyne

Saxifraga veitchiana
(4)
(Saxifragaceae)

Common name: Saxifrage
Height: 1ft (30cm)
Spread: Indefinite
Aspect: Full or half shade
Soil: Moist, well-drained,
humus-rich
Hardiness: Zone 7
Propagation: Seed, in
autumn; division, in spring

Stoloniferous, evergreen ground cover from
China. Leaves rounded, crenate, matt green,
red-brown below. Flowers in loose panicles,
tiny, white, in late spring and early summer.

Scabiosa atropurpurea
(Dipsacaceae)

Common name: Sweet
scabious
Height: 36in (90cm)
Spread: 10in (25cm)
Aspect: Sun
Soil: Well-drained, fertile
Hardiness: Zone 7
Propagation: Seed, when ripe
or in spring; division, in
spring

A short-lived perennial from S Europe.
Leaves basal, spoon-shaped, and stem,
pinnatifid, midgreen. Flowers solitary,
perfumed, dark purple, in summer.

Scabiosa caucasica
'Clive Greaves' A.G.M.
(Dipsacaceae)

Common name: Caucasian
scabious
Height: 2ft (60cm)
Spread: 2ft (60cm)
Aspect: Sun
Soil: Well-drained, fertile
Hardiness: Zone 4
Propagation: Seed, when ripe
or in spring; division, in
spring

A selected form of a hardy, clump-forming
perennial from the Caucasus. Leaves lance-
shaped, gray-green. Flowers solitary, domed,
double, lavender, all summer if deadheaded.

Scabiosa columbaria
var. ochroleuca
(Dipsacaceae)

Common name: Dove
scabious
Height: 30in (75cm)
Spread: 36in (90cm)
Aspect: Sun
Soil: Well-drained, fertile
Hardiness: Zone 6
Propagation: Seed, when ripe
or in spring; division, in
spring

Perennial from Eurasia. Leaves basal, and
stem, pinnatifid, grayish-green. Flowers
solitary, lemon-yellow, from summer to
early autumn. Superb for flower-arranging.

Schoenoplectus lacustris
subsp. tabernaemontani
'Zebrinus'

Common names: None
Height: 3ft (1m)
Spread: 2ft (60cm)
Aspect: Sun
Soil: Wet, or marginal aquatic
Hardiness: Zone 7
Propagation: Division, from
spring to summer

Rhizomatous perennial. Stems from
rhizome leafless, gray-green, banded
creamy-white. Flowers brown, spikelets,
in clusters, from early to late summer.

Schizostylis coccinea
f. alba
(Iridaceae)

Common name: Crimson-flag
Height: 2ft (60cm)
Spread: 1ft (30cm)
Aspect: Sun
Soil: Moist to wet, well-
drained, fertile
Hardiness: Zone 6
Propagation: Seed or division,
both in spring

Rhizomatous evergreen from southern
Africa. Leaves erect, narrow-linear, pointed,
midgreen. Flowers in spikes, open cups,
white, in autumn. Soon becomes congested.

Schizostylis coccinea
'Major' A.G.M.
(Iridaceae)

Common name: Crimson-flag
Height: 2ft (60cm)
Spread: 1ft (30cm)
Aspect: Sun
Soil: Moist to wet, well-
drained, fertile
Hardiness: Zone 6
Propagation: Seed or division,
both in spring

Rhizomatous evergreen from southern
Africa. Leaves erect, sword-shaped, midgreen. Flowers in spikes, open cups, red, in
autumn. Becomes congested rapidly.

Schizostylis coccinea
'Professor Barnard'
(Iridaceae)

Common name: Crimson-flag
Height: 2ft (60cm)
Spread: 1ft (30cm)
Aspect: Sun
Soil: Moist to wet, well-
drained, fertile
Hardiness: Zone 6
Propagation: Seed or division,
both in spring

Rhizomatous evergreen. Flowers large,
deep dusky pink. Leaves erect, sword-
shaped, midgreen. Rapidly becomes
overcrowded; lift and divide regularly.

Saxifrages such as 'Southside Seedling' need sharply drained soil; their low clumps of rosetted leaves suit a stone trough or a rock garden.

**Schizostylis coccinea
'Sunrise' A.G.M.
(Iridaceae)**

Common name: Crimson-flag
Height: 2ft (60cm)
Spread: 1ft (30cm)
Aspect: Sun
Soil: Moist to wet, well-
drained, fertile
Hardiness: Zone 6
Propagation: Division, in
spring

Selected form of rhizomatous evergreen,
with large, salmon-pink flowers in autumn.
Leaves evergreen, erect, pointed, midgreen.
Rapidly becomes congested.

**Scilla natalensis
(Hyacinthaceae/Liliaceae)**

Common name: Natal squill
Height: 4ft (1.2m)
Spread: 4in (10cm)
Aspect: Sun or half shade
Soil: Well-drained, fertile,
humus-rich
Hardiness: Zone 9
Propagation: Seed, when ripe;
offsets, when dormant

Bulbous perennial from South Africa. Leaves
basal, lance-shaped, midgreen. Bears tall
racemes of up to 100 small, flat, lilac-blue,
pink, or white flowers, in summer.

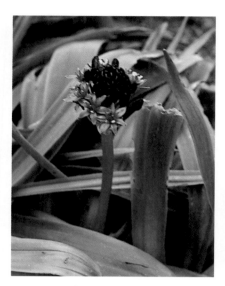

**Scilla peruviana
(Hyacinthaceae/Liliaceae)**

Common name: Peruvian
squill
Height: 18in (45cm)
Spread: 12in (30cm)
Aspect: Sun or half shade
Soil: Well-drained, fertile,
humus-rich
Hardiness: Zone 8
Propagation: Seed, when ripe;
offsets, when dormant

Bulbous Mediterranean plant; named for
the ship it came to Britain on, the *Peru*.
Leaves in basal clusters, lance-shaped.
Flowers deep blue stars in conical racemes.

**Scopolia carniolica
(Solanaceae)**

Common names: None
Height: 18in (45cm)
Spread: 24in (60cm)
Aspect: Half shade
Soil: Moist, well-drained,
humus-rich
Hardiness: Zone 5
Propagation: Seed, in autumn
or spring; division, in spring

A poisonous, rhizomatous perennial from
Europe and the Caucasus. Leaves ovate,
veined, wrinkled, midgreen. Flowers
solitary, pendent, brown-purple bells, spring.

**Scrophularia auriculata
'Variegata'
(Scrophulariaceae)**

Common name: Figwort
Height: 30in (75cm)
Spread: 2ft (60cm)
Aspect: Half shade
Soil: Moist to wet or
marginal aquatic
Hardiness: Zone 5
Propagation: Division, in
spring

Perennial from Europe. Leaves large, ovate,
wrinkled, toothed, pale green, marked pink
and cream. Flowers insignificant, in cymes,
yellowish-green, in summer to autumn.

**Scutellaria incana
(Labiatae/Lamiaceae)**

Common name: Skullcap
Height: 4ft (1.2m)
Spread: 2ft (60cm)
Aspect: Sun or half shade
Soil: Sharply drained,
alkaline, fertile
Hardiness: Zone 5
Propagation: Seed, in spring;
division, in spring or autumn

A perennial from the U.S.A. Leaves ovate,
toothed, hairy, crenate, sage-gray. Flowers
in corymbs, tubular, 2-lipped, blue, in
summer, and again later if deadheaded.

**Scutellaria integrifolia
(Labiatae/Lamiaceae)**

Common name: Hyssop
skullcap
Height: 2ft (60cm)
Spread: 1ft (30cm)
Aspect: Sun or half shade
Soil: Sharply drained,
alkaline, fertile
Hardiness: Zone 5
Propagation: Seed, in spring;
division, in spring or autumn

A perennial from the eastern U.S.A. Leaves
ovate, hairy, midgreen. Flowers tubular,
2-lipped, lilac-blue, in racemes, in late
spring to early summer.

**Sedum acre
(Crassulaceae)**

Common name: Goldmoss
Height: 2in (5cm)
Spread: 32in (80cm)
Aspect: Sun
Soil: Sharply drained,
alkaline, fertile
Hardiness: Zone 5
Propagation: Seed, in
autumn; softwood cuttings of blind shoots,
in early summer

Creeping, evergreen perennial from Turkey,
North Africa, and Europe. Leaves
triangular, light green. Flowers in cymes,
yellow-green stars, over a long period in

SEDUM (Crassulaceae)
Stonecrop

A wide genus of some 400 species, encompassing annuals, biennials, deciduous, semievergreen, and evergreen perennials, subshrubs, and shrubs from both hemispheres. Their habitats in the wild vary from mountainous areas, where most are found, to arid regions of South America. As a result, they vary widely from dwarf, rock-garden plants (the predominant type) to fairly tall plants, eminently suitable for beds or borders. Some of the smaller species can be quite invasive. Stonecrops prefer sun, but some will tolerate light shade. They are drought-tolerant, and prefer light, well-drained soils; the border types will grow in almost all soils, but become lush and need to be staked if grown in over-fertile conditions. The foliage of stonecrops is of a thick, fleshy, succulent nature, although the arrangement and form of the leaves is very variable. The flowers appear in summer and autumn. They are mostly 5-petalled and star-shaped, and borne in usually terminal corymbs, panicles, or cymes. The flowers are beloved of butterflies, especially those of *Sedum spectabile*. Unfortunately, slugs and snails are also fond of the leaves. All parts of the plants are poisonous, and contact with the sap may cause skin irritation.

Sedum acre
'Aureum'
(Crassulaceae)

Common name: Goldmoss stonecrop
Height: 4in (10cm)
Spread: 8in (20cm)
Aspect: Sun
Soil: Well-drained, alkaline, fertile
Hardiness: Zone 5
Propagation: Softwood cuttings of blind shoots, in early summer

A form of the species in which the leaves and flowers are bright yellow. Very good for a scree garden or the front of a border, and a superb backdrop for butterflies.

Sedum aizoon
'Euphorbioides'
(Crassulaceae)

Common name: Aizoon stonecrop
Height: 14in (35cm)
Spread: 12in (30cm)
Aspect: Sun
Soil: Well-drained, alkaline
Hardiness: Zone 7
Propagation: Softwood cuttings of blind shoots, in early summer

A rhizomatous, herbaceous perennial from Japan and China. Leaves ovate, toothed, dark green. Flowers in terminal clusters, star-shaped, orange-yellow, in summer.

Sedum alboroseum
'Mediovariegatum'
(Crassulaceae)

Common name: Stonecrop
Height: 18in (45cm)
Spread: 12in (30cm)
Aspect: Sun
Soil: Well-drained, alkaline
Hardiness: Zone 4
Propagation: Softwood cuttings of blind shoots, in early summer

Also known as *S. erythrostictum*; from Asia. Leaves ovate, cream, margined green. Flowers in terminal clusters, greenish-white stars, in late summer.

Sedum populifolium
(Crassulaceae)

Common name: Poplar sedum
Height: 12in (30cm)
Spread: 18in (45cm)
Aspect: Sun
Soil: Well-drained, alkaline
Hardiness: Zone 4
Propagation: Softwood cuttings of blind shoots, in early summer

A deciduous perennial from Siberia. Leaves ovate, toothed, pale green. Flowers scented, in many-flowered cymes, pinkish-white, star-shaped, in late summer and early autumn.

Sedum
'Ruby Glow' A.G.M.
(Crassulaceae)

Common name: Stonecrop
Height: 12in (30cm)
Spread: 18in (45cm)
Aspect: Sun
Soil: Well-drained, alkaline
Hardiness: Zone 7
Propagation: Softwood cuttings of blind shoots, in early summer

Hybrid perennial. Leaves elliptic, toothed, purple-green. Flowers star-shaped, ruby-colored, in loose, many-flowered cymes, from summer to early autumn.

Sedum rupestre
(Crassulaceae)

Common names: None
Height: 6in (15cm)
Spread: 2ft (60cm)
Aspect: Sun
Soil: Well-drained, alkaline
Hardiness: Zone 4
Propagation: Softwood cuttings of blind shoots, in early summer

An evergreen, mat-forming ground cover from the mountains of Europe. Leaves linear, gray-green. Flowers in terminal cymes, star-shaped, yellow, in summer.

Sedum spectabile A.G.M. (Crassulaceae)

Common name: Showy
sedum
Height: 18in (45cm)
Spread: 18in (45cm)
Aspect: Sun
Soil: Well-drained, alkaline
Hardiness: Zone 4
Propagation: Softwood
cuttings of blind shoots,
in early summer

Clump-forming perennial from Japan and
China. Leaves fleshy, ovate, toothed, light
green. Flowers in dense, flat-topped cymes,
star-shaped, pink, late summer to autumn.

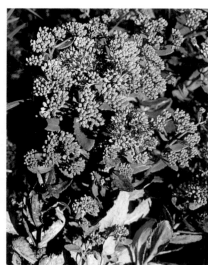

Sedum telephium 'Abbeydore' (Crassulaceae)

Common name: Orpine
Height: 2ft (60cm)
Spread: 1ft (30cm)
Aspect: Sun
Soil: Well-drained, alkaline
Hardiness: Zone 4
Propagation: Softwood
cuttings of blind shoots,
in early summer

Cultivar of a rhizomatous perennial.
Leaves oblong, toothed, gray-green.
Flowers star-shaped, dusky pink, in dense
cymes, in late summer to early autumn.

Sedum telephium 'Arthur Branch' (Crassulaceae)

Common name: Orpine
Height: 2ft (60cm)
Spread: 1ft (30cm)
Aspect: Sun
Soil: Well-drained, alkaline
Hardiness: Zone 4
Propagation: Softwood
cuttings of blind shoots,
in early summer

Cultivar of a rhizomatous perennial from
Eurasia and the Far East. Leaves oblong,
toothed, light green. Flowers dusky red, in
dense cymes, late summer to early autumn.

Sedum telephium subsp. maximum 'Atropurpureum' A.G.M. (Crassulaceae)

Common name: Orpine
Height: 2ft (60cm)
Spread: 18in (45cm)
Aspect: Sun
Soil: Well-drained, alkaline
Hardiness: Zone 4
Propagation: Softwood
cuttings of blind shoots,
in early summer

A form of the species with dark purple
stems and glaucous, dark purple leaves.
Flowers in cymes, star-shaped, purple-red,
in late summer and early autumn.

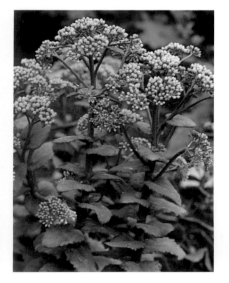

Sedum telephium subsp. ruprechtii (Crassulaceae)

Common name: Orpine
Height: 2ft (60cm)
Spread: 18in (45cm)
Aspect: Sun
Soil: Well-drained, alkaline
Hardiness: Zone 4
Propagation: Softwood
cuttings of blind shoots,
in early summer

A naturally occurring form of the orpine
with glaucous, blue-green leaves and
creamy-pink, star-shaped flowers, in late
summer and early autumn.

Selaginella kraussiana A.G.M. (Selaginellaceae)

Common name: None
Height: 1in (2.5cm)
Spread: Indefinite
Aspect: Half shade
Soil: Well-drained, acidic,
humus-rich, fertile
Hardiness: Zone 9
Propagation: Spores, in
warmth as soon as ripe;
division, in spring

A tender, evergreen, mat-forming perennial
from the Azores and southern Africa.
Stems covered in pinnatisect foliage of
bright green.

Semiaquilegia ecalcarata (Ranunculaceae)

Common names: None
Height: 12in (30cm)
Spread: 8in (20cm)
Aspect: Sun or half shade
Soil: Well-drained, acidic,
humus-rich
Hardiness: Zone 6
Propagation: Seed, when ripe

A short-lived perennial from China.
Leaves 2-ternate, midgreen, purple below.
Flowers in loose panicles, pendent, pink
bells, in early summer.

Sempervivum arachnoideum A.G.M. (Crassulaceae)

Common name: Spiderweb
houseleek
Height: 4in (10cm)
Spread: 12in (30cm)
Aspect: Sun
Soil: Very sharply drained,
humus-rich
Hardiness: Zone 5
Propagation: Seed, in spring;
offsets, in spring to early summer

Evergreen, rosette-forming succulent from
the Alps. Leaves fleshy, obovate, green or
red, in cobwebbed rosettes. Flowers in flat
cymes, on leafy stems, pink, in summer.

Senecio cineraria
(Asteraceae/Compositae)

Common name: Silver
groundsel
Height: 2ft (60cm)
Spread: 2ft (60cm)
Aspect: Sun
Soil: Well-drained, fertile
Hardiness: Zone 8
Propagation: Seed, in spring;
semiripe cuttings, in summer

An evergreen, Mediterranean subshrub.
Leaves ovate, pinnatisect, felted, silver-
gray. Flowers in loose corymbs, mustard
yellow, in summer.

Senecio pulcher
(Asteraceae/Compositae)

Common name: Showy
groundsel
Height: 2ft (60cm)
Spread: 18in (45cm)
Aspect: Sun
Soil: Well-drained, fertile
Hardiness: Zone 8
Propagation: Seed, in spring;
semiripe cuttings, in summer

Perennial from Argentina, Uruguay, and
Brazil. Leaves basal, elliptic, and stem,
lance-shaped, toothed. Flowers in solitary
corymbs, carmine-purple, in late autumn.

Senecio viravira
A.G.M.
(Asteraceae/Compositae)

Common name: Argentine
groundsel
Height: 2ft (60cm)
Spread: 3ft (90cm)
Aspect: Sun
Soil: Well-drained, fertile
Hardiness: Zone 8
Propagation: Seed, in spring;
semiripe cuttings, in summer

Evergreen subshrub from Argentina. Leaves
deeply pinnatisect, with 5 to 9 silver-white
leaflets. Flowers of disc florets only, in loose
corymbs, off-white, summer to autumn.

Serratula seoanei
(Asteraceae/Compositae)

Common names: None
Height: 12in (30cm)
Spread: 8in (20cm)
Aspect: Sun
Soil: Well-drained
Hardiness: Zone 7
Propagation: Seed, in autumn
or spring; offsets, in spring

Perennial from Europe. Leaves pinnate,
toothed, midgreen. Flowers purple-pink,
cornflowerlike, on branched stems, solitary
or in panicles, in autumn to winter.

Seseli gummiferum
(Apiaceae/Umbelliferae)

Common names: None
Height: 3ft (1m)
Spread: 2ft (60cm)
Aspect: Sun
Soil: Well-drained, fertile
Hardiness: Zone 6
Propagation: Seed or division,
both in autumn or spring

From the Crimea and Aegean. Leaves 2- or
3-pinnatisect, segments wedge-shaped,
hairy, glaucous-green. Flowers in umbels of
up to 60, pinkish-white or red, in summer.

Sesleria glauca
(Graminae/Poaceae)

Common names: None
Height: 12in (30cm)
Spread: 8in (20cm)
Aspect: Sun or half shade
Soil: Well-drained, fertile
Hardiness: Zone 6
Propagation: Seed, in spring
or autumn; division, in spring

An evergreen, perennial grass from
Eurasia. Leaves narrow, linear, glaucous
green. Flowers in dense, cylindrical
panicles, greenish-white.

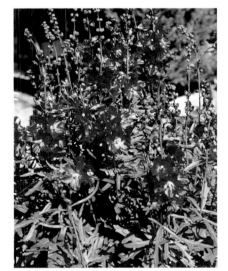

Sidalcea
'Croftway Red'
(Malvaceae)

Common name: Checker-
mallow
Height: 3ft (90cm)
Spread: 18in (45cm)
Aspect: Sun
Soil: Moist, well-drained,
acidic, fertile
Hardiness: Zone 6
Propagation: Division, in
spring or autumn

A hybrid perennial. Leaves round, lobed,
midgreen. Flowers in racemes, rich
pinkish-red, in early and midsummer.
Good for flower arrangements.

Sidalcea
'Elsie Heugh'
(Malvaceae)

Common name: Checker-
mallow
Height: 3ft (90cm)
Spread: 18in (45cm)
Aspect: Sun
Soil: Moist, well-drained,
acidic, fertile
Hardiness: Zone 6
Propagation: Division, in
spring or autumn

Hybrid perennial. Leaves round, shallowly
lobed, midgreen. Flowers in racemes, large,
satiny, lilac-pink, with frilled petals, in
early and midsummer.

Sidalcea
'William Smith' A.G.M.
(Malvaceae)

Common name: Checker-
mallow
Height: 3ft (90cm)
Spread: 18in (45cm)
Aspect: Sun
Soil: Moist, well-drained,
acidic, fertile
Hardiness: Zone 6
Propagation: Division, in
spring or autumn

A hybrid perennial. Leaves round,
shallowly lobed, midgreen. Flowers borne
in upright racemes, deep pink, in early and
midsummer.

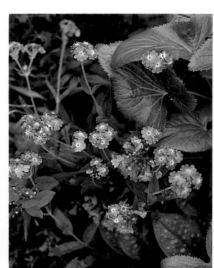

Silene dioica
(Caryophyllaceae)

Common name: Red campion
Height: 30in (75cm)
Spread: 18in (45cm)
Aspect: Sun or half shade
Soil: Well-drained, alkaline,
fertile
Hardiness: Zone 6
Propagation: Seed, in
autumn; basal cuttings, in
spring

Clump-forming European perennial. Leaves
obovate, dark green. Flowers in branched
cymes, round, deep pink with white base
and notched petals, in spring and summer.

Silene dioica
'Thelma Kay'
(Caryophyllaceae)

Common name: Red campion
Height: 32in (80cm)
Spread: 18in (45cm)
Aspect: Sun or half shade
Soil: Well-drained, alkaline,
fertile
Hardiness: Zone 6
Propagation: Rooted
offshoots, from midsummer
to autumn

Cultivar of the red campion with
variegated foliage and double flowers in
late spring to midsummer. Does not self-
seed as much as the single form.

Silene uniflora
'Druett's Variegated'
(Caryophyllaceae)

Common name: Bladder
campion
Height: 8in (20cm)
Spread: 8in (20cm)
Aspect: Sun
Soil: Well-drained, alkaline,
fertile
Hardiness: Zone 3
Propagation: Rooted
offshoots, from midsummer to autumn

Cultivar of a creeping, semievergreen,
coastal plant. Leaves lance-shaped, fleshy,
cream and green. Flowers white, solitary
or in clusters, petals deeply cut, in summer.

Silene uniflora
'Robin Whitebreast'
(Caryophyllaceae)

Common name: Bladder
campion
Height: 8in (20cm)
Spread: 12in (30cm)
Aspect: Sun
Soil: Well-drained, alkaline,
fertile
Hardiness: Zone 3
Propagation: Rooted
offshoots, from midsummer to autumn

Crawling, hybrid perennial. Leaves
shaped, fleshy, green. Flowers
or in clusters, white with a green
summer.

Silphium laciniatum
(Asteraceae/Compositae)

Common name: Compass-
plant
Height: 10ft (3m)
Spread: 2ft (60cm)
Aspect: Sun or half shade
Soil: Moist, fertile, deep,
heavy
Hardiness: Zone 4
Propagation: Seed, when ripe;
division, in spring

Ovate, bristly, toothed, midgreen leaves,
pointing north-south to minimize exposure
to sun. Terminal corymbs of dark-centered,
yellow daisies, midsummer to early autumn.

Sisyrinchium angustifolium
(Iridaceae)

Common name: Common
blue-eyed grass
Height: 20in (50cm)
Spread: 6in (15cm)
Aspect: Sun
Soil: Well-drained, alkaline,
fertile
Hardiness: Zone 3
Propagation: Seed, in spring;
division, in spring or autumn

A clump-forming perennial from North
America. Leaves linear, midgreen. Flowers
solitary, single, blue with a yellow throat,
in summer.

Sisyrinchium
'Californian Skies'
(Iridaceae)

Common name: Blue-eyed
grass
Height: 6in (15cm)
Spread: 4in (10cm)
Aspect: Sun
Soil: Well-drained, alkaline,
fertile
Hardiness: Zone 8
Propagation: Division, in
spring or autumn

Short-lived, rhizomatous hybrid. Leaves
basal, sword-shaped, gray-green. Flowers
large, flat, blue, dark-centered, in clusters,
surrounded by bracts, spring and summer.

Sisyrinchium californicum
Brachypus Group
(Iridaceae)

Common name: Yellow-eyed
grass
Height: 2ft (60cm)
Spread: 6in (15cm)
Aspect: Sun
Soil: Well-drained, alkaline,
fertile
Hardiness: Zone 8
Propagation: Seed, in spring;
division, in spring or autumn

A rhizomatous perennial from North
America. Leaves sword-shaped, gray-green.
Flowers small, solitary stars, yellow with
dark veins, in succession, in summer.

Sisyrinchium idahoense
'Album'
(Iridaceae)

Common name: Idaho blue-
eyed grass
Height: 6in (15cm)
Spread: 6in (15cm)
Aspect: Sun
Soil: Well-drained, alkaline,
fertile
Hardiness: Zone 3
Propagation: Seed, in spring;
division, in spring or autumn

A rhizomatous perennial from the U.S.A.
Leaves narrowly linear, midgreen.
Flowers star-shaped, white with yellow
throats, in summer.

Sisyrinchium
'Quaint and Queer'
(Iridaceae)

Common name: Blue-eyed
grass
Height: 8in (20cm)
Spread: 8in (20cm)
Aspect: Sun
Soil: Well-drained, alkaline,
fertile
Hardiness: Zone 7
Propagation: Division, in
spring or autumn

A hybrid, rhizomatous perennial. Leaves
basal, narrowly linear, midgreen. Flowers
small, star-shaped, yellow, brown, and
purple, in summer.

Sisyrinchium striatum
(Iridaceae)

Common names: None
Height: 3ft (90cm)
Spread: 1ft (30cm)
Aspect: Sun
Soil: Well-drained, alkaline,
fertile
Hardiness: Zone 8
Propagation: Seed, in spring;
division, in spring or autumn

Rhizomatous evergreen from Argentina and
Chile. Leaves basal, linear, stiff, gray-green.
Flowers in clusters, stemless, pale yellow
cups, early to midsummer. Black seed heads.

Sisyrinchium striatum
'Aunt May'
(Iridaceae)

Common names: None
Height: 3ft (90cm)
Spread: 1ft (30cm)
Aspect: Sun
Soil: Well-drained, alkaline,
fertile
Hardiness: Zone 8
Propagation: Division, in
spring or autumn

A form of the species with leaves striped
green and cream. Yellow, stemless flowers
in clusters in early to midsummer, followed
by attractive seed heads.

Smilacina racemosa
A.G.M.
(Convallariaceae/Liliaceae)

Common names: False
Solomon's seal; wild spikenard
Height: 1m (3ft)
Spread: 2ft (60cm)
Aspect: Full or half shade
Soil: Moist, well-drained,
acidic, humus-rich, fertile
Hardiness: Zone 4
Propagation: Seed, in
autumn; division, in spring

Rhizomatous woodlander. Leaves ovate to
lance-shaped, midgreen. Flowers scented,
creamy-white stars, in terminal racemes, in
spring, sometimes followed by red berries.

Solenopsis axillaris
(Campanulaceae)

Common names: None
Height: 1ft (30cm)
Spread: 1ft (30cm)
Aspect: Sun
Soil: Well-drained, fertile
Hardiness: Zone 9
Propagation: Seed, in warmth
in spring; softwood cuttings,
in summer

A tender perennial from Australia. Leaves
ovate, pinnatisect, leaflets narrow, midgreen. Flowers small, star-shaped, pale
blue, abundant, from spring to autumn.

Solidago
'Goldenmosa' A.G.M.
(Asteraceae/Compositae)

Common name: Goldenrod
Height: 32in (80cm)
Spread: 18in (45cm)
Aspect: Sun
Soil: Sharply drained, fertile
Hardiness: Zone 4
Propagation: Division, in
autumn or spring

Woody hybrid. Leaves wrinkled, midgreen,
lance-shaped. Flowers tiny, yellow, in one-
sided, conical panicles, late summer and
autumn. Deadhead to prevent self-seeding.

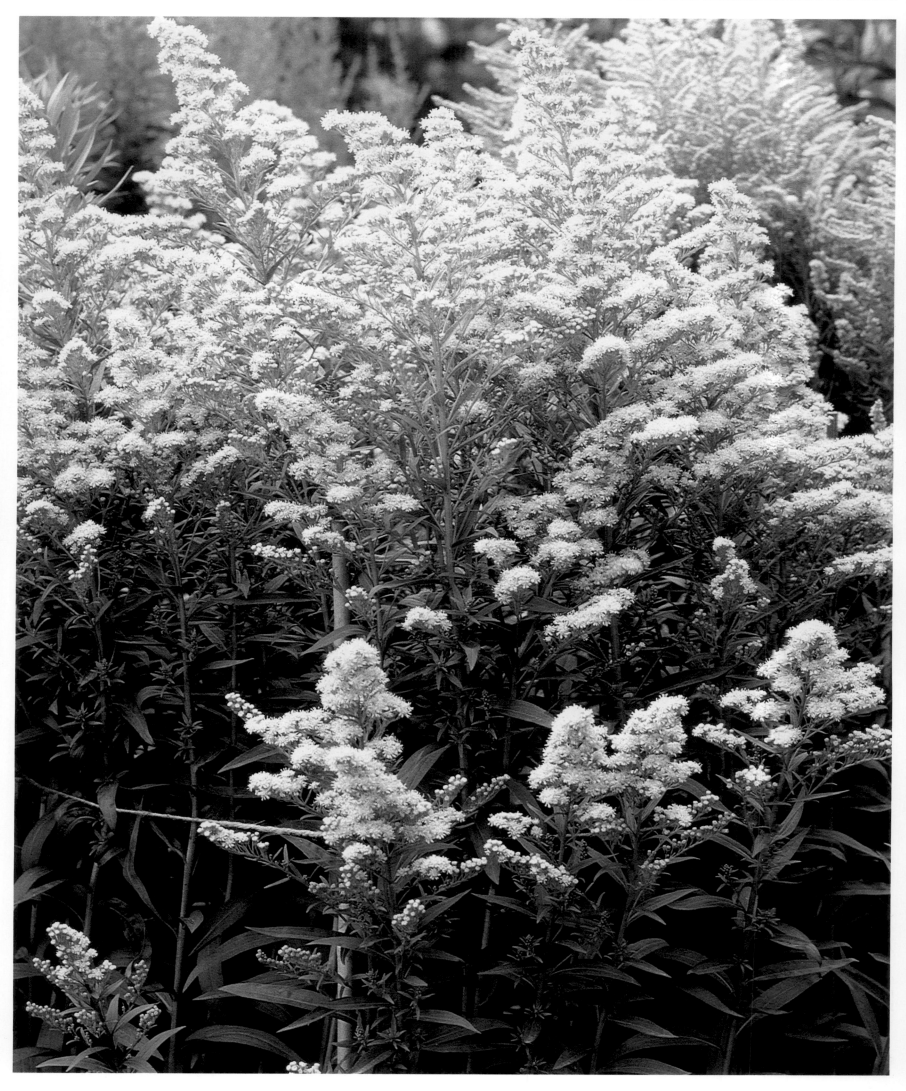

Golden rods such as Solidago elongata are impressive in gardens that can accommodate their tendency to abundant self-seeding.

x *Solidaster luteus*
(Asteraceae/Compositae)

Common name: Hybrid
goldenrod
Height: 3ft (1m)
Spread: 1ft (30cm)
Aspect: Sun
Soil: Well-drained, fertile
Hardiness: Zone 6
Propagation: Basal cuttings
or division, both in spring

Intergeneric garden hybrid. Leaves lance-shaped to linear. Flowers small, yellow, daisylike, in panicles, midsummer to autumn. Deadhead to prevent self-seeding.

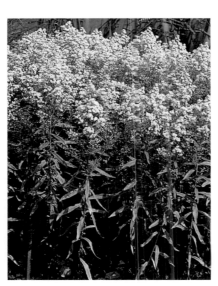

x *Solidaster luteus*
'Lemore' A.G.M.
(Asteraceae/Compositae)

Common name: Hybrid
goldenrod
Height: 32in (80cm)
Spread: 12in (30cm)
Aspect: Sun
Soil: Well-drained, fertile
Hardiness: Zone 6
Propagation: Division, in
spring

Selected form of intergeneric garden hybrid, with panicles of small, daisylike flowers of pale lemon. Leaves lance-shaped to linear. Deadhead to prevent self-seeding.

Sparaxis elegans
(Iridaceae)

Common name: Wand-flower
Height: 18in (45cm)
Spread: 4in (10cm)
Aspect: Sun
Soil: Well-drained, fertile
Hardiness: Zone 9
Propagation: Seed, when ripe;
offsets, when dormant

Cormous perennial from South Africa. Leaves basal, in fans, sword-shaped, bright green. Flowers in spikes, wide funnels, red, orange, or white, in spring and summer.

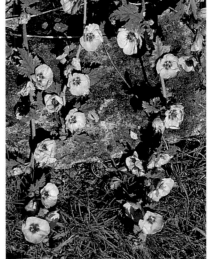

Sphaeralcea fendleri
(Malvaceae)

Common name: Prarie
mallow
Height: 32in (80cm)
Spread: 24in (60cm)
Aspect: Sun
Soil: Sharply drained, fertile
Hardiness: Zone 8
Propagation: Seed, in spring;
softwood cuttings, in summer

Sprawling subshrub from the U.S.A. Leaves ovate, 3-lobed, toothed, gray-green. Flowers in axillary panicles, pink saucers, in summer. Prune to keep compact.

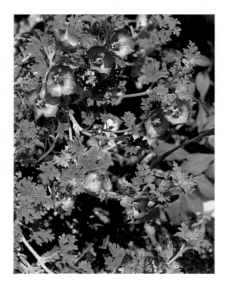

Sphaeralcea munroana
(Malvaceae)

Common name: Prarie
mallow
Height: 32in (80cm)
Spread: 36in (90cm)
Aspect: Sun
Soil: Well-drained, fertile
Hardiness: Zone 8
Propagation: Seed, in spring;
softwood cuttings, in summer

Sprawling perennial. Leaves ovate to diamond-shaped, 3- to 5-lobed, gray-green. Flowers in axillary panicles, salmon-pink saucers, over a very long period in summer.

Spiranthes gracilis
(Orchidaceae)

Common name: Nodding
Ladies'-tresses
Height: 30in (75cm)
Spread: 4in (10cm)
Aspect: Half shade
Soil: Moist, well-drained,
humus-rich, fertile
Hardiness: Zone 3
Propagation: Division, when
dormant

A hardy, tuberous, terrestrial orchid from North America. Leaves basal, ovate, mid-green. Flowers in spiral racemes, small, white, perfumed, in autumn.

Stachys byzantina
(Labiatae/Lamiaceae)

Common names: Lamb's-ears; woolly betony
Height: 18in (45cm)
Spread: 2ft (60cm)
Aspect: Sun
Soil: Well-drained, fertile
Hardiness: Zone 5
Propagation: Seed, in autumn
or spring; division, in spring

Mat-forming perennial. Leaves in basal rosettes, oblong, veined, densely white-woolly. Flowers in spikes, pink-purple, woolly, from early summer to autumn

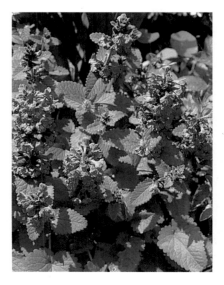

Stachys macrantha
(Labiatae/Lamiaceae)

Common names: None
Height: 2ft (60cm)
Spread: 1ft (30cm)
Aspect: Sun or half shade
Soil: Well-drained, fertile
Hardiness: Zone 5
Propagation: Seed, in autumn
or spring; division, in spring

Leaves ovate, scalloped, veined, wrinkled, deep green. Flowers in dense spikes, hooded, purplish-pink, from early summer to early autumn.

Stachys macrantha
'Superba'
(Labiatae/Lamiaceae)

Common names: None
Height: 2ft (60cm)
Spread: 1ft (30cm)
Aspect: Sun or half shade
Soil: Well-drained, fertile
Hardiness: Zone 5
Propagation: Seed, in autumn
or spring; division, in spring

A form of the species with dense spikes of
purplish, hooded flowers. Leaves ovate,
scalloped, veined, wrinkled, deep green.
Top-heavy, especially in rain; needs staking.

Stachys monieri
(Labiatae/Lamiaceae)

Common names: None
Height: 20in (50cm)
Spread: 18in (45cm)
Aspect: Sun
Soil: Well-drained, fertile
Hardiness: Zone 5
Propagation: Seed, in autumn
or spring; division, in spring

A perennial from the Alps and Pyrenees.
Leaves in basal rosette, ovate, crinkled,
glossy, dark green. Flowers in spikes, pale
pink, white, or deep pink, in late summer.

Stachys officinalis
(Labiatae/Lamiaceae)

Common name: Common
betony
Height: 2ft (60cm)
Spread: 1ft (30cm)
Aspect: Sun or half shade
Soil: Well-drained, fertile
Hardiness: Zone 5
Propagation: Seed, in autumn
or spring; division, in spring

Perennial from Europe. Leaves in rosettes,
ovate, veined, wrinkled, scalloped, midgreen. Flowers in dense spikes, purplish-
red, white, or pink, all summer.

Stipa gigantea
A.G.M.
(Graminae/Poaceae)

Common name: Giant feather
grass
Height: 8ft (2.5m)
Spread: 4ft (1.2m)
Aspect: Sun
Soil: Well-drained, fertile,
light
Hardiness: Zone 8
Propagation: Seed or division,
both in spring

Evergreen grass from the Iberian peninsula.
Leaves long, linear, inrolled, midgreen.
Flowers silvery, green-purple spikes,
turning gold, in panicles in summer.

Stokesia laevis
(Asteraceae/Compositae)

Common name: Stokesia
Height: 2ft (60cm)
Spread: 18in (45cm)
Aspect: Sun
Soil: Moist, well-drained,
acidic, light, fertile
Hardiness: Zone 5
Propagation: Seed, in
autumn; division, in spring

Rosette-forming evergreen. Leaves basal,
lance-shaped, spiny, with white midribs.
Flowers solitary, cornflowerlike, purplish-
pink, center paler, midsummer to autumn.

Stokesia laevis
'Alba'
(Asteraceae/Compositae)

Common name: White
Stokesia
Height: 2ft (60cm)
Spread: 18in (45cm)
Aspect: Sun
Soil: Moist, well-drained,
acidic, light, fertile
Hardiness: Zone 5
Propagation: Seed, in
autumn; division, in spring

Form of the species with cornflowerlike,
solitary, white flowers from midsummer to
autumn. Leaves in basal rosette, evergreen,
lance-shaped, spiny, with white midribs.

Strelitzia reginae
A.G.M.
(Musaceae/Strelitziaceae)

Common name: Queen's
Bird-of-paradise
Height: 6ft (1.8m)
Spread: 3ft (90cm)
Aspect: Sun or half shade
Soil: Moist, well-drained,
humus-rich, fertile
Hardiness: Zone 9
Propagation: Seed or division,
both in spring

Evergreen from South Africa. Leaves oblong
to lance-shaped, midgreen. Flowers have
green spathes, flushed purple-red, yellow
calyces, blue corollas, in winter to spring.

Strobilanthes
atropurpureus
(Acanthaceae)

Common names: None
Height: 4ft (1.2m)
Spread: 3ft (90cm)
Aspect: Sun or half shade
Soil: Sharply drained, fertile
Hardiness: Zone 5
Propagation: Seed or basal
or softwood cuttings, all in
warmth in spring

A perennial from N India. Leaves large,
ovate, toothed, dark green. Flowers
tubular, indigo-blue, borne in dense spikes,
in summer.

Stylophorum diphyllum
(Papaveraceae)

Common name: Celandine
poppy
Height: 1ft (30cm)
Spread: 1ft (30cm)
Aspect: Full or half shade
Soil: Moist, humus-rich,
fertile
Hardiness: Zone 7
Propagation: Seed, in
autumn; division, in spring

Perennial woodlander. Leaves pinnatisect,
with 5 to 7 hairy, midgreen, obovate
leaflets. Flowers yellow, poppylike, in
terminal umbels, intermittently in summer.

Stylophorum lasiocarpum
(Papaveraceae)

Common names: None
Height: 18in (45cm)
Spread: 12in (30cm)
Aspect: Full or half shade
Soil: Moist, humus-rich,
fertile
Hardiness: Zone 7
Propagation: Seed, in
autumn; division, in spring

Perennial woodlander from China. Leaves
pinnatifid, with 4 to 7 oblong, toothed
lobes, midgreen. Flowers in terminal
clusters, yellow, poppylike, in summer.

Symphyandra armena
(Campanulaceae)

Common name: Ring
bellflower
Height: 18in (45cm)
Spread: 12in (30cm)
Aspect: Sun or half shade
Soil: Well-drained, fertile
Hardiness: Zone 7
Propagation: Seed, when ripe
or in spring

Rhizomatous plant from Turkey and Iran.
Leaves heart-shaped, velvety-hairy, toothed,
midgreen. Flowers in corymbs, pendent,
tubular, pale blue, long period in summer.

Symphytum
'Goldsmith'
(Boraginaceae)

Common name: Comfrey
Height: 1ft (30cm)
Spread: 1ft (30cm)
Aspect: Sun or half shade
Soil: Moist, fertile
Hardiness: Zone 5
Propagation: Division,
in spring; root cuttings,
in early winter

Rhizomatous ground cover. Leaves ovate to
lance-shaped, dark green, variegated cream
and gold. Flowers in cymes, pale blue, mid-
and late spring. Toxic and skin-irritant.

Symphytum ibericum
(Boraginaceae)

Common name: Comfrey
Height: 16in (40cm)
Spread: Indefinite
Aspect: Sun or half shade
Soil: Moist, fertile
Hardiness: Zone 5
Propagation: Seed, in autumn
or spring; division, in spring

Invasive, rhizomatous plant. Leaves ovate,
wrinkled, veined, midgreen. Flowers
tubular, pendent, white or pale yellow, in
cymes, in late spring. Toxic and irritant.

Symphytum ibericum
'Langthornes Pink'
(Boraginaceae)

Common name: Comfrey
Height: 16in (40cm)
Spread: 18in (45cm)
Aspect: Sun or half shade
Soil: Moist, fertile
Hardiness: Zone 5
Propagation: Division, in
spring; root cuttings, in
early winter

Form of the species with pendent, tubular,
pink flowers, in cymes, in late spring.
Leaves ovate, wrinkled, veined, midgreen.
Poisonous, skin-irritant, but low-allergen.

Symphytum
'Lambrook Sunrise'
(Boraginaceae)

Common name: Comfrey
Height: 22in (55cm)
Spread: 12in (30cm)
Aspect: Sun or half shade
Soil: Moist, fertile
Hardiness: Zone 5
Propagation: Division, in
spring; root cuttings, in
early winter

A form which is non-invasive, and has
leaves of acid yellow. Flowers in cymes,
tubular, blue, in spring, making a lovely
contrast to the foliage. Toxic and irritant.

Symphytum orientale
(Boraginaceae)

Common names: Comfrey
Height: 28in (70cm)
Spread: 18in (45cm)
Aspect: Sun or half shade
Soil: Moist, fertile
Hardiness: Zone 5
Propagation: Seed, in autumn
or spring; division, in spring

Rhizomatous perennial from Europe. Leaves
ovate-oblong, densely hairy, midgreen.
Flowers in many-flowered cymes, pendent,
tubular, white, in summer. Toxic, irritant.

Symphytum × *uplandicum*
(Boraginaceae)

Common name: Comfrey
Height: 6ft (1.8m)
Spread: 4ft (1.2m)
Aspect: Sun or half shade
Soil: Moist, fertile
Hardiness: Zone 5
Propagation: Seed, in autumn
or spring; division, in spring

A rhizomatous hybrid of garden origin.
Leaves basal, elliptic to lance-shaped,
midgreen. Flowers in cymes, lilac-blue,
from late spring to late summer.

Symphytum × *uplandicum*
'Axminster Gold'
(Boraginaceae)

Common name: Comfrey
Height: 6ft (1.8m)
Spread: 4ft (1.2m)
Aspect: Sun or half shade
Soil: Moist, well-drained
Hardiness: Zone 5
Propagation: Division, in
spring; root cuttings, in early
winter

A variegated and noninvasive form of this
garden hybrid, with elliptic to lance-shaped
leaves margined pale gold. Flowers white,
in cymes, from late spring to late summer.

Symphytum × *uplandicum*
'Variegatum' A.G.M.
(Boraginaceae)

Common name: Comfrey
Height: 6ft (1.8m)
Spread: 4ft (1.2m)
Aspect: Sun or half shade
Soil: Moist, fertile
Hardiness: Zone 5
Propagation: Division, in
spring; root cuttings, in early
winter

A noninvasive cultivar of this hybrid, with
elliptic to lance-shaped leaves variegated
heavily in yellow. Flowers in cymes, lilac,
from late spring to late summer.

Tanacetum coccineum
'Brenda' A.G.M.
(Asteraceae/Compositae)

Common names: Painted
daisy; pyrethrum
Height: 30in (75cm)
Spread: 18in (45cm)
Aspect: Sun
Soil: Sharply drained
Hardiness: Zone 5
Propagation: Division or
basal cuttings, both in spring

Clump-forming. Leaves basal, 2-pinnatisect,
10–14 lance-shaped, toothed leaflets. Single,
solitary, yellow-centered, cerise daisies, early
summer, again if deadheaded. Skin irritant.

Tanacetum coccineum
'Eileen May Robinson' A.G.M.
(Asteraceae/Compositae)

Common names: Painted
daisy; pyrethrum
Height: 30in (75cm)
Spread: 18in (45cm)
Aspect: Sun
Soil: Sharply drained
Hardiness: Zone 5
Propagation: Division or basal
cuttings, both in spring

Clump-forming. Leaves pinnatisect, 10–14
lance-shaped, toothed segments. Solitary,
single daisies, rich pink, yellow discs, early
summer, again if deadheaded. Skin irritant.

Tanacetum coccineum
'James Kelway' A.G.M.
(Asteraceae/Compositae)

Common names: Painted
daisy; pyrethrum
Height: 30in (75cm)
Spread: 18in (45cm)
Aspect: Sun
Soil: Sharply drained
Hardiness: Zone 5
Propagation: Division or
basal cuttings, both in spring

Short-lived. Leaves pinnatisect, 10–14 lance-
shaped, toothed segments. Solitary, single
daisies, deep crimson, yellow discs, in early
summer, again if deadheaded. Skin irritant.

Tanacetum coccineum
'Snow Cloud'
(Asteraceae/Compositae)

Common names: Painted
daisy; pyrethrum
Height: 2ft (60cm)
Spread: 18in (45cm)
Aspect: Sun
Soil: Sharply drained
Hardiness: Zone 5
Propagation: Division or
basal cuttings, both in spring

Short-lived. Leaves pinnatisect, 10–14 lance-
shaped, toothed segments. Solitary, single
white daisies, yellow centers, in early
summer, again if deadheaded. Skin irritant.

Tanacetum parthenium
'Aureum'
(Asteraceae/Compositae)

Common name: Feverfew
Height: 2ft (60cm)
Spread: 1ft (30cm)
Aspect: Sun
Soil: Sharply drained
Hardiness: Zone 5
Propagation: Seed or division,
both in spring

Aromatic herb. Leaves basal and stem,
hairy, ovate, pinnatisect, golden-yellow.
Flowers in dense corymbs, small, single,
white, daisylike, with yellow discs, summer.

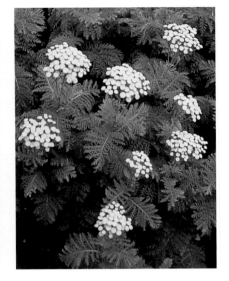

Tanacetum vulgare
(Asteraceae/Compositae)

Common name: Common tansy
Height: 3ft (90cm)
Spread: 18in (45cm)
Aspect: Sun
Soil: Sharply drained
Hardiness: Zone 4
Propagation: Seed or division, both in spring

Invasive perennial from Europe. Leaves aromatic, pinnate. up to 12 lance-shaped, toothed leaflets, midgreen. Flowers in flat corymbs, bright yellow buttons, in summer.

Telekia speciosa
(Asteraceae/Compositae)

Common names: None
Height: 6ft (1.8m)
Spread: 3ft (90cm)
Aspect: Half shade
Soil: Moist
Hardiness: Zone 6
Propagation: Seed, when ripe; division, in spring

Woodlander. Leaves ovate, toothed, midgreen, aromatic. Flowers in sprays, single, with bracts, ray florets narrow, yellow, late summer and early autumn.

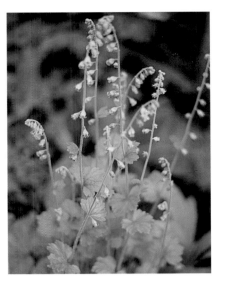

Tellima grandiflora
(Saxifragaceae)

Common name: Alaska fringecup
Height: 30in (75cm)
Spread: 12in (30cm)
Aspect: Sun or half shade
Soil: Moist, humus-rich
Hardiness: Zone 6
Propagation: Seed or division, both in spring

Rosette-forming ground cover for shade. Leaves heart-shaped, hairy, lobed, scalloped. Flowers greenish-white, in terminal racemes on hairy stems, late spring to midsummer.

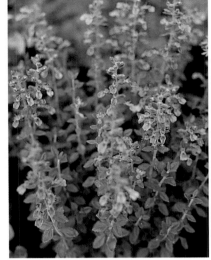

Teucrium x lucidrys
(Labiatae/Lamiaceae)

Common name: Wall germander
Height: 20in (50cm)
Spread: 12in (30cm)
Aspect: Sun
Soil: Well-drained, alkaline, poor
Hardiness: Zone 5
Propagation: Seed, when ripe; softwood or semi-ripe cuttings, in summer

Subshrub from Eurasia and North Africa. Leaves aromatic, ovate-obovate, toothed, dark green. Flowers in racemes, in whorls, tubular, purplish-pink, summer to autumn.

Teucrium x lucidrys
'Variegata'
(Labiatae/Lamiaceae)

Common name: Variegated wall germander
Height: 20in (50cm)
Spread: 12in (30cm)
Aspect: Sun
Soil: Well-drained, alkaline, poor
Hardiness: Zone 5
Propagation: Softwood or semi-ripe cuttings, both in summer

Subshrub cultivar with aromatic, ovate-obovate, toothed, cream and green leaves. Flowers tubular, purplish-pink, in whorled racemes. Excellent ground cover.

Thalictrum aquilegiifolium
'White Cloud'
(Ranunculaceae)

Common name: Meadow-rue
Height: 3ft (1m)
Spread: 18in (45cm)
Aspect: Half shade
Soil: Moist, humus-rich
Hardiness: Zone 6
Propagation: Seed, when ripe; division, in spring

Architectural, rhizomatous perennial. Leaves columbine-like, 2-pinnate, leaflets obovate, midgreen. Flowers in flat-topped panicles, in clusters, white, fluffy, in early summer.

Thalictrum delavayi
A.G.M.
(Ranunculaceae)

Common name: Meadow-rue
Height: 5ft (1.5m)
Spread: 2ft (60cm)
Aspect: Half shade
Soil: Moist, humus-rich
Hardiness: Zone 6
Propagation: Seed, when ripe or in spring

Rhizomatous perennial from Tibet to China. Leaves 2- or 3-pinnate, lobes 3-lobed. Pink, fluffy flowers on widely branching stems, in panicles, midsummer to early autumn.

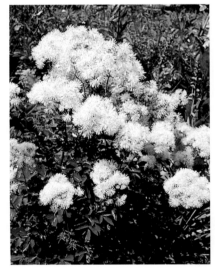

Thalictrum delavayi
'Album'
(Ranunculaceae)

Common name: Meadow-rue
Height: 5ft (1.5m)
Spread: 2ft (60cm)
Aspect: Half shade
Soil: Moist, humus-rich
Hardiness: Zone 6
Propagation: Division, in spring

Form of the species with white, fluffy flowers in panicles on widely branching stems, midsummer to early autumn. Leaves 2- or 3-pinnate.

Planted in paving crevices, mat-forming thyme cultivars such as 'Doone Valley' will release their scent when they are stepped upon.

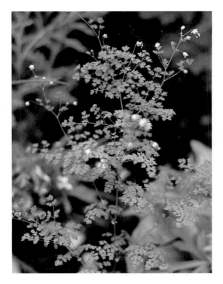

**Thalictrum delavayi
'Hewitt's Double' A.G.M.
(Ranunculaceae)**

Common name: Meadow-rue
Height: 5ft (1.5m)
Spread: 2ft (60cm)
Aspect: Half shade
Soil: Moist, humus-rich
Hardiness: Zone 6
Propagation: Division, in
spring

Sterile form with flowers that lack stamens
but have many sepals, making the flower a
rounded pompon, rich mauve in color,
from midsummer to early autumn.

**Thalictrum flavum
(Ranunculaceae)**

Common name: Yellow
meadow-rue
Height: 36in (90cm)
Spread: 18in (45cm)
Aspect: Half shade
Soil: Moist, humus-rich
Hardiness: Zone 6
Propagation: Seed, when ripe
or in spring

Rhizomatous perennial from Eurasia.
Leaves 2- or 3-pinnate, leaflets obovate,
midgreen. Flowers scented, in panicles,
with yellow sepals and stamens, in summer.

**Thalictrum flavum
subsp. glaucum A.G.M.
(Ranunculaceae)**

Common name: Yellow
meadow-rue
Height: 3ft (1m)
Spread: 2ft (60cm)
Aspect: Sun
Soil: Humus-rich
Hardiness: Zone 6
Propagation: Seed, when ripe
or in spring

Subspecies with 2- or 3-pinnate, glaucous
foliage. Bears large panicles of pale lemon-
yellow flowers in summer. An excellent
flower for cutting.

**Thalictrum minus
adiantifolium
(Ranunculaceae)**

Common name: Meadow-rue
Height: 32in (80cm)
Spread: 12in (30cm)
Aspect: Half shade
Soil: Moist, humus-rich
Hardiness: Zone 6
Propagation: Seed, when ripe
or in spring

Rhizomatous plant. Leaves 3- or 4-pinnate,
leaflets ovate, lobed, glaucous, midgreen.
Flowers in panicles, insignificant, yellow, in
summer. Grown for its fernlike foliage.

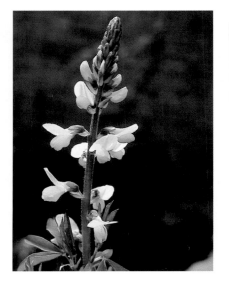

**Thermopsis lanceolata
(Leguminosae/Papilionaceae)**

Common names: None
Height: 32in (80cm)
Spread: 12in (30cm)
Aspect: Sun or half shade
Soil: Well-drained, humus-
rich, fertile
Hardiness: Zone 3
Propagation: Seed, in spring

Rhizomatous perennial from Siberia to
Japan. Leaves 3-palmate, leaflets ovate,
light green. Flowers in racemes, lupinlike,
yellow, from spring to midsummer.

**Thymus x citriodorus
'Silver Queen' A.G.M.
(Labiatae/Lamiaceae)**

Common name: Lemon-
scented thyme
Height: 12in (30cm)
Spread: 18in (45cm)
Aspect: Sun
Soil: Well-drained, alkaline
Hardiness: Zone 7
Propagation: Division, in
spring

Evergreen subshrub of garden origin. Leaves
lance-shaped, lemon-scented when bruised,
midgreen, variegated cream. Flowers in
irregular heads, pale pink, in summer.

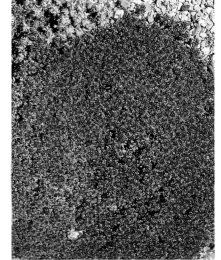

**Thymus serpyllum
var. coccineus A.G.M.
(Labiatae/Lamiaceae)**

Common name: Mother-of-
thyme
Height: 4in (10cm)
Spread: 12in (30cm)
Aspect: Sun
Soil: Well-drained, alkaline
Hardiness: Zone 5
Propagation: Division, in
spring

Aromatic, evergreen subshrub from Europe.
Leaves aromatic, linear-elliptic, dark green.
Flowers crimson-red, in summer. Excellent
in a scree or a raised bed.

**Tiarella cordifolia
A.G.M.
(Saxifragaceae)**

Common name: Allegheny
foam flower
Height: 1ft (30cm)
Spread: 2ft (60cm)
Aspect: Full or half shade
Soil: Any protected from
winter wet, but prefers moist,
humus-rich
Hardiness: Zone 3
Propagation: Seed, when ripe or in spring;
division, in spring

Rhizomatous, woodland perennial from
North America. Leaves ovate, light green.
Flowers in racemes, fluffy, white, in
summer. Spreads by stolons.

Tiarella wherryi
A.G.M.
(Saxifragaceae)

Common name: Foam flower
Height: 8in (20cm)
Spread: 8in (20cm)
Aspect: Full or half shade
Soil: Any, but prefers moist,
humus-rich
Hardiness: Zone 6
Propagation: Seed, when ripe
or in spring; division, in
spring

Rhizomatous perennial from the U.S.A.
Leaves ovate, hairy, 3-lobed, light green.
Flowers in racemes, white, tinged pink, in
late spring and early summer.

Tolmeia menziesii
A.G.M.
(Saxifragaceae)

Common name: Piggy-back
plant
Height: 2ft (60cm)
Spread: 2m (6ft)
Aspect: Full shade
Soil: Moist, humus-rich
Hardiness: Zone 7
Propagation: Seed, in autumn;
division, in spring

Rhizomatous ground cover. Leaves reniform,
lobed, veined, toothed, light green. Flowers
small, purple-brown, scented, in one-sided
racemes, late spring and early summer.

TRADESCANTIA (Commelinaceae)
Spiderwort

A genus of some 60 or so species, all perennial, from North,
Central, and South America. The genus is well-known for the
tender species, often grown as house- or conservatory plants,
but there are also hardy types suitable for borders. Their
natural habitats are scrub or woodland, so they are fairly
tolerant of any soil as long as it is not waterlogged, and will
do well in sun or partial shade. The varieties in cultivation
are hybrids, and go by the name *Tradescantia* x *andersoniana*.
Their leaves are green, often flushed with purple, narrowly
lance-shaped and slightly fleshy, and they bear flowers in
white and shades of pink, blue, and purple. *Tradescantia*
flowers are 3-petalled and saucer-shaped. They are
individually short-lived, but are borne in succession over a
long season from summer to autumn, especially if deadheaded.
They can be disappointing if not carefully positioned, because
the flowers nestle down in the leaves, and may not be seen to
their best advantage from any great distance. Despite being
quite dwarf, *Tradescantia* sometimes need to be staked. They
are fairly long-lived and become large in time, and so benefit
from regular division. They are low-allergen plants, but
contact with the sap may irritate the skin.

Tradescantia x *andersoniana*
'Isis' A.G.M.
(Commelinaceae)

Common name: Spiderwort
Height: 2ft (60cm)
Spread: 2ft (60cm)
Aspect: Sun or half shade
Soil: Moist, fertile
Hardiness: Zone 5
Propagation: Division, in
spring or autumn

Clump-forming hybrid. Leaves narrow,
lance-shaped, pointed, midgreen. Flowers
3-petalled, dark blue, in paired, terminal
cymes, early summer to early autumn.

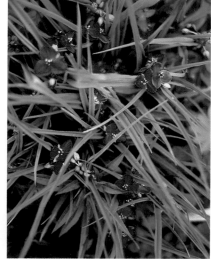

Tradescantia x *andersoniana*
'Karminglut'
(Commelinaceae)

Common name: Spiderwort
Height: 2ft (60cm)
Spread: 2ft (60cm)
Aspect: Sun or half shade
Soil: Moist, fertile
Hardiness: Zone 5
Propagation: Division, in
spring or autumn

Clump-forming hybrid. Leaves narrow,
pointed, lance-shaped, midgreen. Flowers
3-petalled, carmine-red, in paired, terminal
cymes, early summer to early autumn.

Tradescantia x *andersoniana*
'Osprey' A.G.M.
(Commelinaceae)

Common name: Spiderwort
Height: 2ft (60cm)
Spread: 2ft (60cm)
Aspect: Sun or half shade
Soil: Moist, fertile
Hardiness: Zone 5
Propagation: Division, in
spring or autumn

A hybrid, clump-forming perennial. Leaves
narrow, pointed, lance-shaped, midgreen.
Flowers in paired, terminal cymes, large,
white, from early summer to early autumn.

Tradescantia x *andersoniana*
'Purewell Giant'
(Commelinaceae)

Common name: Spiderwort
Height: 2ft (60cm)
Spread: 2ft (60cm)
Aspect: Sun or half shade
Soil: Moist, fertile
Hardiness: Zone 5
Propagation: Division, in
spring or autumn

Clump-forming hybrid. Leaves narrow,
lance-shaped, midgreen. Flowers in paired,
terminal cymes, large, 3-petalled, purple-
red, from early summer to early autumn.

Tradescantia x andersoniana
'Zwanenburg Blue'
(Commelinaceae)

Common name: Spider wort
Height: 2ft (60cm)
Spread: 2ft (60cm)
Aspect: Sun or half shade
Soil: Moist, fertile
Hardiness: Zone 5
Propagation: Division, in
spring or autumn

Clump-forming hybrid. Leaves narrow,
pointed, lance-shaped, midgreen. Flowers
in paired, terminal cymes, 3-petalled, large,
dark blue, early summer to early autumn.

Tradescantia ohiensis
(Commelinaceae)

Common name: Ohio
spiderwort
Height: 3ft (90cm)
Spread 2ft (60cm)
Aspect: Sun or half shade
Soil: Moist, fertile
Hardiness: Zone 7
Propagation: Seed, when ripe;
division, in autumn or spring

A perennial species from the U.S.A. Leaves
narrow, lance-shaped, midgreen. Flowers
in pairs in terminal cymes, blue, white,
purple or pink, in spring.

Tricyrtis formosana
A.G.M.
(Convallariaceae/Liliaceae)

Common name: Toad-lily
Height: 30in (75cm)
Spread: 18in (45cm)
Aspect: Sun or half shade
Soil: Moist, well-drained,
humus-rich
Hardiness: Zone 7
Propagation: Seed, when ripe;
division, in early spring

Rhizomatous, stoloniferous plant. Leaves
inverse lance-shaped, veined, glossy. Cymes
of upward-facing, pinkish stars, spotted
purple, early autumn. For a raised bed.

Tricyrtis hirta
(Convallariaceae/Liliaceae)

Common name: Hairy toad-
lily
Height: 30in (75cm)
Spread: 2ft (60cm)
Aspect: Sun or half shade
Soil: Moist, well-drained,
humus-rich
Hardiness: Zone 5
Propagation: Seed, when ripe;
division, in early spring

Rhizomatous plant. Leaves lance-shaped,
hairy, veined, light green. Flowers white,
purple-spotted stars, late summer to
midautumn. Seen at best in a raised site.

Tricyrtis latifolia
(Convallariaceae/Liliaceae)

Common name: Toad-lily
Height: 30in (75cm)
Spread: 3ft (90cm)
Aspect: Sun or half shade
Soil: Moist, well-drained,
humus-rich
Hardiness: Zone 5
Propagation: Seed, when ripe;
division, in spring or autumn

Rhizomatous, clump-forming plant. Leaves
ovate, veined, glossy green. Branched cymes
of yellow stars, spotted brown, in early to
midsummer. Seen best in a raised site.

Tricyrtis ohsumiensis
(Convallariaceae/Liliaceae)

Common name: Toad-lily
Height: 8in (20cm)
Spread: 12in (30cm)
Aspect: Half or full shade,
protected from midday sun
Soil: Moist, well-drained,
humus-rich
Hardiness: Zone 5
Propagation: Seed, when ripe;
division, in spring or autumn

Rhizomatous, clump-forming plant. Leaves
lance-shaped, veined, glossy, light green,
scorched by hot sun. Flowers yellow
saucers, spotted brown, in early autumn.

Trifolium pannonicum
(Leguminosae/Papilionaceae)

Common name: Hungarian
clover
Height: 3ft (90cm)
Spread: 3ft (90cm)
Aspect: Sun
Soil: Moist, well-drained,
fertile
Hardiness: Zone 5
Propagation: Seed, division or
separation of plantlets, all in spring

Perennial from E Europe. Leaves palmate,
basal leaves obovate, stem leaves inverse
lance-shaped, midgreen. Flowers cloverlike, creamy-yellow, in summer.

Trifolium repens
(Leguminosae/Papilionaceae)

Common name: White clover
Height: 12in (30cm)
Spread: 20in (50cm)
Aspect: Sun
Soil: Moist, well-drained,
fertile
Hardiness: Zone 4
Propagation: Seed, division or
separation of plantlets, all in
spring

Selected form of the lawn weed, and
equally invasive. Leaves 3-foliate, leaflets
toothed, midgreen. Flowers cloverlike,
perfumed, pink, from spring to autumn.

TRILLIUM (Liliaceae/Ttrilliaceae)
Trinity flower • Wake-robin • Wood lily

A genus of some 30 species of rhizomatous woodland plants, the majority of them originating in North America, but some native to the Himalayas and northeast Asia. They bloom in the spring, and bear their leaves, tepals, and petals in threes, hence the name. The leaves, borne in an apical whorl, range from lance- to diamond-shaped, and are veined and often marbled with purple or silver. The flowers are cup- or funnel-shaped and often stalkless, growing directly above the leaves. All species like some degree of shade and an acidic soil, except for *Trillium rivale*, which prefers a sunny position and alkaline soil. All like a moisture-retentive, humus-rich, woodland type of soil, and should be mulched annually with leaf mold. They are extremely resentful of disturbance or damage to the roots, so site them carefully on first planting, and avoid digging around them. They require some patience: divisions may be slow to establish, and plants grown from seed take several years to reach flowering size. In all, these can be demanding plants, but the rewards are generous. They are soundly perennial, and would make good cut flowers, except that one has perforce to cut the leaves at the same time, and this is harmful to the plants, so best avoided.

Trillium chloropetalum var. *giganteum* A.G.M. (Liliaceae/Trilliaceae)

Common name: Giant trillium
Height: 16in (40cm)
Spread: 8in (20cm)
Aspect: Full or half shade
Soil: Moist, well-drained, deep, acidic, humus-rich
Hardiness: Zone 6
Propagation: Seed, as soon as ripe; division, after flowering

A rhizomatous perennial. Leaves ovate to diamond-shaped, dark green, marbled gray or maroon. Flowers scented, brown-purple, among or above the leaves, in spring.

Trillium chloropetalum var. *giganteum* A.G.M. (Liliaceae/Trilliaceae)

Common names: Giant trillium
Height: 16in (40cm)
Spread: 8in (20cm)
Aspect: Full or half shade
Soil: Moist, well-drained, deep, acidic, humus-rich
Hardiness: Zone 6
Propagation: Seed, as soon as ripe; division, after flowering

This rhizomatous plant has a both a purple form (*left*) and this white form. Leaves ovate to diamond-shaped, dark green, marbled gray or maroon.

Trillium cuneatum (Liliaceae/Trilliaceae)

Common name: Whippoorwill flower
Height: 2ft (60cm)
Spread: 1ft (30cm)
Aspect: Full or half shade
Soil: Moist, well-drained, deep, acidic, humus-rich
Hardiness: Zone 6
Propagation: Seed, as soon as ripe; division, after flowering

Rhizomatous perennial from the southeast U.S.A. Leaves rounded, midgreen, marked silver. Flowers scented, maroon, borne above the leaves in spring.

Trillium erectum A.G.M. (Liliaceae/Trilliaceae)

Common names: Berthroot, purple trillium
Height: 20in (50cm)
Spread: 12in (30cm)
Aspect: Full or half shade
Soil: Moist, well-drained, deep, acidic, humus-rich
Hardiness: Zone 4
Propagation: Seed, as soon as ripe; division, after flowering

A rhizomatous perennial from E North America. Leaves ovate, midgreen. Flowers deep red-purple, borne above the leaves in spring. Smell described as like a wet dog.

Trillium grandiflorum A.G.M. (Liliaceae/Trilliaceae)

Common name: Snow trillium
Height: 16in (40cm)
Spread: 18in (45cm)
Aspect: Full or half shade
Soil: Moist, well-drained, deep, acidic, humus-rich
Hardiness: Zone 5
Propagation: Seed, as soon as ripe; division, after flowering

Rhizomatous perennial from E North America. Leaves ovate, dark green. Flowers pure white, fading to pink, borne above the leaves in spring and summer.

Trillium luteum A.G.M. (Liliaceae/Trilliaceae)

Common name: Yellow trillium
Height: 16in (40cm)
Spread: 12in (30cm)
Aspect: Full or half shade
Soil: Moist, well-drained, deep, acidic, humus-rich
Hardiness: Zone 5
Propagation: Seed, as soon as ripe; division, after flowering

Rhizomatous perennial from the southeast U.S.A. Leaves ovate, midgreen. Flowers lemon-scented, upright, yellow, borne above the leaves in spring.

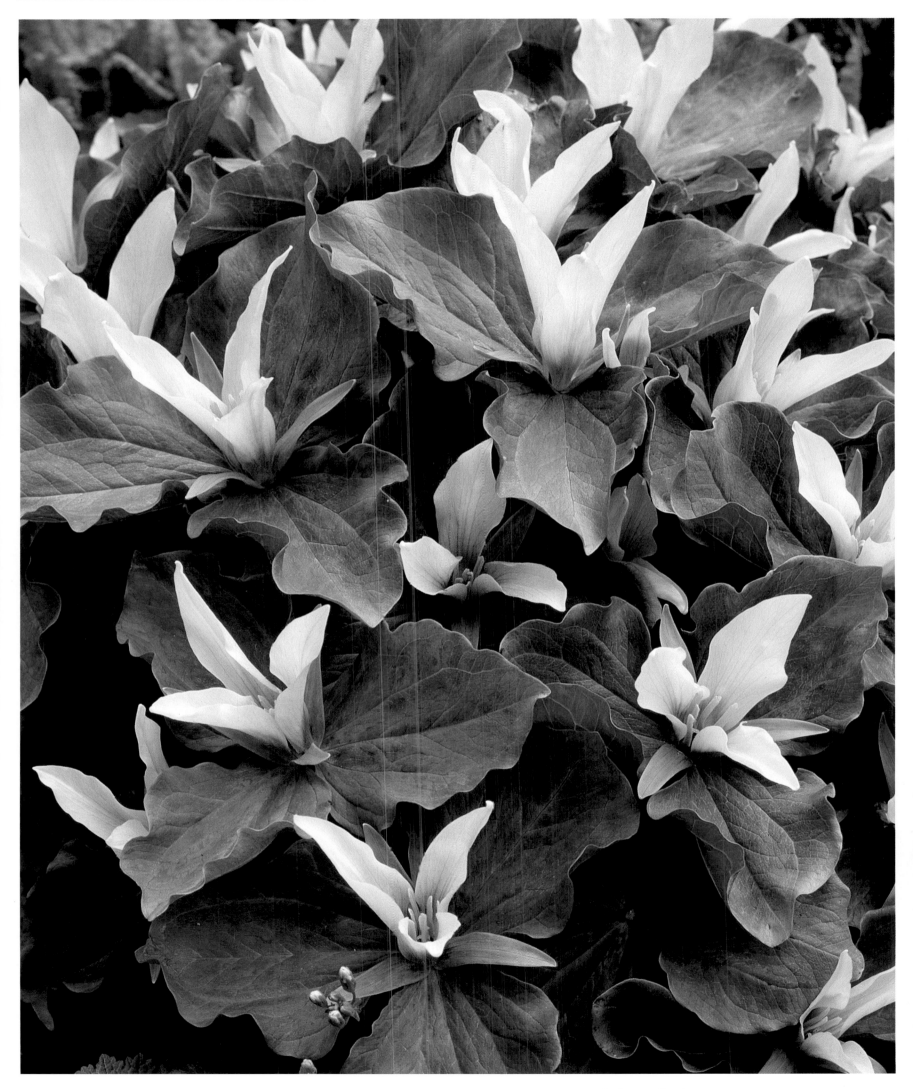

Once established, Trillium chloropetalum makes a superb display in a moist, shady woodland setting.

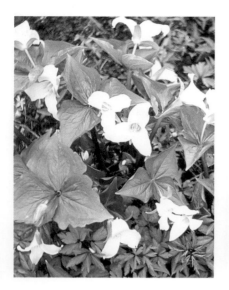

Trillium ovatum
(Liliaceae/Trilliaceae)

Common name: Pacific
trillium
Height: 20in (50cm)
Spread: 8in (20cm)
Aspect: Full or half shade
Soil: Moist, well-drained,
deep, acidic, humus-rich
Hardiness: Zone 5
Propagation: Seed, as soon as
ripe; division, after flowering

Rhizomatous plant from western North
America. Leaves diamond-shaped, deep
green. Flowers upright, pure white, petals
ovate, borne above the leaves in spring.

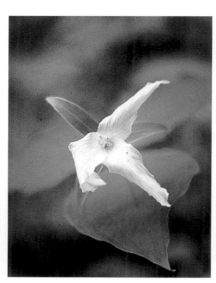

Trillium pusillum
(Liliaceae/Trilliaceae)

Common name: Dwarf
trillium
Height: 6in (15cm)
Spread: 4in (10cm)
Aspect: Full or half shade
Soil: Moist, well-drained,
deep, acidic, humus-rich
Hardiness: Zone 6
Propagation: Seed, as soon as
ripe; division, after flowering

Rhizomatous perennial from eastern North
America. Leaves lance-shaped, dark green.
Flowers small, white, borne among the
leaves, in spring.

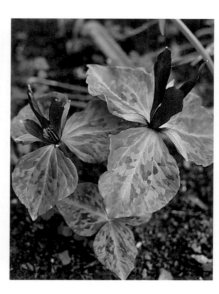

Trillium sessile
(Liliaceae/Trilliaceae)

Common name: Toad trillium
Height: 12in (30cm)
Spread: 8in (20cm)
Aspect: Full or half shade
Soil: Moist, well-drained,
deep, acidic, humus-rich
Hardiness: Zone 4
Propagation: Seed, as soon as
ripe; division, after flowering

Rhizomatous plant from the U.S.A. Leaves
rounded, dark green, marbled gray, silver
and maroon. Flowers upright, maroon-red,
petals lance-shaped, above the leaves, spring.

Trillium vaseyi
(Liliaceae/Trilliaceae)

Common name: Sweet
trillium
Height: 26in (65cm)
Spread: 12in (30cm)
Aspect: Full or half shade
Soil: Moist, well-drained,
deep, acidic, humus-rich
Hardiness: Zone 6
Propagation: Seed, as soon as
ripe; division, after flowering

A rhizomatous perennial from the southeast U.S.A. Leaves rhombic, dark green.
Flowers held horizontally, perfumed, dark
red-purple, in spring.

Tritonia disticha
subsp. *rubrolucens*
(Iridaceae)

Common names: None
Height: 3ft (90cm)
Spread 6in (15cm)
Aspect: Sun
Soil: Sharply drained
Hardiness: Zone 9
Propagation: Seed, in warmth
when ripe; offsets, when
dormant

Cormous perennial from southern Africa.
Leaves basal, linear, erect, lance-shaped,
midgreen. Flowers open, pink funnels in
one-sided spikes, from mid- to late summer.

Trollius acaulis
(Ranunculaceae)

Common name: Globeflower
Height: 12in (30cm)
Spread: 6in (15cm)
Aspect: Sun or half shade
Soil: Moist or wet, deep,
humus-rich, fertile
Hardiness: Zone 6
Propagation: Seed, as soon
as ripe or in spring; division,
after flowering

Clump-forming waterside perennial. Leaves
5- to 7-palmate, leaflets 3-lobed, toothed,
midgreen. Flowers solitary, single, yellow
saucers, in spring. Poisonous.

Trollius chinensis
'Imperial Orange'
(Ranunculaceae)

Common name: Globeflower
Height: 36in (90cm)
Spread: 18in (45cm)
Aspect: Sun or half shade
Soil: Moist or wet, deep,
humus-rich, fertile
Hardiness: Zone 5
Propagation: Seed, as soon
as ripe or in spring; division,
after flowering

Cultivar of a clump-forming bog plant.
Leaves basal, large, 5 lance-shaped, toothed
lobes, and smaller stem. Flowers solitary,
bowl-shaped, orange, in summer. Poisonous.

Trollius x cultorum
'Lemon Queen'
(Ranunculaceae)

Common name: Globeflower
Height: 36in (90cm)
Spread: 18in (45cm)
Aspect: Sun or half shade
Soil: Moist or wet, deep,
humus-rich, fertile
Hardiness: Zone 5
Propagation: Seed, as soon
as ripe or in spring; division,
after flowering

Hybrid cultivar. Leaves basal, large, 5-lobed,
lobes lance-shaped, toothed; smaller stem
leaves. Flowers large, solitary, pale yellow,
globular, midspring to midsummer. Toxic.

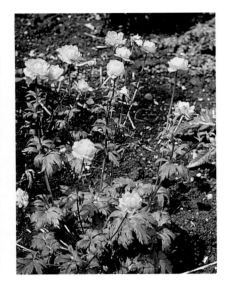

Trollius × cultorum
'Orange Princess' A.G.M.
(Ranunculaceae)

Common name: Globeflower
Height: 3ft (90cm)
Spread: 18in (45cm)
Aspect: Sun or half shade
Soil: Moist or wet, deep,
humus-rich, fertile
Hardiness: Zone 5
Propagation: Seed, as soon as
ripe or in spring: division,
after flowering

Clump-forming hybrid. Leaves large basal,
smaller stem, 5-lobed, lobes lance-shaped,
toothed, glossy. Flowers solitary, orange
bowls, midspring to midsummer. Poisonous.

Trollius europaeus
(Ranunculaceae)

Common name: Common
globeflower
Height: 3ft (90cm)
Spread: 18in (45cm)
Aspect: Sun or half shade
Soil: Moist or wet, deep,
humus-rich, fertile
Hardiness: Zone 5
Propagation: Seed, as soon as
ripe or in spring; division, after flowering

Clump-forming species. Leaves 5-lobed,
segments wedge-shaped, toothed,
midgreen. Flowers solitary, spherical,
yellow, early to midsummer. Poisonous.

Trollius yunnanensis
(Ranunculaceae)

Common name: Globeflower
Height: 28in (70cm)
Spread: 12in (30cm)
Aspect: Sun or half shade
Soil: Moist or wet, deep,
humus-rich, fertile
Hardiness: Zone 5
Propagation: Seed, as soon as
ripe or in spring; division,
after flowering

A clump-forming bog plant. Leaves 3- to
5-lobed, segments ovate, toothed, glossy.
Flowers solitary, yellow saucers, from late
spring to early summer. Poisonous.

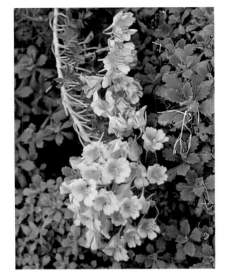

Tropaeolum polyphyllum
(Tropaeolaceae)

Common name: Wreath
nasturtium
Height: 4in (10cm)
Spread: 4ft (1.2m)
Aspect: Sun
Soil: Well-drained, humus-rich
Hardiness: Zone 8
Propagation: Division, in
early spring; basal or stem
cuttings, in spring or early summer

Trailing, rhizomatous, herbaceous plant for
a sunny wall. Leaves up to 9 lobes, glaucous.
Flowers yellow, over a long period in
summer. Spreads a long way underground.

Tuberaria lignosa
(Cistaceae)

Common names: None
Height: 1ft (30cm)
Spread: 3ft (90cm)
Aspect: Sun
Soil: Well-drained
Hardiness: Zone 8
Propagation: Seed, in early
spring

A spreading, rosette-forming perennial
from the Mediterranean. Leaves ovate,
hairy, dull green. Flowers in loose cymes,
bright yellow, all summer.

Tulbaghia cepacea
(Alliaceae/Liliaceae)

Common names: None
Height: 24in (60cm)
Spread: 8in (20cm)
Aspect: Sun
Soil: Well-drained, humus-
rich, fertile
Hardiness: Zone 8
Propagation: Seed, when
ripe or in spring; division,
in spring

Rhizomatous plant from southern Africa.
Leaves narrow, linear, grayish-green. Flowers
soft purple-pink, night-scented, tubular, in
umbels, from late spring to summer.

Tulbaghia cominsii
(Alliaceae/Liliaceae)

Common names: None
Height: 10in (25cm)
Spread: 4in (10cm)
Aspect: Sun
Soil: Well-drained, humus-
rich, fertile
Hardiness: Zone 8
Propagation: Seed, when
ripe or in spring; division,
in spring

Rhizomatous perennial from South Africa.
Leaves narrowly linear, glaucous, midgreen.
Flowers in terminal scapes, white, night-
scented, in spring to summer.

Tulbaghia violacea
(Alliaceae/Liliaceae)

Common names: None
Height: 2ft (60cm)
Spread: 1ft (30cm)
Aspect: Sun
Soil: Well-drained, humus-
rich, fertile
Hardiness: Zone 7
Propagation: Seed, when
ripe or in spring; division,
in spring

Rhizomatous perennial from South Africa.
Leaves narrow, linear, grayish-green.
Flowers in terminal umbels, scented, from
summer to autumn.

TULIPA (Liliaceae)
Tulip

A genus of some 100 species from Europe, Asia and the Middle East, especially Central Asia. All are hardy, bulbous perennials. They prefer sun but will take light shade, and must have a well-drained soil but seem to prefer heavy soils to light ones. Tulips are grown for their showy flowers, which are usually terminal and upright, with six tepals. They vary from cup- or bowl-shaped to goblet-shaped, some with long, very narrow tepals, or lilylike or star-shaped; some are fringed. There is a wide range of colors and bicolors. The leaves are usually basal, broadly ovate, and sometimes wavy-edged or channeled. The bulbs should be planted 6in (15cm) deep in the autumn. Cultivars benefit from being lifted and ripened every year once the leaves have died down. The Greigii and Kaufmanniana groups and the species can be left in the ground all year; mark the position to avoid damaging the bulbs by infill planting. These also benefit from being lifted and divided every few years, and this should be done as soon as the foliage dies down; mice love tulip bulbs, so store lifted bulbs out of their reach and protect newly planted bulbs from disturbance. Contact with any part may cause skin irritation, and all parts are mildly poisonous if ingested.

Tulipa
'Apeldoorn' (4)
(Liliaceae)

Common names: None
Height: 2ft (60cm)
Spread: Nil
Aspect: Sun
Soil: Well-drained, fertile
Hardiness: Zone 5
Propagation: Offsets, after flowering

A Darwin hybrid tulip with flowers of cherry-red outside, signal-red with yellow-edged black marks inside, and with black anthers, in midspring.

Tulipa
'Bright Gem' (15)
(Liliaceae)

Common names: None
Height: 14in (35cm)
Spread: Nil
Aspect: Sun
Soil: Well-drained
Hardiness: Zone 5
Propagation: Offsets, after flowering

A Miscellaneous Group tulip with flowers of sulfur-yellow, flushed orange, and orange-bronze basal marks, in early and midspring.

Tulipa clusiana var.
chrysantha A.G.M (15)
(Liliaceae)

Common names: Clusius tulip
Height: 1ft (30cm)
Spread: Nil
Aspect: Sun
Soil: Well-drained, fertile
Hardiness: Zone 6
Propagation: Seed, in autumn; offsets, after flowering

A species from Iran to the Himalayas. Leaves linear, glaucous, gray-green. Flowers bowl-shaped, yellow, tinged red-brown outside, in early and midspring.

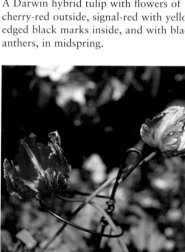

Tulipa
'Keizerskroon' A.G.M. (1)
(Liliaceae)

Common names: None
Height: 1ft (30cm)
Spread: Nil
Aspect: Sun
Soil: Well-drained, fertile
Hardiness: Zone 5
Propagation: Offsets, after flowering

A Single Early Group tulip with cup-shaped, scarlet flowers with broad margins of bright yellow, in midspring. Leaves broadly ovate, midgreen.

Tulipa
'Fantasy' A.G.M. (10)
(Liliaceae)

Common names: None
Height: 22in (55cm)
Spread: Nil
Aspect: Sun
Soil: Well-drained, fertile
Hardiness: Zone 5
Propagation: Offsets, after flowering

A Parrot Group tulip. Flowers cup-shaped, salmon-pink streaked green, with fringed edges, in late spring. Excellent border plant and a good cut flower.

CLASSIFIED LIST AND INTERNATIONAL REGISTER OF TULIP NAMES by Koninklijke Algemeene Vereeniging voor Bloembollencultuur, 1996

Group 1 Single Early Group

Group 2 Double Early Group

Group 3 Triumph Group

Group 4 Darwin Hybrid Group

Group 5 Single late, including Darwin Group and Cottage Group

Group 6 Lily-Flowered Group

Group 7 Fringed Group

Group 8 Viridiflora Group

Group 9 Rembrandt Group

Group 10 Parrot Group

Group 11 Double Late Group

Group 12 Kaufmanniana Group

Group 13 Fosteriana Group

Group 14 Greigii Group

Group 15 Miscellaneous

The flowers of Tulipa sylvestris *are unusual in that they are scented, and also in being pendent in bud, turning upward as they open.*

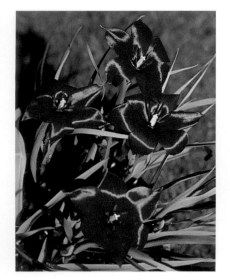

Tulipa linifolia
A.G.M (15)
(Liliaceae)

Common names: None
Height: 8in (20cm)
Spread: Nil
Aspect: Sun
Soil: Well-drained, fertile
Hardiness: Zone 5
Propagation: Seed, in
autumn; offsets, after
flowering

Species from Afghanistan, Uzbekistan, and
Iran. Leaves linear, sickle-shaped, grey-
green. Flowers red with black-purple bases,
bowl-shaped, in early and midspring.

Tulipa
'Monte Carlo' (2)
(Liliaceae)

Common names: None
Height: 1ft (30cm)
Spread: Nil
Aspect: Sun
Soil: Well-drained, fertile
Hardiness: Zone 5
Propagation: Offsets, after
flowering

A Double Early Group tulip with bowl-
shaped flowers of sulfur-yellow, with small
"feather" markings of red at the tips of the
tepals, in midspring.

Tulipa
'Oranje Nassau' A.G.M. (2)
(Liliaceae)

Common names: None
Height: 1ft (30cm)
Spread: Nil
Aspect: Sun
Soil: Well-drained, fertile
Hardiness: Zone 5
Propagation: Offsets, after
flowering

A Double Early Group tulip with open,
bowl-shaped flowers of blood-red, flushed
fiery-red, in midspring. Good for growing
in a container.

Tulipa praestans
'Fusilier' A.G.M. (15)
(Liliaceae)

Common name: Leather-bulb
tulip
Height: 1ft (30cm)
Spread: Nil
Aspect: Sun
Soil: Well-drained, fertile
Hardiness: Zone 5
Propagation: Offsets, after
flowering

Selected form of a species from Kazakhstan
and Tajikistan. Leaves lance-shaped, keeled,
downy grey-green. Flowers in clusters,
bright red, in early to midspring.

Tulipa
'Red Riding Hood' A.G.M.
(14) (Liliaceae)

Common names: None
Height: 8in (20cm)
Spread: Nil
Aspect: Sun
Soil: Well-drained, fertile
Hardiness: Zone 5
Propagation: Offsets, after
flowering

A Greigii Group tulip. Leaves broad, gray-
green, spotted maroon-blue. Flowers
carmine red outside, scarlet-red inside,
with black bases, in early spring.

Tulipa saxatilis
Bakeri Group (15)
(Liliaceae)

Common name: Cliff tulip
Height: 14in (35cm)
Spread: Nil
Aspect: Sun
Soil: Well-drained, fertile
Hardiness: Zone 6
Propagation: Offsets, after
flowering

Selection of a Mediterranean tulip. Leaves
linear, shiny, midgreen. Flowers pink with
yellow bases, margined white, fragrant,
mid- and late spring. Spreads by runners.

Tulipa sprengeri
A.G.M. (15)
(Liliaceae)

Common names: None
Height: 20in (50cm)
Spread: Nil
Aspect: Sun or half shade
Soil: Well-drained
Hardiness: Zone 5
Propagation: Seed, in
autumn; offsets, after
flowering

Species from Turkey, but extinct in the wild.
Leaves linear, shiny, midgreen. Flowers red
or orange, in early summer. Will naturalize,
and has attractive seed pods, shown here.

Tulipa tarda
A.G.M. (15)
(Liliaceae)

Common names: None
Height: 6in (15cm)
Spread: Nil
Aspect: Sun
Soil: Well-drained, fertile
Hardiness: Zone 5
Propagation: Seed, in
autumn; offsets, after
flowering

A species from Central Asia. Leaves lance-
shaped, arching, shiny, bright green.
Flowers in clusters, perfumed, white, with
yellow bases, in early and midspring.

Tulipa
'Toronto' A.G.M. (14)
(Liliaceae)

Common names: None
Height: 8in (20cm)
Spread: Nil
Aspect: Sun
Soil: Well-drained, fertile
Hardiness: Zone 5
Propagation: Offsets, after
flowering

A Greigii Group tulip with broad, ovate
leaves, marked bluish-maroon. Flowers
pinkish-red, tinged vermilion outside and
tangerine inside, in midspring.

Tulipa turkestanica
A.G.M. (15)
(Liliaceae)

Common names: None
Height: 1ft (30cm)
Spread: Nil
Aspect: Sun
Soil: Well-drained, fertile
Hardiness: Zone 5
Propagation: Seed, in
autumn; offsets, after
flowering

A species from Central Asia and China.
Leaves linear, gray-green. Flowers star-
shaped, white with yellow centers, in early
to midspring.

Tulipa urumiensis
A.G.M. (15)
(Liliaceae)

Common names: None
Height: 6in (15cm)
Spread: Nil
Aspect: Sun
Soil: Well-drained, fertile
Hardiness: Zone 5
Propagation: Seed, in
autumn; offsets, after
flowering

A Miscellanous Group tulip from Iran.
Leaves linear, midgreen. Flowers star-
shaped, yellow, flushed lilac or brown
outside, in pairs or solitary, in early spring.

Tweedia caerulea
A.G.M.
(Asclepiadaceae)

Common names: None
Height: 36in (1m)
Spread: 8in (20cm)
Aspect: Sun
Soil: Moist, well-drained,
fertile
Hardiness: Zone 10
Propagation: Seed, in spring;
softwood cuttings, in summer

A twining, evergreen subshrub from Brazil.
Leaves oblong, downy, pale green. Flowers
in 3- or 4-flowered cymes, sky-blue aging
to purple, from summer to early autumn.

Umbilicus rupestris
(Crassulaceae)

Common names: Navelwort;
pennywort
Height: 16in (40cm)
Spread: 6in (15cm)
Aspect: Sun or half shade
Soil: Sharply drained
Hardiness: Zone 7
Propagation: Seed, in spring
or autumn

A perennial from Europe. Leaves rounded,
succulent, depressed in center, midgreen.
Flowers in spikes, small, tubular, greenish-
white, in summer. Good wall plant.

Uncinia rubra
(Cyperaceae)

Common name: Hook sedge
Height: 12in (30cm)
Spread: 16in (40cm)
Aspect: Sun or half shade
Soil: Moist, well-drained,
fertile
Hardiness: Zone 8
Propagation: Seed, in spring;
division, in early summer

An evergreen grass from New Zealand.
Leaves flat, linear, pointed, rich red.
Flowers dark brown to black, in spikes,
in mid- to late summer.

Urospermum delachampii
(Asteraceae/Compositae)

Common names: None
Height: 16in (40 cm)
Spread: 24in (60cm)
Aspect: Sun
Soil: Sharply drained, fertile
Hardiness: Zone 6
Propagation: Seed, in spring
or autumn; division, in spring

A perennial from the Mediterranean.
Leaves obovate, toothed, gray-green.
Flowers dandelion-like, lemon-yellow,
in summer.

Uvularia grandiflora
A.G.M.
(Convallariaceae/Liliaceae)

Common name: Big
merrybells
Height: 32in (80cm)
Spread: 24in (60cm)
Aspect: Full or half shade
Soil: Moist, well-drained,
humus-rich, fertile
Hardiness: Zone 4
Propagation: Seed, when ripe;
division, in spring

Rhizomatous, spreading woodlander. Ovate,
perfoliate, leaves. Flowers yellow, tubular,
pendent, solitary or paired, on arching
stems, mid and late spring. Red berries.

Valeriana officinalis
subsp. *sambucifolia*
(Valerianaceae)

Common name: Common
valerian
Height: 6ft (2m)
Spread: 30in (75cm)
Aspect: Sun or half shade
Soil: Moist
Hardiness: Zone 4
Propagation: Seed, division or
basal cuttings, all in spring

Rhizomatous plant from Europe. Leaves
aromatic, pinnate; up to 9 pairs of lance-
shaped, toothed, leaflets. Flowers white,
salverform, in rounded cymes, all summer.

Valeriana phu
'Aurea'
(Valerianaceae)

Common name: Valerian
Height: 5ft (1.5m)
Spread: 2ft (60cm)
Aspect: Sun or half shade
Soil: Moist
Hardiness: Zone 6
Propagation: Seed, division or
basal cuttings, all in spring

Rhizomatous perennial from the Caucasus.
Leaves aromatic, simple or pinnatifid, first
yellow, then lime- then midgreen. Flowers
in corymbs, white, salverform, in spring.

Valeriana montana
(Valerianaceae)

Common name: Dwarf
valerian
Height: 16in (40cm)
Spread: 8in (20cm)
Aspect: Sun or half shade
Soil: Moist, alkaline, fertile
Hardiness: Zone 5
Propagation: Seed, division or
basal cuttings, all in spring

Rhizomatous perennial from the mountains
of Europe. Leaves basal, entire, elliptic, and
stem, ovate. Flowers in corymbs, white,
salverform, late spring or early summer.

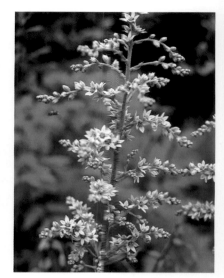

Veratrum album
(Liliaceae/Melianthiaceae)

Common name: False
hellebore
Height: 6ft (2m)
Spread: 2ft (60cm)
Aspect: Sun or half shade
Soil: Moist, well-drained,
deep, fertile
Hardiness: Zone 5
Propagation: Seed when ripe;
division, in autumn or spring

Rhizomatous plant. Leaves broad, elliptic,
pleated, shiny. Flowers in many-branched
panicles, white stars, early and midsummer.
Very poisonous. Slugs can decimate it.

Veratrum nigrum
A.G.M.
(Liliaceae/Melianthiaceae)

Common name: False
hellebore
Height: 4ft (1.2m)
Spread: 2ft (60cm)
Aspect: Sun or half shade
Soil: Moist, well-drained,
deep, fertile
Hardiness: Zone 6
Propagation: Seed, when ripe;
division, in autumn or spring

Rhizomatous plant. Leaves broad, elliptic,
pleated, shiny, light green. Flowers offensive-
smelling, small, brown-black, in panicles.
Very toxic, highly allergenic, and irritant.

VERBASCUM (Scrophulrriaceae)
Mullein

A genus of over 350 species, from Europe, Asia and North
Africa. Most of the species are biennial, but there are also
annuals, perennials, and some subshrubs; the perennial
members are short-lived, often dying after flowering. Some
are evergreen, but most are not. They grow for the most part
in open scrubland or on dry hillsides, but a few are found in
open woods. They like a sunny position and sharp drainage.
They generally form a basal clump or rosette of large, soft,
leaves, which may be simple, lobed, or toothed, and produce
one or more dense spikes of saucer-shaped flowers. The
flowers are individually short-lived, but they are borne in
succession over a long season. The flowers of hybrid cultivars
tend to be larger and more showy than those of species.
Many mulleins are quite tall, and they may need to be staked.
All self-sow freely, and the seedlings of the named varieties
will not come true, so they should be deadheaded. The larger
species can be left to naturalize in gravel or in wild gardens,
where they make impressive architectural plants and benefit
from the support of other plants. The smaller types are good
for rock gardens, screes, or even walls. All mulleins are
unfortunately prone to powdery mildew.

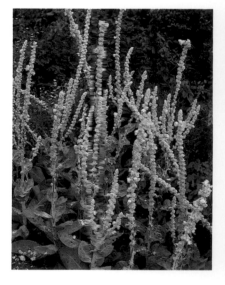

Verbascum bombyciferum
A.G.M.
(Scrophulariaceae)

Common name: Mullein
Height: 6ft (1.8m)
Spread: 3ft (90cm)
Aspect: Sun
Soil: Sharply drained,
alkaline, poor
Hardiness: Zone 6
Propagation: Seed or division,
both in spring; root cuttings,
in winter

Short-lived evergreen from Turkey. Leaves
basal, densely white-woolly, silky-hairy.
Flowers sulfur-yellow, saucer-shaped, in
spikes, in clusters, in summer.

Verbascum chaixii (Scrophulariaceae)

Common name: Chaix mullein
Height: 3ft (90cm)
Spread: 18in (45cm)
Aspect: Sun
Soil: Sharply drained, alkaline, poor
Hardiness: Zone 5
Propagation: Seed or division, both in spring; root cuttings, in winter

Species from Europe. Leaves basal, ovate, hairy, and stem, rounded. Flowers in slim panicles on white-woolly stems, pale yellow saucers, from mid- to late summer.

Verbascum chaixii 'Album' (Scrophulariaceae)

Common name: Chaix mullein
Height: 3ft (90cm)
Spread: 2ft (60cm)
Aspect: Sun
Soil: Sharply drained, alkaline, poor
Hardiness: Zone 5
Propagation: Seed or division, both in spring; root cuttings, in winter

Leaves basal, ovate, hairy, midgreen, and stem, rounded. Flowers on white-woolly stems, in slim panicles, white saucers with mauve centres, from mid- to late summer.

Verbascum dumulosum A.G.M. (Scrophulariaceae)

Common name: Mullein
Height: 10in (25cm)
Spread: 16in (40cm)
Aspect: Sun
Soil: Sharply drained, alkaline, poor
Hardiness: Zone 8
Propagation: Seed or division, both in spring; root cuttings, in winter

Evergreen subshrub from Turkey. Leaves elliptic, hairy-felted, gray-green. Flowers on white-downy stems, in short racemes, yellow saucers, late spring to early summer.

Verbascum chaixii 'Gainsborough' A.G.M. (Scrophulariaceae)

Common name: Chaix mullein
Height: 4ft (1.2m)
Spread: 1ft (30cm)
Aspect: Sun
Soil: Sharply drained, alkaline, poor
Hardiness: Zone 6
Propagation: Division, in spring; root cuttings, in winter

A hybrid mullein. Leaves in basal rosettes, ovate, wrinkled, gray-green. Flowers in long panicles, soft yellow saucers, from early to late summer.

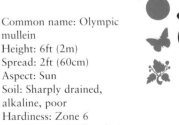

Verbascum 'Helen Johnson' A.G.M. (Scrophulariaceae)

Common name: Mullein
Height: 3ft (90cm)
Spread: 1ft (30cm)
Aspect: Sun
Soil: Sharply drained, alkaline, poor
Hardiness: Zone 7
Propagation: Division, in spring; root cuttings, in winter

Evergreen, hybrid mullein. Leaves ovate, wrinkled, downy, gray-green. Flowers in erect spikes, pinkish-brown saucers, from early to late summer.

Verbascum 'Jackie' (Scrophulariaceae)

Common name: Mullein
Height: 3ft (90cm)
Spread: 18in (45cm)
Aspect: Sun
Soil: Sharply drained, alkaline, poor
Hardiness: Zone 6
Propagation: Division, in spring; root cuttings, in winter

Rosette-forming, hybrid mullein. Leaves ovate, downy, gray-green. Flowers in erect spikes, buff-pink saucers with a purple eye, in summer.

Verbascum nigrum (Scrophulariaceae)

Common name: Dark mullein
Height: 3ft (90cm)
Spread: 2ft (60cm)
Aspect: Sun
Soil: Sharply drained, alkaline, poor
Hardiness: Zone 5
Propagation: Seed or division, both in spring; root cuttings, in winter

Rosette-forming species. Leaves basal, ovate, and stem, rounded, mid- to dark-green. Slim racemes of clustered flowers, dark yellow saucers, midsummer to early autumn.

Verbascum olympicum (Scrophulariaceae)

Common name: Olympic mullein
Height: 6ft (2m)
Spread: 2ft (60cm)
Aspect: Sun
Soil: Sharply drained, alkaline, poor
Hardiness: Zone 6
Propagation: Seed or division, both in spring; root cuttings, in winter

Rosette-forming species. Leaves broad, lance-shaped, gray-white woolly. Flowers in panicles, clustered, golden-yellow saucers, from early to late summer. May then die.

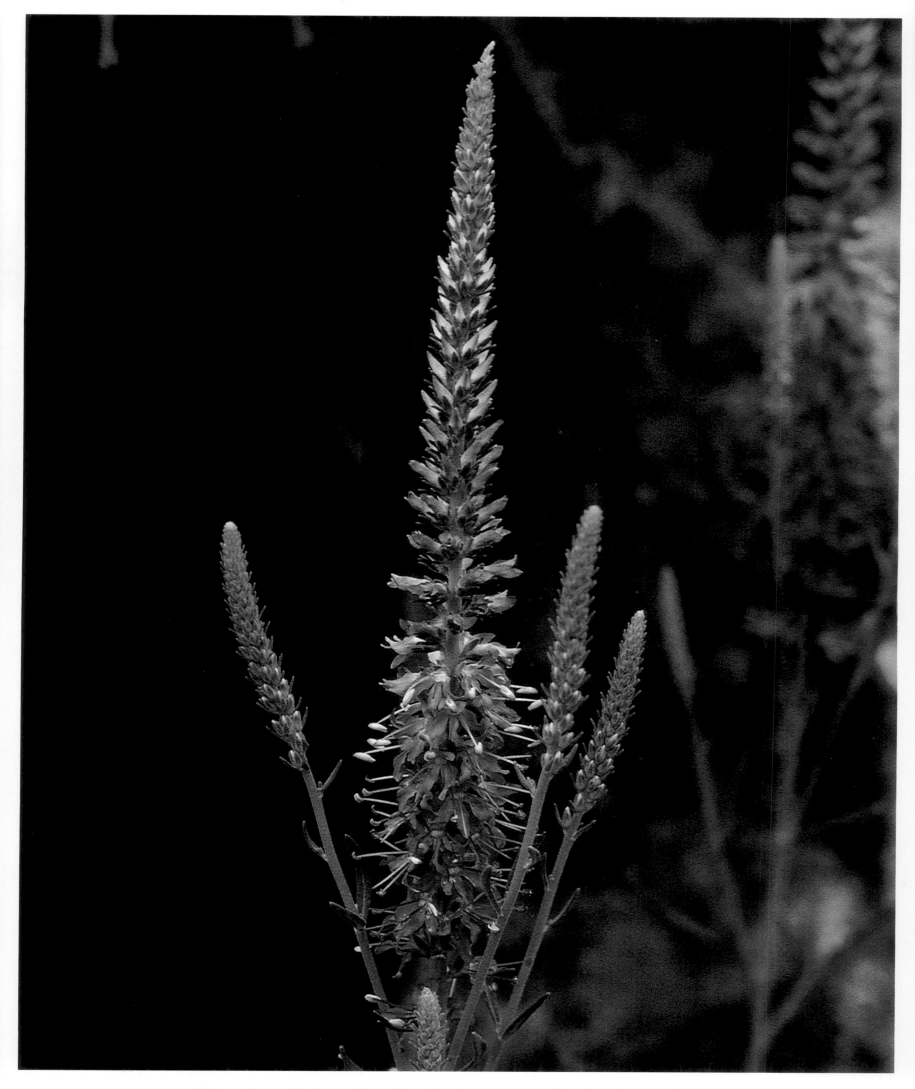

Native to Europe, Turkey, and Central Asia, Veronica spicata *is excellent for rock or gravel gardens.*

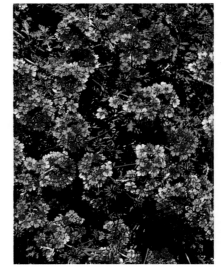

Verbena bonariensis
(Verbenaceae)

Common names: None
Height: 6ft (2m)
Spread: 75cm (30in)
Aspect: Sun
Soil: Moist, well-drained,
fertile
Hardiness: Zone 8
Propagation: Seed or division,
both in spring

Clump-forming plant. Leaves few, oblong,
wrinkled, stem-clasping, midgreen. Flowers
in cymes, purple-lilac salvers, midsummer
to early autumn. Excellent butterfly plant.

Verbena hastata
'Alba'
(Verbenaceae)

Common name: White blue
vervain
Height: 4ft (1.2m)
Spread: 2ft (60cm)
Aspect: Sun
Soil: Moist, well-drained,
fertile
Hardiness: Zone 3
Propagation: Seed or division,
both in spring

Clump-forming plant from North America.
Leaves lance-shaped, toothed, pointed,
midgreen. Flowers in stiff panicles, white,
salverform. early summer to early autumn.

Verbena
'Homestead Purple'
(Verbenaceae)

Common names: Hybrid
verbena
Height: 18in (45cm)
Spread: 20in (50cm)
Aspect: Sun
Soil: Moist, well-drained,
fertile
Hardiness: Zone 8
Propagation: Division in spring or autumn;
stem-tip cuttings, in late summer

Hybrid cultivar. Leaves ovate, toothed,
rough, dark green. Flowers in tight
panicles, tiny, salverform, purple, all
summer to autumn.

Verbena
'Sissinghurst' A.G.M.
(Verbenaceae)

Common name: Hybrid
verbena
Height: 18in (45cm)
Spread: (20in (50cm)
Aspect: Sun
Soil: Moist, well-drained,
fertile
Hardiness: Zone 8
Propagation: Division, in autumn or
spring; stem-tip cuttings, in late summer

A hybrid cultivar. Leaves ovate, toothed,
rough, midgreen. Flowers tiny, salverform,
cherry-red, in tight panicles, from summer
to autumn.

Veronica
'Blue Spire'
(Scrophulariaceae)

Common names: None
Height: 3ft (90cm)
Spread: 2ft (60cm)
Aspect: Sun or half shade
Soil: Moist, well-drained,
humus-rich, fertile
Hardiness: Zone 6
Propagation: Division, in
autumn or spring

A hybrid perennial. Leaves lance-shaped,
toothed, pointed, midgreen. Flowers in
dense, erect racemes, tubular, deep blue,
in late summer and early autumn.

Veronica gentianoides
A.G.M.
(Scrophulariaceae)

Common name: Gentian
speedwell
Height: 18in (45cm)
Spread: 18in (45cm)
Aspect: Sun or half shade
Soil: Moist, well-drained,
humus-rich, fertile
Hardiness: Zone 4
Propagation: Seed, in
autumn; division, in autumn or spring

Rosette-forming perennial from Turkey and
the Ukraine. Leaves broad, lance-shaped,
thick, dark green. Flowers pale blue cups,
in erect racemes, in early summer.

Veronica
'Ray of Fire'
(Scrophulariaceae)

Common names: None
Height: 30in (75cm)
Spread: 2ft (60cm)
Aspect: Sun or half shade
Soil: Moist, well-drained,
humus-rich, fertile
Hardiness: Zone 5
Propagation: Division, in
autumn or spring

A hybrid, mat-forming perennial. Leaves
lance-shaped, pointed, midgreen. Flowers
in dense, terminal panicles, pinkish-red,
tubular, in late summer and autumn.

Veronica spicata
subsp. *incana* A.G.M.
(Scrophulariaceae)

Common name: Spike
speedwell
Height: 1ft (30cm)
Spread: 1ft (30cm)
Aspect: Sun or half shade
Soil: Moist, well-drained,
humus-rich, fertile
Hardiness: Zone 3
Propagation: Seed, in
autumn; division, in autumn or spring

A mat-forming perennial from Eurasia and
Turkey. Leaves linear, toothed, silver-hairy.
Flowers in dense, terminal racemes, bright
blue stars, from early to late summer.

Veronica spicata 'Rotfuchs' (Scrophulariaceae)

Common name: Spike speedwell
Height: 1ft (30cm)
Spread: 1ft (30cm)
Aspect: Sun or half shade
Soil: Moist, well-drained, humus-rich, fertile
Hardiness: Zone 3
Propagation: Division, in spring or autumn; stem-tip cuttings, in summer

A hybrid, mat-forming perennial. Leaves linear, toothed, midgreen. Flowers in dense, terminal racemes, deep pink stars, from early to late summer.

Veronicastrum virginicum f. album (Scrophulariaceae)

Common name: Culver's root
Height: 6ft (2m)
Spread: 18in (45cm)
Aspect: Sun or half shade
Soil: Moist, humus-rich, fertile
Hardiness: Zone3
Propagation: Seed, in autumn; division, in spring

Perennial from North America. Leaves lance-shaped, toothed, pointed, dark green. Flowers white, tubular, in slim, dense racemes, from midsummer to early autumn.

Veronicastrum virginicum 'Pink Glow' (Scrophulariaceae)

Common name: Culver's-root
Height: 6ft (2m)
Spread: 18in (45cm)
Aspect: Sun or half shade
Soil: Moist, humus-rich, fertile
Hardiness: Zone 3
Propagation: Division, in spring

Selected form of the species. Leaves lance-shaped, toothed, pointed, dark green. Soft pink, tubular flowers, in dense racemes, from midsummer to early autumn.

Vinca major (Apocynaceae)

Common name: Big periwinkle
Height: 18in (45cm)
Spread: Indefinite
Aspect: Sun or half shade
Soil: Moisture-retentive
Hardiness: Zone 7
Propagation: Division, from autumn to spring

Evergreen, trailing, Mediterranean ground-cover subshrub. Leaves ovate, shiny, dark green. Flowers starry, violet-blue, over long period from mid-spring to autumn. Toxic.

Vinca major 'Variegata' A.G.M. (Apocynaceae)

Common name: Variegated big periwinkle
Height: 18in (45cm)
Spread: Indefinite
Aspect: Sun or half shade
Soil: Moisture-retentive
Hardiness: Zone 7
Propagation: Division, from autumn to spring

Evergreen, trailing, Mediterranean ground cover subshrub. Leaves ovate, dark green margined cream; good for cutting. Flowers lilac-blue, starry, from spring to autumn.

Vinca minor (Apocynaceae)

Common names: Myrtle; periwinkle
Height: 8in (20cm)
Spread: Indefinite
Aspect: Sun or half shade
Soil: Moisture-retentive
Hardiness: Zone 4
Propagation: Division, from autumn to spring

Trailing, evergreen subshrub from Eurasia, not invasive like V. major. Leaves ovate, dark green. Flowers reddish-purple, blue or white, all summer long.

VIOLA (Violaceae)
Viola • Pansy • Violetta

A genus of some 500 species from habitats the world over. The genus has given rise, by interbreeding, to three main types of plant: garden pansies, violas and violettas. The garden pansies, *Viola × wittrockiana*, have arisen from the crossing of several species. They are biennial or at best a very short-lived perennial, with unscented or only faintly scented flowers with a "face," and single-stemmed roots. The violas or tufted pansies are perennial, with rounded, usually scented flowers with rays of a contrasting, often deeper color, and multiple-stemmed roots. The violettas are perennial, sweetly scented, with oval flowers with a yellow center but no rays, and a multi-stemmed root system. Other forms include South American species that have rosettes of leaves like those of a sempervivum; these are very difficult in cultivation, and best left to the enthusiast. There are ten subdivisions in all, but only the violas (Va) and violettas (Vtta) are of interest and covered here. All forms of *Viola* like full sun or partial shade, and moist, well-drained but moisture-retentive soil. They all have a long flowering season, and can be made even more prolific by deadheading. Many of the species violas are unfortunately short-lived.

Viola biflora
(Va)
(Violaceae)

Common name: Twin-flowered violet
Height: 3in (8cm)
Spread: 8in (20cm)
Aspect: Half shade
Soil: Moist, humus-rich, fertile
Hardiness: Zone 4
Propagation: Seed, as soon as ripe or in spring

Dwarf, creeping, rhizomatous species from Eurasia and North America. Leaves heart-shaped, toothed, pale green. Flowers pale yellow, dark-veined, late spring and summer.

Viola cornuta
A.G.M. (Va)
(Violaceae)

Common names: Horned violet; tufted pansy
Height: 6in (15cm)
Spread: 16in (40cm)
Aspect: Sun or half shade
Soil: Moist, humus-rich, fertile
Hardiness: Zone 7
Propagation: Division or stem-tip cuttings, both in spring or autumn

A rhizomatous, evergreen species. Leaves ovate, toothed, midgreen. Flowers scented, lilac-blue, lower petals marked white, from spring to summer, twice if sheared over.

Viola cornuta
Alba Group A.G.M. (Va)
(Violaceae)

Common name: Tufted pansy; white horned violet
Height: 6in (15cm)
Spread: 18in (45cm)
Aspect: Sun or half shade
Soil: Moist, humus-rich, fertile
Hardiness: Zone 7
Propagation: Division or stem-tip cuttings, both in spring or autumn

White form of evergreen, rhizomatous species, flowering in spring and summer, twice if sheared over. Flowers pure white. Leaves ovate, toothed, midgreen.

Viola
'Columbine' (Va)
(Violaceae)

Common names: None
Height: 8in (20cm)
Spread: 12in (30cm)
Aspect: Sun or half shade
Soil: Moist, well-drained, fertile
Hardiness: Zone 7
Propagation: Division or stem-tip cuttings, both in spring or autumn

A compact, hybrid viola. Leaves ovate, toothed, midgreen. Flowers lilac and white, streaked purple, held high above the foliage, in spring and summer.

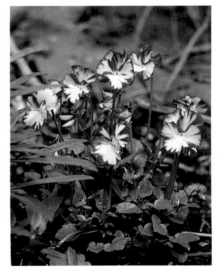

Viola
'Jackanapes' A.G.M. (Va)
(Violaceae)

Common names: None
Height: 8in (20cm)
Spread: 18in (45cm)
Aspect: Sun or half shade
Soil: Moist, well-drained, fertile
Hardiness: Zone 7
Propagation: Division or stem-tip cuttings, both in spring or autumn

Vigorous, evergreen hybrid. Leaves ovate, toothed, midgreen. Flowers have upper 3 petals chocolate-colored, lower 3 yellow, streaked purple, in spring and summer.

Viola
'Jeannie Bellew' (Va)
(Violaceae)

Common names: None
Height: 8in (20cm)
Spread: 18in (45cm)
Aspect: Sun or half shade
Soil: Moist, well-drained, fertile
Hardiness: Zone 7
Propagation: Division or stem-tip cuttings, both in spring or autumn

A hybrid viola cultivar. Leaves ovate, toothed, midgreen. Flowers of pale yellow are borne among the leaves in spring and summer.

Viola
'Maggie Mott' A.G.M. (Va)
(Violaceae)

Common names: None
Height: 1ft (30cm)
Spread: 1ft (30cm)
Aspect: Sun or half shade
Soil: Moist, well-drained, fertile
Hardiness: Zone 7
Propagation: Division or stem-tip cuttings, both in spring or autumn

Hybrid viola. Leaves ovate, toothed, midgreen. Flowers perfumed, soft silvery-mauve, with a pale cream center, in spring and summer. A very popular old variety.

Viola
'Rebecca' (Vtta)
(Violaceae)

Common names: None
Height: 6in (15cm)
Spread: 8in (20cm)
Aspect: Sun or half shade
Soil: Moist, well-drained, fertile
Hardiness: Zone 7
Propagation: Division or stem-tip cuttings, both in spring or autumn

A hybrid violetta. Leaves ovate, toothed, mid-green. Flowers scented, creamy-white, flecked and streaked with violet around the edges, in spring and summer.

Given its favored conditions in a rock garden or wall, Zauschneria californica will bear abundant flowers from late summer into early autumn.

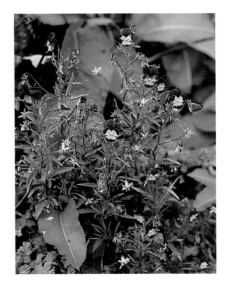

Viola tricolor (Va)
(Violaceae)

Common name: Johnny-
jump-up
Height: 5in (12cm)
Spread: 6in (15cm)
Aspect: Sun or half shade
Soil: Moist, well-drained,
fertile
Hardiness: Zone 4
Propagation: Seed, as soon as
ripe or in spring

Short-lived, evergreen species. Leaves
ovate, toothed, midgreen. Flowers have
dark purple upper petals and yellow,
streaked lower petals. Self-seeds plentifully.

Viola
'Zoe' (Vtta)
(Violaceae)

Common names: None
Height: 6in (15cm)
Spread: 8in (20cm)
Aspect: Sun or half shade
Soil: Moist, well-drained,
fertile
Hardiness: Zone 7
Propagation: Division or
stem-tip cuttings, both in
spring or autumn

A hybrid violetta cultivar. Leaves ovate,
toothed, midgreen. Flowers perfumed,
mauve and white with a yellow eye, in
spring and summer.

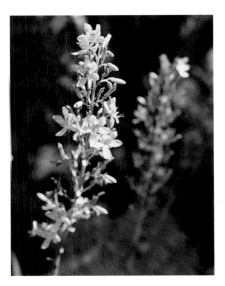

Wachendorfia paniculata
(Haemodoraceae)

Common name: Redroot
Height: 6ft (1.8m)
Spread: 18in (45cm)
Aspect: Sun or half shade
Soil: Moist, well-drained,
humus-rich fertile
Hardiness: Zone 8
Propagation: Seed in warmth
or separated tubers, both in
spring

Tuberous, evergreen perennial from South
Africa. Leaves basal, broad, linear, veined,
midgreen. Flowers in dense panicles,
yellow, starry, in early summer.

Watsonia borbonica
subsp. *ardernei*
(Iridaceae)

Common name: Bugle-lily
Height: 5ft (1.5m)
Spread: 4in (10cm)
Aspect: Sun
Soil: Well-drained, humus-
rich, fertile
Hardiness: Zone 9
Propagation: Seed, in warmth
in autumn; division, in spring

A tender, cormous perennial from South
Africa. Leaves narrow, sword-shaped,
midgreen. Flowers in spikes of up to 20,
white, rarely pink, in summer.

Watsonia densiflora
(Iridaceae)

Common name: Bugle-lily
Height: 5ft (1.5m)
Spread: 4in (10cm)
Aspect: Sun
Soil: Well-drained, humus-
rich, fertile
Hardiness: Zone 9
Propagation: Seed, in warmth
in autumn; division, in spring

A tender, cormous perennial from South
Africa. Leaves narrow, sword-shaped,
midgreen. Flowers in spikes of up to 30,
red or orange-red, in summer.

Watsonia marginata
(Iridaceae)

Common name: Bugle-lily
Height: 6ft (2m)
Spread: 6in (15cm)
Aspect: Sun
Soil: Well-drained, humus-
rich, fertile
Hardiness: Zone 9
Propagation: Seed, in warmth
in autumn; division, in spring

A tender, cormous perennial from South
Africa. Leaves sword-shaped, midgreen.
Flowers in spikes, tubular, mauve-pink, in
spring and early summer.

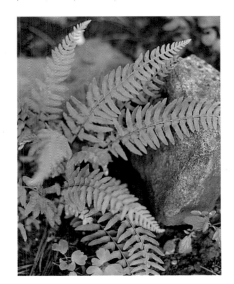

Woodsia polystichoides
A.G.M.
(Aspidiaceae/Dryopteridaceae)

Common name: Holly-fern
woodsia
Height: 12in (30cm)
Spread: 16in (40cm)
Aspect: Half shade
Soil: Moist, sharply drained,
fertile
Hardiness: Zone 4
Propagation: Spores, in warmth
when ripe; division, when dormant

A deciduous, rhizomatous, terrestrial fern
from high regions of East Asia. Fronds
lance-shaped, pinnate, with 15–30 pairs of
oblong pinnae, pale green.

Woodwardia radicans
A.G.M
(Blechnaceae)

Common name: European
chain fern
Height: 6ft (1.8m)
Spread: 10ft (3m)
Aspect: Half shade
Soil: Wet, fertile
Hardiness: Zone 8
Propagation: Bulbils or
spores, in warmth in early autumn;
division, in spring

Evergreen fern from Europe and islands of
the Atlantic. Fronds pinnate, lance-shaped,
dark green; pinnae ovate, pinnatifid, with
lance-shaped, toothed segments.

Yucca filamentosa
A.G.M
(Agavaceae)

Common name: Adam's
needle
Height: 30in (75cm)
Spread: 5ft (1.5m)
Aspect: Sun
Soil: Well-drained
Hardiness: Zone 7
Propagation: Seed in warmth
or rooted suckers, both in
spring; root cuttings, in winter

Evergreen shrub. Leaves in basal rosettes,
inversely lance-shaped, fringed, dark green.
Flowers in short-stemmed, upright panicles,
nodding, white bells, mid- to late summer.

Yucca flaccida
'Ivory' A.G.M.
(Agavaceae)

Common name: Spanish
bayonet
Height: 2ft (60cm)
Spread: 5ft (1.5m)
Aspect: Sun
Soil: Well-drained
Hardiness: Zone 7
Propagation: Seed in warmth
or rooted suckers, both in
spring; root cuttings, in winter

Evergreen shrub. Leaves in basal rosettes,
lance-shaped, dark blue-green, fringed.
Flowers in panicles, nodding creamy-white
bells, in mid- and late summer.

Yucca gloriosa
'Variegata' A.G.M.
(Agavaceae)

Common name: Mount-lily
yucca
Height: 6ft (2m)
Spread: 6ft (2m)
Aspect: Sun
Soil: Well-drained
Hardiness: Zone 7
Propagation: Seed in warmth
or rooted suckers, both in
spring; root cuttings, in winter

Evergreen shrub. Leaves in basal rosettes,
arching, lance-shaped, pointed, green, edged
yellow. Flowers in panicles, white pendent
bells, from late summer to autumn.

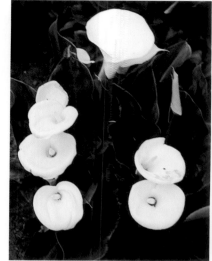

Zantedeschia aethiopica
A.G.M.
(Araceae)

Common name: Common
calla
Height: 3ft (90cm)
Spread: 2ft (60cm)
Aspect: Sun
Soil: Moist or marginal
aquatic, humus-rich
Hardiness: Zone 8
Propagation: Seed, in warmth
when ripe; division, in spring

A rhizomatous perennial from southern
Africa. Leaves arrow-shaped, glossy-green.
Bears large, pure white spathes with yellow
spadices from late spring to mid-summer.

Zantedeschia elliottiana
A.G.M.
(Araceae)

Common name: Golden
calla
Height: 3ft (90cm)
Spread: 10in (25cm)
Aspect: Sun
Soil: Moist, humus-rich
Hardiness: Zone 9
Propagation: Seed, in warmth
when ripe; division, in spring

Tender rhizomatous perennial of unknown
source. Leaves basal, heart-shaped, dark
green, spotted white. Spathes and spadices
golden yellow, in summer.

Zantedeschia
Elliottiana hybrids
(Araceae)

Common name: Golden
calla
Height: 2ft (60cm)
Spread: 8in (20cm)
Aspect: Sun
Soil: Moist, humus-rich
Hardiness: Zone 9
Propagation: Division, in
spring

Tender, rhizomatous perennial hybrids from
Z. elliottiana. Leaves basal, heart-shaped,
dark green, unspotted. Spathes in a variety
of shades of red, orange and yellow.

Zantedeschia rehmannii
A.G.M.
(Araceae)

Common name: Pink calla
Height: 16in (40cm)
Spread: 11in (28cm)
Aspect: Sun
Soil: Moist, humus-rich
Hardiness: Zone 9
Propagation: Seed, in warmth
when ripe; division, in spring

A tender, rhizomatous perennial from
southern Africa. Leaves basal, lance-
shaped, dark green. Spathe pink, spadix
yellow, in summer.

Zauschneria californica
(Onagraceae)

Common name: California-
fuchsia
Height: 12in (30cm)
Spread: 20in (50cm)
Aspect: Sun
Soil: Well-drained, fertile
Hardiness: Zone 8
Propagation: Seed or basal
cuttings, both in spring

Rhizomatous evergreen from California.
Leaves lance-shaped, hairy, gray-green.
Flowers in racemes, tubular, scarlet, long
periods in late summer and early autumn.

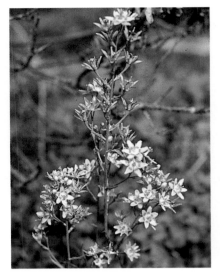

Zauschneria californica
subsp. *cana*
(Onagraceae)

Common name: California-fuchsia
Height: 2ft (60cm)
Spread: 18in (45cm)
Aspect: Sun
Soil: Well-drained, fertile
Hardiness: Zone 8
Propagation: Seed or basal cuttings, both in spring

Deciduous, rhizomatous perennial from California. Leaves linear, gray woolly-hairy. Flowers in racemes, tubular, vermilion; long period from late summer to early autumn.

Zephyranthes candida
(Amaryllidaceae)

Common name: Autumn zephyr-lily
Height: 8in (20cm)
Spread: 3in (8cm)
Aspect: Sun
Soil: Moist, well-drained
Hardiness: Zone 9
Propagation: Seed, in warmth when ripe; offsets, in spring

Tender, bulbous perennial from Argentina. Leaves basal, grassy, upright, midgreen. Flowers solitary, crocus-like, white, over a long period from summer to early autumn.

Zephyranthes flavissima
(Amaryllidaceae)

Common name: Autumn zephyr-lily
Height: 8in (20cm)
Spread: 3in (8cm)
Aspect: Sun
Soil: Moist, well-drained
Hardiness: Zone 8
Propagation: Seed, in warmth when ripe; offsets, in spring

A bulbous perennial from South America. Leaves grassy, linear, midgreen. Flowers solitary, crocus-like, yellow goblets, from summer to autumn.

Zigadenus elegans
(Liliaceae/Melianthaceae)

Common name: Mountain deathcamus
Height: 28in (70cm)
Spread: 8in (20cm)
Aspect: Sun or half shade
Soil: Moist, well-drained deep, fertile
Hardiness: Zone 3
Propagation: Seed, in warmth when ripe; offsets, in spring

A bulbous perennial from North America. Leaves basal, grassy, gray-green. Flowers in many-flowered spikes, small, greenish-white, starry, in mid- and late summer.

Appendices

THE APPENDICES BELOW list genera and species of perennials that share certain characteristics. These lists provide instant reference for the gardener looking for plants to suit specific growing conditions or plants with desirable attributes such as a long flowering season, perfumed flowers, or attractive seed heads. The selections also list plants to avoid if, for example, a child-friendly garden is required, free from poisonous plants, or if a household member is prone to allergies and therefore favors low-allergen plants. Detailed information on the plants in these appendices can be found by referring to the individual entry in the Plant Directory on pages 26–289.

Long-flowering perennials

Acanthus
Achillea
Aeonium
Alcea
Alchemilla
Alstroemeria
Althaea
Anchusa
Anemone x hybrida
Anemone multifida
Anisodontea capensis
Anthemis
Arctotis
Argyranthemum
Aster x frikartii 'Monch'
Astrantia
Begonia grandis
Bellis
Calceolaria
Campanula
Canna
Catananche

Centranthus
Chrysogonum virginianum
Commelina coelestis
Coreopsis
Corydalis ochroleuca
Cosmos atrpsanguineus
Crepis incana
Crocosmia
Dahlia
Dianthus deltoides
Diascia
Dicentra
Epilobium
Eremurus
Erigeron
Erodium
Erysimum
Eucomis
Fragaria
Fuchsia
Gaillardia
Gaura

Gazania
Geranium
Geum
Helenium
Helianthemum
Helichrysum italicum
Hieracium
Hemerocallis
Hosta
Iris japonica
Lavatera
Leucanthemum x superbum
Linaria purpurea
Linum perenne
Liriope
Lychnis coronaria
Lysimachia punctata
Lythrum
Malva moschata
Meconopsis cambrica
Melissa officinalis
Mertensia

Mimulus
Mirabilis jalapa
Monarda
Neirembergia
Nemesia denticulata
Nepeta
Nerine
Oenothera
Omphalodes
Origanum
Osteospermum
Pelargonium
Penstemon
Phlox 'Chattahoochee'
Phuopsis
Phygelius
Potentilla
Pratia
Pulmonaria
Rhodanthemum
Rhodohypoxis
Romneya

Roscoea
Rudbeckia
Salvia
Scabiosa
Senecio cirevira
Solenopsis axillaris
Sphaeralcee
Stachys
Symphyandra
Symphytum armena
Teucrium
Tradescantia x andersoniana
Tuberaria lignosa
Tulbaghia
Verbascum
Verbena
Viola
Zauschneria

Evergreen perennials

Achillea (some)
Aciphylla
Agapanthus (some)
Agave
Alchemilla
Alyssum saxatile
Anthemis
Arabis
Armeria
Asarum
Asplenium
Astilbe glaberrima
Aubrieta
Bergenia
Blechnum
Campanla porschkiana
Carex
Celmisia

Cerastium
Chrysogonum virginianum
Cortaderia
Dianella
Dianthus
Dicksonia
Dierama
Draba
Dryopteris (some)
Epimedium (some)
Erigeron glaucus
Eryngium (some)
Erysimum
Euphorbia (most)
Fascicularia
Festuca (some)
Gazania
Geum

Helleborus
Heuchera (most)
x Heucherella
Iris douglasiana
Iris 'Holden Clough'
Iris innominata
Iris japonica
Iris pallida
Juncus
Kniphofia (some)
Lavandula
Lewisia
Libertia
Limonium
Liriope
Luzula
Mitchella repens
Moraea

Morina
Orthrosanthus
Parahebe
Pelargonium
Phlomis
Phormium
Plectranthus ciliatus
Polygala chamaebuxus
Polypodium (some)
Polystichium (some)
Pulmonaria (most)
Reineckia
Salvia africana-lutea
Salvia leucantha
Santolina chamaecyparissus
Saxifraga stolonifera
Saxifraga veitchiana
Sedum acre

Sedum rupestre
Selaginella
Sempervivum arachnoideum
Seslera
Sisyrinchium
Stacorys
Stipa gigantea
Strelitzia reginae
Tanacetum
Tellima
Tulbaghia
Tweedia caerulea
Umeria
Valeriana
Vinca
Woodsia (some)
Woodwardia some
Yucca

Shade-loving perennials

Actaea
Ajuga
Alchemilla
Anemone x hybrida
Anemone nemorosa

Aquilegia
Arum italicum
Aruncus
Asplenium scolopodendrium
Aster macrophyllus

Astilbe
Athyrium filix-femina
Begonia grandis
Bergenia
Blechnum

Brunnera
Campanula latifolia
Cardamine
Cardiocrinum
Carex

Chaerophyllum
Chelidonium
Chrysogonum
Cicerbita
Cimicifuga

Clintonia	Dodecatheon	Hylomecon	Osmunda	Sesleria
Codonopsis	Doronicum	Iris foetidissima	Ourisia	Smilacina
Convallaria	Dryopteris	Kirengeshoma palmata	Paeonia (some)	Spiranthes
Cortusa	Eomecon	Lamium	Paris	Stipa
Corydalis	Epimedium	Leucojum	Podophyllum	Stylophorum
Cyclamen	Epipactis	Lilium martagon	Polygonatum	Symphytum
Cypripedium	Eupatorium	Liriope	Polygonum	Tellima
Dactylorhiza	Euphorbia some	Lunaria	Polypodium	Tiarella
Davallia	Gentiana asclepiadea	Luzula	Polystichium	Trillium
Dicentra	Geranium some	Meconopsis	Primula	Uvularia
Dicksonia	Helleborus	Milium	Pulmonaria	Vinca
Digitalis	× Heucherella	Mitchella	Saxifraga some	
Diphylleia	Hosta	Myrrhis	Scopolia	
Disporum	Hyacinthoides	Nomocharis	Selaginella	

Drought-tolerant perennials

Acanthus	Claytonia	Gladiolus	Megacarpaea	Rhodanthemum
Achillea	Commelina	Glaucium	Melianthus	Rhodiola
Agapanthus	Convolvulus	Grindelia	Melissa	Rhodohypoxis
Agave	Crambe	Hedysarum	Nepeta	Rosularia
Aloe	Crepis	Hieracium	Nerine	Scabiosa
Anemone nemorosa	Cynara	Hyacinthus	Oenothera (some)	Scilla
Anisodontea	Dicentra	Ipheion	Onosma	Sedum
Anomatheca	Dichelostemma	Iris (some)	Ophiopogon	Silene
Anthericum	Digitalis	Ixia	Origanum	Stachys
Aristaea	Diplarrhena	Knautia	Ornithogalum	Stipa
Artemesia	Dracunculus	Lamium	Othonna	Stokesia
Arthropodium	Echinops	Lathyrus	Oxalis	Symphytum (some)
Arum	Echium	Lavandula	Papaver	Thalictrum
Asarina	Elsholtzia	Lavatera	Pentas	Tiarella
Asphodelus	Elymus	Leonotis	Perovskia	Trifolium
Asteriscus	Eranthis	Leptinella	Phaenosperma	Tritonia
Ballota	Eremurus	Lewisia	Phlomis	Tulbaghia
Begonia grandis	Eriophyllum	Lilium (some)	Phyteuma	Umbilicus
Buglossoides	Erodium	Limonium	Pilosella	Verbascum
Buphthalmum	Eucomis	Linaria	Plantago	Verbena
Bupleurum	Francoa	Linum	Polypodium	Wachendorfia
Camassia	Fritillaria	Lotus	Polystichium	
Carex	Galanthus	Luzula	Pulsatilla	
Catananche	Galega	Lychnis	Puschkinia	
Centaurea	Galtonia	Malvastrum	Rehmannia	
Chiastophyllum	Geranium (most)	Marrubium	Reineckia	

Perennials for acid soils

Anemonopsis macrophylla	Iris chrysographes	Iris uromovii	Meconopsis punicea	Primula juliae
Blechnum	Iris douglasiana	Kirengeshoma palmata	Meconopsis regia	Primula prolifera
Celmisia	Iris ensata	Lilium formosanum	Meconopsis × sheldonii	Primula pulverulenta
Cornus canadensis	Iris graminea	Lilium grayi	Mitchella	Primula rosea
Cypripedium	Iris innominata	Lilium lancifolium	Narcissus (some)	Primula veris
Dianella	Iris laevigata	Lilium pumilum	Ophiopogon	Primula vialii
Dodecatheon	Iris missouriensis	Lilium speciosum	Osmunda	Reineckia carnea
Erythronium	Iris pallida	Lithodora diffusa	Plantago	Sarracenia
Galax urceolata	Iris pumila	Maianthemum bifolium	Podophyllum	Sidalcea
Gentiana (autumn-flowering)	Iris sibirica	Meconopsis betonicifolia	Primula bulleyana	Smilacina racemosa
Hacquetia	Iris spuria	Meconopsis chelidoniifolia	Primula capitata	Trillium
Hylomecon	Iris tenax	Meconopsis grandis	Primula denticulata	Uvularia
Iris 'Brighteyes'	Iris tridentata	Meconopsis napaulensis	Primula japonica	Viola pedata

Perennials for cut flowers

Achillea	Bergenia	Echinops ritro	Monarda	Solidago
Aconitum	Campanula	Gaillardia	Narcissus	Stachys
Agapanthus	Catananche	Galanthus	Paeonia officinalis	Strelitzia
Anaphalis	Convallaria	Gentiana	Paradisea	Tanacetum
Anchusa	Crocosmia	Gypsophila	Phlox paniculata	Tulipa
Anemone × hybrida	Delphinium	Helianthus	Platycodon	Viola odorata
Aquilegia	Dianthus	Helleborus	Polemonium	Zantedeschia
Aster novae-angliae	Dicentra	Iris	Polygonatum × hybridum	
Aster novae-belgii	Digitalis	Leucanthemum	Ranunculus	
Astilbe	Doronicum	Liatris	Rudbeckia	
Astrantia major	Echinacea	Lilium	Schizostylis	

Perennials with perfumed flowers

Asphodeline lutea
Begonia grandis
Cardiocrinum giganteum
Clematis heracleifolia
Convallaria majalis
Cosmos atrosanguineus
Crambe
Crinum x powellii
Cyclamen
Dianthus
Dictamnus
Erysimum

Filipendula
Galanthus
Galtonia candicans
Hedychium
Hemerocallis (some)
Hesperis matrionalis
Hosta 'Honeybells'
Hosta plantaginea
Hosta 'Sweet Susan'
Hyacinthoides non-scripta
Hyacinthus orientalis
Ipheion

Iris chrysographes
Iris graminea
Iris pallida
Iris reticulata
Lathyrus odoatus
Lilium 'African Queen'
Lilium candidum
Lilium formosanum
Lilium grayi
Lilium henryi
Lilium monadelphum
Lilium Pink Perfection Group

Lilium pumilum
Lilium regale
Lunaria rediviva
Mirabilis jalapa
Muscari armeniacum
Narcissus jonquilla
Nymphaea
Ornithogalum arabicum
Paeonia lactiflora
Paradisea
Phlox maculata
Phlox paniculata (some)

Primula auricula
Primula vulgaris
Romneya coulteri
Sedum populifolium
Spiranthes
Tulbaghia
Tulipa sylvestris
Verbena bonariensis
Verbena x hybrida
Viola odorata

Aquatic and marginal perennials

Alisma plantago-aquatica
Butomus umbellatus
Caltha palustris
Carex
Cyperus
Houttuynia

Iris ensata
Iris 'Holden Clough'
Iris laevigata
Iris pseudacorus
Iris sibirica
Juncus spiralis

Lobelia cardinalis
Lythrum salicaria
Mimulus
Myosotis scorpiodes
Nymphaea
Nymphoides

Peltiphyllum peltatum
Phormium tenax
Pontederia cordata
Ranunculus aquatilis
Ranunculus lingua
Sagittaria

Saururus cernuus
Schoenoplectus lacustris
Scirpus
Scrophularia auriculata
Zantedeschia

Bog garden perennials

Aruncus dioicus
Astilbe
Caltha
Cardamine
Cardiocrinum
Cimicifuga simplex
Eupatorium
Filipendula
Fritillaria meleagris

Geum rivale
Glyceria
Gunnera
Hemerocallis
Hosta
Houttuynia
Iris ensata
Iris laevigata
Iris pseudacorus

Iris sibirica
Kirengeshoma
Leucojum
Ligularia
Lobelia cardinalis
Lychnis flos-cuculi
Lysimachia
Lythrum
Mimulus

Monarda
Onoclea
Osmunda
Parnassia
Polygonum
Primula (many)
Ranunculus aconitifolius
Ranunculus lingua
Rheum

Rodgersia
Sanguisorba obtusa
Sarracenia
Schizostylis
Symphytum x uplandicum
Trollius
Uvularia
Woodsia
Woodwardia

Perennials with attractive seed heads

Acanthus
Achillea
Aconitum
Agapanthus
Alchemilla
Allium
Alstroemeria
Althaea
Anaphalis
Anemone x hybrida
Artemesia
Asphodeline
Asphodelus

Astilbe
Baptisia
Cardiocrinum
Catananche
Cautleya
Centaurea
Cimicifuga simplex
Clematis (some)
Crambe maritima
Dierama
Diplarrhena
Echinops
Eremurus

Eryngium
Eupatorium
Euphorbia some
Filipendula
Galtonia
Gillenia
Glaucium
Gypsophila
Hyacinthoides
Incarvillea
Iris (some)
Lathyrus vernus
Lychnis (some)

Malva
Monarda
Moraea
Morina
Nectaroscordum siculum
Paeonia (some)
Papaver orientale
Paradisea
Paris
Phlomis
Phormium
Pulsatilla
Rheum

Rodgersia
Rumex
Scabiosa (some)
Sedum (some)
Sisyrinchium striatum
Stokesia
Thalictrum
Veratrum
Veronicastrum

Perennials for ground cover

Acaena
Acanthus
Achillea
Adiantum
Aegopodium podagraria
Ajuga
Alchemilla
Alyssum
Anaphalis
Anemone x hybrida
Antennaria
Anthemis
Anthericum
Arabis
Arenaria
Arisarum
Armeria
Artemesia
Aruncus

Aster macrophyllus
Astilbe
Astrantia
Aubrieta
Ballota
Bergenia
Blechnum
Brunnera
Buphthalmum
Calamintha
Campanula carpatica
Campanula latiloba
Centaurea
Cerastium tomentosum
Chiastophyllum oppositifolium
Chrysanthemum yezoense
Claytonia sibirica
Convallaria
Corydalis

Crambe
Crocosmia
Cyclamen
Darmera
Dianthus
Dicentra
Dryopteris filix-mas
Epimedium
Erigeron glaucus
Eriogonum umbellatum
Eriophyllum lanatum
Erodium carviflorum
Erodium manescauii
Euphorbia polychroma
Euphorbia griffithii
Filipendula
Fragaria
Geranium (most)
Geum

Gypsophila
Helianthemum
Helleborus
Hemerocallis
Heuchera
x Heucherella
Hosta (all)
Houttuynia
Hypericum
Iberis
Iris (some)
Lamium
Limonium
Liriope
Lithodora diffusa
Lysimachia nummularia
Maianthemum
Mentha
Mitella

Nepeta
Omphalodes
Onoclea sensibilis
Ophiopogon
Osmunda
Othonna
Ourisia
Oxalis acetosella
Persicaria
Phlomis
Physalis
Polygonatum
Polygonum
Potentilla
Prunella grandiflora
Pulmonaria
Ranunculus aconitifolius
Rheum
Rodgersia

Saponaria
Saxifraga stolonifera
Saxifraga × urbium
Sedum

Smilacina
Stachys macrantha
Symphytum ibericum
Tellima

Teucrium × lucidrys
Thymus
Tiarella
Tolmiea

Trollius
Veronica
Vinca
Viola

Zauschneria

Perennials with aromatic foliage

Achillea filipendula
Achillea millefolium
Artemesia
Cedronella canariensis
Chamaemelum nobile
Dictamnus albus
Elsholtzia stauntonii

Filipendula ulmaria
Foeniculum vulgare
Geranium incanum
Geranium macrorrhizum
Helichrysum italicum
Houttuynia cordata
Hyssopus officinalis

Lavandula
Leptinella denayi
Malva moschata
Melissa officinalis
Mellitis melissophyllum
Menika × gracilis
Monarda (all)

Morina longifolia
Myrrhis odorata
Nepeta
Origanum vulgare
Perovskia
Phuopsis stylosa
Rosmarinus

Ruta graveolens
Salvia oficinalis
Santolina chamaecyparissus
Tanacetum parthenium
Tanacetum vulgare
Teucrium × lucidrys
Thymus

Architectural perennials

Acanthus
Aciphylla
Aeonium
Amicia
Angelica archangelica
Cortaderia selloana
Crambe cordifolia
Cynara cardunculus

Darmera peltata
Dierama
Echinops
Echium
Eremurus
Eupatorium
Ferula
Hedychium

Helianthus
Heliopsis
Inula magnifica
Kniphofia
Leonotis
Ligularia
Macleaya
Meconopsis grandis

Meconopsis napaulensis
Meconopsis paniculata
Melianthus major
Nectaroscordum siculum
Ostrowskia magnifica
Paeonia (some)
Phormium tenax
Phygelius

Rheum
Ricinus
Rodgersia
Strelitzia
Telekia speciosa
Thalictrum

Perennials which have berries after flowering

Actaea alba
Actaea rubra
Arisaema ssp.
Arum italicum
Clintonia umbellulata

Convallaria majalis
Cornus canadensis
Dianella nigra
Dianella tasmanica
Diphyleia cymosa

Disporum smithii
Dracunculus vulgaris
Fragaria
Fuchsia
Iris foetidissima

Mitchella repens
Pachyphragma macrophyllum
Paeonia mascula subsp. triternata
Phytolacca americana
Phytolacca polyandra

Podophyllum hexandrum
Polygonatum × hybridum
Smilacina racemosa
Uvularia grandiflora

Low-allergen perennials

Acanthus mollis
Aegopodium podagraria
Agapanthus campanulatus
Ajuga reptans
Alcea rosea
Alchemilla mollis
Allium
Anchusa azurea
Anemone × hybrida
Armeria maritima
Aquilegia
Aruncus dioicus
Asphodeline lutea
Astilbe
Astrantia
Baptisia australis
Bergenia
Brunnera
Camassia

Campanula persicifolia
Cardamine
Corydalis
Crambe
Crocosmia
Delphinium
Dicentra
Dierama
Digitalis
Dryas
Epilobium
Epimedium
Eremurus
Eryngium
Filipendula
Foeniculum
Galtonia
Gentiana asclepiadea
Geranium ssp.

Geum
Gladiolus
Glycyrrhiza
Helianthemum
Hemerocallis
Heuchera
× Heucherella
Houttuynia
Hyssopus
Iberis
Iris sibirica
Kirengeshoma palmata
Kniphofia
Lamium
Linum
Liriope
Lysimachia
Lythrum
Macleaya

Melissa
Mentha
Mertensia pulmonarioides
Monarda
Nepeta
Omphalodes
Origanum
Paeonia
Papaver
Penstemon
Phlox paniculata
Physostegia virginiana
Platycodon grandiflorus
Polemonium caeruleum
Potentilla
Prunella
Pulmonaria
Rodgersia
Rosmarinus

Salvia
Saxifraga
Scabiosa
Schizostylis
Scrophularia aquatica
Sidalcea
Sisyrinchium striatum
Stachys
Symphytum
Thalictrum
Tellima
Tiarella
Tradescantia × andersoniana
Trollius × cultorum
Valeriana
Verbena
Veronica
Vinca
Viola

High-allergen perennials

Achillea millefolium
Aconitum spp.
Alstroemeria spp.
Anaphalis spp.
Anemone nemorosa
Angelica archangelica
Arctotis
Argyranthemum frutesens
Armoracia rusticana
Arnica montana
Artemesia spp.
Arum spp.
Aster spp.

Bellis perennis
Caltha palustris
Catananche caerulea
Centurea spp.
Chamaemelum nobile
Chelidonum majus
Coreopsis spp.
Cortaderia selloana
Dactylis spp.
Dianthus spp.
Dictamnus albus
Echinacea purpurea
Echinops spp.

Elymus spp.
Erigeron spp.
Erysimum spp.
Euphorbia spp.
Festuca spp.
Gaillardia spp.
Gazania spp.
Gerbera
Hakonechloa spp.
Helenium autumnale
Helianthus spp.
Helictotrichon sempervirens
Helleborus spp.

Heracleum mantegazzanium
Holcus spp.
Hordeum jubatum
Imperata cylindrica
Lathyrus odoratus
Lavandula angustifolia
Ligularia spp.
Lilium spp.
Lupinus spp.
Microseris ringens
Milium spp.
Osteospermum spp.
Pennisetum orientale

Persicaria spp.
Phaenosperma
Phalaris arundinacea
Pilosella
Plantago spp.
Primula (many)
Pulsatilla vulgaris
Ranunculus spp.
Ruta graveolens
Rumex spp.
Santolina chamaecyparissus
Senecio jacobea
Sesleria

Solidago spp.
x Solidaster

Stipa gigantea
Stokesia laevis

Uncinia
Veratrum spp.

Zantedeschia aethiopica

Perennials which attract butterflies

Ajuga	Centranthus	Erigeron	Lavandula	Scabiosa
Arabis	Cephalaria	Eryngium	Lunaria	Sedum
Armeria	Chrysanthemum	Helenium	Melissa	Solidago
Aubrieta	Coreopsis	Hesperis	Mentha	Thymus
Aster	Dahlia	Hyssopus	Nepeta	
Aurinia	Echinacea	Iberis	Phlox paniculata	
Calamintha	Echinops	Knautia	Saponaria	

Perennials which attract bees

Allium	Coreopsis	Galega	Ligularia	Rudbeckia
Alstroemeria	Cosmos	Galtonia	Lupinus	Salvia
Althaea	Crocus	Gypsophila	Lythrum	Scabiosa
Anchusa	Dahlia	Helenium	Malva	Sedum
Anemone	Doronicum	Helianthemum	Mellitis	Senecio
Asclepias	Echinacea	Helianthus	Mirabilis	Sidalcea
Calamintha	Echinops	Heliopsis	Monarda	Stachys
Camassia	Epilobium	Hyacinthus	Nepeta	Thymus
Campanula	Eranthis	Hyssopus	Oenothera	Verbascum
Centaurea	Eryngium	Iberis	Origanum	Veronica
Clematis	Fuchsia	Inula	Polemonium	
Colchicum	Galanthus	Lavandula	Potentilla	

Perennials for seaside gardens

Achillea	Centaurea	Glaucium	Morina	Schizostylis
Acanthus	Centranthus	Gypsophila	Myosotidium	Scrophularia
Alstroemeria	Crambe	Heuchera	Nerine	Sedum
Amaryllis belladonna	Crocosmia	Hieracium	Oenothera	Senecio
Anaphalis	Cynoglossum	Iris	Origanum	Sisyrinchium
Anchusa	Dianthus	Kniphofia	Osteospermum	Stachys
Anemone	Dierama	Lathyrus	Penstemon	Stokesia
Anthemis	Echinacea	Lavatera	Perovskia	Tritonia
Anthericum	Echinops	Libertia	Phormium	Veronica
Armeria	Erigeron	Limonium	Phygelius	Viscaria
Artemisia	Erodium	Linaria	Physostegia	Yucca
Aster (dwarf)	Eryngium	Lupinus	Potentilla	Zantedeschia
Bergenia	Euphorbia	Lychnis flos-jovis	Pulsatilla	
Campanula (dwarf)	Fascicularia	Melissa	Romneya coulteri	
Catananche	Filipendula	Mertensia virginica	Salvia	
Celmisia	Geranium	Mimulus	Scabiosa	

Rabbit-proof perennials

Acanthus	Cortaderia	Geranium	Lysimachia	Rosmarinus
Aconitum	Corydalis	Hedychium	Malva	Ruta
Agapanthus	Crinum	Helenium	Melissa	Saxifraga geum
Alchemilla	Crocosmia	Helianthus	Miscanthus	Saxifraga x umbrosa
Anaphalis	Cyclamen	Helleborus	Narcissus	Sedum
Anemone	Cynara	Hemerocallis	Nepeta	Stachys olympica
Aquilegia	Dahlia	Hosta	Omphalodes	Tellima
Aster	Delphinium	Houttuynia	Orchis	Tradescantia
Astilbe	Digitalis	Iris	Paeonia	Trillium
Bergenia	Doronicum	Kirengeshoma	Papaver	Trollius
Brunnera	Epimedium	Kniphofia	Phormium	Tulipa
Campanula lactiflora	Eranthis	Lamium	Phytolacca	Verbena
Campanula latifolia	Eupatorium	Lavatera	Polygonatum	Vinca
Cardiocrinum	Euphorbia	Leucojum	Polygonum	Yucca
Clematis	Fuchsia	Liriope	Pulmonaria	Zantedeschia
Colchicum	Galanthus	Lupinus	Rheum	
Convallaria	Gentiana asclepiadea	Luzula	Romneya	

Deer-resistant perennials

Acanthus	Agapanthus	Allium	Aquilegia	Arum
Aconitum	Agave	Amaryllis	Artemisia	Astilbe

Campanula
Carex
Centaurea
Ceratostigma
Clematis
Cortaderia
Crinum
Crocosmia
Delphinium
Dicentra
Digitalis
Epimedium

Euphorbia
Ferns
Festuca glauca
Filipendula
Gaillardia
Geranium
Helianthus
Helichrysum
Helleborus
Hosta
Iris
Kniphofia

Lavendula
Leucanthemum × superbum
Leucojum
Liriope
Lupinus
Lychnis coronaria
Melianthus
Melissa
Melittis
Mentha
Mirabilis
Myosotis

Narcissus
Nepeta
Origanum
Paeonia
Papaver
Polygonatum
Potentilla
Pulmonaria
Romneya coulteri
Rudbeckia
Salvia
Satureja

Scabiosa
Sisyrinchium
Tellima
Thalictrum
Tiarella
Trillium
Veratrum
Vinca
Yucca

Poisonous perennials

All parts are poisonous, unless specified

Aconitum
Actaea
Amaryllis
Anemone blanda
Anemone nemorosa
Anemone ranunculoides
Anemone rivularis
Aquilegia
Arisaema

Arnica
Arum
Asclepias
Calla palustris (fruits)
Chaerophyllum hirsutum 'Roseum'
Colchicum
Cyclamen persicum
Convallaria majalis (seeds)
Coriaria terminalis (fruits)
Crinum × powellii
Delphinium

Dendranthema weyrichii
Dendranthema yezoense
Dicentra
Dictamnus
Digitalis
Echium
Eranthis
Euphorbia
Galanthus
Helenium
Helleborus
Iris

Lathyrus (seeds)
Lupinus (seeds)
Narcissus (bulb)
Nuphar lutea
Ornithogalum
Paeonia
Paris quadrifolia (fruits)
Physalis alkengi
Phytolacca
Podophyllum
Polygonatum × hybridum
Ranunculus ficaria

Ricinus (seeds)
Rumex
Scopolia (root)
Sedum
Senecio
Symphytum
Trollius europaeus
Tulipa
Veratrum
Vinca

Perennials which may cause skin irritation

Aconitum
Alstroemeria
Amsonia
Aquilegia
Arisaema
Arum
Borago
Caltha
Chamaemelum

Chelidonum
Cichorium
Clematis
Delphinium
Dendranthema
Dicentra
Echium
Euphorbia
Helenium

Helianthus
Helleborus
Heracleum
Hyacinthus
Iris
Lobelia
Macleaya
Myosotis
Narcissus

Onosma
Ornithogalum
Pelargonium
Pentaglottis
Persicaria
Phytolacca
Podophyllum
Primula elatior
Primula obconica

Pulmonaria
Ranunculus
Rumex
Ruta
Symphytum
Tanacetum
Tradescantia × andersoniana
Tulipa
Veratrum

Perennials which seed freely

Achillea millefolium
Alchemilla mollis
Allium christophii
Anthericum
Antirrhinum
Aquilegia (all)
Asphodeline
Asplenium
Aster novae-belgii
Astrantia major
Bellis
Brunnera
Bupleurum
Campanula latifolium
Campanula persicifolia
Campanula trachelium

Centaurea montana
Cephalaria
Chelidonum
Cicerbita
Cirsium
Corydalis lutea
Corydalis ochroleuca
Crepis
Cynara
Digitalis (most)
Echinops
Echium
Epilobium
Erigeron compositus
Erodium
Euphorbia characias

Galtonia
Geranium pratense
Geranium pyrenaicum 'Bill Wallis'
Glaucium
Helleborus orientalis
Hesperis matronalis
Hieracium
Isatis tinctoria
Juncus
Lamium galeobdolon
Lamium maculatum
Linaria
Lotus
Lychnis chalcedonica
Lychnis coronaria

Lychnis flos-cuculi
Lythrum salicaria
Lythrum virgatum
Malva
Marrubium supinum
Meconopsis cambrica
Melissa officinalis
Milium effusum
Myrrhis odorata
Nectaroscordum siculum
Oenothera fruticosa
Oxalis acetosella
Papaver
Parahebe
Pentaglottis
Phytolacca

Pilosella
Plantago
Polemonium
Pulmonaria
Rumex
Senecio cineraria
Senecio uniflora
Sisyrinchium
× Solidaster
Telekia
Valeriana
Verbascum
Verbena

Short-lived perennials

Achillea ptarmica
Aethionema
Agastache
Alcea
Anagallis
Anchusa
Antirrhinum
Aquilegia
Arabis
Asarina procumbens
Baptisia australis
Begonia grandis

Belamcanda chinensis
Bupleurum falcatum
Calamintha nepeta
Campanula pulla
Campanula pyramidalis
Carlina acaulis
Catananche aerulea
Claytonia
Coreopsis
Crepis
Delphinium Pacific hybrids
Dianthus

Diascia
Dicentra speciabilis
Dictamnus albus
Erigeron
Erinus
Eryngium giganteum
Erysimum
Gaillardia
Gaura
Glaucium
Gypsophila
Hedysarum

Hesperis
Isatis tinctoria
Lavatera
Leontopodium
Linum
Lobelia
Lotus
Lupinus
Lychnis × arkwrightii
Lychnis coronaria
Malva
Matthiola

Meconopsis betonicifolia
Meconopsis grandis
Megacarpaea
Mimulus
Oenothera
Orthrosanthus
Papaver atlanticum
Papaver croceum
Papaver 'Fireball'
Papaver fourei
Papaver rupifragum
Polemonium

Primula capitata
Rehmannia
Rudbeckia
Salvia argentea

Salvia coccinea
Salvia pratensis
Sanguisorba albiflora
Scabiosa atropurpurea

Semiaquilegia ecalcarata
Senecio cineraria
Silene dioica
Silene uniflora

Sisyrinchium
Stylophorum
Symphyandra
Tanacetum

Verbascum bombiciferum
Viola

Invasive perennials

Acanthus hungaricus
Acanthus mollis
Acanthus spinosus
Achillea ptarmica
Aegopodium podagraria
Anemone × hybrida
Arisarum proboscideum
Arum italicum
Aruncus dioicus
Campanula persicifolia
Campanula pulla
Campanula rotundifolia
Campanula takesimana
Cardamine pentaphyllos
Cardamine pratensis
Ceratostigma plumbaginoides
Chamaemelum nobile
Cirsium rivulare

Commelina coelestis
Convallaria
Convolvulus altheoides
Cornus canadensis
Dicentra 'Pearl Drops'
Eomecon chionanthum
Epilobium angustifolium
Galium odoratum
Geranium himalayense
Gladiolus papilio
Glyceria maxima
Helianthus decapetalus
Helianthus doronicoides
Helianthus 'Lemon Queen'
Lamium galeobdolon
Houttuynia cordata
Hylomecon japonicum
Inula hookeri

Leonotis dysophyllus
Leonotis leonurus
Lilium bulbiferum
Linaria triornithophora
Lotus corniculatus
Lysimachia ciliata
Lysimachia nummularia
Lysimachia punctata
Maianthemum bifolium
Malvastrum lateritium
Mentha × gracilis
Mertensia implicissima
Mertensia pulmonarioides
Milium effusum
Muscari armeniacum
Myosotis scorpioides
Nectaroscordum siculum
Oenothera speciosa

Ornithogalum nutans
Ornithogalum thyrsoides
Ornithogalum tetraphylla
Oxalis acetosella
Oxalis pes-caprae
Oxalis tetraphylla
Persicaria affinis
Persicaria capitata
Petasites japonicus
Phygelius aequalis
Physalis alkengi
Physostegia virginiana
Plectranthus ciliatus
Pontederia cordata
Pratia pedunculata
Prunella grandiflora
Ranunculus acris
Ranunculus ficaria

Ranunculus repens
Sanguisorba canadensis
Sanguisorba obtusa
Sanguisorba officinalis
Sanguisorba tenuifolia
Saponaria officinalis
Saxifraga × urbium
Scopolia carniolica
Symphytum ibericum
Symphytum orientale
Symphytum × uplandicum
Telekia speciosa
Tiarella cordifolia
Tricyrtis formosana
Tricyrtis latifolia
Trifolium repens

Perennials which require to be lifted and divided regularly

Achillea
Aster amellus
Aster ericoides
Aster thomsonii
Astilbe
Bergenia
Camassia
Campanula persicifolia

Campanula pulla
Coreopsis
Crocosmia
Crocus
Doronicum
Dracunculus
Erigeron
Fritillaria imperialis

Geum
Gladiolus communis
Gladiolus papilio
Helenium
Helianthus
Heliopsis
Hemerocallis
Heuchera

Liatris
Muscari
Narcissus
Nerine
Ophiopogon
Ornithogalum
Phlox paniculata
Polygonatum × hybridum

Schizostylis
Sisyrinchium
Stachys byzantina
Tradescantia × andersoniana

Perennials which resent transplantation

Aciphylla
Aconitum
Agapanthus
Alstroemeria
Anemone × hybrida
Angelica
Anthemis
Aquilegia
Aristaea
Asclepias
Baptisia
Brunsvigia
Campanula lactiflora

Catananche
Centranthus
Cephalaria
Chaerophyllum
Claytonia
Clivia
Crambe
Crepis
Crinum
Cynara
Dictamnus
Dierama
Echinops

Echium
Eriogonum
Eryngium
Euphorbia
Fascicularia
Ferula
Foeniculum
Galega
Gentiana
Gerbera
Glaucium
Glycyrrhiza
Gypsophila

Hacquetia
Hedysarum
Hesperis
Isatis
Incarvillea
Lathyrus
Limonium
Linum
Lupinus
Megacarpaea
Mertensia
Myrrhis
Oenothera

Ostrowskia magnifica
Paeonia
Papaver orientale
Pentaglottis
Platycodon
Pulsatilla
Scabiosa
Thermopsis
Trillium
Tropaeolum polyphyllum

BIBLIOGRAPHY

General Reference:

Berry, S. and Bradley, S. *Best Plants for your Garden* Anness Publishing. London. 1996.

Bird, R. *The Complete Book of Hardy Perennials* Ward Lock. London. 1993.

Bloom, A. *Alan Bloom's Selected Garden Plants* Jarrold. Norwich. 1968.

Bremness, L. Contributing Editor *Herbs D.K. Pocket Encyclopaedia* Dorling Kindersley London. 1990.

Brickell, C. Editor-in-chief: *The Royal Horticultural Society Gardeners' Encyclopedia of Plants and Flowers* Dorling Kindersley. London, 1994.

Brickell, C. Editor-in-chief. *The Royal Horticultural Society A-Z Encyclopedia of Garden Plants* Dorling Kindersley. London, 1997.

Cooke, I. *The Plantfinder's Guide to Tender Perennials* David & Charles. Newton Abbot. 1998.

Elliott, J. *The Smaller Perennials* B.T. Batsford. London. 1997.

Godet, J-D. *Plants and Flowers of Great Britain and Europe* Arboris Press. Bern. 1991.

Griffiths, M. *Index of Garden Plants* derived from *The New Royal Horticultural Society Dictionary of Gardening* Macmillan Press. Basingstoke. 1994.

Harris, T.Y. *Alpine Plants of Australia* Watson Ferguson. Brisbane. 1970.

Hessayon, D.G. *The Bulb Expert* Expert Books. London. 1995.

Hessayon, D.G. *The Flower Expert* Expert Books. London 1997.

Hessayon, D.G. *The Rock and Water Garden Expert* Expert Books. London. 1997.

Heywood, V.H. Consultant Editor. *Flowering Plants of the World* Oxford University Press. 1978.

Jellito, L and Schacht, W. *Hardy Herbaceous Perennials* in two volumes Third Edition revised by Schacht, W. and Fessler, A., Timber Press Inc. Portland, Oregon. 1990.

Kidd, M.M. *South African Wild Flower Guide No 3* Cape Peninsula. 2nd Ed. Oxford University Press. 1996.

Kohlein, F. and Menzel, P. *The Encyclopaedia of Plants for Garden Situations* B.T. Batsford, Ltd. London. 1994.

Lancaster, R. *What Perennial Where?* Dorling Kindersley London. 1997.

Mathew, B. *The Larger Bulbs* B.T. Batsford. London. 1978.

Onderstall, J. *South African Wild Flower Guide No 4* Transvaal Lowveld and Escarpment. Botanical Society of South Africa. 1984.

Parker, H. Editor. *Perennials. A Royal Horticultural Society Plant Guide* Dorling Kindersley. London. 1996.

Philipson, W.R. and Hearn, D. *Rock Garden Plants of the Southern Alps* The Caxton Press. Christchurch. 1962.

Phillip, C. *The Plant Finder 1999/2000 Edition* The Royal Horticultural Society. Dorling Kindersley. London.

Phillips, R. and Rix, M. *Bulbs* Pan Books. London. 1989.

Phillips, R. and Rix, M. *Herbs* Pan Books. London. 1990.

Phillips, R. and Rix, M. *Perennials* In two volumes: I *Early-flowering*; II *Late-flowering* Pan Books. London. 1991.

Phillips, R. and Rix, M. *Shrubs* Pan Books. London. 1989.

Press, B. and Gibbons, B. *Wild Flowers of Britain and Europe* New Holland. London. 1993.

Redgrove, H. Editor. *An Illustrated Handbook of Bulbs and Perennials* Cassell. London. 1991.

Rice, G. *Hardy Perennials* Viking. London. 1995.

Rickett, H.W. *Wild Flowers of the United States Vol. 2 The Southeastern States* McGraw-Hill. New York. 1967.

Segall, B. Consultant. *Botanica; the Illustrated A-Z of over 10,000 garden plants, and how to grow them* Mynah. N.S.W., Australia. 1997.

Thomas, G.S. *Cuttings from my Garden Notebooks* John Murray. London. 1998.

Thomas, G.S. *Perennial Garden Plants, or The Modern Florilegium* J.M. Dent. London 1990.

Trehane, P. et. al. *International Code of Nomenclature for Cultivated Plants* Quarterjack Publishing. 1995.

Walters et. al. *The European Garden Flora*, in five volumes. Cambridge University Press. 1984-1998.

Books on Cultivation:

Anderton, E. and Park, R. *Growing Gladioli* Christopher Helm. London. 1989.

Bath, T. and Jones, J. *The Gardener's Guide to Growing Hardy Geraniums* David & Charles. Newton Abbot. 1994.

Bird, R. *The Cultivation of Hardy Perennials* B.T. Batsford, London, 1994.

Grenfell, D. *The Gardener's Guide to Growing Hostas* David & Charles. Newton Abbot. 1996.

Jefferson-Brown, M. and Howland, H. *The Gardener's Guide to Growing Lilies* David & Charles. Newton Abbot. 1995.

Mathew, B. *Growing Bulbs: the Complete Practical Guide* B.T. Batsford. London. 1997.

Pratt, K. and Jefferson-Brown, M. *The Gardener's Guide to Growing Fritillaries* David & Charles. Newton Abbot. 1997.

Rice, G. and Strangman, E. *The Gardener's Guide to Growing Hellebores* David & Charles. Newton Abbot. 1994.

Smith, F.C. *Growing Carnations and Pinks* Ward Lock. London. 1994.

Stebbings, G. *The Gardener's Guide to Growing Irises* David & Charles. Newton Abbot. 1997.

Books on General Topics:

Bird, R. *Woodland Gardening* Souvenir Press. London. 1992.

Bird, R. Editor and Compiler. *Plantsmen on Plants* The Hardy Plant Society. 1990.

Boddy, F.A. *Foliage Plants* David & Charles. Newton Abbot. 1973.

Boisset, C. and Walker, J. *The Garden Designer. Selecting Plants.* Reed International Books London. 1994.

Chatto, B. *The Dry Garden.* J.M.Dent. London. 1978.

Cooke, I. *The Plantfinder's Guide to Tender Perennials* David & Charles. Newton Abbot. 1998.

Evans, A. *The Peat Garden and its Plants* J.M.Dent. London. 1974.

Ferguson, N. *Right Plant, Right Place* Aura Books. 1996.

Genders, R. *The Scented Flora of the World* Robert Hale. London. 1994.

Grounds, R. *The Plantfinder's Guide to Ornamental Grasses* David & Charles. Newton Abbot. 1998.

Frohne, D. and Pfander, H.J. *A Colour Atlas of Poisonous Plants* Wolfe Publishing. 1983.

Howes, F.N. *Plants and Beekeeping* Faber & Faber. London and Boston. 1979.

Huntingdon, L. *Creating a Low-allergen Garden* Mitchell Beazley. London. 1998.

Jones, David L. *Encyclopaedia of Ferns* Thomas C. Lothian. Port Melbourne, 1987.

Lloyd, C. *Foliage Plants* Collins, London. 1973.

Lloyd, C. *The Well-tempered Garden* Collins, London. 1973.

Marion Merrell Dow. *Hayfever in the Garden.* 1994.

Paterson, A. *Plants for Shade* J.M. Dent. London. 1981.

Raven, J. *A Botanist's Garden* Collins. London. 1971.

Rice, G. *The Planting Planner* Macmillan. London. 1996.

Rogers, Barbara R. *The Dried Flower Encyclopaedia* Simon & Schuster. London. 1988.

Royal Horticultural Society, The *Award of Garden Merit Plants.* 1994.

Royal Horticultural Society, The *Award of Garden Merit Plants* First Supplement. 1994.

Royal Horticultural Society, The *A.G.M. Plants.* 1999.

Scott, G.H. *Bulbs: how to select, grow and enjoy* H.P. Books. Los Angeles. 1982.

Stary, F. and Berger, Z. *Poisonous Plants* Magna Books. Leicester. 1995.

Taylor, J. *Collecting Garden Plants* J.M. Dent. London.1988.

Taylor, J. *The Milder Garden* J.M. Dent. London 1990.

Thomas, G.S. *Colour in the Winter Garden* Weidenfeld and Nicolson. London. 1994.

Thomas, G.S. *Plants for Ground Cover* J.M.Dent and Sons Ltd. London. 1990.

Verey, R. *The Flower Arranger's Garden* Conran Octopus. London. 1992.

Monographs on Individual Families:

Barker, D.G. *Epimediums and other herbaceous Berberidaceae* The Hardy Plant Society. 1996.

Cribb, P. and Bailes, C. *Hardy Orchids* Christopher Helm. London. 1989.

Grey-Wilson, C. Poppies: *The Poppy Family in the Wild and in Cultivation* B.T. Batsford. London. 1993.

Ingram, T. *Umbellifers* The Hardy Plant Society. 1993.

Innes, C. *The World of Iridaceae* Holly Gate International Ltd. Ashington. 1985.

Kellaway, D. *Clematis and the Ranunculaceae* Pavilion Books. London. 1994.

Kohlein, F. *Saxifrages and related Genera* B. T. Batsford. London. 1984.

Reed, D. Editor. *Lilies and Related Plants* The Royal Horticultural Society Lily Group 1988/9.

Stocks, A. *Saxifragaceae* The Hardy Plant Society. 1995.

Monographs on Individual Genera:

Anderton, E.W. and Park, R., *Growing Gladioli* Christopher Helm, London, 1989.

Bartlett, M. *Gentians* Blandford Press. Poole. 1975.

Bath, T. and Jones, J. *The gardener's guide to growing Hardy Geraniums* David & Charles. Newton Abbot. 1994.

Bird, R. *Border Pinks* The Crowood Press. Marlborough. 1997.

Bird, R. *Lilies; an Illustrated Identifier and Guide to Cultivation* Apple Press. London. 1991.

Blanchard, J.W. *Narcissus; A Guide to Wild Daffodils* Alpine Garden Society. 1990.

Bond, S. *Hostas* Ward Lock. London. 1994.

Case, Frederick W., Jnr. and Case, Roberta B. *Trilliums* Timber Press. Portland, Oregon. 1997.

Clapham, S. *Primulas* David & Charles. Newton Abbot. 1971.

Clark, D. *The Hardy Fuchsia Guide* Oakleigh Publications. Monkswood. 1992.

Cobb, J.L.S. *Meconopsis* Christopher Helm. London. 1989.

Cohen, V.A. *A Guide to the Pacific Coast Irises* British Iris Society. 1967.

Cooper, A. *Pentstemons* Power Publications. Ferndown. 1996.

Crook, H.C. *Campanulas and Bellflowers in Cultivation* Blandford Press. London. 1959.

Davies, D. *Alliums: The Ornamental Onions* B.T. Batsford. London. 1992.

Erhardt, W. *Hemerocallis: Daylilies* B.T. Batsford. London. 1992.

Fuller, R. *Pansies, Violas and Violettas: The Complete Guide* The Crowood Press. Marlborough. 1990.

Goldblatt, P. *The Genus Watsonia* National Botanic Gardens, South Africa. 1989.

Green, R. *Asiatic Primulas: A Gardener's Guide* Alpine Garden Society. Pershore. 1976.

Grenfell, D. *The Gardener's Guide to Growing Hostas* David & Charles. Newton Abbot. 1996.

Grenfell, D. *The Gardener's Guide to Growing Daylilies* David & Charles. Newton Abbot 1998.

Grenfell, D. *Hostas* The Hardy Plant Society. 1993.

Hewitt, J. *Pulmonarias* The Hardy Plant Society. 1994.

Ingwersen, W. *The Dianthus* Collins. London. 1949.

Jacobs, D.L. and Jacobs, R.L. *Trilliums in Woodland and Garden* Eco-Gardens Decatur, Ga. USA.

Jefferson-Brown, M. and Howland, H. *The Gardener's Guide to Growing Lilies* David & Charles. Newton Abbot. 1995.

Jones, Joy, et. al. *Hardy Geraniums* The Hardy Plant Society. 1993.

Kohlein, F. *Iris* Christopher Helm. London. 1981.

Lewis, P. and Lynch, M. *Campanulas* Christopher Helm. London. 1989.

Liden, M. and Zetterlund, H. *Corydalis* Alpine Garden Society. Pershore. 1997.

Linnegar, S and Hewitt, J. *Irises A Wisley Handbook,* Royal Horticultural Society. Cassell. London. 1990.

Mann-Taylor, J. *Phlomis.* N.C.C.P.G. Wisley. 1998.

Matthew, B. *The Iris* B.T. Batsford. London. 1981.

Picton, Paul, *The Gardener's Guide to Growing Asters* David & Charles. Newton Abbot. 1999

Pradhan, U.C. *Himalayan Cobra Lilies: Their Botany and Culture* Primulaceae Books. Darjeeling. 1990.

Pratt, K. and Jefferson-Brown, M. *The Gardener's Guide to Growing Fritillaries* David & Charles. Newton Abbot. 1997.

Puttock, A.G. *Primulas* John Gifford. London. 1957.

Rice, G. and Strangman, E. *The Gardener's Guide to Growing Hellebores* David & Charles. Newton Abbot. 1994.

Robinson, M. *Primulas: The Complete Guide* The Crowood Press. Marlborough. 1996.

Snoeijer, Wim, *Agapanthus; a review* Gouda, The Netherlands 1998.

Stebbings, G. *The Gardener's Guide to Growing Irises* David & Charles. Newton Abbot. 1997.

Sutton, J. *The Gardener's Guide to Growing Salvias* David & Charles. Newton Abbot. 1999.

Swindells, P. *A Plantsman's Guide to Primulas* Ward Lock. London. 1989.

Taylor, J.M. *Phlomis; the neglected genus* N.C.C.P.G. Wisley. 1998.

Turner, R. *Euphorbias: A Gardener's Guide* B.T. Batsford. London. 1995.

Way, D. *Pentstemons* The Hardy Plant Society. 1996.

Way, D. and James, P., *The Gardener's Guide to Growing Pentstemons* David & Charles. Newton Abbot. 1998.

White, S. *Origanum* N.C.C.P.G. Wisley. 1998.

Yeo, C. *Salvias* Pleasant View Nursery, Newton Abbot. 1995.

Yeo, C. *Salvias 2* Pleasant View Nursery, Newton Abbot. 1997

Yeo, P.F. *Hardy Geraniums* Croom Helm. London and Sydney. 1985.

INDEX

Picture Credits

All photographs by Marshall Craigmyle, except:

Heather Angel 1, 2, 6, 13, 14, 15, 16, 19, 20, 26, 32, 53, 64, 94, 99, 103, 110, 132, 135, 160, 169, 190, 220, 234, 273

Salamander Picture Library 9, 12, 22, 23, 42, 47, 57, 71, 76, 83, 89, 119, 124, 146, 153, 166, 173, 178, 185, 198, 203, 209, 215, 227, 239, 245, 250, 255, 262, 268, 277, 282, 286

Maps by Eugene Fleury © Salamander Books Ltd.

Zonal Temperature Ranges

ZONE 1: Below -50°F (Below -44°C)
ZONE 2: -50° to -40°F (-44° to -37°C)
ZONE 3: -40° to -30°F (-37° to -32°C)
ZONE 4: -30° to -20°F (-32° to -27°C)
ZONE 5: -20° to -10°F (-27° to -22°C)
ZONE 6: -10° to 0°F (-22° to -16°C)
ZONE 7: -0° to +10°F (-16° to -10°C)
ZONE 8: +10° to +20°F (-10° to -5°C)
ZONE 9: +20° to +32°F (-5° to 0°C)
ZONE 10: +32° to +40°F (0° to +5°C)
ZONE 11: Above +40°F (Above +5°C)

HARDINESS ZONES